THE WRITTEN WORLD

THE WRITTEN WORLD

WORLD

Reading and Writing in Social Contexts

Susan Miller

University of Utah

HARPER & ROW, PUBLISHERS, NEW YORK

Cambridge, Philadelphia, San Francisco, London,
Mexico City, São Paulo, Singapore, Sydney

For Nathaniel Miller and Gavi Price:
Young readers of the world create its best future.

A list of acknowledgments appears on pages 597–600, which is hereby made part of this copyright page.

Sponsoring Editor: Lucy Rosendahl
Project Editor: Carla Samodulski
Text Design and Text Art: Caliber Design Planning Inc.
Cover Design: 20/20 Services Inc.
Production Manager: Jeanie Berke
Production Assistant: Paula Roppolo
Compositor: ComCom Division of Haddon Craftsmen, Inc.
Printer and Binder: R. R. Donnelley & Sons Company
Cover Printer: N.E.B.C.

The Written World: Reading and Writing in Social Contexts

Library of Congress Cataloging-in-Publication Data

The written world: reading and writing in social contexts/[compiled by] Susan
    Miller.
        p. cm.
    Includes indexes.
    ISBN 0-06-044526-2 (student ed.)
    ISBN 0-06-044523-8 (teacher ed.)
    1. Readers—Social sciences. 2. College readers. 3. English
language—Rhetoric. I. Miller, Susan, date.
PE1127.S6W75 1989
808'.0427—dc19   88-24660
                        CIP

88 89 90 91 9 8 7 6 5 4 3 2 1

Brief
Contents

Contents

2. Visible Language   74

3 The Writer's Contexts: From Self to Community   157

Curricular and Thematic Contents

History: Methods and Results

Languages and Meanings

Men and Women

Natural Settings

Past and Future

Poetry and Drama

Politics and Government

Reading and Writing: Methods and Results

Science: Methods and Results

Technology and Media

Stories and Plots

Young and Old: Perspectives

To
the Teacher

We use anthologies of readings for many purposes in our writing courses. Anthologies include materials that extend our students' range of reading experience as we use them to teach methods of critical reading. They allow students, as a classroom community, to share a fund of topics and rhetorical models they can discuss and question. They provide points of departure for the wide variety of writing assignments we make. They lead students to their own analyses of content and persuasive strategies; to imitations of style, form, or voice; and to many forms of personal response.

The Written World aims to meet these needs, but I have selected its contents, designed its arrangement, and composed its apparatus with something more in mind. I want to offer what many other anthologies lack—sustained attention to the contexts of both writing and reading. Students need to understand that ordinary but active human processes both take life from and result in writing and reading. In this book, I have persistently asked students to think about the origins and effects of reading and writing, both their own and others'. They are invited to appreciate how diverse and complex the reasons for writing can be.

Consequently, *The Written World* works against a flatly textual approach that removes the selections from their own contexts and purposes. It doesn't suggest that students simply receive a text as an example of "good writing." Instead, it encourages them to see the cultural and individual energies that produced a text and to realize how these are at work in its words. While it is never entirely possible to complete this sort of recovery, I want to insure that students' own reasons for writing, and their ways of doing so, are not isolated from the class materials designed to expand them.

In order to do this, I have highlighted some basic human uses for writing in distinct communities of readers and writers and have organized them into five categories. These uses include telling stories, making public arguments and policy, creating documents and preserving cultural wisdom, enriching our singular and social selves, finding distinct ways of talking and thinking about a subject, and monitoring the distinctly literary pitfalls and play within written worlds. I have entitled the chapters "Written Voices: Writing to Record Stories and Statements of Public Policy," "Visible Language," "The Writer's Contexts: From Self to Community," "Written Worlds," and "Writing about Writing: Diversions and Dangers," respectively.

These categories roughly follow the history of literacy, which has been entirely intertwined with the changing nature and scope of reading communities. That is, changes in composing and its technologies have increased opportunities for writers to expand and change the written world, finally making it possible to create separate fields of writing and to write commentaries on other writing. Neither reading nor writing has ever been a static set of "operations" on words, for both have acquired new connotations as manuscript culture, print culture, competitive publishing, democratic educational opportunities, and competing media have evolved. As these developments created interdependent communities of readers and writers, they also changed the nature of these communities. Each distinct moment has both challenged us and enriched the complex, specific ways in which we now map an originally sketchy universe of writing.

I have ordered these uses of writing and reading, and the forms they have taken, chronologically. This arrangement does not require you to teach your course as a sequential history, but it does allow students to see how printed words shape our constantly changing personal, public, and self-referential worlds. The text of Homer is no less sophisticated than a contemporary novel like *Riddley Walker,* but culturally unified Homeric audiences certainly preceded the sophisticated and solitary readers of Russell Hoban's futuristic fiction, which is composed in a style that reflects on writing itself. Thus, the two selections result from different imaginative perspectives on what composition can do, both from the writer's and from the readers' or listeners' points of view. While a speech may be no less well formed than a case study, the motive for composing a persuasive public address preceded the motive for writing to contribute specialized data to members of an international academic discipline.

I realize that the history of writing and reading has been incremental, not strictly sequential. Each of the five major divisions of this book includes a mixture of examples from past and present that allows the instructor to focus on a variety of themes. I have done this both to give you flexibility and to enable students to see the continuity from earlier uses for writing to current ones. For instance, the examples of an ongoing conversation about "character" in Chapter 4 include selections by Aristotle and Joan Didion that raised new issues for consideration by the established community of readers and writers. These two selections, and those with them, comment on one another, showing a textual community around the issues of individuality and the self. In each of the other chapters, I have organized the examples in categories that represent common motives, writing situations, or imagined audiences, so that students can see reading and writing as specific, consequential processes that they may use themselves to understand and change their own experience.

I hope that these functional, recursive categories will highlight purpose and activate reading in a way that other anthologies do not. Whenever the writing in question is more complex than a grocery list, asking the question "What is this piece of writing *doing*?" generally produces two groups of responses. The more familiar reactions may take up textual issues like authorial voice, format and organization, kinds of evidence, and language and style. But a second set of answers, often avoided in textual approaches, also results. These reactions describe a reading's best possible outcome from its author's viewpoint; the responses, both implied and actual, of its readers, the personal and social situation in which the writing occurred, and the student's possible analogous writing in a similar set of circumstances.

The apparatus of this book doesn't ignore the first set of answers. Both the questions for individual analysis and the suggestions for writing call for fairly close, traditional analyses of language and form, and direct the student to deal with the text itself. But these questions are also part of a larger drama of reading. Each chapter provides a brief introduction that explains the purposes and processes that its selections share. Individual headnotes explicitly address the motives and situation from which a piece was written in order to connect an author's motives with the student's experience. Often, headnotes also suggest ways of reading that direct attention to the writer's purposes and to readers' responses to the selection.

The questions following the readings fall into three groups that roughly follow a common sequence for teaching. "Rereading and Independent Analysis" questions ask for investigations of language, structure, and other prominent features of a selection. These are suggested as old-fashioned homework that can be brought to bear on later class discussions and writing, but they might also guide classes on specific textual features. They often direct students to make notes or write brief statements, so that writing will sustain reading, not follow later as only a "product."

"Suggested Discussion and Group Activities" often rely on evidence compiled in response to analysis questions, as do the suggestions for writing. These prompts for discussion engage students in group and class projects that will allow them to bring their individual interpretations to a group for response and modification. For some teachers, these may be the center of work for each piece. The final "Writing Suggestions" are not meant to be make-work but instead call on the student to apply readings and individual experience to both private and public written forms. These are organized into "Response," "Analysis," and "Finding a Purpose" assignments. These suggestions often specify a situation, audience, and genre so the students may take a controlling rhetorical stance and thereby see themselves taking meaningful action through writing, whether by exploring, persuading, or explaining.

I have included selections at various levels of difficulty, from both past and present, so that teachers can explore contextual reading with various groups of students. I hope this wide range of selections will introduce collegiate reading and writing in ways that usefully precede their later practice in specialized academic settings. I have been especially concerned to provide what strictly "cross-curricular" collections usually overlook: information about how separate texts may together form a textual community with identifiable customs and purposes. In my experience, this fundamental issue is not prominent enough in introductions that focus on textual rather than contextual issues.

The selections include many familiar examples, but I have also attempted to expand the reading canon, for what I hope are obvious reasons. The unusual selections here are meant to enhance traditional views of quality and significance, to give you flexibility, and to increase opportunities for the readings to interpret each other.

In everything, I have tried to show students how reading and writing are connected, mutually supportive activities. Following George Hillock's essay, "What Works in Teaching Composition," as well as my own teaching experience, I have avoided rigid "natural process" and "presentational" attitudes. Students are encouraged to learn the actual processes that writers use, but they are also expected to gain information and use it as they work with this book. The exercises therefore take a flexible "environmental" stance, suggesting various specific tasks and requiring students to see their reading as a source as well as a model. I have aimed for a reasoned mixture of limited, staged analytic tasks; modeling; and various peer and teacher collaborations. In concert with the text's arrangement, there are questions about changing contexts for reading and writing, and at times an exercise will refer the student to other selections. The questions address particular problems that unite the selections with their writers', and readers', historical, social, and literary expectations.

There is now widespread support for understanding and teaching that language constructs experience as often as it preserves it. I hope this anthology will help those who have become uncomfortable with existing texts that focus on the value of readings but do not reawaken the desires and situations that first invested the pieces with value. *The Written World* aims to show students that reading and writing contain many ongoing conversations determined by, resumed, and joined for many reasons.

Acknowledgments

This collection is the result of so many minds and hands that I cannot claim even the credit due an editor without immediately qualifying that claim. For suggesting selections, I am especially grateful to Dean Rehberger, who has followed this project from its beginning, and to my brother, Jack Miller. In addition, I want to thank my colleagues at the University of Utah who suggested some of the selections and have been invaluable collaborators in many other ways: Meg Brady, Ray Freeze, Karen Lawrence, Richard Price, Mark Strand, Michael Rudick, Jeri Schneider, and Barry Weller.

Barry Weller, Pam Hunt, Nicole Hoffman, and Regina Oost contributed invaluable editing and proofreading; Carla Samodulski has been the best project editor imaginable. My greatest thanks go to Lucy Rosendahl, whose editorial faith and friendship are a gift.

I would also like to thank the following manuscript reviewers: Charles Davis, University of Arizona; Robert DiYanni, Pace University; Diane Dowdey, Texas A&M University; Cynthia Frazer, Old Dominion University; George Haich, Georgia State University; John Hanes, Duquesne University; Joseph Harris, Temple University; David Hoddeson, Rutgers University; Clayton Hudnall, University of Hartford; George Kennedy, Washington State University; Elizabeth Larsen, West Chester University; Richard L. Larson, Lehman College; Cleo Martin, University of Iowa; Thomas E. Martinez, Villanova University; Elizabeth McPherson; Patricia Morgan, Louisiana State University; William Powers, Michigan Technological University; John Ramage, Montana State University; Charles Schuster, University of Wisconsin (Milwaukee); Margot Soven, La Salle College; Joseph F. Trimmer, Ball State University.

Susan Miller

To
the Student

The Uses of Writing: Actions Through Language

If you think of writing as something you do in an English course (perhaps you like it, perhaps you don't), you probably also separate writing from reading, which you do in many situations. My purpose in gathering the group of readings in this collection has been to help put these two activities—writing and reading—together, to show you how *your* writing has everything to do with the reading you do in this course or anywhere.

When I say this, I don't mean "writing" as something to be "corrected," but as an action. This book's title, *The Written World,* is meant to suggest that written words serve two important purposes. They are ways to save thoughts and record events, but they are first ways to think and act. They create their own universe of language, entwined with daily experience. As the unique species that uses language, we fulfill some of our most important purposes entirely *in* language, by writing and reading. Both activities have become common enough over their history to allow us, as individuals and as socially organized groups, to use them in many important ways. They communicate and preserve ideas, they allow us to investigate shared events and problems, they establish laws and communicate beliefs, and they permit us to know ourselves better.

You may not at first see how these purposes for written language actually affect you, a student whose writing and reading appear so different from the writing and reading you are assigned. What I have in mind, therefore, is to show you through this collection some actual uses of writing, and to invite you to read and write for similar reasons. The many kinds of writing represented here have everything to do with you. They established our shared communities by fixing beliefs and social structures that still affect us. They communicated some of our most enduring ways of looking at the world that is not written, but lived in every day. They gave individuals a way to realize their own best (and worst) selves by using written language to try on roles and reach out to others. And they became specialized written "conversations" that we enter and leave, gatherings in language that enrich us and give us a chance to leave our mark on them.

In the first three chapters of this book, the purposes for writing include the following actions:

1. Telling stories and making public speeches to unite communities and to explore basic human problems
2. Creating documents that preserve the laws and wisdom of distinct cultures
3. Exploring the self in privacy, in the special dialogue of a letter, or in widely shared reflections on community experience

These three purposes are not neatly separable, as you will see when you read. But by putting them in categories, I hope to show you how writing and reading serve specific human needs to organize and share common experiences.

The last two chapters show more specialized purposes for writing, purposes that it has taken centuries for writing to accomplish. Continuing written conversations have become specialized, so that a group of written statements may stake out a particular subject or problem, or may represent specialized methods for asking and answering questions, similar to those that define the fields in which you take courses. Or, as the final chapter shows, writing and reading may be playful, and at times dangerous, activities that comment on other writing and reading.

These five uses by no means exhaust the reasons that people write, but they do clarify how writing has been and is a way of making something happen in a specific time, place, and situation. These readings show that writing exists to help us accomplish something for ourselves, for those we know, and for others who participate in our many roles and interests. In order to do these things, writers use many methods of composing. They think and talk a lot before they actually write, but they also use notes and written doodles to get ideas about what to say. And they share "rules"—agreements about conventional forms of finished writing. "Errors" that get corrected reveal contracts in the groups who use these rules, decisions made over time that assure that written words—which usually don't have their writer around to explain them—will make the best possible sense.

Of course, all of these conditions for reading and writing apply to you. I point them out because writing—and reading—are never merely exercises. They are ways to achieve a new understanding, to change a situation, to continue to build knowledge others can use, and to entertain and regulate ourselves. They deserve, therefore, our most versatile attitudes and actions.

When you read, you connect your own moment of reading to the original situation in which a piece was written. A newly meaningful experience results. The uses of writing are never entirely fixed because each time someone else reads, say, an article or story, written words are revitalized in the new situation of the reader. When you write, your ideas, your knowledge, and your reasons for writing grow from ideas that others have used and purposes that others have had. In both reading and writing, you make new contributions to a written conversation that started before you joined it, within that conversation's established but elastic limits of meaning.

Your reading and writing are, therefore, related to each other—practicing one process helps you accomplish more with the other. With this book, I want to alert you to the possibilities for changing and enlarging your own world by using all of the resources in the written world.

Looking for Purpose as You Read

Since it is not enough for you only to hear that writing and reading are actions rather than exercises, I want to be specific about the ways in which you can approach the selections in this book. As you read a piece of writing, keep the following ideas in mind to help discover the purpose and the kind of action that the writer was taking.

1. Identify the Context

"Context" is the whole situation around a piece of writing. It is the actual and imagined "place" where a particular text is located. To find the context of a selection, look for the qualities of this situation that distinguish it from the situations that produced other texts. Before you can understand a reading's "message," you need to know when, where, and why it was written. Use the introductions and headnotes in this book to help get a sense of the goals a writer had in mind for a specific group of readers. Think of yourself as one of those readers and try to answer these questions:

- What was the purpose of this selection from the writer's point of view? What outcomes did the writer hope for?
- In what time and place would these outcomes best be realized?
- Whom do you imagine to be the author and "ideal" reader of this selection?
- If you were making a movie of this written action, what would its setting be?

2. Get a Sense of the Whole Before You Focus on the Parts

Before you actually read a selection, use your answers to the first questions about context to help you predict a selection's content. Look over the whole piece before you settle in to read one paragraph or sentence at a time. Read only the first paragraph, and try to guess what will follow. You might try writing a brief note about what you would write if you were in this writer's situation and shared this purpose. How would you have continued after this beginning?

Read the first sentence in each paragraph, and the last few paragraphs in their entirety, to make a mental outline that will help you understand and remember the whole piece. Then, before you read closely, try to predict the kinds of examples and evidence the writer might choose to support the points in your outline.

3. Read Actively

Successful writing carries its readers along so that they subordinate individual details to their grasp of the whole. But as a reader whose purpose is to understand *how* this wholeness was achieved, you will need to reread, looking for the ways in which a piece of writing "works." Ask yourself these questions:

- What are the most important points this selection makes?
- What kind of evidence—examples, facts, logical reasoning—makes you trust these ideas?
- In what pattern is this content presented? Can you find the reasons that an author chose a particular order of arrangement?

Writing for Your Readers

Any community that understands distinct written meanings shares habits of expression and a common vocabulary. The familiarity of this language allows the group to cooperate. Just as you need to know something about the habits of specific communities to understand the purpose of a reading, you also need to keep your own community's expectations in mind as you write. Every class you take is a small community of readers and writers who have a purpose for being there and expectations about what sort of approach, content, and results they will find. In your writing course, you can learn ways to control the effect your writing will have in many contexts by testing your writing against your classmates' and teacher's responses.

First, of course, you want ways to guide your own writing processes. Here is where the connection between reading and writing becomes most clear. The same questions that help you understand what you read can help as you write. They can guide you as you plan, write drafts, and revise, processes that often go on all at once. You will need to think about, answer, and reanswer the following questions, since the act of writing itself will change your direction and sense of the whole.

Purpose: What is my purpose? What would be the best outcome of this piece of writing? What information, new ideas, and perspectives will my readers have after they read? What will this piece of writing *do*?

Readers: What role am I taking for my readers? Whom do I imagine to be the ideal reader for this writing? What does this ideal reader want and need from my writing?

Setting: In what specific setting do I imagine this writing accomplishing its purpose? What are my limits of time, place, and possibility?

Approach and support: Considering my purpose, role, and reader, what is the best sort of evidence I can use to make my point? What do I need to include to accomplish my purpose? In what order should I present this material so the reader will follow my ideas?

Language: Do my sentences and vocabulary fit all of these choices? Have I chosen a level of diction, references to specific facts, and interesting comparisons that contribute to my purpose in this setting? Does each sentence clearly contribute to the reader's understanding of what I want to accomplish?

Answering these questions can help you learn to act like a "writer"—a person who uses writing for many specific reasons. Your answers will change even while you are writing, and may change again after you get responses from others. But your successful finished writing will be held together by your control of each of these elements of the whole.

Susan Miller

A View of Culture and Community Language

 The Madness of Dark

This prologue to *The Written World,* a view of writing that shows us many common assumptions about written language, provides a good introduction to the nature of the written world. Its "author," an aging Eskimo woman, talked as her words were recorded. She understood the world before reading and writing determined our habits of thinking and ways of taking action. She dealt with the ways that memories create a cultural heritage, describing a primarily oral world of spoken and remembered tales, where knowledge was passed on from individual to individual, often in ways that now seem indirect and difficult.

The Eskimo woman was interviewed by Robert Coles, a psychiatrist who often asks people to tell stories of change and its results. (Another of Coles's interviews is included in Chapter 4.) The old woman talked about how her memories and ways of thinking differ from those that her grandchildren are learning in school from the new, "lower forty-eight." She reminded Coles not to separate young from old Eskimos. She warned that he may misunderstand how much the children still identify with their ancestors' customs and habits. "We are all together here. We are all wondering what will come next," she told him.

The old woman does not write herself, nor does she separate, categorize, and analyze "change." When she does make a point, she asks her listener to understand it by hearing and understanding the stories in her memories, not by hearing a "statement." She focuses on counting and "explaining" as ways of thought that she does not need and has doubts about. Her ideas have not been formed by reading, but she is nonetheless sophisticated about how new patterns of organization and ways of transmitting the community's history will affect her culture.

Reading and writing are intimidating to the Eskimo woman. They are new technologies that directly affect her world by changing its traditional concepts about past and future. She is talking to a visitor, giving examples in stories about her father, missionaries, and nature. But her life is given to us through Coles's perspective as an observer who collects information and writes it down for a wide audience of readers in many times and places who may never know one another but who can share this experience. As you read, try to identify with the Eskimo woman and with Coles. Think about how new technologies both disturb and enlarge your own everyday experience. How does the Eskimo woman stand in for each of us as we learn unfamiliar patterns and rules for organizing and interpreting our actions? How does Coles stand in for you as you try to share with others what you hear and learn by writing?

Sometimes the old Eskimo woman sits down and looks for many minutes 1 at a rug of polar bear skin. She remembers when her husband and her brother-in-law and her young nephew brought that particular bear home. She remembers how big it was, the biggest she has ever seen, and she has seen a few in her time. She remembers how glad she was to have the skin. It is so cold, the winter floor. One can take the extremes of winter weather, but there is a "weak spot" in everyone, she insists, and for her, it has always been the feet. They make her tremble all over when they are cold. Does the visitor from the "lower forty-eight" remember what it was like when he took in an especially cold drink, or savored hard ice cream too long in his mouth? The headache that comes, the shivering in the chest, the lump of chill in the stomach—they are the body's way of saying no, stop, please be more thoughtful. Likewise, the woman's feet on a hard, frigid floor send waves of agitation up her legs, through her torso, to her head. She specifies the anatomical stages, comments on how fidgety her feet get as they pursue warmth—anywhere it is available, usually the bed—how trembling or even writhing her body gets, anxious indeed for relief from the source of marked irritation; how pointedly her eyes do their work, eventually transmitting their important message: go there, and your agony will be over.

There is, of course, something else for the old woman to stare at, 2 when she is of a mind to sit and look (and look and look); there is the snow. In the summer, the snow has gone—but in the summer she claims never to sit and stare. In the fall (which begins in September, and yields to winter in October, or November at the very latest) she takes up again what she once called her "position." She possesses a linguist's (and philosopher's) sense of what she has in mind: "These are the long days, the long months. The sun has its position; I have mine—the chair. I can't keep track of time, the way my children do, or my grandchildren. Even though the sun has left us, my grandson comes home from school and tells his mother what day it is. He looks at me afterward, because he knows that I will smile. I may be away from them, in the middle of my thoughts, but I know when to come back and smile. Without my smile, the boy would be disappointed. He would not be so sure of himself. To be sure of yourself, you have to see someone else smile—let you know that not everyone does things the way you do! My grandson counts the days in a month. I don't know how old I am. He thinks I am kidding him when I shrug my shoulders and say I am many winters old. He asks me, to have fun, how many. I tell him more than he would care to count up. He is sure I have done the counting. But I haven't.

"Once he asked me how many *summers* I've lived. I told him a winter or two worth of summers. He was so interested in those *numbers* they teach the children at school, he repeated his question—as if what I'd said had nothing to do with what he asked. I didn't repeat myself—and he surprised me. He *had* heard me—and understood me. He told me that he wished he could just forget all the arithmetic he was learning and play in the winters and go hunting and fishing in the summers. I told him that young people are going to have a new life. They are learning a lot, and some of them will go to the lower forty-eight and learn more. And the white men don't push our young people around the way they used to push us around. They are changing, the white people. When I sit and think of *them,* I get lost to the world. I don't hear my own daughter speaking to me." 3

The white people have always perplexed, if not dumbfounded, her. She has tried hard, many times, to figure them out—especially when she has been sitting in the chair. But they are no obsessions of hers. They startle her, occasionally, with their arrival in her mind; soon enough, however, she gets rid of them. It is just that, as she experiences it—a hasty housecleaning, a dismissal of sorts: "I don't like to be bothered when I'm sitting in my chair. I want to rest. I want to remember. The greatest joy for me, now, is remembering. I would be lonely if I couldn't remember. I remember my whole life. I will sit and look out the window, and suddenly I'm a young girl, and my father is holding my hand, and teaching me how to use the knife with the fish we've caught. My favorite time was with him; he would wake me up every morning, with his hand on my shoulder. I'd see his smile. He never told me to get up. My daughter tells her children to get up. We didn't talk as much then as people do now. I've caught the sickness—it's the sickness of words; no wonder I keep *saying* what I remember! I may die talking! It will serve me right! 4

"I will wake up, and I will see my father. He is with me. He has never left me. He will be touching my shoulder, or maybe squeezing it. He always squeezed when he was afraid I was not paying attention, or I was too much asleep. Once we went fishing, and I was moving too much. He put the line down, and he came over to me. He held my hands in his, so that they would be as still as possible. Then, just as he was going back to his line, he squeezed my shoulder. I knew what he meant. He meant that I should not forget what he'd just done—and he was afraid I would, so it's best to remind me. The other day I was going to fry some potatoes for my grandchildren, but I felt tired, and my eyes caught the large bag of potato 5 chips. The young people of our village like potato chips more than any-thing else—except the Cokes they use afterwards, to wash their tongues of all the salt. I put the potatoes down, and decided not to use the stove. I picked up the bag of potato chips. But I let go of it before I really had done more than hold it in my hands. My father had seen me, and squeezed my shoulder.

"He died a long time ago. I don't know how long. Even my daughter 6 has a number; she says thirty years—when she was a girl as old as one of my grandsons. He has a number, too. He is twelve, he tells me. So what! All these numbers. What do they have to do with life? Does the sun have numbers for itself? The bears and caribou? The fish? The snow that greets us, stays with us, goes away crying? I watch the snow cry. My grandson says it is melting. I say no, it is crying. Who likes to leave? My father died with tears in his eyes. I wiped them away, and put them to my mouth. He has been with me ever since! He used to take me to watch the snow melt. He said it was sad to see it leave, even though we were going to have a good time in the summer.

"I don't sit here and wait for the summer. I am still surprised when 7 I hear my grandchildren say that they are counting the days until summer. Why count? Each year they talk like that. Each year I smile! I want to tell them to become more like their Eskimo ancestors, but I feel my father's squeeze on my shoulder; he always said that an Eskimo will never stop being an Eskimo, even if he goes to the lower forty-eight, and comes back here dressed up like a white man from Fairbanks. An Eskimo is born to be an Eskimo, and he may talk like the white man (my grandchildren do, more and more), but he will never stop being part of our people.

"I remember one time a missionary was visiting us. I was a girl, but 8 I was almost a woman. He kept telling me I should be 'good.' I didn't know what he meant. Out of the corner of my eye I saw the dogs, pointing their noses. Their heads were very high. They weren't moving, just standing there. Then, they started to go around and around in a circle. I wanted to go get my father. He was in the village. Did he know a storm was coming? I told the missionary, finally, that we were in danger, and we'd better go get my mother, who was with my aunt, and my father. The missionary looked up at the sky. It was clear. He said that there was no storm coming. I said there was, I knew there was. He wanted to know how I knew. I told him: the dogs. He asked me to explain. I did. He laughed. He told me I was superstitious. It was the first time I heard the word, and I didn't know what he was talking about. How often I would hear that word over the years. The Eskimos were always hearing, then, that they were superstitious. But I knew what I knew! I told the missionary that I had to leave, right away. He said I wasn't being a good Eskimo; I was leaving *him!* I asked him to come along with me. He did. We reached my mother, and she joined us, and we found my father, and we went home. I remember seeing some clouds in the sky, as we came home. The dogs were beginning to howl. They were hungry, but not howling hungry. They were upset with us. Why weren't we doing something faster to protect ourselves from the storm? A dog keeps a close eye on his neighbors—people.

"Before we could do anything, the missionary had to leave; other- 9 wise, to be polite, we would have to stand there talking with him. My father called me away to the back of our house, and said I should pretend to get sick. He told me to hold my stomach and come to him and say it hurts. I waited for him to go back to the minister, and then I came over and did what my father wanted me to do. The minister excused himself and left—after my father excused himself because he wanted to take me in the house and look after me. My mother could tell that my father and I had figured out a way to send the minister off. We watched him leaving, and suddenly the storm came upon us—like lightning in the summer. The wind pushed at us; it wanted to sweep us away. My father realized that the minister might not make it back to his church. I went with my father on the sled, to get the minister. We caught up with him, but he wanted to keep moving. He said we shouldn't worry. God would look after him. I was only a child, and I had no right to say anything. But I did. I said that the wind is God's breath, and we have to be careful, because when he blows that hard, he means for us to go inside and wait until he's decided to stop. The minister told me I was superstitious, again! Then he went on, and we went back home.

"We stayed inside for a long, long time—over a week, my grandchil- 10 dren would say. It was a bad storm, but we had a good time. I helped my mother sew. We had enough food. The baby cried, but the wind was noisier than the baby. It was very hard to clear a path from the house to the shed. Later, we heard that the minister had died on his way back to the church. The storm had taken his spirit. My mother believed that the storm lasted such a long time because the minister was trying to break away from the storm; the longer his spirit fought with the wind, the worse the wind became. When the wind left us, it went to the mountains, far inland. That is where the minister's spirit is. Our ancestors are there, and I'm sure they are looking after the minister. I hope he doesn't wave his finger at them, the way he did at me when I was a girl. I can see him now, pointing at me and telling me I should listen carefully to everything he said. My grandmother told me that the white man never listens to anyone, but he expects everyone to listen to him. So, we listen! The wind isn't a good listener! The wind wants to speak, and we know how to listen. My father always told me that an Eskimo is a listener. We have survived here because we know how to listen. The white people in the lower forty-eight talk. They are like the wind; they sweep over everything. I used to think we would survive them, too. But I'm not so sure. When I look at my grandchildren, I am not sure at all!"

She worries a lot about those grandchildren. They talk so much; they 11 expect so much. And they have received so much—too much by far, for her taste. Still, she is not a bitter, cynical woman, all too smugly self-righteous about her generation, her kind of life, as opposed to the way others live and, no doubt, will continue to live. More than anything else, she clings to the winter, ironically, as a source of hope. The Alaska winter will be the same for Eskimos, generation after generation of them. So long as there are Arctic winters, there will be Eskimos, or so she believes. Even the white people, with their pipelines and machinery and airplanes and navy stations and radar and helicopters and television sets and radio-telephones and bricks and mortar and electricity and loudspeakers and record players and (again and again she brings them up) snowmobiles; even the white people, with their motorboats and automatic rifles and telescopes and magnifying glasses and binoculars and medicines and portable X-ray machines and needles and freezers and frozen foods and cellophane bags and canned goods—even the white people bow to the winter, hide during it, run from it, acknowledge its sovereignty. There is not the slightest question in her mind that the winter is lord and master over all the acreage of "creation" she has ever seen. And it will fight to the finish, that winter, if ever seriously challenged.

She is afraid that, ultimately, the white people of "mainland" U.S.A. 12 are headed for such a futile confrontation. She is no authority on twentieth-century technology, but she knows it is ever expanding, and she is certainly no innocent about those who wield that technology. There are moments, there are stretches of time (one had best not attempt to quantify them through even indirect questions) when she becomes at once grim, gloomy, apprehensive, agitated, and more than a little apocalyptic. She endows the visitors from the lower forty-eight states with a zeal and ambition that are themselves as potentially apocalyptic in character as her notion of what finally will take place during some (as yet distant, she hopes and believes) winter, when a struggle will be fought for the heart and soul of the Arctic.

"My father was the first one in our village to drink. I don't know why 13 he did. The missionary said, often, that he knew why. But white people do a lot of talking, and they believe themselves, *always*. Often we don't believe them—but we listen. Oh, sometimes we *seem* to listen! Eskimos don't 'understand' as much as white people. I used to argue with the missionary, when he told me that he wanted to 'explain' his religion to my people. I would say that if he just let us come to his church, and ask us to pray, then we *would* believe. Why not? But the more he had those 'classes,' and the more he gave his 'talks,' and his 'sermons,' the more we became captured by him—and not real believers. But he meant us no harm. And he was against liquor.

"I have been against liquor all my life. A glass of wine is enough for 14 anyone! I told my father he was treating himself like a ghost. He was *making* himself a ghost. The ghosts are the bad spirits. They wander all over. They have no home. I think they are mostly men. Men who drink! I may have had a man's spirit in me for a long while, but it wasn't a ghost!

And finally, I was left alone; the spirit left me. I can remember the moment—and the many days that came before that moment. I felt the fists, hitting me in the belly. I felt the hands, pulling at my chest, trying to reach my mouth, so that they could get out. I tried to help. I didn't want my body to be a jail! I reached into my mouth with my own hands, hoping to touch the hands of the spirit. I vomited and vomited. But no luck—for days, no luck. That is why I cut myself. I sat down one day and remembered what my grandfather had told me. He said that if you let your blood run, you make yourself better. If there are spirits in you that want to go, they will leave with the blood. I had been counting on my stomach to do the work!

"After the blood began to run, I felt better. I let it run and run. I   15
didn't touch the blood. I took the cup and left it outside, near our place where we keep caribou meat. It snowed that night. I threw up one more time. It was the worst time. My chest and stomach hurt so bad that I started crying. The missionary said I should cry when my husband left us, but that is the missionary's thinking: death. I told him I was happy for my husband. I expect to be with him soon. It is a man's right to go exploring first. A woman follows. If I had not cut myself, I would have left first—a long time ago. Either the man's spirit in me would go, or I would go. It was either the spirit would take me, or I would release the spirit! Once the spirit had left me, I was free to stay here. Afterward, I stopped going out hunting—well, most of the time. I wasn't as fast a runner. I walked slower. I used to walk so fast, when I was a girl, my mother told me I was being chased. I guess the spirit was pushing me! When the spirit left, I could slow down a lot. And here I am, so quiet that I wonder what my legs are thinking! No wonder they have become weak. No wonder they send me all those complaints—sighs and groans and cries. I hear the minister use those words—the sighs and groans and cries of Jesus Christ and His disciples. My feet have been my disciples, and I have not been as nice to them as I have been to strangers from the lower forty-eight!"

A faint smile. A twinkle of her wide-open eyes. A prolonged silence.   16
She lifts her right arm, uses the hand to push back her hair, gray but not white. She wonders whether she will live to have all-white hair. Probably not. She remembers her grandmother's hair—remembers the pride of the old grandmother: not a touch of black. If only that would be the case with her! She is sure her "spirit" would be especially fond of an all-white head of hair. In her more fanciful moments, she dares specify where her "spirit" is—what its color is, and how it makes do, so to speak: "I woke up this morning and I thought of some geese. I saw them at night in my sleep. They were circling over this house. I think they wanted me to join them! They made so much noise. I waved at them, then I began to worry that they would wake everyone up, so I motioned to them that they should quiet down or fly away. They stayed, circling around and around. I got dizzy looking at them. I think I woke up for a few seconds, but I went right back to sleep, and there they were again. This time, one of the geese, all

white, came close to me and I saw the eyes, and I was sure I was getting an invitation: come with us! I think my spirit was almost ready to fly away with the geese. Maybe it would have entered that white goose."

She is not very good at telling *how* that might happen—the transmi-   17 gration of her soul, as a visitor might want to put it. She is not ready to affirm (to her grandchildren, never mind to a stranger) that such an event *will* happen, or even *can* happen. She merely wonders out loud whether there might not be a "spirit" in a person, and whether that "spirit" might not wander about the Arctic, and occasionally settle for a spell of residence within an animal, a bird, a fish. Let those who want to "study" her, figure her out, know her every thought, not to mention her "beliefs," "customs," "rituals," guess what she "really" banks on, or swears by. She herself smiles, looks off—her eyes reaching for a bird, moving with the bird's movements, leaving the bird reluctantly when it has escaped her field of vision. There is the madness of the darkness, she may well be thinking, and the madness of questions, definitions, conclusions, words and more words. So a stranger dares presume—after hearing the woman's grandson say that she once told him that birds are enviably able to move, to travel, to fly, to see so much and yet be quiet about all they have looked at and come to know: the routes, the pathways, the cycles of weather, the refuges or opportunities which the earth, the sun, the trees, the wind all offer.

Questions

Rereading and Independent Analysis

1. Reread the Eskimo woman's account and list each of the stories she tells about herself and her people. Then review the parts of the account told by Robert Coles. How does he tell his "story" of talking to the woman? List some similarities between the way he tells a story about her and the ways she tells about herself. Then look for differences. Find a few examples that represent differences in their vocabulary and sentence length. How do you account for their different choices?

2. How would you state the woman's most basic idea? Note each of the places in the account where she compares or contrasts Eskimos and whites, the past and the present, young and old. How do these comparisons verify your statement of her message to Coles?

Suggested Discussion and Group Activities

1. Interview a classmate about important knowledge that his or her grandparents have passed on. How does the woman's statement that "we are all together" apply to the person you interviewed? Then, as a class, put together your results. Determine ways that your community is like and different from the Eskimo woman's in relying on the experience and wisdom of older people.

2. How are the Eskimo woman's attitudes toward children like, and different from, the attitudes of older people you know? Do these older

people share her view of change? How is her place in her community similar to or different from theirs?

3. The Eskimo woman relies on natural cycles and rhythms to explain her world, avoiding "separations and categories" that she associates with white culture. She thinks of the seasons, not of statistics about the weather. In groups or as a class, look for places in her account that demonstrate her special sense of cause and result, time, and reasoning. Try explaining some of her points from the "white," or "civilized," point of view that she objects to, showing how psychology, science, or education might give different explanations of her stories.

4. As a class or in groups, identify three or four kinds of stories that you were told as a child. For example, you may have heard about the way your family came to this country, how your parents met, or some outstanding family accomplishment. Once you have identified similar stories, make some generalizations about the importance of stories. What functions do they serve in the family and the larger community?

Writing Suggestions

Response

Recall and tell a classmate or class group one of your family's favorite stories or legends. Then work with your listeners to see if you can discover a point or moral to the story. Write your story for your classmates, using this event and its general point to tell specifically about your family's influences on your life now. Make it clear why this story is told and retold in your family—what important lesson is it preserving?

Analysis

Using your "Independent Analysis" work, write a comparison of the two ways of telling about events used by Coles and the Eskimo woman. Show how they represent "old and new" or "story and explanation" perspectives. Your comparison should be suitable for a brief introduction to the selection for students.

Finding a Purpose

Write a scene with dialogue, taking the point of view of an "old" person who is explaining to a "new" scientist how life was before an alien group came to your community.

Written Voices: Writing to Record Stories and Statements of Public Policy

INTRODUCTION

Before writing came to be used at different times and places in the ancient world, human memory was so well developed that long epic tales like Homer's *Iliad* and *Odyssey* and other important oral works were easily enough passed on for centuries. Memory and repeated tellings still preserve such important spoken material in cultures that do not rely on the written word.

Writing made it possible to record these public recitations, but we need to remember that speech preceded and was independent of a written record. Works were composed by the composer's relying on his memory of a store of traditional ideas and on the standard forms for the kind of work—such as a story or a speech—that the composer was forming. An orator (an experienced public speaker) might have a scribe write down what he had said and send it to others who would read and memorize it. (The Roman orator Cicero once apologized to a friend for not "writing" to him sooner, giving as his reason that he had had a sore throat.) Important and complex parts of stories might be written as aids to memory, but the spoken word remained most important in communicating.

Now, of course, we often use writing as a way to think on paper. We write before we speak, and we learn stories and public statements by reading rather than listening. Nonetheless, the purposes of stories and speeches are often best understood by "hearing" the tone and "voice" that determined their significance in specific times and places. To understand the intention and original impact of these compositions for listeners, we need to imagine their first delivery to a group of listeners.

Early narratives and speeches observed well-defined patterns that allowed their listeners to follow and remember their meaning. These patterns still guide the movement and organization of our tales and public addresses. Since a traditional story is a continuous action whose "actors" and setting unify it and give it a point, separate events in this action must also be unified. One thing must believably follow another; characters must respond to other characters and to their situations. In stories that are interesting and well told, conflicts between characters and their interests develop, and characters meet in increasingly complex oppositions until an outcome is determined.

Speeches generally follow a five-part pattern. They include a "narration" to establish the context and give the speaker's credentials to speak about a subject; a statement of the speaker's position (a "thesis"); evidence to support this thesis; reasons why opposing positions do not solve the problem at hand; and a conclusion (the *peroration*—after the oration) that sums up and tells what the speaker's ideas will mean for the audience.

Both of these ancient patterns allow an audience to enter into the context of the story or speech, put themselves in the place of the story's "hero" or the speaker, follow the actions and ideas, and take a result with them back into ordinary experience. As you read these selections, you will understand their purposes better if you put yourself in the place of a listener whose life could be affected by the narrator or speaker and the situation addressed.

TELLING A STORY

 Odysseus' Homecoming
(Homer)

The ancient Greek stories of the Trojan War, the *Iliad,* and of the Greek hero Odysseus' ten-year journey home after victory, the *Odyssey,* united preliterate Mediterranean culture for centuries. These stories were recited as epic poems; they were written down in the versions we still read long after their composing and repeated retellings. Examination of their language has revealed that they were composed during the very act of recitation. The poets used a number of traditional devices that enabled them to make long, rich narratives from relatively limited verbal formulas, such as fixed rhythmical patterns, standard vocabulary, and repeatable descriptive phrases. They had no need for a written text during their performances.

Evidently, these epic stories were continuously transmitted over many centuries exclusively through speech. We cannot know the poet or poets who shaped the *Iliad* and the *Odyssey* into the forms we have now, but Greeks traditionally identified the poet with Homer, a blind singer of these songs about heroes and their adventures with gods and supernatural forces. Each poem was also shaped by conventions that define an *epic* as a type *(genre):* They begin in the middle of the action, then return to explain earlier events; they tell of the great deeds of heroes; they include intervention by the gods; they were "told" in segments that could be listened to by an audience in one sitting.

In this excerpt from the *Odyssey,* Odysseus and his men leave Troy after its defeat to return to Ithaca, where Odysseus' wife, Penelope, and son, Telemakhos, wait faithfully, beset by rivals for Odysseus' kingdom and his bed. Along the way, Odysseus' craftiness often saves him and his men from threatened disasters, as when he devises a way to blind the one-eyed giant, the "outrageous and lawless" Cyclops, and escape.

Penelope and Telemakhos are as resourceful as Odysseus. During her husband's absence, Penelope has put off all her persistent suitors, promising to choose one when she finishes weaving a tapestry but delaying the choice by unraveling the day's work each night. Odysseus returns in disguise so he can discover the status of his kingdom and reassure himself about his family's good faith. When he is recognized by his faithful dog as the suitors are demanding Penelope's decision, he overthrows them in combat, firmly reestablishing his honor.

Throughout the *Odyssey,* story tellings are treated as events in the narrative. Identification of strangers, hospitality, concord, and resolution are achieved in the communion of listening to the hero's accounts of himself. Consequently, the story of Odysseus' life becomes the story of any hero's life. It is the image of its listeners' cultural values and idealized history. To understand better the importance of such an epic tale, we might imagine gatherings where the *Odyssey* was recited. It was a "song" for entertainment, but it and other epic poems also explained their audience's confrontations with experience. The gods' erratic interventions in human destiny explained sudden events that broke regular patterns of nature. The community drew strength from its shared knowledge of the old "wisdom" and "history," which showed its ancestors' heroic courage in the face of unpredictability. Even as we read today, we participate in some of these implications, identifying with heroes who overcame uncertainty and with families who remain unsure of how struggles have affected them.

This English translation of the *Odyssey* by Robert Fitzgerald illustrates traits of composition that are suitable to spoken rather than written story telling. The translation imitates the oral patterns of the poem. Repetitions, labels, regular rhythm, and descriptive asides all helped a "singer" to compose the next part of the story in his head while reciting the words.

The old nurse went upstairs exulting,
with knees toiling, and patter of slapping feet,
to tell the mistress of her lord's return,
and cried out by the lady's pillow:

"Wake, 5
wake up, dear child! Penélopê, come down,

see with your own eyes what all these years you longed for!
Odysseus is here! Oh, in the end, he came!
And he has killed your suitors, killed them all
who made his house a bordel and ate his cattle   10
and raised their hands against his son!"

                                    Penélopê said:

"Dear nurse . . . the gods have touched you.
They can put chaos into the clearest head
or bring a lunatic down to earth. Good sense   15
you always had. They've touched you. What is this
mockery you wake me up to tell me,
breaking in on my sweet spell of sleep?
I had not dozed away so tranquilly
since my lord went to war, on that ill wind   20
to Ilion.

                       Oh, leave me! Back down stairs!
If any other of my women came in babbling
things like these to startle me, I'd see her
flogged out of the house! Your old age spares you that."   25

Eurýkleia said:

"Would I play such a trick on you, dear child?
It is true, true, as I tell you, he has come!
That stranger they were baiting was Odysseus.
Telémakhos knew it days ago—   30
cool head, never to give his father away,
till he paid off those swollen dogs!"

The lady in her heart's joy now sprang up
with sudden dazzling tears, and hugged the old one,
crying out: 35

                        "But try to make it clear!
If he came home in secret, as you say,
could he engage them singlehanded? How?
They were all down there, still in the same crowd."

To this Eurýkleia said: 40

                            "I did not see it,
I knew nothing; only I heard the groans
of men dying. We sat still in the inner rooms
holding our breath, and marvelling, shut in,
until Telémakhos came to the door and called me—   45
your own dear son, sent this time by his father!
So I went out, and found Odysseus
erect, with dead men littering the floor
this way and that. If you had only seen him!

It would have made your heart glow hot!—a lion   50
splashed with mire and blood.

                                       But now the cold

corpses are all gathered at the gate,
and he has cleansed his hall with fire and brimstone,
a great blaze. Then he sent me here to you.   55
Come with me: you may both embark this time
for happiness together, after pain,
after long years. Here is your prayer, your passion,
granted: your own lord lives, he is at home,
he found you safe, he found his son. The suitors   60
abused his house, but he has brought them down."

The attentive lady said:

                                       "Do not lose yourself

in this rejoicing: wait: you know
how splendid that return would be for us,   65
how dear to me, dear to his son and mine;
but no, it is not possible, your notion
must be wrong.

                            Some god has killed the suitors,

a god, sick of their arrogance and brutal   70
malice—for they honored no one living,
good or bad, who ever came their way.
Blind young fools, they've tasted death for it.
But the true person of Odysseus?
He lost his home, he died far from Akhaia."   75

The old nurse sighed:

                          "How queer, the way you talk!

Here he is, large as life, by his own fire,
and you deny he ever will get home!
Child, you always were mistrustful!   80
But there is one sure mark that I can tell you:
that scar left by the boar's tusk long ago.
I recognized it when I bathed his feet
and would have told you, but he stopped my mouth,
forbade me, in his craftiness.   85

                                  Come down,

I stake my life on it, he's here!
Let me die in agony if I lie!"

                              Penélopê said:

"Nurse dear, though you have your wits about you,   90
still it is hard not to be taken in
by the immortals. Let us join my son, though,

and see the dead and that strange one who killed them."
She turned then to descend the stair, her heart
in tumult. Had she better keep her distance   95
and question him, her husband? Should she run
up to him, take his hands, kiss him now?
Crossing the door sill she sat down at once
in firelight, against the nearest wall,
across the room from the lord Odysseus.   100
                                        There

leaning against a pillar, sat the man
and never lifted up his eyes, but only waited
for what his wife would say when she had seen him.
And she, for a long time, sat deathly still   105
in wonderment—for sometimes as she gazed
she found him—yes, clearly—like her husband,
but sometimes blood and rags were all she saw.
Telémakhos' voice came to her ears:
                                   "Mother, 110

cruel mother, do you feel nothing,
drawing yourself apart this way from Father?
Will you not sit with him and talk and question him?
What other woman could remain so cold?
Who shuns her lord, and he come back to her   115
from wars and wandering, after twenty years?
Your heart is hard as flint and never changes!"

Penélopê answered:

                            "I am stunned, child.
I cannot speak to him. I cannot question him.   120
I cannot keep my eyes upon his face.
If really he is Odysseus, truly home,
beyond all doubt we two shall know each other
better than you or anyone. There are
secret signs we know, we two."   125

                                   A smile
came now to the lips of the patient hero, Odysseus,
who turned to Telémakhos and said:

"Peace: let your mother test me at her leisure.
Before long she will see and know me best.   130
These tatters, dirt—all that I'm caked with now—
make her look hard at me and doubt me still.
As to this massacre, we must see the end.
Whoever kills one citizen, you know,
and has no force of armed men at his back,   135
had better take himself abroad by night

and leave his kin. Well, we cut down the flower of Ithaka,
the mainstay of the town. Consider that."

Telémakhos replied respectfully:

                         "Dear Father, 140

enough that you yourself study the danger,
foresighted in combat as you are,
they say you have no rival.

                             We three stand

ready to follow you and fight. I say   145
for what our strength avails, we have the courage."

And the great tactician, Odysseus, answered:

                                 "Good.

Here is our best maneuver, as I see it:
bathe, you three, and put fresh clothing on,   150
order the women to adorn themselves,
and let our admirable harper choose a tune
for dancing, some lighthearted air, and strum it.
Anyone going by, or any neighbor,
will think it is a wedding feast he hears.   155
These deaths must not be cried about the town
till we can slip away to our own woods. We'll see
what weapon, then, Zeus puts into our hands."

They listened attentively, and did his bidding,
bathed and dressed afresh; and all the maids   160
adorned themselves. Then Phêmios the harper
took his polished shell and plucked the strings,
moving the company to desire
for singing, for the sway and beat of dancing,
until they made the manor hall resound   165
with gaiety of men and grace of women.
Anyone passing on the road would say:

"Married at last, I see—the queen so many courted.
Sly, cattish wife! She would not keep—not she!—
the lord's estate until he came."   170

                             So travellers'

thoughts might run—but no one guessed the truth.
Greathearted Odysseus, home at last,
was being bathed now by Eurýnomê
and rubbed with golden oil, and clothed again   175
in a fresh tunic and a cloak. Athena
lent him beauty, head to foot. She made him
taller, and massive, too, with crisping hair

in curls like petals of wild hyacinth
but all red-golden. Think of gold infused   180
on silver by a craftsman, whose fine art
Hephaistos taught him, or Athena: one
whose work moves to delight: just so she lavished
beauty over Odysseus' head and shoulders.
He sat then in the same chair by the pillar,   185
facing his silent wife, and said:

                                                    "Strange woman,

the immortals of Olympos made you hard,
harder than any. Who else in the world
would keep aloof as you do from her husband   190
if he returned to her from years of trouble,
cast on his own land in the twentieth year?

Nurse, make up a bed for me to sleep on.
Her heart is iron in her breast."

                                                      Penélopê 195

spoke to Odysseus now. She said:

                                                    "Strange man,

if man you are . . . This is no pride on my part
nor scorn for you—not even wonder, merely.
I know so well how you—how he—appeared   200
boarding the ship for Troy. But all the same . . .

Make up his bed for him, Eurýkleia.
Place it outside the bedchamber my lord
built with his own hands. Pile the big bed
with fleeces, rugs, and sheets of purest linen."   205

With this she tried him to the breaking point,
and he turned on her in a flash raging:

"Woman, by heaven you've stung me now!
Who dared to move my bed?
No builder had the skill for that—unless   210
a god came down to turn the trick. No mortal
in his best days could budge it with a crowbar.
There is our pact and pledge, our secret sign,
built into that bed—my handiwork
and no one else's!   215
                                     An old trunk of olive

grew like a pillar on the building plot,
and I laid out our bedroom round that tree,
lined up the stone walls, built the walls and roof,
gave it a doorway and smooth-fitting doors.   220

Then I lopped off the silvery leaves and branches,
hewed and shaped that stump from the roots up
into a bedpost, drilled it, let it serve
as model for the rest. I planed them all,
inlaid them all with silver, gold and ivory,   225
and stretched a bed between—a pliant web
of oxhide thongs dyed crimson.

                                     There's our sign!
I know no more. Could someone's else's hand
have sawn that trunk and dragged the frame away?"   230

Their secret! as she heard it told, her knees
grew tremulous and weak, her heart failed her.
With eyes brimming tears she ran to him,
throwing her arms around his neck, and kissed him,
murmuring: 235

                         "Do not rage at me, Odysseus!
No one ever matched your caution! Think
what difficulty the gods gave: they denied us
life together in our prime and flowering years,
kept us from crossing into age together.   240
Forgive me, don't be angry. I could not
welcome you with love on sight! I armed myself
long ago against the frauds of men,
impostors who might come—and all those many
whose underhanded ways bring evil on!   245
Helen of Argos, daughter of Zeus and Leda,
would she have joined the stranger, lain with him,
if she had known her destiny? known the Akhaians
in arms would bring her back to her own country?
Surely a goddess moved her to adultery,   250
her blood unchilled by war and evil coming,
the years, the desolation; ours, too.
But here and now, what sign could be so clear
as this of our own bed?
No other man has ever laid eyes on it—   255
only my own slave, Aktoris, that my father
sent with me as a gift—she kept our door.
You make my stiff heart know that I am yours."

Now from his breast into his eyes the ache
of longing mounted, and he wept at last,   260
his dear wife, clear and faithful, in his arms,
longed for
        as the sunwarmed earth is longed for by a swimmer
spent in rough water where his ship went down

under Poseidon's blows, gale winds and tons of sea.   265
Few men can keep alive through a big surf
to crawl, clotted with brine, on kindly beaches
in joy, in joy, knowing the abyss behind:
and so she too rejoiced, her gaze upon her husband,
her white arms round him pressed as though forever.   270
The rose Dawn might have found them weeping still
had not grey-eyed Athena slowed the night
when night was most profound, and held the Dawn
under the Ocean of the East. That glossy team,
Firebright and Daybright, the Dawn's horses   275
that draw her heavenward for men—Athena
stayed their harnessing.

                                        Then said Odysseus:

"My dear, we have not won through to the end.
One trial—I do not know how long—is left for me   280
to see fulfilled. Teirêsias' ghost forewarned me
the night I stood upon the shore of Death, asking
about my friends' homecoming and my own.

But now the hour grows late, it is bed time,
rest will be sweet for us; let us lie down."   285

To this Penélopê replied:

                                              "That bed,

that rest is yours whenever desire moves you,
now the kind powers have brought you home at last.
But as your thought has dwelt upon it, tell me: 290
what is the trial you face? I must know soon;
what does it matter if I learn tonight?"

The teller of many stories said:

                                        "My strange one,
must you again, and even now,   295
urge me to talk? Here is a plodding tale;
no charm in it, no relish in the telling.
Teirêsias told me I must take an oar
and trudge the mainland, going from town to town,
until I discover men who have never known   300
the salt blue sea, nor flavor of salt meat—
strangers to painted prows, to watercraft
and oars like wings, dipping across the water.
The moment of revelation he foretold
was this, for you may share the prophecy: 305
some traveller falling in with me will say:
'A winnowing fan, that on your shoulder, sir?'

There I must plant my oar, on the very spot,
with burnt offerings to Poseidon of the Waters:
a ram, a bull, a great buck boar. Thereafter   310
when I come home again, I am to slay
full hekatombs to the gods who own broad heaven,
one by one.

                                            Then death will drift upon me
from seaward, mild as air, mild as your hand,   315
in my well-tended weariness of age,
contented folk around me on our island.
He said all this must come."

                                                       Penélopê said: 320

"If by the gods' grace age at least is kind,
we have that promise—trials will end in peace."

So he confided in her, and she answered.
Meanwhile Eurýnomê and the nurse together
laid soft coverlets on the master's bed,
working in haste by torchlight. Eurýkleia   325
retired to her quarters for the night,
and then Eurýnomê, as maid-in-waiting,
lighted her lord and lady to their chamber
with bright brands.

                              She vanished.   330
                              So they came
into that bed so steadfast, loved of old,
opening glad arms to one another.
Telémakhos by now had hushed the dancing,
hushed the women. In the darkened hall   335
he and the cowherd and the swineherd slept.

The royal pair mingled in love again
and afterward lay revelling in stories:
hers of the siege her beauty stood at home
from arrogant suitors, crowding on her sight,   340
and how they fed their courtship on his cattle,
oxen and fat sheep, and drank up rivers
of wine out of the vats.

                              Odysseus told
of what hard blows he had dealt out to others   345
and of what blows he had taken—all that story.
She could not close her eyes till all was told.

His raid on the Kikonês, first of all,
then how he visited the Lotos Eaters,
and what the Kyklops did, and how those shipmates,   350

pitilessly devoured, were avenged.
Then of his touching Aiolos's isle
and how that king refitted him for sailing
to Ithaka; all vain: gales blew him back
groaning over the fishcold sea. Then how   355
he reached the Laistrygonians' distant bay
and how they smashed his ships and his companions.
Kirkê, then: of her deceits and magic,
then of his voyage to the wide underworld
of dark, the house of Death, and questioning   360
Teirêsias, Theban spirit.

                                 Dead companions,

many, he saw there, and his mother, too.
Of this he told his wife, and told how later
he heard the choir of maddening Seirênês,   365
coasted the Wandering Rocks, Kharybdis' pool
and the fiend Skylla who takes toll of men.
Then how his shipmates killed Lord Hêlios' cattle
and how Zeus thundering in towering heaven
split their fast ship with his fuming bolt,   370
so all hands perished.

                              He alone survived,

cast away on Kalypso's isle, Ogýgia.
He told, then, how that nymph detained him there
in her smooth caves, craving him for her husband,   375
and how in her devoted lust she swore
he should not die nor grow old, all his days,
but he held out against her.

                                 Last of all

what sea-toil brought him to the Phaiákians;   380
their welcome; how they took him to their hearts
and gave him passage to his own dear island
with gifts of garments, gold and bronze . . .

                             Remembering,

he drowsed over the story's end. Sweet sleep   385
relaxed his limbs and his care-burdened breast.

Other affairs were in Athena's keeping.
Waiting until Odysseus had his pleasure
of love and sleep, the grey-eyed one bestirred
the fresh Dawn from her bed of paling Ocean   390
to bring up daylight to her golden chair,
and from his fleecy bed Odysseus
arose. He said to Penélopê:

                                 "My lady,

what ordeals have we not endured! Here, waiting   395

you had your grief, while my return dragged out—
my hard adventures, pitting myself against
the gods' will, and Zeus, who pinned me down
far from home. But now our life resumes:
we've come together to our longed-for bed.   400
Take care of what is left me in our house;
as to the flocks that pack of wolves laid waste
they'll be replenished: scores I'll get on raids
and other scores our island friends will give me
till all the folds are full again.   405
                                                        This day

I'm off up country to the orchards. I must see
my noble father, for he missed me sorely.
And here is my command for you—a strict one,
though you may need none, clever as you are.   410
Word will get about as the sun goes higher
of how I killed those lads. Go to your rooms
on the upper floor, and take your women. Stay there
with never a glance outside or a word to anyone."

Fitting cuirass and swordbelt to his shoulders,   415
he woke his herdsmen, woke Telémakhos,
ordering all in arms. They dressed quickly,
and all in war gear sallied from the gate,
led by Odysseus.
                                        Now it was broad day 420

but these three men Athena hid in darkness,
going before them swiftly from the town.

Questions

Rereading and Independent Analysis

1. Mark the points in the dialogue between Odysseus and Penelope where you notice changes as the two reestablish their marriage after 20 years apart. How did the poet move the action ahead from one point to another in this process?

2. List the adjectives, descriptive comparisons, and other language that you think would be helpful in remembering this story as it is told. Then classify the list according to the aids to memory that the headnote describes—formulas, repetitions, and rhythm, for instance.

Suggested Discussion and Group Activities

1. What is Penelope's first response to Odysseus' return? Why does Athena transform him? How does Odysseus' transformed appearance affect Penelope's responses? Can you compare this transformation and its results to a sudden change in a person's looks or actions that you have noticed?

2. What is the significance of Odysseus' "command" to Penelope the morning after their reunion? In view of her adventures in his absence, how does this command reveal his character? What generalizations about the nature of "homecomings" can you draw from this incident and the couple's other conversations?

Writing Suggestions

Response

Try writing the dialogue for a modern scene in a play or film in which two people you have known who were once close to each other are reunited after ten or more years apart. First establish the characters' personalities by writing short sketches of what they were like in the past. Then visualize the setting for the reunion conversation before you write their words.

Analysis

Write an essay in which you show how the characters' story telling in this section of the *Odyssey* completes the adventure. What is the purpose for each of the stories told? In what order are these purposes met? What is the significance of placing them in this order? Your essay should introduce other readers of this selection to the ways that story telling helps bring people together.

Finding a Purpose

Write the story of an adventure you have had, using some of the devices common in epic poems. Begin in the middle of the action before explaining how you got there. Attribute some of the causes of the action to "gods" or forces beyond human control. Use a repetitive list of descriptive words and phrases to describe your characters and the setting of the story. Tell the story in language that will emphasize your heroism and the great consequences of this action. You are writing an "imitation" of an epic; you need not be precise about taking devices from Homer, but try to capture the spirit and form of the epic in telling a story for your community of friends.

From London—September 22, 1940
Edward R. Murrow

Edward R. Murrow (1908–1965) had a long, prominent career as a broadcast journalist. His career and involvement in public life began early, when he was president of the National Student Federation of America and traveled to England. He became well known during the height of radio journalism, when radio reports were the only way to receive immediate information from Europe about World War II and its aftermath. In 1938 he reported from

Vienna about Hitler's startling invasion of Austria. That first broadcast from
Vienna was also the first time that a multiple hookup—from Vienna, Paris,
Rome, and New York—delivered news to a radio audience, creating a sense
of sharing important but distant events.

This immediacy was the outstanding characteristic of Murrow's reports from London, a city he loved, during its nightly bombings. He began
broadcasting there in 1938, soon creating a trademark with his opening
words: "This is London." Each of his reports created a standard that American journalists who find themselves in the middle of critical events still aim
for—to tell what is happening now, how it is meaningful to America, and
how typical people feel about it.

Murrow, like Benjamin Franklin in earlier examples of American
printed journalism, helped create the importance of "public opinion" and
of involved citizens as the two major constituents of American political
action and decision making. As you read, keep in mind that in his time, radio
was the only way to make distant events vivid to the public at home. Try
to imagine yourself listening with your family or friends to a report of similar
importance in your world.

September 13, 1940

This is London at 3:30 in the morning. This has been what might be called   1
a "routine night"—air-raid alarm at about nine o'clock and intermittent
bombing ever since. I had the impression that more high explosives and
few incendiaries have been used tonight. Only two small fires can be seen
on the horizon. Again the Germans have been sending their bombers in
singly or in pairs. The antiaircraft barrage has been fierce but sometimes
there have been periods of twenty minutes when London has been silent.
Then the big red buses would start up and move on till the guns started
working again. That silence is almost hard to bear. One becomes accustomed to rattling windows and the distant sound of bombs, and then there
comes a silence that can be felt. You know the sound will return. You wait,
and then it starts again. That waiting is bad. It gives you a chance to
imagine things. I have been walking tonight—there is a full moon, and the
dirty-gray buildings appear white. The stars, the empty windows, are
hidden. It's a beautiful and lonesome city where men and women and
children are trying to snatch a few hours' sleep underground.

In the fashionable residential districts I could read the TO LET signs   2
on the front of big houses in the light of the bright moon. Those houses
have big basements underneath—good shelters—but they're not being
used. Many people think they should be.

The scale of this air war is so great that the reporting of it is not easy.   3
Often we spend hours traveling about this sprawling city, viewing damage, talking with people and occasionally listening to the bombs come
down, and then more hours wondering what you'd like to hear about these
people who are citizens of no mean city. We've told you about the bombs,
the fires, the smashed houses and the courage of the people. We've read
you the communiqués and tried to give you an honest estimate of the

wounds inflicted upon this, the best bombing target in the world. But the business of living and working in this city is very personal—the little incidents, the things the mind retains, are in themselves unimportant, but they somehow weld together to form the hard core of memories that will remain when the last all clear has sounded. That's why I want to talk for just three or four minutes about the things we haven't talked about before; for many of these impressions it is necessary to reach back through only one long week. There was a rainbow bending over the battered and smoking East End of London just when the all clear sounded one afternoon. One night I stood in front of a smashed grocery store and heard a dripping inside. It was the only sound in all London. Two cans of peaches had been drilled clean through by flying glass, and the juice was dripping down onto the floor.

Talking from a studio with a few bodies lying about on the floor, 4 sleeping on mattresses, still produces a strange feeling, but we'll probably get used to that. Today I went to buy a hat—my favorite shop had gone, blown to bits. The windows of my shoe store were blown out. I decided to have a haircut; the windows of the barbershop were gone, but the Italian barber was still doing business. Someday, he said, we smile again, but the food it doesn't taste so good since being bombed. I went on to another shop to buy flashlight batteries. I bought three. The clerk said, "You needn't buy so many. We'll have enough for the whole winter." But I said, "What if you aren't here?" There were buildings down in that street, and he replied, "Of course we'll be here. We've been in business here for a hundred and fifty years."

September 18, 1940

There are no words to describe the thing that is happening. Today I talked 5 with eight American correspondents in London. Six of them had been forced to move. All had stories of bombs, and all agreed that they were unable to convey through print or the spoken word an accurate impression of what's happening in London these days and nights.

I may tell you that Bond Street has been bombed, that a shop selling 6 handkerchiefs at $40 the dozen has been wrecked, that these words were written on a table of good English oak which sheltered me three times as bombs tore down in the vicinity. But you can have little understanding of the life in London these days—the courage of the people, the flash and roar of the guns rolling down streets where much of the history of the English-speaking world has been made, the stench of air-raid shelters in the poor districts. These things must be experienced to be understood.

September 22, 1940

I'm standing again tonight on a rooftop looking out over London, feeling 7 rather large and lonesome. In the course of the last fifteen or twenty

minutes there's been considerable action up there, but at the moment
there's an ominous silence hanging over London. But at the same time a
silence that has a great deal of dignity. Just straightaway in front of me the
searchlights are working. I can see one or two bursts of antiaircraft fire far
in the distance. Just on the roof across the way I can see a man wearing
a tin hat, a pair of powerful night glasses to his eyes, scanning the sky.
Again, looking in the opposite direction, there is a building with two
windows gone. Out of one window there waves something that looks like
a white bed sheet, a window curtain swinging free in this night breeze.
It looks as though it were being shaken by a ghost. There are a great many
ghosts around these buildings in London. The searchlights straightaway,
miles in front of me, are still scratching that sky. There's a three-quarter
moon riding high. There was one burst of shellfire almost straight in the
Little Dipper.

Down below in the streets I can see just that red and green wink of 8
the traffic lights; one lone taxicab moving slowly down the street. Not a
sound to be heard. As I look out across the miles and miles of rooftops and
chimney pots, some of those dirty-gray fronts of the buildings look almost
snow-white in this moonlight here tonight. And the rooftop spotter across
the way swings around, looks over in the direction of the searchlights,
drops his glasses and just stands there. There are hundreds and hundreds
of men like that standing on rooftops in London tonight watching for fire
bombs, waiting to see what comes out of this steel-blue sky. The searchlights now reach up very, very faintly on three sides of me. There is a flash
of a gun in the distance but too far away to be heard.

Questions

Rereading and Independent Analysis

1. Underline each of the personal pronouns in this piece. Then write
a sentence or two explaining how they link Murrow to his listeners. How
do they contribute to the feeling of being with Murrow at the time?

2. Make a list of the specific, concrete details of physical experience
that Murrow mentions. Which of these details create pictures in your mind
of things you have heard and seen yourself?

Discussion and Group Activities

1. Bring in examples of important news stories in your local newspaper. In groups, compare Murrow's report and its techniques to these
examples of writing about major local events. Find specific differences and
similarities—for instance, in the use of pronouns. Why do you think your
examples of contemporary reporting are less personal? Do they share
Murrow's purpose or do they fulfill a different need?

2. Would you say that Murrow's reporting is objective or subjective?
How does it balance "facts" against "opinions"? Is it a reporter's job to
include opinion in such a report? What is lost and gained by including

opinion? How does this report differ from obvious political propaganda? What do you think its effect on its listeners was?

Writing Suggestions

Response

Make notes about Murrow's report, jotting down your reactions as you read. How do you connect this report with other news you have seen, heard, and read about combat? What feelings do you experience and how do you relate them to your more peaceful daily life?

Analysis

Write an essay for students of correspondence reporting, showing how Murrow made himself a bridge between his fellow Americans and the people of London and how he used details to make those safe at home feel involved. How did he persuade radio listeners to agree with his judgment about events without relying on techniques of propaganda?

Finding a Purpose

Choose an event you have witnessed and want to tell others about so that they will feel as you did when it happened. Write a report of it that would be suitable for a broadcast, including specific details from your observation and the actual results of the event, so that your listeners can experience the feelings you had at the time. Read your report aloud to the class or in a group so they can tell you whether you vividly recreated the event.

 # No Name Woman
Maxine Hong Kingston

When we read "the story" of a person whose family and cultural roots have been transplanted, we are almost always reading two stories. One is like the surface story of "No Name Woman" told here; the other is the unstated story of the teller, who is making sense of a dislocated and renewed life. Maxine Hong Kingston (b. 1940) has written two books with such dual tellings, *The Woman Warrior* and *China Men*. In them, she has taught us to see a particularly Chinese perspective on relocations from the Orient to the West. She has explained her family's original culture, while reminding us that the United States has also been partially constructed by Chinese, as it has been by people from many other "different" patterns of life. Her purpose in these books is to help us unite opposed cultures and states of mind by understanding her consciousness of separated, but universal, meanings.

"No Name Woman" contains three surface stories: the story of the sister who killed herself, the story of the mother trying to explain Chinese ways to her daughter, and the story of the daughter's struggle to understand. Within the three stories are events whose "reality" shifts from country to country and time to time. But this selection also tells one unified account of individual women making sense of events they have not caused and cannot control. Reading this account carefully will help you understand a family story's power. Such tales explain why we all react to events with different responses, determining their significance for ourselves and using perspectives that arise from our own experiences. Your reading will also raise the questions of why Kingston writes these stories and how they help her make sense of the two worlds in which she inevitably lives.

"You must not tell anyone," my mother said, "what I am about to tell you. 1 In China your father had a sister who killed herself. She jumped into the family well. We say that your father has all brothers because it is as if she had never been born.

"In 1924 just a few days after our village celebrated seventeen hurry- 2 up weddings—to make sure that every young man who went 'out on the road' would responsibly come home—your father and his brothers and your grandfather and his brothers and your aunt's new husband sailed for America, the Gold Mountain. It was your grandfather's last trip. Those lucky enough to get contracts waved good-bye from the decks. They fed and guarded the stowaways and helped them off in Cuba, New York, Bali, Hawaii. 'We'll meet in California next year,' they said. All of them sent money home.

"I remember looking at your aunt one day when she and I were 3 dressing; I had not noticed before that she had such a protruding melon of a stomach. But I did not think, 'She's pregnant,' until she began to look like other pregnant women, her shirt pulling and the white tops of her black pants showing. She could not have been pregnant, you see, because her husband had been gone for years. No one said anything. We did not discuss it. In early summer she was ready to have the child, long after the time when it could have been possible.

"The village had also been counting. On the night the baby was to 4 be born the villagers raided our house. Some were crying. Like a great saw, teeth strung with lights, files of people walked zigzag across our land, tearing the rice. Their lanterns doubled in the disturbed black water, which drained away through the broken bunds. As the villagers closed in, we could see that some of them, probably men and women we knew well, wore white masks. The people with long hair hung it over their faces. Women with short hair made it stand up on end. Some had tied white bands around their foreheads, arms, and legs.

"At first they threw mud and rocks at the house. Then they threw 5 eggs and began slaughtering our stock. We could hear the animals scream their deaths—the roosters, the pigs, a last great roar from the ox. Familiar wild heads flared in our night windows; the villagers encircled us. Some of the faces stopped to peer at us, their eyes rushing like searchlights. The hands flattened against the panes, framed heads, and left red prints.

"The villagers broke in the front and the back doors at the same time, 6
even though we had not locked the doors against them. Their knives
dripped with the blood of our animals. They smeared blood on the doors
and walls. One woman swung a chicken, whose throat she had slit, splat-
tering blood in red arcs about her. We stood together in the middle of our
house, in the family hall with the pictures and tables of the ancestors
around us, and looked straight ahead.

"At that time the house had only two wings. When the men came 7
back, we would build two more to enclose our courtyard and a third one
to begin a second courtyard. The villagers pushed through both wings,
even your grandparents' rooms, to find your aunt's, which was also mine
until the men returned. From this room a new wing for one of the younger
families would grow. They ripped up her clothes and shoes and broke her
combs, grinding them underfoot. They tore her work from the loom. They
scattered the cooking fire and rolled the new weaving in it. We could hear
them in the kitchen breaking our bowls and banging the pots. They overturned the great waist-high earthenware jugs; duck eggs, pickled fruits,
vegetables burst out and mixed in acrid torrents. The old woman from the
next field swept a broom through the air and loosed the spirits-of-the-
broom over our heads. 'Pig.' 'Ghost.' 'Pig,' they sobbed and scolded while
they ruined our house.

"When they left, they took sugar and oranges to bless themselves. 8
They cut pieces from the dead animals. Some of them took bowls that
were not broken and clothes that were not torn. Afterward we swept up
the rice and sewed it back up into sacks. But the smells from the spilled
preserves lasted. Your aunt gave birth in the pigsty that night. The next
morning when I went for the water, I found her and the baby plugging
up the family well.

"Don't let your father know that I told you. He denies her. Now that 9
you have started to menstruate, what happened to her could happen to
you. Don't humiliate us. You wouldn't like to be forgotten as if you had
never been born. The villagers are watchful."

Whenever she had to warn us about life, my mother told stories that 10
ran like this one, a story to grow up on. She tested our strength to establish
realities. Those in the emigrant generations who could not reassert brute
survival died young and far from home. Those of us in the first American
generations have had to figure out how the invisible world the emigrants
built around our childhoods fit in solid America.

The emigrants confused the gods by diverting their curses, mislead- 11
ing them with crooked streets and false names. They must try to confuse
their offspring as well, who, I suppose, threaten them in similar ways—
always trying to get things straight, always trying to name the unspeakable. The Chinese I know hide their names; sojourners take new names
when their lives change and guard their real names with silence.

Chinese-Americans, when you try to understand what things in you 12
are Chinese, how do you separate what is peculiar to childhood, to poverty, insanities, one family, your mother who marked your growing with

stories, from what is Chinese? What is Chinese tradition and what is the movies?

If I want to learn what clothes my aunt wore, whether flashy or 13
ordinary, I would have to begin, "Remember Father's drowned-in-the-well sister?" I cannot ask that. My mother has told me once and for all the useful parts. She will add nothing unless powered by Necessity, a river-bank that guides her life. She plants vegetable gardens rather than lawns; she carries the odd-shaped tomatoes home from the fields and eats food left for the gods.

Whenever we did frivolous things, we used up energy; we flew high 14
kites. We children came up off the ground over the melting cones our parents brought home from work and the American movie on New Year's Day—*Oh, You Beautiful Doll* with Betty Grable one year, and *She Wore a Yellow Ribbon* with John Wayne another year. After the one carnival ride each, we paid in guilt; our tired father counted his change on the dark walk home.

Adultery is extravagance. Could people who hatch their own chicks 15
and eat the embryos and the heads for delicacies and boil the feet in vinegar for party food, leaving only the gravel, eating even the gizzard lining—could such people engender a prodigal aunt? To be a woman, to have a daughter in starvation time was a waste enough. My aunt could not have been the lone romantic who gave up everything for sex. Women in the old China did not choose. Some man had commanded her to lie with him and be his secret evil. I wonder whether he masked himself when he joined the raid on her family.

Perhaps she encountered him in the fields or on the mountain where 16
the daughters-in-law collected fuel. Or perhaps he first noticed her in the marketplace. He was not a stranger because the village housed no stran-gers. She had to have dealings with him other than sex. Perhaps he worked an adjoining field, or he sold her the cloth for the dress she sewed and wore. His demand must have surprised, then terrified her. She obeyed him; she always did as she was told.

When the family found a young man in the next village to be her 17
husband, she stood tractably beside the best rooster, his proxy, and pro-mised before they met that she would be his forever. She was lucky that he was her age and she would be the first wife, an advantage secure now. The night she first saw him, he had sex with her. Then he left for America. She had almost forgotten what he looked like. When she tried to envision him, she only saw the black and white face in the group photograph the men had had taken before leaving.

The other man was not, after all, much different from her husband. 18
They both gave orders: she followed. "If you tell your family, I'll beat you. I'll kill you. Be here again next week." No one talked sex, ever. And she might have separated the rapes from the rest of living if only she did not have to buy her oil from him or gather wood in the same forest. I want her fear to have lasted just as long as rape lasted so that the fear could have been contained. No drawnout fear. But women at sex hazarded birth and

hence lifetimes. The fear did not stop but permeated everywhere. She told the man, "I think I'm pregnant." He organized the raid against her.

On nights when my mother and father talked about their life back 19 home, sometimes they mentioned an "outcast table" whose business they still seemed to be settling, their voices tight. In a commensal tradition, where food is precious, the powerful older people made wrongdoers eat alone. Instead of letting them start separate new lives like the Japanese, who could become samurais and geishas, the Chinese family, faces averted but eyes glowering sideways, hung on to the offenders and fed them leftovers. My aunt must have lived in the same house as my parents and eaten at an outcast table. My mother spoke about the raid as if she had seen it, when she and my aunt, a daughter-in-law to a different household, should not have been living together at all. Daughters-in-law lived with their husbands' parents, not their own; a synonym for marriage in Chinese is "taking a daughter-in-law." Her husband's parents could have sold her, mortgaged her, stoned her. But they had sent her back to her own mother and father, a mysterious act hinting at disgraces not told me. Perhaps they had thrown her out to deflect the avengers.

She was the only daughter; her four brothers went with her father, 20 husband, and uncles "out on the road" and for some years became western men. When the goods were divided among the family, three of the brothers took land, and the youngest, my father, chose an education. After my grandparents gave their daughter away to her husband's family, they had dispensed all the adventure and all the property. They expected her alone to keep the traditional ways, which her brothers, now among the barbarians, could fumble without detection. The heavy, deep-rooted women were to maintain the past against the flood, safe for returning. But the rare urge west had fixed upon our family, and so my aunt crossed boundaries not delineated in space.

The work of preservation demands that the feelings playing about in 21 one's guts not be turned into action. Just watch their passing like cherry blossoms. But perhaps my aunt, my forerunner, caught in a slow life, let dreams grow and fade and after some months or years went toward what persisted. Fear at the enormities of the forbidden kept her desires delicate, wire and bone. She looked at a man because she liked the way the hair was tucked behind his ears, or she liked the question-mark line of a long torso curving at the shoulder and straight at the hip. For warm eyes or a soft voice or a slow walk—that's all—a few hairs, a line, a brightness, a sound, a pace, she gave up family. She offered us up for a charm that vanished with tiredness, a pigtail that didn't toss when the wind died. Why, the wrong lighting could erase the dearest thing about him.

It could very well have been, however, that my aunt did not take 22 subtle enjoyment of her friend, but, a wild woman, kept rollicking company. Imagining her free with sex doesn't fit, though. I don't know any women like that, or men either. Unless I see her life branching into mine, she gives me no ancestral help.

To sustain her being in love, she often worked at herself in the 23 mirror, guessing at the colors and shapes that would interest him, changing them frequently in order to hit on the right combination. She wanted him to look back.

On a farm near the sea, a woman who tended her appearance reaped 24 a reputation for eccentricity. All the married women blunt-cut their hair in flaps about their ears or pulled it back in tight buns. No nonsense. Neither style blew easily into heart-catching tangles. And at their weddings they displayed themselves in their long hair for the last time. "It brushed the backs of my knees," my mother tells me. "It was braided, and even so, it brushed the backs of my knees."

At the mirror my aunt combed individuality into her bob. A bun 25 could have been contrived to escape into black streamers blowing in the wind or in quiet wisps about her face, but only the older women in our picture album wear buns. She brushed her hair back from her forehead, tucking the flaps behind her ears. She looped a piece of thread, knotted into a circle between her index fingers and thumbs, and ran the double strand across her forehead. When she closed her fingers as if she were making a pair of shadow geese bite, the string twisted together catching the little hairs. Then she pulled the thread away from her skin, ripping the hairs out neatly, her eyes watering from the needles of pain. Opening her fingers, she cleaned the thread, then rolled it along her hairline and the tops of her eyebrows. My mother did the same to me and my sisters and herself. I used to believe that the expression "caught by the short hairs" meant a captive held with a depilatory string. It especially hurt at the temples, but my mother said we were lucky we didn't have to have our feet bound when we were seven. Sisters used to sit on their beds and cry together, she said, as their mothers or their slave removed the bandages for a few minutes each night and let the blood gush back into their veins. I hope that the man my aunt loved appreciated a smooth brow, that he wasn't just a tits-and-ass man.

Once my aunt found a freckle on her chin, at a spot that the almanac 26 said predestined her for unhappiness. She dug it out with a hot needle and washed the wound with peroxide.

More attention to her looks than these pullings of hairs and pickings 27 at spots would have caused gossip among the villagers. They owned work clothes and good clothes, and they wore good clothes for feasting the new seasons. But since a woman combing her hair hexes beginnings, my aunt rarely found an occasion to look her best. Women looked like great sea snails—the corded wood, babies, and laundry they carried were the whorls on their backs. The Chinese did not admire a bent back; goddesses and warriors stood straight. Still there must have been a marvelous freeing of beauty when a worker laid down her burden and stretched and arched.

Such commonplace loveliness, however, was not enough for my aunt. 28 She dreamed of a lover for the fifteen days of New Year's, the time for families to exchange visits, money, and food. She plied her secret comb. And sure enough she cursed the year, the family, the village, and herself.

Even as her hair lured her imminent lover, many other men looked 29
at her. Uncles, cousins, nephews, brothers would have looked, too, had
they been home between journeys. Perhaps they had already been restraining their curiosity, and they left, fearful that their glances, like a field
of nesting birds, might be startled and caught. Poverty hurt, and that was
their first reason for leaving. But another, final reason for leaving the
crowded house was the never-said.

She may have been unusually beloved, the precious only daughter, 30
spoiled and mirror gazing because of the affection the family lavished on
her. When her husband left, they welcomed the chance to take her back
from the in-laws; she could live like the little daughter for just a while
longer. There are stories that my grandfather was different from other
people, "crazy ever since the little Jap bayoneted him in the head." He
used to put his naked penis on the dinner table, laughing. And one day he
brought home a baby girl, wrapped up inside his brown western-style
greatcoat. He had traded one of his sons, probably my father, the youngest,
for her. My grandmother made him trade back. When he finally got a
daughter of his own, he doted on her. They must have all loved her, except
perhaps my father, the only brother who never went back to China,
having once been traded for a girl.

Brothers and sisters, newly men and women, had to efface their 31
sexual color and present plain miens. Disturbing hair and eyes, a smile like
no other, threatened the ideal of five generations living under one roof.
To focus blurs, people shouted face to face and yelled from room to room.
The immigrants I know have loud voices, unmodulated to American tones
even after years away from the village where they called their friendships
out across the fields. I have not been able to stop my mother's screams in
public libraries or over telephones. Walking erect (knees straight, toes
pointed forward, not pigeon-toed, which is Chinese-feminine) and speaking in an inaudible voice, I have tried to turn myself American-feminine.
Chinese communication was loud, public. Only sick people had to whisper. But at the dinner table, where the family members came nearest one
another, no one could talk, not the outcasts nor any eaters. Every word
that falls from the mouth is a coin lost. Silently they gave and accepted
food with both hands. A preoccupied child who took his bowl with one
hand got a sideways glare. A complete moment of total attention is due
everyone alike. Children and lovers have no singularity here, but my aunt
used a secret voice, a separate attentiveness.

She kept the man's name to herself throughout her labor and dying; 32
she did not accuse him that he be punished with her. To save her insemi-
nator's name she gave silent birth.

He may have been somebody in her own household, but intercourse 33
with a man outside the family would have been no less abhorrent. All the
village were kinsmen, and the titles shouted in loud country voices never
let kinship be forgotten. Any man within visiting distance would have
been neutralized as a lover—"brother," "younger brother," "older

brother"—one hundred and fifteen relationship titles. Parents researched birth charts probably not so much to assure good fortune as to circumvent incest in a population that has but one hundred surnames. Everybody has eight million relatives. How useless then sexual mannerisms, how dangerous.

As if it came from an atavism deeper than fear, I used to add "brother" silently to boys' names. It hexed the boys, who would or would not ask me to dance, and made them less scary and as familiar and deserving of benevolence as girls.

But, of course, I hexed myself also—no dates. I should have stood up, both arms waving, and shouted out across libraries, "Hey, you! Love me back." I had no idea, though, how to make attraction selective, how to control its direction and magnitude. If I made myself American-pretty so that the five or six Chinese boys in the class fell in love with me, everyone else—the Caucasian, Negro, and Japanese boys—would too. Sisterliness, dignified and honorable, made much more sense.

Attraction eludes control so stubbornly that whole societies designed to organize relationships among people cannot keep order, not even when they bind people to one another from childhood and raise them together. Among the very poor and the wealthy, brothers married their adopted sisters, like doves. Our family allowed some romance, paying adult brides' prices and providing dowries so that their sons and daughters could marry strangers. Marriage promises to turn strangers into friendly relatives—a nation of siblings.

In the village structure, spirits shimmered among the live creatures, balanced and held in equilibrium by time and land. But one human being flaring up into violence could open up a black hole, a maelstrom that pulled in the sky. The frightened villagers, who depended on one another to maintain the real, went to my aunt to show her a personal, physical representation of the break she had made in the "roundness." Misallying couples snapped off the future, which was to be embodied in true offspring. The villagers punished her for acting as if she could have a private life, secret and apart from them.

If my aunt had betrayed the family at a time of large grain yields and peace, when many boys were born, and wings were being built on many houses, perhaps she might have escaped such severe punishment. But the men—hungry, greedy, tired of planting in dry soil, cuckolded—had had to leave the village in order to send food-money home. There were ghost plagues, bandit plagues, wars with the Japanese, floods. My Chinese brother and sister had died of an unknown sickness. Adultery, perhaps only a mistake during good times, became a crime when the village needed food.

The round moon cakes and round doorways, the round tables of graduated size that fit one roundness inside another, round windows and rice bowls—these talismans had lost their power to warn this family of the law: a family must be whole, faithfully keeping the descent line by having sons to feed the old and the dead, who in turn look after the family. The villagers came to show my aunt and her lover-in-hiding a broken house. The villagers were speeding up the circling of events because she was too shortsighted to see that her infidelity had already harmed the village, that waves of consequences would return unpredictably, sometimes in disguise, as now, to hurt her. This roundness had to be made coin-sized so that she would see its circumference: punish her at the birth of her baby. Awaken her to the inexorable. People who refused fatalism because they could invent small resources insisted on culpability. Deny accidents and wrest fault from the stars.

After the villagers left, their lanterns now scattering in various directions toward home, the family broke their silence and cursed her. "Aiaa, we're going to die. Death is coming. Death is coming. Look what you've done. You've killed us. Ghost! Dead ghost! Ghost! You've never been born." She ran out into the fields, far enough from the house so that she could no longer hear their voices, and pressed herself against the earth, her own land no more. When she felt the birth coming, she thought that she had been hurt. Her body seized together. "They've hurt me too much," she thought. "This is gall, and it will kill me." With forehead and knees against the earth, her body convulsed and then relaxed. She turned on her back, lay on the ground. The black well of sky and stars went out and out and out forever; her body and her complexity seemed to disappear. She was one of the stars, a bright dot in blackness, without home, without a companion, in eternal cold and silence. An agoraphobia rose in her, speeding higher and higher, bigger and bigger; she would not be able to contain it; there would be no end to fear. [40]

Flayed, unprotected against space, she felt pain return, focusing her body. This pain chilled her—a cold, steady kind of surface pain. Inside, spasmodically, the other pain, the pain of the child, heated her. For hours she lay on the ground, alternately body and space. Sometimes a vision of normal comfort obliterated reality: she saw the family in the evening gambling at the dinner table, the young people massaging their elders' backs. She saw them congratulating one another, high joy on the mornings the rice shoots came up. When these pictures burst, the stars drew yet further apart. Black space opened. [41]

She got to her feet to fight better and remembered that old-fashioned women gave birth in their pigsties to fool the jealous, pain-dealing gods, who do not snatch piglets. Before the next spasms could stop her, she ran to the pigsty, each step a rushing out into emptiness. She climbed over the fence and knelt in the dirt. It was good to have a fence enclosing her, a tribal person alone. [42]

Laboring, this woman who had carried her child as a foreign growth that sickened her every day, expelled it at last. She reached down to touch the hot, wet, moving mass, surely smaller than anything human, and could feel that it was human after all—fingers, toes, nails, nose. She pulled it up on to her belly, and it lay curled there, butt in the air, feet precisely tucked [43] one under the other. She opened her loose shirt and buttoned the child inside. After resting, it squirmed and thrashed and she pushed it up to her breast. It turned its head this way and that until it found her nipple. There, it made little snuffling noises. She clenched her teeth at its preciousness, lovely as a young calf, a piglet, a little dog.

She may have gone to the pigsty as a last act of responsibility: she 44 would protect this child as she had protected its father. It would look after her soul, leaving supplies on her grave. But how would this tiny child without family find her grave when there would be no marker for her anywhere, neither in the earth nor the family hall? No one would give her a family hall name. She had taken the child with her into the wastes. At its birth the two of them had felt the same raw pain of separation, a wound that only the family pressing tight could close. A child with no descent line would not soften her life but only trail after her, ghostlike, begging her to give it purpose. At dawn the villagers on their way to the fields would stand around the fence and look.

Full of milk, the little ghost slept. When it awoke, she hardened her 45 breasts against the milk that crying loosens. Toward morning she picked up the baby and walked to the well.

Carrying the baby to the well shows loving. Otherwise abandon it. 46 Turn its face into the mud. Mothers who love their children take them along. It was probably a girl; there is some hope of forgiveness for boys.

"Don't tell anyone you had an aunt. Your father does not want to 47 hear her name. She has never been born." I have believed that sex was unspeakable and words so strong and fathers so frail that "aunt" would do my father mysterious harm. I have thought that my family, having settled among immigrants who had also been their neighbors in the ancestral land, needed to clean their name, and a wrong word would incite the kinspeople even here. But there is more to this silence: they want me to participate in her punishment. And I have.

In the twenty years since I heard this story I have not asked for details 48 nor said my aunt's name; I do not know it. People who can comfort the dead can also chase after them to hurt them further—a reverse ancestor worship. The real punishment was not the raid swiftly inflicted by the villagers, but the family's deliberately forgetting her. Her betrayal so maddened them, they saw to it that she would suffer forever, even after death. Always hungry, always needing, she would have to beg food from other ghosts, snatch and steal it from those whose living descendants give them gifts. She would have to fight the ghosts massed at crossroads for the buns a few thoughtful citizens leave to decoy her away from village and home so that the ancestral spirits could feast unharassed. At peace, they could act like gods, not ghosts, their descent lines providing them with paper suits and dresses, spirit money, paper houses, paper automobiles, chicken, meat, and rice into eternity—essences delivered up in smoke and flames, steam and incense rising from each rice bowl. In an attempt to make the Chinese care for people outside the family, Chairman Mao encourages us now to give our paper replicas to the spirits of outstanding soldiers and workers, no matter whose ancestors they may be. My aunt remains forever hungry. Goods are not distributed evenly among the dead.

My aunt haunts me—her ghost drawn to me because now, after fifty 49 years of neglect, I alone devote pages of paper to her, though not origamied into houses and clothes. I do not think she always means me well. I am telling on her, and she was a spite suicide, drowning herself in the drinking water. The Chinese are always very frightened of the drowned one, whose weeping ghost, wet hair hanging and skin bloated, waits silently by the water to pull down a substitute.

Questions

Rereading and Independent Analysis

1. Reread the essay, marking its parts according to the places where you see changes in the time, place, and the viewpoint from which events are told. Then list events in their order according to "actual" time, not the order in which they were told. What is the result of telling events in another order? How do the changes in perspective you first marked support the choice of another order of telling?

2. List the details used to explain and define "femininity" according to two distinct categories: "in America" and "in China." Then write a summary statement that tells the crucial difference between the two concepts of women that are presented here.

Suggested Discussion and Group Activities

1. Twice, Kingston's mother says "you must not tell" this story. Why is she afraid of its telling? Why is Kingston telling it? As a class or in groups, make a list of the kinds of stories that we avoid telling. What do these categories tell you about the power of stories to shape your world?

2. In what ways is this story universal? How does it allow all of us to apply to ourselves the situations that each of its characters encounters? With which particular experiences in Kingston's story can you identify?

Writing Suggestions

Response

1. More than once, Kingston tells us that she is not sure of the facts she tells or the reasons for them. Write a response to this story, explaining how you react to its vague elements. How does the order of events contribute to its vagueness? What are the implications of "ghosts" from the past and Kingston's uncertainty about what is "true"? What is the lesson you learn from Kingston's account?

2. This story is a good example of a family history about traditions that have been handed down privately to instruct young people about the

dangers of adult experiences. Write a narrative in which you explain a parallel bit of family education, a private teaching that warned you about adult life.

Analysis

Write a narrative essay for your classmates or another group whose members have not known you over a long time. In your essay, explain how your current school or work community defines a personal characteristic (femininity, masculinity, "good student," or another one you choose). Show how this definition contrasts with the way your family or the community where you grew up defined it and tell how this difference affects you.

 # The Poem
Mark Strand

Mark Strand (b. 1934) is one of America's most important poets. He has published six books of poetry and numerous translations and anthologies. His first book of short stories, *Mr. and Mrs. Baby,* was published in 1985; he has written art criticism, columns on photography for *Vogue* magazine, and essays. Strand teaches poetry and poetry writing and lectures and reads his poetry across the country. He says that his poems often begin in sounds and words he hears, and that they always depend on a voice and the way that voice will be heard, not on visual, silent reading.

His "Poem" is two imagined letters between a poet and a farmer. The poet fears that his poems are not read; the farmer writes to thank him for the poems, telling small stories of the people and nature around him. In these letters, Strand reverses the usual importance credited to poet and reader. The farmer tells us about the content of a poem we have not actually heard as he interests us in the peculiar details of his own life. His feelings are fresher than the poet's conventional wish to have his work read and remembered.

This prose poem comments on the relationships among writers and readers, speakers and hearers. Strand shows the power of a poem, and of any story, to reach us and help us begin a dialogue with the imagined voice we hear. In Strand's poem, we are directed to hear the honest voices of poet and farmer, who are stimulated by their imagined views of each other. We never see "the poem" that is imagined in these letters, but we do experience its vivid power to unite a poet and a reader.

Dear Reader, though I spend my days and nights in hiding, wanting your 1
attention and fearing it will be no more than the sad interest success finds in failure, my faith in you has never been shaken, for only in you do my poems have life. There is no limit to what you make possible. That is why

I have wanted, for the longest time, to give you something. Accept the enclosed poem as an attempt to present the self I have so long hidden.

Dear Poet, thank you for the poem. I like the part about the bird and the 2 part about the tree. And I like it when you talk about the hard, cold ground and the hard, cold stars, like the woman's stare which was hard and cold and the man's arms which were that way too. Knowledge for some of us who live on the farm is hard to come by, especially knowledge of how things really are, so to read your poems gives us hope. What is tenderness anyway, if it can't be relied on to teach us a little something. After all, the world is cold and hard and almost everyone has problems. The farmer next door wears a costume. And my wife has her doubts about me. But that is neither here nor there. What matters—and you put it so well—is that the bird is in the tree. Still, we must strive, which is what you must have meant when you said "The fish leaps unnetted into sunrise." Who cares if it's salmon or trout? *The big thing is* the fish leaps. It is that sort of observation which makes such a difference. Just yesterday the farmer next door told me a terrible story—never mind what it was—to amuse me. Such daily occurrences may relax us into states of well-being, but they don't build character. I was left with an empty feeling all over, so I went to the kitchen and picked up your poem again. My breath quickened when I realized that the fish you mentioned must have been heading upstream to lay its eggs, and that the bird had flown into the tree to avoid the hard, cold ground and the stare of the woman sitting next to the muscular man. We live in need of such uplift, and I for one thank you for providing it. Don't hesitate to write me again. Sincerely yours,

Questions

Rereading and Independent Analysis

1. Reread "The Poem" aloud. Copy those sentences whose words and phrasing slow your voice as you say them. What is the effect of these sentences?

2. The poem that "The Poem" is about is never actually seen. Make a list of what you know of its details from reading these letters. Then try to write a summary of the poem as you imagine it.

Suggested Discussion and Group Activities

1. What does the Poet mean by saying that he is "in hiding" but "wanting your attention"? What "success" and "failure" is he referring to? Why is it "only in you" that his poems "have life"? What sort of "life" do they have?

2. The Reader's letter to the Poet is much longer than the Poet's letter to the Reader. In groups, sort out what the Reader expresses about himself. What do we learn about his life? What relation does the (absent)

poem have to these facts? How does the Reader himself create this relationship?

Writing Suggestions

Response

"The Poem" tells stories about the Poet and the Reader and the content of the poem. But these stories are not in Strand's writing so much as in your own careful reading of its letters. Write a response to "The Poem" in which you tell these stories as you see them from your reading. Then compare your written versions of these stories with those of your classmates. As a class, make some generalizations about the reader's or listener's part in any story telling. How does the audience for any story help to shape the meaning of the story?

Analysis

Write an essay for your classmates in which you explain how readers always participate in the stories they read by actively relating them to their own experience. Use Strand's "Poem" and other examples to show how readers' responses always contribute to the meaning of any story.

Finding a Purpose

Write a letter responding to the Reader's letter in which you comment directly on the Reader's responses to the poem. Explain the Reader's "success" in understanding the poem's actual purpose. Be as imaginative as you wish in your references to what the Poet had in mind, and try to write with his tone and voice.

SPEAKING IN PUBLIC

 # Mark Antony's Funeral Oration
William Shakespeare

One of the most famous public speeches lives for us now only in the form of a scene from a play, *Julius Caesar,* by William Shakespeare (1564–1616). Although this speech was mentioned often in ancient histories, no written copy of it remains. But its fame shows how the educated citizen-soldier of Rome was also a skilled orator who could compose and deliver effective speeches, often without having to write them down at all.

Shakespeare was a student of ancient oratory. He thoroughly understood the conventions of composition and language in traditional funeral orations in praise of the dead. He had also read ancient Roman accounts of Mark Antony's speech, which, at the actual funeral, reversed the crowd's approval of killing Caesar just as it does in this dramatic version. Antony began by having a herald read decrees of honors that the Senate had given Caesar. Next, the senators' oath of loyalty to Caesar was read. Then Antony commented on favors Caesar had done for those who had just killed him. According to the ancient accounts, Antony arranged to have voices cry out from the corpse and closed his speech by holding Caesar's bloody clothes in his hands. The crowd rioted.

Shakespeare's tragedy of Julius Caesar is in many ways a parallel tragedy of Brutus the betrayer, who first doubts whether he should join the conspirators planning to murder Caesar for his ambition. Brutus finally joins the plot on the basis of false evidence left at his door. Remembering his family's overthrow of an earlier Roman tyrant, Brutus joins in stabbing Caesar. Caesar dies wondering how Brutus, whose reputation for honor is strong, could have betrayed him.

Reading the entire scene from the play, which includes Brutus' own defensive speech, allows us to compare Brutus' self-defeat through an ineffective formal and mechanical presentation to Antony's success through skill and subtlety. As you read the scene, imagine the tone and emphasis that each of these speakers would have employed at each stage. Try to recreate the atmosphere after this assassination, and imagine your own sense of risk and determination if you were Antony.

ACT III*

SCENE II. *The Forum.*

[*Enter* BRUTUS *and* CASSIUS, *and a throng of*
CITIZENS.]

CITS: We will be satisfied. Let us be satisfied.
BRU: Then follow me, and give me audience, friends.
    Cassius, go you into the other street,
    And part the numbers.
    Those that will hear me speak, let 'em stay here,   5
    Those that will follow Cassius, go with him,
    And public reasons shall be rendered
    Of Caesar's death.
1. CIT: I will hear Brutus speak.
2. CIT: I will hear Cassius, and compare their reasons
    When severally we hear them rendered.   10

[*Exit* CASSIUS, *with some of the* CITIZENS.]

[BRUTUS *goes into the pulpit.*]

3. CIT: The noble Brutus is ascended. Silence!
BRU: Be patient till the last.
    Romans, countrymen, and lovers! Hear me for my cause, and be silent, that you may hear. Believe me for mine honor, and have respect to mine honor,[15] that you may believe. Censure me in your

* Superscript numbers indicate line numbers.

wisdom, and awake your senses, that you may the better judge. If there be any in this assembly, any dear friend of Caesar's, to him I say that Brutus' love to Caesar was no less than his. If then that friend[20] demand why Brutus rose against Caesar, this is my answer—not that I loved Caesar less, but that I loved Rome more. Had you rather Caesar were living, and die all slaves, than that Caesar were dead, to live all freemen? As Caesar loved me, I weep[25] for him; as he was fortunate, I rejoice at it; as he was valiant, I honor him. But as he was ambitious, I slew him. There is tears for his love, joy for his fortune, honor for his valor, and death for his ambition. Who is here so base that would be a bondman? If[30] any, speak, for him have I offended. Who is here so rude that would not be a Roman? If any, speak, for him have I offended. Who is here so vile that will not love his country? If any, speak, for him have I offended. I pause for a reply.   37

ALL: None, Brutus, none.

BRU: Then none have I offended. I have done no more to Caesar than you shall do to Brutus. The question of his death is enrolled in the Capitol, his glory not extenuated, wherein he was worthy,[42] nor his offenses enforced, for which he suffered death.

[*Enter* ANTONY *and others, with* CAESAR's *body.*]

Here comes his body, mourned by Mark Antony, who, though he had no hand in his death, shall receive the benefit of his dying, a place in the[47] commonwealth—as which of you shall not? With this I depart—that, as I slew my best lover for the good of Rome, I have the same dagger for myself when it shall please my country to need my death.

ALL: Live, Brutus! Live, live!   53

1. CIT: Bring him with triumph home unto his house.

2. CIT: Give him a statue with his ancestors.

3. CIT: Let him be Caesar.

4. CIT: Caesar's better parts
    Shall be crowned in Brutus.

1. CIT: We'll bring him to his house with shouts and clamors.   58

BRU: My countrymen————

2. CIT: Peace! Silence! Brutus speaks.

1. CIT: Peace, ho!

BRU: Good countrymen, let me depart alone,
    And, for my sake, stay here with Antony.   61
    Do grace to Caesar's corpse, and grace his speech
    Tending to Caesar's glories, which Mark Antony
    By our permission is allowed to make.
    I do entreat you, not a man depart,   65
    Save I alone, till Antony have spoke.

                                                                [*Exit.*]

1. CIT: Stay, ho, and let us hear Mark Antony!
3. CIT: Let him go up into the public chair.
 We'll hear him. Noble Antony, go up.   69
ANT: For Brutus' sake, I am beholding to you.

          [*Goes into the pulpit.*]

4. CIT: What does he say of Brutus?
3. CIT: He says, for Brutus' sake,
 He finds himself beholding to us all.
4. CIT: 'Twere best he speak no harm of Brutus here.
1. CIT: This Caesar was a tyrant.
3. CIT: Nay, that's certain.
 We are blest that Rome is rid of him.   75
2. CIT: Peace! Let us hear what Antony can say.
ANT: You gentle Romans———
ALL: Peace, ho! Let us hear him.
ANT: Friends, Romans, countrymen, lend me your ears.
 I come to bury Caesar, not to praise him.
 The evil that men do lives after them,   80
 The good is oft interrèd with their bones.
 So let it be with Caesar. The noble Brutus
 Hath told you Caesar was ambitious.
 If it were so, it was a grievous fault,
 And grievously hath Caesar answered it.   85
 Here, under leave of Brutus and the rest—
 For Brutus is an honorable man,
 So are they all, all honorable men—
 Come I to speak in Caesar's funeral.
 He was my friend, faithful and just to me.   90
 But Brutus says he was ambitious,
 And Brutus is an honorable man.
 He hath brought many captives home to Rome,
 Whose ransoms did the general coffers fill.
 Did this in Caesar seem ambitious?   95
 When that the poor have cried, Caesar hath wept—
 Ambition should be made of sterner stuff.
 Yet Brutus says he was ambitious,
 And Brutus is an honorable man.
 You all did see that on the Lupercal   100
 I thrice presented him a kingly crown,
 Which he did thrice refuse. Was this ambition?
 Yet Brutus says he was ambitious,
 And, sure, he is an honorable man.
 I speak not to disprove what Brutus spoke,   105
 But here I am to speak what I do know.
 You all did love him once, not without cause.

What cause withholds you then to mourn for him?
O judgment, thou art fled to brutish beasts,
And men have lost their reason! Bear with me,
My heart is in the coffin there with Caesar,   111
And I must pause till it come back to me.
1. CIT: Methinks there is much reason in his sayings.
2. CIT: If thou consider rightly of the matter,
    Caesar has had great wrong.
3. CIT: Has he, masters?   115
    I fear there will a worse come in his place.
4. CIT: Marked ye his words? He would not take the crown,
    Therefore 'tis certain he was not ambitious.
1. CIT: If it be found so, some will dear abide it.
2. CIT: Poor soul! His eyes are red as fire with weeping.   120
3. CIT: There's not a nobler man in Rome than Antony.
4. CIT: Now mark him, he begins again to speak.
ANT: But yesterday the word of Caesar might
    Have stood against the world. Now lies he there,
    And none so poor to do him reverence.   125
    O masters, if I were disposed to stir
    Your hearts and minds to mutiny and rage,
    I should do Brutus wrong and Cassius wrong,
    Who, you all know, are honorable men.
    I will not do them wrong; I rather choose   130
    To wrong the dead, to wrong myself and you,
    Than I will wrong such honorable men.
    But here's a parchment with the seal of Caesar—
    I found it in his closet—'tis his will.
    Let but the commons hear this testament—   135
    Which, pardon me, I do not mean to read—
    And they would go and kiss dead Caesar's wounds
    And dip their napkins in his sacred blood,
    Yea, beg a hair of him for memory,
    And, dying, mention it within their wills,   140
    Bequeathing it as a rich legacy
    Unto their issue.
4. CIT: We'll hear the will. Read it, Mark Antony.
ALL: The will, the will! We will hear Caesar's will.
ANT: Have patience, gentle friends. I must not read it.   145
    It is not meet you know how Caesar loved you.
    You are not wood, you are not stones, but men;
    And, being men, hearing the will of Caesar,
    It will inflame you, it will make you mad.
    'Tis good you know not that you are his heirs,   150
    For if you should, oh, what would come of it!
4. CIT: Read the will. We'll hear it, Antony.
    You shall read us the will, Caesar's will.

ANT: Will you be patient? Will you stay awhile?
    I have o'ershot myself to tell you of it. 155
    I fear I wrong the honorable men
    Whose daggers have stabbed Caesar. I do fear it.
4. CIT: They were traitors—honorable men!
ALL: The will! The testament!
2. CIT: They were villains, murderers. The will! Read the will. 160
ANT: You will compel me then to read the will?
    Then make a ring about the corpse of Caesar,
    And let me show you him that made the will.
    Shall I descend? And will you give me leave?
ALL: Come down. 165
2. CIT: Descend.

                    [He comes down from the pulpit.]

3. CIT: You shall have leave.
4. CIT: A ring. Stand round.
1. CIT: Stand from the hearse, stand from the body. 169
2. CIT: Room for Antony, most noble Antony.
ANT: Nay, press not so upon me. Stand far off.
ALL: Stand back. Room! Bear back.
ANT: If you have tears, prepare to shed them now.
    You all do know this mantle. I remember
    The first time ever Caesar put it on. 175
    'Twas on a summer's evening, in his tent,
    That day he overcame the Nervii.
    Look, in this place ran Cassius' dagger through.
    See what a rent the envious Casca made.
    Through this the well-belovèd Brutus stabbed, 180
    And as he plucked his cursèd steel away,
    Mark how the blood of Caesar followed it,
    As rushing out of doors, to be resolved
    If Brutus so unkindly knocked, or no.
    For Brutus, as you know, was Caesar's angel. 185
    Judge, O you gods, how dearly Caesar loved him!
    This was the most unkindest cut of all,
    For when the noble Caesar saw him stab,
    Ingratitude, more strong than traitors' arms,
    Quite vanquished him. Then burst his mighty heart,
    And, in his mantle muffling up his face, 191
    Even at the base of Pompey's statuë,
    Which all the while ran blood, great Caesar fell.
    Oh, what a fall was there, my countrymen!
    Then I, and you, and all of us fell down, 195
    Whilst bloody treason flourished over us.
    Oh, now you weep, and I perceive you feel
    The dint of pity. These are gracious drops. 198

Kind souls, what weep you when you but behold
Our Caesar's vesture wounded? Look you here—
Here is himself, marred, as you see, with traitors.
1. Cit: Oh, piteous spectacle!
2. Cit: Oh, noble Caesar!
3. Cit: Oh, woeful day!
4. Cit: Oh, traitors, villains!   205
1. Cit: Oh, most bloody sight!
2. Cit: We will be revenged.
All: Revenge! About! Seek! Burn! Fire! Kill! Slay!
    Let not a traitor live!
Ant: Stay, countrymen.   210
1. Cit: Peace there! Hear the noble Antony.
2. Cit: We'll hear him, we'll follow him, we'll die with him.
Ant: Good friends, sweet friends, let me not stir you up
    To such a sudden flood of mutiny.   215
    They that have done this deed are honorable.
    What private griefs they have, alas, I know not,
    That made them do it. They are wise and honorable,
    And will, no doubt, with reasons answer you
    I come not, friends, to steal away your hearts.   220
    I am no orator, as Brutus is,
    But, as you know me all, a plain blunt man
    That love my friend; and that they know full well
    That gave me public leave to speak of him.
    For I have neither wit, nor words, nor worth,   225
    Action, nor utterance, nor the power of speech,
    To stir men's blood. I only speak right on,
    I tell you that which you yourselves do know,
    Show you sweet Caesar's wounds, poor poor dumb mouths,
    And bid them speak for me. But were I Brutus,   230
    And Brutus Antony, there were an Antony
    Would ruffle up your spirits, and put a tongue
    In every wound of Caesar that should move
    The stones of Rome to rise and mutiny.
All: We'll mutiny.   235
1. Cit: We'll burn the house of Brutus.
3. Cit: Away, then! Come, seek the conspirators.
Ant: Yet hear me, countrymen, yet hear me speak.
All: Peace, ho! Hear Antony. Most noble Antony!
Ant: Why, friends, you go to do you know not what.   240
    Wherein hath Caesar thus deserved your loves?
    Alas, you know not. I must tell you, then—
    You have forgot the will I told you of.
All: Most true, the will! Let's stay and hear the will.   244
Ant: Here is the will, and under Caesar's seal.

To every Roman citizen he gives,
To every several man, seventy-five drachmas.
2. CIT: Most noble Caesar! We'll revenge his death.
3. CIT: Oh, royal Caesar!
ANT: Hear me with patience.   250
ALL: Peace, ho!
ANT: Moreover, he hath left you all his walks,
His private arbors and new-planted orchards,
On this side Tiber. He hath left them you,
And to your heirs forever—common pleasures,   255
To walk abroad and recreate yourselves.
Here was a Caesar! When comes such another?
1. CIT: Never, never. Come, away, away!
We'll burn his body in the holy place,
And with the brands fire the traitors' houses.   260
Take up the body.
2. CIT: Go fetch fire.
3. CIT: Pluck down benches.
4. CIT: Pluck down forms, windows, anything.

[*Exeunt* CITIZENS *with the body.*]

ANT: Now let it work. Mischief, thou art afoot,
Take thou what course thou wilt.   266

[*Enter a* SERVANT.]   How now, fellow?

SERV: Sir, Octavius is already come to Rome.
ANT: Where is he?
SERV: He and Lepidus are at Caesar's house.
ANT: And thither will I straight to visit him.   270
He comes upon a wish. Fortune is merry,
And in this mood will give us anything.
SERV: I heard him say Brutus and Cassius
Are rid like madmen through the gates of Rome.
ANT: Belike they had some notice of the people,
How I had moved them. Bring me to Octavius.

[*Exeunt.*]

Questions

Rereading and Independent Analysis

1. Contrast Brutus' speech with Antony's by looking carefully at the
kinds of sentences each speaker used most often. Do they make statements, insist on agreement, or ask questions? List the number of times
each speaker chooses one of these forms. What effect do these sentence
choices have on listeners?

2. Reread Antony's speech, marking each use of contrast, or *antithesis* (saying one thing followed directly by its opposite). How do these oppositions help Antony achieve his goal despite the other Senators' desire to restrain him? How do these contrasts affect the crowd?

Suggested Discussion and Group Activities

1. How does Antony control the order of his points and manipulate the crowd so that he appears reluctant "to praise" Caesar? In groups, list in order the points he makes and their probable effect. Try rearranging the order of these points. How could a different order have changed the effect on the crowd?

2. The citizens speaking at the beginning of the scene pledge to listen to both sides of the question, "comparing reasons." Compare and contrast the "reasons" Brutus offers with those Antony unfolds. Which set of reasons do you find more persuasive? Why?

Writing Suggestions

Response

Recall a speech or public event where what you heard had an especially powerful effect on you. Describe the speech or event and try to recall your feelings at the time. What characteristics of this speech or public event contributed to its emotional impact on the audience?

Analysis

1. Imagine that you are in a situation like Antony's—you must reverse a crowd's view of the benefits of a public action that they have previously favored. As preparation for your speech, write a comparative evaluation of the strategies used by Antony and Brutus. Analyze their uses of the word *honor* and other features of their speeches such as the order of their points and the ways they control or fail to control the crowd's emotions and reasoning. Keep in mind that you will have something at stake when you make your own speech. You want to avoid Brutus' mistakes and imitate Antony's strategy.

2. Choose one of the long sections of Antony's speech and show how it was designed to affect its Roman audience. Show how this portion of the speech is a stage in the change Antony made in the crowd's attitude. Point out specific places where Antony appeals to the audience or where he reminds them of Caesar's goodness. How does he control his language to create an emotional response from the audience? Show how each line in the section you choose contributes to the result of the entire speech. (See "The Gettysburg Address" and "The Rhetoric of the Kennedy Address," below, for help.)

Finding a Purpose

Imagine that you are a time-traveling reporter, transported to ancient Rome to broadcast this scene to your classmates. Write a script for yourself in which you make the situation and the power of these speeches clear to your listeners, who are unused to hearing and evaluating funeral orations.

 # "The Gettysburg Address"
Gilbert Highet

Although Lincoln's "Gettysburg Address" was publicly delivered at a memorial dedication on the battlefield, both its timely composition by Lincoln and its newspaper reports to readers who were first curious and then moved placed its impact well within the written world. As Gilbert Highet (1906–1978) says in this account of the speech's reception and power, Lincoln's words had little effect when he delivered them, perhaps because the speech was so brief in comparison to Edward Everett's longer comments. Newspaper reporters attending the ceremonies gave Lincoln little attention, but later, when editors across the country had time to read what he had said, they recognized his exactness and appropriateness.

Lincoln's speech shows how a speaker raised in a local community tradition could recall common themes and devices from an entire culture's well-known readings. Lincoln's struggle to obtain an education has been well documented. He gave careful attention to each of the few books he could obtain, trying to absorb as much as he could, and made his reading a working part of himself. He read books aloud throughout his life to gain a sense of their voice and impact on a listener. As Highet points out, Lincoln did not need to "look up" the speech's many verbal devices (for instance, parallelism and antithesis) or artificially contrive its rhythmic language patterns and imitations (Highet calls them "adaptations") of the Bible and earlier American speeches.

Lincoln was a virtuoso debater who could be direct and clear or general and vague, depending on his political aims. As he composed this speech, he automatically took clear, traditional references and oratorical devices from his memory because they were the most suitable rhythms and language for this memorial occasion. Their simple power supported his purpose—to reunite the country by recalling its common shared experiences of life and death.

Fourscore and seven years ago our fathers brought forth on this continent, a new nation, conceived in Liberty, and dedicated to the proposition that all men are created equal. 1

Now we are engaged in a great civil war, testing whether that nation or any nation so conceived and so dedicated, can long endure. We are met on a great battle-field of that war. We have come to dedicate a portion of that field, as a final resting place for those who here gave their lives that that nation might live. It is altogether fitting and proper that we should do this. 2

But, in a larger sense, we can not dedicate—we can not conse- 3
crate—we can not hallow—this ground. The brave men, living and dead,
who struggled here, have consecrated it, far above our poor power to
add or detract. The world will little note, nor long remember, what we
say here, but it can never forget what they did here. It is for us the living, rather, to be dedicated here to the unfinished work which they who
fought here have thus far so nobly advanced. It is rather for us to be
here dedicated to the great task remaining before us—that from these
honored dead we take increased devotion to that cause for which they
gave the last full measure of devotion—that we here highly resolve that
these dead shall not have died in vain—that this nation, under God, shall
have a new birth of freedom—and that government of the people, by
the people, for the people, shall not perish from the earth.

Fourscore and seven years ago . . . 1

These five words stand at the entrance to the best-known monument 2
of American prose, one of the finest utterances in the entire language and
surely one of the greatest speeches in all history. Greatness is like granite:
it is molded in fire, and it lasts for many centuries.

Fourscore and seven years ago . . . . It is strange to think that Presi- 3
dent Lincoln was looking back to the 4th of July 1776, and that he and his
speech are now further removed from us than he himself was from George
Washington and the Declaration of Independence. Fourscore and seven
years before the Gettysburg Address, a small group of patriots signed the
Declaration. Fourscore and seven years after the Gettysburg Address, it
was the year 1950,[1] and that date is already receding rapidly into our
troubled, adventurous, and valiant past.

Inadequately prepared and at first scarcely realized in its full impor- 4
tance, the dedication of the graveyard at Gettysburg was one of the supreme moments of American history. The battle itself had been a turning
point of the war. On the 4th of July 1863, General Meade repelled Lee's
invasion of Pennsylvania. Although he did not follow up his victory, he had
broken one of the most formidable aggressive enterprises of the Confederate armies. Losses were heavy on both sides. Thousands of dead were left
on the field, and thousands of wounded died in the hot days following the
battle. At first, their burial was more or less haphazard; but thoughtful
men gradually came to feel that an adequate burying place and memorial
were required. These were established by an interstate commission that
autumn, and the finest speaker in the North was invited to dedicate them.
This was the scholar and statesman Edward Everett of Harvard. He made
a good speech—which is still extant: not at all academic, it is full of close
strategic analysis and deep historical understanding.

Lincoln was not invited to speak, at first. Although people knew him 5
as an effective debater, they were not sure whether he was capable of
making a serious speech on such a solemn occasion. But one of the impressive things about Lincoln's career is that he constantly strove to *grow.* He

[1] In November 1950 the Chinese had just entered the war in Korea.

was anxious to appear on that occasion and to say something worthy of it. (Also, it has been suggested, he was anxious to remove the impression that he did not know how to behave properly—an impression which had been strengthened by a shocking story about his clowning on the battlefield of Antietam the previous year.) Therefore when he was invited he took considerable care with his speech. He drafted rather more than half of it in the White House before leaving, finished it in the hotel at Gettysburg the night before the ceremony (not in the train, as sometimes reported), and wrote out a fair copy next morning.

There are many accounts of the day itself, 19 November 1863. There 6 are many descriptions of Lincoln, all showing the same curious blend of grandeur and awkwardness, or lack of dignity, or—it would be best to call it humility. In the procession he rode horseback: a tall lean man in a high plug hat, straddling a short horse, with his feet too near the ground. He arrived before the chief speaker, and had to wait patiently for half an hour or more. His own speech came right at the end of a long and exhausting ceremony, lasted less than three minutes, and made little impression on the audience. In part this was because they were tired, in part because (as eye-witnesses said) he ended almost before they knew he had begun, and in part because he did not speak the Address, but read it, very slowly, in a thin high voice, with a marked Kentucky accent, pronouncing "to" as "toe" and dropping his final R's.

Some people of course were alert enough to be impressed. Everett 7 congratulated him at once. But most of the newspapers paid little attention to the speech, and some sneered at it. The *Patriot and Union* of Harrisburg wrote, "We pass over the silly remarks of the President; for the credit of the nation we are willing . . . that they shall no more be repeated or thought of"; and the London *Times* said, "The ceremony was rendered ludicrous by some of the sallies of that poor President Lincoln," calling his remarks "dull and commonplace." The first commendation of the Address came in a single sentence of the Chicago *Tribune,* and the first discriminating and detailed praise of it appeared in the Springfield *Republican,* the Providence *Journal,* and the Philadelphia *Bulletin.* However, three weeks after the ceremony and then again the following spring, the editor of *Harper's Weekly* published a sincere and thorough eulogy of the Address, and soon it was attaining recognition as a masterpiece.

At the time, Lincoln could not care much about the reception of his 8 words. He was exhausted and ill. In the train back to Washington, he lay down with a wet towel on his head. He had caught smallpox. At that moment he was incubating it, and he was stricken down soon after he reentered the White House. Fortunately it was a mild attack, and it evoked one of his best jokes: he told his visitors, "At last I have something I can give to everybody."

He had more than that to give to everybody. He was a unique person, 9 far greater than most people realize until they read his life with care. The wisdom of his policy, the sources of his statesmanship—these were things too complex to be discussed in a brief essay. But we can say something about the Gettysburg Address as a work of art.

A work of art. Yes: for Lincoln was a literary artist, trained both by 10 others and by himself. The textbooks he used as a boy were full of difficult exercises and skillful devices in formal rhetoric, stressing the qualities he practiced in his own speaking: antithesis, parallelism, and verbal harmony. Then he read and reread many admirable models of thought and expression: the King James Bible, the essays of Bacon, the best plays of Shakespeare. His favorites were *Hamlet, Lear, Macbeth, Richard III,* and *Henry VIII,* which he had read dozens of times. He loved reading aloud, too, and spent hours reading poetry to his friends. (He told his partner Herndon that he preferred getting the sense of any document by reading it aloud.) Therefore his serious speeches are important parts of the long and noble classical tradition of oratory which begins in Greece, runs through Rome to the modern world, and is still capable (if we do not neglect it) of producing masterpieces.

The first proof of this is that the Gettysburg Address is full of quota- 11 tions—or rather of adaptations—which give it strength. It is partly religious, partly (in the highest sense) political: therefore it is interwoven with memories of the Bible and memories of American history. The first and the last words are Biblical cadences. Normally Lincoln did not say "fourscore" when he meant eighty; but on this solemn occasion he recalled the important dates in the Bible—such as the age of Abram when his first son was born to him, and he was "fourscore and six years old."[2] Similarly he did not say there was a chance that democracy might die out: he recalled the somber phrasing of the Book of Job—where Bildad speaks of the destruction of one who shall vanish without a trace, and says that "his branch shall be cut off; his remembrance shall perish from the earth."[3] Then again, the famous description of our State as "government of the people, by the people, for the people" was adumbrated by Daniel Webster in 1830 (he spoke of "the people's government, made for the people, made by the people, and answerable to the people") and then elaborated in 1854 by the abolitionist Theodore Parker (as "government of all the people, by all the people, for all the people"). There is good reason to think that Lincoln took the important phrase "under God" (which he interpolated at the last moment) from Weems, the biographer of Washington; and we know that it had been used at least once by Washington himself.

Analyzing the Address further, we find that it is based on a highly 12 imaginative theme, or group of themes. The subject is—how can we put it so as not to disfigure it?—the subject is the kinship of life and death, that mysterious linkage which we see sometimes as the physical succession of

---

[2] Gen. 16.16; cf. Exod. 7.7.
[3] Job 18.16–17; cf. Jer. 10.11, Micah 7.2.

birth and death in our world, sometimes as the contrast, which is perhaps a unity, between death and immortality. The first sentence is concerned with birth:

Our *fathers brought forth* a *new* nation, *conceived* in liberty.

The final phrase but one expresses the hope that

this nation, under God, shall have a *new birth* of freedom.

And the last phrase of all speaks of continuing life as the triumph over death. Again and again throughout the speech, this mystical contrast and kinship reappear: "those who *gave their lives* that that nation might *live*," "the brave men *living* and *dead*," and so in the central assertion that the dead have already consecrated their own burial place, while "it is for us, the *living*, rather to be dedicated . . . to the great task remaining." The Gettysburg Address is a prose poem; it belongs to the same world as the great elegies, and the adagios of Beethoven.

Its structure, however, is that of a skillfully contrived speech. The 13 oratorical pattern is perfectly clear. Lincoln describes the occasion, dedicates the ground, and then draws a larger conclusion by calling on his hearers to dedicate themselves to the preservation of the Union. But within that, we can trace his constant use of at least two important rhetorical devices.

The first of these is *antithesis:* opposition, contrast. The speech is full 14 of it. Listen:

The world will little *note*
             nor long *remember*   what *we say* here
but   it can never *forget*   what *they did* here.

And so in nearly every sentence: "brave men, *living* and *dead*"; "to *add* or *detract.*" There is the antithesis of the Founding Fathers and the men of Lincoln's own time:

Our *fathers brought forth* a new nation . . .
now *we* are testing whether that nation . . . can *long endure.*

And there is the more terrible antithesis of those who have already died and those who still live to do their duty. Now, antithesis is the figure of contrast and conflict. Lincoln was speaking in the midst of a great civil war.

The other important pattern is different. It is technically called *trico-* 15 *lon*—the division of an idea into three harmonious parts, usually of increasing power. The most famous phrase of the Address is a tricolon:

government of the people
              by the people
       and   for the people.

The most solemn sentence is a tricolon:

> we cannot dedicate
> we cannot consecrate
> we cannot hallow this ground.

And above all, the last sentence (which has sometimes been criticized as too complex) is essentially two parallel phrases, with a tricolon growing out of the second and then producing another tricolon: a trunk, three branches, and a cluster of flowers. Lincoln says that it is for his hearers to be dedicated to the great task remaining before them. Then he goes on,

> that from these honored dead

—apparently he means "in such a way that from these honored dead"—

> we take increased devotion to that cause.

Next, he restates this more briefly:

> that we here highly resolve . . .

And now the actual resolution follows, in three parts of growing intensity:

> that these dead shall not have died in vain
> that this nation, under God, shall have a new birth of freedom

and that (one more tricolon)

> government of the people
>   by the people
>   and   for the people
> shall not perish from the earth.

Now, the tricolon is the figure which, through division, emphasizes basic harmony and unity. Lincoln used antithesis because he was speaking to a people at war. He used the tricolon because he was hoping, planning, praying for peace.

No one thinks that when he was drafting the Gettysburg Address, 16 Lincoln deliberately looked up these quotations and consciously chose these particular patterns of thought. No, he chose the theme. From its development and from the emotional tone of the entire occasion, all the rest followed, or grew—by that marvelous process of choice and rejection which is essential to artistic creation. It does not spoil such a work of art to analyze it as closely as we have done; it is altogether fitting and proper that we should do this: for it helps us to penetrate more deeply into the rich meaning of the Gettysburg Address, and it allows us the very rare privilege of watching the workings of a great man's mind.

W. E. Barton, *Lincoln at Gettysburg* (Bobbs-Merrill, 1930).
R. P. Basler, "Abraham Lincoln's Rhetoric," *American Literature* 11 (1939–40), 167–82.
L. E. Robinson, *Abraham Lincoln as a Man of Letters* (Chicago, 1918).

Questions

Rereading and Independent Analysis

1. Review Highet's definitions of devices before rereading the speech. Then mark each example of antithesis and tricolon. Compose two sentences of your own that use each of these devices.

2. Make a topical outline of Highet's essay. How does Lincoln's form follow the classical pattern for arranging the parts of a public address? Where is the break between the "narration," or background, and Lincoln's thesis? (See the Introduction to this chapter for help.) How does Lincoln use comparisons and transitions to further his purpose of unifying the country?

Suggested Discussion and Group Activities

1. In groups, find the grammatical subject, verb, and object in each sentence of the address. Then decide how the changes from one subject to another in Lincoln's sentences also separate the themes that support his purpose. How do these details of grammatical change fit the speech's themes and points?

2. Consider the drama Highet describes: the speech's poor reception, Lincoln's illness, the aftermath of the battle itself. How does Highet use these elements in his literary analysis of the speech as evidence for his positive evaluation of it? Must we know this context to understand completely the speech's impact? Why?

Writing Suggestions

Response

After reviewing your answers to the analysis and discussion questions above, write a short statement of how you see the relationships among the grammatical devices and sentence patterns and the messages in your writing. You needn't be sophisticated in your response, but try to express how the power of a speech like Lincoln's depended on details and how you approach similar details in your own writing. Are you intimidated by what you read? How can you use it to help you write better?

Analysis

Highet concludes by stating: "Lincoln used antithesis because he was speaking to a people at war. He used the tricolon because he was hoping, planning, praying for peace." After underlining Lincoln's references to life and death, write an essay in which you show how Lincoln also used these (and other) devices to develop that unifying theme of life and death. Your essay should be useful to other students who have read Highet's piece.

Finding a Purpose

Choose any subject, setting, and audience you wish and write a brief memorial talk. You may wish to commemorate a sports event, the end of a school term, or a personal event. Don't limit yourself to sad events like a battle. Begin with a reference to the past, then state the situation now. Tell how the future will be determined by the event whose passing you are marking.

 Prospects in the Arts and Sciences
J. Robert Oppenheimer

J. Robert Oppenheimer (1904–1967) was the leader of the team of scientists who completed the research for, and testing of, the first nuclear weapon, at laboratories in Los Alamos, New Mexico. He was in large measure the father of the atomic bomb that the United States dropped on Japan in 1945 to end World War II. After the war, Oppenheimer continued research and served as director for the Institute for Advanced Studies in Princeton, New Jersey. This speech to an audience of reporters was delivered at Columbia University's Bicentennial Anniversary celebration in December 1954.

The title of this speech may not appeal to you. Its language and the dispassionate phrasing of the speech itself are not as dramatic as the language of other memorable speeches. But the context in which Oppenheimer spoke reveals the urgency behind these words, both for Oppenheimer and for us. In the year the speech was delivered, 1954, Oppenheimer was suspected of security leaks and, partially owing to the false reports of another physicist, Edward Teller, was relieved of his post in the Atomic Energy Commission. That year many other scientists and artists were also unfairly suspected and accused of anti-American activities; many of them were defamed and destroyed when their names appeared on the infamous "black lists."

In addition, the consequences of using nuclear weapons against Japan were becoming visible to scientists like Oppenheimer. At that time the dangers of nuclear warfare were not so clearly terrifying in the eyes of the general public as they are now; most Americans still believed that their independent military strength protected them and that they could help, or war against, other countries without consequences for the entire human community. They did not want to hear disturbing contradictions of this belief, even in the name of "free speech."

Consequently, Oppenheimer's address, on issues that he felt deeply about, appeared quite radical at the time. Nonetheless, he bravely spoke out about the inevitability of change, the independence of science from politics, the special worlds of scientists and artists, and the new need, brought on by nuclear weapons, to define a "community" in global rather than national or political terms. Each of these ideas was likely to bring down charges of "communism" on anyone willing to voice them publicly. As you read, imagine yourself having the nerve to make equally unpopular evaluations in these circumstances. Decide also whether Oppenheimer's ideas are still radical or if his predictions have been confirmed.

In the natural sciences these are, and have been, and are most surely likely 1
to continue to be, heroic days. Discovery follows discovery, each both
raising and answering questions, each ending a long search, and each
providing the new instruments for new search.

There are radical ways of thinking unfamiliar to common sense, 2
connected with it by decades or centuries of increasingly specialized and
unfamiliar experience. There are lessons how limited, for all its variety,
the common experience of man has been with regard to natural phenomenon, and hints and analogies as to how limited may be his experience with
man.

Every new finding is a part of the instrument kit of the sciences 3
for further investigation and for penetrating into new fields. Discoveries
of knowledge fructify technology and the practical arts, and these in
turn pay back refined techniques, new possibilities for observation and
experiment.

In any science there is a harmony between practitioners. A man may 4
work as an individual, learning of what his colleagues do through reading
or conversation; or he may be working as a member of a group on problems whose technical equipment is too massive for individual effort. But
whether he is part of a team or solitary in his own study, he, as a professional, is a member of a community.

His colleagues in his own branch of science will be grateful to him 5
for the inventive or creative thoughts he has, will welcome his criticism.
His world and work will be objectively communicable and he will be quite
sure that, if there is error in it, that error will not be long undetected. In
his own line of work he lives in a community where common understanding combines with common purpose and interest to bind men together
both in freedom and in cooperation.

This experience will make him acutely aware of how limited, how 6
precious is this condition of his life; for in his relations with a wider society
there will be neither the sense of community nor of objective understanding. He will sometimes find, it is true, in returning to practical undertak-
ings, some sense of community with men who are not expert in his science,
with other scientists whose work is remote from his, and with men of
action and men of art.

The frontiers of science are separated now by long years of study, by 7
specialized vocabularies, arts, techniques and knowledge from the common heritage even of a most civilized society, and anyone working at the
frontier of such science is in that sense a very long way from home and
a long way, too, from the practical arts that were its matrix and origin, as
indeed they were of what we today call art.

The specialization of science is an inevitable accompaniment of prog- 8
ress; yet it is full of dangers, and it is cruelly wasteful, since so much that
is beautiful and enlightening is cut off from most of the world. Thus it is
proper to the role of the scientist that he not merely find new truth and
communicate it to his fellows, but that he teach, that he try to bring the

most honest and intelligible account of new knowledge to all who will try to learn.

This is one reason—it is the decisive organic reason—why scientists 9 belong in universities. It is one reason why the patronage of science by and through universities is its most proper form; for it is here, in teaching, in the association of scholars, and in the friendships of teachers and taught, of men who by profession must themselves be both teachers and taught, that the narrowness of scientific life can best be moderated and that the analogies, insights and harmonies of scientific discovery can find their way into the wider life of man.

In the situation of the artist today there are both analogies and 10 differences to that of the scientist; but it is the differences which are the most striking and which raise the problems that touch most on the evil of our day.

For the artist it is not enough that he communicate with others who 11 are expert in his own art. Their fellowship, their understanding and their appreciation may encourage him; but that is not the end of his work, nor its nature.

The artist depends on a common sensibility and culture, on a com- 12 mon meaning of symbols, on a community of experience and common ways of describing and interpreting it. He need not write for everyone or paint or play for everyone. But his audience must be man, and not a specialized set of experts among his fellows.

Today that is very difficult. Often the artist has an aching sense of 13 great loneliness, for the community to which he addresses himself is largely not there; the traditions and the history, the myths and the common experience, which it is his function to illuminate and to harmonize and to portray, have been dissolved in a changing world.

There is, it is true, an artificial audience maintained to moderate 14 between the artist and the world for which he works: the audience of the professional critics, popularizers and advertisers of art. But though, as does the popularizer and promoter of science, the critic fulfills a necessary present function, and introduces some order and some communication between the artist and the world, he cannot add to the intimacy and the directness and the depth with which the artist addresses his fellow men.

To the artist's loneliness there is a complementary great and terrible 15 barrenness in the lives of men. They are deprived of the illumination, the light and the tenderness and insight of an intelligible interpretation, in contemporary terms, of the sorrows and wonders and gaeties and follies of man's life.

This may be in part offset, and is, by the great growth of technical 16 means for making the art of the past available. But these provide a record of past intimacies between art and life; even when they are applied to the writing and painting and composing of the day, they do not bridge the gulf between a society too vast and too disordered and the artist trying to give meaning and beauty to its parts.

In an important sense, this world of ours is a new world, in which the   17
unity of knowledge, the nature of human communities, the order of society, the order of ideas, the very notions of society and culture have
changed and will not return to what they have been in the past. What is
new is new not because it has never been there before, but because it has
changed in quality.

One thing that is new is the prevalence of newness, the changing   18
scale and scope of change itself, so that the world alters as we walk in it,
so that the years of man's life measure not some small growth or rearrange-
ment or moderation of what he learned in childhood, but a great upheaval.

What is new is that in one generation our knowledge of the natural   19
world engulfs, upsets and complements all knowledge of the natural world
before. The techniques, among which and by which we live, multiply and
ramify, so that the whole world is bound together by communication,
blocked here and there by the immense synopses of political tyranny.

The global quality of the world is new: our knowledge of and sympa-   20
thy with remote and diverse peoples, our involvement with them in practical terms and our commitment to them in terms of brotherhood. What
is new in the world is the massive character of the dissolution and corruption of authority, in belief, in ritual and in temporal order.

Yet this is the world that we have come to live in. The very difficulties   21
which it presents derive from growth in understanding, in skill, in power.
To assail the changes that have unmoored us from the past is futile, and,
in a deep sense, I think it is wicked. We need to recognize the change and
learn what resources we have.

Again I will turn to the schools, and, as their end and as their center,   22
the universities. For the problem of the scientist is in this respect not
different from that of the artist, nor of the historian. He needs to be a part
of the community, and the community can only, with loss and peril, be
without him. Thus it is with a sense of interest and hope that we see a
growing recognition that the creative artist is a proper charge on the
university, and the university a proper home for him: that a composer or
a poet or a playwright or painter needs the toleration, understanding, the
rather local and parochial patronage that a university can give; and that
this will protect him to some extent from the tyranny of man's communication and professional promotion.

For here there is an honest chance that what the artist has of insight   23
and of beauty will take root in the community and that some intimacy and
some human bonds can mark his relations with his patrons. For a university rightly and inherently is a place where the individual man can form
new syntheses, where the accidents of friendship and association can open
a man's eyes to a part of science or art which he had not known before,
where parts of human life, remote and perhaps superficially incompatible
one with the other, can find in men their harmony and their synthesis.

The truth is that this is indeed inevitably and increasingly an open,   24
and inevitably and increasing an eclectic world. We know too much for

one man to know much, we live too variously to live as one. Our histories and traditions—the very means of interpreting life—are both bonds and barriers among us. Our knowledge separates as well as it unites; our orders disintegrate as well as bind; our art brings us together and sets us apart. The artist's loneliness, the scholar's despairing, because no one will any longer trouble to learn what he can teach, the narrowness of the scientist, these are not unnatural insignia in this great time of change.

This is a world in which each of us, knowing his limitations, knowing 25 the evils of superficiality and the terrors of fatigue, will have to cling to what is close to him, to what he knows, to what he can do, to his friends and his tradition and his love, lest he be dissolved in a universal confusion and know nothing and love nothing.

Both the man of science and the man of art live always at the edge 26 of mystery, surrounded by it; both always, as the measure of their creation, have had to do with the harmonization of what is new and what is familiar, with the balance between novelty and synthesis, with the struggle to make partial order in total chaos.

This cannot be an easy life. We shall have a rugged time of it to keep 27 our minds open and to keep them deep, to keep our sense of beauty and our ability to make it, and our occasional ability to see it, in places remote and strange and unfamiliar.

But this is, as I see it, the condition of man; and in this condition we 28 can help, because we can love one another.

Questions

Rereading and Independent Analysis

1. Make a topical outline of Oppenheimer's speech, using his words and your own brief paraphrases (rewordings) to create a summary of the points he made.

2. Oppenheimer did not use traditional forms of address to gain his listeners' confidence. His speech uses neither "I" nor "we" to establish links with its audience. Reread the speech, marking the content that contributes to belief in his points. What evidence does Oppenheimer give for his assertions? Given the situation in which he spoke, how was this evidence especially suitable for gaining his listeners' acceptance of his points?

Suggested Discussion and Group Activities

1. Take the position of a member of Oppenheimer's audience who disagrees with his ideas. What specific evidence would you use to refute (argue against) his predictions about the future?

2. This speech was given before NASA's space explorations had begun, before the development of lasers, before the computer revolution, before it was known that some cancers are viruses, before the United States established relations with mainland China, before a woman ran for national executive office in the United States, and before the passage of the civil

rights amendment to the Constitution. In groups, determine how Oppenheimer's themes and statements forecast these events and others like them.

Writing Suggestions

Response

Write a personal statement in which you explore your own timidity about speaking up for what you believe in. Have you ever felt you should have said something but didn't, or spoken up despite your fears about how others might respond? Try to make some generalizations about your feelings so you can understand reasons for your attitudes.

Analysis

1. Write an editorial commentary on Oppenheimer's speech for a newspaper. Explain his definition of "community" as both small groups of people who interact daily and cross-cultural, global groups. Take into account your readers' possible objections to what Oppenheimer said. Try to persuade your readers that this speech has unified these seemingly opposed ideas of community.

2. Write an essay explaining to another student why this essay should not be dismissed as "boring" but read as an example of a speaker's wisdom in choosing language and examples that fit the situation he is in and his purpose. Show the student why alternative choices would have undermined Oppenheimer's speech, not made it more powerful.

Finding a Purpose

This speech repeatedly addresses the problem of the individual's relationship to society. It describes the individual's responsibility to be both independent and concerned with larger interests. Write an essay in which you personally address this idea, using examples of people you know who demonstrate this responsibility in their work. Explain this principle to a group of potential athletes, actors, astronauts, or others who work alone but who are also part of groups with unified purposes. How can one be both independent and part of a group?

The Rhetoric of the Kennedy Address
The New Yorker

John F. Kennedy, who was elected president in 1960, was assassinated as he campaigned for a second term of office. His presidency symbolized a time of renewed enthusiasm and vigor in American life, a period of confidence and social action proclaimed by this inaugural address. Hopes for and fears of the many new powers humans had acquired were frequently expressed at the time. Kennedy, however, was able to instill a sense of commitment and responsibility for others that no leader since his time has succeeded in doing with such force.

The New Yorker's commentary on Kennedy's inaugural address praised his renewal of the art of effective speech making (rhetoric) at the same time that the study of rhetoric was being renewed at many universities. In concert with a long tradition of similar statements, this essay complains that we have only a few powerful speakers now, so it is both nostalgic and hopeful that eloquent speech will again be in fashion. The essay does not analyze the speech part by part but instead summarizes some principles of rhetoric and shows how Kennedy used them successfully.

Equally important, the essay extends the significance of Kennedy's speech beyond its momentary political context. We and other readers of this national weekly magazine can re-hear the speech by reading the magazine's analysis. The New Yorker essay links Kennedy and the inaugural address to a long tradition in politics and education. It makes the brief event of inaugurating a new American President part of a larger pattern of historical development.

VICE-PRESIDENT JOHNSON, MR. SPEAKER, MR. CHIEF JUSTICE, PRESIDENT EISENHOWER, VICE-PRESIDENT NIXON, PRESIDENT TRUMAN, REVEREND CLERGY, FELLOW CITIZENS:

We observe today not a victory of party but a celebration of freedom— 1 symbolizing an end as well as a beginning—signifying renewal as well as change. For I have sworn before you and Almighty God the same solemn oath our forebearers prescribed nearly a century and three-quarters ago.

The world is very different now. For man holds in his mortal hands 2 the power to abolish all forms of human poverty and all forms of human life. And yet the same revolutionary beliefs for which our forebearers fought are still at issue around the globe—the belief that the rights of man come not from the generosity of the state but from the hand of God.

We dare not forget today that we are the heirs of that first revolu- 3 tion. Let the word go forth from this time and place, to friend and foe alike, that the torch has been passed to a new generation of Americans— born in this century, tempered by war, disciplined by a hard and bitter peace, proud of our ancient heritage—and unwilling to witness or permit the slow undoing of those human rights to which this nation has always been committed, and to which we are committed today at home and around the world.

Let every nation know, whether it wishes us well or ill, that we   4 shall pay any price, bear any burden, meet any hardship, support any friend, oppose any foe to assure the survival and the success of liberty.

This much we pledge—and more.   5

To those old allies whose cultural and spiritual origins we share, we   6 pledge the loyalty of faithful friends. United, there is little we cannot do in a host of co-operative ventures. Divided, there is little we can do—for we dare not meet a powerful challenge at odds and split asunder.

To those new states whom we welcome to the ranks of the free, we   7
pledge our word that one form of colonial control shall not have passed
away merely to be replaced by a far more iron tyranny. We shall not always expect to find them supporting our view. But we shall always hope
to find them strongly supporting their own freedom—and to remember
that, in the past, those who foolishly sought power by riding the back of
the tiger ended up inside.

To those people in the huts and villages of half the globe struggling   8
to break the bonds of mass misery, we pledge our best efforts to help
them help themselves, for whatever period is required—not because the
Communists may be doing it, not because we seek their votes, but because it is right. If a free society cannot help the many who are poor, it
cannot save the few who are rich.

To our sister republics south of our border, we offer a special   9
pledge—to convert our good words into good deeds—in a new alliance
for progress—to assist free men and free governments in casting off the
chains of poverty. But this peaceful revolution of hope cannot become
the prey of hostile powers. Let all our neighbors know that we shall join
with them to oppose aggression or subversion anywhere in the Americas.
And let every other power know that this hemisphere intends to remain
the master of its own house.

To that world assembly of sovereign states, the United Nations, our   10
last best hope in an age where the instruments of war have far outpaced
the instruments of peace, we renew our pledge of support—to prevent it
from becoming merely a forum for invective—to strengthen its shield of
the new and the weak—and to enlarge the area in which its writ may
run.

Finally, to those nations who would make themselves our adver-   11
sary, we offer not a pledge but a request: that both sides begin anew the
quest for peace, before the dark powers of destruction unleashed by science engulf all humanity in planned or accidental self-destruction.

We dare not tempt them with weakness. For only when our arms   12
are sufficient beyond doubt can we be certain beyond doubt that they
will never be employed.

But neither can two great and powerful groups of nations take   13
comfort from our present course—both sides overburdened by the cost of
modern weapons, both rightly alarmed by the steady spread of the
deadly atom, yet both racing to alter that uncertain balance of terror
that stays the hand of mankind's final war.

So let us begin anew—remembering on both sides that civility is   14
not a sign of weakness, and sincerity is always subject to proof. Let us
never negotiate out of fear. But let us never fear to negotiate.

Let both sides explore what problems unite us instead of belabor-   15
ing those problems which divide us.

Let both sides, for the first time, formulate serious and precise   16
proposals for the inspection and control of arms—and bring the absolute
power to destroy other nations under the absolute control of all nations.

Let both sides seek to invoke the wonders of science instead of its   17
terrors. Together let us explore the stars, conquer the deserts, eradicate
disease, tap the ocean depths, and encourage the arts and commerce.

Let both sides unite to heed in all corners of the earth the com-   18
mand of Isaiah—to "undo the heavy burdens . . . [and] let the oppressed
go free."

And if a beachhead of co-operation may push back the jungle of   19
suspicion, let both sides join in creating a new endeavor, not a new balance of power, but a new world of law, where the strong are just and
the weak secure and the peace preserved.

All this will not be finished in the first one hundred days. Nor will   20
it be finished in the first one thousand days, nor in the life of this administration, nor even perhaps in our lifetime on this planet. But let us
begin.

In your hands, my fellow citizens, more than mine, will rest the   21
final success or failure of our course. Since this country was founded,
each generation of Americans has been summoned to give testimony to
its national loyalty. The graves of young Americans who answered the
call to service surround the globe.

Now the trumpet summons us again—not as a call to bear arms,   22
though arms we need—not as a call to battle, though embattled we are—
but a call to bear the burden of a long twilight struggle, year in and year
out, "rejoicing in hope, patient in tribulation"—a struggle against the
common enemies of man: tyranny, poverty, disease, and war itself.

Can we forge against these enemies a grand and global alliance,   23
North and South, East and West, that can assure a more fruitful life for
all mankind? Will you join in that historic effort?

In the long history of the world, only a few generations have been   24
granted the role of defending freedom in its hour of maximum danger. I
do not shrink from this responsibility—I welcome it. I do not believe that
any of us would exchange places with any other people or any other generation. The energy, the faith, the devotion which we bring to this endeavor will light our country and all who serve it—and the glow from
that fire can truly light the world.

And so, my fellow Americans: ask not what your country can do for   25
you—ask what you can do for your country.

My fellow citizens of the world: ask not what America will do for   26
you, but what together we can do for the freedom of man.

Finally, whether you are citizens of America or citizens of the   27
world, ask of us here the same high standards of strength and sacrifice
which we ask of you. With a good conscience our only sure reward, with
history the final judge of our deeds, let us go forth to lead the land we
love, asking His blessing and His help, but knowing that here on earth
God's work must truly be our own.

As rhetoric has become an increasingly dispensable member of the liberal 1
arts, people have abandoned the idea, held so firmly by the ancient Greeks
and Romans, that eloquence is indispensable to politics. Perhaps President
Kennedy's achievements in both spheres will revive a taste for good oratory—a taste that has been alternately frustrated by inarticulateness and
dulled by bombast. There have been a few notable orators in our day—
most recently, Adlai Stevenson—but they have been the exceptions, and
it has taken Mr. Kennedy's success as a politician to suggest that the power
to "enchant souls through words" (Socrates) may soon be at a premium
once more. Whatever the impact of the Inaugural Address on contemporary New Frontiersmen, we find it hard to believe that an Athenian or
Roman citizen could have listened to it unmoved, or that Cicero, however
jealous of his own reputation, would have found reason to object to it.

We are all familiar by now with the generally high praise the Presi- 2
dent received for his first speech, but before the responsibility for a final
judgment is yielded to Time it would be a shame not to seek the opinion
of a couple of true professionals. Both Aristotle and Cicero, the one a
theorist and the other a theorizing orator, believed that rhetoric could be
an art to the extent that the orator was, first, a logician, and, second, a
psychologist with an appreciation and understanding of words. Cicero felt,
further, that the ideal orator was the thoroughly educated man. (He would
be pleased by Mr. Kennedy's background with its strong emphasis on
affairs of state: the philosopher-orator-statesman.) Of the three types of
oratory defined by the ancients—political, forensic, and display (in which
audience participation was limited to a judgment of style)—the political
was esteemed most highly, because it dealt with the loftiest of issues:
namely, the fate of peoples, rather than of individuals. ("Now the trumpet
summons us again . . . against the common enemies of man. . . .") The ideal
speech was thought to be one in which three kinds of persuasion were
used by the speaker: logical, to present the facts of the case and construct
an argument based on them; emotional, to reach the audience psychologically; and "ethical," to appeal to the audience by establishing one's own
integrity and sincerity. The Inaugural Address, being a variation on the
single theme of man's rights and obligations, is not primarily logical, although it contains no illogic; it is an appeal to men's souls rather than to
their minds. During the Presidential campaign, Mr. Kennedy tested and
patented an exercise in American psychology that proved to be all the
emotional appeal he required for the inaugural speech: "And so, my fellow
Americans, ask not what your country can do for you, ask what you can
do for your country." His ethical persuasion, or indication of his personal
probity, consisted of an extension of that appeal: ". . . ask of us here the
same high standards of strength and sacrifice which we ask of you."

Aristotle recognized only one (good) style, while Cicero thought that 3
there were three styles—the plain, the middle, and the grand. To Aristotle, who considered it sufficient for a style to be clear and appropriate,
avoiding undue elevation (whence bombast) and excessive lowliness, it

would have seemed that Mr. Kennedy had achieved the Golden Mean. The formality of the Inaugural Address ("To that world assembly of sovereign states, the United Nations . . .") is appropriate to the subject; the language ("In your hands, my fellow citizens, more than mine, will rest the final success or failure of our course") is clear and direct. Cicero's ideal orator was able to speak in all three styles, in accordance with the demands of his subject, and in that respect Mr. Kennedy filled the role by speaking plainly on the practical ("All this will not be finished in the first one hundred days"), by speaking formally but directly on the purpose of national defense ("For only when our arms are sufficient beyond doubt can we be certain beyond doubt that they will never be employed"), and by speaking grandly on the potential accomplishments of the movement toward the New Frontier ("The energy, the faith, the devotion which we bring to this endeavor will light our country and all who serve it—and the glow from that fire can truly light the world").

The address, however, is largely in the grand style, which is charac- 4 terized by Cicero as the ultimate source of emotional persuasion, through figures of speech and a certain degree of dignified periodic rhythm, not iambic ("The world is very different now. For man holds in his mortal hands the power to abolish all forms of human poverty and all forms of human life"). The oration is so rich in figures of speech—the many metaphors include a torch, a beachhead, jungles, a trumpet, a tiger—that we can imagine students of the future studying it for examples of antithesis ("If a free society cannot help the many who are poor, it cannot save the few who are rich"), personification (". . . the hand of mankind's final war"), and anaphora ("Not as a call to bear arms, though arms we need; not as a call to battle, though embattled we are . . ."). "Battle" and "embattled"— an excellent example of paronomasia.*

And so we leave the speech to the students of rhetoric, having in- 5 voked for Mr. Kennedy the blessings of Aristotle and Cicero, and for ourself the hope that he has reestablished the tradition of political eloquence.

* Figures of speech: Definitions
1) antithesis: balancing opposing ideas and words ("the *many* . . . are *poor;* the *few* are *rich*"); 2) personification: giving human traits to nonhuman beings (the *hand* of . . . war); 3) anaphora: repeating introductory words or clauses ("not as . . . ," "not as. . ."); 4) paronomasia: repeating a root word with a slight change in sound, sense, or affix ("battle" and "embattled").

Questions

Rereading and Independent Analysis

1. Make a topical outline of Kennedy's speech. What idea unifies it throughout? How did Kennedy expand on and explore that theme in the subdivisions of the speech?

2. Make a chart in which you identify and categorize the figures of

speech that the essay identifies in its last paragraph. (Use a dictionary to expand the definitions given in the footnote.) What devices did Kennedy use most?

Suggested Discussion and Group Activities

1. Which of the ideas Kennedy proposed in this speech are still influential in United States politics and public policy? Do his proposals appear realistic from your perspective now?

2. The *New Yorker* demonstrates that Kennedy gave a polished speech, a good example of the art of rhetoric, but it does not comment specifically on Kennedy's content. What details of the essay tell you that the magazine approved of the speech's message?

3. Would it be possible to use the techniques the *New Yorker* found in the speech to persuade people to accept unsuitable, dishonest, or ill-conceived ideas? In groups, select currently influential ideas that you think are poorly formed and state them in language and forms like those that Kennedy used. Use ideas in national and local politics that you disagree with because of their logic or consequences. Do these ideas become more persuasive when they are stated in "rhetorical" language? Why?

4. Bring to class an example of a more recent speech that you think was especially effective because of its powerful language and presentation. In groups, explain why you rate it highly.

Writing Suggestions

Response

Write a response to Kennedy's address in which you react to his points as though you were able to interrupt and answer what he said. Explain why his statements appeal to your sense of our country's needs now or why you disagree with them. What results do you think they would have if we adopted them in our current situation? Would you want Kennedy to be President now?

Analysis

Write a few sentences that argue for public action or an attitude you believe in, using figures of speech you identify in Kennedy's inaugural address. Then write a paragraph or two using these sentences. Ask one or more of your classmates to judge whether or not you would persuade them to agree with you about your policies. Follow their suggestions for revision. Then as a class select two or three examples of the most persuasive sentences.

Finding a Purpose

In small groups, do some reading about the 1960s and the results of the Kennedy "spirit" to expand your knowledge of the period. You will need to compare trends and leaders in the 1960s with those today in order to explain the differences between the two eras; therefore, you can divide your work to gather both old and new information. After you have assigned this reading and note taking, prepare a joint outline and draft of a retrospective column for your school or local paper. Then, together, write the column, in which you discuss Kennedy as a hero figure in his time and the reception you think he might receive today.

I Have a Dream
Martin Luther King

Martin Luther King, Jr. (1929–1968) was the leader of the nonviolent American civil rights revolution in the 1960s. King, the son of a black minister and a minister himself, was a master of one of public speaking's special forms, the sermon. Because of this mastery and his use of it in all his public speaking and writing, he was able to change American attitudes, law, and personal interactions. He mobilized both black and white groups, notably the Southern Christian Leadership Conference, to act through passive resistance, economic boycott, and political pressure. His followers gradually but emphatically changed racial interactions in this country. He was awarded the Nobel Peace Prize in honor of these accomplishments.

This speech was delivered at a peaceful demonstration in August 1963 on the steps of the Lincoln Memorial in Washington, D.C. Two hundred thousand blacks and whites had gathered there after long marches from the South and other parts of the country, setting up tents on the grounds of the Washington Monument to focus attention on black demands for change in civil rights laws. Many black and white leaders led the group in songs, and several people gave speeches. But King's address, delivered in the cadences of his preaching and interrupted often by approving audience responses, was the high point of the entire event.

As always in the best of his statements, King was able to argue the case of poor and minority groups without inciting mob violence. He spoke and wrote effectively to inspire lengthy, sometimes dangerous, individual and group action. John F. Kennedy was President at the time. Both he and King were shot by assassins within six years of each other, a fate King had often predicted for himself. As you read, imagine the scene of this speech and the possibility of violence from its approving audience, and from those who opposed King.

Five score years ago, a great American, in whose symbolic shadow we 1
stand today, signed the Emancipation Proclamation. This momentous decree came as a great beacon light of hope to millions of Negro slaves who had been seared in the flames of withering injustice. It came as a joyous daybreak to end the long night of their captivity.

But one hundred years later, the Negro still is not free. One hundred 2
years later, the life of the Negro is still sadly crippled by the manacles of segregation and the chains of discrimination.

One hundred years later, the Negro lives on a lonely island of poverty 3
in the midst of a vast ocean of material prosperity. One hundred years
later, the Negro is still languishing in the corners of American society and
finds himself an exile in his own land. So we have come here today to
dramatize a shameful condition.

In a sense we have come to our nation's capital to cash a check. When 4
the architects of our republic wrote the magnificent words of the Constitution and the Declaration of Independence, they were signing a promissory
note to which every American was to fall heir. This note was a promise
that all men, yes, black men as well as white men, would be guaranteed
the unalienable rights of life, liberty, and the pursuit of happiness.

It is obvious today that America has defaulted on this promissory note 5
insofar as her citizens of color are concerned. Instead of honoring this
sacred obligation, America has given the Negro people a bad check, which
has come back marked "insufficient funds."

But we refuse to believe that the bank of justice is bankrupt. We 6
refuse to believe that there are insufficient funds in the great vaults of
opportunity of this nation. So we have come to cash this check—a check
that will give us upon demand the riches of freedom and the security of
justice.

We have also come to this hallowed spot to remind America of the 7
fierce urgency of now. This is no time to engage in the luxury of cooling
off or to take the tranquilizing drug of gradualism. Now is the time to make
real the promises of democracy. Now is the time to rise from the dark and
desolate valley of segregation to the sunlit path of racial justice. Now is the
time to lift our nation from the quicksands of racial injustice to the solid
rock of brotherhood. Now is the time to make justice a reality for all of
God's children.

It would be fatal for the nation to overlook the urgency of the move- 8
ment and to underestimate the determination of the Negro. This sweltering summer of the Negro's legitimate discontent will not pass until there
is an invigorating autumn of freedom and equality. 1963 is not an end but
a beginning. Those who hope that the Negro needed to blow off steam and
will now be content will have a rude awakening if the nation returns to
business as usual.

There will be neither rest nor tranquility in America until the Negro 9
is granted his citizenship rights. The whirlwinds of revolt will continue to
shake the foundations of our nation until the bright day of justice emerges.

But there is something that I must say to my people who stand on 10
the warm threshold which leads into the palace of justice. In the process
of gaining our rightful place we must not be guilty of wrongful deeds.

Let us not seek to satisfy our thirst for freedom by drinking from the 11
cup of bitterness and hatred. We must forever conduct our struggle on the
high plane of dignity and discipline. We must not allow our creative
protest to degenerate into physical violence. Again and again we must rise
to the majestic heights of meeting physical force with soul force.

The marvelous new militancy which has engulfed the Negro commu- 12 nity must not lead us to a distrust of all white people, for many of our white brothers, as evidenced by their presence here today, have come to realize that their destiny is tied up with our destiny and they have come to realize that their freedom is inextricably bound to our freedom. We cannot walk alone.

And as we walk, we must make the pledge that we shall always march ahead. We cannot turn back. There are those who are asking the devotees of civil rights, "When will you be satisfied?" We can never be satisfied as long as the Negro is the victim of the unspeakable horrors of police brutality. 13

We can never be satisfied as long as our bodies, heavy with the fatigue of travel, cannot gain lodging in the motels of the highways and the hotels of the cities. We cannot be satisfied as long as the Negro's basic mobility is from a smaller ghetto to a larger one. 14

We can never be satisfied as long as our children are stripped of their selfhood and robbed of their dignity by signs stating "for whites only." We cannot be satisfied as long as a Negro in Mississippi cannot vote and a Negro in New York believes he has nothing for which to vote. No, we are not satisfied, and we will not be satisfied until justice rolls down like waters and righteousness like a mighty stream. 15

I am not unmindful that some of you have come here out of excessive trials and tribulation. Some of you have come fresh from narrow jail cells. Some of you have come from areas where your quest for freedom left you battered by the storms of persecution and staggered by the winds of police brutality. You have been the veterans of creative suffering. Continue to work with the faith that unearned suffering is redemptive. 16

Go back to Mississippi; go back to Alabama; go back to South Carolina; go back to Georgia; go back to Louisiana; go back to the slums and ghettos of the Northern cities, knowing that somehow this situation can, and will be changed. Let us not wallow in the valley of despair. 17

So I say to you, my friends, that even though we must face the difficulties of today and tomorrow, I still have a dream. It is a dream deeply rooted in the American dream that one day this nation will rise up and live out the true meaning of its creed—we hold these truths to be self evident, that all men are created equal. 18

I have a dream that one day on the red hills of Georgia, sons of former slaves and sons of former slave-owners will be able to sit down together at the table of brotherhood. 19

I have a dream that one day, even the state of Mississippi, a state sweltering with the heat of injustice, sweltering with the heat of oppression, will be transformed into an oasis of freedom and justice. 20

I have a dream my four little children will one day live in a nation where they will not be judged by the color of their skin but by content of their character. I have a dream today! 21

I have a dream that one day, down in Alabama, with its vicious racists, with its governor having his lips dripping with the words of inter- 22 position and nullification, that one day, right there in Alabama, little black boys and black girls will be able to join hands with little white boys and white girls as sisters and brothers. I have a dream today!

    I have a dream that one day every valley shall be exalted, every hill   23
and mountain shall be made low, the rough places shall be made plain, and the crooked places shall be made straight and the glory of the Lord will be revealed and all flesh shall see it together.

    This is our hope. This is the faith that I go back to the South with.   24

    With this faith we will be able to hew out of the mountain of despair,   25
a stone of hope. With this faith, we will be able to transform the jangling discords of our nation into a beautiful symphony of brotherhood.

    With this faith we will be able to work together, to pray together, to   26
struggle together, to go to jail together, to stand up for freedom together, knowing that we will be free one day. This will be the day when all of God's children will be able to sing with new meaning—"my country 'tis of thee, sweet land of liberty, of thee I sing; land where my fathers died, land of the pilgrim's pride; from every mountain side, let freedom ring"— and if America is to be a great nation, this must become true.

    And so let freedom ring from the prodigious hilltops of New Hamp-   27
shire.

    Let freedom ring from the mighty mountains of New York.   28

    Let freedom ring from the heightening Alleghenies of Pennsylvania.   29

    Let freedom ring from the snow-capped Rockies of Colorado.   30

    Let freedom ring from the curvaceous slopes of California.   31

    But not only that.   32

    Let freedom ring from Stone Mountain of Georgia.   33

    Let freedom ring from Lookout Mountain of Tennessee.   34

    Let freedom ring from every hill and molehill of Mississippi, from   35
every mountainside, let freedom ring.

    And when this happens, and when we allow freedom to ring, when   36
we let it ring from every village and hamlet, from every state and city, we will be able to speed up that day when all of God's children—black men and white men, Jews and Gentiles, Catholics and Protestants—will be able to join hands and to sing in the words of the old Negro spiritual, "Free at last, free at last; thank God Almighty, we are free at last."

Questions

Rereading and Independent Analysis

    1. The words "five score years ago" echo the beginning of the "Gettysburg Address." Starting here, King frequently quoted from or imitated important American documents. Reread the speech, underlining passages that seem familiar and noting their sources where you can. How do these references contribute to the speech's purpose? How do they make it authoritative?

    2. In this speech, King translated the name *civil rights movement* into the concrete image of actual movement. List all of the words that indicate motion in the speech. How do they work together to state a theme? Write a sentence that summarizes this theme.

Suggested Discussion and Group Activities

1. Read portions of the speech aloud, either alone or by taking turns in a group. After listening to it, do you think it is more effective in its spoken or written form? How do its quotations and references contribute to its power when it is spoken aloud?

2. One of the speech's most frequent techniques is the use of *metaphor,* a brief comparison of two unlike objects or ideas (for example, "You are a chicken"). Choose any five sequential paragraphs of the speech and identify the metaphors they include. How do these comparisons, including those that suggest motion, support King's argument?

Writing Suggestions

Response

1. King says that the presence of white people at this event showed that they "have come to realize that their destiny is tied up with our destiny and they have come to realize that their freedom is inextricably bound to our freedom." Do you agree with the principle expressed here? Is the destiny of a majority always tied up with the destiny of minority groups? Write a few paragraphs in which you explain your position about this question. Explain your position with examples of minority-majority relations in your school or community.

2. The change in racial relations is only one example of the major shifts in American political, family, and social life in this century. Choose an area of such change that has affected your life—for example, urbanization, new technology, or women's rights. Explain the results of this change to a reader who has not experienced it. Include any negative reaction to the change ("backlash") that you think the change has caused.

Analysis

Imagine that you are a foreign correspondent in Washington, writing a dispatch to your home newspaper in a major foreign city about this speech. Pictures of the occasion will be sent, but you must write a summary of the speech's contents to accompany them. Write the summary, telling what King said to a foreign audience and showing why it was significant.

Finding a Purpose

In the sense that a well-known speaker's audience is a public who may resist change, we might conclude that "speaking in public" is dangerous. Lincoln, Kennedy, and King, who are represented in this chapter, were all shot by members of the public they wanted to influence. Socrates, the ancient Greek teacher, was indicted and executed by his countrymen for promoting dangerous ideas.

Write an essay in which you explain to students of politics and public speaking how new ideas can be dangerous to the traditional customs and beliefs of a community. What is at stake in holding on to traditional public customs and beliefs? Why do you think that new ideas can create terrible anger toward speakers who argue for them?

CHAPTER 2

Visible Language

INTRODUCTION

Because written words are relatively permanent, one of their chief characteristics is that they can take on many meanings after they are written. Writing fixes the precise language of laws, contracts, proclamations, manifestos, negotiations, or wise sayings, so generations of readers turn to written records for authority. Our community roots are in such documents. We read them repeatedly to find support for our social, political, religious, and community actions.

But, to extend the metaphor, while these documents are roots, each reading of them also produces a new plant. By interpreting and reinterpreting documents, we revive their original situations and purposes. We reopen the special written "conversation" in which they were conceived, either to agree with it or to modify it. Written documents are paradoxical—their very permanence and authority invite us to question their intentions and to reform them to fit new needs and purposes. They are simultaneously the record of past community agreements and the living moments of ongoing social processes.

This chapter highlights three purposes for such highly visible writing. "Letters of the Law" includes writing that has become the foundation of long religious, legal, and political traditions. Generations have turned to these written words for guidance, for the principles they preserve have endured beyond their moments of composition. As a reader, you will understand these documents best if you contrast the original times and places that produced them with the many situations in which they are still applied.

The second section, "Renewing Social Contracts," includes examples of equally visible writing that changes or renews particular agreements about the relations between people. The examples included here are taken from specific and significant historical settings, but they have standardized forms that are always important. Because they give public authority and status to our decisions, we use these forms as we pass new laws, propose new systems of interaction, resolve conflicts, negotiate, and sign contracts.

The third section, "Sayings and Inscriptions," includes writing whose importance derives from its frequent repetition and from its actual physical locations. Short, easily remembered bits of wisdom and advice become like charms. We invoke them as semimagical formulas for explanation and guidance in common human situations. "A penny saved is a penny earned," one of Benjamin Franklin's bits of wisdom in *Poor Richard's Almanac,* is hardly "true," but its perfectly balanced, repetitive form has made it a common part of the language.

We give some writing our thoughtful attention because it has been placed where it will strike us forcibly. An inscription on a monument, a bit of graffiti, and a headline take much of their meaning from the places where we see them. Groups of words have significance in their visually arresting physical contexts, so we read their contents with a sense of the importance that they may fulfill or ironically undercut.

The specific language and vocabulary in all of these selections is especially important. As you read any of them, you should be aware of their special preservative purpose. They show writers attempting to cast wide but very economical networks of meaning to include a multitude of situations and assure others of the importance of their statements.

LETTERS OF THE LAW

 # The Ten Commandments

The biblical story of how the Jewish people established their special pact ("covenant") with God may be so familiar to you that you do not think of it as taking place in a specific situation whose elements had much to do with the words you now read. But the account shows the Jews reacting to their situation as any people might have. After they escaped slavery in Egypt and ventured into the desert, physical needs were their first concerns. Their very real insecurities about making a new life in an alien environment led them repeatedly to test the power of their deliverer, Moses. They asked why he had brought them to the desert if they were only going to die there of hunger and thirst, and they questioned the strange identity of the God Moses had brought to them. Moses needed to establish that this God was the only true

God and convince his people that He was unlike the many different gods of other places and tribes. Unlike the Greek gods, who casually participated in human life, the Hebrew God was not to be worshiped as an idol, statue, or in human form, and was not to be given a name.

This written monument to the important consequences of leaving Egypt shows Moses explaining his agreement with God to save his people and the conditions of that agreement. He must persuade his people to believe in a being who will not appear to them in recognizable forms but who will not abandon them so long as they believe He is their God. Because he needs support, Moses asks God for a *sign* of His superiority. His talk with God on Mt. Sinai, which established the agreement with a God that the people seriously questioned, was *"sign*ified" by the stone tablets inscribed with the Ten Commandments.

The commandments are an easily remembered list for people who cannot read but who can count on their fingers. But as laws governing the Jews' relations with God and with other people, their "neighbors," they are more than a list of rules or precepts that must be obeyed. They are also a visible agreement between God and the Jews, an inscribed list that will substitute for an image.

The commandments provide for patterns of behavior that are not given justification or explanation because God exists before reasons and explanations. When the Jews finally hear the voice of God, proof of His existence and power, they ask Moses to speak for Him because they are so frightened. God insists that they not fashion altars from metal or hewn stones, so that they will always remember His integration with nature. He does not want His image subjected to human shaping, and the commandments insist that they do not lightly use the name He does allow them to speak.

The commandments are also a memorial to the tribal culture of the Jews. As you read them, imagine their setting, one where "neighbor," "ox," and basic human crimes are vivid issues. Try to imagine the need for this particular list of precepts in a tribal group who must face the problems of gathering family units into a community of "neighbors."

16 On the morning of the third day there were thunders and lightnings, and a thick cloud upon the mountain, and a very loud trumpet blast, so that all the people who were in the camp trembled. [17]Then Moses brought the people out of the camp to meet God; and they took their stand at the foot of the mountain. [18]And Mount Sinai was wrapped in smoke, because the LORD descended upon it in fire; and the smoke of it went up like the smoke of a kiln, and the whole mountain quaked greatly. [19]And as the sound of the trumpet grew louder and louder, Moses spoke, and God answered him in thunder. [20]And the LORD came down upon Mount Sinai, to the top of the mountain; and the LORD called Moses to the top of the mountain, and Moses went up. [21]And the LORD said to Moses, "Go down and warn the people, lest they break through to the LORD to gaze and many of them perish. [22]And also let the priests who come near to the LORD consecrate themselves, lest the LORD break out upon them." ²³And Moses said to the LORD, "The people cannot come up to Mount Sinai; for thou thyself didst charge us, saying, 'Set bounds about the mountain, and consecrate it.' " ²⁴And the LORD said to him, "Go down, and come up bringing Aaron with you; but do not let the priests and the people break through to come up to the LORD, lest he break out against them." ²⁵So Moses went down to the people and told them.

20 And God spoke all these words, saying,

2 "I am the LORD your God, who brought you out of the land of Egypt, out of the house of bondage.

3 "You shall have no other gods before me.

4 "You shall not make yourself a graven image, or any likeness of anything that is in heaven above, or that is in the earth beneath, or that is in the water under the earth; ⁵you shall not bow down to them or serve them; for I the LORD your God am a jealous God, visiting the iniquity of the fathers upon the children to the third and the fourth generation of those who hate me, ⁶but showing steadfast love to thousands of those who love me and keep my commandments.

7 "You shall not take the name of the LORD your God in vain; for the LORD will not hold him guiltless who takes his name in vain.

8 "Remember the sabbath day, to keep it holy. ⁹Six days you shall labor, and do all your work; ¹⁰but the seventh day is a sabbath to the LORD your God; in it you shall not do any work, you, or your son, or your daughter, your manservant, or your maidservant, or your cattle, or the sojourner who is within your gates; ¹¹for in six days the LORD made heaven and earth, the sea, and all that is in them, and rested the seventh day; therefore the LORD blessed the sabbath day and hallowed it.

12 "Honor your father and your mother, that your days may be long in the land which the LORD your God gives you.

13 "You shall not kill.

14 "You shall not commit adultery.

15 "You shall not steal.

16 "You shall not bear false witness against your neighbor.

17 "You shall not covet your neighbor's house; you shall not covet your neighbor's wife, or his manservant, or his maidservant, or his ox, or his ass, or anything that is your neighbor's."

18 Now when all the people perceived the thunderings and the lightnings and the sound of the trumpet and the mountain smoking, the people were afraid and trembled; and they stood afar off. ¹⁹and said to Moses, "You speak to us, and we will hear; but let not God speak to us, lest we die." ²⁰And Moses said to the people, "Do not fear; for God has come to prove you, and that the fear of him may be before your eyes, that you may not sin."

Questions

Rereading and Independent Analysis

1. Classify the commandments into groups determined by the areas of public and private life that they address. If all you knew about the biblical Jews was what you could learn from this list, how would you describe them? What are the concerns and interests of this community?

2. Try rewriting any of the commandments in more modern language, including more details. What is gained and lost in your rewriting? Would your rewritten "commandments" be suitable for a memorable list? Why or why not?

Suggested Discussion and Group Activities

1. Is this list of rules still applicable to contemporary urban patterns of interaction? Why? Explain why you think a longer, more elaborate description of principles would be more, or less, effective now.

2. Give examples of personal and public "lists" you know about or have made yourself. What are some purposes for making lists? Can you see these purposes for making lists at work in the commandments? How do their brevity, order, and repetitiveness achieve these purposes?

3. If you had to make a list of principles and rules to govern your class, what issues would it address? In groups or as a class, identify five to ten problems you would like to solve, and decide on the best language for making them clear and memorable.

Writing Suggestions

Response

Write a few paragraphs in which you explain your reaction to formal "rules" like those that an organization or your family imposes on you. How do you respond to having definite limits on your actions? What benefits do you find in knowing what is expected of you? What happens when you do not follow the rules?

Analysis

The Ten Commandments suggest that the people who received them were multidimensional. The commandments portray the Jews as having equally important exterior lives of action and interior lives of thought and feeling. Write an essay explaining how this belief that people have both "inside" and "outside" facets still appears in our views of success. How does your image of a "well-rounded" life, of a fulfilling career, or of being a valuable member of a family or other group include private as well as visible values and achievements?

You might begin your thinking by listing the specific qualities and achievements that you think of as important for success in one or another of these areas (e.g., family or career). Then classify the list according to whether its elements could always be seen by others or might only be known to the person who holds them. Use your two lists to show how "complete" success requires a person to have more than one dimension. How is a one-dimensional person limited?

Finding a Purpose

Imagine that you must organize and govern a specific community you know—for example, people of a certain age, way of life, or occupation. Make a list of no more than ten rules that will accomplish the comprehensive regulation that the Ten Commandments achieved. Be sure to address directly your chosen group's special problems.

Now write a document that heads this list with a brief explanation of your purpose for making it. Make your document suitable for posting where it can be read easily by all members of your group.

 # Magna Carta

As Americans we take for granted that our government will consider problems, make laws about them, enforce these laws, and treat us all equally in these actions. In addition, we expect to participate in this governance, either directly or through representation. We know that we have rights ensuring our freedom to act and that there are limits to what the government may require us to do. We also know that if we break laws, we will become subject to a legal process (called "due process of law") and that evidence against us is required before we may be brought to a trial, where a jury of citizens will consider the evidence before we are judged. We assume that these principles apply equally to us all.

But what we take for granted, know, assume, and expect about living by such principles of law did not always exist. We in the United States live under a legal arrangement about our rights that was impossible in countries where a king or other absolute ruler governed with a free hand. The arbitrary personal privilege of a king and others he might designate with authority once meant that a citizen could at any time be subject to special taxes, sudden judgments, and other unevenly applied interference with personal action.

This was the situation that produced the document we know as Magna Carta, or "great charter." In the time between the Norman Conquest of England in 1066 and the day King John affixed his seal to this charter, the scattered barons who ruled local areas of England became increasingly angry about the strong centralized government under the king. In order to increase revenues to the crown, the barons were required to pay heavy taxes, ransoms, and other fees gathered from judicial fines and other sources. Military taxes were also levied to support various wars, and the crown insisted on its right to control church property as well.

The barons were not alone in their dissatisfaction. Other groups, notably supporters of the church, were also disgusted by the unfairness of the privileges given to royal officers. By Easter week of 1215, the barons had drawn up a charter describing their proper liberties. King John rejected it out of hand. In May, the barons formally rejected royal power, refused John's suggestion of arbitration, and began plans to march together in revolt on London. John, who knew that too many interest groups were against him to assure his winning a fight, sent a message that he would "freely accede" to the barons' charter; he met with them on June 15, 1215, at Runnymede, a meadow on the Thames near Windsor.

The document King John signed says nothing of the *principles* of rule of law that it later came to support. It was immediate, practical, and to the point in each of its 63 articles. But the document itself, copied in Latin and sent to cathedrals in all parts of England, demonstrated the change King John had been forced to agree to by unlettered local rulers. Its words were devised by men who probably could not write themselves but who had scribes record the agreement.

These written words became the basis for a monumental principle of just governance that has established human rights throughout the world. It became the ground on which the American Declaration of Independence, Constitution, and Bill of Rights rest. As you read, you will not need to have studied specific points of English history to realize how the ideas in this document are part of our way of life. These articles named freedoms we now think of as normal: the freedom of the church (if not its separation from the state), easy access into and out of the country, the consent of the governed to laws, reasonable judicial procedures, and requirements for trial by one's peers and punishment appropriate to the offense. The charter's controls on the power of government over personal property and its embryonic idea of equal justice for all have become basic elements of the American concept of the state.

These principles have been refined, extended, and debated when specific laws in England and the United States have been passed or changed. Magna Carta was the basic document on which such modifications were made. We may no longer be concerned with some of the charter's original statements. For example, Chapter 54, which prohibits women from asking any champion to fight for them in a trial by combat, was intended to prevent them from having an unfair advantage by choosing the best warrior available to defeat specific opponents in legal contests. But we still adhere to the principle of fairness that underlies this statement, even though competition between knightly champions appears to us to be a romantic view of how to settle a legal dispute.

The language and presentation of this document are unfamiliar, but they are not barriers to your understanding its significance or to imagining the urgent situation in which it was written. As you read the Preamble, keep in mind the purpose of the entire document: to proclaim King John's new wishes. The king's many titles, the names of those he consulted, and the form of what follows were all designed to create a royal action-in-words, the most official and forceful sort of statement possible at the time.

Preamble
John, by the grace of God, King of England, Lord of Ireland, Duke of Normandy and Aquitaine, and Count of

Anjou: To the Archbishops, Bishops, Abbots, Earls, Barons, Justiciaries, Foresters, Sheriffs, Reeves, Ministers, and all Bailiffs and others, his faithful subjects, Greeting. Know ye that in the presence of God, and for the health of Our soul, and the souls of Our ancestors and heirs, to the honor of God, and the exaltation of Holy Church, and amendment of Our kingdom, by the advice of Our reverend Fathers, Stephen, Archbishop of Canterbury, Primate of all England, and Cardinal of the Holy Roman Church; Henry, Archbishop of Dublin; William of London, Peter of Winchester, Jocelin of Bath and Glastonbury, Hugh of Lincoln, Walter of Worcester, William of Coventry, and Benedict of Rochester, Bishops; Master Pandulph, the Pope's subdeacon and familiar; Brother Aymeric, Master of the Knights of the Temple in England; and the noble persons, William Marshal, Earl of Pembroke; William, Earl of Salisbury; William, Earl of Warren; William, Earl of Arundel; Alan de Galloway, Constable of Scotland; Warin Fitz-Gerald, Peter Fitz-Herbert, Hubert de Burgh, Seneschal of Poitou, Hugh de Neville, Matthew Fitz-Herbert, Thomas Basset, Alan Basset, Philip Daubeny, Robert de Roppelay, John Marshal, John Fitz-Hugh, and others, Our liegemen:

The English Church shall be free; grant of liberties to free men of the kingdom

1   We have, in the first place, granted to God, and by this Our present Charter confirmed for Us and Our heirs forever—That the English Church shall be free and enjoy her rights in their integrity and her liberties untouched. And that We will this so to be observed appears from the fact that We of Our own free will, before the outbreak of the dissensions between Us and Our barons, granted, confirmed, and procured to be confirmed by Pope Innocent III the freedom of elections, which is considered most important and necessary to the English Church, which Charter We will both keep Ourself and will it to be kept with good faith by Our heirs forever. We have also granted to all the free men of Our kingdom, for Us and Our heirs forever, all the liberties underwritten, to have and to hold to them and their heirs of Us and Our heirs.

Reliefs for inheritance

2   If any of Our earls, barons, or others who hold of Us in chief by knight's service shall die, and at the time of his death his heir shall be of full age and owe a relief, he shall have his inheritance by ancient relief; to wit, the heir or heirs of an earl of an entire earl's barony, £100; the heir or heirs of a baron of an entire barony, £100; the heir or heirs of a knight of an entire knight's fee, 100s. at the most; and he that owes less shall give less, according to the ancient custom of fees.

Heir under age 3 If, however, any such heir shall be under age and in ward, he shall, when he comes of age, have his inheritance without relief or fine.

. . . .

Rights of widows 7 A widow, after the death of her husband, shall immediately and without difficulty have her marriage portion and inheritance. She shall not give anything for her marriage portion, dower, or inheritance which she and her husband held on the day of his death, and she may remain in her husband's house for forty days after his death, within which time her dower shall be assigned to her.

Remarriage of widows 8 No widow shall be compelled to marry so long as she has a mind to live without a husband, provided, however, that she give security that she will not marry without Our assent, if she holds of Us, or that of the lord of whom she holds, if she holds of another.

. . . .

Liberties of London and other towns 13 The City of London shall have all her ancient liberties and free customs, both by land and water. Moreover, We will and grant that all other cities, boroughs, towns, and ports shall have all their liberties and free customs.

Calling of council to consent to aids 14 For obtaining the common counsel of the kingdom concerning the assessment of aids (other than in the three cases aforesaid) or of scutage, We will cause to be summoned, severally by Our letters, the archbishops, bishops, abbots, earls, and great barons; We will also cause to be summoned, generally, by Our sheriffs and bailiffs, all those who hold lands directly of Us, to meet on a fixed day, but with at least forty days' notice, and at a fixed place. In all letters of such summons We will explain the cause thereof. The summons being thus made, the business shall proceed on the day appointed, according to the advice of those who shall be present, even though not all the persons summoned have come.

. . . .

Fines to be measured by the offense; livelihoods not to be destroyed 20 A free man shall be amerced for a small fault only according to the measure thereof, and for a great crime according to its magnitude, saving his position; and in like manner a merchant saving his trade, and a villein saving his tillage, if they should fall under Our mercy. None of these amercements shall be imposed except by the oath of honest men of the neighborhood.

Same for barons 21   Earls and barons shall be amerced only by their peers, and only in proportion to the measure of the offense.

Same for clergymen 22   No amercement shall be imposed upon a clerk's lay property, except after the manner of the other persons aforesaid, and without regard to the value of his ecclesiastical benefice.

. . . .

Compensation for taking of private property 28   No constable or other of Our bailiffs shall take corn or other chattels of any man without immediate payment, unless the seller voluntarily consents to postponement of payment.

. . . .

No taking of horses without consent 30   No sheriff or other of Our bailiffs, or any other man, shall take the horses or carts of any free man for carriage without the owner's consent.

No taking of wood without consent 31   Neither We nor Our bailiffs will take another man's wood for Our castles or for any other purpose without the owner's consent.

. . . .

Uniform weights and measures 35   There shall be one measure of wine throughout Our kingdom, and one of ale, and one measure of corn, to wit, the London quarter, and one breadth of dyed cloth, russets, and haberjets, to wit, two ells within the selvages. As with measures so shall it also be with weights.

. . . .

No man to be put to his trial upon unsupported accusation 38   In the future no bailiff shall upon his own unsupported accusation put any man to trial without producing credible witnesses to the truth of the accusation.

Free men guaranteed "law of the land" 39   No free man shall be taken, imprisoned, disseised, outlawed, banished, or in any way destroyed, nor will We proceed against or prosecute him, except by the lawful judgment of his peers and by the law of the land.

Guarantee of equal justice 40   To no one will We sell, to none will We deny or delay, right or justice.

. . . .

Freedom to leave and reenter the kingdom 42   In the future it shall be lawful (except for a short period in time of war, for the common benefit of the realm) for anyone to leave and return to Our kingdom safely and securely by land and water, saving his fealty to

Us. Excepted are those who have been imprisoned or outlawed according to the law of the land, people of the
country at war with Us, and merchants, who shall be dealt
with as aforesaid.

. . . .

Women's
appeals

54 No one shall be arrested or imprisoned upon a
woman's appeal for the death of any person other than her
husband.

. . . .

Liberties to be
granted to lesser
tenants

60 All the customs and liberties aforesaid, which We
have granted to be enjoyed, as far as in Us lies, by Our
people throughout Our kingdom, let all Our subjects,
whether clerks or laymen, observe, as far as in them lies,
toward their dependents.

Questions

Rereading and Independent Analysis

1. The Preamble to Magna Carta contains a series of lists: John's
titles, the categories of people addressed, those who actually and symboli-
cally bear witness to this proclamation, and the word indicating what this
document accomplishes. After marking the Preamble to indicate breaks
among the lists, circle the word that tells what the document will do.

2. The articles of Magna Carta have a twofold significance: they both
recognized past customs and established a government with newly limited
power. For each of the articles here, write a brief explanation of the
condition or practice that you think it changed.

3. Classify the articles into three groups: governmental powers, personal powers, and the new rights they represent.

Suggested Discussion and Group Activities

1. Do you have any trouble understanding the intention of any of
these articles? As a class, identify the problems you have and discuss the
possible implications of unclear articles with your classmates. Try to reach
agreement about the situation these articles were correcting and the
change that would result.

2. What kind of community and way of life is this list of agreements
suited to? How can you tell from the document that the barons were rural
and relatively unlettered?

3. In groups, discuss your most basic assumptions about your rights
as a member of any group or community. What are some connections
between Magna Carta and modern American ways of acting in national,
local, and even small-group situations? How do your class discussions and
work in small groups demonstrate these connections?

Writing Suggestions

Response

Imagine that you are with the barons meeting the king in 1215. Write a personal letter expressing your feelings as you watch John agree to sign the charter. Mention the changes this event will make.

Analysis

One of the earliest copies of Magna Carta is kept in the British Museum in London for visitors to see. On the basis of your reading, write a brief explanation of the document that would be suitable for handing out to visitors from all over the world. Tell a broad group from many places about the charter's origins and its role as a living force in the lives of millions of people.

Finding a Purpose: Research

Individually or in groups, do some research in your library to gather information about similar "foundational" documents that have guided the laws and organizations of people. Look for similar statements in other cultures, such as the Orient, the Muslim world, Israel. Then prepare a descriptive catalog of these documents. Collaborate on a general introduction explaining their purposes, similarities, and differences. Add a brief explanation of each document you found, telling its time of composition, what you know of the circumstances that brought it about, and its influence.

The Declaration of Independence: First Draft and Final Version

It is amazing that the United States came to exist because 13 separately settled colonies were able to agree that they had to separate themselves from British rule and were willing to band together to establish a new country and fight for its right to exist. The extraordinary nature of this accomplishment gives us a sense of the power of the Declaration of Independence. After years of difficult government conducted over the great distance and many months it took to cross the Atlantic, of fighting wars for a country that the colonists had never seen, and of paying taxes to support a king with little interest in the colonists' problems, the "United Colonies" came together. They gathered representatives to discuss two issues: whether or not to strike out on their own as a new nation, and how to get along with one another if they did. Both matters were controversial among the new Americans, whose leaders were heavily influenced by more than one eighteenth-century definition of the social contract on which governments are based.

If the colonies were to declare independence, the statement proclaiming it had to be written by a representative group and written so well that it would persuade both its English and American readers of the justice of this enormous act. The Declaration must justify rebellion against a ruler whose authority was thought to come from God. When the idea of writing this document was formed, the colonies had already been at war with England for months and had sent representatives to a Continental Congress meeting in Philadelphia. Richard Henry Lee (ancestor of the Confederate general Robert E. Lee) proposed such a resolution of independence on June 7, 1776, but a vote was postponed until July. A committee was appointed to draft a document that could be voted on, with representatives from Massachusetts (John Adams), Pennsylvania (Benjamin Franklin), Virginia (Thomas Jefferson), Connecticut (Roger Sherman), and New York (Robert Livingston). This committee gave the task to Thomas Jefferson (1743–1826) who was writing many of the important explanations of the colonies' position. To justify separation from England, he quickly set out to produce a statement that would persuasively explain common ideas about a country's integrity and a people's rights. What was at stake was not only a principle but also the opinions of other countries whose support the colonists would need if they were to win the war and continue to exist as a country.

As you read the Declaration, you will notice that its structure is much like that of the persuasive speeches in the first chapter. The document establishes the position (or *ethos*) of the new country first by appealing to principles all accept. Then, starting with the second paragraph, it states its thesis—that the colonists have a right and duty to overthrow bad government. If it is true ("self-evident") that all men have certain rights under law, and if these rights are denied, then "all men" must consider themselves not to be governed by law. Next, the Declaration narrates the reasons that justify this position. In this section, the document is a list of specific grievances, made more powerful by parallel construction of the sentences and phrasing in the list. The document then goes on to refute possible objections, explaining that the colonists have taken every opportunity to discuss, negotiate, and establish good relations with the king. In the final section, the Declaration fulfills its title: it *declares* the colonies to be free and independent as a consequence of the logic of the argument.

The Declaration was not conceived as a speech, but it clearly demonstrates how a single speaker addressing a visible audience of listeners can be replaced by a "document" that will persuade readers across time and space. "The opinions of mankind" is the "audience" for this writing, which has become so important that the original is kept in the National Archives, on view for all in a permanently sealed case.

This national enshrinement may prevent us from noticing, however, that Jefferson wrote the Declaration with the help of the committee, who offered spoken and written comments on its phrasing and content to produce the language we now read. The draft included here is probably the second version of the document, which was submitted to the Continental Congress. In addition, two days of heated debate, especially about the list of grievances, resulted in many more changes than the committee had made in Jefferson's work. The Congress especially edited the last part of the document, returning to the wording of Richard Lee's June 7 resolution. These changes are important signs that the Declaration was written to be a powerful *document.* Each word was carefully considered as a message to readers who were far distant from the knowledge, feelings, and events that its writers knew intimately. Both the content and the style of the document were inspected so that there would be no doubt that its framers' insistent complaints were not personal statements of particular prejudices, but absolute truth.

Original Draft of the Declaration of Independence

*A Declaration of the Representatives of the
United States of America, in General Congress assembled.*

When in the course of human events it becomes necessary for a people 1
to advance from that subordination in which they have hitherto remained, & to assume among the powers of the earth the equal & independant station to which the laws of nature & of nature's god entitle them, a decent respect to the opinions of mankind requires that they should declare the causes which impel them to the change.

We hold these truths to be sacred & undeniable; that all men are 2
created equal & independant, that from that equal creation they derive rights inherent & inalienable, among which are the preservation of life, & liberty, & the spirit of happiness; that to secure these ends, governments are instituted among men, deriving their just powers from the consent of the governed; that whenever any form of government shall become destructive of these ends, it is the right of the people to alter or to abolish it, & to institute new government, laying it's foundation on such principles & organising it's powers in such form, as to them shall seem most likely to effect their safety & happiness. prudence indeed will dictate that governments long established should not be changed for light & transient causes: and accordingly all experience hath shewn that mankind are more disposed to suffer while evils are sufferable, than to right themselves by abolishing the forms to which they are accustomed. but when a long train of abuses & usurptions, begun at a distinguished period, & pursuing invariably the same object, evinces a design to subject them to arbitrary power, it is their right, it is their duty, to throw off such government & to provide new guards for their future security. such has been the patient sufferance of these colonies; & such is now the necessity which constrains them to expunge their former systems of government. the history of his present majesty, is a history of unremitting injuries and usurpations, among which no one fact stands single or solitary to contradict the uniform tenor of the rest, all of which have in direct object the establishment of an absolute tyranny over these states. to prove this, let facts be submitted to a candid world, for the truth of which we pledge a faith yet unsullied by falsehood.

he has refused his assent to laws the most wholesome and necessary for
the public good:

he has forbidden his governors to pass laws of immediate & pressing importance, unless suspended in their operation till his assent should be obtained; and when so suspended, he has neglected utterly to attend to them.

he has refused to pass other laws for the accommodation of large districts of people unless those people would relinquish the right of representation, a right inestimable to them, & formidable to tyrants alone:[1]

he has dissolved Representative houses repeatedly & continually, for opposing with manly firmness his invasions on the rights of the people:

he has refused for a long space of time to cause others to be elected, whereby the legislative powers, incapable of annihilation, have returned to the people at large for their exercise, the state remaining in the mean time exposed to all the dangers of invasion from without, &, convulsions within:

he has suffered the administration of justice totally to cease in some of these colonies, refusing his assent to laws for establishing judiciary powers:

he has made our judges dependant on his will alone, for the tenure of their offices, and amount of their salaries:

he has erected a multitude of new offices by a self-assumed power, & sent hither swarms of officers to harrass our people & eat out their substance:

he has kept among us in times of peace standing armies & ships of war:

he has affected[2] to render the military, independent of & superior to the civil power:

he has combined with others to subject us to a jurisdiction foreign to our constitutions and unacknoledged by our laws; giving his assent to their pretended acts of legislation, for quartering large bodies of armed troops among us;

> for protecting them by a mock-trial from punishment for any murders they should commit on the inhabitants of these states;
> for cutting off our trade with all parts of the world;
> for imposing taxes on us without our consent;
> for depriving us of the benefits of trial by jury

he has endeavored to prevent the population of these states for that purpose obstructing the laws for naturalization of foreigners; refusing to pass others to encourage their migrations hither; & raising the conditions of new appropriations of lands

---

[1] At this point in the manuscript a strip containing the following clause is inserted: "He called together legislative bodies at places unusual, unco[mfortable & distant from] the depository of their public records for the sole purpose of fatiguing [them into compliance] with his measures:" Missing parts in the Library of Congress text are supplied from the copy made by Jefferson for George Wythe. This copy is in the New York Public Library. The fact that this passage was omitted from John Adams's transcript suggests that it was not a part of Jefferson's original rough draft.

[2] Tried.

for transporting us beyond seas to be tried for pretended offences:

for taking away our charters & altering fundamentally the forms of our governments;

for suspending our own legislatures & declaring themselves invested with power to legislate for us in all cases whatsoever:

he has abdicated government here, withdrawing his governors, & declaring us out of his allegiance & protection:

he has plundered our seas, ravaged our coasts, burnt our towns & destroyed the lives of our people:

he is at this time transporting large armies of foreign mercenaries to compleat the works of death, desolation & tyranny, already begun with circumstances of cruelty & perfidy unworthy the head of a civilized nation:

he has endeavored to bring on the inhabitants of our frontiers the merciless Indian savages, whose known rule of warfare is an undistinguished destruction of all ages, sexes, & conditions of existence:

he has incited treasonable insurrections of our fellow-citizens, with the allurements of forfeiture & confiscation of our property:

he has waged cruel war against human nature itself, violating it's most sacred rights of life & liberty in the persons of a distant people who never offended him, captivating & carrying them into slavery in another hemisphere, or to incur miserable death in their transportion thither. this piratical warfare, the opprobrium of *infidel* powers, is the warfare of the CHRISTIAN king of Great Britain. determined to keep open a market where MEN should be bought & sold; he has prostituted his negative for suppressing every legislative attempt to prohibit or to restrain this execrable commerce: and that this assemblage of horrors might want no fact of distinguished die, he is now exciting those very people to rise in arms among us, and to purchase that liberty of which *he* has deprived them, by murdering the people upon whom *he* also obtruded them; thus paying off former crimes committed against the *liberties* of one people, with crimes which he urges them to commit against the *lives* of another.

in every stage of these oppressions we have petitioned for redress in the most humble terms; our repeated petitions have been answered by repeated injury. a prince whose character is thus marked by every act which may define a tyrant, is unfit to be the ruler of a people who mean to be free. future ages will scarce believe that the hardiness of one man, adventured within the short compass of twelve years only, on so many acts of tyranny without a mask, over a people fostered & fixed in principles of liberty.

Nor have we been wanting in attentions to our British brethren. we [3] have warned them from time to time of attempts by their legislature to extend a jurisdiction over these our states. we have reminded them of the circumstances of our emigration & settlement here, no one of which could warrant so strange a pretension: that these were effected at the expence of our own blood & treasure, unassisted by the wealth or the strength of Great Britain: that in constituting indeed our several forms of government, we had adopted one common king, thereby laying a foundation for perpetual league & amity with them; but that submission to their [Parliament, was no Part of our Constitution, nor ever in Idea, if History may be] credited: and we appealed to their native justice & magnanimity, as to the ties of our common kindred to disavow these usurpations which were likely to interrupt our correspondence & connection. they too have been deaf to the voice of justice & of consanguinity, & when occasions have been given them, by the regular course of their laws, of removing from their councils the disturbers of our harmony, they have by their free election re-established them in power. at this very time too they are permitting their chief magistrate to send over not only soldiers of our common blood, but Scotch & foreign mercenaries to invade & deluge us in blood. these facts have given the last stab to agonizing affection, and manly spirit bids us to renounce for ever these unfeeling brethren. we must endeavor to forget our former love for them, and to hold them as we hold the rest of mankind, enemies in war, in peace friends. we might have been a free & a great people together; but a communication of grandeur & of freedom it seems is below their dignity. be it so, since they will have it: the road to glory & happiness is open to us too; we will climb it in a separate state, and acquiesce in the necessity which pronounces our everlasting Adieu!

We therefore the representatives of the United States of America in 4 General Congress assembled do, in the name & by authority of the good people of these states, reject and renounce all allegiance & subjection to the kings of Great Britain & all others who may hereafter claim by, through, or under them; we utterly dissolve & break off all political connection which may have heretofore subsisted between us & the people or parliament of Great Britain; and finally we do assert and declare these colonies to be free and independant states, and that as free & independant states they shall hereafter have power to levy war, conclude peace, contract alliances, establish commerce, & to do all other acts and things which independant states may of right do. And for the support of this declaration we mutually pledge to each other our lives, our fortunes, & our sacred honour.

The Declaration of Independence.—1776.

IN CONGRESS, JULY 4, 1776.

The Unanimous Declaration of the thirteen U. S. of America.

When, in the course of human events, it becomes necessary for one people 1 to dissolve the political bands which have connected them with another, and to assume among the Powers of the earth, the separate and equal station to which the Laws of Nature and of Nature's God entitle them, a decent respect to the opinions of mankind requires that they should declare the causes which impel them to the separation.

We hold these truths to be self-evident, that all men are created 2 equal, that they are endowed by their Creator with certain unalienable Rights; that among these are Life, Liberty, and the pursuit of Happiness. That to secure these rights, Governments are instituted among Men, deriving their just powers from the consent of the governed; That whenever any Form of Government becomes destructive of these ends, it is the Right of the People to alter or to abolish it, and to institute new Government, laying its foundations on such principles and organizing its powers in such form, as to them shall seem most likely to effect their Safety and Happiness. Prudence, indeed, will dictate that Governments long established should not be changed for light and transient causes; and accordingly all experience hath shown, that mankind are more disposed to suffer, while evils are sufferable, than to right themselves by abolishing the forms to which they are accustomed. But when a long train of abuses and usurpations, pursuing invariably the same Object, evinces a design to reduce them under absolute Despotism, it is their right, it is their duty, to throw off such Government, and to provide new Guards for their future security. Such has been the patient sufferance of these Colonies; and such is now the necessity which constrains them to alter their former systems of Government. The history of the present King of Great Britain is a history of repeated injuries and usurpations, all having in direct object the establishment of an absolute Tyranny over these States. To prove this let facts be submitted to a candid world.

He has refused his Assent to Laws the most wholesome and necessary 3 for the public good.

He has forbidden his Governors to pass Laws of immediate and 4 pressing importance, unless suspended in their operation till his Assent should be obtained; and when so suspended, he has utterly neglected to attend to them.

He has refused to pass other Laws for the accommodation of large 5 districts of people, unless those people would relinquish the right of Representation in the Legislature, a right inestimable to them and formidable to tyrants only.

He has called together legislative bodies at places unusual, uncom- 6 fortable and distant from the depository of their Public Records, for the sole purpose of fatiguing them into compliance with his measures.

He has dissolved Representative Houses repeatedly, for opposing 7 with manly firmness his invasions on the rights of the people.

He has refused for a long time, after such dissolutions, to cause others 8 to be elected, whereby the Legislative Powers, incapable of Annihilation, have returned to the People at large for their exercise; the State remaining in the meantime exposed to all the dangers of invasion from without, and convulsions within.

He has endeavoured to prevent the population of these States; for 9
that purpose obstructing the Laws for Naturalization of Foreigners; refusing to pass others to encourage their migration hither, and raising the
conditions of new Appropriations of Lands.

He has obstructed the Administration of Justice, by refusing his As- 10
sent to Laws for establishing Judiciary Powers.

He has made Judges dependent on his Will alone, for the tenure of 11
their offices, and the amount and payment of their salaries.

He has erected a multitude of New Offices, and sent hither swarms 12
of Officers to harass our People and eat out their substance.

He has kept among us, in times of peace, Standing Armies without 13
the Consent of our legislature.

He has affected to render the Military independent of and superior 14
to the Civil Power.

He has combined with others to subject us to a jurisdiction foreign 15
to our constitution, and unacknowledged by our laws; giving his Assent to
their acts of pretended Legislation:

For quartering large bodies of armed troops among us: 16

For protecting them, by a mock Trial, from Punishment for any 17
Murders which they should commit on the Inhabitants of these States:

For cutting off our Trade with all parts of the world: 18

For imposing taxes on us without our Consent: 19

For depriving us, in many cases, of the benefits of Trial by Jury; 20

For transporting us beyond Seas to be tried for pretended offences. 21

For abolishing the free System of English Laws in a neighbouring 22
Province, establishing therein an Arbitrary government, and enlarging its
Boundaries, so as to render it at once an example and fit instrument for
introducing the same absolute rule into these Colonies:

For taking away our Charters, abolishing our most valuable Laws, 23
and altering fundamentally the Forms of our Government:

For suspending our own Legislature, and declaring themselves in- 24
vested with Power to legislate for us in all cases whatsoever.

He has abdicated Government here, by declaring us out of his Pro- 25
tection, and waging War against us.

He has plundered our seas, ravaged our Coasts, burned our towns, 26
and destroyed the lives of our people.

He is at this time transporting large armies of foreign mercenaries 27
to complete the works of death, desolation and tyranny, already begun
with circumstances of Cruelty and perfidy scarcely paralleled in the most
barbarous ages, and totally unworthy the Head of a civilized nation.

He has constrained our fellow Citizens taken Captives on the high 28
Seas to bear Arms against their Country, to become the executioners of
their friends and Brethren, or to fall themselves by their Hands.

He has excited domestic insurrection amongst us, and has en- 29
deavoured to bring on the inhabitants of our frontiers, the merciless

Indian Savages, whose known rule of warfare is an undistinguished destruction of all ages, sexes and conditions.

In every stage of these oppressions We have Petitioned for Redress 30 in the most humble terms: Our repeated Petitions have been answered only by repeated injury. A Prince, whose character is thus marked by every act which may define a Tyrant, is unfit to be the ruler of a free People.

Nor have we been wanting in attention to our British brethren. We 31 have been warned from time to time of attempts by their legislature to extend an unwarrantable jurisdiction over us. We have reminded them of the circumstances of our emigration and settlement here. We have appealed to their native justice and magnanimity, and we have conjured them by the ties of our common kindred to disavow these usurpations, which would inevitably interrupt our connections and correspondence. They too have been deaf to the voice of justice and of consanguinity. We must, therefore, acquiesce in the necessity, which denounces our Separation, and hold them, as we hold the rest of mankind, Enemies in War, in Peace, Friends.

We, therefore, the Representatives of the United States of America, 32 in General Congress Assembled, appealing to the Supreme Judge of the world for the rectitude of our intentions, do in the Name, and by Authority of the good People of these Colonies, solemnly publish and declare, That these United Colonies are, and of right ought to be, Free and Independent States; That they are Absolved from all Allegiance to the British Crown, and that all political connection between them and the State of Great Britain is, and ought to be, totally dissolved; and that as Free and Independent States, they have full Power to levy War, conclude Peace, contract Alliances, establish Commerce, and to do other Acts and Things which Independent States may of right do. And for the support of this Declaration, with a firm reliance on the Protection of Divine Providence, we mutually pledge to each other our Lives, our Fortunes and our sacred Honour.

John Hancock,
President.

NEW HAMPSHIRE.
Josiah Bartlett,
Wm. Whipple,
Matthew Thornton.

MASSACHUSETTS BAY.
Samuel Adams,
John Adams,
Robt. Treat Paine,
Eldridge Gerry.

RHODE ISLAND.
Step. Hopkins,
William Ellery.

CONNECTICUT.
Roger Sherman,
Samuel Huntington,
Wm. Williams.
Oliver Wolcott.

NEW YORK.
Wm. Floyd,
Phil. Livingston,
Frans. Lewis,
Lewis Morris.

NEW JERSEY.
Richd. Stockton,
Jno. Witherspoon,
Fras. Hopkinson.
John Hart,
Abra. Clark.

PENNSYLVANIA.
Robt. Morris,
Benjamin Rush,
Benja. Franklin.
John Morton,
George Clymer,
Jas. Smith,
Geo. Taylor,
James Wilson.
Geo Ross.

DELAWARE.
Cæsar Rodney,
George Read,
Tho. McKean.

MARYLAND.
Samuel Chase,
Wm. Paca,
Thos. Stone,
Charles Carroll of Carollton.

VIRGINIA,
George Whyte,
Richard Henry Lee.
Th. Jefferson,
Benja. Harrison,
Thos. Nelson, Jr.,
Francis Lightfoot Lee.
Carter Braxton.

NORTH CAROLINA.
Wm. Hooper,
Joseph Hewes,
John Penn.

SOUTH CAROLINA.
Edward Rutledge,
Thos. Heyward, Junr.,
Thomas Lynch, Junr.,
Arthur Middleton.

GEORGIA.
Button Gwinnett,
Lyman Hall,
George Walton.

Questions

Rereading and Independent Analysis

1. Review the Introduction to Chapter 1 and the headnote here. Then reread the draft and the Declaration, marking the places where the argument makes new points in separate sections. Compare these sections in both versions. Are they the same? Were any major changes made in the logic of the final version of the Declaration? Now write a brief summary of the document, a one-paragraph statement of the points it makes in logically connected form.

2. *Parallelism* is the repetition of words, phrases, and grammatical structures within sentences and longer units of writing. Read the section of the Declaration in which the colonies' grievances against the king are listed. Make a list of the uses of parallelism in this section. What effect does each of these repeated structures have? Now examine the draft of the Declaration. What changes were made in it to make parallelism more or less prominent?

Suggested Discussion and Group Activities

1. Leaving the colonists' grievances against King George aside, how might you go about refuting the Declaration? Specifically, how could you disagree with the first two paragraphs? Are their assumptions true and of consequence?

2. A "declaration of independence" suggests complete freedom from agreements, custom, and established systems. What evidence can you find in the Declaration that its writers did not want to produce anarchy or destroy orderly government? How does the document maintain a balance between freedom and order?

3. Divide your class into two groups—supporters of the draft of the Declaration and supporters of the final version. In each group, contrast the two versions to show why the version you support is superior. Particularly explain the exclusions in the final version—why was it politically better (or worse, if you support the draft) to exclude some parts of the draft?

Writing Suggestions

Response

Treat one of your earlier papers for this course or another one as a draft. Form your group into a committee whose job it is to make suggestions for change that will enhance the paper's fulfillment of its purpose. Look particularly for ways to rewrite its sentences to make them more powerful statements.

Analysis

1. Write your own declaration of independence, following the pattern of argument in the Declaration. Choose any person or group from which to declare yourself independent.

2. Imagine that you are King George or one of his ministers of state and that you must write a refutation of the Declaration for the same readers to whom the colonists were appealing. A refutation follows the form of a speech, but it disagrees by making some or all of the following points: The opponent's proposal is based on untrue statements; the opponent's proposed solution is impractical; the opponent's solution is not the best one in this case; the solution is unnecessary to resolve the difficulties; the solution is in fact against the purposes for which it was proposed. You need not include each of these possible weaknesses, but include as many as you think you could reasonably apply to the Declaration and the situation between the king and the colonies.

Finding a Purpose

Choose a partner or a small group of classmates to work with and follow the process that the authors of the Declaration followed to write a proposal that you know will be controversial. You might address an issue that concerns your class or your school, or you might propose a new local law. After you have worked with your group, submit the document to other classmates for their objections and suggestions about how to make it more effective. Keep in mind that the document's success depends on how readers react to its words and presentation.

Preamble to the Constitution and the Bill of Rights

Both the Preamble to the American Constitution and its Bill of Rights, written four years later, state principles of government that early statesmen needed to establish to clarify the nature of their new country. The Preamble to the Constitution emerged, like the Declaration of Independence, out of controversy and disagreement. The survival of the country, so diverse in population and geographically difficult to travel through, was never taken for granted. From 1776 until 1788, the year in which the Constitution was sent to the separate states for ratification, early statesmen carried on long oral and written debates about governing principles and practices.

This background of argument is not visible in the bold Preamble, which is a written monument to the unity and purpose of the country. A "preamble" is a device used in both ordinary speech and in documents. It differs from the typical "introduction" by more officially establishing the cause for making a statement. It asserts the "voice" of a public individual or group who wants to be "heard" very widely. It is useful to compare the Preamble to the Constitution to the first part of Magna Carta, which was a much more personal document whose speaker and intended audience were more limited than those of the American Constitution. In both, however, the purpose is to establish a voice that will carry farther than immediate personal meetings.

The Bill of Rights is not a conclusion to the Constitution, but was added to it in 1791 because many of the states insisted that the country's most important document should be clearer about the particular rights of the states and individuals in relation to national government. Like the Declaration, the Bill of Rights was drafted by a committee with a leader, in this case James Madison.

The Bill of Rights reminds us of a typical process of composing in which the writers often decide to clarify by adding material that in fact guides our reading of an entire work. The principles in the Bill of Rights were, many argued at the time, already intended in the original Constitution. By stating them, however, the Constitution became a document with its own glossary (list of terms and definitions). These statements do not specifically change articles of the Constitution, but they have become a persistent instrument for change and extension. "Freedom of speech," for instance, has been applied in many areas of individual expression that are not strictly "speech." This process of continuing redefinition has meant that "no law respecting an establishment of religion," or "the right of the people to keep and bear Arms" have continued to be living, recurring issues that we address anew in each era.

Preamble

We the People of the United States, in Order to form a more perfect Union, establish Justice, insure domestic Tranquility, provide for the common defence, promote the general Welfare, and secure the Blessings of Liberty to ourselves and our Posterity, do ordain and establish this Constitution for the United States of America.

Bill of Rights

Articles in addition to, and amendment of, the constitution of the United States of America, proposed by Congress, and ratified by the legislatures of the several states, pursuant to the fifth article of the original constitution.

Article I

Congress shall make no law respecting an establishment of religion, or prohibiting the free exercise thereof; or abridging the freedom of speech, or of the press; or the right of the people peaceably to assemble, and to petition the Government for a redress of grievances.

Article II

A well regulated Militia, being necessary to the security of a free State, the right of the people to keep and bear Arms, shall not be infringed.

Article III

No Soldier shall, in time of peace be quartered in any house, without the consent of the Owner, nor in time of war, but in a manner to be prescribed by law.

Article IV

The right of the people to be secure in their persons, houses, papers, and effects, against unreasonable searches and seizures, shall not be violated, and no Warrants shall issue, but upon probable cause, supported by Oath or affirmation, and particularly describing the place to be searched, and the persons or things to be seized.

Article V

No person shall be held to answer for a capital, or otherwise infamous crime, unless on a presentment or indictment of a Grand Jury, except in cases arising in the land or naval forces, or in the Militia, when in actual service in time of War or public danger; nor shall any person be subject for the same offence to be twice put in jeopardy of life or limb; nor shall be compelled in any criminal case to be a witness against himself; nor be deprived of life, liberty, or property, without due process of law; nor shall private property be taken for public use, without just compensation.

Article VI

In all criminal prosecutions, the accused shall enjoy the right to a speedy and public trial, by an impartial jury of the State and district wherein the crime shall have been committed, which district shall have been previously ascertained by law, and to be informed of the nature and cause of the accusation; to be confronted with the witnesses against him; to have compulsory process for obtaining witnesses in his favor, and to have the Assistance of Counsel for his defence.

Article VII

In Suits at common law, where the value in controversy shall exceed twenty dollars, the right of trial by jury shall be preserved, and no fact tried by a jury, shall be otherwise reexamined in any Court of the United States, than according to the rules of the common law.

Article VIII

Excessive bail shall not be required, nor excessive fines imposed, nor cruel and unusual punishments inflicted.

Article IX

The enumeration in the Constitution, of certain rights, shall not be construed to deny or disparage others retained by the people.

Article X

The powers not delegated to the United States by the Constitution, nor prohibited by it to the States, are reserved to the States respectively, or to the people.

Questions

Rereading and Independent Analysis

1. The Preamble is one complete sentence. Analyze it grammatically, identifying its subject, main verb or predicate, and subordinate structures. Explain how the order of the content in these grammatical parts supports its purpose. Then make a list of all of the verbs used in the Preamble. How do these verbs support its intention?

2. Analyze each of the amendments in the Bill grammatically. Find each subject, main verb, and object. Then analyze each of the amendments to find who is acting in each, what action is taken, and what the result of the action is. Match your two lists: are the subjects and actors, verbs and actions, and objects and results expressed by the same words? Where they are not, try rewriting the sentence to place the actor in the subject position, the action in the verb position, and the goal of the action in the object (or complement) position of the sentence. How does this rewriting clarify the document?

3. Classify the Bill's amendments according to the principles established, governmental functions mentioned, and actions described.

Suggested Discussion and Group Activities

1. Use a dictionary to discover the meaning and connotations of the word *preamble.* When is a preamble appropriate as the beginning of a long piece of writing or a speech? What relationship to readers does it establish? As a class or in groups, compare the Preamble to introductions to other documents you select, for instance Magna Carta and the Declaration of Independence. How does a preamble differ from an ordinary introduction? What is lost from a document without a preamble?

2. Make a list of the separate purposes for the Constitution described in its Preamble. Then compare your list to the statements in the Bill of Rights. Do you think the Bill was necessary to complete the original purposes for the Constitution? What might be the results of not stating the conditions for governing in the Bill?

3. We do not often think consciously of our rights, but their importance in our everyday lives is obvious. How are your assumptions about what you may do as a citizen based on the Preamble and the Bill of Rights? Do these documents give complete freedom or suggest limits on it? What are these limits?

Writing Suggestions

Response

Write a Bill of Rights of your own, stating ten principles that you think every individual in the world, not just those in a particular country, should have. Take into account that your list should apply to people under many different forms of government.

Analysis

1. Write a one-sentence imitation of the Preamble. Begin with a personal pronoun. Follow the grammatical form of the Preamble, explaining the reasons for any action you choose before you close with the main verb or verbs in the predicate.

2. Write an essay in which you explain to people in another country the purposes of the American Constitution as established by its Preamble and the Bill of Rights. Give examples of how these purposes are fulfilled in laws and local customs.

Finding a Purpose

Individually or in collaboration with your classmates, prepare a pamphlet for newcomers to the United States in which you explain how the Constitution will affect their everyday life. You should give examples of the aspects of life the newcomer will find affected, perhaps classifying them into private and public categories. Make these statements positive and inviting. Identify a particular person or group who will read your explanation.

RENEWING SOCIAL CONTRACTS

 Massachusetts High School Law, 1827

You may assume that the system of schooling you have participated in is "normal" and has been roughly the same throughout American history. In the 13 original colonies, however, there were various customs regarding education that depended on the social and economic circumstances of the colonists. In Virginia, for instance, the large sizes of farms and plantations generally meant that private tutorial lessons were common because travel to centralized schools was too difficult. In Massachusetts, geography and trade, as well as Puritan influences, produced small townships where trade and industry dominated. "Public" schools attended by the members of a local church congregation were more common than tutors. Therefore, the state of Massachusetts passed this law, the first of its kind in America, to require that towns and districts provide high schools that everyone could attend.

The law's importance as a model is unquestionable. It defined the subjects to be taught in postprimary instruction and the distribution of this curriculum in rural and city settings throughout much of the country. The law was not enforced immediately, even though it also required payment for public education. In 1837 Horace Mann became chair of the Massachusetts Board of Education and began to ensure the law's enforcement, but by 1840 there were still only 18 high schools in the state. By 1860, there were more than 100. Mann, a champion of universal education, argued effectively that the European model that divided educational opportunities according to social class was inferior to the "Massachusetts model" of providing all citizens with equal opportunity to learn and improve their state in life. "Education," he said, "is the great equalizer of the conditions of men." This ideal has guided American education since his time.

As you read, you will notice that the law does not require students to attend school for the prescribed terms, but instead addresses the necessity of providing a teacher and of teaching specific subjects for specific lengths of time. Look for ways that the law's language strives to make its provisions precise and applicable in the future. Where do you see the influence of this law in your own education?

Be it enacted, That each town or district within this Commonwealth, containing fifty families, or householders, shall be provided with a teacher or teachers, of good morals, to instruct children in orthography, reading, writing, English grammar, geography, arithmetic, and good behavior, for such term of time as shall be equivalent to six months for one school in each year; and every town or district containing one hundred families or householders, shall be provided with such teacher or teachers, for such term of time as shall be equivalent to eighteen months, for one school in each year. In every city, town, or district, containing five hundred families, or householders, shall be provided with such teacher or teachers for such term of time as shall be equivalent to twenty-four months, shall also be provided with a master of good morals, competent to instruct, in addition to the branches of learning aforesaid, in the history of the United States, bookkeeping by single entry, geometry, surveying, algebra; and shall employ such master to instruct a school in such city, town, or district, for the benefit of all the inhabitants thereof, at least ten months in each year, exclusive of vacations, in such convenient places, or alternately at such places in such city, town, or district, as said inhabitants, at their meeting in March, or April, annually, shall determine; and in every city, or town, and district, containing four thousand inhabitants, such master shall be competent in addition to all the foregoing branches, to instruct the Latin and Greek languages, history, rhetoric, and logic.

Questions

Rereading and Independent Analysis

1. The language of this law is that of a legal action that applies throughout a state and in all times. Reread the law, underlining specific words, phrases, and sentences that show that this was not a casual statement but one intended to be precise and directive.

2. How do specific features of the law establish a pattern of action? List the provisions of the law in categories according to its requirements: Who is affected? What must they do? Where? When? How?

Suggested Discussion and Group Activities

1. Why do you think this law was necessary at the time? Are its provisions necessary now, or are too many people involved in education to make it possible to close the public school system? What reasons might there be for revoking such laws?

2. How did this model law establish a distinct way of life in the United States? What expectations does it place on American parents and children? Has education been the "great equalizer" that Horace Mann said it would be?

3. As a class, form a legislative committee that will consider proposals for laws about any aspect of education. Choose two to five proposals, work in groups to put them into effective language, and then debate their effectiveness and wide applicability for an entire locale or state.

Writing Suggestions

Response

Write a few paragraphs in which you describe what your life would be like without public schools. How do you think you would have learned the basic subjects of reading, writing, mathematics, and history without an organized legal system of schooling? If you had not learned these things, what would you be doing now? Do you think public schools have done an adequate job preparing you for your current activities and educational pursuits? Why?

Analysis

Write an essay in which you show how the curriculum available in your high school was more suitable than the one prescribed by this law. When comparing the old Massachusetts plan with the curriculum in your school, you should address not only the content of the curriculum but also the number of choices that your high school permitted you to make. You are writing to persuade a public group such as your state Board of Education, so explain why having such choices of subjects is a better way to arrange high school teaching today. To support these choices, be sure to adopt an informed and fair point of view.

Finding a Purpose

Write a law to establish a new institution that you think is necessary to improve life in your community or the country as a whole. You should use language as precise and directive as the language exemplified by this law. Arrange the points you make as this law arranged its points, being precise about who will be affected and where, when, and how.

"Bourgeois and Proletarians" from *The Communist Manifesto*
Karl Marx and Friedrich Engels

The definitions of *bourgeois* and *proletarians* created by Marx and Engels in the *Communist Manifesto* (1848) show how old terms can be given powerful new meanings that establish a new reality in the lives of millions of people. Karl Marx (1818–1883) was a German social theorist whose ideas were so threatening to existing European governments that he lived as an impoverished nomad, moving from one country to another on the Continent and finally to London. There his friend Friedrich Engels (1820–1895) supported him and contributed to the book that became (along with *Das Kapital,* 1867) the bible of the Bolshevik revolution.

The revolution, which overturned centuries of feudal and merchant domination in Russia and spread its principles over half the world, occurred in 1917. Although Marx had been relatively unknown in his lifetime, his writings became the basis for the intellectual debate that accompanied vast social and industrial changes in the late nineteenth and early twentieth centuries. This writing affected the ordinary lives of millions of workers. While you may think of Marxism as a dangerous threat to the American economic system, its prominence has indirectly influenced working conditions throughout the world.

This section of *The Communist Manifesto* defines the "bourgeois" as those who own property, whether this property is land or industrial tools such as ships and factories. This class, which Marx says evolved historically from the "burghers," or tradesmen, in the earliest towns, is held responsible for having transformed personal and local communities into impersonal dependencies based only on "cash payment." The workers, or "proletariat," work only for money. They see no results from their labor and live in a series of profit-determined interruptions brought on by the bourgeois' constant revolutionizing of the instruments of production. People thereby become instruments themselves, not respected individuals working to provide other individuals with needed goods and services.

Marx describes this economic reduction of people into classes as a straightforward process over time. He insists that revolution is "inevitable" because two forces confronting each other in increasingly vivid opposition will clash and, he theorizes, bring on a new order—communism. Thus his view of history is *teleological,* that is, it assumes that events move in a purposeful direction that cannot be stopped. He thinks that change always has purpose and direction, and he believes in an inevitable synthesis of oppositions, or reformation, as the predetermined outcome of a conflict.

Marx's views are, of course, easy enough to criticize. They are extremely simplistic, reducing individuals to parts of a group who think alike only because of their earnings. His views also ignore the possibilities of legislation to correct inequities through a system of negotiations between opposing groups with mutual interests, and of using foresight and goodwill to prevent disasters. In fact, Marx's theories have not described an "inevitable" course of history in countries whose traditions permit individual mobility and retain open communication across classes.

But Marxism nonetheless plausibly explains many of the daily conditions of people in many nations. While the publication of this document was not immediately considered particularly important, it has directly and indirectly created the political situations that millions of individuals live in today. Its descriptions, written to inspire revolution, clearly call for revisions of social contracts. They radically altered preindustrial and newly industrial nations during the period when Marx wrote. The moral outrage he expressed has touched all of the economies of the world. As you read, notice the language that Marx uses both to reason with and excite his readers.

A specter is haunting Europe—the specter of communism. All the powers 1
of old Europe have entered into a holy alliance to hunt down and exorcise
this specter: Pope and Tsar, Metternich and Guizot, French Radicals and
German police-spies.

Where is the party in opposition that has not been denounced as 2
communistic by its opponents in power? Where the opposition that has
not hurled back the branding reproach of communism against the more
advanced opposition parties, as well as against its reactionary adversaries?

Two things result from this fact: 3

I. Communism is already acknowledged by all European powers to
be itself a *power.*

II. It is high time that Communists should openly, in the face of the whole world, publish their views, their aims, their tendencies, and meet this nursery tale of the *specter of communism* with a manifesto of the party itself.

To this end, Communists of various nationalities have assembled in ⁴ London and sketched the following *Manifesto,* to be published in the English, French, German, Italian, Flemish, and Danish languages.

I
Bourgeois and Proletarians¹

The history of all hitherto existing society² is the history of class struggles. ⁵

Freeman and slave, patrician and plebeian, lord and serf, guildmas- ⁶ ter³ and journeyman, in a word, oppressor and oppressed, stood in constant opposition to one another, carried on an uninterrupted, now hidden, now open fight, a fight that each time ended, either in a revolutionary reconstitution of society at large, or in the common ruin of the struggling classes.

In the earlier epochs of history, we find almost everywhere a compli- ⁷ cated arrangement of society into various orders, a manifold gradation of social rank. In ancient Rome we have patricians, knights, plebeians, slaves; in the Middle Ages, feudal lords, vassals, guildmasters, journeymen, apprentices, serfs; and in almost all of these particular classes, again, other subordinate gradations.

The modern bourgeois society that has sprouted from the ruins of ⁸ feudal society has not done away with class antagonisms. It has only established new classes, new conditions of oppression, new forms of struggle in place of the old ones.

Our epoch, the epoch of the bourgeoisie, shows, however, this dis- ⁹ tinctive feature: it has simplified the class antagonisms. Society as a whole is more and more splitting up into two great hostile camps, into two great classes directly facing each other: *bourgeoisie* and *proletariat.*

---

¹ By bourgeois is meant the people in the class of modern capitalists, owners of the means of social production and employers of wage labor. By proletarians, the people in the class of modern wage laborers who, having no means of production of their own, are reduced to selling their labor power in order to live.

² That is, all *written* history. In 1847, the prehistory of society, the social organization existing previous to recorded history, was all but unknown. Since then, Haxthausen discovered common ownership of land in Russia, Maurer proved it to be the social foundation from which all Teutonic races started in history, and by and by village communities were found to be, or to have been the primitive form of society everywhere from India to Ireland. The inner organization of this primitive communistic society was laid bare, in its typical form, by Morgan's crowning discovery of the true nature of the *gens* and its relation to the *tribe.* With the dissolution of these primeval communities society begins to be differentiated into separate and finally antagonistic classes. I have attempted to retrace this process of dissolution in: *Der Ursprung der Familie, des Privateigenthums und des Staats.* [*The Origin of the Family, Private Property, and the State*], 2nd edition, Stuttgart, 1886. [*Note by Engels in the edition of 1888.*]

³ Guildmaster, that is, a full member of a guild, a master within, not a head of a guild. [*Note by Engels in the edition of 1888.*]

From the serfs of the Middle Ages sprang the chartered burghers of 10 the earliest towns. From these burghers the first elements of the bourgeoisie were developed.

The discovery of America, the rounding of the Cape, opened up fresh 11 ground for the rising bourgeoisie. The East-Indian and Chinese markets, the colonization of America, trade with the colonies, the increase in the means of exchange and in commodities generally, gave to commerce, to navigation, to industry, an impulse never before known, and thereby, to the revolutionary element in the tottering feudal society, a rapid development.

The feudal system of industry, under which industrial production 12 was monopolized by closed guilds, now no longer sufficed for the growing wants of the new markets. The manufacturing system took its place. The guildmasters were pushed on one side by the manufacturing middle class; division of labor between the different corporate guilds vanished in the face of division of labor in each single workshop.

Meanwhile the markets kept on growing; demand went on rising. 13 Manufacturing no longer was able to keep up with this growth. Then, steam and machinery revolutionized industrial production. The place of manufacture was taken by the giant, *modern industry;* the place of the industrial middle class, by industrial millionaires, the leaders of whole industrial armies, the modern bourgeois.

Modern industry has established the world market, for which the 14 discovery of America paved the way. This market has given an immense development to commerce, to navigation, to communication by land. This development has, in its turn, reacted on the extension of industry; and in proportion as industry, commerce, navigation, railways extended, in the same proportion the bourgeoisie developed, increased its capital, and pushed into the background every class handed down from the Middle Ages.

We see, therefore, how the modern bourgeoisie is itself the product 15 of a long course of development, of a series of revolutions in the modes of production and of exchange.

Each step in the development of the bourgeoisie was accompanied 16 by a corresponding political advance of that class. An oppressed class under the sway of the feudal nobility, an armed and self-governing association in the medieval commune:[4] here an independent urban republic (as in Italy and Germany); there taxable "third estate" of the monarchy (as in France); afterward, in the period of manufacturing proper, serving either

---

[4] "Commune" was the name taken, in France, by the nascent towns even before they had wrested from their feudal lords and masters local self-government and political rights as the "Third Estate." Generally speaking for the economical development of the bourgeoisie, England is here taken as the typical country; for its political development, France. [*Note by Engels in the edition of 1888.*]

This was the name given their urban communities by the townsmen of Italy and France, after they had purchased or wrested their initial rights of self-government from their feudal lords. [*Note by Engels in the edition of 1890.*]

the semi-feudal or the absolute monarchy as a counterpoise against the nobility, and, in fact, a cornerstone of the great monarchies in general, the bourgeoisie has at last, since the establishment of modern industry and of the world market, conquered for itself, in the modern representative state, exclusive political sway. The executive of the modern state is but a committee for managing the common affairs of the whole bourgeoisie.

The bourgeoisie, historically, has played a most revolutionary part. 17

The bourgeoisie, wherever it has got the upper hand, has put an end 18 to all feudal, patriarchal, idyllic relations. It has pitilessly torn asunder the motley feudal ties that bound man to his "natural superiors," and has left remaining no other bond between man and man than naked self-interest and callous "cash payment." It has drowned the most heavenly ecstasies of religious fervor, of chivalrous enthusiasm, of philistine sentimentalism, in the icy water of egotistical calculation. It has resolved personal worth into exchange value, and in place of the numberless indefeasible chartered freedoms, has set up that single, unconscionable freedom—free trade. In one word, for exploitation, veiled by religious and political illusions, it has substituted naked, shameless, direct, brutal exploitation.

The bourgeoisie has stripped of its halo every occupation hitherto 19 honored and looked up to with reverent awe. It has converted the physician, the lawyer, the priest, the poet, the man of science, into its paid wage laborers.

The bourgeoisie has torn away from the family its sentimental veil, 20 and has reduced the family relation to a mere money relation.

The bourgeoisie has disclosed how it came to pass that the brutal 21 display of vigor in the Middle Ages, which reactionaries so much admire, found its fitting complement in the laziest indolence. It has been the first to show what man's activity can bring about. It has accomplished wonders far surpassing Egyptian pyramids, Roman aqueducts, and Gothic cathedrals; it has conducted expeditions that put to shame all former Exoduses of nations and crusades.

The bourgeoisie cannot exist without constantly revolutionizing the 22 instruments of production, and thereby the relations of production, and with them the whole relations of society. Conservation of the old modes of production in unaltered form, was, on the contrary, the first condition of existence for all earlier industrial classes. Constant revolutionizing of production, uninterrupted disturbance of all social conditions, everlasting uncertainty and agitation distinguish the bourgeois epoch from all earlier ones. All fixed, fast-frozen relations, with their train of ancient and venerable prejudices and opinions are swept away, all new-formed ones become antiquated before they can ossify. All that is solid melts into air, all that is holy is profaned, and man is at last compelled to face his real conditions of life, and his mutual relations with sober eye.

The need of a constantly expanding market for its products chases 23 the bourgeoisie over the whole surface of the globe. It must nestle everywhere, settle everywhere, establish connections everywhere.

The bourgeoisie has through its exploitation of the world market 24 given a cosmopolitan character to production and consumption in every country. To the great chagrin of reactionaries, it has drawn from under the feet of industry the national ground on which it stood. All old-established national industries have been destroyed or are daily being destroyed. They are dislodged by new industries, whose introduction becomes a life and death question for all civilized nations, by industries that no longer work up indigenous raw material, but raw material drawn from the remotest zones; industries whose products are consumed, not only at home, but in every quarter of the globe. In place of the old wants, satisfied by the productions of the country, we find new wants, requiring for their satisfaction the products of distant lands and climates. In place of the old local and national seclusion and self-sufficiency, we have intercourse in every direction, universal inter-dependence of nations. And as in material, so also in intellectual production. The intellectual creations of individual nations become common property. National one-sidedness and narrow-mindedness become more and more impossible, and from the numerous national and local literatures, there emerges a world literature.

The bourgeoisie, by the rapid improvement of all instruments of 25 production, by the immensely facilitated means of communication, draws all, even the most backward, nations into civilization. The cheap prices of its commodities are the heavy artillery with which it batters down all Chinese walls, with which it forces the underdeveloped nations' intensely obstinate hatred of foreigners to capitulate. It compels all nations, on pain of extinction, to adopt the bourgeois mode of production; it compels them to introduce what it calls civilization into their midst, *i.e.*, to become bourgeois themselves. In one word, it creates a world in its own image.

The bourgeoisie has subjected rural areas to the rule of cities. It has 26 created enormous cities, has greatly increased the urban population as compared with the rural, and has thus rescued a considerable part of the population from the idiocy of rural life. Just as it has made the country dependent on the cities, so has it made barbarian and semi-underdeveloped countries dependent on the civilized ones, nations of peasants on nations of bourgeois, the East on the West.

The bourgeoisie keeps more and more doing away with the scattered 27 state of the population, of the means of production, and of property. It has agglomerated population, centralized means of production, and has concentrated property in a few hands. The necessary consequence of this was political centralization. Independent, or but loosely connected, provinces with separate interests, laws, governments, and systems of taxation became lumped together into one nation, with one government, one code of laws, one national class-interest, one frontier, and one customs-tariff.

The bourgeoisie, during its rule of scarcely one hundred years, has 28 created more massive and more colossal productive forces than have all preceding generations together. Subjection of Nature's forces to man, machinery, application of chemistry to industry and agriculture, steam-navigation, railways, electric telegraphs, clearing of whole continents for cultivation, canalization of rivers, whole populations conjured out of the ground—what earlier century had even a presentiment that such productive forces slumbered in the lap of social labor?

We see then: the means of production and of exchange, on whose 29 foundation the bourgeoisie built itself up, were generated in feudal society. At a certain stage in the development of these means of production and of exchange, the conditions under which feudal society produced and exchanged, the feudal organization of agriculture and manufacturing industry, in one word, the feudal relations of property became no longer compatible with the already developed productive forces; they became so many fetters. They had to be burst asunder; they were burst asunder.

Into their place stepped free competition, accompanied by a social 30 and political constitution adapted to it, and by the economical and political sway of the bourgeois class.

A similar movement is going on before our own eyes. Modern bour- 31 geois society with its relations of production, of exchange and of property, a society that has conjured up such gigantic means of production and of exchange, is like the sorcerer, who is no longer able to control the powers of the subterranean world which he has called up by his spells. For many decades now the history of industry and commerce has been but the history of the revolt of modern productive forces against modern conditions of production, against the property relations that are the conditions for the existence of the bourgeoisie and of its rule. It is enough to mention the commercial crises that by their periodical return put on trial, each time more threateningly, the existence of the entire bourgeois society. In these crises a great part not only of the existing products, but also of the previously created productive forces, are periodically destroyed. In these crises there breaks out an epidemic that, in all earlier epochs, would have seemed an absurdity—the epidemic of over-production. Society suddenly finds itself put back into a state of momentary barbarism; it appears as if a famine, a universal war of devastation had cut off the supply of every means of subsistence; industry and commerce seem to be destroyed; and why? Because there is too much civilization, too much means of subsistence, too much industry, too much commerce. The productive forces at the disposal of society no longer tend to further the development of the conditions of bourgeois property; on the contrary, they have become too powerful for these conditions, by which they are fettered, and so soon as they overcome these fetters, they bring disorder into the whole of bourgeois society, endanger the existence of bourgeois property. The conditions of bourgeois society are too narrow to comprise the wealth created by them. And how does the bourgeoisie get over these crises? On the one hand by enforced destruction of a mass of productive forces; on the other, by the conquest of new markets, and by the more thorough exploitation of the old ones. That is to say, by paving the way for more extensive and more destructive crises, and by diminishing the means whereby crises are prevented.

The weapons with which the bourgeoisie felled feudalism to the 32 ground are now turned against the bourgeoisie itself.

But not only has the bourgeoisie forged the weapons that bring death 33 to itself; it has also called into existence the men who are to wield those weapons—the modern working class—the proletarians.

In proportion as the bourgeoisie, *i.e.*, capital, is developed, in the 34 same proportion is the proletariat, the modern working class, developed— a class of laborers, who live only so long as they find work, and who find work only so long as their labor increases capital. These laborers, who must sell themselves piecemeal, are a commodity, like every other article of commerce, and are consequently exposed to all the vicissitudes of competition, to all the fluctuations of the market.

Owing to the extensive use of machinery and to division of labor, the 35 work of the proletarians has lost all individual character, and, consequently, all charm for the workman. He becomes an appendage of the machine, and it is only the most simple, most monotonous, and most easily acquired knack that is required of him. Hence, the cost of production of a workman is restricted, almost entirely, to the means of subsistence that he requires for his maintenance, and for the propagation of his race. But the price of a commodity, and therefore also of labor,[5] is equal to its cost of production. In proportion, therefore, as the repulsiveness of the work increases, the wage decreases. What is more, in proportion as the use of machinery and division of labor increases, in the same proportion the burden of toil also increases, whether by prolongation of the working hours, by increase of the work exacted in a given time or by increased speed of the machinery, etc.

Modern industry has converted the little workshop of the patriarchal 36 master into the great factory of the industrial capitalist. Masses of laborers, crowded into the factory, are organized like soldiers. As privates of the industrial army they are placed under the command of a perfect hierarchy of officers and sergeants. Not only are they slaves of the bourgeois class, and of the bourgeois state; they are daily and hourly enslaved by the machine, by the foreman, and, above all, by the individual bourgeois manufacturer himself. The more openly this despotism proclaims gain to be its end and aim, the more petty, the more hateful, and the more embittering it is.

The less the skill and exertion of strength implied in manual labor, 37 in other words, the more modern industry becomes developed, the more is the labor of men superseded by that of women. Differences in age and sex have no longer any distinctive social validity for the working class. All are instruments of labor, more or less expensive to use, according to their age and sex.

No sooner is the exploitation of the laborer by the manufacturer, so 38

[5] Subsequently Marx pointed out that the worker does not sell his labor but his labor power. See in this connection Engels' introduction to Marx's *Wage Labor and Capital*, 1891, in K. Marx and F. Engels, *Selected Works*, Eng. ed., Vol. I, Moscow, 1951, pp. 66–73.—*Ed.*

far, at an end, that he receives his wages in cash, than he is set upon by the other portions of the bourgeoisie, the landlord, the shopkeeper, the pawnbroker, etc.

The lower strata of the middle class—the small tradespeople, shop- 39 keepers, and retired tradesmen generally, the handicraftsmen, and farmers—all these sink gradually into the proletariat, partly because their diminutive capital does not suffice for the scale on which modern industry is carried on, and is swamped in the competition with large capitalists, partly because their specialized skill is rendered worthless by new methods of production. Thus the proletariat is recruited from all classes of the population.

The proletariat goes through various stages of development. With its 40 birth begins its struggle with the bourgeoisie. At first the contest is carried on by individual laborers, then by the workers of a factory, then by the members of one trade, in one locality, against the individual bourgeois who directly exploits them. They direct their attacks not against the bourgeois conditions of production, but against the instruments of production themselves; they destroy imported wares that compete with their labor, they smash machinery to pieces, they set factories ablaze, they seek to restore by force the vanished status of the workman of the Middle Ages.

At this stage the laborers still form an incoherent mass scattered over 41 the whole country, and broken up by their mutual competition. If the workers unite at all this is not yet the consequence of their own initiative, but of the union of the bourgeoisie, which class, in order to attain its own political ends, is compelled to set the whole proletariat in motion, and is moreover still able to do so. At this stage, therefore, the proletarians do not fight their enemies, but the enemies of their enemies, the remnants of absolute monarchy, the landowners, the nonindustrial bourgeoisie, the petty bourgeoisie. Thus the whole historical movement is concentrated in the hands of the bourgeoisie; every victory so obtained is a victory for the bourgeoisie.

But with the development of industry the proletariat not only in- 42 creases in number; it becomes concentrated in greater masses, its strength grows, and it feels that strength more. The various interests and conditions of life within the ranks of the proletariat are more and more equalized, in proportion as machinery obliterates all distinctions of labor, and nearly everywhere reduces wages to the same low level. The growing competition among the bourgeoisie, and the resulting commercial crises, make the wages of the workers ever more fluctuating. The unceasing improvement of machinery, ever more rapidly developing, makes their livelihood more and more precarious; the collisions between individual workmen and individual bourgeoisie take more and more the character of collisions between two classes. Thereupon the workers begin to form combinations (trade unions) against the bourgeoisie; they club together in order to keep up the rate of wages; they found permanent associations in order to make provision beforehand for these occasional revolts. Here and there the contest breaks out into riots.

From time to time the workers are victorious, but only for a time. 43 The real fruit of their battles lies not in the immediate result, but in the ever-expanding union of the workers. This union is helped by the improved means of communication that are created by modern industry and that place the workers of different localities in contact with one another. It was just this contact that was needed to centralize the numerous local struggles, all of the same character, into one national struggle between classes. But every class struggle is a political struggle. And that union, to attain which the burghers of the Middle Ages, with their miserable highways, required centuries, the modern proletarians, thanks to railways, achieve in a few years.

This organization of the proletarians into a class, and consequently 44 into a political party, is continually being upset again by the competition among the workers themselves. But it constantly rises up again, stronger, firmer, mightier. It compels legislative recognition of particular interests of the workers, by taking advantage of the divisions among the bourgeoisie itself. Thus was the ten-hours' bill in England carried.

Moreover, collisions between the classes of the old society advance, 45 in many ways, the course of development of the proletariat. The bourgeoisie finds itself involved in a constant battle. At first with the aristocracy; later on, with those portions of the bourgeoisie itself, whose interests have become antagonistic to the progress of industry; at all times, with the bourgeoisie of foreign countries. In all these battles it sees itself compelled to appeal to the proletariat, to ask for its help, and thus, to drag it into the political arena. The bourgeoisie itself, therefore, supplies the proletariat with its own elements of political and general education, in other words, it furnishes the proletariat with weapons for fighting the bourgeoisie.

Further, as we have already seen, entire sections of the ruling classes 46 are, by the advance of industry, precipitated into the proletariat, or are at least threatened in their conditions of existence. These also supply the proletariat with fresh elements of enlightenment and progress.

Finally, in times when the class struggle nears the decisive hour, the 47 process of dissolution going on within the ruling class, in fact within the whole range of old society, assumes such a violent, glaring character, that a small section of the ruling class cuts itself adrift, and joins the revolutionary class, the class that holds the future in its hands. Just as, therefore, at an earlier period, a section of the nobility went over to the bourgeoisie, so now a portion of the bourgeoisie goes over to the proletariat, and in particular, a portion of the bourgeois ideologists, who have raised themselves to the level of comprehending theoretically the historical movement as a whole.

Of all the classes that stand face to face with the bourgeoisie today, 48 the proletariat alone is a really revolutionary class. The other classes decay and finally disappear in the face of modern industry; the proletariat is its ·special and essential product.

The lower middle class, the small manufacturer, the shopkeeper, the 49 artisan, the peasant, all these fight against the bourgeoisie, to save from

extinction their existence as fractions of the middle class. They are therefore not revolutionary, but conservative. What is more, they are reactionary, for they try to roll back the wheel of history. If by chance they are
revolutionary, they are so only in view of their impending transfer into the
proletariat, they thus defend not their present, but their future interests,
they desert their own standpoint to place themselves at that of the proletariat.

The "dangerous class,"[6] the social scum, that passively rotting mass 50
thrown off by the lowest layers of old society, may, here and there, be
swept into the movement by a proletarian revolution; its conditions of life,
however, prepare it far more for the part of a bribed tool of reactionary
intrigue.

The living conditions of the old society at large are already virtually 51
swamped by the living conditions of the proletariat. The proletarian is
without property; his relation to his wife and children has no longer anything in common with the bourgeois family relations; modern industrial
labor, modern subjection to capital, the same in England as in France, in
America as in Germany, has stripped him of every trace of national character. Law, morality, religion, are to him so many bourgeois prejudices,
behind which lurk in ambush just as many bourgeois interests.

All the preceding classes that got the upper hand sought to fortify 52
their already acquired status by subjecting society at large to their conditions of appropriation. The proletarians cannot become masters of the
productive forces of society, except by abolishing their own previous
mode of appropriation, and thereby also every other previous mode of
appropriation. They have nothing of their own to secure and to fortify;
their mission is to destroy all previous securities for, and insurances of,
individual property.

All previous historical movements were movements of minorities, or 53
in the interest of minorities. The proletarian movement is the self-con-
scious, independent movement of the immense majority, in the interest
of the immense majority. The proletariat, the lowest stratum of our present society, cannot stir, cannot raise itself up, without the whole superin-
cumbent strata of official society being sprung into the air.

Though not in substance, yet in form, the struggle of the proletariat 54
with the bourgeoisie is at first a national struggle. The proletariat of each
country must, of course, first of all settle matters with its own bourgeoisie.

In depicting the most general phases of the development of the 55
proletariat, we traced the more or less veiled civil war, raging within
existing society, up to the point where that war breaks out into open
revolution, and where the violent overthrow of the bourgeoisie lays the
foundation for the sway of the proletariat.

Hitherto, every form of society has been based, as we have already 56
seen, on the antagonism of oppressing and oppressed classes. But in order

---

[6] The "Lumpenproletariat" in German.—*Ed.*

to oppress a class, certain conditions must be assured to it under which it can, at least, continue its slavish existence. The serf, in the period of serfdom, raised himself to membership in the commune, just as the petty bourgeois, under the yoke of feudal absolutism, managed to develop into a bourgeois. The modern laborer, on the contrary, instead of rising with the progress of industry, sinks deeper and deeper below the conditions of existence of his own class. He becomes a pauper, and pauperism develops more rapidly than population and wealth. And here it becomes evident that the bourgeoisie is unfit any longer to be the ruling class in society, and to impose its conditions of existence upon society as an overriding law. It is unfit to rule because it is incompetent to assure an existence to its slave within his slavery, because it cannot help letting him sink into such a state, that it has to feed him, instead of being fed by him. Society can no longer live under this bourgeoisie, in other words, its existence is no longer compatible with society.

The essential condition for the existence, and for the sway of the 5 bourgeois class, is the formation and augmentation of capital; the condition for capital is wage labor. Wage labor rests exclusively on competition between the laborers. The advance of industry, whose involuntary promoter is the bourgeoisie, replaces the isolation of the laborers, due to competition, by their revolutionary combination, due to association. The development of modern industry, therefore, cuts from under its feet the very foundation on which the bourgeoisie produces and appropriates products. What the bourgeoisie, therefore, produces, above all, is its own grave-diggers. Its fall and the victory of the proletariat are equally inevitable.

Questions

Rereading and Independent Analysis

1. A "manifesto" both explains principles and excites readers to act on them. Its language is chosen to further both of these purposes. Reread this selection, underlining specific words and passages that are written to inspire action as well as belief. What would be the effect of omitting or changing these passages by using less colorful language? Try rewriting a few of your underlined sections to make them less emotional.

2. The Marxist dialectical view of history is that progress results from action (thesis), reaction (antithesis), and conflict leading to a new mixture of ideas (synthesis). Mark the parts of this selection that show Marx's commitment to this view of history.

Suggested Discussion and Group Activities

1. Using *only* this passage as evidence, describe why communism as a theory would be opposed to American democratic values. How would it influence your way of life? Cite specific places in the selection that show these influences.

2. What arguments would you use to oppose the case that Marx and Engels made here? Where would you obtain your evidence for these arguments? What sources of support did these authors rely on? What groups and individuals would be persuaded by the arguments you would use to oppose Marx and Engels? Why do you think so?

Writing Suggestions

Response

Describe your feelings as you read and think about this selection. Do you think Marx made a sensible case, or do you find yourself opposed to him? Where do you think your reactions come from? Personal experience? Learning in school? Media? What in this document itself do you find persuasive or mistaken?

Analysis

This document was intended to persuade its readers to change some of the basic structures of their society, and it was influential in bringing about just that result. Write an analysis of the points and language in the selection, explaining why it has worked as effective persuasion. Point out specific features of its appeals to logic and to emotion. Who would its most and least receptive readers be? Who would not be persuaded? Why?

Finding a Purpose

Imagine that you have been chosen by your class to respond to someone who objects to Marx and wants to know why it is worthwhile to read *The Communist Manifesto*. Identify a person or group whom you think of as potentially critical of anyone's reading this document, and write an explanation of the value of reading it based primarily on the points made in the document itself. Show in examples what this reading has taught you about how others think, and explain the value of that learning.

 # Civil War Surrender Documents
Gen. Ulysses S. Grant and Gen. Robert E. Lee

Ulysses S. Grant (1822–1885) and Robert E. Lee (1807–1870) commanded the armies of the North and South, respectively, during the Civil War (1861–1865), but they had more in common than being commanders of large armies. Both were well-educated military tacticians and experienced soldiers in the United States Army. Both had campaigned in Mexico. Both men were astute students of their nation's troubled politics and leaders whose military skill was matched by their ability to inspire their men. Grant, who was born in Illinois and had attended West Point, later became the eighteenth

President of the United States. Lee, whose father was Lighthorse Harry Lee, a prominent commander during the Revolutionary War and a close associate of George Washington and James Madisons', had also attended West Point. Lee might have been the North's best tactician if his loyalty to Virginia and his family had not led him to join the forces of the Confederate States when they seceded from the Union in 1861.

Although the actual conflict broke out in 1861, its underlying debates began as early as arguments about states' rights written immediately after the congressional proposal of the Constitution. The 13 original colonies, which had banded together against the British to free themselves from distant and unresponsive rule, were nonetheless individually settled and had separate governments whose interests differed widely. In general, the North's Puritan, manufacturing interests and the South's Anglican, agrarian interests created very different economic and social situations. These differences were visible in arguments about slavery but went beyond that issue. The Civil War, actual secession and physical conflict, was the last resort after a series of failed debates, agreements, and compromises designed to keep the interests of both regions within the compass of the United States Constitution's unification of the states. When Lincoln spoke at Gettysburg (see Chapter 1) after the first decisive Northern victory, his question about whether "a nation so conceived . . . could long endure" was not trivial. The endurance of the *United* States had always been open to question. It was reasonable to imagine divided countries sharing the same continent. The South's insistence on "states' rights," which supported its lax attitude toward enforcing national civil rights legislation well into this century, made union questionable.

Grant and Lee were in roles that the course of the war had reversed at the time of the surrender described in this selected correspondence. In the beginning, Lee's brilliant leadership and that of his fellow Confederate generals had made it appear that the South could win. But after Gettysburg, and especially after Gen. William Sherman's successful march through the center of the South's lines of transportation and supply, the South's resources were depleted. After that, the South was increasingly unable to match the North in battle. Lee's 1865 surrender of the Army of Northern Virginia at Appomattox Courthouse was decisive, though the hostility continued for another year. These two men, writing on the move from one flimsy tent to another were, after years of questions and then armed battle, finally answering Lincoln's question by writing "union" and *United* States permanently. Their letters renew the contract among the states that was first imagined in the Declaration of Independence.

As you read this correspondence, you will see clearly its crucial nature as well as the dignity of two men who respect each other and two battle-worn armies of individual soldiers. The understatement and precise formal address each man uses in this negotiation contrast sharply with their surroundings. These two generals in tents, moving through farm fields and surrounded by wounded, had at stake the fate of their respective nations and the possibility for healing both political and physical wounds. These brief notes preserve a clear picture of the implications of this particular peace, settled in a rural courthouse, which, under the circumstances, was the most dignified place that could be found.

The letters also demonstrate the particular communication situation that existed before the invention of electronic devices. Although the generals were not more than a few minutes' drive from each other by today's timing, these letters vividly remind us that distance made letters a useful way to negotiate, delay, and reconsider. As in all similar diplomatic encounters, Grant and Lee chose their words carefully, saying very little beyond what was necessary to accomplish their purpose. This correspondence reflects changing conditions on the battlefield, the difficulty of making final decisions, and the process of transferring power from one person to another in an orderly way.

Headquarters Armies of the United States,

April 7, 1865—5 P.M.

General R. E. Lee,
Commanding C. S. Army:

General:
The result of the last week must convince you of the hopelessness of further resistance on the part of the Army of Northern Virginia in this struggle. I feel that it is so, and regard it as my duty to shift from myself the responsibility of any further effusion of blood by asking of you the surrender of that portion of the C. S. Army known as the Army of Northern Virginia.

Very respectfully, your obedient servant,

U. S. Grant,
Lieutenant-General,
Commanding Armies of the United States.

April 7, 1865.

Lieut. Gen. U. S. Grant,
Commanding Armies of the United States:

General:
I have received your note of this date. Though not entertaining the opinion you express of the hopelessness of further resistance on the part of the Army of Northern Virginia, I reciprocate your desire to avoid useless effusion of blood, and therefore, before considering your proposition, ask the terms you will offer on condition of its surrender.

R. E. LEE.
General.

Headquarters Armies of the United States,

April 9, 1865.

General R. E. Lee,
Commanding C. S. Army:

General:

Your note of yesterday is received. As I have no authority to treat on the subject of peace the meeting proposed for 10 A. M. to-day could lead to no good. I will state, however, general, that I am equally anxious for peace with yourself, and the whole North entertain the same feeling. The terms upon which peace can be had are well understood. By the South laying down their arms they will hasten that most desirable event, save thousands of human lives, and hundreds of millions of property not yet destroyed. Sincerely hoping that all our difficulties may be settled without the loss of another life, I subscribe myself,

Very respectfully, your obedient servant.

U. S. Grant,
Lieutenant-General, U. S. Army.

April 9, 1865.

Lieut. Gen. U. S. Grant,
Commanding U. S. Armies:

General:

I received your note of this morning on the picket-line, whither I had come to meet you and ascertain definitely what terms were embraced in your proposal of yesterday with reference to the surrender of this army. I now request an interview in accordance with the offer contained in your letter of yesterday for that purpose.

Very respectfully, your obedient servant.

R. E. Lee,
General.

April 9, 1865.

Lieut. Gen. U. S. Grant,
Commanding U. S. Armies:

General:

I ask a suspension of hostilities pending the adjustment of the terms of the surrender of this army, in the interview requested in any former communication to-day.

Very respectfully, your obedient servant,

R. E. Lee,
General.

Headquarters Army of Northern Virginia,

April 9, 1865.

Lieut. Gen. U. S. Grant,
Commanding U. S. Armies:

General:

I sent a communication to you to-day from the picket-line, whither I had gone in hopes of meeting you in pursuance of the request contained in my letter of yesterday. Major-General Meade informs me that it would probably expedite matters to send a duplicate through some other part of your lines. I therefore request an interview, at such time and place as you may designate, to discuss the terms of the surrender of this army in accordance with your offer to have such an interview, contained in your letter of yesterday.

Very respectfully, your obedient servant,

R. E. Lee,
General.

Headquarters Armies of the United States,

April 9, 1865.

General R. E. Lee,
Commanding C. S. Army:

Your note of this date is but this moment (11.50 A. M.) received. In consequence of my having passed from the Richmond and Lynchburg road to the Farmville and Lynchburg road I am at this writing about four miles west of Walker's Church, and will push forward to the front for the purpose of meeting you. Notice sent to me on this road where you wish the interview to take place will meet me.

Very respectfully, your obedient servant,

U. S. Grant,
Lieutenant-General.

Headquarters Armies of the United States,

Appomattox Court-House, Va., April 9, 1865.

General R. E. Lee,
Commanding C. S. Army:

General:

In accordance with the substance of my letter to you of the 8th instant, I propose to receive the surrender of the Army of Northern

Virginia on the following terms, to wit: Rolls of all the officers and men to be made in duplicate—one copy to be given to an officer to be designated by me, the other to be retained by such officer or officers as you may designate; the officers to give their individual paroles not to take up arms against the Government of the United States until properly exchanged, and each company or regimental commander sign a like parole for the men of their commands. The arms, artillery, and public property to be parked and stacked, and turned over to the officers appointed by me to receive them. This will not embrace the side-arms of the officers, nor their private horses or baggage. This done, each officer and man will be allowed to return to their homes, not to be disturbed by United States authority so long as they observe their paroles and the laws in force where they may reside.

Very respectfully,

U. S. Grant,
Lieutenant-General.

Headquarters Army of Northern Virginia,

April 9, 1865.

Lieut. Gen. U. S. Grant,
Commanding Armies of the United States:

General:
I have received your letter of this date containing the terms of surrender of the Army of Northern Virginia as proposed by you. As they are substantially the same as those expressed in your letter of the 8th instant, they are accepted. I will proceed to designate the proper officers to carry the stipulations into effect.

Very respectfully, your obedient servant,

R. E. Lee,
General.

Questions

Rereading and Independent Analysis

1. Each of these letters accomplished one small step toward the outcome. Make a list of the purposes and results of each letter. Then write a short paragraph in which you explain Grant's and Lee's goals in each letter. Say how each man's goals were parallel to and in contrast with those of the other in each exchange.

2. The delicacy of these negotiations is clear from the carefully chosen language each man employs in each sentence. Make lists of the passages whose purposes are to (a) make statements, (b) make appeals, (c) offer

reasons or explanations. Then underline the words that show these particular purposes for each item on your lists.

Suggested Discussion and Group Activities

1. These letters demonstrate the concept of *persona,* a writer's choice of a particular role and stance toward a subject and a reader. Nothing personal is said in this correspondence, but it displays a "character" for each participant. What are the qualities of these chosen characters? What elements of the letters establish the image you have of each man? What are Grant's and Lee's complex concerns? Why do you think that their politeness to each other is genuine?

2. Did this relatively polite and unemotional negotiation toward the end of the Civil War characterize the future of relations between all of the regions of the country? How do the North and South as well as other areas of the country emphasize their separations by remaining distant and polite? Are the United States genuinely "united," or are they in many ways a collection of separate countries? Give examples of differences between regions of the country that you know about and the ways these differences are allowed to continue without open quarrels. How can a country be both united and separate at the same time?

Writing Suggestions

Response

Imagine that you are a secretary with each general, copying a final version of the letters that must be sent immediately. What are your feelings as you read the words in each pair of letters? Write an entry for the journal you keep with you describing the important changes these brief letters will make.

Analysis

The format of these letters is precise; their headings and closings are never shortened, even though they were written during battle. Write an essay in which you explain to a student of diplomacy the importance of following prescribed forms in diplomatic correspondence, using these letters to exemplify your points.

Finding a Purpose

1. Choose any pair of correspondents you know of who have or who might have written letters that effected great change (for example, Caesar and Mark Antony, Odysseus and Penelope, President Reagan and former President Nixon, your mayor and governor). Write a correspondence between these two people that might have accomplished specific public goals.

2. In small groups or pairs, compose letters from Grant and Lee that they might have sent to each other soon after the meeting at Appomattox. Before you write, be sure you have a clear idea of the *persona* you think each of these men would have adopted.

Proceedings of the Navajo Treaty Council

Gen. William T. Sherman and Barboncito

Navajo lands in the United States are now spread over northern Arizona and parts of Utah and New Mexico, but this tribe once thought of itself as free to roam across the whole Southwest. Barboncito, the Navajo chief of the Coyote Pass clan, who negotiated this treaty with Gen. William T. Sherman in 1868, says that "when the Navajo were first created four mountains and four rivers" encompassed their land. "We were never to move east of the Rio Grande or west of the San Juan rivers." Until the United States Army and homesteading farmers moved west, the Navajos had moved throughout this vast area as the seasons and hunting required, trading with other tribes and acquiring horses and sheep from the Spaniards who settled Mexico.

In 1863 one of the legendary "heroes" of the westward movement, Kit Carson, was ordered to round up the scattered Navajo and relocate them on a government reserve on the Pecos River. Many Navajos died during this relocation, which they refer to as the "Long Walk." Of the 9000 who were alive when they reached the reserve, 2000 subsequently died of pneumonia and dysentery brought on by starvation rations, salty water, and unfamiliar ways of life.

Many of the Navajos soon began to sneak back to their homelands. After the Civil War, when westward expansion and homesteading took on new energy, the federal government sent a peace commission to Fort Sumner, the military post on the reserve, to negotiate yet another move. The government was willing to return a portion of the Navajo lands held before relocation in return for a peaceful move. This commission, led by General Sherman, established one of the first treaties with Indians that still in any way shapes their lives. All earlier negotiations between the United States and Native Americans had been—and continued to be—ignored, broken, or changed by the government and settlers.

The treaty negotiations recorded in this Navajo document took place over three days of talks. The Navajos were, of course, unused to planting by European agricultural methods and unable to grow corn when they tried. When they were permitted to hunt, they often made trouble for white settlers. The whites, believing in "Manifest Destiny," or their right to rule and migrate to expand the country, interpreted the Navajos' customs and presence as a tiresome interruption and a threat to the whites' right of progress. Both sides had a great deal at stake.

These council proceedings consequently represent complex and lengthy discussion between two peoples who have great cause to mistrust each other and who hold equally ignorant, hard-earned prejudices against their adversaries. General Sherman began by asking why the Navajos had not, after centuries of nomadic life, succeeded in becoming stable farmers like eastern residents of Virginia and Ohio. Barboncito, who was born in Canyon de Chelly, patiently explained, stating the view that it generally costs any culture some abrupt scrapes in order to change: "I thought at one time

the whole world was the same as my own country, but I got fooled in it."
He used simple, eloquent words that the Navajos continue to repeat: "I hope
to God you will not ask me to go to any other country except my own." You
may know little of the West or its Native Americans, but as you read you
will find it easy to sympathize with the sense of dislocation Barboncito
expressed.

Proceedings of a Council between General W. T. Sherman and Samuel F.
Tappan Commissioners on the part of the United States and the Chiefs and
Head men of the Navajo Tribe of Indians held at the Reservation known
as Bosque Redondo at Fort Sumner in the Territory of New Mexico on the
28th day of May 1868.
Indian Chiefs Present:
     Delgadito
     Barboncito
     Manuelito
     Largo
     Herrero
     Armijo
     Torivio
Jesus Alviso Indian Interpreter and James Sutherland Spanish Interpreter.

General Sherman Said:
The Commissioners are here now for the purpose of learning and knowing 1
all about your condition and we wish to hear from you the truth and
nothing but the truth. We have read in our books and learned from our
officers that for many years whether right or wrong the Navajos have been
at war with us and that General Carleton had removed you here for the
purpose of making you agriculturists—with that view the Government of
the United States gave you money and built this fort to protect you until
you were able to protect yourselves. We find you have done a good deal
of work here in making acequias,* but we find you have no farms, no herds
and are now as poor as you were four years ago when the Government
brought you here. That before we discuss what we are to do with you, we
want to know what you have done in the past and what you think about
your reservation here.

Barboncito said:
The bringing of us here has caused a great decrease of our numbers, many 2
of us have died, also a great number of our animals. Our Grand-fathers had
no idea of living in any other country except our own and I do not think
it right for us to do so as we were never taught to. When the Navajos were
first created four mountains and four rivers were pointed out to us, inside
of which we should live, that was to be our country and was given to us

---

* *Acequias* are irrigation canals.

by the first woman of the Navajo tribe. It was told to us by our forefathers, that we were never to move east of the Rio Grande or west of the San Juan rivers and I think that our coming here has been the cause of so much death among us and our animals. That our God when he was created (the woman I spoke of) gave us this piece of land and created it specially for us and gave us the whitest of corn and the best of horses and sheep. You can see them (pointing to the other chiefs) ordinarily looking as they are, I think that when the last of them is gone the world will come to an end.—It is true we were brought here, also true we have been taken good care of since we have been here—As soon as we were brought here, we started into work making acequias (and I myself went to work with my party) we made all the Adobes you see here, we have always done as we were told to, if told to bring ashes from the hearth we would do so, carry water and herd stock, we never refused to do anything we were told to do. This ground we were brought on, it is not productive, we plant but it does not yield, all the stock we brought here have nearly all died. Because we were brought here we have done all we could possibly do, but found it to be labor in vain, and have therefore quit it, for that reason we have not planted or tried to do anything this year. It is true we put seed in the ground but it would not grow two feet high, the reason I cannot tell, only I think this ground was never intended for us, we know how to irrigate and farm, still we cannot raise a crop here, we know how to plant all kinds of seed, also how to raise stock and take care of it. The Commissioners can see themselves that we have hardly any sheep or horses, nearly all that we brought here have died and that has left us so poor that we have no means wherewith to buy others—There are a great many among us who were once well off now they have nothing in their houses to sleep on except gunny sacks, true some of us have a little stock left yet, but not near what we had some years ago, in our old country, for that reason my mouth is dry and my head hangs in sorrow to see those around me who were at one time well off so poor now, when we had a way of living of our own, we lived happy, we had plenty of stock, nothing to do but look at our stock, and when we wanted meat nothing to do but kill it. (Pointing to the chiefs present) they were once rich. I feel sorry at the way I am fixed here, I cannot rest comfortable at night, I am ashamed to go to the Commissary for my food, it looks as if somebody was waiting to give it to me since the time I was very small until I was a man when I had my father and mother to take care of I had plenty and since that time I have always followed my father's advice and still keep it. viz: to live at peace with everybody. I want to tell the Commissioners I was born at the lower end of Canon de Chelly. We have been living here five winters. The first year we planted corn, it yielded a good crop but a worm got in the corn and destroyed nearly all of it, the second year the same, the third year it grew about two feet high when a hail storm completely destroyed all of it. We have done all we possibly could to raise a crop of corn and pumpkins but we were disappointed. I thought at one time the whole world was the same as my own country but I got fooled in it, outside my own country we cannot raise a crop, but in it we can raise a crop almost anywhere, our families and stock there increase, here they decrease, we know this land does not like us neither does the water. They have all said this ground was not intended for us, for that reason none of us have attempted to put in seed this year, I think now it is true what my forefathers told me about crossing the line of my own country. It seems that whatever we do here causes death, some work at the Acequias take sick and die, others die with the hoe in their hands, they go to the river to their waists and suddenly disappear, others have been struck and torn to pieces by lightning. A Rattlesnake bite here kills us, in our own country a Rattlesnake before he bites gives warning which enables us to keep out of its way and if bitten we readily find a cure—here we can find no cure. When one of our big men die, the cries of the women causes the tears to roll down on to my moustache. I then think of my own country. I think the Commissioners have seen one thing, when we came here there was plenty of mesquite root which we used for fuel now there is none nearer than the place where I met the Commissioners 25 miles from here and in the winter many die from cold and sickness and overworking in carrying wood such a long distance on their backs, for that reason we cannot stay contented where we now are. Some years ago I could raise my head and see flocks of cattle in any direction, now I feel sorry I cannot see any; I raise my head and can see herds of stock on my right and left, but they are not mine, it makes me feel sorry thinking of the time when I had plenty. I can scarcely endure it, I think that all nations round here are against us (I mean Mexicans and Indians) the reason is that we are a working tribe of Indians, and if we had the means we could support ourselves far better than either Mexican or Indian. The Comanches are against us I know it for they came here and killed a good many of our men. In our own country we knew nothing about the Comanches. Last winter I heard said that there was a Commission coming here, now I am happy it has arrived for I expect to hear from that Commission today the object of its coming here. We have all declared that we do not want to remain here any longer. If I can complete my thoughts today I will give the General my best thanks and think of him as my father and mother. As soon as I heard of your coming I made three pair of moccasins and have worn out two pair of them since, as you see yourselves I am strong and hearty and before I am sick or older I want to go and see the place where I was born, now I am just like a woman, sorry like a woman in trouble. I want to go and see my own country. If we are taken back to our own country, we will call you our father and mother, if you should only tie a goat there we would all live off it, all of the same opinion. I am speaking for the whole tribe, for their animals from the horse to the dog, also the unborn, all that you have heard now is the truth and is the opinion of the whole tribe. It appears to me that the General commands the whole thing as a god. I hope therefore he will do all he can for the Indian, this hope goes in at my feet and out at my mouth. I am speaking to you (General

Sherman) now as if I was speaking to a spirit and I wish you to tell me when you are going to take us to our own country.

General Sherman said:
I have listened to all you have said of your people and believe you have 3 told us the truth. You are right, the world is big enough for all the people it contains and all should live at peace with their neighbors. All people love the country where they were born and raised, but the Navajos are very few indeed compared with all the people in the world, they are not more than seven leaves to all the leaves you have ever seen—still we want to do to you what is right—right to you—and right to us as a people: If you will live in peace with your neighbors, we will see that your neighbors will be at peace with you—The government will stand between you and other Indians and Mexicans. We have got a map here which if Barboncito can understand I would like to show him a few points on it, show him his own country, places inhabited by other Indians, the four mountains spoken of and old Fort Defiance. For example tell him that in our country nearly every family raises a crop or works at a trade for example everybody does something for a living, those who work hard get rich, those who are lazy are poor, also in the upper country the ground is high and requires irrigation, in the lower country there is plenty of water and corn for example can be raised without irrigation. For many years we have been collecting Indians on the Indian Territory south of the Arkansas and they are now doing well and have been doing so for many years. We have heard you were not satisfied with this reservation and we have come here to invite some of your leading men to go and see the Cherokee country and if they liked it we would give you a reservation there. There we will give you cattle to commence with and corn, it being much cheaper there than here; give you schools to educate your children in english or spanish and take care of you until such time as you will be able to protect yourselves. We do not want you to take our word for it but send some of your wisest men to see for themselves. If you do not want that we will discuss the other proposition of going back to your own country and if we agree we will make a boundary line outside of which you must not go except for the purpose of trading—we must have a clearly defined boundary line and know exactly where you belong to, you must live at peace and must not fight with other Indians. If people trouble you, you must go to the nearest military post and report to the Commanding Officer who will punish those who trouble you. The Army will do the fighting, you must live at peace, if you go to your own country the Utes will be the nearest Indians to you, you must not trouble the Utes and the Utes must not trouble you. If however the Utes or Apaches come into your country with bows and arrows and guns you of course can drive them out but must not follow beyond the boundary line. You must not permit any of your young men to go to the Ute or Apache country to steal—neither must they steal from Mexicans. You can come to the Mexican towns to trade. Any Navajo can

now settle in this Territory and he will get a piece of land not occupied, but he will be subject to the laws of the country. Our proposition now is to send some of you at the Government expense to the Indian Territory south of Kansas or if you want to go to your own country you will be sent but not to the whole of it, only a portion which must be well defined.

Barboncito said:
I hope to God you will not ask me to go to any other country except my 4 own. It might turn out another Bosque Redondo. They told us this was a good place when we came but it is not.

General Sherman said:
We merely made the proposition to send you to the Lower Arkansas 5 country for you to think seriously over it. Tomorrow at 10 o'clock I want the whole tribe to assemble at the back of the Hospital and for you then to delegate ten of your men to come forward and settle about the boundary line of your own country which will be reduced to writing and signed by those ten men.

Barboncito said:
I am very well pleased with what you have said, and if we go back to our 6 own country, we are willing to abide by whatever orders are issued to us, we do not want to go to the right or left, but straight back to our own country.

General Sherman said:
This is all we have to say to-day to-morrow we will meet again.   7

 The Council accordingly adjourned until to-morrow the 29th instant 8 at 10 o'clock A.M.

Fort Sumner, New Mexico
May 29th, 1868

The Council met according to adjournment. Present the Commissioners 9 on the part of the United States Government. On the part of the Indians the Navajo nation or tribe.

General Sherman said:
We have come from our Capital, Washington, where our Government 10 consists of a President and a great Council. We are empowered to do now what is necessary for your good, but what we do must be submitted to our Great Father in Washington. We heard that you were not satisfied with this Reservation, that your crops failed for three years and that you wanted to go somewhere else. We know that during the time you have been here the Government has fed and done for you what was considered necessary to make you a thriving people; Yesterday we had a long talk with your

principal chiefs and then told them, that any Navajo could go wherever he pleased in this territory and settle with his family but if he did he would be subject to the laws of the Territory as a citizen, or we would remove you as a nation or tribe to the lower Canadian and Arkansas if you were pleased to go there—but if neither of these propositions suited you, we would discuss the other proposition of sending you to your own country west of the Rio Grande. Barboncito yesterday insisted strongly on going back to his own country in preference to the other two propositions. We then asked him and all the Navajos to assemble here today and for them to select (10) ten of their number as delegates with whom we would conclude terms of treaty. We want to know if these ten men have been chosen; the ten men then stood up, viz:

Delgadito
Barboncito
Manuelito
Largo
Herrero
Chiqueto
Murerto de Hombre
Hombro
Narbono
Armijo

and the Navajos upon being asked if satisfied with these ten men, unanimously responded—Yes— We will now consider these ten men your principal men and we want them to select a chief the remaining to compose his Council for we cannot talk to all the Navajos. Barboncito was unanimously elected Chief—now from this time out you must do as Barboncito tells you, with him we will deal and do all for your good. When we leave here and [you] go to your own country you must do as he tells you and when you get to your country you must obey him or he will punish you, if he has not the power to do so he will call on the soldiers and they will do it. You must all keep together on the march. Must not scatter for fear some of your young men might do wrong and get you all into trouble. All these things will be put down on paper and tomorrow these ten men will sign that paper and now we want to know about the country you want to go to. We heard Barboncito yesterday, if there are any others who differ from him, we would like to hear them, we want also to hear if you want schools in your country—

Blacksmiths or Carpenters Shops. We want to put everything on paper so that hereafter there may be no misunderstanding between us, we want to know if the whole Navajo nation is represented by those present and if they will be bound by the acts of these ten men—unanimous response of yes.

Barboncito said:
What you have said to me now I never will forget. It is true I never liked 1
this place, and feel sorry for being here, from here I would like to go back

the same road we came by way of Teralote, Bernal, Tijeras and Taralto.
All the people on the road are my friends. After I cross the Rio Grande
river I want to visit the Pueblo villages, I want to see the Pueblo Indians
to make friends with them. I then want to go to Canon de Chelly leaving
Pueblo village Laguna to the left. I will take all the Navajos to Canon de
Chelly leave my own family there—taking the rest and scattering them
between San Mateo mountain and San Juan river. I said yesterday this was
the heart of the Navajo country. In this place there is a mountain called
the Sierra Chusque or mountain of agriculture from which (when it rains)
the water flows in abundance creating large sand bars on which the Navajos plant their corn; it is a fine country for stock or agriculture—there is
another mountain called the Mesa Calabasa where these beads which we
wear on our necks have been handed down from generation to generation
and where we were told by our forefathers never to leave our own country. For that reason I want to go back there as quick as possible and not
remain here another day. When the Navajos go back to their own country
I want to put them in different places, it would not do to put them all
together as they are here, if separated they would be more industrious.
There is one family whose intention I do not know, the (Cibollettas) I do
not know whether or not they want to go back to their own country.

General Sherman said:
If the "Cibollettas" choose they can go and live among the Mexicans in this   12
Territory but if they do they will not be entitled to any of the advantages
of the treaty.

Barboncito said:
I merely wished to mention it for if they remain with the Mexicans I   13
cannot be held responsible for their conduct. You spoke to me yesterday
about putting us on a reservation with a boundary line. I do not think it
right to confine us to a certain part we want to have the privilege of going
outside the line to hunt and trade.

General Sherman said:
You can go outside the line to hunt—you can go to Mexican towns to trade   14
but your farms and homes must be inside the boundary line beyond which
you have no claim to the land.

Barboncito said:
That is the way I like to be and return the Commissioners my best thanks.   15
After we get back to our country it will brighten up again and the Navajos
will be as happy as the land, black clouds will rise and there will be plenty
of rain. Corn will grow in abundance and everything look happy. Today
is a day that anything black or red does not look right everything should
be white or yellow representing the flower and the corn. I want to drop
this conversation now and talk about Navajo children held as prisoners by
Mexicans. Some of those present have lost a brother or a sister and I know
that they are in the hands of the Mexicans. I have seen some myself.

General Sherman said:
About their children being held as Peons by Mexicans—you ought to know 16
that there is an Act of Congress against it. About four years ago we had
slaves and there was a great war about it, now there are none. Congress
our great council passed a law prohibiting peonage in New Mexico. So that
if any Mexican holds a Navajo in peonage he (the Mexican) is liable to be
put in the penitentiary. We do not know that there are any Navajos held
by Mexicans as Peons but if there are, you can apply to the judges of the
Civil Courts and the Land Commissioners. They are the proper persons
and they will decide whether the Navajo is to go back to his own people
or remain with the Mexican. That is a matter with which we have nothing
to do. What do you say about schools, Blacksmiths and Carpenter Shops
for the purpose of teaching your children.

Barboncito said:
We would like to have a blacksmith Shop as a great number of us can work 17
at the trade, we would like a carpenter's Shop and if a school was established among us I am satisfied a great number would attend it. I like it very
well. Whatever orders you leave here you may rely upon their being
obeyed.

General Sherman said:
Whatever we promise to do you can depend upon being done.   18

Colonel Samuel F. Tappan asked:
How many Navajos are among the Mexicans now?   19
Answer: Over half of the tribe.   20
Question: How many have returned within the five years?   21
Answer: Cannot tell.   22

General Sherman said:
We will do all we can to have your children returned to you. Our govern- 23
ment is determined that the enslavement of the Navajos shall cease and
those who are guilty of holding them as peons shall be punished.

   All are free now in this country to go and come as they please if 24
children are held in peonage the courts will decide; you can go where any
Navajos are and General Getty will give you an order or send a soldier and
if the Navajo peons wishes to go back or remain he can please himself, we
will not use force, the courts must decide.

   Tomorrow we will meet with those ten men chosen and enter into 25
business with them committing it to writing which they must sign.

   The Council then adjourned until 9 o'clock tomorrow the 30th in- 26
stant.

Fort Sumner N.M.
May 30th, 1868

The Council met according to adjournment. Present the Commissioners 27
on the part of the United States and on the part of the Navajo Tribe the

ten chiefs or headmen chosen by the tribe at yesterday's council as their representatives.

General Sherman said:
We are now ready to commence business, we have it all written down on   28
paper and settled and when agreed on, we will have three copies made, one for you, one to keep ourselves and one to send to Washington. We do not consider it complete until we have all signed our names to it. I will now read it to you and any changes that may be considered necessary will be made.

The treaty was then read by General Sherman and interpreted to the   29
Indians and approved by them.

Then General Sherman said:
We have marked off a reservation for you, including the Canon de Chelly   30
and part of the valley of the San Juan, it is about (100) one hundred miles square. It runs as far south as Canon Bonito and includes the Chusca mountain but not the Mesa Calabesa you spoke of; that is the reservation we suggest to you, it also includes the Ceresca mountain and the bend of the San Juan river, not the upper waters.

Barboncito said:
We are very well pleased with what you have said and well satisfied with   31
that reservation. It is the very heart of our country and is more than we ever expected to get.

We wish now to have Narbono Segundo and Ganado Mucho admit-   32
ted as members of our council in addition to the ten elected yesterday which was agreed to.

General Sherman then asked:
How would old Fort Defiance suit you as a site for your agency?   33

Answer—Very Well.   34

Ganado Mucho said:
After what the Commissioners have said, I do not think anybody has   35
anything to say. After we go back to our own country it will be the same as it used to be. We have never found any person heretofore who told us what you now have and when we return to our own country we will return you our best thanks. We understand the good news you have told us, to be right and we like it very much; we have been waiting for a long time to hear the good words you have now told us, about going back to our own country and I will not stop talking until I have told all the tribe the good news.

General Sherman said:
Now we will adjourn until Monday the 1st day of June 1868 at 9 o'clock   36
A.M. when we will meet and sign the treaty.

The Council accordingly adjourned until Monday the 1st day of June 37 1868 at 9 o'clock A.M.

Questions

Rereading and Independent Analysis

1. These proceedings are presented as a dialogue, but in fact each man made long position statements, not conversational exchanges. This is not an exact record of speech, with all of its hesitations and repetitions, but neither is it what each man "wrote" for publication. Choose any two long speeches, one by each participant, and rewrite them so they are more suitable for reading. Insert paragraph markers where you think they are appropriate, and rewrite sentences that you think are too long because they are meant to represent speech.

2. Reread General Sherman's speeches, making a list of words and phrases you think he chose to adjust white cultural customs and definitions so that Barboncito and the other Navajos would understand them. Then rewrite these words and phrases in the form that you think he might have used in negotiations with white Americans. How would you generalize about the differences in the two versions?

Suggested Discussion and Group Activities

1. General Sherman reveals his attitude toward the Navajos and his ignorance of cultural differences throughout these proceedings. Characterize his attitudes, using examples from the speeches to demonstrate your generalizations. Are such attitudes common today among the majority toward any culturally different groups? What forces do you think bring about and eventually lessen such attitudes?

2. Imagine that you have a reason to relocate suddenly to a part of the country you are totally unfamiliar with. What would be your most important problems? How might people already there react to your problems? What would be your first reactions to a new situation? Your later reactions?

3. Divide your class into two groups, white soldiers and Navajos, or any two groups of culturally different people who must negotiate with each other. In your groups, make a list of the cultural issues you think you would have to research before you could successfully communicate with the other group.

Writing Suggestions

Response
Reread the proceedings, writing brief summaries of the main points in each speech and adding to these points the reaction you might have had if you had been in the listener's place. In your role as a listener, how positively or negatively does each speaker affect you?

Analysis

These proceedings show a process of mutual persuasion whose outcome is in doubt—a negotiation. Write an analysis in which you indicate methods of persuasion that each man used, pointing out specific devices that seem intended to create understanding and elicit cooperation from the other side. Your analysis should be useful to others who must negotiate, even in daily life, so point out the various appeals that each man used. What were the sources of trust? What were the threats that were spoken or implied? What was each side offering? What was each willing to give to the other side? What effect did the length of the statements have?

Finding a Purpose

Both speakers in these proceedings rely on comparisons to explain and give force to their positions. Analyze these comparisons in a report to the diplomatic corps that will help others who negotiate with people whose customs they find extremely strange and whose way of life they disapprove of. Cite specific examples of metaphors, similes, and other imaginative comparisons that create the tone and effect of each speaker's attempt to persuade the other.

Two Marriage Contracts: The Ways of the World

Whenever people agree about changing their present legal, social, and property status, they enter into a contract, an agreement that has the force of law. Most commonly, we think of a contract as a real estate transaction or a sale of services, such as an entertainer's contract to appear on a particular show or an athlete's commitment to play for a team. But, as the *Nichols Cyclopedia of Legal Forms* (1975 ed.) says, "Marriage is a legal relationship, contractual in nature, and is generally subject to statutory provisions of the several jurisdictions." Two people who decide to marry establish the specific terms of their marriage—how their property will be shared, what they promise to do for each other, how they will live, and any other conditions of their marriage that will not oppose established laws.

Usually, couples marry according to the agreements sanctioned by organized religions. They agree, for instance, that their marriage means that they will "love, comfort, and cherish" each other and endow each other with "all [their] worldly goods." But such an agreement, like any other, takes place in reference to civil laws that require the parties to record publicly that they have agreed to these conditions. That is why marriage requires a state license, a public permit to make a legal commitment. Marriage also implies that two people are willing to be responsible for each other so that their household will not become a burden to the state. They affirm that they are willing for their property to be shared or disposed of under conditions that a state's laws prescribe for married people.

The marriage contracts that follow are of two kinds. The first, taken from *Nichols Cyclopedia,* is one of a long series of contracts that apply to marriage. Others include declarations of marriage (which are more like the marriage "ceremony" in a church, where the couple "declares" that they are married), agreements about property arrangements, "life estate termination on remarriage," "notice of refusal to pay debts of spouse," "reconciliation agreements," "separation agreements," and a host of others that apply in every imaginable change of single or married status. The purpose of contracts to marry, as you will see, is primarily to make a public and binding record of intentions.

The second contract in this selection is less fanciful than you may at first think. The two lovers in William Congreve's (1670–1729) comedy *The Way of the World* (1700) are discussing their marriage in what appears to be only a joking way. But the conditions they establish in this scene are like those in traditional "antenuptial agreements," agreements made before marriage to set limits on the freedoms and property rights of those marrying. Congreve's lovers establish conditions that are funny because they raise issues we often dispute but usually do not think of as being important enough to negotiate in marriages.

But the form of their conversation, a negotiation about the implications of marriage, has always been typical and still is when the two parties have established patterns of life and property they wish to maintain. The custom of having marriages arranged by parents or lawyers, which is common in many cultures, is abrogated here by Mrs. Millamant and Mirabell, who make their own arrangements. As you read, notice how Millamant and Mirabell represent themselves to each other and to the audience of the play. Their expectations and desires and the conditions they want to impose wittily reveal issues that are often disputed in any close living arrangement.

Contract and Declaration of Marriage

II. Forms[23]

6.380 Contract to marry.[24]

In consideration of the mutual promises herein contained,[25] _____ hereby agrees to marry _____ on or before the _____ day of _____, 19—, and _____ agrees to marry _____ on or before said day.

[23] Certificate of physician as to blood test of applicant for marriage license is generally required; consult applicable statute.

[24] Construction of contract to marry. 12 Am Jur2d, Breach of Promise, § 2. Common-law marriage, see 55 CJS 816–819; 52 Am Jur2d, Marriage, §§ 42–46.

In some states statutes govern the content and execution of a contract of marriage.

[25] Measure and elements of damages for breach of contract to marry, see note in 73 ALR2d 553.

Tax Note   For gift tax purposes, a consideration not reducible to a money value, as love and affection, promise of marriage, etc., is to be wholly disregarded and the entire value of the property transferred constitutes the amount of the gift. See Beveridge Fed Gift Tax § 3.03.

6.381 Declaration of marriage.

A. [Date]
In the city and county of _____, state of _____, on the _____ day of
_____, 19—, I _____, of the city and county of _____, state of
_____, aged _____ years, do here, in the presence of Almighty God,
take _____ of the state of _____ to be my lawful and wedded husband,
and do hereby acknowledge and declare myself to be the wife of _____
of the state of _____.

[Date]
In the city and county of _____, state of _____, on the _____ day of
_____, 19—, I _____, of the state of _____, aged _____ years, do
here, in the presence of Almighty God, take _____ of the city of _____,
state of _____, to be my lawful and wedded wife, and do hereby acknowledge myself to be the husband of _____.

_____

B. [Place and date]
This is to certify that we, _____ and _____, both of _____, state of
_____, do hereby acknowledge ourselves before the undersigned wit-
nesses to be man and wife.

[Signature]

Signed in the presence of _____.

C. This agreement, made at _____ this _____ day of _____, 19—,
between _____ residing at _____, party of the first part, and _____,
residing at _____, party of the second part.

Witnesseth, that the parties hereto at the place and on the date aforesaid, agree to and hereby do marry one unto the other. The party of the
first part agrees to love, comfort and cherish the party of the second part,
and to keep unto him as her lawful husband forever; and the party of the
second part agrees to love, comfort and cherish the party of the first part
as his lawful wife forever. The party of the first part does hereby become
the lawful wedded wife of the party of the second part, and the party of
the second part does hereby become the lawful wedded husband of the
party of the first part; all to the same effect and extent as if their marriage
had been solemnized before a clergyman or a proper magistrate.

In witness whereof, etc.

Tax Note For the purpose of the personal exemption allowed as a deduction in computing
taxable income by Sec 151, Int Rev Code of 1954, the determination whether an individual
is married shall be made as of the close of his taxable year, except that if his spouse dies during
his taxable year such determination shall be made as of the time of such death. Sec 153, Int
Rev Code of 1954. See Mertens Law of Federal Income Taxation § 32.10.

From *The Way of the World*
William Congreve

Act IV, Scene 5

. . . .

MRS. MILLAMANT: Vanity! No—I'll fly, and be followed to the last mo-
    ment. Though I am upon the very verge of matrimony, I expect you
    should solicit me as much as if I were wavering at the grate of a
    monastery, with one foot over the threshold. I'll be solicited to the
    very last—nay, and afterwards.   5
MIRABELL: What, after the last?
MRS. MILLAMANT: Oh, I should think I was poor and had nothing to
    bestow, if I were reduced to an inglorious ease and freed from the
    agreeable fatigues of solicitation.
MIRABELL: But do not you know that when favors are conferred upon   10
    instant[1] and tedious solicitation, that they diminish in their value,
    and that both the giver loses the grace, and the receiver lessens his
    pleasure?
MRS. MILLAMANT: It may be in things of common application; but never,
    sure, in love. Oh, I hate a lover that can dare to think he draws a   15
    moment's air, independent of the bounty of his mistress. There is not
    so impudent a thing in nature as the saucy look of an assured man,
    confident of success. The pedantic arrogance of a very husband has
    not so pragmatical[2] an air. Ah! I'll never marry unless I am first made
    sure of my will and pleasure.   20
MIRABELL: Would you have 'em both before marriage? or will you be
    contented with the first now, and stay for the other till after grace?
MRS. MILLAMANT: Ah! don't be impertinent.—My dear liberty, shall I
    leave thee? my faithful solitude, my darling contemplation, must I
    bid you then adieu? Ay-h adieu—my morning thoughts, agreeable   25
    wakings, indolent slumbers, all ye *douceurs,* ye *sommeils du matin,*[3]
    adieu.—I can't do't, 'tis more than impossible.—Positively, Mirabell,
    I'll lie abed in a morning as long as I please.
MIRABELL: Then I'll get up in a morning as early as I please.
MRS. MILLAMANT: Ah? Idle creature, get up when you will—and d'ye   30
    hear, I won't be called names after I'm married; positively, I won't
    be called names.
MIRABELL: Names!
MRS. MILLAMANT: Aye, as wife, spouse, my dear, joy, jewel, love, sweet-
    heart, and the rest of that nauseous cant, in which men and their   35

[1] Urgent.
[2] Officious.
[3] Sweetnesses, morning naps (i.e., beauty sleep).

wives are so fulsomely familiar—I shall never bear that. Good Mirabell, don't let us be familiar or fond, nor kiss before folks, like my
Lady Fadler and Sir Francis; nor go to Hyde Park together the first
Sunday in a new chariot, to provoke eyes and whispers, and then
never to be seen there together again, as if we were proud of one 40
another the first week, and ashamed of one another ever after. Let
us never visit together, nor go to a play together; but let us be very
strange and well-bred. Let us be as strange as if we had been married
a great while, and as well-bred as if we were not married at all.

MIRABELL: Have you any more conditions to offer? Hitherto your de- 45
mands are pretty reasonable.

MRS. MILLAMANT: Trifles—as liberty to pay and receive visits to and from
whom I please; to write and receive letters, without interrogatories
or wry faces on your part; to wear what I please, and choose conversation with regard only to my own taste; to have no obligation upon me 50
to converse with wits that I don't like, because they are your acquaintance: or to be intimate with fools, because they may be your
relations.—Come to dinner when I please; dine in my dressingroom
when I'm out of humor, without giving a reason. To have my closet
inviolate; to be sole empress of my tea-table, which you must never 55
presume to approach without first asking leave. And lastly, wherever
I am, you shall always knock at the door before you come in. These
articles subscribed, if I continue to endure you a little longer, I may
by degrees dwindle into a wife.

MIRABELL: Your bill of fare is something advanced in this latter ac- 60
count.—Well, have I liberty to offer conditions—that when you are
dwindled into a wife, I may not be beyond measure enlarged into a
husband?

MRS. MILLAMANT: You have free leave. Propose your utmost; speak and
spare not.   65

MIRABELL: I thank you.—*Imprimis*[4] then, I covenant that your acquaintance be general; that you admit no sworn confidante or intimate of
your own sex—no she-friend to screen her affairs under your countenance, and tempt you to make trial of a mutual secrecy. No decoy-
duck to wheedle you—a fop scrambling to the play in a mask—[5] then 70
bring you home in a pretended fright, when you think you shall be
found out—and rail at me for missing the play and disappointing the
frolic which you had, to pick me up and prove my constancy.

MRS. MILLAMANT: Detestable *imprimis!* I go to the play in a mask!

MIRABELL: *Item,* I article, that you continue to like your own face, as long 75
as I shall; and while it passes current with me, that you endeavor not
to new-coin it. To which end, together with all vizards for the day,

---

[4] In the first place.
[5] In the original, "to wheedle you a fop-scrambling to the play in a mask," which may be
correct in the sense: wheedle you to the theater to scramble after a fop.

I prohibit all masks for the night, made of oiled-skins and I know not what—hogs' bones, hares' gall, pig-water, and the marrow of a roasted cat. In short, I forbid all commerce with the gentlewoman in 80 what-d'ye-call-it Court. *Item,* I shut my doors against all bawds with baskets, and pennyworths of muslin, china, fans, atlases,[6] etc.—*Item,* when you shall be breeding—

MRS. MILLAMANT: Ah! name it not.

MIRABELL: Which may be presumed, with a blessing on our endeavors— 85

MRS. MILLAMANT: Odious endeavors!

MIRABELL: I denounce against all strait lacing, squeezing for a shape, till you mould my boy's head like a sugar-loaf, and instead of a man-child, make me father to a crooked billet. Lastly, to the dominion of the tea-table I submit—but with proviso, that you exceed not in your 90 province, but restrain yourself to native and simple tea-table drinks, as tea, chocolate, and coffee; as likewise to genuine and authorized tea-table talk—such as mending of fashions, spoiling reputations, railing at absent friends, and so forth—but that on no account you encroach upon the men's prerogative, and presume to drink healths, or 95 toast fellows: for prevention of which I banish all foreign forces, all auxiliaries to the tea-table, as orange-brandy, all aniseed, cinnamon, citron, and Barbadoes waters, together with ratafia, and the most noble spirit of clary,[7] but for cowslip wine, poppy water, and all dormitives, those I allow.—These provisos admitted, in other things 100 I may prove a tractable and complying husband.

MRS. MILLAMANT: O horrid provisos! filthy strong-waters! I toast fellows! odious men! I hate your odious provisos.

MIRABELL: Then we're agreed. Shall I kiss your hand upon the contract? And here comes one to be a witness to the sealing of the deed.   105

---

[6] An atlas is a variety of satin (Summers).

[7] *Orange-brandy* is brandy flavored with orange peel; *aniseed,* a cordial so flavored; *cinnamon* is used for the same purpose; *citron* is citron water, a brandy so flavored; *Barbadoes waters* is a cordial flavored with orange and lemon peelings; *ratafia* is a cordial flavored with the kernels of peach, cherry, apricot, or almond; *clary* is composed of brandy, sugar, clary-flowers and cinnamon.

Questions

Rereading and Independent Analysis

1. Make lists of the specific requirements that Mrs. Millamant ("Mrs." is an eighteenth-century title of respect) and Mirabell each have for marriage. Can you generalize about their separate concerns about marriage? What principle guides each of them? Write a brief statement of purpose for each of them.

2. Underline the words and phrases in the Congreve scene that indicate that the two lovers think of themselves as engaging in a discussion with legal, though humorous, implications.

Suggested Discussion and Group Activities

1. What are the benefits of thinking of marriage as a legal instead of only a romantic agreement? Are there disadvantages for the couple involved? Do you think that love rather than agreements should be the only basis for marriage? Why or why not? How might the ages of the people marrying determine the best choice?

2. What other interpersonal relationships can you think of that might benefit from clear agreements before they are begun? Should parents and children, or neighbors, negotiate the conditions of their togetherness? What issues would be addressed in arranging these relationships? Decide on these individually or in groups, and then share your lists as a class. What issues come up on more than one or two of the lists? Why do you think that these issues might create problems in these and many kinds of relationships?

Writing Suggestions

Response

Write a short narrative about a major change that has taken place in your life and the worries you had before you made the change. Were your fears justified? Could you have made any agreement before you entered the new situation that would have allowed you to avoid problems? Why would you have wanted to write a contract first, or why are you glad you weren't limited by one?

Analysis

Write a contract between two people, specifying its conditions clearly, in language that you think would be legally acceptable as the terms of an agreement about a personal action or venture. You can choose an unlikely possibility (discovering gold or oil, opening the first McDonald's on the moon) and clearly spell out the conditions you want to establish with a partner before you attempt to write the contract in clear, unambiguous language. Use the model contract here to help you frame your contract precisely.

Finding a Purpose

1. Try writing a humorous dialogue in the same light tone as the one in Congreve's play. In your dialogue, show two people pretending that they do not want to accomplish something they really do want—a trip, a move to another place, a purchase, or another joint project. Be sure to set the scene for the conversation and define the characters of the speakers. In class, have two of your classmates read your dialogue aloud to see if the words fit the speakers.

2. Write a proposal to a specific person to join you in an important new action. In your proposal, spell out the benefits this person will receive, the plans you have, and the conditions you expect to set. Give your proposal to a classmate to determine if it is persuasive.

SAYINGS AND INSCRIPTIONS

Common sayings and public inscriptions share qualities that make them a special kind of visible community language, separated from their individual authors and the precise context that motivated their writing. They are generally brief statements that define a concept, give advice, or draw attention to the places where they are found. Whether they are read and remembered depends on their visible forms, which are often repetitive and rely on word play—figurative language, rhymes, puns, or *double entendre* (words that have two meanings that reflect on each other). To appreciate sayings and inscriptions, you must look for the messages implied when all of their structural elements are taken together.

Sayings

Sayings are "pro-verbs," "words put forth," as typical responses or truths that people say and call on in common situations. They are found in the Bible and many later works, like the advice of Polonius in Shakespeare's (1564–1616) *Hamlet,* Benjamin Franklin's (1706–1790) *Poor Richard's Almanac,* or William Blake's (1757–1827) "Proverbs of Hell." They may contain the wisdom of people who do not have formal education but who do have experience and insight. You will find many of these examples familiar. Sayings invite both imitations and parody; their standard forms suggest both continuity and humor. Polonius, for instance, has no idea of the implications of the complex actions in *Hamlet.* His ignorance of the tensions around him gives an ironic context to his epigrammatic advice to his son, which he speaks with straightforward certainty as Laertes leaves for Paris. Little that Polonius says stands up to careful review, but its memorable language has nonetheless allowed it to be quoted often without reference to its irony in the play.

Franklin's establishment of the popular press in America sowed the first seeds of the distinctly American force of "public opinion." He also contributed "Poor Richard"—his view of a wise, concerned, involved, and rational citizen who can accurately judge events—to the American "character." The *Almanac,* which sold 10,000 copies a year, was the first popular guide to agriculture, economy, right action, and virtue in America. Interspersed among the practical information, Franklin's homely maxims urged the colonists to become capitalists, persuading them with parallelism, contrast, and repetition. Blake, a Romantic poet, included the "Proverbs of Hell" in his *Marriage of Heaven and Hell,* whose title shows his paradoxical intent. He reverses common wisdom about the nature of "good" and "bad," raising the steep problem of deciding whether any straightforward, simple statement can be absolutely "true."

Inscriptions

Inscriptions often become "sayings," but they are distinguished by their physical settings on monuments and other permanent structures. They interest us because they draw attention to the almost absolute separation between the first writer and the permanent form of the writing. For instance,

Percy Bysshe Shelley's (1792–1822) poem "Ozymandias" is both an important example of his art and a comment on his fear of disappearing forever as writer who only "writ on water." "Ozymandias" transfers this fear to the bleak desert, where a statue inscribed with a warning is found and described only by a nameless traveler. The reporter quotes the ironic words on the statue, demanding attention, fear, and "despair." This sonnet shows how the supposed "permanence" of writing depends, always, on its being noticed, found significant, and passed on. The good will of readers, not the insistence of writers, will determine its power.

The nameless authors of graffiti do assure their thoughts of some permanence, but anonymously. They use public places to write on, telling us that a thoughtful, witty, and opinionated person wants to send a message through irregular channels. "Graffiti" (the word derives from the Italian word for "scratch") have been found from sources as early as 350 B.C. They are usually one of two kinds—public messages in more or less private places we visit regularly or announcements of private opinions found on walls, buildings, or fences.

Newspaper headlines are a special category of inscriptions. They are attention getters, serving as catchy titles to make readers interested in what follows. Headline writing takes place within limits: Headlines must draw attention, be simple and brief, and convey the sense of the story to follow. They also must use only the number of letters that will fit above the column or columns they head. The selections here, collected by the Columbia University School of Journalism, all went wrong as a result of these limits.

 # Proverbs, Chapter 15

A soft answer turns away wrath, but a harsh word stirs up anger.   1
The tongue of the wise dispenses knowledge, but the mouths of fools
    pour out folly.   2
The eyes of the LORD are in every place, keeping watch on the evil
    and the good.   3
A gentle tongue is a tree of life, but perverseness in it breaks the
    spirit.   4
A fool despises his father's instruction, but he who heeds admonition is
    prudent.   5
In the house of the righteous there is much treasure, but trouble
    befalls the income of the wicked.   6
The lips of the wise spread knowledge; not so the minds of fools.   7
The sacrifice of the wicked is an abomination to the LORD, but the
    prayer of the upright is his delight.   8

The way of the wicked is an abomination to the LORD, but he loves
him who pursues righteousness.   9

There is severe discipline for him who forsakes the way; he who hates
reproof will die.   10

Sheol and Abaddon lie open before the LORD, how much more the
hearts of men!   11

A scoffer does not like to be reproved; he will not go to the wise. 12

A glad heart makes a cheerful countenance, but by sorrow of heart the
spirit is broken.   13

The mind of him who has understanding seeks knowledge, but the
mouths of fools feed on folly.   14

All the days of the afflicted are evil, but a cheerful heart has a
continual feast.   15

Better is a little with the fear of the LORD than great treasure and
trouble with it.   16

Better is a dinner of herbs where love is than a fatted ox and hatred
with it.   17

A hot-tempered man stirs up strife, but he who is slow to anger quiets
contention.   18

The way of a sluggard is overgrown with thorns, but the path of the
upright is a level highway.   19

A wise son makes a glad father, but a foolish man despises his
mother.   20

Folly is a joy to him who has no sense, but a man of understanding
walks aright.   21

Without counsel plans go wrong, but with many advisers they
succeed.   22

To make an apt answer is a joy to a man, and a word in season, how
good it is!   23

The wise man's path leads upward to life, that he may avoid Sheol
beneath.   24

The LORD tears down the house of the proud, but maintains the
widow's boundaries.   25

The thoughts of the wicked are an abomination to the LORD, the
words of the pure are pleasing to him.   26

He who is greedy for unjust gain makes trouble for his household, but
he who hates bribes will live.   27

The mind of the righteous ponders how to answer, but the mouth of
the wicked pours out evil things.   28

The LORD is far from the wicked, but he hears the prayer of the
righteous.   29

The light of the eyes rejoices the heart, and good news refreshes the
bones.   30

He whose ear heeds wholesome admonition will abide among the
wise.   31

He who ignores instruction despises himself, but he who heeds
　　admonition gains understanding.　　　　　　　　　　　　　　32
The fear of the LORD is instruction in wisdom, and humility goes
　　before honor.　　　　　　　　　　　　　　　　　　　　　　33

From "Proverbs of Hell"
William Blake

In seed time learn, in harvest teach, in winter enjoy.
Drive your cart and your plow over the bones of the dead.
The road of excess leads to the palace of wisdom.
Prudence is a rich ugly old maid courted by Incapacity.
He who desires but acts not, breeds pestilence.　　　　　　　　5
The cut worm forgives the plow.
Dip him in the river who loves water.
A fool sees not the same tree that a wise man sees.
He whose face gives no light, shall never become a star.
Eternity is in love with the productions of time.　　　　　　　10
The busy bee has no time for sorrow.
The hours of folly are measur'd by the clock, but of wisdom: no clock
　　can measure.
All wholsom food is caught without a net or a trap.
Bring out number, weight, & measure in a year of dearth.
No bird soars too high, if he soars with his own wings.　　　　15
A dead body revenges not injuries.
The most sublime act is to set another before you.
If the fool would persist in his folly he would become wise.
Folly is the cloke of knavery.
Shame is Pride's cloke.　　　　　　　　　　　　　　　　　20

Prisons are built with stones of Law, Brothels with bricks of Religion.
The pride of the peacock is the glory of God.
The lust of the goat is the bounty of God.
The wrath of the lion is the wisdom of God.
The nakedness of woman is the work of God.　　　　　　　　25
Excess of sorrow laughs. Excess of joy weeps.
The roaring of lions, the howling of wolves, the raging of the stormy
　　sea, and the destructive sword, are portions of eternity too great
　　for the eye of man.
The fox condemns the trap, not himself.
Joys impregnate. Sorrows bring forth.
Let man wear the fell of the lion, woman the fleece of the sheep.　　30
The bird a nest, the spider a web, man friendship.

The selfish smiling fool & the sullen frowning fool shall be both
    thought wise, that they may be a rod.
What is now proved was once only imagin'd.

Polonius' Advice to Laertes from *Hamlet*
William Shakespeare

ACT I

SCENE III. *A room in Polonius's house.*

Enter LAERTES *and* OPHELIA.

LAER: My necessaries are embark'd, farewell;
    And, sister, as the winds give benefit
    And convoy is assistant, do not sleep,
    But let me hear from you.
OPH: Do you doubt that?   5
LAER: For Hamlet and the trifling of his favours,
    Hold it a fashion and a toy in blood,
    A violet in the youth of primy nature,
    Forward, not permanent, sweet, not lasting,   10
    The (perfume and) suppliance of a minute;
    No more.
OPH: No more but so?
LAER: Think it no more:
    For nature crescent does not grow alone   15
    In thews and bulk, but, as (this) temple waxes,
    The inward service of the mind and soul
    Grows wide withal. Perhaps he loves you now,
    And now no soil nor cautel doth besmirch
    The virtue of his (will); but you must fear,   20
    His greatness weigh'd, his will is not his own;
    For he himself is subject to his birth.
    He may not, as unvalued persons do,
    Carve for himself, for on his choice depends
    The (sanity) and health of the whole state;   25
    And therefore must his choice be circumscrib'd
    Unto the voice and yielding of that body
    Whereof he is the head. Then, if he says he loves you,
    It fits your wisdom so far to believe it   30
    As he in his (particular act and place)

May give his saying deed; which is no further
Than the main voice of Denmark goes withal.
Then weigh what loss your honour may sustain
If with too credent ear you list his songs,   35
Or lose your heart, or your chaste treasure open
To his unmast'red importunity.
Fear it, Ophelia, fear it, my dear sister,
And keep within the rear of your affection,
Out of the shot and danger of desire.   40
The chariest maid is prodigal enough,
If she unmask her beauty to the moon.
Virtue itself scapes not calumnious strokes.
The canker galls the infants of the spring
Too oft before the buttons be disclos'd,   45
And in the morn and liquid dew of youth
Contagious blastments are most imminent.
Be wary then; best safety lies in fear;
Youth to itself rebels, though none else near.

OPH: I shall th' effect of this good lesson keep,   50
As watchman to my heart. But, good my brother,
Do not, as some ungracious pastors do,
Show me the steep and thorny way to heaven,
Whilst, like a puff'd and reckless libertine,
Himself the primrose path of dalliance treads,   55
And recks not his own rede.

LAER: O, fear me not.

                                        [*Enter* POLONIUS.]

I stay too long; but here my father comes.
A double blessing is a double grace;   60
Occasion smiles upon a second leave.

POL: Yet here, Laertes? Aboard, aboard, for shame!
The wind sits in the shoulder of your sail,
And you are stay'd for. There; my blessing with you!   65
And these few precepts in thy memory
See thou character. Give thy thoughts no tongue,
Nor any unproportion'd thought his act.
Be thou familiar, but by no means vulgar.   70
The friends thou hast, and their adoption tried,
Grapple them to thy soul with hoops of steel;
But do not dull thy palm with entertainment
Of each (new)-hatch'd, unfledg'd comrade. Beware
Of entrance to a quarrel; but being in,   75
Bear 't that the opposed may beware of thee.
Give every man thine ear, but few thy voice;
Take each man's censure, but reserve thy judgment.
Costly thy habit as thy purse can buy,

But not express'd in fancy; rich, not gaudy;   80
For the apparel oft proclaims the man,
And they in France of the best rank and station
Are most select and generous in that.
Neither a borrower nor a lender be;
For loan oft loses both itself and friend,   85
And borrowing dulls the edge of husbandry.
This above all: to thine own self be true,
And it must follow, as the night the day,   90
Thou canst not then be false to any man.

 # From *Poor Richard's Almanac, 1749*
Benjamin Franklin

JANUARY

Advice to Youth

First, Let the Fear of HIM who form'd thy Frame,
Whose Hand sustain'd thee e'er thou hadst a Name,
Who brought thee into Birth, with Pow'r of Thought
Receptive of immortal Good, be wrought
Deep in thy Soul. His, not thy own, thou art;   5
To him resign the Empire of thy Heart.
His Will, thy Law; His Service, thy Employ;
His Frown, thy Dread, his Smile be all thy Joy.
Wealth and Content are not always Bed-fellows.
Wise Men learn by others harms; Fools by their own.   10

FEBRUARY

Wak'd by the Call of Morn, on early Knee,
Ere the World thrust between thy God and thee,
Let thy pure Oraisons, ascending, gain
His Ear, and Succour of his Grace obtain,
In Wants, in Toils, in Perils of the Day,   15
And strong Temptations that beset thy Way.
Thy best Resolves then in his Strength renew
To walk in Virtue's Paths, and Vice eschew.
The end of Passion is the beginning of Repentance.
Words may shew a man's Wit, but Actions his Meaning.   20

MARCH

To HIM intrust thy Slumbers, and prepare
The fragrant Incense of thy Ev'ning Prayer.

But first tread back the Day, with Search severe,
And *Conscience,* chiding or applauding, hear.
Review each Step; *Where, acting, did I err?*   25
Omitting, where? Guilt either Way infer.
Labour this Point, and while thy Frailties last,
Still let each following Day correct the last.
'T is a well spent penny that saves a groat.
Many Foxes grow grey, but few grow good.   30
Presumption first blinds a Man, then sets him a running.

APRIL

LIFE is a shelvy Sea, the Passage fear,
And not without a skilful Pilot steer.
Distrust thy Youth, experienc'd Age implore,
And borrow all the Wisdom of Threescore.   35
But chief a Father's, Mother's Voice revere;
'T is Love that chides, 't is Love that counsels here.
Thrice happy is the Youth, whose pliant Mind
To all a Parent's Culture is resign'd.
A cold April, The Barn will fill.   40
Content makes poor men rich; Discontent makes rich
        Men poor.
Too much plenty makes Mouth dainty.

MAY

O, well begun, Virtue's great Work pursue,
Passions at first we may with Ease subdue;   45
But if neglected, unrestrain'd too long,
Prevailing in their Growth, by Habit Strong,
They've wrapp'd the Mind, have fix'd the stubborn Bent,
And Force of Custom to wild Nature lent;
Who then would set the crooked Tree aright,   50
As soon may wash the tawny Indian white.
If Passion drives, let Reason hold the Reins.
Neither trust, nor contend, nor lay wagers, nor lend;
And you'll have peace to your Lives end.
Drink does not drown Care, but waters it, and makes it   55
        grow faster.
Who dainties love, shall Beggars prove.

JUNE

Industry's bounteous Hand may *Plenty* bring,
But wanting *frugal Care,* 't will soon take wing.
Small thy Supplies, and scanty in their Source,   60

'Twixt *Av'rice* and Profusion steer thy Course.
Av'rice is deaf to Want's Heart-bursting Groan,
Profusion makes the Beggar's Rags thy own:
Close Fraud and Wrong from griping Av'rice grow,
From rash *Profusion* desp'rate Acts and Woe.   65
A Man has no more Goods than he gets Good by.
Welcome, Mischief, if thou comest alone.
Different Sects like different clocks, may be all near the
      matter, 'tho they don't quite agree.

JULY

Honour the softer Sex; with courteous Style,   70
And Gentleness of Manners, win their Smile;
Nor shun their virtuous Converse; but when Age
And Circumstance consent, thy Faith engage
To some discreet, well-natur'd, chearful Fair,
One not too stately for the Household Care,   75
One form'd in Person and in Mind to please,
To season Life, and all its Labours ease.
If your head is wax, don't walk in the Sun.
Pretty & Witty will wound if they hit ye.
Having been poor is no shame, but being ashamed of   80
      it, is.

AUGUST

Gaming, the Vice of Knaves and Fools, detest,
Miner of Time, of Substance and of Rest;
Which, in the Winning or the Losing Part,
Undoing or undone, will wring the Heart: 85
Undone, self-curs'd, thy Madness thou wilt rue;
Undoing, Curse of others will pursue
Thy hated Head. A Parent's, Household's Tear,
A Neighbour's Groan, and *Heav'n's* displeasure fear.
'T is a laudable Ambition, that aims at being better than   90
      his Neighbours.
The wise Man draws more Advantage from his Enemies,
      than the Fool from his Friends.

SEPTEMBER

Wouldst thou extract the purest Sweet of Life,
Be nor Ally nor Principal in Strife.   95
A Mediator there, thy Balsam bring,
And lenify the Wound, and draw the Sting;
On *Hate* let *Kindness* her warm Embers throw,
And mould into a Friend the melting Foe.

The weakest Foe boasts some revenging Pow'r;   100
The weakest Friend some serviceable Hour.
All would live long, but none would be old.
Declaiming against Pride, is not always a Sign of
    Humility.
Neglect kills Injuries, Revenge increases them.   105

OCTOBER

In Converse be reserv'd, yet not morose,
In Season grave, in Season, too, jocose.
Shun Party-Wranglings, mix not in Debate
With Bigots in Religion or the State.
No Arms to Scandal or Detraction lend,   110
Abhor to wound, be fervent to defend.
Aspiring still to know, a Babbler scorn,
But watch where Wisdom opes her golden Horn.
9 Men in 10 are suicides.
Doing an Injury puts you below your Enemy; Revenging one makes
    you but even with him; Forgiving it sets you above him.

NOVEMBER

In quest of Gain be just: A Conscience clear
Is Lucre, more than Thousands in a Year;
Treasure no Moth can touch, no Rust consume;   120
Safe from the Knave, the Robber, and the Tomb.
Unrighteous Gain is the curs'd Seed of Woe,
Predestin'd to be reap'd by them who sow;
A dreadful Harvest! when th' avenging Day
Shall like a Tempest, sweep the Unjust away.   125
Most of the Learning in use, is of no great Use.
Great Good-nature, without Prudence, is a great Misfortune.
Keep Conscience clear, Then never fear.

DECEMBER

But not from Wrong alone thy Hand restrain,   130
The *Appetite* of Gold demands the Rein.
What Nature asks, what Decency requires,
Be this the Bound that limits thy Desires:
This, and the gen'rous godlike Pow'r to feed
The Hungry, and to warm the Loins of *Need:*   135
To dry Misfortune's Tear, and scatter wide
Thy Blessings, like the Nile's o'erflowing Tide.
A man in a Passion rides a mad Horse.
Reader farewel, all Happiness attend thee; May each New-Year, better
    and richer find thee.   140

HOW TO GET RICHES

The Art of getting Riches consists very much in THRIFT. All Men are not equally qualified for getting Money, but it is in the Power of every one alike to practice this Virtue.

He that would be beforehand in the World, must be beforehand with his Business: It is not only ill Management, but discovers a slothful Disposition, to do that in the Afternoon, which should have been done in the Morning.

Useful Attainments in your Minority will procure Riches in Maturity, of which Writing and Accounts are not the meanest.

Learning, whether Speculative or Practical, is, in Popular or Mixt Governments, the Natural Source of Wealth and Honour.

PRECEPT I

In Things of moment, on thy self depend,
Nor trust too far thy Servant or thy Friend:
With private Views, thy Friend may promise fair,
And Servants very seldom prove sincere.

155

PRECEPT II

What can be done, with Care perform to Day,
Dangers unthought-of will attend Delay;
Your distant Prospects all precarious are,
And Fortune is as fickle as she's fair.

160

PRECEPT III

Nor trivial Loss, nor trivial Gain despise;
Molehills, if often heap'd, to Mountains rise:
Weigh every small Expence, and nothing waste,
Farthings long sav'd, amount to Pounds at last.

 Ozymandias
Percy Bysshe Shelley

I MET a traveller from an antique land
Who said: Two vast and trunkless legs of stone
Stand in the desert. Near them, on the sand,
Half sunk, a shattered visage lies, whose frown,
And wrinkled lip, and sneer of cold command,
Tell that its sculptor well those passions read
Which yet survive, stamped on these lifeless things,

5

The hand that mocked them and the heart that fed;
And on the pedestal these words appear:
"My name is Ozymandias, king of kings: 10
Look on my works, ye Mighty, and despair!"
Nothing beside remains. Round the decay
Of that colossal wreck, boundless and bare,
The lone and level sands stretch far away.

 # Writing on the Wall: Graffiti

For those who think life is a joke, just think of the punchline.
(Ladies' room, Bennington College, Bennington, Vermont.)

Sockitome, Socrates!
(Arlington County Public Library, Arlington, Virginia. Cited in American Library Association Bulletin, April, 1969.)

Norman Mailer is the master of the single entendre.
(Ladies' room, Limelight Restaurant, Greenwich Village, New York City.)

God, I suspect you of being a left-wing intellectual.
(Condorcet, Paris, May, 1968.)

I'm a Marxist, Groucho type.
(Nanterre, May, 1968.)

Artists are misunderstood. Not by people, but by themselves.

There were two big beautiful elm trees in front of the student union at Cornell University, but this year the Dutch elm disease struck one. There is now only one big elm tree, and one 6-foot-high stripped stump where graffiti appeared almost instantaneously.

This is the Math tree, it has ordered pairs and square roots.
(Cornell, 1969)

Dear Johnny if you don't see my message on this wall then you know I wasn't here.

The world is flat. Class of 1491.
(Princeton University, Princeton, New Jersey, 1970)

Everyone hates me because I'm paranoid.

[*below*]

Just because you're paranoid, don't think they don't hate you.

[*below*]

Everyone is paranoid because they all know I hate them.
    (Wisconsin—White Library)

South Dakota: Where men are men and the sheep are nervous.

[*below*]

North Dakota: Where men are sheep and the women are nervous.

[*below*]

Washington D.C.: Where politicians are bought, the people are nervous, and your secretaries tell.
    (Indiana—Swain Hall)

. . . .

$E = Mc^2$

[*below*]

Good, Albert. Next time please submit your work papers.

[*below*]

"Work Papers": $E = Mc^2$ ~~$E = Mb^2$~~ ~~$E = Mc^2$~~
    (Wisconsin—Humanities)

. . . .

World's Shortest List:

[*below*]

Creative Accountants

[*below*]

Good American Cars

[*below*]

Qualified Campus Security Officers

[*below*]

Chicanos I Have Met While Yachting

[*below*]

Italian War Heroes

[*below*]

Graffitists Who Can Spell Rite

[*below*]

This List Two Months Ago

[*below*]

Consecutive Winning Seasons at Iowa
  (Iowa—Phillips)

. . . .

I wanted to be a pathologist, but it was a deadend job.

[*below*]

I wanted to be a surgeon, but I wasn't cut out for it.

[*below*]

I wanted to be a plumber, but it wasn't fitting.

[*below*]

I wanted to be an electrician, but the idea shocked me.

[*below*]

I wanted to be in the Air Force, but the idea bombed.

 Squad Helps Dog Bite Victim:
Headlines and News

SQUAD HELPS DOG BITE VICTIM

Grant County (Wis.) *Herald Independent* 4/29/76

CORECTION

The Mountain Echo (Yellville, Ark) 5/15/75

Planes must clear mountains first
CRASH PROMPTS CHANGE IN RULES

Rocky Mountain News, Denver 2/6/75

WAR DIMS HOPES FOR PEACE

Wisconsin State Journal, 12/27/65

CHESTER MORRILL, 92, WAS FED SECRETARY

The Washington Post 4/21/78

COMPLAINTS ABOUT NBA REFEREES GROWING UGLY

Chicago Sun-Times 5/23/79

MAN ROBS, THEN KILLS HIMSELF

The Washington Post 12/19/75

AN ITALIAN SINNER will be served at 5:30 P.M. at the Essex Center United Methodist Church.

Vermonter 10/16/77

The Assembly passed and sent to the Senate a bill requiring dog owners in New York City to clean up after their pets, on penalty of a $100 fine. The bill also applies to Buffalo.

The New York Times 5/24/77

STIFF OPPOSITION EXPECTED TO CASKETLESS FUNERAL PLAN

The Toronto Star 4/7/76

Joining Wallace on stage were new School Committeewoman Elvira Pixie Palladino and Boston City Councilman Albert (Dapper) O'Neil, both active opponents of court-ordered busing and Wallace's wife Cornelia.

The Boston Globe 1/10/76

BLUE SKIES UNLESS IT'S CLOUDY

San Francisco Chronicle 5/29/71

FARMER BILL DIES IN HOUSE

The Atlanta Constitution 4/13/78

SCHOOL BOARD AGREES TO DISCUSS EDUCATION

Philadelphia *Evening Bulletin* 10/8/74

TUNA BITING OFF WASHINGTON COAST

Seattle Post-Intelligencer 8/3/79

Questions

Rereading and Independent Analysis

1. Choose five of the sayings from Proverbs, "The Proverbs of Hell," Polonius' speech, and *Poor Richard's Almanac*. (Use at least one from each selection.) Analyze each grammatically, identifying its subject, verb, and object or complement. Then analyze each to show (a) its use of parallelism (repeated grammatical features), (b) repetition in the length of the words and rhythm of its parts, (c) repeated sounds, and (d) any figures of speech (e.g., metaphors and similes). Based on your analysis, what generalization can you make about the form of a saying? Are they composed to be heard or to be read? Why do you think so?

2. Reread one of the selections of sayings to discover how its statements are organized into a whole. How does it progress from one statement to another, or from one section to another? What topics are addressed? Identify the problem or situation that the selection "covers" as a whole.

3. Choose a selection of sayings or inscriptions and rewrite it in direct prose. Your revision should make clear what the selection is saying in language that you and your classmates will find familiar.

4. A sentence element is said to "squint" when it serves two functions at once, usually to the confusion of the reader. Reread the graffiti and newspaper headlines, marking each word or phrase that "squints" in them. Write down the two possible meanings or senses of the words you marked. Try to identify the grammatical function of each squinting word in the selections.

Suggested Discussion and Group Activities

1. As a class or in small groups, make a collection of common wisdom that you have heard in your family or community. As a group, examine the collection to draw conclusions about the language and forms in which it is preserved and passed on. Give examples of features in your collection that are like the language and form of the selections here.

2. What features of your collection of common wisdom (question 1) reveal characteristics of the community that it came from? What problems does it address? How does it emphasize a particular social, religious, or political point of view? For instance, does it indicate, like the Proverbs, that the people live in the country? Find evidence to support the point that "folk wisdom" arises from particular groups in specific places, times, and situations.

3. Contrast the implied advice in Blake's "Proverbs of Hell" to that in the other examples of sayings. Find contrasts between the distinct tone

and the "personality" Blake takes on and those in other sayings. As a group, decide whether Blake specifically opposes the values of the other selections. How would you define Blake's perspective? Why do you agree or disagree with it?

4. Although inscriptions are common on buildings, books, and many other places, we regularly overlook them. Make a collection of inscriptions from the places and objects in your city and on your campus. What generalizations can you make about the purposes that these writings were intended to serve? What would be lost if they all disappeared?

5. Newspaper headlines share many of the characteristics of titles, yet they are not used for exactly the same purposes. Choose any page of a newspaper you usually read and bring the headlines to class. Suggest alternative titles for the stories that you think their writers might have used if they had none of the limits imposed by the headline form. What effect does the headline have on your reading of its story? Discuss the various groups of readers who might need and prefer the longer titles.

Writing Suggestions

Response

What is your most common reaction to taking advice? Write a journal entry in which you tell about a particular instance of taking or giving advice and the results of it.

Analysis

1. Write ten sentences in which you aim to create "sayings"—advice, definitions, or comments written in imitation of the grammatical forms, patterns of repetition, parallelism, and other techniques used in the selections.

2. Write an essay in which you compare *and* contrast Blake's "Proverbs of Hell" and those of one of the other selections. Show how the sentence forms in Blake and another selection are similar, and how Blake's paradoxical meanings take some of their force from this common form. Contrast the different situations, beliefs, and habits of the people each selection would appeal to.

3. Reread Polonius' advice to Laertes carefully. Then write an essay in which you use specific examples from all of the sayings to explain the truth *or* the falsehood of the statement, "to thine own self be true/And it must follow . . . Thou canst not then be false to any man." Is this common wisdom? Is it valid? Do precepts from all of the selections support or deny it? That is, does being true to yourself guarantee that you cannot be false to others or different from what they remember about you?

4. Write an essay in which you explain how Shelley's poem "Ozymandias" comments on all of the other sayings and inscriptions in this section. Carefully show what each part of the poem means, and then show how its irony also applies to the value we place on other advice, wisdom, and beliefs that were meant to be permanent and universal.

Finding a Purpose

1. In a letter to one or both of your parents or another person of your choice, offer thanks for advice and counsel given you. Describe the situations in which you have benefited from this help.

2. Choose three or four signs you commonly see in public places. Rewrite them for different groups of readers: children, older people, tourists, or any other group you choose. Then write a proposal to your local government persuading them to provide alternative versions of these common signs for readers who might not understand the present versions. Include your revisions as examples of alternatives.

3. All of the selections in this chapter raise questions about the permanence of writing versus the impermanence of speech. They show us the difference between two definitions of "memory": the private memories we use daily to conduct our lives, and public memory, the lasting collection of ideas formed by community events that gives us a sense of continuity.

Write a letter or report to an important person you know of from history, using examples from this chapter or from other sources to assure the person that writing has created a public memory that makes his or her words, actions, or ideas significant.

CHAPTER

3

The Writer's Contexts: From Self to Community

INTRODUCTION

Being "able to write" has had many meanings since ancient times when writing was a highly specialized craft requiring many tools. At first, this complex craft was delegated to slave-secretaries who wrote down the words that their employers orally composed. For centuries, being "literate" meant *knowing* the important literature and documents of a culture, but not necessarily being able to read them. Literate people usually had heard these important records repeated many times. But after the Bible was printed in the 1450s, being able to read increasingly became the primary definition of "literacy." Only recently has the democratic idea of education in both reading and writing for everyone become widespread. We now expect to read and to write for ourselves, not to hear others read or recite to us.

With this recent change in the meaning of literacy, a development that has depended on the accessibility of writing materials, the purposes of the act of writing have multiplied. Effective writers are not necessarily people who publish or "author" important works. Any of us who readily uses writing for many reasons can be an effective writer. We may write privately to explore our thoughts and learn what we feel and believe. We may write letters and notes to communicate conveniently with distant correspondents. We can also use writing to reflect on community experience. Our explorations of personal and public events integrate our own lives into broader community perspectives.

We may sometimes approach writing hesitantly, as though it were still the early technological chore that required stiff parchment and eight different tools to make marks and erasures. But the ease of writing today, whether by hand or machine, allows us to move smoothly from private to public use. We can begin with private notes and jottings in self-exploration, then make drafts that are about as polished as a letter to a close friend would be, and finally, revising and editing as much as we wish as we go along, produce a finished document for publication. As we write, we play many different roles. We may first be talking to ourselves, then to someone who knows us, and finally to a broader, distant group of readers who will only know us from the printed page.

The selections in this chapter are divided according to these roles. They demonstrate ways that writers have revealed themselves as private individuals and as community figures. We find writers whose private expressions are as powerful as the public statements about experience that others make. As these published selections show, writing extends even casual thought, giving us the advantage of being able to read about and rethink our own experiences. We can write about any subject, not just predetermined topics that others have thought important. When we do address traditional topics and situations, we can write from distinct personal perspectives, relating our own time, place, and individual history to enduring subjects and relationships.

The writers represented here, whether they thought of their writing as private or public, wrote to re-live, explore, preserve, and test their experiences. Each of these selections reveals ways that writing helps us make sense of experience. As you read them, you will share moments that could have been lost if the writers had not had the desire to translate observations and memories into written words.

WRITERS ALONE

 ## The Journal of Julia, A.D. 4
John Williams

John Williams (b. 1922), who has taught creative writing at the University of Denver and has won many awards for his novels and poetry, is the author of Augustus, *an historical novel that includes the fictional diary of Augustus Caesar's daughter, Julia. In Williams's novel, which won the National Book Award for Fiction in 1973, Augustus's life is told through the letters, depositions, and written testimony of actual and invented characters around him during his rise and reign. Augustus's daughter, Julia, is sent to exile on Pandateria, a sparsely populated island in the Mediterranean. She has been banned from life in Rome as a result of her public immorality. Two years after* her exile begins, she starts a diary, presented here as what she might have written if the actual Julia had kept such a record.

Keeping such a journal would have been thought strange in her time. Early writers did not imagine composing words that would not reach a reader or a listener. The first artfully composed speech was always guided by considerations of its audience. Because of the technical difficulty of writing down spoken words, few individuals learned the skill. The Greeks assigned the act of writing to "craft-literates"—slaves who recorded what others composed.

The Romans, as Julia points out here, were well educated but deeply prejudiced against contemplative activities. Although they did actually write for themselves without slaves, they were taught to write for public, not private, ends. As Julia muses on the problems of an exiled writer who will receive no response to her words, she describes her education in composition as it would actually have been taught in early Greek and Roman schools or by tutors. She reveals how this education relied on careful study of the texts of great surviving literature, which was used as the basis for mastering grammar, composition, and public speaking. As you read, evaluate Julia's difficulties in writing only for her own reading. Do you share these problems in keeping diaries and journals?

Outside my window, the rocks, gray and somber in the brilliance of the 1 afternoon sun, descend in a huge profusion toward the sea. This rock, like all the rock on this island of Pandateria, is volcanic in origin, rather porous and light in weight, upon which one must walk with some caution, lest one's feet be slashed by hidden sharpnesses. There are others on this island, but I am not allowed to see them. Unaccompanied and unwatched, I am permitted to walk a distance of one hundred yards to the sea, as far as the thin strip of black-sand beach; and to walk a like distance in any direction from this small stone hut that has been my abode for five years. I know the body of this barren earth more intimately than I have known the contours of any other, even that of my native Rome, upon which I lavished an intimacy of almost forty years. It is likely that I shall never know another place.

On clear days, when the sun or the wind has dispersed the mists that 2 often rise from the sea, I look to the east; and I think that I can sometimes see the mainland of Italy, perhaps even the city of Naples that nestles in the safety of her gentle bay; but I cannot be sure. It may be only a dark cloud that upon occasion smudges the horizon. It does not matter. Cloud or land, I shall not approach closer to it than I am now.

Below me, in the kitchen, my mother shouts at the one servant we 3 are allowed. I hear the banging of pots and pans, and the shouting again; it is a futile repetition of every afternoon of these years. Our servant is mute; and though not deaf, it is unlikely that she even understands our Latin tongue. Yet indefatigably my mother shouts at her, in the unflagging optimism that her displeasure will be felt and will somehow matter. My mother, Scribonia, is a remarkable woman; she is nearly seventy-five, yet she has the energy and the will of a young woman, as she goes about setting in some peculiar order a world that has never pleased her, and berating it for not arranging itself according to some principle that has evaded them both. She came with me here to Pandateria, not, I am sure, out of any maternal regard, but out of a desperate pursuit of a condition that would confirm once again her displeasure with existence. And I allowed her to accompany me out of what I believe was an appropriate indifference.

I scarcely know my mother. I saw her upon few occasions when I was 4 a child, even less frequently when I was a girl, and we met only at more or less formal social gatherings when I was a woman. I was never fond of her; and it gives me now some assurance to know, after these five years of enforced intimacy, that my feeling for her has not changed.

I am Julia, daughter of Octavius Caesar, the August; and I write these 5 words in the forty-third year of my life. I write them for a purpose of which the friend of my father and my old tutor, Athenodorus, would never have approved; I write them for myself and my own perusal. Even if I wished it otherwise, it is unlikely that any eyes save my own shall see them. But I do not wish it otherwise. I would not explain myself to the world, and I would not have the world understand me; I have become indifferent to us both. For however long I may live in this body, which I have served with much care and art for so many years, that part of my life which matters is over; thus I may view it with the detached interest of the scholar that Athenodorus once said I might have become, had I been born a man and not the daughter of an Emperor and god.

—Yet how strong is the force of old habit! For even now, as I write 6 these first words in this journal, and as I know that they are written to be read only by that strangest of all readers, myself, I find myself pausing in deliberation as I seek the proper topic upon which to found my argument, the appropriate argument itself, the constitution of the argument, the effective arrangement of its parts, and even the style in which those parts are to be delivered. It is myself whom I would persuade to truth by the force of my discourse, and myself whom I would dissuade. It is a foolishness, yet I believe not a harmful one. It occupies my day at least as fully as does the counting of the waves that break over the sand upon the rocky coast of this island where I must remain.

Yes: it is likely that my life is over, though I believe I did not fully 7 apprehend the extent to which I knew the truth of that until yesterday, when I was allowed to receive for the first time in nearly two years a letter from Rome. My sons Gaius and Lucius are dead, the former of a wound received in Armenia and the latter of an illness whose nature no one knows on his way to Spain, in the city of Marseilles. When I read the letter, a numbness came upon me, which in a removed way I judged to have resulted from the shock of the news; and I waited for the grief which I imagined would ensue. But no grief came; and I began to look upon my life, and to remember the moments that had spaced it out, as if I were not concerned. And I knew that it was over. To care not for one's self is of little moment, but to care not for those whom one has loved is another matter. All has become the object of an indifferent curiosity, and nothing is of consequence. Perhaps I write these words and employ the devices that I have learned so that I may discover whether I may rouse myself from this great indifference into which I have descended. I doubt that I shall be able to do so, any more than I should be able to push these massive rocks down the slope into the dark concern of the sea. I am indifferent even to my doubt.

I am Julia, daughter of Gaius Octavius Caesar, the August, and I was 8 born on the third day of September in the year of the consulship of Lucius Marcius and Gaius Sabinus, in the city of Rome. My mother was that Scribonia whose brother was father-in-law to Sextus Pompeius, the pirate whom my father destroyed for the safety of Rome two years after my birth. . . .

That is a beginning of which even Athenodorus, my poor 9 Athenodorus, would have approved.

For the past several years, since shortly after my arrival upon this 10 island of Pandateria, it has been my habit to arise before dawn and to observe the first glimmer of light in the east. It has become nearly a ritual, this early vigil; I sit without moving at an eastern window, and measure the light as it grows from gray to yellow to orange and red, and becomes at last no color but an unimaginable illumination upon the world. After the light has filled my room, I spend the morning hours reading one or another of those books from the library that I was allowed to bring with me here from Rome. The indulgence of my library was one of the few allowed me; yet of all that might have been, it is the one that has made this exile the most nearly endurable. For I have returned to that learning which I abandoned many years ago, and it is likely that I should not have done so had not I been condemned to this loneliness; I sometimes can almost believe that the world in seeking to punish me has done me a service it cannot imagine.

It has occurred to me that this early vigil and this study is a regimen 11 that I became used to many years ago, when I was little more than a child.

When I was twelve years old, my father decided that it was time for 12 me to forgo my childhood studies, and put myself in the care of his old teacher, Athenodorus. Before that, I had, in addition to the kind of education imposed upon my sex by Livia, merely been exercised in the reading and composition of Greek and Latin, which I found remarkably easy, and in arithmetic, which I found easy but dull. It was a leisurely kind of learning, and my tutor was at my disposal at any hour of the day, with no very rigid schedule that I had to follow.

But Athenodorus, who gave me my first vision of a world outside 13 myself, my family, and even of Rome, was a stern and unrelenting master. His students were few—the sons of Octavia, both adopted and natural; Livia's sons, Drusus and Tiberius; and the sons of various relatives of my

father. I was the only girl among them, and I was the youngest. It was
made clear to all of us by my father that Athenodorus was the master; and
despite whatever name and power the parents of his students might have,
Athenodorus's word in all matters was final, and that there was no recourse
beyond him.

We were made to arise before dawn and to assemble at the first hour 14
at Athenodorus's home, where we recited the lines from Homer or Hesiod
or Aeschylus that we had been assigned the day before; we attempted
compositions of our own in the styles of those poets; and at noon we had
a light lunch. In the afternoon, the boys devoted themselves to exercises
in rhetoric and declamation, and to the study of law; such subjects being
deemed inappropriate for me, I was allowed to use my time otherwise, in
the study of philosophy, and in the elucidation of whatever poems, Latin
or Greek, that I chose, and in composition upon whatever matters struck
my fancy. Late in the afternoon, I was allowed to return to my home, so
that I might perform my household duties under the tutelage of Livia. It
was a release that became increasingly irksome to me.

For as within my body there had begun to work the changes that led 15
me to womanhood, there began to work also in my mind the beginnings
of a vision that I had not suspected before. Later, when we became
friends, Athenodorus and I used to talk about the Roman distaste for any
learning that did not lead to a practical end; and he told me that once,
more than a hundred years before my birth, all teachers of literature and
philosophy were, by a decree of the Senate, expelled from Rome, though
it was a decree that could not be enforced.

It seems to me that I was happy, then, perhaps as happy as I have 16
been in my life; but within three years that life was over, and it became
necessary for me to become a woman. It was an exile from a world that
I had just begun to see.

Questions

Rereading and Independent Analysis

1. In this excerpt from Julia's diary, she mentions seeking "the
proper topic upon which to found my argument." *Topics* are particular
possibilities for developing a subject. We can compare, contrast, and classify elements of the subject and others like it, discuss its similarities to and
differences from other subjects, describe its past and future, define it, and
relate its causes and effects. Julia's subject is herself. Reread these passages
from the diary, making a list as you go of the "topics" she used to explain
herself. These are not her "content" but the angles on herself that she used
to develop her narrative.

2. This passage describes aspects of Julia's education, both in school
and in the political world of her family. Make a list of the subjects she
learned in this dual education, and then make notes for a short paragraph
about how this education seems to have shaped the adult she is now. Apart

from making her a writer, what has been the result of her education, in actions as well as in knowledge? Use your answer as the controlling idea in your paragraph.

Suggested Discussion and Group Activities

1. Julia says that her education in composition was for public speaking and writing, not for private writing for herself. As a class, make a list of all the uses you have for reading and writing. Then discuss the differences between Julia's view of these purposes and the views of your class. In what ways have uses for reading and writing broadened over time? What does Julia's exiled state contribute to expanding her own uses of reading and writing? (Compare, for example, the selection by Malcolm X, below.)

2. Compare the actual curriculum Julia describes in her formal schooling to the subjects you have studied. Would her schooling be as useful to you as the curriculum you have taken? Discuss the relative advantages of the two courses of study.

Writing Suggestions

Response

Imagine that you are exiled to an island where you have no contact with the outside world. Write a journal entry, imagining it to be composed only for yourself. Explain how you came to be where you are, how you feel about exile, and what you do with your time. Then rewrite this entry as a letter to the people who have exiled you, asking for reconsideration of your case. Be sure to make it clear who the reader of the letter will be.

Analysis

Write an essay explaining to another reader how Williams achieved the lifelike qualities of this fictional diary. What features of its actual printing, its formal devices, its language, and its content persuade you to believe that a real Julia actually wrote this ancient record? Draw some useful generalizations for the reader about how to achieve this credibility in other kinds of writing.

Finding a Purpose

1. At the end of this entry, Julia comments on Rome's unsuccessful decree exiling all teachers of literature and philosophy. Write a humorous position paper to your local government explaining why a similar decree should be passed in your state. Use some of the same reasons that the Romans might have had for removing those who can make students too thoughtful and "well educated."

2. Write a description of a place you have visited for someone who has never been there. In your description, make the place vivid by including details that show the reader its geography and physical conditions, its atmosphere, and some specific problems and pleasures that this particular place gives to a visitor.

From *A Writer's Diary*
Virginia Woolf

Virginia Woolf (1882–1941) has become an important model for women
who want to contribute to the written world. The men in her family—
including her grandfather, William Thackeray, the novelist; her father, Leslie
Stephen, the historian; and her husband, Leonard Woolf, the social critic—
were all accomplished literary figures who would have presented a formidable challenge even to a male who wanted to match them. But Woolf, like
other women, also had to overcome traditional prejudices against women
writers, whose work might be ignored merely because a woman had written
it, it was thought to be "womanish," or it addressed subjects that men had
not addressed in their writing.

Woolf wrote often about this problem and the position a woman
writer might take about working while at the same time remaining "feminine." This theme comes up both in her essays *(The Common Reader, The
Death of the Moth)* and her novels *(Mrs. Dalloway, To the Lighthouse,
Orlando, The Waves).* Whether you are a man or a woman, you will be able
to imagine her situation as you read her writing: feeling isolated in the
attempt to overcome prejudices against writers whose perspectives traditionally have not been recognized.

Leonard Woolf in 1953 published portions of the diaries Virginia
Woolf had kept for 26 years. His selections omit personal references that
could have distressed living people and instead focus on his wife's concerns
about her writing. He explained that she wrote her diaries and her other
work in bound volumes of blank paper, made for her at the Hogarth Press,
their joint publishing house. As you read, you will see several themes: being
in the mood to write, needing special ways of writing, overcoming blocks
to writing, and enjoying the rewards of success. Try to determine the ideal
reader for these entries. Who were Woolf's readers? How does she present
writing as a way to grow and overcome problems?

Thursday, August 18th, 1921

Nothing to record; only an intolerable fit of the fidgets to write away. Here   1
I am chained to my rock; forced to do nothing; doomed to let every worry,
spite, irritation and obsession scratch and claw and come again. This is a
day that I may not walk and must not work. Whatever book I read bubbles
up in my mind as part of an article I want to write. No one in the whole
of Sussex is so miserable as I am; or so conscious of an infinite capacity of
enjoyment hoarded in me, could I use it. The sun streams (no, never
streams; floods rather) down upon all the yellow fields and the long low
barns; and what wouldn't I give to be coming through Firle woods, dirty
and hot, with my nose turned home, every muscle tired and the brain laid
up in sweet lavender, so sane and cool, and ripe for the morrow's task.
How I should notice everything—the phrase for it coming the moment
after and fitting like a glove; and then on the dusty road, as I ground my

pedals, so my story would begin telling itself; and then the sun would be down; and home, and some bout of poetry after dinner, half read, half lived, as if the flesh were dissolved and through it the flowers burst red and white. There! I've written out half my irritation. I hear poor L. driving the lawn mower up and down, for a wife like I am should have a latch to her cage. She bites! And he spent all yesterday running round London for me. Still if one is Prometheus, if the rock is hard and the gadflies pungent, gratitude, affection, none of the nobler feelings have sway. And so this August is wasted.

Only the thought of people suffering more than I do at all consoles; 2 and that is an aberration of egotism, I suppose. I will now make out a time table if I can to get through these odious days.

Poor Mdlle. Lenglen, finding herself beaten by Mrs. Mallory, flung 3 down her racquet and burst into tears. Her vanity I suppose is colossal. I daresay she thought that to be Mdlle. Lenglen was the greatest thing in the world; invincible, like Napoleon. Armstrong, playing in the test match, took up his position against the gates and would not move, let the bowlers appoint themselves, the whole game became farcical because there was not time to play it out. But Ajax in the Greek play was of the same temper—which we all agree to call heroic in him. But then everything is forgiven to the Greeks. And I've not read a line of Greek since last year, this time, too. But I shall come back, if it's only in snobbery; I shall be reading Greek when I'm old; old as the woman at the cottage door, whose hair might be a wig in a play, it's so white, so thick. Seldom penetrated by love for mankind as I am, I sometimes feel sorry for the poor who don't read Shakespeare, and indeed have felt some generous democratic hum-bug at the Old Vic, when they played Othello and all the poor men and women and children had him there for themselves. Such splendour and such poverty. I am writing down the fidgets, so no matter if I write nonsense. Indeed, any interference with the normal proportions of things makes me uneasy. I know this room too well—this view too well—I am getting it all out of focus, because I can't walk through it.

Wednesday, November 28th

Father's birthday. He would have been 96, 96, yes, today; and could 4 have been 96, like other people one has known: but mercifully was not. His life would have entirely ended mine. What would have happened? No writing, no books;—inconceivable.

I used to think of him and mother daily; but writing the *Lighthouse* 5 laid them in my mind. And now he comes back sometimes, but differently. (I believe this to be true—that I was obsessed by them both, unhealthily; and writing of them was a necessary act.) He comes back now more as a contemporary. I must read him some day. I wonder if I can feel again, I hear his voice, I know this by heart?

So the days pass and I ask myself sometimes whether one is not 6 hypnotised, as a child by a silver globe, by life; and whether this is living. It's very quick, bright, exciting. But superficial perhaps. I should like to take the globe in my hands and feel it quietly, round, smooth, heavy, and so hold it, day after day. I will read Proust I think. I will go backwards and forwards.

As for my next book, I am going to hold myself from writing till I have 7 it impending in me: grown heavy in my mind like a ripe pear; pendant, gravid, asking to be cut or it will fall. *The Moths* still haunts me, coming, as they always do, unbidden, between tea and dinner, while L. plays the gramophone. I shape a page or two; and make myself stop. Indeed I am up against some difficulties. Fame to begin with. *Orlando* has done very well. Now I could go on writing like that—the tug and suck are at me to do it. People say this was so spontaneous, so natural. And I would like to keep those qualities if I could without losing the others. But those qualities were largely the result of ignoring the others. They came of writing exteriorly; and if I dig, must I not lose them? And what is my own position towards the inner and the outer? I think a kind of ease and dash are good;—yes: I think even externality is good; some combination of them ought to be possible. The idea has come to me that what I want now to do is to saturate every atom. I mean to eliminate all waste, deadness, superfluity: to give the moment whole; whatever it includes. Say that the moment is a combination of thought; sensation; the voice of the sea. Waste, deadness, come from the inclusion of things that don't belong to the moment; this appalling narrative business of the realist: getting on from lunch to dinner: it is false, unreal, merely conventional. Why admit anything to literature that is not poetry—by which I mean saturated? Is that not my grudge against novelists? that they select nothing? The poets succeeding by simplifying: practically everything is left out. I want to put practically everything in: yet to saturate. That is what I want to do in *The Moths.* It must include nonsense, fact, sordidity: but made transparent. I think I must read Ibsen and Shakespeare and Racine. And I will write something about them; for that is the best spur, my mind being what it is; then I read with fury and exactness; otherwise I skip and skip; I am a lazy reader. But no: I am surprised and a little disquieted by the remorseless severity of my mind: that it never stops reading and writing; makes me write on Geraldine Jewsbury, on Hardy, on Women—is too professional, too little any longer a dreamy amateur.

Tuesday, December 18th

L. has just been in to consult about a 3rd edition of *Orlando.* This has 8 been ordered; we have sold over 6,000 copies; and sales are still amazingly brisk—150 today for instance; most days between 50 and 60; always to my surprise. Will they stop or go on? Anyhow my room is secure. For the first time since I married, 1912–1928—16 years, I have been spending money. The spending muscle does not work naturally yet. I feel guilty; put off buying, when I know that I should buy; and yet have an agreeable luxurious sense of coins in my pocket beyond my weekly 13/- which was always running out, or being encroached upon.

Questions

Rereading and Independent Analysis

1. What references and brief comments in this selection reveal that these entries were written for Woolf herself, not for other readers? Look up as many of these personally understood references (e.g., "chained to my rock," Prometheus, Ajax) as you can find. What group of readers might be able to understand this diary without special help?

2. Underline all of the references Woolf makes to her actual writing processes. Then write a short paragraph or make notes in which you describe her actions as a writer and her feelings about writing. How do her statements compare to your view of yourself as a writer?

Suggested Discussion and Group Activities

1. Like all of us, Woolf was strongly influenced by important people in her life. Discuss the implications of her statement about her father's death: "but mercifully was not [96 years old]. His [long] life would have entirely ended mine." Even without gathering more information about Woolf's relationship with her father, tell why you think this statement might be made by many children of successful parents, no matter what sex they are. What sorts of burdens (as well as help) can be gained from parents who are successful?

2. Woolf refers to having, and to writing, "the fidgets." Describe how your own approach to writing sometimes shows signs of similar "fidgets." What exactly is Woolf referring to? As a class or in groups, describe the thoughts, distractions, and false starts you have when you write. How do you overcome them?

Writing Suggestions

Response

1. Over the next few weeks, keep a writing journal. Record your feelings about the writing you do in and out of school; the processes you go through before, during, and after writing; and your understanding of the ways you think of, expand, and change the ideas you put down.

2. Write a letter to your grandparents, explaining fully how your parents strongly influenced your ability to accomplish something important to you. Tell them how grateful you are for this help.

Analysis

Use your response to the second "Rereading" question above to prepare an essay describing the writing processes that Woolf revealed. Compare these processes with those that other writers in this chapter tell of. Choose one or more of the other selections (e.g., by Malcolm X, William Allen, and/or Carol Sternhell) to explain common ways that people who think of themselves as writers go about the actual process of writing. How do they define what it means to be a "writer"? Include reference to their other idiosyncratic activities.

Finding a Purpose

Use the material that you gathered in your writing journal (above) to write a report to your class about your own writing processes. Present your information in categories (e.g., times and places you write; your tools, purposes, feelings) to make your writing process clear for a reader. Draw some conclusions about what you learned from observation. Then, read your classmates' reports and ask them questions about points you find unclear or especially interesting. As a class, what sort of "writing profile" would your group have? What are high and low points for this group of writers? What processes do you share with writers represented in this chapter? What might you learn from them to make your writing more enjoyable?

The Source of Originality
Dorothea Brande

Dorothea Brande (1893–1948) first published *Becoming a Writer* in 1934. The book begins with her apology for adding to the already plentiful advice for those who want to publish their writing. As a successful teacher of writing for publication, she disliked books about tricks of the trade and was apprehensive about the usefulness of typical "creative" writing classes. Nonetheless, she taught such classes and wrote about what she saw as a writer's most important problems. Long before popular psychology emphasized how subconscious feelings and motives affect our abilities to say what we mean, she addressed how we can overcome common blocks to writing: anxiety, uncertainty, resistance to writing itself, and distorted self-images that make us try to write as though we were someone other than ourselves.

Brande's essay on originality demonstrates an important change over the last two centuries in what it means to be a writer. Good writing is no longer thought of as only conventional imitations that follow "great" authors in the public stream of literature. Two important influences on writing have helped change ideas about individual creativity. First, now the "individual self" can be made available to large audiences because we have a large publishing industry and mass literacy, instead of a small production of books for a very restricted readership. Second, the purposes of writing have been expanded by the revolutionary perspectives of the Romantic poets who wrote in the nineteenth century. They questioned traditional forms and broke with customs about the writer's proper subjects, the way writers present their subjects and how much these subjects can, or should, stand in for more public "reality." Both of these influences placed a high value on being "original." They created an image of writers as people who work alone, often in opposition to the community of readers that will read their work. Brande's discussion frankly considers the pressures that our relatively new belief in individual, isolated creativity puts on young writers. She offers suggestions useful to us all about how to handle this pressure. As you read, think about how accurate she is in describing problems you have experienced when you write anything, not just fiction or other "creative" pieces.

It is a commonplace that every writer must turn to himself to find most 1 of his material; it is such a commonplace that a chapter on the subject is likely to be greeted with groans. Nevertheless it must be written, for only a thorough understanding of the point will clear away the misapprehensions as to what constitutes "originality."

The Elusive Quality

Every book, every editor, every teacher will tell you that the great key to 2 success in authorship is originality. Beyond that they seldom go. Sometimes they will point out to the persistent inquirer someone whose work shows the "originality" that they require, and those free examples are often responsible for some of the direst mistakes that young writers fall into. "Be original, like William Faulkner," an editor will say, meaning only to enforce his advice by an instance; or "Look at Mrs. Buck; now if you could give me something like that—!" And the earnest inquirer, quite missing the point of the exhortation, goes home and tries with all his might to turn out what I have already complained of: "a marvelous Faulkner story," or "a perfect Pearl Buck novel." Once in a long while—a very long while, if my experience as editor and teacher counts for anything—the imitative writer actually finds in his model some quality so congenial that he is able to turn out an acceptable story on the same pattern. But for one who succeeds there are hundreds who fail. I could find it in my heart to wish that everyone who cut his coat by another man's pattern would find the result a crass failure. For originality does not lie down that road.

It is well to understand as early as possible in one's writing life that 3 there is just one contribution which every one of us can make: we can give into the common pool of experience some comprehension of the world as it looks to each of us. There is one sense in which everyone is unique. No one else was born of your parents, at just that time of just that country's history; no one underwent just your experiences, reached just your conclusions, or faces the world with the exact set of ideas that you must have. If you can come to such friendly terms with yourself that you are able and willing to say precisely what you think of any given situation or character, if you can tell a story as it can appear only to you of all the people on earth, you will inevitably have a piece of work which is original.

Now this, which seems so simple, is the very thing that the average 4 writer cannot do. Partly because he has immersed himself in the writing of others since he was able to read at all, he is sadly apt to see the world through someone else's eyes. Occasionally, being imaginative and pliable, he does a very good job of it, and we have a story which is near enough to an original story to seem good, or not to show too plainly that it is derivative. But often those faults in comprehension, those sudden misunderstandings of one's own fictional characters, come from the fact that the author is not looking at the persons of his own creation with his own eyes; he is using the eyes of Mr. Faulkner, of Mr. Hemingway, of D. H. Lawrence or Mrs. Woolf.

Originality Not Imitation

The virtue of those writers is precisely that they have refused to do what 5 their imitators do so humbly. Each of them has had a vision of the world and has set out to transcribe it, and their work has the forthrightness and vigor of all work that comes from the central core of the personality without deviation or distortion. There is always a faint flavor of humbug about a Dreiserian story written by some imitator of Mr. Dreiser, or one of those stark mystical Laurentian tales not directly fathered by D. H. Lawrence; but it is exceedingly hard to persuade the timid or hero-worshipping young writer that this must always be so.

The "Surprise Ending"

When the pitfall of imitation is safely skirted, one often finds that in the 6 effort to be original an author has pulled and jerked and prodded his story into monstrous form. He will plant dynamite at its crisis, turn the conclusion inside out, betray a character by making him act uncharacteristically, all in the service of the God of Originals. His story may be all compact of horror, or, more rarely, good luck may conquer every obstacle hands down; and if the teacher or editor protests that the story has not been made credible, its author will murmur *"Dracula"* or "Kathleen Norris," and will be unconvinced if told that the minimum requirement for a good story has not been met: that he has not shown that he, the author, truly and consistently envisages a world in which such events could under any circumstances come to pass, as the authors whom he is imitating certainly do.

Honesty, the Source of Originality

So these stories fail from their own inconsistency, although the author has 7 at his command, in the mere exercise of stringent honesty, the best source of consistency for his own work. If you can discover what you are like, if you can discover what you truly believe about most of the major matters of life, you will be able to write a story which is honest and original and unique. But those are very large "ifs," and it takes hard digging to get at the roots of one's own convictions.

Very often one finds a beginner who is unwilling to commit himself 8 because he knows just enough about his own processes to be sure that his beliefs of today are not likely to be his beliefs of tomorrow. This operates to hold him under a sort of spell. He waits for final wisdom to arrive, and since it tarries he feels that he cannot commit himself in print. When this is a real difficulty, and not simply (as it sometimes is) a neurotic excuse to postpone writing indefinitely, you will find a writer who can turn out a sketch, a half-story with no commitments in it, but seldom more. Obviously what such a writer needs is to be made to realize that his case is not isolated; that we all continue to grow, and that in order to write at all we must write on the basis of our present beliefs. If you are unwilling to write from the honest, though perhaps far from final, point of view that represents your present state, you may come to your deathbed with your contribution to the world still unmade, and just as far from final conviction about the universe as you were at the age of twenty.

Trust Yourself

There are only so many dramatic situations in which man can find him- 9 self—three dozen, if one is to take seriously *The Thirty-six Dramatic Situations* of Georges Polti—and it is not the putting of your character in the central position of a drama which has never been dreamed of before that will make your story irresistible. Even if it were possible to find such a situation it would be an almost heartbreaking feat to communicate it to your readers, who must find some recognizable quality in the story they read or be hopelessly at sea. How *your* hero meets his dilemma, what *you* think of the impasse—those are the things which make your story truly your own; and it is your own individual character, unmistakably showing through your work, which will lead you to success or failure. I would almost be willing to go so far as to say that there is no situation which is trite in itself; there are only dull, unimaginative, or uncommunicative authors. No dilemma in which a man can find himself will leave his fellows unmoved if it can be fully presented. There is, for instance, a recognizable thematic likeness between *The Way of All Flesh, Clayhanger,* and *Of Human Bondage.* Which of them is trite?

"Your Anger and My Anger"

Agnes Mure MacKenzie, in *The Process of Literature,* says, "Your loving 10 and my loving, your anger and my anger, are sufficiently alike for us to be able to call them by the same names: but in our experience and in that of any two people in the world, they will never be quite completely identical"; if that were not literally true there would be neither basis nor opportunity for art. And again, in a recent issue of the *Atlantic Monthly,* Mrs. Wharton, writing *The Confessions of a Novelist,* declares: "As a matter of fact, there are only two essential rules: one, that the novelist should deal only with what is within his reach, literally or figuratively (in most cases the two are synonymous), and the other that the value of a subject depends almost wholly on what the author sees in it, and how deeply he is able to see into it."

By returning to those quotations from time to time you may at last 11 persuade yourself that it is your insight which gives the final worth to your writing, and that there is no triteness where there is a good, clear, honest mind at work.

One Story, Many Versions

Very early in my classes I set out to prove this by direct demonstration. 12 I ask for synopses of stories reduced to the very bones of an outline. Of those that are offered I choose the "tritest." In one class this was offered: "A spoiled girl marries and nearly ruins her husband by her attitude toward money." I confess that when I read this aloud to my pupils my heart misgave me. I could foresee, myself, only one elaboration of it, with one possible variation which would only occur to those who could perform the rather sophisticated feat of "dissociation" upon it—those, that is, who could discover what their immediate response to the idea was, and then deliberately alter their first association into its opposite. The class was asked to write for ten minutes, expanding the sentence into a paragraph or two, as if they were going to write a story on the theme. The result, in a class of twelve members, was twelve versions so different from each other that any editor could have read them all on the same day without realizing that the point of departure was the same in each.

We had, to begin with, a girl who was spoiled because she was a golf 13 champion, and who, since she was an amateur, nearly ruined her husband by traveling around to tournaments. We had a story of a politician's daughter who had entertained her father's possible supporters and who entertained her husband's employer too lavishly, leading him to think that his young right-hand man was too sure of promotion. We had a story of a girl who had been warned that young wives were usually too extravagant, and who consequently pinched and pared and cut corners till she wore out her husband's patience. Before the second variation was half-read the class was laughing outright. Each member realized that she, too, had seen the situation in some purely personal light, and that what seemed so inevitable to her was fresh and unforeseen to the others. I wish I could conclude this anecdote by saying that I never again heard one of them complain that the only idea she could think of was too platitudinous to use, but this story really happened.

Nevertheless it is true that not even twins will see the same story idea 14
from the same angle. There will always be differences of emphasis, a
choice of different factors to bring about the dilemma and different actions
to solve it. If you can once believe this thoroughly you can release for your
immediate use any idea which has enough emotional value to engage your
attention at all. If you find yourself groping for a theme you may take this
as a fair piece of advice, simple as it sounds: "You can write about anything
which has been vivid enough to cause you to comment upon it." If a
situation has caught your attention to that extent, it has meaning for you,
and if you can find what that meaning is you have the basis for a story.

Your Inalienable Uniqueness

Every piece of writing which is not simply the purveying of straightfor- 15
ward information—as a recipe or a formula is, for example—is an essay in
persuasion. You are persuading your reader, while you hold his attention,
to see the world with your eyes, to agree with you that this is a stirring
occasion, that that situation is essentially tragic, or that another is deeply
humorous. All fiction is persuasive in this sense. The author's conviction
underlies all imaginative representation of whatever grade.

Since this is so, it behooves you to know what you do believe of most 16
of the major problems of life, and of those minor problems which you are
going to use in your writing.

A Questionnaire

Here are a few questions for a self-examination which may suggest others 17
to you. It is by no means an exhaustive questionnaire, but by following
down the other inquiries which occur to you as you consider these, you
can come by a very fair idea of your working philosophy:

Do you believe in a God? Under what aspect? (Hardy's "President of the 18
    Immortals," Wells' "emerging God"?)
Do you believe in free will or are you a determinist? (Although an artist-
    determinist is such a walking paradox that imagination staggers at
    the notion.)
Do you like men? Women? Children?
What do you think of marriage?
Do you consider romantic love a delusion and a snare?
Do you think the comment "It will all be the same in a hundred years"
    is profound, shallow, true or false?
What is the greatest happiness you can imagine? The greatest disaster?

And so on. If you find that you are balking at definite answers to the 19
great questions, then you are not yet ready to write fiction which involves
major issues. You must find subjects on which you are capable of making
up your mind, to serve as the groundwork of your writing. The best books

emerge from the strongest convictions—and for confirmation see any bookshelf.

Questions

Rereading and Independent Analysis

1. Use a good dictionary to look up the meanings of the words *original* and *creative*. Then review Brande's chapter, making a chart in which you show how many different ways she defines and illustrates these words. What is the meaning of "originality" that she wants young writers to keep in mind?

2. Write short answers to the questions with which Brande closes, just for yourself. Then write another version, to read aloud in class. In what specific ways do the two versions differ?

Suggested Discussion and Group Activities

1. Brande wrote this advice primarily for people who want to write fiction. How could you apply her points to any kind of writing, including the writing you do in personal letters and diaries and the writing you do for school courses?

2. Brande stresses how everyone is unique and how our experiences of "common" emotions are different. She says, "if that were not literally true there would be neither basis nor opportunity for art." But imagine a world in which this *is not* literally true. If we all had the same sense of what an emotion means and shared only a few ways to tell about it, what would become of the basis and opportunity for art, and for any kind of critical or scientific thinking?

3. Come to class with your own try at a sentence similar to the one Brande used as the "tritest" story outline. In groups, pick out the sentence that you agree is the most worn out and trite. What qualities does the winner have? Why is it difficult to write a "good" but trite story outline? (You might look for sources in William Allen's "A Whole Society of Loners and Dreamers" [below] and in the library for *It Was a Dark and Stormy Night*, a collection of bad first sentences for novels.)

4. Do your writing textbooks address the same issues Brande discusses here? Compare her treatment of personal perspectives in writing to the advice in other books you have read.

Writing Suggestions

Response

Write an essay for your classmates in which you tell the differences between your answers to Brande's list of questions (Question 2, "Rereading") when you wrote them for yourself and the version you wrote for reading in class. Your purpose is to enlarge Brande's discussion of a writer's honesty. Explain your feelings about stating your private ideas and feelings in a public setting.

Analysis

Write an essay in which you describe a time when you did something you thought to be creative and original. In your essay, describe the event and then go on to generalize from it about the nature of creativity. Use Brande's points as you support your generalizations.

Finding a Purpose

1. Write a story or summary of a story based on your group's choice of the tritest idea brought to class (Question 3, "Suggested Discussion"). Then, in groups or as a class, compare your elaborations of the outline with your classmates' versions. Identify three to five stories you think are outstanding. Then tell what qualities distinguish them as the best.

2. In your group, write a section to add to a textbook about writing in which you explain how writers work both alone and in a group. Your advice should explain helpfully what "originality" means and also should tell how other people help writers before, during, and after a piece of writing is being made. Use examples from Brande and other selections to demonstrate your points directly and economically. Then trade your group's work among other groups and decide on a final version as a class. Keep in mind the brevity and clarity necessary in textbook descriptions.

 # Saved!
Malcolm X

The statement that reading and writing change people's lives sounds like nothing more than a bit of common wisdom, probably thought up by English teachers. But no story of learning to write makes these words more vivid than the one Malcolm X (1925–1965) told in his *Autobiography* (1964). This black leader in the civil rights movement of the 1950s and 1960s began life as street-smart Malcolm Little, a petty criminal. He learned to use his anger against racial injustice effectively only after he educated himself—first literally, then more broadly—in the words of public power.

His description of "a homemade education" also shows firsthand how reading and writing are equal to each other. Malcolm X equated learning to write with learning to read as he slowly taught himself both processes in prison. Without teacher or support, he began alone, reading the dictionary and copying its words. He continued by reading the history, philosophy, and literature to which he would eventually contribute himself.

Like all autobiographies, this one is a "fiction." It is not a minute-by-minute record but an account based on personal memory of important moments and encounters that helped make a broadly applicable "sense" of one life. This account was written with the assistance of Alex Haley, the author of *Roots,* who participated in forming its influential image of Malcolm X's life. It not only told about Malcolm X but also became an example for many, a symbol of black power and the power of individual blacks to participate in and change their larger community. After his release from prison, Malcolm X became one of the most celebrated and controversial representatives of the Black Muslim movement. He was shot in New York in 1965, probably, but not certainly, by American Black Muslims who disagreed with his views. As you read, notice his determination about learning to write so that you can get a sense of the concentration he brought to any cause.

It was because of my letters that I happened to stumble upon starting to 1 acquire some kind of a homemade education.

I became increasingly frustrated at not being able to express what I 2 wanted to convey in letters that I wrote, especially those to Mr. Elijah Muhammad.[1] In the street, I had been the most articulate hustler out there—I had commanded attention when I said something. But now, trying to write simple English, I not only wasn't articulate, I wasn't even functional. How would I sound writing in slang, the way I would *say* it, something such as, "Look, daddy, let me pull your coat about a cat, Elijah Muhammad—"

Many who today hear me somewhere in person, or on television, or 3 those who read something I've said, will think I went to school far beyond the eighth grade. This impression is due entirely to my prison studies.

It had really begun back in the Charlestown Prison, when Bimbi first 4 made me feel envy of his stock of knowledge. Bimbi had always taken charge of any conversations he was in, and I had tried to emulate him. But every book I picked up had few sentences which didn't contain anywhere from one to nearly all of the words that might as well have been in Chinese. When I just skipped those words, of course, I really ended up with little idea of what the book said. So I had come to the Norfolk Prison Colony still going through only book-reading motions. Pretty soon, I would have quit even these motions, unless I had received the motivation that I did.

I saw that the best thing I could do was get hold of a dictionary—to 5 study, to learn some words. I was lucky enough to reason also that I should try to improve my penmanship. It was sad. I couldn't even write in a straight line. It was both ideas together that moved me to request a dictionary along with some tablets and pencils from the Norfolk Prison Colony school.

I spent two days just riffling uncertainly through the dictionary's 6 pages. I'd never realized so many words existed! I didn't know *which* words I needed to learn. Finally, just to start some kind of action, I began copying.

In my slow, painstaking, ragged handwriting, I copied into my tablet 7 everything printed on that first page, down to the punctuation marks.

I believe it took me a day. Then, aloud, I read back, to myself, 8

[1] Elijah Muhammad was a leader of the Black Muslims (The Temple of Islam) in the 1940s, 1950s, and 1960s.

everything I'd written on the tablet. Over and over, aloud, to myself, I read my own handwriting.

I woke up the next morning, thinking about those words—im- 9 mensely proud to realize that not only had I written so much at one time, but I'd written words that I never knew were in the world. Moreover, with a little effort, I also could remember what many of these words meant. I reviewed the words whose meanings I didn't remember. Funny thing, from the dictionary first page right now, that "aardvark" springs to my mind. The dictionary had a picture of it, a long-tailed, long-eared, burrowing African mammal, which lives off termites caught by sticking out its tongue as an anteater does for ants.

I was so fascinated that I went on—I copied the dictionary's next 10 page. And the same experience came when I studied that. With every succeeding page, I also learned of people and places and events from history. Actually the dictionary is like a miniature encyclopedia. Finally the dictionary's A section had filled a whole tablet—and I went on into the B's. That was the way I started copying what eventually became the entire dictionary. It went a lot faster after so much practice helped me to pick up handwriting speed. Between what I wrote in my tablet, and writing letters, during the rest of my time in prison I would guess I wrote a million words.

I suppose it was inevitable that as my word-base broadened, I could 11 for the first time pick up a book and read and now begin to understand what the book was saying. Anyone who has read a great deal can imagine the new world that opened. Let me tell you something: from then until I left that prison, in every free moment I had, if I was not reading in the library, I was reading on my bunk. You couldn't have gotten me out of books with a wedge. Between Mr. Muhammad's teachings, my correspondence, my visitors—usually Ella and Reginald—and my reading of books, months passed without my even thinking about being imprisoned. In fact, up to then, I never had been so truly free in my life.

The Norfolk Prison Colony's library was in the school building. A 12 variety of classes was taught there by instructors who came from such places as Harvard and Boston universities. The weekly debates between inmate teams were also held in the school building. You would be astonished to know how worked up convict debaters and audiences would get over subjects like "Should Babies Be Fed Milk?"

Available on the prison library's shelves were books on just about 13 every general subject. Much of the big private collection that Parkhurst had willed to the prison was still in crates and boxes in the back of the library—thousands of old books. Some of them looked ancient: covers faded, old-time parchment-looking binding. Parkhurst, I've mentioned, seemed to have been principally interested in history and religion. He had the money and the special interest to have a lot of books that you wouldn't have in general circulation. Any college library would have been lucky to get that collection.

As you can imagine, especially in a prison where there was heavy 14 emphasis on rehabilitation, an inmate was smiled upon if he demonstrated an unusually intense interest in books. There was a sizable number of well-read inmates, especially the popular debaters. Some were said by many to be practically walking encyclopedias. They were almost celebrities. No university would ask any student to devour literature as I did when this new world opened to me, of being able to read and *understand*.

I read more in my room than in the library itself. An inmate who was 15 known to read a lot could check out more than the permitted maximum number of books. I preferred reading in the total isolation of my own room.

When I had progressed to really serious reading, every night at about 16 ten P.M. I would be outraged with the "lights out." It always seemed to catch me right in the middle of something engrossing.

Fortunately, right outside my door was a corridor light that cast a 17 glow into my room. The glow was enough to read by, once my eyes adjusted to it. So when "lights out" came, I would sit on the floor where I could continue reading by that glow.

At one-hour intervals the night guards paced past every room. Each 18 time I heard the approaching footsteps, I jumped into bed and feigned sleep. And as soon as the guard passed, I got back out of bed onto the floor area of that light-glow, where I would read for another fifty-eight minutes—until the guard approached again. That went on until three or four every morning. Three or four hours of sleep a night was enough for me. Often in the years in the streets I had slept less than that.

The teachings of Mr. Muhammad stressed how history had been 19 "whitened"—when white men had written history books, the black man simply had been left out. Mr. Muhammad couldn't have said anything that would have struck me much harder. I had never forgotten how when my class, me and all of those whites, had studied seventh-grade United States history back in Mason, the history of the Negro had been covered in one paragraph, and the teacher had gotten a big laugh with his joke, "Negroes' feet are so big that when they walk, they leave a hole in the ground."

This is one reason why Mr. Muhammad's teachings spread so swiftly 20 all over the United States, among *all* Negroes, whether or not they became followers of Mr. Muhammad. The teachings ring true—to every Negro. You can hardly show me a black adult in America—or a white one, for that matter—who knows from the history books anything like the truth about the black man's role. In my own case, once I heard of the "glorious history of the black man," I took special pains to hunt in the library for books that would inform me on details about black history.

I can remember accurately the very first set of books that really 21 impressed me. I have since bought that set of books and I have it at home for my children to read as they grow up. It's called *Wonders of the World*. It's full of pictures of archeological finds, statues that depict, usually, non-European people.

I found books like Will Durant's *Story of Civilization.* I read H. G. 22
Wells' *Outline of History. Souls of Black Folk* by W. E. B. Du Bois gave
me a glimpse into the black people's history before they came to this
country. Carter G. Woodson's *Negro History* opened my eyes about black
empires before the black slave was brought to the United States, and the
early Negro struggles for freedom.

J. A. Rogers' three volumes of *Sex and Race* told about race-mixing 23
before Christ's time; about Aesop being a black man who told fables; about
Egypt's Pharaohs; about the great Coptic Christian Empires; about Ethio-
pia, the earth's oldest continuous black civilization, as China is the oldest
continuous civilization.

Mr. Muhammad's teaching about how the white man had been 24
created led me to *Findings In Genetics* by Gregor Mendel. (The dictionary's G section was where I had learned what "genetics" meant.) I really
studied this book by the Austrian monk. Reading it over and over, especially certain sections, helped me to understand that if you started with
a black man, a white man could be produced; but starting with a white
man, you never could produce a black man—because the white chromosome is recessive. And since no one disputes that there was but one Original Man, the conclusion is clear.

During the last year or so, in the *New York Times,* Arnold Toynbee 25
used the word "bleached" in describing the white man. His words were:
"White (i.e. bleached) human beings of North European origin. . . ." Toynbee also referred to the European geographic area as only a peninsula of
Asia. He said there is no such thing as Europe. And if you look at the globe,
you will see for yourself that America is only an extension of Asia. (But at
the same time Toynbee is among those who have helped to bleach history.
He has written that Africa was the only continent that produced no history. He won't write that again. Every day now, the truth is coming to
light.)

I never will forget how shocked I was when I began reading about 26
slavery's total horror. It made such an impact upon me that it later became
one of my favorite subjects when I became a minister of Mr. Muhammad's.
The world's most monstrous crime, the sin and the blood on the white
man's hands, are almost impossible to believe. Books like the one by
Frederick Olmstead opened my eyes to the horrors suffered when the
slave was landed in the United States. The European woman, Fannie
Kimball, who had married a Southern white slaveowner, described how
human beings were degraded. Of course I read *Uncle Tom's Cabin.* In
fact, I believe that's the only novel I have ever read since I started serious
reading.

Parkhurst's collection also contained some bound pamphlets of the 27
Abolitionist Anti-Slavery Society of New England. I read descriptions of
atrocities, saw those illustrations of black slave women tied up and flogged
with whips; of black mothers watching their babies being dragged off,
never to be seen by their mothers again; of dogs after slaves, and of the

fugitive slave catchers, evil white men with whips and clubs and chains and guns. I read about the slave preacher Nat Turner, who put the fear of God into the white slavemaster. Nat Turner wasn't going around preaching pie-in-the-sky and "non-violent" freedom for the black man. There in Virginia one night in 1831, Nat and seven other slaves started out at his master's home and through the night they went from one plantation "big house" to the next, killing, until by the next morning 57 white people were dead and Nat had about 70 slaves following him. White people, terrified for their lives, fled from their homes, locked themselves up in public buildings, hid in the woods, and some even left the state. A small army of soldiers took two months to catch and hang Nat Turner. Somewhere I have read where Nat Turner's example is said to have inspired John Brown to invade Virginia and attack Harper's Ferry nearly thirty years later, with thirteen white men and five Negroes.

I read Herodotus, "the father of History," or, rather, I read about 28 him. And I read the histories of various nations, which opened my eyes gradually, then wider and wider, to how the whole world's white men had indeed acted like devils, pillaging and raping and bleeding and draining the whole world's non-white people. I remember, for instance, books such as Will Durant's *The Story of Oriental Civilization,* and Mahatma Gandhi's accounts of the struggle to drive the British out of India.

Book after book showed me how the white man had brought upon 29 the world's black, brown, red, and yellow peoples every variety of the sufferings and exploitation. I saw how since the sixteenth century, the so-called "Christian soldier" white man began to ply the seas in his lust for Asian and African empires, and plunder, and power. I read, I saw, how the white man never has gone among the non-white peoples bearing the Cross in the true manner and spirit of Christ's teachings—meek, humble, and Christlike.

I perceived, as I read, how the collective white man had been actu- 30 ally nothing but a piratical opportunist who used Faustian machinations to make his own Christianity his initial wedge in criminal conquests. First, always "religiously," he branded "heathen" and "pagan" labels upon ancient non-white cultures and civilizations. The stage thus set, he then turned upon his non-white victims his weapons of war.

I read how, entering India—half a *billion* deeply religious brown 31 people—the British white man, by 1759, through promises, trickery and manipulations, controlled much of India through Great Britain's East India Company. The parasitical British administration kept tentacling out to half of the sub-continent. In 1857, some of the desperate people of India finally mutinied—and, excepting the African slave trade, nowhere has history recorded any more unnecessary bestial and ruthless human carnage than the British suppression of the non-white Indian people.

Over 115 million African blacks—close to the 1930's population of 32 the United States—were murdered or enslaved during the slave trade. And I read how when the slave market was glutted, the cannibalistic white powers of Europe next carved up, as their colonies, the richest areas of the black continent. And Europe's chancelleries for the next century played a chess game of naked exploitation and power from Cape Horn to Cairo.

Ten guards and the warden couldn't have torn me out of those books. 33 Not even Elijah Muhammad could have been more eloquent than those books were in providing indisputable proof that the collective white man had acted like a devil in virtually every contact he had with the world's collective non-white man. I listen today to the radio, and watch television, and read the headlines about the collective white man's fear and tension concerning China. When the white man professes ignorance about why the Chinese hate him so, my mind can't help flashing back to what I read, there in prison, about how the blood forebears of this same white man raped China at a time when China was trusting and helpless. Those original white "Christian traders" sent into China millions of pounds of opium. By 1839, so many of the Chinese were addicts that China's desperate government destroyed twenty thousand chests of opium. The first Opium War was promptly declared by the white man. Imagine! Declaring *war* upon someone who objects to being narcotized! The Chinese were severely beaten, with Chinese-invented gunpowder.

The Treaty of Nanking made China pay the British white man for the 34 destroyed opium: forced open China's major ports to British trade; forced China to abandon Hong Kong; fixed China's import tariffs so low that cheap British articles soon flooded in, maiming China's industrial development.

After a second Opium War, the Tientsin Treaties legalized the ravag- 35 ing opium trade, legalized a British-French-American control of China's customs. China tried delaying that Treaty's ratification; Peking was looted and burned.

"Kill the foreign white devils!" was the 1901 Chinese war cry in the 36 Boxer Rebellion. Losing again, this time the Chinese were driven from Peking's choicest areas. The vicious, arrogant white man put up the famous signs, "Chinese and dogs not allowed."

Red China after World War II closed its doors to the Western white 37 world. Massive Chinese agricultural, scientific, and industrial efforts are described in a book that *Life* magazine recently published. Some observers inside Red China have reported that the world never has known such a hate-white campaign as is now going on in this non-white country where, present birth-rates continuing, in fifty more years Chinese will be half the earth's population. And it seems that some Chinese chickens will soon come home to roost, with China's recent successful nuclear tests.

Let us face reality. We can see in the United Nations a new world 38 order being shaped, along color lines—an alliance among the non-white nations. America's U.N. Ambassador Adlai Stevenson complained not long ago that in the United Nations "a skin game" was being played. He was right. He was facing reality. A "skin game" *is* being played. But Ambassador Stevenson sounded like Jesse James accusing the marshal of carrying a gun. Because who in the world's history ever has played a worse "skin game" than the white man?

Mr. Muhammad, to whom I was writing daily, had no idea of what 39 a new world had opened up to me through my efforts to document his teachings in books.

When I discovered philosophy, I tried to touch all the landmarks of 40 philosophical development. Gradually, I read most of the old philosophers, Occidental and Oriental. The Oriental philosophers were the ones I came to prefer; finally, my impression was that most Occidental philosophy had largely been borrowed from the Oriental thinkers. Socrates, for instance, traveled in Egypt. Some sources even say that Socrates was initiated into some of the Egyptian mysteries. Obviously Socrates got some of his wisdom among the East's wise men.

I have often reflected upon the new vistas that reading opened to 41 me. I knew right there in prison that reading had changed forever the course of my life. As I see it today, the ability to read awoke inside me some long dormant craving to be mentally alive. I certainly wasn't seeking any degree, the way a college confers a status symbol upon its students. My homemade education gave me, with every additional book that I read, a little bit more sensitivity to the deafness, dumbness, and blindness that was afflicting the black race in America. Not long ago, an English writer telephoned me from London, asking questions. One was, "What's your alma mater?" I told him, "Books." You will never catch me with a free fifteen minutes in which I'm not studying something I feel might be able to help the black man.

Yesterday I spoke in London, and both ways on the plane across the 42 Atlantic I was studying a document about how the United Nations proposes to insure the human rights of the oppressed minorities of the world. The American black man is the world's most shameful case of minority oppression. What makes the black man think of himself as only an internal United States issue is just a catch-phrase, two words, "civil rights." How is the black man going to get "civil rights" before first he wins his *human* rights? If the American black man will start thinking about his *human* rights, and then start thinking of himself as part of one of the world's great peoples, he will see he has a case for the United Nations.

I can't think of a better case! Four hundred years of black blood and 43 sweat invested here in America, and the white man still has the black man begging for what every immigrant fresh off the ship can take for granted the minute he walks down the gangplank.

But I'm digressing. I told the Englishman that my alma mater was 44 books, a good library. Every time I catch a plane, I have with me a book that I want to read—and that's a lot of books these days. If I weren't out here every day battling the white man, I could spend the rest of my life reading, just satisfying my curiosity—because you can hardly mention anything I'm not curious about. I don't think anybody ever got more out of going to prison than I did. In fact, prison enabled me to study far more intensively than I would have if my life had gone differently and I had attended some college. I imagine that one of the biggest troubles with colleges is there are too many distractions, too much panty-raiding, fraternities, and boola-boola and all of that. Where else but in a prison could I have attacked my ignorance by being able to study intensely sometimes as much as fifteen hours a day?

Questions

Rereading and Independent Analysis

1. Reread this selection to find the particular words and phrases that contribute to your image of the adult Malcolm X, who was writing at what turned out to be the end of his life. Then write a few sentences in which you identify the *purpose* of this writing (its intended outcome), the ideal *reader* that Haley and Malcolm X had in mind, and the intended *message* implied by the book's level of diction.

2. Make a list of specific, changing reasons for learning to read and write that Malcolm X reveals here. Then write a generalization about these motives. Are they entirely practical or do they show a mixture of external and internal influences? Does he learn to want knowledge for its own sake as well as for other reasons? What is the implication of the title of this selection, "Saved!"?

3. Three times in this selection, Malcolm X refers to white people as "devils." Review the way evidence for this metaphoric claim accumulated for him. How does he persuade you of the fairness of this label?

Suggested Discussion and Group Activities

1. Compare the progress of Malcolm X's self-education to the stages of learning that school curricula provide most students. How do the two patterns differ? What are differences in your attitudes toward learning, as a student who has been "taught" instead of learning on your own?

2. In groups, review the selection to discover how its comparisons create its tone. For instance, references to "carnage," to "Chinese chickens coming home to roost," and to Jesse James establish a pattern of *allusions* (references to events and people outside the narrative). How do these and other comparisons show the perspective of the author(s)? How do they tell us how the ideal reader of the *Autobiography* should respond to the facts? What is their persuasive function?

3. Bring to class one of the books that Malcolm X mentions. Based on your reading of it, discuss the fairness of his claim that white history distorts or ignores the reality of the treatment of nonwhites in specific situations.

4. If Malcolm X had lived until now, would he have felt that the patterns he protested have changed? Cite examples from recent local and national political events that support your conclusion.

Writing Suggestions

Response

Write a few paragraphs about your response to Malcolm X's anger. Do you feel that his anger is unwarranted? Do you think that you share responsibility for the social problems he discusses? Do you respond with your own anger? Use the issues Malcolm X brings up, not other experience, as you write.

Analysis

Malcolm X says that a dictionary is like a small encyclopedia because it teaches more than the meaning of words. Go to your library and find *The Oxford English Dictionary* in the reference section. Copy the definition of a word whose meaning is new to you. Then write a short report for the class that tells how this word has changed and acquired new meanings over time.

Finding a Purpose

1. Imagine that you are isolated as Malcolm X was in prison. Write a brief section of your own imagined "Autobiography," explaining how you spent your time in a way that changed you. (You can stock your imaginary place with books, tools, or any other resources you want.)

2. Based on your own observations and reading, write an essay about "The Politics of Reading and Writing." Your purpose is to explain the differences between people who read and *understand* in your culture and those who do not, showing their differing powers to change established patterns in society. Use your reading of Malcolm X's account to support your case. You may want to focus on a particular group (a minority, women, older people, factory workers) in your discussion of these two categories, or on particular kinds of reading and writing. Your intended readers are people who do not think that extensive reading or the ability to write are very important.

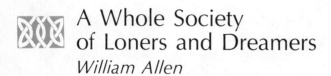

A Whole Society
of Loners and Dreamers
William Allen

William Allen teaches creative writing at Ohio State University. He studied writing at the University of Iowa, where he wrote this essay for *Saturday Review,* a national magazine. He has published novels, stories, and an account of the rampant murder spree of Charles Starkweather. In that book (*Starkweather,* 1976) Allen described the mass murderer from information he gathered personally from people involved in the crimes. He was able to identify with his subject, a young man of his age who was a victim of the popular vision of a loner, a rebel without a cause.

In this essay, Allen looks positively at "loners and dreamers." Writing in 1972 from the perspective of a student enrolled in one of the country's most important writing programs, Allen captures the feelings of isolation and competition that both young and experienced writers can testify to. He plays the ignorant but appealing dreams of a young boy learning to write on his own off against the humorous but obviously useless mail-order writing school. As you read, try to remember similar feelings of isolation and hope from your childhood. Allen's essay shows how many people change their youthful dreams into sophisticated perceptions without losing their first determination to accomplish difficult goals. But it does this primarily by constructing a distinct *persona* for the young character of Allen, a boy who was both innocent and aware at the same time.

IOWA CITY, Iowa—On Sunday afternoons here, if you're tired of taking 1
walks in the country and fighting off the green-bellied hogflies, your next best choice is thumbing magazines at the downtown drugstore. One Sunday not long ago, when I ran out of anything else to thumb, I started looking through one of those magazines geared toward helping new writers achieve success. I used to pore over them a lot when I was a teen-ager, and the first thing I noticed now was that the ads haven't changed much over the past fifteen years:

"IMAGINE MAKING $5,000 A YEAR WRITING IN YOUR SPARE 2
TIME! Fantastic? Not at all. . . . Hundreds of People Make That Much or More Every Year—and Have Fun Doing It!"

"TO PEOPLE WHO WANT TO WRITE FOR PROFIT BUT CAN'T 3
GET STARTED. Have You Natural Writing Ability? Now a Chance to Test Yourself—FREE!"

"I FIRE WRITERS . . . with enthusiasm for developing God-given 4
talent. You'll 'get fired' too with my 48-lesson home study course. Over-the-shoulder coaching . . . personalized critiques. Amazing sales opportunity the first week. Write for my FREE STARTER KIT."

The ad that struck me the most showed a picture of a handsome and 5
darkly serious young man sitting on a hill, picking his teeth with a weed, and gazing out over the countryside. The caption read: DO YOU HAVE THE "FAULTS" THAT COULD MEAN YOU WERE MEANT TO BE A WRITER? The ad went on to list the outstanding characteristics of writers. They are dreamers, loners, bookworms. They are too impractical, too intense, too idealistic.

When I was fourteen and had just started trying to write, I saw an 6
ad much like this and was overwhelmed by it. That fellow on the hill was just like me, I thought. It was a tremendous feeling to discover that I might not be alone—that there was a whole society of loners and dreamers, that they were called writers, and that by sending off for a free writing IQ test I could find out by return mail if I qualified to climb the hill and chew straw with them.

I took that test and blew the top off it. The writing school said I   7
demonstrated a rare creative potential unlike anything they had seen in
years. They did wonder, though, if I had what it took to stick with them
through long months of arduous training to develop my raw talent. If I
really did have that kind of fortitude, the next step would be to send in
some actual samples of my writing.

Spurred, I sent off everything I had ever written—two stories of   8
about 200 words each. One was about some unidentified creatures who
lived in dread of an unidentified monster who came around every week
or so to slaughter as many of them as he could. Some of the persecuted
creatures had the option of running, hopping, scurrying, or crawling to
safety, but the others, for some unexplained reason, couldn't move and
had just to stand there and take it. There was a description of the monster's
roaring approach. Then the last line hit the reader like a left hook: "The
lawn mower ran swiftly over . . . ."

The other story I have preserved these many years: 9

The Race
Two gleaming hot rods stand side by side, poised and tensed—eager to   10
scream down the hot asphalt track, each secretly confident that he will
be the supreme victor. The time is drawing close now; in just a few minutes the race will be on.

There is a last minute check of both cars . . . everything is ready. A   11
yell rings out for everyone to clear the track. The flagman raises the
starting flag above his head, pauses for a second, and with a downward
thrust of the flag, he sends the cars leaping forward with frightening
speed.

They fly down the track, side by side, neither able to take the lead.   12
They are gaining speed with every second. Faster and faster they go, approaching the half-way mark with incredible momentum. . . .

Wait! Something is wrong—one of the cars is going out of control   13
and skidding toward the other car! The rending sound of ripping metal
and sliding tires cuts through the air as the two autos collide and spin
crazily off the track.

For a moment the tragic panorama is hidden by a self-made cur-   14
tain of dust, but it isn't a second before the curtain is pulled away by the
wind, revealing the horrible sight. There are the two hot rods, one
turned over, both broken and smashed. All is quiet. . . .

Two small children, a boy and a girl, get up from the curb where   15
they have been sitting. They eye each other accusingly as they walk
slowly across the street where the two broken toy cars lay silent. . . .
"Woman driver," grumbles the little boy.
The End

The correspondence school's copy desk quickly replied that the writ-   16
ing samples confirmed my aptitude test results and that they looked forward to working with me to the point of publication and beyond. I

couldn't imagine what could be beyond publication but finally figured out they meant to handle my work later as agent-representative. They praised my choice of subject matter, sense of drama, and powerful surprise endings—all of which they said indicated I could sell to the sci-fi market. This made sense, because science fiction was all I had ever read voluntarily except for *Comic Classics* and, as a child, *Uncle Wiggily.* The school was particularly impressed by my style, which they said was practically poetry, in places. They made reference to my use of alliteration ("rending sound of ripping metal") and of metaphor ("self-made curtain of dust . . . pulled away by the wind").

They were quick to make clear, however, that what I had here were only germs of stories. They needed to be expanded to publishable lengths and had to have better character development—particularly the one about the bugs and grass being slaughtered by the lawn mower. They said a good writer could give even an insect an interesting personality. 17

The next step was to send them $10 for each of the two stories—the standard fee for detailed, over-the-shoulder copy-desk criticism. Then after these stories had been redone and rushed off for publication, I should enroll in their thirty-six-lesson course, in which I would be taught the ins and outs of plotting, characterization, point of view, theme, tone, and setting. The fee was $10 a lesson, and after my successful completion of the course they would then handle my literary properties, protect my legal rights, etc., for the regular 10 per cent. 18

At this point I began to wonder if I might be going in over my head. I was getting only a dollar a week from my folks and didn't understand half of what the writing school was talking about. In English class I had heard of such terms as "alliteration," "tone," and "point of view" but had no clear idea what they meant. Also I felt like an imposter. I had given my age as twenty-one. Of course, I was strutting because at fourteen I was doing better than anybody they had worked with in years, but I wondered if I could keep it up. "Rending sound of ripping metal" was genius, but could I crank out lines like that on a daily basis? I decided to try. 19

First I wrote them that I was a little short of cash this month and asked if, just to get started, it would be all right to work on one story for $10 instead of two for $20. They replied that that would be fine—just send in the ten bucks so they could get rolling. 20

Meanwhile I hadn't been able to get even that much money together. I approached my family and was turned down flat because my father thought there was something unhealthy about people who wanted to write. He was bothered by the school's remark that my writing was like poetry. "If you were a girl, it might be different," he said, and showed me a copy of *Men's Adventure.* "Look here, why don't you get one of these two ninety-eight worm ranches? Or one of these small-game boomerangs?" 21

After a few days of trying to drum up work around the neighborhood, I realized I wasn't going to be able to pull it off and decided just not to 22 write back. But in a week I got a curt note saying they wanted to help me, were trying to be patient, but I was going to have to be more responsible. They said that writing was 1 per cent inspiration and 99 per cent perspiration and wondered if in my case the figures might be reversed.

This both goaded and scared me. I wrote back that on account of 23 unexpected medical expenses I could afford to give them only $5 at first. Could they possibly let me have a cut rate? They replied that it was strictly against their policy, but in view of my undeniably vast potential the copy-desk team had voted to go along with me just this once—send the $5.

By mowing lawns and selling bottles, I had by this time scraped 24 together $3, but there my earning potential dropped sharply. Another week went by, and I made only 48 cents more. Then a letter arrived stamped in red, front and back: URGENT! IMPORTANT! DO NOT DIS-CARD! It said I had violated an agreement based on mutual trust and had exactly twenty-four hours to send in the $5. Without exactly spelling it out, they gave the impression that legal action might be taken. The letter ended: "Frankly, Mr. Allen, we're about at our wits' end with you."

I was hurt as well as shaken. I felt that I just didn't have what it takes. 25 If there ever had been a chance of my climbing that hill and sitting with that elite group of loners and dreamers, it was gone now. I had my mother write them that I had suddenly been struck down with polio and was unable even to write my name, much less take their course. I hung onto the little money I had in case I had to give it to them to avoid a lawsuit, but I didn't hear from them after that. In a few weeks I relaxed and mailed off for the $2.98 worm ranch.

Questions

Rereading and Independent Analysis

1. The humor of this essay depends largely on the *persona,* or mask, that Allen creates to represent himself at the age of 14. Review the essay, marking the young Allen's particularly funny responses to the situation he gets into. What principles did the young would-be writer act on?

2. What is the effect of withholding until the middle of this essay the detail about the age that Allen told the writer's school he was? How would your reading have changed if you had known earlier what the boy had told them? Find other examples where the order in which a story is told controls your responses to it.

Suggested Discussion and Group Activities

1. What is the significance of the title of Allen's piece? How does the idea of "a whole society" of writers unify the essay? Review the essay as a class to find the places where this image is brought up. How does it provide connections among the essay's points?

2. In groups, analyze the two stories Allen sent to the writers' school. Why did the young Allen write "The End" at the end of "The Race"?

Explain why the school made the comments about them that they did. If you have them, bring in examples of your own writing when you were younger to compare with Allen's youthful attempts. What qualities do they share?

3. Have you ever had any contact with mail-order lessons or "free" offers? How do these encounters remind you of Allen's experience? How likely is it that the school Allen wrote to actually wrote the letters he describes? Why? Why do you think Allen wrote this essay? What benefits are there from telling this sort of story about ourselves?

Writing Suggestions

Response
Try writing an ad for a mail-order offer of any service or product you choose. Without being entirely dishonest, exaggerate your claims. Then trade ads with a classmate and write a letter of response to one of his or her ads, explaining why you cannot send in your money just now, even though you want to participate.

Analysis
Write an essay in which you explain how Allen achieved his humorous purpose. Explain how misrepresentation and exaggeration characterize the writing of both the mail-order house and the young Allen. Your reader is someone who has read Allen's essay but thinks it was meant seriously.

Finding a Purpose
Using Allen's essay as a model, tell a similar story about yourself or someone you know. Use the difference between your current knowledge of "how things work" and an earlier innocence to explain a situation that could have been upsetting at the time but seems humorous to you now.

From *The Black Notebooks*
Toi Derricotte

Toi Derricotte (b. 1941) is a black woman who has been a teacher and a writer. She has published several books, including *The Empress of the Death House* and *The Black Notebooks,* as well as other poetry and articles in magazines. She keeps her diaries as records of particular times in her life that seemed to have common themes arising from particular problems. For her, diaries are less difficult to approach than blank paper waiting for a poem: "Sitting down to write in my diary, I feel doors opening."

The Black Notebooks records a time when the other doors outside her were only ajar. In 1974 she and her husband had moved to Upper

Montclair, New Jersey, a well-kept suburb of New York City. Derricotte is a very light-skinned black, whose encounters in this previously segregated white neighborhood took on special irony—and difficulty because of her pale skin. She has said that these diaries were painfully slow to write, because they preserve "the most revolting aspects of my inner life."

Racial differences are so visible and definitive in history and in current social attitudes that Derricotte's personal diaries are a valuable source for understanding the situations of people who must deal with these differences frequently. But their sadness for all of us results from the universal sense of embarrassment or shame that can arise when we must reveal an important but undesirable fact about ourselves that has not been obvious to others. Derricotte's diaries have been her way of dealing with these feelings. As you read, look for connections to your own experience of feeling, and being, different from others. Derricotte's expectations, her neighbors' expectations, and social patterns tie these entries together, revealing a universal theme of disappointment and self-doubt resulting from prejudice.

July 1977

1 Yesterday I put my car in the shop. The neighborhood shop. When I went to pick it up I held a conversation with the man who worked on it. I told him I had been afraid to leave the car there at night with the keys in it. "Don't worry," he said. "You don't have to worry about stealing in Upper Montclair as long as the niggers don't move in." I couldn't believe it. I hoped I had heard him wrong. "What did you say?" I asked. He repeated the same thing without hesitation.

2 In the past my anger would have swelled quickly. I would have blurted out something, hotly demanded he take my car down off the rack immediately though he had not finished working on it, and taken off in a blaze. I love that reaction. The only feeling of power one can possibly have in a situation in which there is such a sudden feeling of powerlessness is to "do" something, handle the situation. When you "do" something, everything is clear. But for some reason yesterday, I, who have been more concerned lately with understanding my feelings than in reacting, repressed my anger. Instead of reacting, I leaned back in myself, dizzy with pain, fear, sadness, and confused.

3 I go home and sit with myself for an hour, trying to grasp the feeling—the odor of self-hatred, the biting stench of shame.

December 1977

4 About a month ago we had the guy next door over for dinner. He's about twenty-six. The son of a banker. He lived in a camper truck for a year and came home recently with his dog to "get himself together."

5 After dinner we got into a conversation about the Hartford Tennis Club, where he is the swimming instructor. I asked him, hesitantly, but unwilling not to get this firsthand information, if blacks were allowed to join. (Everybody on our block belongs to Hartford, were told about "the

club" and asked to join as soon as they moved in. We were never told about it or asked to join.) Unemotionally, he said, "No. The man who owns the club won't let blacks in." I said, "You mean the people on this block who have had us over to dinner and who I have invited to my home for dinner, the people I have lived next door to for three years, these same people are ones I can't swim in a pool with?" "That's the rule," he said, as if he were stating a fact with mathematical veracity and as if I would have no feelings. He told us about one girl, the daughter of the president of a bank, who worked on the desk at the Hartford Club. When they told her black people couldn't join, she quit her job. I looked at him. He is the swimming instructor at the club.

My husband and I are in marriage counseling with a white therapist. 6 The therapist sees us separately. When I came in upset about that conversation, he said he didn't believe people were like this anymore. He said I would have to try to join the club to tell whether in fact this was true.

Four days ago, the woman down the street called me, asking if my 7 son could baby-sit for her. I like this woman. I don't know why. She is Dutch and has that ruddy coloring, red hair, out of a Rubens painting. Easy to talk to. She and her husband are members of the club and I couldn't resist telling her the story of the guy next door to get her reaction. She said, "Oh, Toi, two years ago, John and I wanted to have you and Bruce be our guests at a dinner party at the club. I was just picking up the phone to call and ask you when Holly called [a woman who lives across the street] and said, 'Do you think that's a good idea? You better check with the Fullers [old members of the club] first before you call Bruce and Toi.' I called Steve and he called a meeting of the executive committee. We met together for four hours. Several of us said we would turn in our resignations unless you could come. But the majority of people felt that it wouldn't be a good idea because you would see all the good things about the club and want to join. And since you couldn't join, it would just hurt you and be frustrating. John and I wanted to quit. I feel very ashamed of myself, but the next summer, when I was stuck in the house with the kids with nothing to do, we joined again."

May 1978

I had a dinner party last week. Saturday night, the first dinner party in 8 over a year. The house was dim & green with plants & flowers, light & orange like a fresh fruit tart, openings of color in darkness, shining, the glass in the dark heart of the house opening out.

& i made sangria with white wine adding strawberries & apples & 9 oranges & limes & lemon slices & fresh squeezed juice in an ice clear pitcher with cubes like glass lighting the taste with sound & color.

& the table was abundant.   10

& they came. one man was a brilliant conversationalist & his wife was 11 happy to offer to help in the kitchen & one woman was quiet & seemed rigid as a fortress & black & stark as night, a wall falling quickly, her brow, that swarthy drop without her, that steep incline away . . . & her husband was a doctor & introduced himself as "dr." & i said "charmed. contessa toinette."

& we were black & white together, we were middle class & we had   12
"been to europe" & the doctors were black & the businessmen were white & the doctors were white & the businessmen were black & the bankers were there too.

& the black people sat on this side of the room & the white people   13
sat on that & they ate cherried chocolates with dainty fingers & told stories.

& soon i found that one couple belonged to the Hartford Club & my   14
heart closed like my eyes narrowing on that corner of the room on that conversation like a beam of light & they said "it isn't our fault. it's the man who owns it." & i was angry & i said it is your fault for you belong & no one made you & suddenly i wanted to belong i wanted them to let me in or die & wanted to go to court to battle to let crosses burn on my lawn let anything happen they will i will go to hell i will break your goddamned club apart don't give me shit anymore.

bruce said it is illegal & if we wanted to we could get in no matter   15
what the man at the top did & everyone is blaming it on that one ugly man & behind him they hide their own ugliness & behind his big fat ass they hide their puny hopes & don't want to be seen so god will pass over their lives & not touch, hide their little house & little dishwasher, hide like the egyptians hid their children from the face of god, hide their soaked brown evil smelling odor dripping ass. and they were saying don't blame me please throwing up their hands begging not to be seen, but i see them, my eye like a cat seeing into x-ray the bird's blood-brain: i will not pass, like god i will not pass over their evil.

the next day bruce & i talk about it. he still doesn't want to pay 200   16
dollars to belong. he says it's not worth it to fight about, he doesn't want to fight to belong to something stupid, would rather save his energy to fight for something important.

important.   17

what is important to me?   18

no large goal like integrating a university. just living here on this   19
cruddy street, taking the street in my heart like an arrow.

Questions

Rereading and Independent Analysis

1. Each diary entry records Derricotte's daily experiences and her reactions to them. Reread them, underlining only those parts of the entries that are her comments on the events and people she encounters. Then notice the placement of these comments in relation to the events that evoke them. What is the effect on a reader of the placement of her

comments? Were these "Notebooks" written only to record events or to shape them to make a sensible pattern? Explain your answer.

2. The last entry from the diary imitates the form of a typical passage from the Old Testament, using coordinate structures and language often found in the Bible. Note the specific places that achieve this effect in the description of the party. What might be Derricotte's reasons for choosing this way to record this event? What kind of reader would be most familiar with it? What qualities does it give to the events it records?

Suggested Discussion and Group Activities

1. Review the metaphors and similes (brief comparisons of unlike things) that Derricotte uses to express her responses to events. Why do you think she would use these brief comparisons (e.g., "taking the street in my heart like an arrow") in her diary as well as in a poem? How do they help her achieve distance from the "revolting" aspects of this period of her life?

2. Exclusion of people in overt and subtle ways is not done only because of racial differences. Discuss other examples in your experience where categories of "insider" and "outsider" have been established. Is this phenomenon most common when people are new? How does it take on larger implications in Derricotte's case?

Writing Suggestions

Response

Derricotte's statement that her diary "opens up" doors for her can be useful advice to all writers. Use a diary or notebook to write about your memory of a painful event. Write your feelings as you remember them, the specific details that you recall, and any other stray thoughts or associations you think of now. First "observe" the event in your mind; then make notes about it. After you have taken time away from these notes, go back to them and treat them as the source material for a story about the experience. Tell the story in the third, rather than first, person.

Analysis

We often use figurative language (metaphors, similes, images) and allusions (brief references) like Derricotte's use of Old Testament forms as ways to make our meanings and feelings more open and accessible to readers. These devices can also be used, however, to give writers, and readers, greater perspective on their immediate thoughts and experiences. They make immediate experience not only more vivid, but also more universal. Write an essay in which you interpret Derricotte's *Notebooks* and imagine her as one intended reader. Show uses of language that allow readers to be close to her experience and to apply it broadly.

Finding a Purpose

Derricotte's feelings of shame and self-hatred arose from the difference between what she appeared to be and what she knew she was. Write a narration in which you tell about an experience whose outcome depended on whether you revealed something about yourself that no one could see unless you told it yourself. Choose a specific audience you would be comfortable telling this story to, one you think would learn from it. (You may want to use your "Response" answer as the basis for this story.)

Bellow's Typewriters and Other Tics of the Trade
Carol Sternhell

Carol Sternhell teaches journalism at New York University. She says in this interview-essay for the *New York Times Book Review* that writers' lives "are both excruciatingly public and intensely private." Because writers work alone, their schedules and tools depend on personal choices that often become superstitiously rigid habits. And because writers' work is entirely public, becoming the property of readers who may never see the writers nor hear their voices, readers are particularly interested in the unseen, secluded writers' ways of working. Readers believe, perhaps, that they will know more about a writer's written words and intentions if they know the precise details of composition.

Sternhell's essay makes a larger point, however, about the relation between the written world and the actual world. Writing gives us another dimension, so vivid that we often think we can step into it, as her young friend Michael tried to do. You already know about that world from reading you have found especially absorbing. But in this essay, you see it from a writer's point of view. The essay describes an intermediate world, between "life" and the printed page, that writers must create for themselves. It shows how the tools of writing are essential signs of a writer's unique space. By pointing out the crucial importance of the tools a writer relies on, the essay reminds us that the physical equipment we use to write reflects both our pace and our vision of the written world we are trying to create.

My favorite story about writing is really a story about reading. A couple 1 of years ago, when my friend Michael was young (he's now 4 years old and sophisticated about the limits of literature), he tried to climb inside a book. Unwilling to believe that so wonderful a world was unreachable, he simply opened the tale to his favorite page, carefully arranged his choice on the floor and stepped in. He tried again and again, certain he would soon get it right, and each time he was left standing out in the cold he cried in bewilderment.

We grown-up readers, accustomed to boundaries and suspicious of 2 magic, have lowered our expectations. Instead of crying, we look for the trick, the hidden springs and pulleys, the key to how it's done. Because the literary process is so mysterious, we become obsessed with concrete details, however petty; we want to picture our favorite authors at their desks, to know whether they "keep bankers' hours," as John Irving said of himself, or sit alone with a yellow pad at 3 A.M., whether they measure their lives in deadlines or type to the beat of some internal drummer. For us, these questions are shortcuts to understanding creativity; to many writers, they're more like wrong turns, irritating and irrelevant. (Or as E. L. Doctorow said when I phoned him, "The whole subject is ridiculous.")

In defense of such questions—since I've just spent most of a month 3 asking them—I would say the novelist's life is particularly opaque. Unlike the rest of us, who generally must accommodate our personal rhythms to the demands of our jobs, writers are alone with time. They determine their own schedules, choose their own work space and create their own systems (to quote Joyce Carol Oates) "of checks and balances, rewards and taboos." Such lives are both excruciatingly public and intensely private: Their work anticipates an audience, yet is performed in isolation. It's not surprising that those of us in the audience seek to penetrate the literary veil. Is writing simply a job, we wonder—or is it a conjuring trick, after all?

To many novelists, the primary practical distinction is between fic- 4 tion writing and anything else they do, from college teaching to book reviewing to vacuuming the rug. John Barth, for instance, writes fiction during the week in his Baltimore home and "something else" on Fridays, which he and his wife spend in their small house on Maryland's eastern shore. His forthcoming collection of essays, "The Friday Book," represents "a year's worth of Friday mornings," Mr. Barth said. He finds the arrangement both convenient—work doesn't have to be moved back and forth— and "refreshing," but notes that the schedule is only approximate: "Fiction in hand can assert its absolute priority."

Saul Bellow owns two old-fashioned Smith Corona typewriters, but 5 they are definitely not interchangeable. "I don't like to use my fiction typewriter for essays," he said.

John Updike has four different studies in his Boston home, all quite 6 small ("I work in what used to be servants' rooms")—one with an easy chair for reading; one with a word processor, good for writing essays and reviews; a third, with "an old steel desk and a view of the sea," where he wrote "The Witches of Eastwick" by hand in soft pencil; and a fourth for answering mail and "talking to interviewers from The Times." Fiction, Mr. Updike said, is so "intimate, chancy and precarious" that it requires the silence of a pencil; machinery is disconcerting because it "comes between you and the work." Worse, he added, equipment can be positively intimidating: "When I turn on the word processor I feel I'm wasting electricity; with the pencil, I'm only wasting my own time."

John Edgar Wideman, whose novel "Sent for You Yesterday" re- 7 cently won the PEN Faulkner Prize, is more likely to switch paper than rooms. "Different writing requires different paper," he said. Long legal

pads may be fine for essays, but "fiction is much more demanding"; generally, Mr. Wideman looks for "a mystical match between writing and format. If things are going well, I won't switch formats. I'm superstitious—I'll
even use the same color pen."

Miss Oates has two studies in her Princeton home, but they represent 8
different stages of creativity rather than different literary forms. The first
is light and airy, all white with plenty of windows and a skylight; the
second contains the more conventional typewriter, desk and books. Miss
Oates, who is likely to amass 1,000 pages of notes before going near a
typewriter, said the glass-enclosed study is "for special things, not for
writing much, but for thinking and taking notes." Beginning a novel is
agonizing, Miss Oates said—"I'm in kind of a white heat or fever"—and
life in the glass study is not pleasant: "When my husband sees me there,
he knows I'm working very hard and am miserable."

Most writers don't have four studies, or two homes, or, like Alix Kates 9
Shulman, a deserted island, but everyone I spoke with had definite ideas
about place. Some, of course, like Ishmael Reed, can work anywhere: "I
write all over the place," Mr. Reed said, "on planes, in airports and hotel
rooms, on match covers and napkins." Others have to be in the same place
every day: Kurt Vonnegut favors the top floor of a Manhattan brownstone,
Stephen King works on the top floor of an old Maine barn, Anne Tyler sits
in a little room "on the same end of the couch each day." Some, like Fay
Weldon, who's fond of writing in her kitchen, enjoy chaos. Isaac Bashevis
Singer works in his living room despite constant interruptions: "I don't
have an office. After breakfast I sit down and write in between one phone
call or another. Sometimes I write a word and the phone rings, then I write
another word and the phone rings." He doesn't get an answering machine,
he explained, "because the people who call me want to hear it from the
horse's mouth." Others require isolation. "I work as far as possible from
the doorbell and phone and anything else that might be going on," said
Alison Lurie, who doesn't even like to read other people's fiction when
she's working on her own.

. . . .

To some novelists, having the right work place is essential. "Four or five 10
years ago," Lynne Sharon Schwartz said, "I worked under a loft bed, in
a space about 5 feet 4 inches high, like a little cell. It was very uncomfortable—I felt the scope of my work was limited by the little space." Now she
writes in a rented Manhattan apartment she uses just for work. "It's like
going to another world. The walls are covered with little sayings and
clippings—it's like the inside of my head. And there's an enormous desk
with nothing on it, like the clean surface of my mind. I go there and don't
think about the rest of my life."

Others, like Mr. Reed, don't care at all. "Where I work matters 11
less to me than to anyone I know," John Irving said. "It comes from

growing up in a large family—if you were going to lay claim to a whole room, you had better have something important to do, something more important than writing fiction." At the moment Mr. Irving works in his dining room—"I feel uncomfortable having a room pretentiously called a studio; I think a wall is enough"—but over the years his work space has varied. "I used to work in a closet," he said. "Then for years I worked in a garden shed in Vermont. I think I'd be uncomfortable in a large space—even a window is probably a bad idea. Why do you need anything else to look at?"

Whatever their space requirements, every one of the authors I inter- 12
viewed made a distinction between their major work—the novels—and all other writing. The most common scheduling solution was to divide the day by time, with mornings reserved for fiction. As Mr. Vonnegut put it, "My spirit is fresh in the morning."

"I generally wake quite early, awakened by thoughts of my subject," 13
Mr. Bellow said. "I lie there quietly, gradually awakening, feeling my way toward the day's work. I work until I'm exhausted—I don't watch the clock—but by one o'clock I'm generally finished; I have nothing further to say. The problem is disposing of the rest of the day." Mr. Bellow teaches a full load of classes at the University of Chicago, but schedules them only in the afternoon: "I make sure my writing gets my best attention."

According to Paule Marshall, the author of "Praisesong for the 14
Widow," mornings are the best time for creative work, in part because "the brain is fresher." Because writing is as much as unconscious as a conscious act, Miss Marshall said, it's important to start soon after awakening "so whatever has happened during sleep is accessible, so you're able to feed on that. Especially when I'm really involved in a novel, I dream about it, and I take the dream to my desk with me."

John Barth, who calls his "work habits very middle class," attends to 15
fiction between breakfast and lunch: "I find if I go back after lunch I can't concentrate; I'm still glazed." Afternoons are reserved for university business—Mr. Barth teaches at Johns Hopkins—and for "fun things to do" like proofreading and editing. "I'm not a binge writer," added Mr. Barth, who believes that novelists are likely to be more patient than other people: "Novelists are used to the longer haul. That's why most novelists are middle-of-the-road politically; in the time it takes us to write a novel, we can change Presidential administrations."

If anyone *is* a binge writer, it's Toni Morrison. "If I permit novel time 16
to operate, life is better for me," she said. "I don't write because I *can*. I wait for the image to be right—then I can't wait to get there. I might write all day every day for 15 days and then not at all for 15 days." When things aren't going well, Miss Morrison added, the only solution is Mr. Barth's prescription—patience. "At times it seems hopeless, it's just not working," she said. "Those times I used to write anything and then throw it out, but that makes me crazy. Now I just have to wait—I haven't found the right door. I can't let it make me sick. All art is knowing when to stop."

The methodical Mr. Barth takes weekends off ("unless I've lost days 17
during the week"), but most of the writers I spoke to were more like
William Kennedy, who has "no certified day of rest" and who, in fact, since
achieving celebrity by winning the Pulitzer Prize for "Ironweed," is
"going berserk" and "would need two secretaries to keep things straight."
To Mr. Kennedy, "all days are the same, all days are work days—I always
feel I'm on constant deadline."

"I work almost constantly," Joseph Heller said. "For a novelist with- 18
out hobbies, weekends don't make much difference. Most people don't
enjoy weekends anyway; they don't know what to do with Sundays." Mr.
Heller writes in spurts—"never more than two hours at a time." He has
never written more than one draft of a novel. "I don't recommend my
method," he said, "but it's the only way I can work. I almost never sit down
to write without knowing the sentence in my mind—I think in very small
segments."

The prolific Stephen King writes 2,500 words every day of the year 19
except Christmas, Thanksgiving, the Fourth of July ("the only day I drink
before five") and his birthday. He does his serious work in the morning to
the beat of "real loud rock 'n' roll music," sleeps, reads or does jigsaw
puzzles during the afternoon, and then works again for fun after dinner.
"In the morning I do what has to be done," he said. "If I've promised
something to somebody, I'd better be at my best. In the morning, I know
what I'm going to write. At night I just goof with it—I'm on my own time,
like some guy who builds ships in bottles. At night it's like playing with a
thread in a mousehole. Lots of nighttime books never get done: I had 500
pages of one, but the thread just got broken."

Even Mr. King seems like a slacker, however, when compared to 20
Joyce Carol Oates. She found my question about her working schedule
incomprehensible. "I'm *always* working," she said. "That's like asking a
person which days they breathe. It's like asking if I eat on Sundays. Writing
is much more interesting to me than eating or sleeping."

Those of us who are more depressed by a blank sheet of paper in 21
the typewriter than by the thought of nuclear war tend to comb literary history for tales of creative torment. The stories I remember are
replete with strangeness, suicide, perversity—Balzac writing in his
monk's habit, Charlotte Brontë scribbling almost in a trance, Joseph
Conrad who, to quote William Styron, "could scarcely approach his
writing desk without feeling he was going to burst into tears." Such
writers are easier to deal with than the cheerfully energetic Dickens,
who reportedly entertained guests with one hand and wrote "Oliver
Twist" with the other.

In fact, however, the novelists I interviewed were strikingly content. 22
The worst part, all agreed, is beginning; the pleasure takes over later,
almost of its own accord. "By now, I'm a little addicted to it," Gail Godwin
said. "If I don't have my two-hour fix in the morning I just don't feel right."
Miss Godwin had just finished a novel when I reached her at her home in

Woodstock, N.Y., and was feeling a bit bereaved: "I loved it so much, I miss it."

Mr. Styron, who finds writing "always a terrible chore" and identifies 23 with Conrad's daily struggle, added, "It's something I almost *never* look forward to—there's a great sense of resistance, of pain. I often have to force myself to do it. Once I've started, though, it's a pleasure. Nine times out of 10 I find it goes very well, and I'm surprised that it caused such resistance. When I finish a good day's work, there's no greater sense of fulfillment."

Miss Oates had also just finished a novel when I spoke to her and was 24 "feeling very relaxed and happy," but said, "What's awful is beginning a new one. The early stages of a novel are extremely painful; the first month or six weeks are terrible. It's a tremendous strain. I become insomniac; my mind is always working. In that stage I take notes any time, even at midnight." The most difficult period, she said, is "when you can't yet do it, but want to desperately"; when that happens, she becomes "very compulsive, very edgy, very distracted—nothing in the world interests me but that work." Rewriting, on the other hand, is "bliss."

Perhaps Miss Shulman best expressed the paradox of creativity. "I do 25 have to force myself, but once I get into it it's a pleasure," she said. "Why is that—why is it that it's so difficult when I *know* what a pleasure it will be? That's the question I'd most like answered."

According to Mr. Styron, the pain comes from the "extraordinary 26 risk," from "plunging into unknown territory not really knowing whether you're going to come out alive." Both Mr. Styron and Miss Oates agreed that the best writing requires the greatest risk. "Really serious writing does come out of anguish," Miss Oates said. "The only necessity for me," Mr. Styron said, "is to find a theme worth dealing with. The best books are the ones where the theme is congruent with the writer's passion. I could no longer write for the sake of inventing a story any more than I could become an Olympic decathlon runner."

Writers who say they "love to write," Mr. Styron said, are likely to 27 be "lying or exaggerating." Most of the novelists I interviewed, however, claimed the joy far outweighed the pain. "I don't think writers should suffer too much," Mr. Singer said. "If you hate it, why do you do it? As a matter of fact, I love it if it goes well." Mr. Bellow agreed. "If it isn't a pleasure, I'm inclined to drop it. If writing something gives more pain than pleasure, there's something wrong with the project."

In the end, writing is both chore and conjuring trick, torment and 28 triumph. As Miss Morrison explained, when her work is going well, she's likely to write all day and night. "Once it's there it's just so glorious I won't stop until it's over."

The really telling moments, however, come on less inspired days. 29 Miss Morrison spoke for many of her colleagues when she said, "It's not always a pleasure, sometimes I don't enjoy it, sometimes I can't even do it—but it's the place where I live, where I really am. It's home."

Questions

Rereading and Independent Analysis

1. As she describes gathering information from interviewing, Sternhell reveals her own process when writing this essay and suggests what kind of work it was for her. Reread the essay to compile these details about her writing process. What do they show about the requirements for writing an essay that contains information from a number of different interviews rather than from written resources?

2. Classify the responses that Sternhell got to her questions according to the topics the essay takes up. Some people appeared to talk about time, some about places, some about tools for writing. Then try to reconstruct the list of questions Sternhell must have asked to gather this information.

Suggested Discussion and Group Activities

1. What generalization can you make from this essay about the special nature of "work" for a writer? Describe other kinds of work or performances that result from the same personal control of time, place, and tools. What do all of these isolated activities have in common?

2. Sternhell's essay raises the issue of habits, which we all have. Describe your most distinctive habits and the special objects you would feel lost without. Are there any you are particularly superstitious about always repeating or using when you want to succeed at something?

3. In groups, make a list of the tools that the group members use while working on the writing that they undertake over a month. Is some of this equipment specialized for certain kinds of writing, or for certain kinds of writers? Into what categories would you classify your list? What do you have in common as a group?

Writing Suggestions

Response

Keep a journal for a week in which you record your activities as you write anything. Note the length of time you spend on writing at various times of day, the actual writing time as opposed to time for thinking and breaks, the tools you use, the settings you write in, and the occasions on which you feel particularly "stuck" or particularly energized. Then use your notes to write an essay for your classmates in which you explain your special approach to writing. Read some of your classmates' essays to discover similarities and differences in your class.

Analysis

1. Alone or in a small group, make a list of questions you would ask an interviewee about how he or she actually accomplishes work, physical activity, or a performance. Then interview someone about his or her work habits. Bring your answers to class and discuss how they might be edited to make an informative essay. Then, as a group, write the essay for readers who are interested in this kind of work.

2. Write an essay in which you describe your own or an older person's particular and idiosyncratic approach to work. You may want to compare yourself to one of your parents. Include details about the physical process like those in this essay so that the reader will be able to picture the work as a step-by-step process.

Finding a Purpose: Research

Do some research in your library to discover how writing tools have changed and multiplied in the last hundred years. Then write a report for your class, explaining how the physical act of writing has grown more (or less) efficient. You should include a statement about how tools have influenced writers and have changed reading habits as well.

PERSON TO PERSON

 # From *Letters to His Son*
Lord Chesterfield

When we read published letters, we are always overhearing a written conversation that was rarely composed with others in mind. But letters that people keep and that eventually are published allow us a special view of one of writing's most immediate purposes, to reach out to those we know across both actual and contrived distances. Usually, of course, we write because we are not with our correspondent. But sometimes, in invitations, notes, and thoughtful longer letters, we write because we want to make our message more permanent. We often keep letters, preserving the perspective that writing gives to words that have special importance.

Philip Dormer Stanhope (1694–1773), fourth earl of Chesterfield, was an English diplomat, statesman, and patron of the arts and father of Philip Stanhope, the illegitimate son to whom he often wrote. We remember Chesterfield in the names of the chair and the topcoat he made fashionable. He wrote this and many other letters to his son to further young Philip's education in "manners"—not just the rules of polite behavior but the habits of mind of a gentleman. Thus, his letters were a handbook for a gentleman.

It is tempting to think of Chesterfield only as a relic of elitist fashion and snobbery, especially because we know how badly he treated Samuel Johnson, a literary hero (see below). But his letters also reveal an eighteenth-century version of present-day, middle-class values. As you read, keep in mind that the distance between father and son represented in these letters was not unusual among members of the nobility, who generally did not see their children frequently. Chesterfield addresses topics that all parents advise their children about, but his sending this advice in letters to a son he seldom

saw put Chesterfield at a distance from the advice that can make his words
appear comic to us now.

BATH, OCTOBER 19, 1748.

Dear Boy,

Having, in my last, pointed out what sort of company you should 1
keep, I will now give you some rules for your conduct in it; rules which
my own experience and observation enable me to lay down and communicate to you with some degree of confidence. I have often given you hints
of this kind before, but then it has been by snatches; I will now be more
regular and methodical. I shall say nothing with regard to your bodily
carriage and address, but leave them to the care of your dancing-master,
and to your own attention to the best models: remember, however, that
they are of consequence.

Talk often, but never long; in that case, if you do not please, at least 2
you are sure not to tire your hearers. Pay your own reckoning, but do not
treat the whole company; this being one of the very few cases in which
people do not care to be treated, every one being fully convinced that he
has wherewithal to pay.

Tell stories very seldom, and absolutely never but where they are 3
very apt, and very short. Omit every circumstance that is not material, and
beware of digressions. To have frequent recourse to narrative betrays
great want of imagination.

Never hold anybody by the button, or the hand, in order to be heard 4
out; for, if people are not willing to hear you, you had much better hold
your tongue than them.

Most long talkers single out some one unfortunate man in company 5
(commonly him whom they observe to be the most silent, or their next
neighbour) to whisper, or at least, in a half voice, to convey a continuity
of words to. This is excessively ill-bred, and, in some degree, a fraud;
conversation-stock being a joint and common property. But, on the other
hand, if one of these unmerciful talkers lays hold on you, hear him with
patience, and at least seeming attention, if he is worth obliging; for nothing will oblige him more than a patient hearing, as nothing would hurt him
more than either to leave him in the midst of his discourse, or to discover
your impatience under your affliction.

Take, rather than give, the tone of the company you are in. If you 6
have parts you will show them, more or less, upon every subject; and, if
you have not, you had better talk sillily upon a subject of other people's
than of your own choosing.

Avoid as much as you can, in mixed companies, argumentative 7
polemical conversations; which, though they should not, yet certainly do,
indispose, for a time, the contending parties towards each other, and, if
the controversy grows warm and noisy, endeavour to put an end to it by

some genteel levity or joke. I quieted such a conversation hubbub once, by representing to them that, though I was persuaded none there present would repeat, out of company, what passed in it, yet I could not answer for the discretion of the passengers in the street, who must necessarily hear all that was said.

Above all things, and upon all occasions, avoid speaking of yourself, 8 if it be possible. Such is the natural pride and vanity of our hearts, that it perpetually breaks out, even in people of the best parts, in all the various modes and figures of the egotism.

Some abruptly speak advantageously of themselves, without either 9 pretence or provocation. They are impudent. Others proceed more artfully, as they imagine, and forge accusations against themselves, complain of calumnies which they never heard, in order to justify themselves, by exhibiting a catalogue of their many virtues. "They acknowledge it may, indeed, seem odd, that they should talk in that manner of themselves; it is what they do not like, and what they never would have done; no, no torture should ever have forced it from them, if they had not been thus unjustly and monstrously accused. But, in these cases, justice is surely due to one's self, as well as to others; and, when our character is attacked, we may say, in our own justification, what otherwise we never would have said." This thin veil of modesty drawn before vanity, is much too transparent to conceal it, even from very moderate discernment.

Others go more modestly and more slyly still (as they think) to work; 10 but, in my mind, still more ridiculously. They confess themselves (not without some degree of shame and confusion) into all the cardinal virtues; by first degrading them into weaknesses, and then owning their misfortune, in being made up of those weaknesses. "They cannot see people suffer, without sympathizing with, and endeavouring to help them. They cannot see people want, without relieving them; though, truly, their own circumstances cannot very well afford it. They cannot help speaking truth, though they know all the imprudence of it. In short, they know that, with all these weaknesses, they are not fit to live in the world, much less to thrive in it. But they are now too old to change, and must rub on as well as they can." This sounds too ridiculous and *outré*, almost for the stage; and yet, take my word for it, you will frequently meet with it upon the common stage of the world. And here I will observe, by the bye, that you will often meet with characters in nature so extravagant, that a discreet poet would not venture to set them upon the stage in their true and high colouring.

This principle of vanity and pride is so strong in human nature, that 11 it descends even to the lowest objects; and one often sees people angling for praise, where, admitting all they say to be true (which, by the way, it seldom is), no just praise is to be caught. One man affirms that he had rode post an hundred miles in six hours: probably it is a lie, but supposing it to be true, what then? Why, he is a very good postboy, that is all. Another asserts, and probably not without oaths, that he has drank six or eight bottles of wine at a sitting; out of charity, I will believe him a liar; for, if I do not, I must think him a beast.

Such, and a thousand more, are the follies and extravagancies, which 12 vanity draws people into, and which always defeat their own purpose, and, as Waller says upon another subject:

Make the wretch the most despised,
Where most he wishes to be prized.

The only sure way of avoiding these evils is never to speak of yourself 13 at all. But when historically you are obliged to mention yourself, take care not to drop one single word, that can directly or indirectly be construed as fishing for applause. Be your character what it will, it will be known; and nobody will take it upon your own word. Never imagine that anything you can say yourself will varnish your defeats, or add lustre to your perfections; but, on the contrary, it may, and nine times in ten will, make the former more glaring, and the latter obscure. If you are silent upon your own subject, neither envy, indignation, nor ridicule will obstruct or allay the applause which you may really deserve; but if you publish your own panegyric, upon any occasion, or in any shape whatsoever, and however artfully dressed or disguised, they will all conspire against you, and you will be disappointed of the very end you aim at.

Take care never to seem dark and mysterious; which is not only a 14 very unamiable character, but a very suspicious one too; if you seem mysterious with others, they will be really so with you, and you will know nothing. The height of abilities is, to have *volto sciolto* and *pensieri stretti;* that is, a frank, open, and ingenuous exterior, with a prudent and reserved interior; to be upon your own guard, and yet, by a seeming natural openness, to put people off theirs. Depend upon it, nine in ten of every company you are in will avail themselves of every indiscreet and unguarded expression of yours, if they can turn it to their own advantage. A prudent reserve is therefore as necessary as a seeming openness is prudent. Always look people in the face when you speak to them; the not doing it is thought to imply conscious guilt; besides that, you lose the advantage of observing by their countenances what impression your discourse makes upon them. In order to know people's real sentiments, I trust much more to my eyes than to my ears; for they can say whatever they have a mind I should hear; but they can seldom help looking what they have no intention that I should know.

Neither retail nor receive scandal willingly; for though the defama- 15 tion of others may for the present gratify the malignity of the pride of our hearts, cool reflection will draw very disadvantageous conclusions from such a disposition; and in the case of scandal, as in that of robbery, the receiver is always thought as bad as the thief.

Mimicry, which is the common and favourite amusement of little low 16 minds, is in the utmost contempt with great ones. It is the lowest and most illiberal of all buffoonery. Pray, neither practise it yourself, nor applaud it in others. Besides that, the person mimicked is insulted; and, as I have often observed to you before, an insult is never forgiven.

I need not, I believe, advise you to adapt your conversation to the 17 people you are conversing with; for I suppose you would not, without this caution, have talked upon the same subject and in the same manner to a Minister of state, a Bishop, a philosopher, a Captain, and a woman. A man of the world must, like the chameleon, be able to take every different hue, which is by no means a criminal or abject, but a necessary complaisance, for it relates only to manners, and not to morals.

One word only as to swearing; and that I hope and believe is more 18 than is necessary. You may sometimes hear some people in good company interlard their discourse with oaths, by way of embellishment, as they think; but you must observe, too, that those who do so are never those who contribute in any degree to give that company the denomination of good company. They are always subalterns, or people of low education; for that practice, besides that it has no one temptation to plead, is as silly and as illiberal as it is wicked.

Loud laughter is the mirth of the mob, who are only pleased with silly 19 things; for true wit or good sense never excited a laugh since the creation of the world. A man of parts and fashion is therefore only seen to smile, but never heard to laugh.

But, to conclude this long letter; all the above-mentioned rules, how- 20 ever carefully you may observe them, will lose half their effect if unaccompanied by the Graces. Whatever you say, if you say it with a supercilious, cynical face, or an embarrassed countenance, or a silly, disconcerted grin, will be ill received. If, into the bargain, *you mutter it, or utter it indistinctly and ungracefully,* it will be still worse received. If your air and address are vulgar, awkward, and *gauche,* you may be esteemed indeed if you have great intrinsic merit; but you will never please, and without pleasing you will rise but heavily. Venus, among the ancients, was synonymous with the Graces, who were always supposed to accompany her; and Horace tells us, that even youth, and Mercury, the god of arts and eloquence, would not do without her.

> —*Parum comis* sine te Juventas
>   Mercuriusque.

They are not inexorable ladies, and may be had if properly and 21 diligently pursued. Adieu!

Questions

Rereading and Independent Analysis

1. Make a list of the topics that Chesterfield takes up in this letter. What specific areas of Philip's life does he address? Beside each item on your list, write the pattern of development used—does he give an exam-

ple, compare, classify, discuss causes and effects, or use other patterns? What kinds of evidence does he use to make his points convincing?

2. Chesterfield begins by saying that he will be "regular and method-ical" in this letter. Outline the sequence of points in the letter. Then write a brief paragraph characterizing the "regularity and method" of the se-quence of the letter. How are its parts related? Does he give the impres-sion that he is explaining parts of a catalog or "life handbook"?

Suggested Discussion and Group Activities

1. Choose the parts of this letter that you think would be practical advice today and those you think are no longer helpful or relevant to a young person's success. How do your choices match those of your class-mates? Where you disagree in class or in groups, defend your decisions with examples.

2. On the basis of this letter, describe the sort of life that Chester-field's son was expected to lead. What kind of education was he receiving? What would he be doing as an adult? In what ways would any college-educated American today expect to have a similar life?

3. Discuss the tone Chesterfield takes. Does it seem suitable in this situation? Why? If you think not, describe a more suitable approach and give a few examples of changes you would make in the letter itself.

Writing Suggestions

Response

Write a few paragraphs of a letter to a friend, telling how you react to advice from your parents and other older members of your family. Do you think that you should be left to find your own ways of handling problems, or would you like to have more help than you usually receive? Do you like to give advice yourself? Why?

Analysis

1. Imagine that you are Chesterfield's son. First make notes based on your reading about the sort of boy you imagine him to be and the way you think he would have approached his father. Then write a letter to your father that answers this letter from him, explaining your responses to his advice. Justify your request that he send you some money in addition to your regular allowance. Remember to write from the perspective of the person you think Philip Stanhope was.

2. Imagine that you are Chesterfield's daughter. Write him a letter explaining why your education must be equal to your brother's in every way. On the basis of what you know from reading about the way he is educating his illegitimate son, persuade him to give you the same support. Request that he begin writing to you with advice similar to that he is sending to your brother. Give good reasons for your request.

Finding a Purpose

Using this letter and Polonius' advice to Laertes (Chapter 2) as evidence, write a contemporary newspaper column on "advice to young people leaving home." Evaluate the advice both fathers give, quoting it where you think it is still valuable. You may choose to list the "important points to remember" or to write a model paternal letter suitable for today's youth.

Letter to the Right Honorable the Earl of Chesterfield
Samuel Johnson

Samuel Johnson (1709–1784) was raised in poverty in rural England and had to leave Oxford University for financial reasons before taking a degree. He came to London in 1737, determined to become a successful writer. He first supported himself by writing for the *Gentleman's Magazine* and other journals, and in 1746 he published a *Plan* for a *Dictionary of the English Language.* The *Plan* asked for subscriptions from patrons, including the wealthy Lord Chesterfield, to support him as he compiled a dictionary that would standardize English spelling and show the development of the language, using examples of the changed meanings of words in new contexts over time.

The *Dictionary* itself appeared nine years later, in 1755. It showed that standard meanings change as we use words in new situations, not as we arbitrarily give them "correct" meanings. The *Dictionary* was widely praised, and it launched Johnson as a self-supporting writer. He later published the moral fable *Rasselas* (1759), an edition of Shakespeare's works (1765), his own magazines *(The Rambler* and *The Idler),* and his *Lives of the Poets* (1779; 1781).

Although Johnson needed, and received, a pension from the king to support himself after his work on the *Dictionary,* he succeeded at making a living from writing because he came to London at the time when the publishing industry and book sales were growing. A writer had new opportunities to earn a living from writing. In the 200 years between the invention of printing and Johnson's time, only favor from patrons like Chesterfield and other donations had allowed authors the time to devote themselves to writing. As a wide market for printed books and magazines developed, patronage became less necessary for an author's survival.

Johnson's London career was an instance of this change. Although he published the *Plan* for the *Dictionary,* as a traditional means of raising support, his later letter to the uncooperative Chesterfield also can be taken as a symbol of the end of the patronage system. Johnson received no support from Chesterfield. When the project was completed, however, Chesterfield began to suggest publicly that he had contributed to it. Johnson expressed his objections to Chesterfield's claims in a letter, which he sent just before the *Dictionary* was published. In 1781 Johnson gave a copy of the letter to James Boswell, his friend and biographer, and Boswell gleefully published it in his *Life of Johnson* (1791). The letter's interest for us is multiple: We appreciate its extraordinarily controlled language; we see from it how letters can allow us to "speak" as we never could in person; and we appreciate the sense of freedom that Johnson's satiric barbs convey as he turns his earlier humiliation by Chesterfield's refusal of aid into a hard-won, dignified sense of superiority.

February 7, 1755.

My Lord

I have been lately informed, by the proprietor of *The World,* that 1 two papers,[1] in which my Dictionary is recommended to the publick, were written by your Lordship. To be so distinguished, is an honour, which, being very little accustomed to favours from the great, I know not well how to receive, or in what terms to acknowledge.

When, upon some slight encouragement, I first visited your Lord- 2 ship, I was overpowered, like the rest of mankind, by the enchantment of your address; and could not forbear to wish that I might boast myself *Le vainqueur du vainqueur de la terre;*—that I might obtain that regard for which I saw the world contending; but I found my attendance so little encouraged, that neither pride nor modesty would suffer me to continue it. When I had once addressed your Lordship in publick, I had exhausted all the art of pleasing which a retired and uncourtly scholar can possess. I had done all that I could; and no man is well pleased to have his all neglected, be it ever so little.

Seven years, my Lord, have now past, since I waited in your outward 3 rooms, or was repulsed from your door; during which time I have been pushing on my work through difficulties, of which it is useless to complain, and have brought it, at last, to the verge of publication, without one act of assistance, one word of encouragement, or one smile of favour. Such treatment I did not expect, for I never had a Patron before.

The shepherd in Virgil grew at last acquainted with Love, and found 4 him a native of the rocks.[2]

Is not a Patron, my Lord, one who looks with unconcern on a man 5 struggling for life in the water, and, when he has reached ground, encumbers him with help? The notice which you have been pleased to take of my labours, had it been early, had been kind; but it has been delayed till I am indifferent, and cannot enjoy it; till I am solitary, and cannot impart it; till I am known, and do not want it. I hope it is no very cynical asperity not to confess obligations where no benefit has been received, or to be

[1] Nos. 100, 101.
[2] Eclogue, 8. 11. 43 ff. Johnson borrows his thrust from the pastoral, a form "easy, vulgar, and therefore disgusting."

unwilling that the Publick should consider me as owing that to a Patron, which Providence has enabled me to do for myself.

Having carried on my work thus far with so little obligation to any 6 favourer of learning, I shall not be disappointed though I should conclude it, if less be possible, with less; for I have been long wakened from that dream of hope, in which I once boasted myself with so much exultation, my Lord,

your Lordship's most humble,
most obedient servant,

SAM: JOHNSON.

Questions

Rereading and Independent Analysis

1. Johnson's style relies heavily on *parallelism* and *antithesis* (contrast). Both of these devices place two words or ideas in a formal relationship to each other in order to restate or reconsider their meanings. Review the letter, marking examples of each technique. Are there places where repeated meanings are used only for effect? Why do you think Johnson made these choices to fulfill his purpose?

2. Reread the letter, one paragraph at a time. Does the tone change as the letter progresses from paragraph to paragraph? Underline uses of the word *Lord* and identify the tone in which you imagine each use of the word was intended. Now read the letter aloud in the tone you "hear" as it unfolds.

Suggested Discussion and Group Activities

1. In groups or in pairs, explain the ironies that Johnson creates in this letter. Where does the letter's meaning depend on the difference between Johnson's expectations and Chesterfield's actions? How does Johnson include the opinions of all people and their expectations about decent behavior? Show how the letter is unified by repeated references to the difference between the "usual" result of an action and the one Johnson experienced.

2. Choose three sentences from the letter that you think display Johnson's sarcasm most pointedly. Discuss the style of each sentence, noting Johnson's use of *parallelism, antithesis,* and other word choices that support its effect.

Writing Suggestions

Response

1. Why do you think Johnson wrote this letter, even after successfully completing the *Dictionary* without Chesterfield's help? Write a few paragraphs explaining why it was justifiable to write and send the letter.

2. Imagine that you are Lord Chesterfield, reading this letter. Then, after looking at the style and tone of Chesterfield's letter to his son (above), write a response to Johnson, aiming for the same sarcastic effect that the letter from Johnson achieved.

Analysis

Write an explanation of Johnson's letter for a reader who does not understand why it was written or why it is not "serious" and straightforward. Include an explanation of the letter's "scene" (its purpose, reader, writer) and the devices that create its sarcasm. Explain why Johnson would have let Boswell publish it.

Finding a Purpose

Imagine that you are James Boswell, Johnson's biographer. Write a summary of the letter Johnson wrote to Chesterfield, telling its main points in straightforward language to introduce its appearance in the biography of Johnson that you are writing. Include enough explanation to make the purpose of the letter clear.

 # A Bloomer Girl on Pike's Peak
Julia Archibald Holmes

One of the ways that Americans learned about life on the frontier during the nineteenth century was by letters written to the writers' friends and relatives that were also published in newspapers and journals. Julia Archibald Holmes (1838–1887), wife of James Holmes, was the first white woman to scale the slopes of Pike's Peak—14,110 feet high—in the Colorado Rockies. She and her husband reached the top on August 5, 1858. This later letter described Holmes's further travels with her husband and her efforts to persuade people that women could appropriately travel in the prairie wilderness. She thought that they must begin wearing more sensible clothes than the billowing skirts that were fashionable at the time.

The letter was first published in the *Sibyl,* a bi-monthly journal that was devoted to reform, especially in women's dress. The editor of the journal, Dr. Lydia Sayer Hasbrouk, allowed republication in other New York newspapers. Julia Holmes wrote "on the run," but she knew that her letters would have fairly wide distribution. This letter was not, then, aimed at only one reader but had a persuasive purpose in support of a cause. As you read it, notice the ways Holmes combined descriptive details with her aim to allow women freedom to move, in all senses, on an equal basis with men.

Fort Union, New Mexico. Jan. 25th, 1859

Sister Sayer—

I think an account of my recent trip will be received with some 1
interest by my sisters in reform, the readers of *The Sibyl*—if not by the
rest of mankind—since I am, perhaps, the first woman who has worn the
"American Costume" across that prairie sea which divides the great frontier of the states from the Rocky Mountains. In company with my husband,
James H. Holmes, and my brother, I traveled in an ox wagon and on foot
upwards of eleven hundred miles during the last three summer months.

We were on our farm on the Neosho River, in Kansas, when news 2
reached us that a company was fitting out in Lawrence for a gold adventure to Pike's Peak. Animated more by a desire to cross the plains and
behold the great mountain chain of North America, than by any expectation of realizing the floating gold stories, we hastily laid a supply of provisions in the covered wagon, and two days thereafter, the 2nd of last June,
were on the road to join the Lawrence company. The next morning we
reached the great Santa Fe Road, and passed the last frontier Post Office,
Council Grove. Here we mailed our last adieus, and felt somewhat sad that
we should hear no more from our friends for so long a time—a period of
six months, it afterward proved, we were to be imprisoned from the world
and friends. Here we learned that the train we were to join had passed
the day before, and we drove as rapidly as staid cattle could travel for the
next fifty miles to overtake it. Several millions of dollars worth of merchandise is transported annually over this road from the Missouri River to New
Mexico, entirely in wagons, and we now met many trains from that Territory, coming to Independence for loads. These teams are composed of
from five to seven pairs of cattle, attached to huge wagons, capable of
carrying seventy to ninety hundred pounds of freight each. Many Americans follow freighting for a living, and have made large fortunes. The price
of freight from Independence to Santa Fe is ten cents per pound, so that
a good team will earn $800 a load. One freighter, an American, residing
in this Territory, (New Mexico), realized last year from a single trip with
eighteen wagons, from Kansas City, Mo. to Salt Lake, the sum of $12,000.

But I am digressing from the subject of my trip. We reached the 3
Cottonwood Creek, crossing the 5th of June, where we found the train
encamped. We were now fairly launched on the waving prairie. A person
who has beheld neither the ocean nor the great, silent, uninhabited plains,
will find it impossible to form any adequate idea of the grandeur of the
scene. With the blue sky overhead, the endless variety of flowers under
foot, it seemed that the ocean's solitude had united with all the landscape
beauties. In such a scene there is a peculiar charm for some minds, which
it is impossible for me to describe; but it made my heart leap for joy.

Finding that we were to have all day to rest, we took our large 4
cooking stove out of the wagon and cooked up provisions for two or three
days.

Nearly all the men were entire strangers to me, and as I was cooking 5
our dinner some of them crowded around our wagon, gazing sometimes
at the stove, which, with its smoke pipe, looked quite as much out of place
as will perhaps the first engine which travels as far away from civilization;
but oftener on my dress, which did not surprise me, for, I presume, some
of them had never seen just such a costume before. I wore a calico dress,
reaching a little below the knee, pants of the same, Indian moccasins on
my feet, and on my head a hat. However much of it lacked in taste, I found
it to be beyond value in comfort and convenience, as it gave me freedom
to roam at pleasure in search of flowers and other curiosities, while the
cattle continued their slow and measured pace.

I was much pleased to learn on my arrival, that the company con- 6
tained a lady, and rejoiced at the prospect of having a female companion
on such a long journey. But my hopes were disappointed. I soon found that
there could be no congeniality between us. She proved to be a woman
unable to appreciate freedom or reform, affected that her sphere denied
her the liberty to rove at pleasure, and confined herself the long days to
feminine impotence in the hot covered wagon. After we had become
somewhat acquainted, she in great kindness gave me her advice.

"If you have a long dress with you, do put it on for the rest of the trip, 7
the men talk so much about you."

"What do they say?" I inquired.   8

"Oh, nothing, only you look so queer with that dress on."   9

"I cannot afford to dress to please their taste," I replied. "I could not 10
positively enjoy a moment's happiness with long skirts on to confine me
to the wagon."

I then endeavored to explain to her the many advantages which the 11
reform dress possesses over the fashionable one but failed to make her
appreciate my views. She had never found her dress to be the least inconvenient, she said; she could walk as much in her dress as she wanted to,
or as was proper for a woman among so many men. I rejoiced that I was
independent of such little views of propriety, and felt that I possessed an
ownership in all that was good or beautiful in nature, and an interest in
any curiosities we might find on the journey as much as if I had been one
of the favored lords of creation.

Soon after we overtook the company a division occurred on the 12
question of keeping the Sabbath. It was Saturday morning, and was
thought necessary for the train to lie over one day and make preparation
for traveling. Two days, however, were considered too long a delay. Some
of the more conscientious christians desired the train to travel that day and
rest the next, Sunday. But it was two days' journey to wood and good water
after leaving the present camp. It was, therefore, decided that we could
not on this journey rest on the seventh day, but must take some time when
we were convenient to wood, good water, and grass for cattle. The next
day we moved on, and every one was looking out for Buffalo. Every
solitary wolf or mound of earth in the distance, was transformed by some
of our most anxious and imaginative hunters into a buffalo. A few short

pursuits of these delusive objects served to render our braves more cautious, and towards the close of the day the cry, "a buffalo! a buffalo!" became less frequent.

After the merits of several different camping grounds had been vigorously discussed by our several leading men, one was finally selected; and the corral made by driving the teams so that the wagons formed a circle enclosing a yard large enough to contain the cattle belonging to the train. The cattle were allowed to feed until dark, and then driven into the corral for safe keeping, and guarded until morning. This was the course pursued throughout the journey. The next morning the camp was aroused at daylight by a chorus of mingled yelling and screeching—music wild and thrilling as only a band of prairie wolves can make. Civilized man has his prototype in the noisy Indian, so the canine domestic has his lupine prototype, which can make comparatively savage sounds. 13

When camped on the Little Arkansas River, as I was searching for different flowers, a few rods from the camp, I cast my eyes across the river, and there within forty yards of me stood a venerable buffalo bull, his eyes in seeming wonder fixed upon me. He had approached me unobserved, behind the trees which lined the bank. His gaze was returned with equal astonishment and earnestness. Much as I had heard and read of the buffalo, I had never formed an adequate idea of their huge appearance. He was larger and heavier than a large ox; his head and shoulders being so disproportionate, he seemed far larger than he really was. He looked the impersonation of a prairie god—the grand emperor of the plain. His countenance expressed terrible majesty and fierceness, and on his chin he wore hair sufficient for the faces of a dozen French emperors. His presence soon became known in camp, and in a few seconds he was coursing westward with our fleetest horses in pursuit. He was overtaken and shot within three or four miles. Buffalo now began to be a common object. 14

One evening we neglected the precaution to cross the stream before camping. During the night a heavy rain came swelling the creek to a depth of twelve or fifteen feet, and flooding the camp, which was pitched on low ground, with several inches of water. The men were thus driven from the tents to the wagons or a more uncomfortable upright position. In consequence of this neglect, we were detained three days. During this time my husband went out buffalo hunting and returned bringing with him a buffalo calf apparently but a week old. It was a great curiosity to all; and, in the fullness of my compassion for the poor little thing, I mixed up a mess of flour and water, which I hoped to make it drink. I approached it with these charitable intentions, when the savage little animal advanced toward me and gave me such a blow with its head as to destroy the center of gravity. His hair was wooly in texture, and of an iron grey color. Unlike the young of our domestic cows, he seldom cried, and when he did only made a faint noise. The buffalo cow as well as the bull is naturally a very timid animal, save when wounded or driven to bay. I learned that the mother of the captured calf made a heroic stand, and presented a beautiful illustration of the triumph of maternal feeling over fear. She was in a herd 15 of many hundred buffaloes, fleeing wildly over the plain before the hunter. After a few miles chase the calf gave signs of fatigue. At its faint cry she would turn and come to the calf, but at sight of the hunter bounded off to the herd. This she did two or three times during a chase of as many miles, the calf falling behind more and more, and his mother wavering between fear for his life and her own, at last her decision was made, and she determined to defend her offspring alone on the prairie. She died in his defence.

While camped here, the company was thrown into great anxiety by   16 a member becoming lost on the prairie. Much search was made and he was given up as dead, when some Cheyenne Indians came into the camp bringing a note from him, stating that he was at a trading post two days in advance. We feasted the Indians in our gratitude. They were large, finely formed, and noble looking men, and but for one sight with which they regaled our eyes they would not have appeared very disgusting. I refer to a habit with them which seems almost too nauseating to write of—that of picking vermin from each other's heads, and eating them with seeming eagerness and gusto.

I commenced the journey with a firm determination to learn to walk.   17 At first I could not walk over three or four miles without feeling quite weary, but by persevering and walking as far as I could every day, my capacity increased gradually, and in the course of a few weeks I could walk ten miles in the most sultry weather without being exhausted. Believing, as I do, in the right of woman to equal privileges with man, I think that when it is in our power we should, in order to promote our own independence, at least, be willing to share the hardships which commonly fall to the lot of man. Accordingly, I signified to the Guardmaster that I desired to take my turn with the others in the duty of guarding the camp, and requested to have my watch assigned with my husband. The captain of the guard was a gentleman formerly from Virginia, who prided himself much upon his chivalry, (and who, to use his own expression, was "conservative up to the eyes,") was of the opinion that it would be a disgrace to the gentlemen of the company for them to permit a woman to stand on guard. He would vote against the question of universal franchise, were it to be submitted to the people, although he was a hero in the struggles of Kansas, and must have witnessed the heroic exertions of many of the women of that Territory to secure for their brothers the boon of freedom. He believes that woman is an angel, (without any sense,) needing the legislation of her brothers to keep her in her place; that restraint removed, she would immediately usurp his position, and then not only be no longer an angel but unwomanly.

After reaching the Great Bend of the Arkansas River, we camped   18 on Walnut Creek, where we found many new varieties of flowers, some of them of exceeding beauty. Among others the sensitive rose, a delicate appearing flower, one of the most beautiful I ever saw, having a fine delicious aroma. It grows on a running vine. In an eastern conser-

vatory it would be the fairy queen among the roses—the queen of
flowers.

Yours,

J. Annie Archibald

Questions

Rereading and Independent Analysis

1. The purposes of this letter are both personal and public. Reread
it, making a list of the purposes that it fulfilled and the audiences it
addressed. How much is description and travel narrative? How much is
argument in favor of a cause? How are the two connected?

2. This narrative is tied together by chronology (movement through
time), punctuated by stories about specific events. Make an outline of the
letter, showing the major and minor topics that it takes up in the order
of the narrative.

3. Do some research in your library about women who were involved in the westward expansion. How common was Julia Holmes's experience? What problems did women typically have when traveling? How
did they adapt to the West?

Suggested Discussion and Group Activities

1. Julia Holmes describes her and her husband's reasons for this trip
at the beginning of the letter. What activities does she mention that could
define the couple as two of the first American tourists? Do you think this
motive was common at the time?

2. Throughout this letter, Holmes promotes reform by raising examples of social restrictions that were overcome because of inconvenience
and necessity. Describe some other changes in "propriety" that you have
seen in your lifetime and others that that you think will occur soon for the
same reasons.

Writing Suggestions

Response

Holmes's letter describes the attitudes of men to women in her time
and gives examples of men's responses to her actions. Write an essay in
which you explain how attitudes like these have changed, and have not
changed, today. What process do changes like these generally follow?
What practical and idealistic considerations determine the success or failure of a widespread change in attitude? Your intended readers should be
a group of people of the opposite sex.

Analysis

Use the material you gathered to answer Question 3, "Rereading,"
as you write an analysis of Holmes's letter. Show how it was and was not

an account of typical experiences women had during the westward expansion. Compare her letter to other accounts you have found, explaining diverse events and forces that created a number of opportunities and problems for women at this time.

Finding a Purpose

Write a letter that you think would be publishable in the Sunday magazine of your local newspaper, describing a trip or an adventure. Write to a specific person, but keep in mind the readership of the paper. Use the same general form that Holmes used, making your points within a chronological narrative. Include details that will appeal to the readers of this particular publication.

 # From *Letters to Bess*
Harry S Truman

These letters were written by Harry S Truman (1884–1972), who was President of the United States from 1945 to 1953. He took office at the death of Franklin D. Roosevelt and won election for himself in 1948. Truman had been a tradesman and farmer in Missouri. He was elected to the United States Senate, where he became known for his direct, simple, and hard-headed approach to complex problems. Truman was never certain that he wanted high public office, and he was never overawed by it or by the people it required him to meet. He and his wife, Bess, the recipient of this letter, were regularly separated during his political career. She was sometimes unwell and was not fond of public life. Their daughter, Margaret, fulfilled many of the functions of a First Lady and has continued in public life as a writer.

While the Trumans were apart, Harry wrote to Bess every day from wherever he was at the time, expressing his constant devotion and love to his family. The letters here, which Bess kept and which were published soon after her death, are from the correspondence that ended in 1959, when they retired together and returned to the house in Independence, Missouri, that had always been the family home.

These letters are an extraordinary record of personal life, which, while influenced by extremely consequential public surroundings, did not lose its intimacy. They contrast with published letters like that of Julia Holmes (above) that were written "personally" but with a larger readership in mind. The letters in this selection were written in 1945, at the time that World War II ended and Truman was negotiating the division of Europe with the United States' British and Soviet allies. The diplomatic missions and political negotiations he undertook at the time shaped the history of the West after the war and determined its continuing alliances and negotiations in Europe.

[The White House]
June 12, 1945

Dear Bess:

Just two months ago today, I was a reasonably happy and contented 1
Vice President. Maybe you can remember that far back too. But things
have changed so much it hardly seems real.

I sit here in this old house and work on foreign affairs, read reports, 2
and work on speeches—all the while listening to the ghosts walk up and
down the hallway and even right in here in the study. The floors pop and
the drapes move back and forth—I can just imagine old Andy and Teddy
having an argument over Franklin. Or James Buchanan and Franklin
Pierce deciding which was the more useless to the country. And when
Millard Fillmore and Chester Arthur join in for place and show the din is
almost unbearable. But I still get some work done. . . .

Write me when you can—I hope every day.   3

Lots of love,

Harry

[The White House]
June 19, 1945

Dear Bess:

Well it looks as if I'm off to Wallgren's at last. That is providing the 4
weather is all right. I'll go to Olympia and rest a few days and then go to
San Francisco on June 25 instead of 22, speak on June 26, and come
directly to Independence. Landing about 1:00 P.M., twenty-seventh. Stay
there until Saturday, thirtieth, and come on back here so I can send the
treaty to Congress on the second of July. The Russians have caused the
delay. But I'm not going to wait any longer.

Hope everything is going well with you. The letter came yesterday 5
afternoon all right. It was promptly given to me—unopened—so you see
I do have some good help. Is Margie solvent? Hope you are too. Give
everybody my best.

Lots of love.

Harry

P.S. Eisenhower's party was a grand success. I pinned a medal on him in 6
the afternoon. He is a nice fellow and a good man. He's done a whale of
a job. They are running him for President, which is O.K. with me. I'd turn
it over to him now if I could.

Berlin
July 20, 1945

Dear Bess:

It was an experience to talk to you from my desk here in Berlin night 7
before last. It sure made me homesick. This is a hell of a place—ruined,

dirty, smelly, forlorn people, bedraggled, hangdog look about them. You never saw as completely ruined a city. But they did it. I am most comfortably fixed and the palace where we meet is one of two intact palaces left standing. . . .

We had a tough meeting yesterday. I reared up on my hind legs and 8 told 'em where to get off and they got off. I have to make it perfectly plain to them at least once a day that so far as this President is concerned Santa Claus is dead and that my first interest is U.S.A., then I want the Jap War won and I want 'em both in it. Then I want peace—world peace and will do what can be done by us to get it. But certainly am not going to set up another [illegible] here in Europe, pay reparations, feed the world, and get nothing for it but a nose thumbing. They are beginning to awake to the fact that I mean business.

It was my turn to feed 'em at a formal dinner last night. Had Church- 9 ill on my right, Stalin on my left. We toasted the British King, the Soviet President, the U.S. President, the two honor guests, the foreign ministers, one at a time, etc. etc. ad lib. Stalin felt so friendly that he toasted the pianist when he played a Tskowsky (you spell it) piece especially for him. The old man loves music. He told me he'd import the greatest Russian pianist for me tomorrow. Our boy was good. His name is List and he played Chopin, Von Weber, Schubert, and all of them.

The ambassadors and Jim Byrnes said the party was a success. Any- 10 way they left in a happy frame of mind. I gave each of them a fine clock, specially made for them, and a set of that good, navy luggage. Well I'm hoping to get done in a week. I'm sick of the whole business—but we'll bring home the bacon.

> Kiss Margie, lots and lots of love,
>
> Harry

Questions

Rereading and Independent Analysis

1. What features of Truman's word choice and style set the tone of these letters? Find specific examples to support your identification of their tone.

2. Who are the people Truman refers to in these letters? For example, "old Andy" and "Teddy." Try to identify as many of these references as you can by using your library and asking people who may remember them.

Suggested Discussion and Group Activities

1. Would you characterize Truman's approach to the presidency as casual, informal, or realistic? Discuss the *rhetorical stance* he takes in these letters toward his office and responsibilities. That is, what does Truman do as he writes to emphasize that he is primarily a husband, a father, and a concerned "local" citizen? What is the purpose of this emphasis?

2. Truman's letters supply examples of the view of "insiders" in any system as opposed to that of "outsiders." What advantages for diplomacy and policy making are there in preventing the public from knowing what "insiders" know? Do you agree with Truman's view of the need for secrecy? Do contemporary "insiders" share Truman's attitude about secrecy, or is it less acceptable now? Cite some examples of recent dealings with political and social problems during which secrecy and freedom of information were important issues. How have specific new communication technologies changed the kinds of information needed to help the public feel secure? Is "showing" more reassuring than telling about a situation?

Writing Suggestions

Response
Write a letter to someone close to you in which you describe an event in your school or work life. Tell about the event from a personal viewpoint, showing how it reminds you of times when you were with the correspondent.

Analysis
Harry Truman might be described as the last American President to hold office in a pretechnological era. Write an essay in which you explain how parts of these letters probably could not or would not have been written were he now in office. Point out how his actions and personal style would now be different because of current media, weaponry, and political considerations.

Finding a Purpose
Choose any historic figure whose official actions were crucial to the future of the nation. Do research to learn details of the person's life and public actions. Write an imaginary personal letter from this person to a relative or a friend, referring to the person's public concerns as well as to personal matters. Where you think it is appropriate for this writer, imitate Truman's mixture of the two concerns.

The Letter
Loren Eiseley

This selection by Loren Eiseley (1907–1977) represents a transition from the letters we have seen so far to another purpose for writing—reflecting on our experiences by writing about them. Eiseley was a hobo in his youth and a student at the University of Pennsylvania. Later he pursued careers as an anthropologist, a naturalist, an essayist, and a poet. Before his death, he held a special chair at the University of Pennsylvania, given to him in recognition of his lifelong project of making connections between the humanities and science. His highly praised writing includes *The Immense Journey, The Invisible Pyramid, Notes of an Alchemist* (poems), and the volume from which this selection is taken, *All the Strange Hours: The Excavation of a Life* (1975).

All the Strange Hours was Eiseley's autobiography, a literary treatment of his difficult early years and their influence on his later life. The book has three parts, whose titles indicate his vision of himself and the changes he underwent: "Days of a Drifter," "Days of a Thinker," and "Days of a Doubter." Eiseley had a remarkable ability to focus on small details like those that make up scientific data, but with the eye of a humanist who also sees their significance and relation to larger human problems. In this selection, a significant letter from a friend that arrives long after this friend has disappointed him becomes a thread that connects the elements of a "lesson" Eiseley learned about trust and change.

As in all autobiographical writing, Eiseley shapes events he experienced to make a point. As you read, notice how he manipulates his perspective, his point of view, and the order in which he tells us about events to explain his life to himself as well as to us. What is the central point of this essay?

"I remember," he had written. That was in 1947, and my hand shook 1 remembering with him. Over a quarter of a century has passed and I have not answered his letter. He was the closest of all my boyhood friends. And if, in the end, I did not respond to his letter, it was not that I intended it so. I sent, in fact, a card saying I was moving to Philadelphia and would write to him later. All this was true. In a little bundle of letters kept in a box and consisting mostly of communications from men long dead, I faithfully preserved his message. Only slowly did I come to realize that something within me was too deeply wounded ever to respond. In the first place, let me state with candor that if I have let nearly thirty years drift by—I last saw Jimmy Dawes when we graduated from grade school—I was forty-one when I received his own first recognition of my existence. He had seen some pieces of mine in a national magazine, *Harper's,* and remembered my name. Perhaps in a sense this balances the equation.

He wrote me as a successful officer in a huge corporate enterprise. 2 He remembered a surprising amount about our childhood activities and he recalled something that touched my naturalist's memories and sent me groping to my book shelf. "I remember," he wrote, "all those squirmy things we collected in jars and buckets and took home to put in the aquariums you made."

He was right even if he was chuckling a little. But he was not content 3 with these boyish memories. He persisted until he came to the explanation, unexpected by me, as to why, though we had lived on into young adulthood in the same community, I had never encountered him after our eighth-grade graduation.

I have said earlier that though in the western towns of those years 4 poor children might attend school with those of another economic level, there came a time when the bridge was automatically withdrawn. This I accepted and never questioned, though much later when I passed my companion's home I used to look up at it a little wistfully. I had once been welcome there—I suppose, looking back, like a dog, a pet good for one's son at a certain stage of life, but not to be confused with the major business of growing up. No, I should not put it so harshly; his mother, his sisters were kind. I know that in their home I saw my first *Atlantic Monthly* in the traditional red-brick covers.

I rarely saw Jimmy Dawes' father, but I knew him as a contained, 5 serious man of business. He ruled a healthy, well-directed household in which one knew that because of the wisdom of father everyone would marry well, be economically secure, and that each child was bound to live happily ever after. Actually, because of the peculiarities of my edge-of-town status, these good people had probably stretched things a little to please their only son, since we played happily together. If I led him to adventures in the fields and ponds around the town, these were no more than an *Atlantic* essayist of the time would have thoroughly approved.

When Jimmy vanished from my ken I suppose I ached a little, but 6 I was adjusted to the inevitable loneliness of my circumstances. There was a very large high school in Lincoln and I never saw him again. Looking back, it is possible he was sent elsewhere. I repeat that the separation was so neatly handled that I never thought of it as more than the usual process of growing up, of being always the aloof observer, never participant, in the success of other families. No, if Jimmy Dawes had written me after all those years merely to wish me well and remember our pond adventures, I would have answered. Not effusively—one comes to accept one's place in life—but to congratulate him upon his success, the fine children of whom he wrote, and to thank him for his interest in my few ephemeral essays. There the matter would have ended. I know he meant well, but having grown up in that ordered household he proceeded, either in tact-less condescension or, more likely, by way of explaining a thirty-year silence, to examine his father's role in the matter.

The social facts of life had left me merely grateful for a few shared 7 years and timid, occasional entrances into a home fantastically different from my own. I had realized, even as a youngster, that Jimmy Dawes was headed for something I would never be. But now here was Jimmy Dawes, after thirty years, telling me with no trace of regret that he had only pursued his father's directive. Father had deemed it time that his son discontinue this enthusiasm for a pond-dipping fox-child and get on with the business of where a properly directed young man should go.

Papa had said it, apparently, right out loud. Oh, it is true that at the 8 end of the letter Jimmy Dawes had suggested, in a belated attempt to mollify my feelings, that perhaps he had himself been responsible in hav-ing taken up with all these matters too enthusiastically. Doubtless father had been right. Fathers, in his world, always were. He managed to tell me that also.

At the end of the letter I found myself shaken over what to Jimmy   9
was a simple fact that I would easily appreciate. Could I now venture pretentiously to Jimmy Dawes, that I was, after all, a social scientist? Could I say that I had long since accepted all that he had to tell me, and then ask him upon what impulse he had chosen to repeat what his father had said? And if you chose to forget your friend, the nagging thought persisted, why are you busy with this resurrection now? Am I made respectable at last by my printed name, because the *Atlantic Monthly* was taken and read in your father's house long ago?

I had liked Jimmy Dawes; that was why his belated emergence was   10
so painful. There was still in that letter some trace of a bounding, youthful eagerness long lost by me. I sent the brief card of acknowledgment, went on my way to Penn, and proceeded to be haunted the rest of my life by his letter. No, not quite. In preparation for eventual retirement I began in the late summer of 1974 to destroy old files. I knew where the letter was, though I had not read it again in all those years. I read it once more, and because Jimmy had been my boyhood chum I reached for the telephone and asked for a number and an address far away. "Sir," the operator's voice came back, "no such name exists at that address."

At heart I knew it would be so, but at least I had finally nerved myself   11
to try. His children would be grown and married. He would be retired and playing golf in Florida, or perhaps reading a vastly changed *Atlantic Monthly,* like his father, in an equally traditional, well-managed home. Slowly, deliberately, I tore up the long-cherished letter. It had served its purpose. Through it I began to remember where part of my interest in the living world began.

On the shelf where I had started to fumble when Jimmy Dawes'   12
letter arrived was an old book, bound in green cloth with a stylized fish in gold stamped on the cover, a book bearing the unimpressive title *The Home Aquarium: How to Care for It.* A man equally obscure had published that book in 1902, five years before I was born. His name was Eugene Smith and whatever else he did in life I do not know. The introduction was written in Hoboken, New Jersey.

The copy I possess is not the one I borrowed and read from the   13
Lincoln City Library while I was still in grade school. So profound had been its influence upon me, however, that in adulthood, after coming East, I had sought for it unsuccessfully in old book stores. One day, in my first year in graduate school, I had been turning over books on a sales' table largely strewn with trivia in Leary's famous old store in Philadelphia, a store now vanished. To my utter surprise there lay three copies with the stamp of the golden fish upon their covers. It was all I could do to restrain myself from purchasing all three. It was the first and last time I ever saw the work in a book store. The name B. W. Griffiths and the date 1903 was inscribed on the fly leaf. To this I added my own scrawled signature and

the date 1933. Now, in the year 1975, I still possess it. I have spoken in
the past of hidden teachers. This book was one such to me.

It is true there had been my early delvings in sandpiles, and so strong 14
is childhood memory, that I can still recollect the precise circumstances
under which I first discovered a trapdoor spider's nest. My amazing, unpredictable mother was the person who explained it to me. How, then, did
this pedestrian work on the home aquarium happen to light up my whole
inner existence?

There were, I think, two very precise reasons having nothing to do 15
with literature as such that intrigued me about this old volume. Most of
the aquarium books of today start with the assumption that you go to a pet
store and buy tanks, thermometers, specialized aeration equipment, and
even your assemblage of flora and fauna "ready made." Smith's book
contained no such assumption. You got the glass, you cut it yourself, you
made bottoms and sides of wood. Then, somewhere, you obtained tar to
waterproof the wood and the joints. Moreover, Smith had given a simple
running account, not alone of easily accessible fresh-water fish, but of local
invertebrates with which aquariums could be stocked.

I genuinely believe that it was from the pages of his book that I first 16
learned about the green fresh-water polyp *Hydra viridis,* so that later I
identified it in one of my own aquariums, not from the wild. In other
words, there had been placed within my hands the possibility of being the
director, the overseer of living worlds of my own. If one has the temperament and takes this seriously one will feel forever afterward responsible
for the life that cannot survive without one's constant attention. One
learns unconsciously about ecological balance, what things may the most
readily survive together, and, if one spends long hours observing, as I later
came to do, one makes one's own discoveries and is not confined to text-
books.

This leads me to the other value gained from Smith's plain little 17
volume. I spent no time, as a midlander, yearning after tropical marine fish
or other exotic specimens. I would have to make my own aquariums and
stock them as well. Furthermore, for a lad inclined as I was, one need not
confine oneself to fish. One could also make smaller aquariums devoted to
invertebrate pond life.

By chance I encountered Smith's book in midwinter and it would be 18
a normal parental expectation that all of this interest in "slippery things"
would have worn itself out while the natural world was asleep under pond
ice. In the flaming heat of enthusiasm, however, I grew determined not
to wait upon nature. I first secured some wood and glass scraps from a
nearby building project and tar from a broken tar barrel. Though I had
no great gifts as a carpenter I did the job by persistence from materials
then strewn casually about every house under construction. I boiled and
applied the warm tar myself. In one triumph, I even made a small aquarium from a cigar box.

In a few days I had enough worlds to start any number of creations. 19

To do so I had to reverse the course of nature. Elders may quail but this is nothing for children. So it was winter? Snow lying thick over the countryside? Ponds under ice? Never mind. I knew where the streams and ponds were. I had also learned that many forms of life hibernate in the mud of ponds. All that was necessary was to improvise a net, again homemade, take a small lard bucket or two, and trudge off to the most accessible Walden.

The countryside was open in those days. On one visit to Lincoln 20 several years ago I thought it might be good to tramp out to that old pond where so many generations of boys had swum, waded, or collected. Forbidding fences warned me away. It was now part of a country club of the sort doubtless frequented by the successors of the parents of Jimmy Dawes. I speak no ill. If a country club had not acquired the pond and landscaped the greens, all would have been filled in by suburban developments in any case. But this was all wild once, and the feeling that is left is somehow lost and bittersweet. The pond is there. It is not the same pond. It is "reserved." It has been tamed for rich men to play beside. Either that or the developers come. One takes one's choice. No. Not really. One has no choice.

On that winter day so long ago I almost lost my life. I arrived at the 21 pond and chopped an experimental hole near the shore where I worked my clumsy mud-dredging apparatus back and forth. My plan was successful. I was drawing up a few sleeping water boatmen, whirligig beetles, and dragonfly larvae, along with other more microscopic animalcules. These I placed in my lard buckets and prepared to go home and begin the stocking of my little aquariums. A forced spring had come early to my captives.

There were skates on a strap hanging around my neck, and before 22 leaving I thought I would take one quick run over the pond. It was a very cold day, the ice firm. I had no reason to anticipate disaster. I made two swift passages out over what I knew to be deeper water. On the second pass, as I stepped up speed, there was a sudden, instantaneous splintering of ice. The leg to which I had just applied skating pressure went hip deep into the water. I came down upon my face. I lay there a moment half stunned. No one was with me. What if the rest of the ice broke? Even if one held on to the edge one would freeze very quickly.

I waited anxiously, trying not to extend the ice-fracture by strug- 23 gling. I was scared enough to yell, but it was useless. No one but a boy infused with the momentary idea of becoming a creator would be out on a day like this. Slowly I slid forward, arms spread, and withdrew my soaking leg from the hole. I must have struck an ice bubble with that one foot. The freezing weather fortunately permitted no general collapse of the ice. In one sweating moment I was safe, but I had to jog all the way home with my closed buckets.

After such an event there was no one's arms in which to fall at home. 24 If one did, there would be only hysterical admonitions, and I would be lucky to be allowed out. Slowly my inner life was continuing to adjust to this fact. I had to rely on silence. It was like creeping away from death out of an ice hole an inch at a time. You did it alone.

Critics, good friends in academia, sometimes ask, as is so frequently the custom, what impelled me to become a writer, what I read, who influenced me. Again, if pressed, I feel as though I were still inching out of that smashed ice bubble. Any educated man is bound to live in the cultural stream of his time. If I say, however, that I have read Thoreau, then it has been Thoreau who has been my mentor; this in spite of the fact that I did not read Thoreau until well into my middle years. Or it is Melville, Poe, anyone but me. If I mention a living writer whom I know, he is my inspiration, my fount of knowledge.

Or it is the editor of my first book who must have taught me this arcane art, because if one writes one must indeed publish a first book and that requires an editor. Or if one remains perplexed and has no answer, then one is stupid and one's work is written by a ghost who is paid well for his silence. In one institution where I taught long ago, it was generally assumed that all of us young science instructors were too manly to engage in this dubious art. Our wives produced our papers.

I myself believe implicitly in what G. K. Chesterton wrote many years ago: "The man who makes a vow makes an appointment with himself at some distant time or place." I think this vow of which Chesterton speaks was made unconsciously by me three separate times in my childhood. These unconscious vows may not have determined the precise mode of whatever achievement may be accorded mine, or what crossroads I may have encountered on the way. I mean to imply simply that when a vow is made one will someday meet what it has made of oneself and, most likely, curse one's failure. In any event, one will meet one's self. Let me tell about the first of those vows. It was a vow to read, and surely the first step to writing is a vow to read, not to encounter an editor.

It so happened that when I was five years old my parents, in a rare moment of doting agreement, looked upon their solitary child and decided not to pack him off to kindergarten in that year. One can call them feckless, kind, or wise, according to one's notions of the result. Surprisingly, I can remember the gist of their conversation because I caught in its implications the feel of that looming weather which, in after years, we know as life.

"Let him be free another year," they said. I remember my astonishment at their agreement. "There'll be all his life to learn about the rest. Let him be free to play just one more time." They both smiled in sudden affection. The words come back from very far away. I rather think they are my mother's, though there is a soft inflection in them. For once, just once, there was total unanimity between my parents. A rare thing. And I pretended not to have heard that phrase "about the rest." Nevertheless when I went out to play in the sunshine I felt chilled.

I did not have to go to kindergarten to learn to read. I had already mastered the alphabet at some earlier point. I had little primers of my own, the see-John-run sort of thing or its equivalent in that year of 1912. Yes, in that fashion I could read. Sometime in the months that followed, my elder brother paid a brief visit home. He brought with him a full adult version of *Robinson Crusoe*. He proceeded to read it to me in spare moments. I lived for that story. I hung upon my brother's words. Then abruptly, as was always happening in the world above me in the lamplight, my brother had departed. We had reached only as far as the discovery of the footprint on the shore.

He left me the book, to be exact, but no reader. I never asked mother 31 to read because her voice distressed me. Her inability to hear had made it harsh and jangling. My father read with great grace and beauty but he worked the long and dreadful hours of those years. There was only one thing evident to me. I had to get on with it, do it myself, otherwise I would never learn what happened to Crusoe.

I took Defoe's book and some little inadequate dictionary I found 32 about the house, and proceeded to worry and chew my way like a puppy through the remaining pages. No doubt I lost the sense of a word here and there, but I mastered it. I had read it on my own. Papa brought me *Twenty Thousand Leagues Under the Sea* as a reward. I read that, too. I began to read everything I could lay my hands on.

Well, that was a kind of vow made to myself, was it not? Not just to 33 handle ABC's, not to do the minimum for a school teacher, but to read books, read them for the joy of reading. When critics come to me again I shall say, "Put Daniel Defoe on the list, and myself, as well," because I kept the vow to read *Robinson Crusoe* and then to try to read all the books in the local library, or at least to examine them. I even learned to scan the papers for what a boy might hopefully understand.

That was 1912 and in the arctic winter of that year three prisoners 34 blasted their way through the gates of the state penitentiary in our town. They left the warden and his deputy dead behind them. A blizzard howled across the landscape. This was long before the time of the fast getaway by car. The convicts were out somewhere shivering in the driving snow with the inevitable ruthless hunters drawing a narrowing circle for the kill.

That night papa tossed the paper on the table with a sigh: "They 35 won't make it," he said and I could see by his eyes he was out there in the snow.

"But papa," I said, "the papers say they are bad men. They killed the 36 warden."

"Yes, son," he said heavily. Then he paused, censoring his words 37 carefully. "There are also bad prisons and bad wardens. You read your books now. Sit here by the lamp. Stay warm. Someday you will know more about people out in the cold. Try to think kindly, until then. These papers," he tapped the one he had brought in, "will not tell you everything. Someday when you are grown up you may remember this."

"Yes, papa," I said, and that was the second vow, though again I did 38 not know it. The memory of that night stayed on, as did the darkness and the howling wind. Long after those fleeing men were dead I would re-enter that year to seek them out. I would dream once more about them. I would be— Never mind, I would be myself a fugitive. When once, just once, through sympathy, one enters the cold, one is always there. One eternally keeps an appointment with one's self, but I was much too young to know.

By the time of the aquarium episode I was several years older. That, 40 too, was a vow, the sudden furious vow that induced me to create spring in midwinter. Record the homely writing of Eugene Smith, placing in my hand a tool and giving me command of tiny kingdoms. When I finally went away to graduate school I left them to the care of my grandmother Corey. I told her just how to manage them. She did so faithfully until her death. I think they brightened her final years—the little worlds we cared for. After the breakup of the house I searched for them. No one could tell me where they were. I would have greatly treasured them in the years remaining. I have never had an aquarium since, though expensive ones are now to be had.

I suppose, if I wrote till midnight and beyond, I could conjure up one 41 last unstable vow—when at nineteen I watched, outwardly unmoved, the letter of my father crumble in the flames. I started, did I not, to explain why a man writes and how there is always supposed to be someone he had derived his inspiration from, following which the good scholar may seek out the predecessor of one's predecessor, until nothing original is left. I have said we all live in a moving stream, as surely as a catfish groping with its whiskers in the muddy dark. I have seized this opportunity nevertheless to ensure that my unhappy parents' part in this dubious creation of a writer is not forgotten, nor the role of my half-brother, who accidentally stimulated me into a gigantic reading effort. As for Eugene Smith, he gave me the gift of wanting to understand other lives, even if he almost stole my own upon that winter pond.

I would like to tell this dead man that I fondled his little handbook 42 as I wrote this chapter. We are not important names, I would like to tell him. His is a very common one and all we are quickly vanishes. But still not quite. That is the wonder of words. They drift on and on beyond imagining. Did Eugene Smith of Hoboken think his book would have a lifelong impact on a boy in a small Nebraska town? I do not think so.

Ironically, one of the senior officers of the firm that published Smith's 43 work asked me not long ago if he could interest me in a project and would I come to lunch. The letter was pleasantly flattering. I wrote the man that I would be glad to lunch with him, though in all honesty I was heavily committed elsewhere. After his original invitation, I was never accorded the dignity of a reply.

Sometimes this is called the world of publishing. It is a pity. I would 44 have liked to tell this important man, over a cocktail, about a man named Smith whose book was published by his very own house before he, this generation's president, had been born. I would have been delighted to inform him that there was a stylized gold fish on the cover, and to what place the book had traveled, and how it had almost drowned, as well as uplifted, a small boy. Alas, this is a foolish dream. The presidents of great companies do not go to luncheons for such purposes. As for me, these strange chances in life intrigue me. I delight or shudder to hear of them.

I am sorry also, Jimmy Dawes, that your letter went unanswered. I 45 genuinely hope that you and your grown-up family are happy. I apologize for the mind-block that descended upon me there in Ohio, that old psychic wound that should have been overlooked had I been stronger. But at the last I tried. Perhaps that is what my parents meant when they said, "There'll be all his life to learn about the rest." I learned part when my father died, the part about the cold. Jimmy Dawes was still in my home town, a few blocks from where I lived, but no note of condolence ever came from him or his family. I kept your letter, Jimmy. Almost thirty years later I tried to call you long distance. And now at last the wound is closing. It is very late.

Questions

Rereading and Independent Analysis

1. In the first part of this essay, Eiseley moves between the perspective of the man who received the letter from Jimmy Dawes and the child who played with Dawes. Reread the first part of the essay, up to its mention of *The Home Aquarium,* marking each paragraph or section to identify its content and point of view. How does the pattern of alternating perspectives help you read the rest of the essay with full understanding?

2. Reread the essay, dividing it into sections according to the major topics Eiseley addresses: the letter, the aquarium, the pond, and learning to write. How are these distinct parts unified by the theme of the "vow," an appointment one makes with oneself and may or may not keep? What references to this idea are there in each of the sections you marked?

Discussion and Group Activities

1. This essay weaves together Eiseley's views of the relation of loneliness to writing—and of loneliness to not writing. Find specific places in the essay where these themes are brought together. As a class or in groups, list characteristics of letters and reasons for letter writing that show how writers of letters respond to and overcome loneliness.

2. Has Eiseley changed, as he describes it here, from the young boy excluded by his friends and his family to a man who is naturally integrated into the world he was once excluded from? What evidence do you find in this essay to support your answer?

Writing Suggestions

Response

Write a letter to someone you have not seen or been in touch with for a long time, explaining why you have not written before. Focus on your memories of the last time you were with the person and how they have stayed with you in other settings.

Analysis

In an autobiographical essay that you would want to publish in one of your favorite magazines, write an explanation for younger people of how a particular book has been important to you. In your essay, describe the book well enough to give your readers a good sense of its contents. Then analyze how it caused you to examine your experience, understand the world, or take specific actions.

Finding a Purpose

You have been invited to review this section of Chapter 3 so that it may be revised, either by expansion or by removing some of its selections. As part of your review, write an overview of the section in which you explain how reading letters like these helps one understand the multiple purposes for writing. Be explicit about the purposes the examples already included demonstrate, and make suggestions about other kinds of letters you would like to see included to show how a dialogue in letters is different from spoken conversation yet is not the same as a statement written for publication.

REFLECTIONS ON COMMUNITY EXPERIENCE

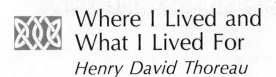

Where I Lived and What I Lived For
Henry David Thoreau

Perhaps the best-known American example of writing to reflect on personal experience is Henry David Thoreau's *Walden.* From July 4, 1845, until September 6, 1847, Thoreau (1817–1862) lived in a hut on Walden Pond, just outside his home town of Concord, Massachusetts. In 1854 he published *Walden,* a carefully crafted account of his life on the pond in which he collapses the two years into a naturalistic account of the pond's changes during the seasons of one year. Thoreau, who attended nearby Harvard, never found a profession (he temporarily taught school with his brother and at another time made pencils). He was a shy, reclusive, and self-directed person. His family and friends were always urging him to develop his obvious talents into decisive actions, but he remained outside the stream of life. He never married, never traveled, never willingly became socialized. His life has become a model for American rugged individualism.

Despite this image, Thoreau did participate in causes, rely on his family, and take an important part in the intellectual life of New England in the early nineteenth century. His essay "Civil Disobedience" (1849) defended his refusal to pay poll tax as a protest against slavery. He visited his family weekly during his stay on the pond, and his mother and sister brought him food and did his laundry while he was roughing it. Most important, he read widely in Eastern philosophy and became an influential friend of Ralph Waldo Emerson, whose Transcendental Club published *The Dial,* an outlet for American academic writing.

In his reflections on his stay on Walden Pond, Thoreau emphasizes themes from his reading. He explains that he went to the woods to discover life in its most stripped-down forms, which we can see in immediate experience, not in events that become important only because they are widely reported and discussed. As you read, notice how carefully Thoreau arranges his materials and selects details to craft his seeming simplicity. Thoreau was clearly writing to shape his experience into a complex statement with larger implications.

I went to the woods because I wished to live deliberately, to front only the essential facts of life, and see if I could not learn what it had to teach, and not, when I came to die, discover that I had not lived. I did not wish to live what was not life, living is so dear; nor did I wish to practise resignation, unless it was quite necessary. I wanted to live deep and suck out all the marrow of life, to live so sturdily and Spartan-like as to put to rout all that was not life, to cut a broad swath and shave close, to drive life into a corner, and reduce it to its lowest terms, and, if it proved to be mean, why then to get the whole and genuine meanness of it, and publish its meanness to the world; or if it were sublime, to know it by experience, and be able to give a true account of it in my next excursion. For most men, it appears to me, are in a strange uncertainty about it, whether it is of the devil or of God, and have *somewhat hastily* concluded that it is the chief end of man here to "glorify God and enjoy him forever." 1

Still we live meanly, like ants; though the fable tells us that we were long ago changed into men; like pygmies we fight with cranes; it is error upon error, and clout upon clout, and our best virtue has for its occasion a superfluous and evitable wretchedness. Our life is frittered away by detail. An honest man has hardly need to count more than his ten fingers, or in extreme cases he may add his ten toes, and lump the rest. Simplicity, simplicity, simplicity! I say, let your affairs be as two or three, and not a hundred or a thousand; instead of a million count half a dozen, and keep your accounts on your thumb-nail. In the midst of this chopping sea of civilized life, such are the clouds and storms and quicksands and thousand-and-one items to be allowed for, that a man has to live, if he would not founder and go to the bottom and not make his port at all, by dead 2 reckoning, and he must be a great calculator indeed who succeeds. Simplify, simplify. Instead of three meals a day, if it be necessary eat but one; instead of a hundred dishes, five; and reduce other things in proportion. Our life is like a German Confederacy, made up of petty states, with its boundary forever fluctuating, so that even a German cannot tell you how it is bounded at any moment. The nation itself, with all its so-called internal improvements, which, by the way, are all external and superficial, is just such an unwieldy and overgrown establishment, cluttered with furniture and tripped up by its own traps, ruined by luxury and heedless expense, by want of calculation and a worthy aim, as the million households in the land; and the only cure for it, as for them, is in a rigid economy, a stern and more than Spartan simplicity of life and elevation of purpose. It lives too fast. Men think that it is essential that the *Nation* have commerce, and export ice, and talk through a telegraph, and ride thirty miles an hour, without a doubt, whether *they* do or not; but whether we should live like baboons or like men, is a little uncertain. If we do not get out sleepers, and forge rails, and devote days and nights to the work, but go to tinkering upon our *lives* to improve *them,* who will build railroads? And if railroads are not built, how shall we get to Heaven in season? But if we stay at home and mind our business, who will want railroads? We do not ride on the railroad; it rides upon us. Did you ever think what those sleepers are that underlie the railroad? Each one is a man, an Irishman, or a Yankee man. The rails are laid on them, and they are covered with sand, and the cars run smoothly over them. They are sound sleepers, I assure you. And every few years a new lot is laid down and run over; so that, if some have the pleasure of riding on a rail, others have the misfortune to be ridden upon. And when they run over a man that is walking in his sleep, a supernumerary sleeper in the wrong position, and wake him up, they suddenly stop the cars, and make a hue and cry about it as if this were an exception. I am glad to know that it takes a gang of men for every five miles to keep the sleepers down and level in their beds as it is, for this is a sign that they may sometime get up again.

Why should we live with such hurry and waste of life? We are determined to be starved before we are hungry. Men say that a stitch in time saves nine, and so they take a thousand stitches to-day to save nine tomorrow. As for *work,* we haven't any of any consequence. We have the Saint Vitus' dance, and cannot possibly keep our heads still. If I should only give a few pulls at the parish bell-rope, as for a fire, that is, without setting the bell, there is hardly a man on his farm in the outskirts of Concord, notwithstanding that press of engagements which was his excuse so many times this morning, nor a boy, nor a woman, I might almost say, but would forsake all and follow that sound, not mainly to save property from the flames, but, if we will confess the truth, much more to see it burn, since burn it must, and we, be it known, did not set it on fire,—or to see it put out, and have a hand in it, if that is done as handsomely; yes, even if it were the parish church itself. Hardly a man takes a half-hour's nap after dinner, but when he wakes he holds up his head and asks, "What's the news?" as if the rest of mankind had stood his sentinels. Some give directions to be waked every half-hour, doubtless for no other purpose; and then, to pay for it, they tell what they have dreamed. After a night's sleep the news is as indispensable as the breakfast. "Pray tell me anything new that has happened to a man anywhere on this globe,"—and he reads it over his coffee and rolls, that a man has had his eyes gouged out this morning on the Wachito River; never dreaming the while that he lives in the dark unfathomed mammoth cave of this world, and has but the rudiment of an eye himself.

For my part, I could easily do without the post-office. I think that 4 there are very few important communications made through it. To speak critically, I never received more than one or two letters in my life—I wrote this some years ago—that were worth the postage. The penny-post is, commonly, an institution through which you seriously offer a man that penny for his thoughts which is so often safely offered in jest. And I am sure that I never read any memorable news in a newspaper. If we read of one man robbed, or murdered, or killed by accident, or one house burned, or one vessel wrecked, or one steamboat blown up, or one cow run over on the Western Railroad, or one mad dog killed, or one lot of grasshoppers in the winter,—we never need read of another. One is enough. If you are acquainted with the principle, what do you care for a myriad instances and applications? To a philosopher all *news*, as it is called, is gossip and they who edit and read it are old women over their tea. Yet not a few are greedy after this gossip. There was such a rush, as I hear, the other day at one of the offices to learn the foreign news by the last arrival, that several large squares of plate glass belonging to the establishment were broken by the pressure,—news which I seriously think a ready wit might write a twelvemonth, or twelve years, beforehand with sufficient accuracy. As for Spain, for instance, if you know how to throw in Don Carlos and the Infanta, and Don Pedro and Seville and Granada, from time to time in the right proportions,—they may have changed the names a little since I saw the papers,—and serve up a bull-fight when other entertainments fail, it will be true to the letter, and give us as good an idea of the exact state or ruin of things in Spain as the most succinct and lucid reports under this head in the newspapers: and as for England, almost the last significant scrap of news from that quarter was the revolution of 1649; and if you have learned the history of her crops for an average year, you never need attend to that thing again, unless your speculations are of a merely pecuniary character. If one may judge who rarely looks into the newspapers, nothing new does ever happen in foreign parts, a French revolution not excepted.

What news! how much more important to know what that is which 5 was never old! "Kieou-he-yu (great dignitary of the state of Wei) sent a man to Khoung-tseu to know his news. Khoung-tseu caused the messenger to be seated near him, and questioned him in these terms: What is your master doing? The messenger answered with respect: My master desires to diminish the number of his faults, but he cannot come to the end of them. The messenger being gone, the philosopher remarked: What a worthy messenger! What a worthy messenger!" The preacher, instead of vexing the ears of drowsy farmers on their day of rest at the end of the week,—for Sunday is the fit conclusion of an ill-spent week, and not the fresh and brave beginning of a new one,—with this one other draggle-tail of a sermon, should shout with thundering voice, "Pause! Avast! Why so seeming fast, but deadly slow?"

Shams and delusions are esteemed for soundest truths, while reality   6 is fabulous. If men would steadily observe realities only, and not allow themselves to be deluded, life, to compare it with such things as we know, would be like a fairy tale and the Arabian Nights' Entertainments. If we respected only what is inevitable and has a right to be, music and poetry would resound along the streets. When we are unhurried and wise, we perceive that only great and worthy things have any permanent and absolute existence, that petty fears and petty pleasures are but the shadow of the reality. This is always exhilarating and sublime. By closing the eyes and slumbering, and consenting to be deceived by shows, men establish and confirm their daily life of routine and habit everywhere, which still is built on purely illusory foundations. Children, who play life, discern its true law and relations more clearly than men, who fail to live it worthily, but who think that they are wiser by experience, that is, by failure. I have read in a Hindoo book, that "there was a king's son, who, being expelled in infancy from his native city, was brought up by a forester, and, growing up to maturity in that state, imagined himself to belong to the barbarous race with which he lived. One of his father's ministers having discovered him, revealed to him what he was, and the misconception of his character was removed, and he knew himself to be a prince. So soul," continues the Hindoo philosopher, "from the circumstances in which it is placed, mistakes its own character, until the truth is revealed to it by some holy teacher, and then it knows itself to be *Brahme.*" I perceive that we inhabitants of New England live this mean life that we do because our vision does not penetrate the surface of things. We think that this *is* which *appears* to be. If a man should walk through this town and see only the reality, where, think you, would the "Milldam" go to? If he should give us an account of the realities he beheld there, we should not recognize the place in his description. Look at a meeting-house, or a court-house, or a jail, or a shop, or a dwelling-house, and say what that thing really is before a true gaze, and they would all go to pieces in your account of them. Men esteem truth remote, in the outskirts of the system, behind the farthest star, before Adam and after the last man. In eternity there is indeed something true and sublime. But all these times and places and occasions are now and here. God himself culminates in the present moment, and will never be more divine in the lapse of all the ages. And we are enabled to apprehend at all what is sublime and noble only by the perpetual instilling and drenching of the reality that surrounds us. The universe constantly and obediently answers to our conceptions; whether we travel fast or slow, the track is laid for us. Let us spend our lives in conceiving then. The poet or the artist never yet had so fair and noble a design but some of his posterity at least could accomplish it.

Let us spend one day as deliberately as Nature, and not be thrown 7 off the track by every nutshell and mosquito's wing that falls on the rails. Let us rise early and fast, or break fast, gently and without perturbation; let company come and let company go, let the bells ring and the children cry,—determined to make a day of it. Why should we knock under and go with the stream? Let us not be upset and overwhelmed in that terrible rapid and whirlpool called a dinner, situated in the meridian shallows. Weather this danger and you are safe, for the rest of the way is down hill. With unrelaxed nerves, with morning vigor, sail by it, looking another way, tied to the mast like Ulysses. If the engine whistles, let it whistle till it is hoarse for its pains. If the bell rings, why should we run? We will consider what kind of music they are like. Let us settle ourselves, and work and wedge our feet downward through the mud and slush of opinion, and prejudice, and tradition, and delusion, and appearance, that alluvion which covers the globe, through Paris and London, through New York and Boston and Concord, through Church and State, through poetry and philosophy and religion, till we come to a hard bottom and rocks in place, which we can call *reality,* and say, This is, and no mistake; and then begin, having a *point d'appui,* below freshet and frost and fire, a place where you might found a wall or a state, or set a lamp-post safely, or perhaps a gauge, not a Nilometer, that future ages might know how deep a freshet of shams and appearances had gathered from time to time. If you stand right fronting and face to face to a fact, you will see the sun glimmer on both its surfaces, as if it were a cimeter, and feel its sweet edge dividing you through the heart and marrow, and so you will happily conclude your mortal career. Be it life or death we crave only reality. If we are really dying, let us hear the rattle in our throats and feel cold in the extremities; if we are alive, let us go about our business.

Time is but the stream I go a-fishing in. I drink at it; but while I drink 8 I see the sandy bottom and detect how shallow it is. Its thin current slides away, but eternity remains. I would drink deeper; fish in the sky, whose bottom is pebbly with stars. I cannot count one. I know not the first letter of the alphabet. I have always been regretting that I was not as wise as the day I was born. The intellect is a cleaver; it discerns and rifts its way into the secret of things. I do not wish to be any more busy with my hands than is necessary. My head is hands and feet. I feel all my best faculties concentrated in it. My instinct tells me that my head is an organ for burrowing, as some creatures use their snout and fore paws, and with it I would mine and burrow my way through these hills. I think that the richest vein is somewhere hereabouts; so by the divining-rod and thin rising vapors I judge; and here I will begin to mine.

Questions

Rereading and Independent Analysis

1. This essay takes the form of an argument to persuade others that "our life is frittered away by detail." Outline the parts of the argument. How does Thoreau establish his character, or *ethos,* at the beginning? Next, how does he support his point? List the "negative details" he uses as examples of subjects that are *not* important and become "frittering detail." Where does he begin making positive assertions, stating his position and supporting it? How does the last paragraph act as a "peroration," the conclusion of the argument that summarizes the character, points, and call to action in the whole essay?

2. Choose one of Thoreau's long paragraphs and analyze its style. That is, describe the grammar of the sentences (subject?/actor?; verb?/action?; object?/goal?). Note sentence parallelism, balance, and use of contrast. How does he proceed from generalizations to supporting details? What figures of speech (such as metaphors, similes, personification, or antithesis) does he use? (Look up definitions of these terms where necessary.) What effect on the reader is he aiming for in this paragraph by using these devices?

Discussion and Group Activities

1. Is Thoreau calling for action or inaction in this essay? Does he suggest that we learn about life by refusing to live it in everyday events, or is he redefining "life" and what living means? Find specific passages that support your judgment.

2. In groups, discuss times when you have felt like withdrawing from your usual surroundings and activities. What were your motives? How do they compare with the reasons Thoreau gives for going to the woods? If you have experienced a similar change in life, describe its effects. Did ordinary experience take on new qualities for you afterwards? What were they?

3. What is the relation between Thoreau's verbal style and the content of his argument? Use examples from your independent analysis (above) to come to a generalization about the style of this essay.

Writing Suggestions

Response

Choose an event from your own past that you have had some time to reflect on. Write an essay explaining its significance to others, beginning with "I [did *x*] because I wanted to discover. . . ." (For example, "I *joined the army* because I wanted to discover *whether a woman could survive boot camp.*") Be sure to clarify the experience for general readers and explain how it caused important changes in your life.

Analysis

Using your answers to Question 2, "Rereading," and to Question 3, "Discussion," write a stylistic analysis of this selection in which you explain how the point Thoreau supported was made more persuasive by his choices of language and verbal patterns. You need not analyze every paragraph of the essay, but expand your previous answers to give a thorough characterization of the style of the entire essay.

Finding a Purpose

Write an essay in which you explain to a friend why leaving his or her current situation would be a good idea because it would help your friend learn to face life with a clearer sense of reality. Use Thoreau's stated and implied arguments to support your own. Your essay is meant to persuade your friend, so use the arrangement of points most common in argument, as described in Question 1, "Rereading," and in the headnote to the Declaration of Independence (Chapter 2). Establish your character as a friend; tell the situation in which you are writing; make your case with evidence from facts, examples, and analogies; conclude with a view of what the changed future might be like.

R.M.S. *Titanic*
Hanson W. Baldwin

The story of the sinking of the "unsinkable" *Titanic* in the North Atlantic on a calm night in 1912 has become a modern moral legend that reminds us of early Greek tragedies in which human reason and pride conflict with inevitably stronger natural forces. Hanson Baldwin (b. 1903), a journalist who worked as an editor for the *New York Times,* published this account in *Harper's* magazine in 1934, 22 years after the tragic event.

Baldwin's brooding reflection on the sudden tragedy is a classical narrative. He wrote not as a reporter who was there but as a moral observer seeing a larger theme in a specific event. Increasingly vivid contacts with the iceberg—beginning with the message received the morning before the crash—mark the initial tension, the defining event, the crisis, and the painful climax of the story, the point at which the two huge inhabitants of the night sea graze each other. (For a review of traditional narrative form, see the introduction to Chapter 1.) In the final stage of this account, the iceberg only shows itself the next day when it and the *Californian,* a ship within sight but not hearing of the sinking *Titanic,* appear in the morning (and mourning) light.

The details and sequence of events in this written narrative were pieced together from reports by the comparatively few survivors who were interviewed later. Baldwin reveals his reflections on these facts in the dramatic tension and irony of his story. As you read, think about the difficulty

of writing about a drama as though you and the reader were there when you
have only heard reports of it. What features of Baldwin's writing create the
power of this account?

The White Star liner *Titanic,* largest ship the world had ever known, sailed   1
from Southampton on her maiden voyage to New York on April 10, 1912.
The paint on her strakes was fair and bright; she was fresh from Harland
and Wolff's Belfast yards, strong in the strength of her forty-six thousand
tons of steel, bent, hammered, shaped and riveted through the three years
of her slow birth.

There was little fuss and fanfare at her sailing; her sister ship, the   2
Olympic—slightly smaller than the *Titanic*—had been in service for some
months and to her had gone the thunder of the cheers.

But the *Titanic* needed no whistling steamers or shouting crowds to   3
call attention to her superlative qualities. Her bulk dwarfed the ships near
her as longshoremen singled up her mooring lines and cast off the turns
of heavy rope from the dock bollards. She was not only the largest ship
afloat, but was believed to be the safest. Carlisle, her builder, had given
her double bottoms and had divided her hull into sixteen watertight compartments, which made her, men thought, unsinkable. She had been built
to be and had been described as a gigantic lifeboat. Her designers' dreams
of a triple-screw giant, a luxurious, floating hotel, which could speed to
New York at twenty-three knots, had been carefully translated from blue
prints and mold-loft lines at the Belfast yards into a living reality.

The *Titanic*'s sailing from Southampton, though quiet, was not   4
wholly uneventful. As the liner moved slowly toward the end of her dock
that April day, the surge of her passing sucked away from the quay the
steamer *New York,* moored just to seaward of the *Titanic*'s berth. There
were sharp cracks as the manila mooring lines of the *New York* parted
under the strain. The frayed ropes writhed and whistled through the air
and snapped down among the waving crowd on the pier; the *New York*
swung toward the *Titanic*'s bow, was checked and dragged back to the
dock barely in time to avert a collision. Seamen muttered, thought it an
ominous start.

Past Spithead and the Isle of Wight the *Titanic* steamed. She called   5
at Cherbourg at dusk and then laid her course for Queenstown. At 1:30
P.M. on Thursday, April 11, she stood out of Queenstown harbor, screaming gulls soaring in her wake, with 2,201 persons—men, women, and
children—aboard.

Occupying the Empire bedrooms and Georgian suites of the first-   6
class accommodations were many well-known men and women—Colonel
John Jacob Astor and his young bride; Major Archibald Butt, military aide
to President Taft, and his friend, Frank D. Millet, the painter; John B.
Thayer, vice-president of the Pennsylvania Railroad, and Charles M. Hays,
president of the Grand Trunk Railway of Canada; W. T. Stead, the English
journalist; Jacques Futrelle, French novelist; H. B. Harris, theatrical man-

ager, and Mrs. Harris; Mr. and Mrs. Isidor Straus; and J. Bruce Ismay, chairman and managing director of the White Star line.

Down in the plain wooden cabins of the steerage class were 706 7 immigrants to the land of promise, and trimly stowed in the great holds was a cargo valued at $420,000: oak beams, sponges, wine, calabashes, and an odd miscellany of the common and the rare.

The *Titanic* took her departure on Fastnet Light and, heading into 8 the night, laid her course for New York. She was due at Quarantine the following Wednesday morning.

Sunday dawned fair and clear. The *Titanic* steamed smoothly toward 9 the west, faint streamers of brownish smoke trailing from her funnels. The purser held services in the saloon in the morning; on the steerage deck aft the immigrants were playing games and a Scotsman was puffing "The Campbells Are Coming" on his bagpipes in the midst of the uproar.

At 9 A.M. a message from the steamer *Caronia* sputtered into the 10 wireless shack:

> CAPTAIN, TITANIC—WESTBOUND STEAMERS REPORT BERGSGROWL-
> ERS AND FIELD ICE IN 42 DEGREES N. FROM 49 DEGREES TO 51 DEGREES
> W. 12TH APRIL.
>
> COMPLIMENTS—
>
> BARR.

It was cold in the afternoon; the sun was brilliant, but the *Titanic*, 11 her screws turning over at 75 revolutions per minute, was approaching the Banks.

In the Marconi cabin Second Operator Harold Bride, earphones 12 clamped on his head, was figuring accounts; he did not stop to answer when he heard MWL, Continental Morse for the nearby Leyland lines *Californian*, calling the *Titanic*. The *Californian* had some message about three icebergs; he didn't bother then to take it down. About 1:42 P.M. the rasping spark of those days spoke again across the water. It was the *Baltic*, calling the *Titanic*, warning her of ice on the steamer track. Bride took the message down and sent it up to the bridge. The officer-of-the-deck glanced at it; sent it to the bearded master of the *Titanic*, Captain E. C. Smith, a veteran of the White Star service. It was lunch time then; the Captain, walking along the promenade deck saw Mr. Ismay, stopped, and handed him the message without comment. Ismay read it, stuffed it in his pocket, told two ladies about the icebergs, and resumed his walk. Later, about 7:15 P.M., the Captain requested the return of the message in order to post it in the chartroom for the information of officers.

Dinner that night in the Jacobean dining room was gay. It was bitter 13 on deck, but the night was calm and fine; the sky was moonless but studded with stars twinkling coldly in the clear air.

After dinner some of the second-class passengers gathered in the 14 saloon, where the Reverend Mr. Carter conducted a "hymn singsong." It was almost ten o'clock and the stewards were waiting with biscuits and coffee as the group sang:

> O, hear us when we cry to Thee
>   For those in peril on the sea.

On the bridge Second Officer Lightoller—short, stocky, efficient— 15 was relieved at ten o'clock by First Officer Murdock. Lightoller had talked with other officers about the proximity of ice; at least five wireless ice warnings had reached the ship; lookouts had been cautioned to be alert; captains and officers expected to reach the field at any time after 9:30 P.M. At twenty-two knots, its speed unslackened, the *Titanic* plowed on through the night.

Lightoller left the darkened bridge to his relief and turned in. Cap- 16 tain Smith went to his cabin. The steerage was long since quiet; in the first and second cabins lights were going out; voices were growing still, people were asleep. Murdock paced back and forth on the bridge, peering out over the dark water, glancing now and then at the compass in front of Quartermaster Hichens at the wheel.

In the crow's nest, Lookout Frederick Fleet and his partner, Leigh, 17 gazed down at the water, still and unruffled in the dim, starlit darkness. Behind and below them the ship, a white shadow with here and there a last winking light; ahead of them a dark and silent and cold ocean.

There was a sudden clang. "Dong-dong. Dong-dong. Dong-dong. 18 Dong!" The metal clapper of the great ship's bell struck out 11:30. Mindful of the warnings, Fleet strained his eyes, searching the darkness for the dreaded ice. But there were only the stars and the sea.

In the wireless room, where Phillips, first operator, had relieved 19 Bride, the buzz of the *Californian*'s set again crackled in to the earphones:

Californian: "Say, old man, we are stuck here, surrounded by ice."*Titanic:* "Shut up, shut up; keep out. I am talking to Cape Race; you are jamming my signals."

Then, a few minutes later—about 11:40 . . .   20

Out of the dark she came, a vast, dim, white, monstrous shape, di- 21 rectly in the *Titanic*'s path. For a moment Fleet doubted his eyes. But she was a deadly reality, this ghastly *thing.* Frantically, Fleet struck three bells—*something dead ahead.* He snatched the telephone and called the bridge:

"Iceberg! Right ahead!"   22
The First Officer heard but did not stop to acknowledge the message. 23
"Hard astarboard!"   24
Hichens strained at the wheel; the bow swung slowly to port. The 25 monster was almost upon them now.

Murdock leaped to the engine-room telegraph. Bells clanged. Far 26
below in the engine room those bells struck the first warning. Danger! The
indicators on the dial faces swung round to "Stop!" Then "Full speed
astern!" Frantically the engineers turned great valve wheels; answered
the bridge bells. . . .

There was a slight shock, a brief scraping, a small list to port. Shell 27
ice—slabs and chunks of it—fell on the foredeck. Slowly the *Titanic*
stopped.

Captain Smith hurried out of his cabin.   28

"What has the ship struck?"   29

Murdock answered, "An iceberg, sir. I hard-astarboarded and re- 30
versed the engines, and I was going to hard-aport around it, but she was
too close. I could not do any more. I have closed the watertight doors."

Fourth Officer Boxhall, other officers, the carpenter, came to the 31
bridge. The Captain sent Boxhall and the carpenter below to ascertain the
damage.

A few lights switched on in the first and second cabins; sleepy passen- 32
gers peered through porthole glass; some casually asked the stewards:

"Why have we stopped?"   33

"I don't know, sir, but I don't suppose it is anything much."   34

In the smoking room a quorum of gamblers and their prey were still 35
sitting round a poker table; the usual crowd of kibitzers looked on. They
had felt the slight jar of the collision and had seen an eighty-foot ice
mountain glide by the smoking-room windows, but the night was calm and
clear, the *Titanic* was "unsinkable"; they hadn't bothered to go on deck.

But far below, in the warren of passages on the starboard side for- 36
ward, in the forward holds and boiler rooms, men could see that the
Titanic's hurt was mortal. In No. 6 boiler room, where the red glow from
the furnaces lighted up the naked, sweaty chests of coal-blackened firemen, water was pouring through a great gash about two feet above the
floor plates. This was no slow leak; the ship was open to the sea; in ten
minutes there were eight feet of water in No. 6. Long before then the
stokers had raked the flaming fires out of the furnaces and had scrambled
through the watertight doors into No. 5 or had climbed up the long steel
ladders to safety. When Boxhall looked at the mail room in No. 3 hold,
twenty-four feet above the keel, the mailbags were already floating about
in the slushing water. In No. 5 boiler room a stream of water spurted into
an empty bunker. All six compartments forward of No. 4 were open to the
sea; in ten seconds the iceberg's jagged claw had ripped a three-hundred-
foot slash in the bottom of the great *Titanic*.

Reports came to the bridge; Ismay in dressing gown ran out on deck 37
in the cold, still, starlit night, climbed up the bridge ladder.

"What has happened?"   38

Captain Smith: "We have struck ice."   39

"Do you think she is seriously damaged?"   40

Captain: "I'm afraid she is."   41

Ismay went below and passed Chief Engineer William Bell fresh 42
from an inspection of the damaged compartments. Bell corroborated the
Captain's statement; hurried back down the glistening steel ladders to his
duty. Man after man followed him—Thomas Andrews, one of the ship's
designers, Archie Frost, the builder's chief engineer, and his twenty assist-
ants—men who had no posts of duty in the engine room but whose traditions called them there.

On deck, in corridor and stateroom, life flowed again. Men, women, 43
and children awoke and questioned; orders were given to uncover the
lifeboats; water rose into the firemen's quarters; half-dressed stokers
streamed up on deck. But the passengers—most of them—did not know
that the *Titanic* was sinking. The shock of the collision had been so slight
that some were not awakened by it; the *Titanic* was so huge that she must
be unsinkable; the night was too calm, too beautiful, to think of death at
sea.

Captain Smith half ran to the door of the radio shack. Bride, partly 44
dressed, eyes dulled with sleep, was standing behind Phillips, waiting.

"Send the call for assistance."   45

The blue spark danced: "CQD—CQD—CQD—CQD—"   46

Miles away Marconi men heard. Cape Race heard it, and the steam- 47
ships *La Provence* and *Mt. Temple.*

The sea was surging into the *Titanic*'s hold. At 12:20 the water burst 48
into the seamen's quarters through a collapsed fore-and-aft wooden bulkhead. Pumps strained in the engine rooms—men and machinery making
a futile fight against the sea. Steadily the water rose.

The boats were swung out—slowly; for the deckhands were late in 49
reaching their stations, there had been no boat drill, and many of the crew
did not know to what boats they were assigned. Orders were shouted; the
safety valves had lifted, and steam was blowing off in a great rushing roar.
In the chart house Fourth Officer Boxhall bent above a chart, working
rapidly with pencil and dividers.

12:15 A.M. Boxhall's position is sent out to a fleet of vessels: "Come 50
at once; we have struck a berg."

To the Cunarder *Carpathia* (Arthur Henry Rostron, Master, New 51
York to Liverpool, fifty-eight miles away): "It's a CQD, old man. Position
41–46 N.; 50–14 W."

The blue spark dancing: "Sinking; cannot hear for noise of steam." 52

12:30 A.M. The word is passed: "Women and children in the boats." 53
Stewards finish waking their passengers below; life preservers are tied on;
some men smile at the precaution. "The *Titanic* is unsinkable." The *Mt.*
Temple starts for the *Titanic*; the *Carpathia,* with a double watch in her
stokeholds, radios, "Coming hard." The CQD changes the course of many
ships—but not of one; the operator of the *Californian,* near by, has just
put down his earphones and turned in.

The CQD flashes over land and sea from Cape Race to New York, 54
newspaper city rooms leap to life and presses whir.

On the *Titanic,* water creeps over the bulkhead between Nos. 5 and 55
6 firerooms. She is going down by the head; the engineers—fighting a
losing battle—are forced back foot by foot by the rising water. Down the
promenade deck, Happy Jock Hume, the bandsman, runs with his instrument.

12:45 A.M. Murdock, in charge on the starboard side, eyes tragic, but 56
calm and cool, orders boat No. 7 lowered. The women hang back, they
want no boat ride on an ice-strewn sea; the *Titanic* is unsinkable. The men
encourage them, explain that this is just a precautionary measure: "We'll
see you again at breakfast." There is little confusion; passengers stream
slowly to the boat deck. In the steerage the immigrants chatter excitedly.

A sudden sharp hiss—a streaked flare against the night; Boxhall sends 57
a rocket toward the sky. It explodes, and a parachute of white stars lights
up the icy sea. "God! Rockets!" The band plays ragtime.

No. 8 is lowered, and No. 5. Ismay, still in dressing gown, calls for 58
women and children, handles lines, stumbles in the way of an officer, is
told to "get the hell out of here." Third Officer Pitman takes charge of No.
5; as he swings into the boat Murdock grasps his hand. "Good-by and good
luck, old man."

No. 6 goes over the side. There are only twenty-eight people in a 59
lifeboat with a capacity of sixty-five.

A light stabs from the bridge; Boxhall is calling in Morse flashes, again 60
and again, to a strange ship stopped in the ice jam five to ten miles away.
Another rocket drops its shower of sparks above the ice-strewn sea and the
dying ship.

1:00 A.M. Slowly the water creeps higher; the fore ports of the *Titanic* 61
are dipping into the sea. Rope squeaks through blocks; lifeboats drop
jerkily seaward. Through the shouting on the decks comes the sound of the
band playing ragtime.

The "Millionaires' Special" leaves the ship—boat No. 1, with a capac- 62
ity of forty people, carries only Sir Cosmo and Lady Duff Gordon and ten
others. Aft, the frightened immigrants mill and jostle and rush for a boat.
An officer's fist flies out; three shots are fired into the air, and the panic is
quelled. . . . Four Chinese sneak unseen into a boat and hide in its bottom.

1:20 A.M. Water is coming into No. 4 boiler room. Stokers slice and 63
shovel as water laps about their ankles—steam for the dynamos, steam for
the dancing spark! As the water rises, great ash hoes rake the flaming coals
from the furnaces. Safety valves pop; the stokers retreat aft, and the
watertight doors clang shut behind them.

The rockets fling their splendor toward the stars. The boats are more 64
heavily loaded now, for the passengers know the *Titanic* is sinking.
Women cling and sob. The great screws aft are rising clear of the sea.
Half-filled boats are ordered to come alongside the cargo ports and take
on more passengers, but the ports are never opened—and the boats are
never filled. Others pull for the steamer's light miles away but never reach
it; the light disappears, the unknown ship steams off.

The water rises and the band plays ragtime.   65

1:30 A.M. Lightoller is getting the port boats off; Murdock the star- 66
board. As one boat is lowered into the sea a boat officer fires his gun along
the ship's side to stop a rush from the lower decks. A woman tries to take
her great Dane into a boat with her; she is refused and steps out of the boat
to die with her dog. Millet's "little smile which played on his lips all
through the voyage" plays no more; his lips are grim, but he waves good-
by and brings wraps for the women.

Benjamin Guggenheim, in evening clothes, smiles and says, "We've 67
dressed up in our best and are prepared to go down like gentlemen."

1:40 A.M. Boat 14 is clear, and then 13, 16, 15, and C. The lights still 68
shine, but the *Baltic* hears the blue spark say, "Engine room getting
flooded."

The *Olympic* signals, "Am lighting up all possible boilers as fast as 69
can."

Major Butt helps women into the last boats and waves good-by to 70
them. Mrs. Straus puts her foot on the gunwale of a lifeboat, then she
draws back and goes to her husband: "We have been together many years;
where you go I will go." Colonel John Jacob Astor puts his young wife in
a lifeboat, steps back, taps cigarette on fingernail: "Good-by, dearie; I'll
join you later."

1:45 A.M. The foredeck is under water, the fo'c'sle head almost 71
awash; the great stern is lifted high toward the bright stars; and still the
band plays. Mr. and Mrs. Harris approach a lifeboat arm in arm.

Officer: "Ladies first, please."   72

Harris bows, smiles, steps back: "Of course, certainly; ladies first."   73

Boxhall fires the last rocket, then leaves in charge of boat No. 2.   74

2:00 A.M. She is dying now; her bow goes deeper, her stern higher. 75
But there must be steam. Below in the stokeholds the sweaty firemen keep
steam up for the flaring lights and the dancing spark. The glowing coals
slide and tumble over the slanted grate bars; the sea pounds behind that
yielding bulkhead. But the spark dances on.

The *Asian* hears Phillips try the new signal—SOS.   76

Boat No. 4 has left now; boat D leaves ten minutes later. Jacques 77
Futrelle clasps his wife: "For God's sake, go! It's your last chance; go!"
Madame Futrelle is half forced into the boat. It clears the side.

There are about 660 people in the boats, and 1,500 still on the sinking 78
Titanic.

On top of the officers' quarters men work frantically to get the two 79
collapsibles stowed there over the side. Water is over the forward part of
A deck now; it surges up the companionways toward the boat deck. In the
radio shack, Bride has slipped a coat and lifejacket about Phillips as the first
operator sits hunched over his key, sending—still sending—"41–46 N.;
50–14 W. CQD—CQD—SOS—SOS—"

The Captain's tired white face appears at the radio-room door: "Men, 80
you have done your full duty. You can do no more. Now, it's every man
for himself." The Captain disappears—back to his sinking bridge, where
Painter, his personal steward, stands quietly waiting for orders. The spark

dances on. Bride turns his back and goes into the inner cabin. As he does so, a stoker, grimed with coal, mad with fear, steals into the shack and reaches for the lifejacket on Phillips' back. Bride wheels about and brains him with a wrench.

2:10 A.M. Below decks the steam is still holding, though the pressure 81 is falling—rapidly. In the gymnasium on the boat deck the athletic instructor watches quietly as two gentlemen ride the bicycles and another swings casually at the punching bag. Mail clerks stagger up the boat-deck stairways, dragging soaked mail sacks. The spark still dances. The band still plays—but not ragtime:

> Nearer my God to Thee,
>   Nearer to Thee . . .

A few men take up the refrain; others kneel on the slanting decks to 82 pray. Many run and scramble aft, where hundreds are clinging above the silent screws on the great uptilted stern. The spark still dances and the lights still flare; the engineers are on the job. The hymn comes to its close. Bandmaster Hartley, Yorkshireman violinist, taps his bow against a bulkhead, calls for "Autumn" as the water curls about his feet, and the eight musicians brace themselves against the ship's slant. People are leaping from the decks into the nearby water—the icy water. A woman cries, "Oh, save me, save me!" A man answers, "Good lady, save yourself. Only God can save you now." The band plays "Autumn":

> God of Mercy and Compassion!
>   Look with pity on my pain . . .

The water creeps over the bridge where the *Titanic*'s master stands; 83 heavily he steps out to meet it.

2:17 A.M. "CQ—" The *Virginian* hears a ragged, blurred CQ, then 84 an abrupt stop. The blue spark dances no more. The lights flicker out; the engineers have lost their battle.

2:18 A.M. Men run about blackened decks; leap into the night; are 85 swept into the sea by the curling wave which licks up the *Titanic*'s length. Lightoller does not leave the ship; the ship leaves him; there are hundreds like him, but only a few who live to tell of it. The funnels still swim above the water, but the ship is climbing to the perpendicular; the bridge is under and most of the foremast; the great stern rises like a squat leviathan. Men swim away from the sinking ship; others drop from the stern.

The band plays in the darkness, the water lapping upwards: 86

> Hold me up in mighty waters,
> Keep my eyes on things above,
> Righteousness, divine atonement,
> Peace and everlas . . .

The forward funnel snaps and crashes into the sea; its steel tons 87 hammer out of existence swimmers struggling in the freezing water.

Streams of sparks, of smoke and steam, burst from the after funnels. The ship upends to fifty—to sixty degrees.

Down in the black abyss of the stokeholds, of the engine rooms, 88 where the dynamos have whirred at long last to a stop, the stokers and the engineers are reeling against hot metal, the rising water clutching at their knees. The boilers, the engine cylinders, rip from their bed plates; crash through bulkheads; rumble—steel against steel.

The *Titanic* stands on end, poised briefly for the plunge. Slowly she 89 slides to her grave—slowly at first, and then more quickly—quickly— quickly.

2:20 A.M. The greatest ship in the world has sunk. From the calm, 90 dark waters, where the floating lifeboats move, there goes up, in the white wake of her passing, "one long continuous moan."

The boats that the *Titanic* had launched pulled safely away from the 91 slight suction of the sinking ship, pulled away from the screams that came from the lips of the freezing men and women in the water. The boats were poorly manned and badly equipped, and they had been unevenly loaded. Some carried so few seamen that women bent to the oars. Mrs. Astor tugged at an oar handle; the Countess of Rothes took a tiller. Shivering stokers in sweaty, coal-blackened singlets and light trousers steered in some boats; stewards in white coats rowed in others. Ismay was in the last boat that left the ship from the starboard side; with Mr. Carter of Philadelphia and two seamen he tugged at the oars. In one of the lifeboats an Italian with a broken wrist—disguised in a woman's shawl and hat— huddled on the floor boards, ashamed now that fear had left him. In another rode the only baggage saved from the *Titanic*—the carry-all of Samuel L. Goldenberg, one of the rescued passengers.

There were only a few boats that were heavily loaded; most of those 92 that were half empty made but perfunctory efforts to pick up the moaning swimmers, their officers and crew fearing that they would endanger the living if they pulled back into the midst of the dying. Some boats beat off the freezing victims; fear-crazed men and women struck with oars at the heads of swimmers. One woman drove her fist into the face of a half-dead man as he tried feebly to climb over the gunwale. Two other women helped him in and stanched the flow of blood from the ring cuts on his face.

One of the collapsible boats, which had floated off the top of the 93 officers' quarters when the *Titanic* sank, was an icy haven for thirty or forty men. The boat had capsized as the ship sank; men swam to it, clung to it, climbed upon its slippery bottom, stood knee-deep in water in the freezing air. Chunks of ice swirled about their legs; their soaked clothing clutched their bodies in icy folds. Colonel Archibald Gracie was cast up there, Gracie who had leaped from the stern as the *Titanic* sank; young Thayer who had seen his father die; Lightoller who had twice been sucked down with the ship and twice blown to the surface by a belch of air; Bride, the second operator, and Phillips, the first. There were many stokers, half-naked; it was a shivering company. They stood there in the icy sea, under the far stars, and sang and prayed—the Lord's Prayer. After a while a lifeboat came and picked them off, but Phillips was dead then or died soon afterward in the boat.

Only a few of the boats had lights; only one—No. 2—had a light that 94 was of any use to the *Carpathia,* twisting through the ice field to the rescue. Other ships were "coming hard" too; one, the *Californian,* was still dead to opportunity.

The blue sparks still danced, but not the *Titanic*'s. *Le Provence* to 95 *Celtic:* "Nobody has heard the *Titanic* for about two hours."

It was 2:40 when the *Carpathia* first sighted the green light from No. 96 2 boat; it was 4:10 when she picked up the first boat and learned that the *Titanic* had foundered. The last of the moaning cries had just died away then.

Captain Rostron took the survivors aboard, boatload by boatload. He 97 was ready for them, but only a small minority of them required much medical attention. Bride's feet were twisted and frozen; others were suffering from exposure; one died, and seven were dead when taken from the boats, and were buried at sea.

It was then that the fleet of racing ships learned they were too late; 98 the *Parisian* heard the weak signals of MPA, the *Carpathia,* report the death of the *Titanic.* It was then—or soon afterward, when her radio operator put on his earphones—that the *Californian,* the ship that had been within sight as the *Titanic* was sinking, first learned of the disaster.

And it was then, in all its white-green majesty, that the *Titanic*'s 99 survivors saw the iceberg, tinted with the sunrise, floating idly, pack ice jammed about its base, other bergs heaving slowly near by on the blue breast of the sea.

Questions

Rereading and Independent Analysis

1. How does Baldwin set the "scene" of this story? Review details of the setting, characters, and themes that he establishes. Reread the first section (through the 9 A.M. message). If you had read only this part, what would you expect to happen later? Use evidence from this section to explain your predictions. How is the tragedy to come forecast in the first part of the report?

2. Baldwin selectively establishes a cast of characters—the groups of people he treats together and individuals who reappear throughout the night. Identify these groups and individuals and make notes about the details Baldwin uses (for example, flicking a cigarette) to give them distinct personalities and make us more and less sympathetic to them.

Suggested Discussion and Group Activities

1. This report raises the question of reliability—the reliability of technology, of individuals and groups, and of nature's forces and patterns.

How does Baldwin balance these different sources of reliability and unreliability in the story? Does he suggest that the sinking was inevitable, or that it could have been avoided? What might have prevented it?

2. Imagine that you are going to make a film based on this story. In groups assigned to various parts of this project, decide how to present it. How would you design the set, cast the characters, and dress them? Would you use color? As a class, compare your decisions and give reasons for your choices.

Writing Suggestions

Response

Write a few paragraphs for your journal in which you describe an event or another story or film you know well to show how it created the same sense of tension and tragedy at its outcome that Baldwin created here. What were your feelings as you witnessed this unfolding action?

Analysis

One of the unifying themes of this report is "communication." Messages that were sent, not sent, ignored, and unheard appear to determine the outcome of the action. Write an analysis of the essay that reveals this theme, showing how communication (and its impossibility) in this situation are symbols of the tragic opposition of man and nature.

Finding a Purpose

Extreme situations like this tragedy rarely occur, but when they do they test the character of those involved. Choose two or three people or groups mentioned in this story and write an essay in which you define "courage" by showing that many different responses to extremity can reveal integrity. Your examples should show how Baldwin's selection of the details of action and their concrete results indicates inner qualities that no one speaks of.

 ## The Trench Scene
Paul Fussell

Paul Fussell's book *The Great War and Modern Memory* (1975) won the 1976 National Book Award, the National Book Critics Circle Award for Criticism, and the Ralph Waldo Emerson Award of Phi Beta Kappa. Fussell (b. 1924) has said that he wrote this book from three perspectives: While *The Great War* is about World War I, it is dedicated to the memory of Sergeant Edward Hudson, who was killed at Fussell's side in France during World War II. But his writing was, he says, stimulated by his desire to understand his own complicated reactions to the Vietnamese War. His book is in every sense a memorial treatment of World War I and all wars.

World War I is often called the worst conflict in history because it combined the fierceness of traditional, individual combat with new, destructive technologies, such as poison gases, whose terrible effects were at first unclear. Fussell's purpose was to place the many literary treatments written during and after the war next to the actual events, to show how these events were surprisingly "literary," or patterned, themselves. His sources were the many detailed accounts and personal memories that the war stimulated, which he wove into a picture of the way it appears to us now, at a distance.

Fussell, who has written several books of literary criticism and scholarship, is John DeWitt Professor of English Literature at Rutgers University. His reflections on war and on the ways it becomes the subject of later stories—from Homer's account of Odysseus to Murrow's reports from London during World War II (see Chapter 1)—are vividly expressed in this examination of events he did not see but learned about from reading. As you read, keep in mind the significance of his title—he is showing how the Great War has become a part of collective modern memory.

1 The idea of "the trenches" has been assimilated so successfully by metaphor and myth ("Georgian complacency died in the trenches") that it is not easy now to recover a feeling for the actualities. *Entrenched,* in an expression like *entrenched power,* has been a dead metaphor so long that we must bestir ourselves to recover its literal sense. It is time to take a tour.

2 From the winter of 1914 until the spring of 1918 the trench system was fixed, moving here and there a few hundred yards, moving on great occasions as much as a few miles. London stationers purveying maps felt secure in stocking "sheets of 'The Western Front' with a thick wavy black line drawn from North to South alongside which was printed 'British Line.' "[1] If one could have gotten high enough to look down at the whole line at once, one would have seen a series of multiple parallel excavations running for 400 miles down through Belgium and France, roughly in the shape of an *S* flattened at the sides and tipped to the left. From the North Sea coast of Belgium the line wandered southward, bulging out to contain Ypres, then dropping down to protect Béthune, Arras, and Albert. It continued south in front of Montidier, Compiègne, Soissons, Reims, Verdun, St. Mihiel, and Nancy, and finally attached its southernmost end to the Swiss border at Beurnevisin, in Alsace. The top forty miles—the part north of Ypres—was held by the Belgians; the next ninety miles, down to the river Ancre, were British; the French held the rest, to the south.

3 Henri Barbusse estimates that the French front alone contained about 6250 miles of trenches.[2] Since the French occupied a little more than half the line, the total length of the numerous trenches occupied by the British must come to about 6000 miles. We thus find over 12,000 miles of trenches on the Allied side alone. When we add the trenches of the Central Powers, we arrive at a figure of about 25,000 miles, equal to a trench sufficient to circle the earth. Theoretically it would have been possible to walk from Belgium to Switzerland entirely below ground, but although the lines were "continuous," they were not entirely seamless:

occasionally mere shell holes or fortified strong-points would serve as a connecting link. Not a few survivors have performed the heady imaginative exercise of envisioning the whole line at once. Stanley Casson is one who, imagining the whole line from his position on the ground, implicitly submits the whole preposterous conception to the criterion of the "normally" rational and intelligible. As he remembers, looking back from 1935,

> Our trenches stood on a faint slope, just overlooking German ground, with a vista of vague plainland below. Away to right and left stretched the great lines of defense as far as eye and imagination could stretch them. I used to wonder how long it would take for me to walk from the beaches of the North Sea to that curious end of all fighting against the Swiss boundary; to try to guess what each end looked like; to imagine what would happen if I passed a verbal message, in the manner of the parlor game, along to the next man on my right to be delivered to the end man of all up against the Alps. Would anything intelligible at all emerge?[3]

Another imagination has contemplated a similar absurd transmission of sound all the way from north to south. Alexander Aitken remembers the Germans opposite him celebrating some happy public event in early June, 1916, presumably either the (ambiguous) German success at the naval battle of Jutland (May 31–June 1) or the drowning of Lord Kitchener, lost on June 5 when the cruiser *Hampshire* struck a mine and sank off the Orkney Islands. Aitken writes, "There had been a morning in early June when a tremendous tin-canning and beating of shell-gongs had begun in the north and run south down their lines to end, without doubt, at Belfort and Mulhausen on the Swiss frontier."[4] Impossible to believe, really, but in this mad setting, somehow plausible.

. . . .

There were normally three lines of trenches. The front-line trench 4 was anywhere from fifty yards or so to a mile from its enemy counterpart. Several hundred yards behind it was the support trench line. And several hundred yards behind that was the reserve line. There were three kinds of trenches: firing trenches, like these; communication trenches, running roughly perpendicular to the line and connecting the three lines; and "saps," shallower ditches thrust out into No Man's Land, providing access to forward observation posts, listening posts, grenade-throwing posts, and machine gun positions. The end of a sap was usually not manned all the time: night was the favorite time for going out. Coming up from the rear, one reached the trenches by following a communication trench sometimes a mile or more long. It often began in a town and gradually deepened. By the time pedestrians reached the reserve line, they were well below ground level.

A firing trench was supposed to be six to eight feet deep and four or 5 five feet wide. On the enemy side a parapet of earth or sandbags rose about two or three feet above the ground. A corresponding "parados" a foot or so high was often found on top of the friendly side. Into the sides of trenches were dug one- or two-man holes ("funk-holes"), and there were deeper dugouts, reached by dirt stairs, for use as command posts and officers' quarters. On the enemy side of a trench was a fire-step two feet high on which the defenders were supposed to stand, firing and throwing grenades, when repelling attack. A well-built trench did not run straight for any distance: that would have been to invite enfilade fire. Every few yards a good trench zig-zagged. It had frequent traverses designed to contain damage within a limited space. Moving along a trench thus involved a great deal of weaving and turning. The floor of a proper trench was covered with wooden duckboards, beneath which were sumps a few feet deep designed to collect water. The walls, perpetually crumbling, were supported by sandbags, corrugated iron, or bundles of sticks or rushes. Except at night and in half-light, there was of course no looking over the top except through periscopes, which could be purchased in the "Trench Requisites" section of the main London department stores. The few snipers on duty during the day observed No Man's Land through loopholes cut in sheets of armor plate.

The entanglements of barbed wire had to be positioned far enough 6 out in front of the trench to keep the enemy from sneaking up to grenade-throwing distance. Interestingly, the two novelties that contributed most to the personal menace of the war could be said to be American inventions. Barbed wire had first appeared on the American frontier in the late nineteenth century for use in restraining animals. And the machine gun was the brainchild of Hiram Stevens Maxim (1840–1916), an American who, disillusioned with native patent law, established his Maxim Gun Company in England and began manufacturing his guns in 1889. He was finally knighted for his efforts. At first the British regard for barbed wire was on a par with Sir Douglas Haig's understanding of the machine gun. In the autumn of 1914, the first wire Private Frank Richards saw emplaced before the British positions was a single strand of agricultural wire found in the vicinity.[5] Only later did the manufactured article begin to arrive from England in sufficient quantity to create the thickets of mock-organic rusty brown that helped give a look of eternal autumn to the front.

The whole British line was numbered by sections, neatly, from right 7 to left. A section, normally occupied by a company, was roughly 300 yards wide. One might be occupying front-line trench section 51; or support trench S 51, behind it; or reserve trench SS 51, behind both. But a less formal way of identifying sections of trench was by place or street names with a distinctly London flavor. *Piccadilly* was a favorite; popular also were *Regent Street* and *Strand;* junctions were *Hyde Park Corner* and *Marble Arch.* Greater wit—and deeper homesickness—sometimes surfaced in the naming of the German trenches opposite. Sassoon remembers "Durley" 's account of the attack at Delville Wood in September, 1916: "Our objective was Pint Trench, taking Bitter and Beer and clearing Ale and Vat, and also Pilsen Lane."[6] Directional and traffic control signs were everywhere in the trenches, giving the whole system the air of a parody modern city, although one literally "underground."

The trenches I have described are more or less ideal, although not so ideal as the famous exhibition trenches dug in Kensington Gardens for the edification of the home front. These were clean, dry, and well furnished, with straight sides and sandbags neatly aligned. R. E. Vernede writes his wife from the real trenches that a friend of his has just returned from viewing the set of ideal ones. He "found he had never seen anything at all like it before."[7] And Wilfred Owen calls the Kensington Gardens trenches "the laughing stock of the army."[8] Explaining military routines to civilian readers, Ian Hay labors to give the impression that the real trenches are identical to the exhibition ones and that they are properly described in the language of normal domesticity a bit archly deployed:

> The firing-trench is our place of business—our office in the city, so to speak. The supporting trench is our suburban residence, whither the weary toiler may betake himself periodically (or, more correctly, in relays) for purposes of refreshment and repose.[9]

The reality was different. The British trenches were wet, cold, smelly, and thoroughly squalid. Compared with the precise and thorough German works, they were decidedly amateur, reflecting a complacency about the British genius for improvisation. Since defense offered little opportunity for the display of pluck or swank, it was by implication derogated in the officers' *Field Service Pocket Book*. One reason the British trench system was so haphazard and ramshackle was that it had originally taken form in accord with the official injunction: "The choice of a [defensive] position and its preparation must be made with a view to economizing the power expended on defense in order that the power of offense may be increased." And it was considered really useless to build solid fortifications anyway: "An occasional shell may strike and penetrate the parápet, but in the case of shrapnel the damage to the parapet will be trifling, while in the case of a shell filled with high explosive, the effect will be no worse on a thin parapet than on a thick one. It is, therefore, useless to spend time and labor on making a thick parapet simply to keep out shell."[10] The repeatedly revived hopes for a general breakout and pursuit were another reason why the British trenches were so shabby. A typical soldier's view is George Coppard's:

> The whole conduct of our trench warfare seemed to be based on the concept that we, the British, were not stopping in the trenches for long, but were tarrying awhile on the way to Berlin and that very soon we would be chasing Jerry across country. The result, in the long term, meant that we lived a mean and impoverished sort of existence in lousy scratch holes.[11]

In contrast, the German trenches, as the British discovered during the attack on the Somme, were deep, clean, elaborate, and sometimes even comfortable. As Coppard found on the Somme, "Some of the [German] dugouts were thirty feet deep, with as many as sixteen bunk-beds, as well as door bells, water tanks with taps, and cupboards and mirrors."[12] They also had boarded walls, floors, and ceilings; finished wooden staircases; electric light; real kitchens; and wallpaper and overstuffed furniture, the whole protected by steel outer doors. Foreign to the British style was a German dugout of the sort recalled by Ernst Jünger:

> At Monchy . . . I was master of an underground dwelling approached by forty steps hewn in the solid chalk, so that even the heaviest shells at this depth made no more than a pleasant rumble when we sat there over an interminable game of cards. In one wall I had a bed hewn out. . . . At its head hung an electric light so that I could read in comfort till I was sleepy. . . . The whole was shut off from the outer world by a dark-red curtain with rod and rings. . . .[13]

As these examples suggest, there were "national styles" in trenches as in other things. The French trenches were nasty, cynical, efficient, and temporary. Kipling remembered the smell of delicious cooking emanating from some in Alsace.[14] The English were amateur, vague, *ad hoc,* and temporary. The German were efficient, clean, pedantic, and permanent. Their occupants proposed to stay where they were.

Normally the British troops rotated trench duty. After a week of "rest" behind the lines, a unit would move up—at night—to relieve a unit in the front-line trench. After three days to a week or more in that position, the unit would move back for a similar length of time to the support trench, and finally back to the reserve. Then it was time for a week of rest again. In the three lines of trenches the main business of the soldier was to exercise self-control while being shelled. As the poet Louis Simpson has accurately remembered:

> Being shelled is the main work of an infantry soldier, which no one talks about. Everyone has his own way of going about it. In general, it means lying face down and contracting your body into as small a space as possible. In novels [*The Naked and the Dead* is an example] you read about soldiers, at such moments, fouling themselves. The opposite is true. As all your parts are contracting, you are more likely to be constipated.[15]

Simpson is recalling the Second War, but he might be recalling the First. While being shelled, the soldier either harbored in a dugout and hoped for something other than a direct hit or made himself as small as possible in a funk-hole. An unlucky sentry or two was supposed to be out in the open trench in all but the worst bombardments, watching through a periscope or loophole for signs of an attack. When only light shelling was in progress, people moved about the trenches freely, and we can get an idea of what life there was like if we posit a typical twenty-four hours in a front-line trench.

The day began about an hour before first light, which often meant at about 4:30. This was the moment for the invariable ritual of morning stand-to (short for the archaic formal command for repelling attack, "Stand to Arms"). Since dawn was the favorite time for launching attacks, at the order to stand-to everyone, officers, men, forward artillery observers, visitors, mounted the fire-step, weapon ready, and peered toward the German line. When it was almost full light and clear that the Germans were not going to attack that morning, everyone "stood down" and began preparing breakfast in small groups. The rations of tea, bread, and bacon, brought up in sandbags during the night, were broken out. The bacon was fried in mess-tin lids over small, and if possible smokeless, fires. If the men were lucky enough to be in a division whose commanding general permitted the issue of the dark and strong government rum, it was doled out from a jar with the traditional iron spoon, each man receiving about two tablespoonsful. Some put it into their tea, but most swallowed it straight. It was a precious thing, and serving it out was almost like a religious ceremonial, as David Jones recalls in *In Parenthesis*, where a corporal is performing the rite:

> O have a care—don't spill the precious
> O don't jog his hand—ministering;
> do take care.
> O please—give the poor bugger elbow room.

Larger quantities might be issued to stimulate troops for an assault, and one soldier remembers what the air smelled like during a British attack: "Pervading the air was the smell of rum and blood."[16] In 1922 one medical officer deposed before a parliamentary committee investigating the phenomenon of "shell shock": "Had it not been for the rum ration I do not think we should have won the war."[17]

During the day the men cleaned weapons and repaired those parts 13 of the trench damaged during the night. Or they wrote letters, deloused themselves, or slept. The officers inspected, encouraged, and strolled about looking nonchalant to inspirit the men. They censored the men's letters and dealt with the quantities of official inquiries brought them daily by runner. How many pipe-fitters had they in their company? Reply immediately. How many hairdressers, chiropodists, bicycle repairmen? Daily "returns" of the amount of ammunition and the quantity of trench stores had to be made. Reports of the nightly casualties had to be sent back. And letters of condolence, which as the war went on became formletters of condolence, had to be written to the relatives of the killed and wounded. Men went to and fro on sentry duty or working parties, but no one showed himself above the trench. After evening stand-to, the real work began.

Most of it was above ground. Wiring parties repaired the wire in 14 front of the position. Digging parties extended saps toward the enemy. Carrying parties brought up not just rations and mail but the heavy engineering materials needed for the constant repair and improvement of the trenches: timbers, A-frames, duckboards, stakes and wire, corrugated iron, sandbags, tarpaulins, pumping equipment. Bombs and ammunition and flares were carried forward. All this ant-work was illuminated brightly from time to time by German flares and interrupted very frequently by machine gun or artillery fire. Meanwhile night patrols and raiding parties were busy in No Man's Land. As morning approached, there was a nervous bustle to get the jobs done in time, to finish fitting the timbers, filling the sandbags, pounding in the stakes, and then returning mauls and picks and shovels to the Quartermaster Sergeant. By the time of stand-to, nothing human was visible above ground anywhere, but every day each side scrutinized the look of the other's line for significant changes wrought by night.

Flanders and Picardy have always been notorious for dampness. It is 15 not the least of the ironies of the war for the British that their trenches should have been dug where the water-table was the highest and the annual rainfall the most copious. Their trenches were always wet and often flooded several feet deep. Thigh-boots or waders were issued as standard articles of uniform. Wilfred Owen writes his mother from the Somme at the beginning of 1917: "The waders are of course indispensable. In 2½ miles of trench which I waded yesterday there was not one inch of dry ground. There is a mean depth of two feet of water."[18] Pumps worked day and night but to little effect. Rumor held that the Germans not only could make it rain when they wanted it to—that is, all the time— but had contrived some shrewd technical method for conducting the water in their lines into the British positions—perhaps piping it under- ground. Ultimately there was no defense against the water but humor. "Water knee deep and up to the waist in places," one soldier notes in his diary. "Rumors of being relieved by the Grand Fleet."[19] One doesn't want to dwell excessively on such discomforts, but here it will do no harm to try to imagine what, in these conditions, going to the latrine was like.

The men were not the only live things in the line. They were accom- 16 panied everywhere by their lice, which the professional delousers in rest positions behind the lines, with their steam vats for clothes and hot baths for troops, could do little to eliminate. The entry *lousy* in Eric Partridge's *Dictionary of Slang and Unconventional English* speaks volumes: "Con- temptible; mean; filthy. . . . Standard English till 20th C, when, especially after the Great War, colloquial and used as a mere pejorative." *Lousy with,* meaning *full of,* was "originally military" and entered the colloquial word-hoard around 1915: "That ridge is lousy with Fritz."

The famous rats also gave constant trouble. They were big and black, 17 with wet, muddy hair. They fed largely on the flesh of cadavers and on dead horses. One shot them with revolvers or coshed them to death with pick-handles. Their hunger, vigor, intelligence, and courage are recalled in numerous anecdotes. One officer notes from the Ypres Salient: "We are fairly plagued with rats. They have eaten nearly everything in the mess, including the table-cloth and the operations orders! We borrowed a large cat and shut it up at night to exterminate them, and found the place empty next morning. The rats must have eaten it up, bones, fur, and all, and dragged it to their holes."[20]

One can understand rats eating heartily there. It is harder to under- [18] stand men doing so. The stench of rotten flesh was over everything, hardly repressed by the chloride of lime sprinkled on particularly offensive sites. Dead horses and dead men—and parts of both—were sometimes not buried for months and often simply became an element of parapets and trench walls. You could smell the front line miles before you could see it. Lingering pockets of gas added to the unappetizing atmosphere. Yet men ate three times a day, although what they ate reflected the usual gulf between the ideal and the actual. The propagandist George Adam announced with satisfaction that "the food of the army is based upon the conclusions of a committee, upon which sat several eminent scientists." The result, he asserted, is that the troops are "better fed than they are at home."[21] Officially, each man got daily:

1 ¼ pounds fresh meat (or 1 pound preserved meat),
1 ¼ pounds bread,
4 ounces bacon,
3 ounces cheese,
½ pound fresh vegetables (or 2 ounces dried),

together with small amounts of tea, sugar, and jam. But in the trenches there was very seldom fresh meat, not for eating, anyway; instead there was "Bully" (tinned corned beef) or "Maconochie" (ma-con'-o-chie), a tinned meat-and-vegetable stew named after its manufacturer. If they did tend to grow tedious in the long run, both products were surprisingly good. The troops seemed to like the Maconochie best, but the Germans favored the British corned beef, seldom returning from a raid on the British lines without taking back as much as they could carry. On trench duty the British had as little fresh bread as fresh meat. "Pearl Biscuits" were the substitute. They reminded the men of dog biscuits, although, together with the Bully beef, they were popular with the French and Belgian urchins, who ran (or more often strolled) alongside the railway trains bringing troops up to the front, soliciting gifts by shouting, "Tom-mee! Bull-ee! Bee-skee!" When a company was out of the line, it fed better. It was then serviced by its company cookers—stoves on wheels—and often got something approaching the official ration, as it might also in a particularly somnolent part of the line, when hot food might come up at night in the large covered containers known as Dixies.

.   .   .   .

To be in the trenches was to experience an unreal, unforgettable [19] enclosure and constraint, as well as a sense of being unoriented and lost. One saw two things only: the walls of an unlocalized, undifferentiated earth and the sky above. Fourteen years after the war J. R. Ackerley was wandering through an unfrequented part of a town in India. "The streets became narrower and narrower as I turned and turned," he writes, "until I felt I was back in the trenches, the houses upon either side being so much of the same color and substance as the rough ground between." That lost feeling is what struck Major Frank Isherwood, who writes his wife in December, 1914: "The trenches are a labyrinth, I have already lost myself repeatedly. . . . you can't get out of them and walk about the country or see anything at all but two muddy walls on each side of you." What a survivor of the Salient remembers fifty years later are the walls of dirt and the ceiling of sky, and his eloquent optative cry rises as if he were still imprisoned there: "To be out of this present, ever-present, eternally present misery, this stinking world of sticky, trickling earth ceilinged by a strip of threatening sky." As the only visible theater of variety, the sky becomes all-important. It was the sight of the sky, almost alone, that had the power to persuade a man that he was not already lost in a common grave.

[1] H.H. Cooper, IWM.

[2] *Under Fire,* trans. W. Fitzwater Wray (1926), p. 25.

[3] *Steady Drummer* (1935), pp. 49–50.

[4] *Gallipoli to the Somme* (1963), p. 97.

[5] *Old Soldiers Never Die* (1933), pp. 44–45.

[6] *Memoirs of an Infantry Officer,* p. 151.

[7] *Letters to His Wife* (1917), p.112.

[8] *Wilfred Owen: Collected Letters,* ed. Harold Owen and John Bell (1967), p. 429.

[9] *The First Hundred Thousand* (New York, 1916), p. 97.

[10] 1914, pp. 88, 91.

[11] *With a Machine Gun to Cambrai,* p. 87.

[12] *Ibid.*

[13] *Copse* 125, trans. Basil Creighton (1930), pp. 18–19.

[14] C. E. Carrington, *The Life of Rudyard Kipling* (New York, 1955), p. 338.

[15] *Air with Armed Men* (1972), p. 114.

[16] H. H. Cooper, IWM.

[17] Quoted by Moore, *The Thin Yellow Line,* p. 203.

[18] Owen and Bell, eds., *Collected Letters,* p. 426.

[19] R. W. Mitchell, IWM.

[20] P. H. Pilditch, IWM.

[21] *Behind the Scenes at the Front* (New York, 1915), pp. 92–93.

Questions

Rereading and Independent Analysis

1. This selection is from a section of Fussell's book entitled "The Troglodyte World." This title associates the trenches with primitive, underground qualities. Reread the selection, making a list of details that stimulate you to see the trenches as a "Troglodyte World." Group the items on your list according to the features of the trenches that Fussell wanted to emphasize.

2. Fussell moves between "straight" presentation of information about the trenches to comments about the images the trenches created

in the memories of those who were in them. Make an outline of this selection, noting its shifts between these perspectives of imagined and actual experience. Does it appear that literary writing comments on realities, the reverse, or both? Why?

Suggested Discussion and Group Activities

1. After reading this selection, which of its sections remain most vivid in your own memory? Discuss specific writing strategies that assure that a reader will remember these particular parts of Fussell's book. Generalize about passages you most often remember from any reading on the basis of the class's responses.

2. Fussell never states a conclusion that he expects you to draw from learning about the reality of the trench "scene." What inferences do you draw from his explanations and details? What conclusion do you think he wanted you to draw?

Writing Suggestions

Response

There is much about Fussell's description of the trenches that can remind us of science fiction books and films. Write your response to the frightening elements in Fussell's account, keeping in mind that he is describing a setting that was experienced by people who were just past adolescence, as many of your class members are. What do you think it would have been like to have been in one of the trenches yourself?

Analysis

1. Choose one of the sources that Fussell cites in his footnotes for further reading. Then write a summary of this source for the class, telling them what further information they would find in it. Bring copies to share with interested classmates.

2. Fussell notes that the trenches of the British, French, and Germans were metaphoric representations of their national "characters" and posture in the war. Choose another example—such as cars, clothes, or music—and write a comparison and contrast essay that relates the categories of this particular object to the kinds of people who might choose it. Your essay should be aimed to amuse as well as inform your classmates.

Finding a Purpose

Reread Fussell's description and write an essay in which you compare it to another selection that deals with war—for instance, the Murrow report from London (Chapter 1) or another account you have read. The purpose of your comparison is to tell your friends what subject matter and attitude toward war they will find when reading each of these presentations of the realities of war. Be sure to cite specific details that capture the flavor of both readings. (If you wish, compare Fussell to one of his sources, or read Michael Herr's *Dispatches,* which is about the Vietnamese War, or find another selection suggested by your teacher.)

The Old Folks Behind Home
Roger Angell

Baseball is, of course, an always changing event, like any sport. In the United States, it is the most important news of the summer to many, who follow both teams and players, run by run and pitch by pitch, from spring training to the World Series in the fall. But Roger Angell (b. 1920), an editor for the *New Yorker* magazine who writes satires, parodies, and poems as well as sports commentary, does not approach baseball as a news reporter. His many essays about it take the perspective of an especially well-informed and contemplative fan who is thinking over what he has seen and learned.

In this selection from his collection of essays, *The Summer Game* (1972), Angell includes in the game the fans who, in retirement in Florida, attend baseball during the winter. They watch young and old players begin another season with memory and hope that characterize the game for us all. As you read, notice that Angell's observations and reported conversations appear to take place, as the practice and the fans' reactions do, at a leisurely rate. This slow pace in Angell's writing recreates the atmosphere that baseball generally evokes. His title, themes, and selection of details contribute to our sense of baseball being a "game" rather than a "contest" in both the mood of the players and the pleasure of its observing fans.

Sarasota, March 20

This winter, a local mortician named Willie Robarts sent Sarasota residents   1
and visitors a mailing of cards printed with his name and with the schedule of baseball games to be played here by the Chicago White Sox, who conduct their spring training in Payne Park, right in the middle of town. This must be interpreted as a pure public service, rather than as an attempt to accelerate business by the exposure of senior citizens (or "senior Americans," as they are sometimes called here) to unbearable excitement; only last night I was informed that a Sarasota heart specialist has ordered one of his patients to attend every Sox game as a therapeutic measure. Big-league ball on the west coast of Florida is a spring sport played by the young for the divertissement of the elderly—a sun-warmed, sleepy exhibition celebrating the juvenescence of the year and the senescence of the fans. Although Florida newspapers print the standings of the clubs in the Grapefruit League every day, none of the teams tries especially hard to win; managers are looking hopefully at their rookies and anxiously at their veteran stars, and by the seventh or eighth inning, no matter what the score, most of the regulars are back in the hotel or driving out to join their families on the beach, their places taken by youngsters up from the minors. The spectators accept this without complaint. Their loyalty to the home club is gentle and unquestioning, and their afternoon pleasure appears scarcely affected by victory or defeat. If this attachment were deeper or more emotional, there would have been widespread distress here three years ago when the Boston Red Sox, who had trained in Sarasota for many years, transferred their spring camp to Scottsdale, Ari-

zona, and the White Sox moved down from Tampa, but the adjustment to the new stocking color, by all accounts, was without trauma. The Beach Club Bar, out on Siesta Key, still displays photographs of Bobby Doerr and Dom DiMaggio and other members of the fine Red Sox teams of the forties, and at the ballpark I spotted a boy of ten or twelve wearing a faded junior-size Red Sox uniform (almost surely a hand-me-down from an older brother), but these are the only evidences of disaffection and memory, and the old gentlemen filing into the park before the game now wear baseball caps with the White Sox insigne above the bill.

Caps are the preferred millinery for both male and female fans in 2 Payne Park—baseball caps, long-billed fishing caps, perforated summer-weights, yachting caps with crossed anchors, old-fashioned John D. Rocke-feller linen jobs. Beneath them are country faces—of retired farmers and small-town storekeepers, perhaps, and dignified ladies now doing their cooking in trailers—wearing rimless spectacles and snap-on dark glasses. This afternoon, Payne Park's little sixteen-row grandstand behind home plate had filled up well before game time (the Dodgers, always a good draw, were here today), and fans on their way in paused to visit with those already in their seats. The ushers greeted the regulars by name, and I saw one of them offering his arm to a very old lady in a blue hairnet and chatting with her as he escorted her slowly to her seat. Just after the national anthem, the loudspeaker announced that a lost wallet had been turned in, and invited the owner to come and claim it—an announcement that I very much doubt has ever been heard in a big-city ballpark.

There were elders on the field, too. Early Wynn, who has spent half 3 of his forty-two years in the major leagues and has won 292 games, started for the Sox. He pitched carefully, slowly wheeling his heavy body on the windup and glowering down on the batters between pitches, his big In-dian-like face almost hidden under his cap. He has a successful construc-tion business in Venice, Florida, south of here, but he wants that three-hundredth game this year; as for the Sox, if they are to be contenders they must have ten or fifteen wins from him. Duke Snider led off the Dodger second. He is as handsome and cheerful-looking as ever—he has the classic ballplayer's face—but he is a bit portly now, and beneath his helmet the sideburns were white. As he stepped up, a man somewhere behind me shouted, "C'mon, Duke! C'mon, Grandpa—belt one!" and a lady just in front of me murmured to her companion, "Now, really, I think that's *very* offensive." (Clapping and small, encouraging cries are heard in Florida parks, but boos and personal epithets are bad form.) Duke's feelings didn't seem hurt; he swung viciously and grounded out to second, running it out fast all the way.

Wynn pitched three innings, shutting out the Dodgers and giving up 4 only two hits, and was succeeded by Herb Score. The crowd was pulling for Score with every pitch; they knew his story, which is the saddest in modern baseball. Although he has entirely recovered from the terrible injury he suffered when he was struck in the face by a line drive hit by Gil MacDougald in 1957, Score's confidence, his control, and, finally, his form have vanished, and he has never again approached the brilliance of 1956, when he won twenty games for the Indians, struck out 263 batters, and finished with an earned-run average of 2.53. Now he is up from the minor leagues, battling for a job. Today, at least, he was getting batters out, but watching him work was a nervous, unhappy business. Most of his pitches were high, and it was difficult to see why the Dodgers weren't hitting him harder. He kept running into bouts of wildness, and his delivery was a painful parody of what it used to be, for his arm would come to a full, hitching halt at the end of his windup, and he appeared to be pushing the ball. He escaped his four innings with only a lone, unearned run scored against him. Meantime, the White Sox were bleeding for runs, too, as they will be all season. They have traded away their power, Minoso and Sievers, for pitching and defense, hoping for a repetition of their 1959 surprise, and the run they scored in the seventh came on two singles and a stolen base—the kind of rally their supporters will have to expect this year.

The tension of a tied, low-scoring game appeared to distract rather 5 than engross the crowd. The sun slid behind the grandstand roof, and there was a great stirring and rustling around me as sweaters were produced and windbreakers zipped up; seats began to be vacated by deserters, and the fans in the upper rows, who had been in the shade all afternoon, came down looking for a warmer perch. Brief bursts of clapping died away, and the only sound was the shrill two-note whistle of infielders encouraging their pitcher. The old people all around me hunched forward, their necks bent, peering out at the field from under their cap bills, and I had the curious impression that I was in a giant aviary. Out in right-field foul ground, members of the Sox' big pitching squad began wind sprints. They stood together in clusters, their uniforms a vivid white in the blaze of late sun, and four or five at a time would break away from the group and make a sudden sandpiper dash along the foot of the distant sea-green wall, all the way into deep center field, where they stopped just as quickly and stood and stared at the game. At last, in the bottom of the twelfth, the White Sox loaded the bases on some sloppy Dodger fielding, and Nellie Fox, his wad of tobacco bulging, delivered the single that broke the bird spell and sent everyone home to supper. *"There,* now," said the woman in front of me, standing up and brushing her skirt. "Wasn't that nice?"

Sarasota, March 21

Watching the White Sox work out this morning at Payne Park reas- 6 sured me that baseball is, after all, still a young man's sport and a cheerful one. Coach Don Gutteridge broke up the early pepper games with a cry of "Ever'body 'round!" and after the squad had circled the field once, the ritual—the same one that is practiced on every high-school, college, and professional ball-field in the country—began. Batters in the cage bunted one, hit five or six, and made room for the next man. Pitchers hit fungoes to the outfielders, coaches on the first and third baselines knocked out grounders to the infield, pepper games went on behind the cage, and the bright air was full of baseballs, shouts, whistles, and easy laughter. There was a raucous hoot from the players around second when a grounder hopped over Esposito's glove and hit him in the belly. Two young boys with fielders' gloves had joined the squad in the outfield, and I saw Floyd Robinson gravely shake hands with them both. Anyone can come to watch practice here, and fans from nearby hotels and cottages wandered in after their breakfasts, in twos and threes, and slowly clambered up into the empty bleachers, where they assumed the easy, ceremonial attitude—feet up on the row in front, elbows on knees, chin in hands. There were perhaps two dozen of us in the stands, and what kept us there, what nailed us to our seats for a sweet, boring hour or more, was not just the *whop!* of bats, the climbing white arcs of outfield flies, and the swift flight of the ball whipped around the infield, but something more painful and just as obvious—the knowledge that we had never made it. We would never know the rich joke that doubled over three young pitchers in front of the dugout; we would never be part of that golden company on the field, which each of us, certainly for one moment of his life, had wanted more than anything else in the world to join.

The Cardinals, who have been having a fine spring, were the visitors 7 this afternoon, and their high spirits infected everyone. Minnie Minoso, grinning extravagantly, exchanged insults with his former White Sox teammates, and Larry Jackson, the big, fast Cardinal right-hander, laughed out loud on the mound when he got Joe Cunningham, who was *his* teammate last year, to miss badly on a big curve in the first inning. Stan Musial had the day off, and Al Lopez, the Sox' manager, had filled his lineup with rookies. My eye was caught by the Chicago shortstop, a kid named Al Weis, who is not on the team's regular roster but who was having a nifty day in the field. He started double plays in the first and second innings, and in the third he made a fine throw from deep short to get Jackson, and then robbed Gotay with a diving spear of a low, hot liner. At the plate, though, he was nervous and uncertain, anxious to succeed in this one short and, to him, terribly important afternoon. He struck out in the first inning and again in the second, stranding two base-runners.

At about this time, I began to pick up a dialogue from the seats 8 directly behind me—a flat, murmurous, continuous exchange in Middle Western accents between two elderly men.

"Look at the skin on my hands, how dry it is," said one.   9

"You do anything for it?" asked the other.   10

"Yes, I got some stuff the doctor gave me—just a little tube of some- 11 thing. It don't help much."

I stole a look at them. They were both in their seventies, at least. Both 12 were sitting back comfortably, their arms folded across their stomachs.

"Watch that ball," said the first. "Is that fair?"   13

"No, it's foul. You know, I haven't seen a homer this year."   14

"Me neither."   15

"Maybe Musial will hit one here tomorrow."   16

The White Sox, down one run after the first inning, could do nothing 17
with Jackson. Weis struck out again in the fifth, made a wild throw to first
in the sixth, and then immediately redeemed himself with another fast
double play. The voices went on.

"This wind melts your ice cream fast, don't it?"   18

"Yes, it does. It feels nice, though. Warm wind."   19

In the top of the eighth, with the bases loaded, Weis grabbed another 20
line drive and doubled up the runner at second base. There were chirps
from the stands.

"It don't seem any time at all since spring training last year."   21

"That's because we're older now. You take my grandson, he's always 22
looking forward to something. Christmas and his birthday and things like
that. That makes the time go slow for him. You and me, we just watch each
day by itself."

"Yes. You know, I didn't hardly think about life at all until I was 23
sixty-five or seventy."

"I know."   24

Weis led off the bottom of the eighth, and popped up to left. He 25
started still another double play in the ninth, but his afternoon was ruined.
The Cardinals won the game, 2–0.

This evening, I looked up Al Weis's record. He is twenty-two years 26
old and was an All-Scholastic player at Farmingdale High, on Long Island.
In his three years in organized baseball, he has played with Holdrege, in
the Nebraska State League; with Lincoln, in the Three-I League; and with
Charleston, in the Sally League. His batting averages in those years—.275,
.231, .261—tell the story: good field, no hit. Time has run out for him this
spring, and it must seem to him that it went too quickly. Next week, he
will report to the White Sox farm camp in Hollywood, Florida, for another
year in the minors.

St. Petersburg, March 22

This is Gerontium, the elders' capital—city of shuffleboard courts, 27
city of sidewalk benches, city of curious signs reading "Youtharama,"
"Smorgarama," and "Biblegraph." Today it was also the baseball capital
of the world, for the game at Al Lang Field was the first encounter between the Yankees and the New York Mets, the new National League
team that sprang—not simply full-grown but middle-aged—out of the
forehead of George Weiss last winter. Some of the spectators' curiosity and
expectancy about this game resembled the unbecoming relish with which
party guests watch a newly divorced couple encountering each other in
public for the first time, for they could watch General Manager Weiss, in
his box behind the home dugout, and Casey Stengel, in the dugout, staring
over at the team that had evicted them so scandalously two years ago. But
there was another, more valid tension to be tasted; one sensed that this
game was a crisis for the Mets—their first chance to discover, against the
all-conquerors, whether they were truly a ball team. A rout, a laughter, a
comedy of ineptitude might destroy them before the season ever began.

St. Petersburg fans are elderly, all right, but they are noisier, keener, 28
and more appreciative than their counterparts to the south. For one thing,
they know more baseball. Al Lang Field has for years been the late-winter
home of two good teams, the Yankees and Cardinals; when the Yankees
moved to new quarters at Fort Lauderdale this year, the Mets moved in to
take their place. I had guessed that this switch of home teams might cause
some confusion of loyalties, but I was wrong. There was a respectable burst
of applause when Mickey Mantle stepped up to the plate in the second
inning, but this was almost immediately smothered by a full roar of pleasure
when Charlie Neal collared Mantle's streaking grounder in short right and
threw him out. Groans and headshakings followed when the Yanks collected three singles and a run off Roger Craig's pitching, but the Mets failed
to collapse. Frank Thomas hit a double in the Mets' half of the inning—the
first hit given up by Bill Stafford, the Yankees' starting pitcher, all spring—
and there was another startled shout a few minutes later when Hodges and
Chacon pulled off a 3-6-3 double play on Maris's bouncer. The Mets not only
belonged, they were winning converts every minute.

The Mets are an attractive team, full of echoes and overtones, and 29
one must believe that George Weiss had designed their clean, honest, but
considerably frayed appearance with great care. Gus Bell, Frank Thomas,
Eddie Bouchee, and Richie Ashburn are former headliners whose mistakes will be forgiven and whose accomplishments will win sentimental
affection. Coach Cookie Lavagetto and pitchers Roger Craig and Clem
Labine will bring the older Dodger fans up to the Polo Grounds this
summer. Neal and Zimmer looked unchanged—Neal intense, withdrawn,
talented, too tightly wound for an ideal infielder, and Zimmer eager and
competitive, angrily trying to make pugnacity compensate for what he
lacks in size, skill, and luck. Gil Hodges still cannot hit pitches over the
outside corners, but his stance and his mannerisms at the plate are a cup
of limeflower tea to those with memories: The bat is held in the left hand
while he fiddles with his eyelashes with his right hand, then settles his
helmet, then tucks up his right pants leg, then sweeps the hand the full
length of the bat, like a duelist wiping blood off a sword, and then at last
he faces the pitcher. Finally, there is Casey himself, a walking pantheon
of evocations. His pinstripes are light blue now, and so is the turtleneck
sweatshirt protruding above his shirt, but the short pants, the hobble, the
muttering lips, and the comic, jerky gestures are unaltered, and today he
proved himself still capable of the winning move.

The Mets went ahead, 3–2, in the sixth inning, on two Yankee errors, 30
two walks, and Zimmer's single. After that, the St. Petersburg fans began
a nervous, fingers-crossed cry of "Keep it *up*, Mets!" and welcomed each
put-out with shouts of incredulity and relief. In the ninth, though, the
Mets' second pitcher, a thin young Negro named Al Jackson, up this year
from Columbus, gave up four singles and the tying run after Neal messed
up a double play. With the winning runs on base, Stengel showed how
much he wanted this game for his team, for he came out to the mound
and relieved Jackson. (Pitchers are almost never yanked in mid-inning in

spring training.) The relief man, Howie Nunn, retired Blanchard on a pop behind second for the last out. More wonders followed. Joe Christopher, another unknown, led off the Mets' ninth with a triple, and after Zimmer had fouled out, Stengel looked into his closet of spare parts, which is far less well stocked than his old Yankee cornucopia, and found Ashburn there. Richie hit the first pitch into right field for the ball game, and George Weiss nodded his head, stood up in his box, and smiled for the first time today.

I doubt whether any of the happy six thousand-odd filing out of Al   31 Lang Field after the game were deluding themselves with dreams of a first-division finish for the Mets this year. The team is both too old and too young for sensible hopes. Its pitchers will absorb some fearful punishment this summer, and Chacon and Neal have yet to prove that they can manage the double play with any consistency. Still, though, the Mets will be playing in the same league with the Houston Colt .45s, another newborn team of castoffs, and with the Phillies, who managed to finish forty-six games out of first place last year and will have eight more games this year in which to disimprove that record. The fight for the National League cellar this summer may be as lively as the fight for the pennant. What cheered *me* as I tramped through the peanut shells and discarded programs and out into the hot late sunlight was not just the score and not just Casey's triumph but a freshly renewed appreciation of the marvelous complexity and balance of baseball. Offhand, I can think of no other sport in which the world's champions, one of the great teams of its era, would not instantly demolish inferior opposition and reduce a game such as the one we had just seen to cruel ludicrousness. Baseball is harder than that; it requires a full season, hundreds and hundreds of separate games, before quality can emerge, and in that summer span every home-town fan, every doomed admirer of underdogs will have his afternoons of revenge and joy.

Questions

Rereading and Independent Analysis

1. Choose one of the reports of a day of spring training and analyze it to discover the theme that Angell uses to unify his observations. How does the description of this particular day make a "statement" without openly stating a "thesis" and explaining or demonstrating its truth in logical form? Look for repeated images and references to time and place.

2. Reread these selections, marking the parts that describe the fans and those that focus on the players and teams. Whose observations are reported in addition to Angell's? What is the effect of these shifts in perspective? In what ways does Angell help you to "see" the scene?

Suggested Discussion and Group Activities

1. Why do you think Angell selected the title of this group of observations, "Old Folks Behind Home"? What does his reflection on winter

baseball have to do with the song, "Old Folks at Home"? How does the theme of his piece reflect the nostalgia of that familiar old song?

2. Angell's emphasis on the links between the players and spectators of baseball suggests a way to write about any event or sport. In groups, make a plan for using this strategy to write about football, basketball, track, gymnastics, or another sports event. In what ways would you link the players to the observers?

Writing Suggestions

Response

In a journal or notebook, write about a time when you watched a sports event or another performance and found it especially moving. Try to capture the details you remember that gave you a strong positive (or negative) feeling about being there.

Analysis

Throughout this essay, Angell uses the metaphor of aging to compare players and fans. Most of the players he mentions are now "too old" to play, and some were aging at the time he wrote. On the other hand, the fans came to these games as a youthful thing to do. Review the selection, day by day, and write an analysis of its comparisons and contrasts of youth and age. Explain how its title, changing points of view, and other details unify the essay around this theme.

Finding a Purpose

Choose a sports or other group activity that involves participants and observers such as a theatrical performance or a rally. Visit it in progress, making notes of your observations and any questions you may have to find specific answers for later. Then write a report like Angell's, in which you make the activity interesting to read about after it is no longer a news item. Assume that your report will be published in a local magazine or newspaper as a "reflection."

 # From *Coming into the Country*
John McPhee

This reflection on modern Alaskan life was written by John McPhee (b. 1931), who studied at Princeton and Cambridge universities and now teaches a course, "The Literature of Fact," at Princeton in addition to writing prolifically. McPhee began his writing career in television, has worked at the *New Yorker* magazine, and has written many observational studies. He is a master of writing timely, semijournalistic pieces that make unfamiliar topics part of common understanding, as he does in this description of Alaskan life from *Coming Into the Country* (1976) or in his book about the geology of the American West (*Basin and Range,* 1982). But he is equally adept at turning topics we think we already know enough about into news by making familiar subjects unfamiliar. In books such as his *Levels of the Game* (1970), which analyzes tennis, or *Oranges* (1967), which describes each part of the citrus industry's processing of that common fruit and its by-products, he demonstrates this second talent. In 1977 McPhee received an award from the American Academy and Institute of Arts and Letters for his many contributions to our understanding of our times.

In this selection, McPhee makes the country's newest, least-established state familiar to readers who have never been there by exploring its similarities to and differences from the older states. As he does this, he depicts a new Alaska created by the energy and money that came into that region with the building of the Alaskan pipeline. Consequently, he also implies that both past and present Alaskan life reveal great contrasts. As you read, notice his use of comparisons and contrasts in specific details to make points.

If Boston was once the most provincial place in America (the story goes 1 that after a six-megaton bomb exploded in Times Square a headline in a Boston paper would say, "HUB MAN KILLED IN NEW YORK BLAST"), Alaska, in this respect, may have replaced Boston. In Alaska, the conversation is Alaska. Alaskans, by and large, seem to know little and to say less about what is going on outside. They talk about their land, their bears, their fish, their rivers. They talk about subsistence hunting, forbidden hunting, and living in trespass. They have their own lexicon. A senior citizen is a pioneer, snow is termination dust, and the N.B.A. is the National Bank of Alaska. The names of Alaska are so beautiful they run like fountains all day in the mind. Mulchatna. Chilikadrotna. Unalaska. Unalakleet. Kivalina. Kiska. Kodiak. Allakaket. The Aniakchak Caldera. Nondalton. Anaktuvuk. Anchorage. Alaska is a foreign country significantly populated with Americans. Its languages extend to English. Its nature is its own. Nothing seems so unexpected as the boxes marked "U.S. Mail," talk and talk about their pipeline—about the big welders from Tulsa ("Animals, sheer animals"), whose power showdowns with the Teamsters so terrified the Teamsters that the Teamsters turned to petroleum jelly. Years in advance, they talked about the royalties the pipeline would bring them, and, to some extent, about the devastation it could bring to Prince William Sound, which, starred with islands, is one of the marine splendors of the subarctic.

"*There* is the real problem—not the possible spills on land but the 2 spills that could happen in Prince William Sound."

In recent time, the entrenched, traditional boomers of Alaska, the 3 develop-it majority, have been challenged by a growing body of people who wonder if the boom philosophy is good for the state. Fairbanks, under the impact of the pipeline, has become (in Willie Hensley's word) "scroungy"—prostitutes, Texans, ticky-tacky. Maybe Alaska should take a more circumspect look before entering such arrangements again. This was the novel body of thought that helped to produce the 1974 election victory of Governor Jay Hammond—fisherman, homesteader, wilderness man. Hammond was hardly a fierce and fighting conservationist. Alaska had not molted. But Hammond's prudent, balanced approach to things was an attempt to reconcile what his first Commerce Commissioner, Langhorne Motley, once called "the Sierra Club syndrome and the Dallas scenario." In the ongoing debate about the new capital, among all the varied reasons for and against the move, those two strands were prominently braided.

"The new capital will be a growth center for Alaska. It will take the 4 pressure off Anchorage."

"In a state this size, if you put everything in one area you detract 5 from the reasons we're all here. The new capital won't be all that far from Anchorage. You put all the people in one place, you create an unattractive state, and you pull out the employment from people who would like to live in the Juneau area."

"Juneau will die." 6

"The people of Alaska have mandated this, and the people of Alaska 7 have darned good judgment."

"I don't think anyone is smart enough to plan a place like that. In 8 Valdez, after the '64 earthquake, up we went and moved the city. Four or five miles, to a safer place. What a mess! The new Valdez is full of cul-de-sacs. What do you do with twenty-five feet of snow at the end of a cul-de-sac? A mess. And I was the mayor."

"Places like that are sterile. Salt Lake is the only planned city worth 9 a damn. Have you ever seen a town planned by an American planner?"

"Savannah was sketched out in England." 10

"The purpose is better government. Move the seat of government to 11 the Susitna Valley and seventy per cent of the population is within driving distance."

"Legislators could drive home for the weekend to Fairbanks, Homer, 12 and anywhere between. To Anchorage they could drive home evenings."

"You want to drive home evenings at fifty below?" 13

"Try flying to Juneau. Socked in. You end up in Seattle." 14

"Lobby groups have an advantage in Juneau. They can afford to stay 15 there, and they are unhampered by people coming down and butting in. They have the legislators to themselves."

"The highway people down there have to fly five hundred miles to 16 see the roads they're working on."

"People voted for the move because they thought the money would 17 be coming in. It won't be there. We have virtually already spent the money from the pipeline. To me, it's that bleak. The state has been taking in about three hundred million a year—from petroleum revenues, highway-fuel revenues, income tax—and it is spending five hundred million. By 1980, Alaska's annual expenditures will be around one billion. The legislature spends money faster than they can get it, and nobody sees where it goes. To try to cover themselves, they hit the oil companies. They enacted a reserves tax on oil that is still in the ground, deductible from future royalties. I guess it's legal, but it sure doesn't sound moral."

"The state parking garage in Fairbanks cost four and a quarter mil- 18 lion—or fourteen thousand dollars a parking slot. So who can pay for a city?"

"Having Juneau the capital provides one more reason for tourists to 19 travel around the state."

"Putting it up here near Anchorage is like putting the barn close to 20 the fields. Better, more responsible people would agree to be legislators. Doctors and lawyers are out of business when they're in Juneau."

"The new city would grow here, grow naturally, the way Alaska will 21 grow."

"Not so fast! The flow of oil will not do everything. We'd better sit 22 back and look at our hole card."

There are those who would say that tens of thousands of barrels of 23 oil erupting from a break in the Trans-Alaska Pipeline would be the lesser accident if, at more or less the same time, a fresh Anchorage were to spill into the bush. While the dream of the capital city plays on in the mind, Anchorage stands real. It is the central hive of human Alaska, and in manner and structure it represents, for all to see, the Alaskan dynamic and the Alaskan aesthetic. It is a tangible expression of certain Alaskans' regard for Alaska—their one true city, the exemplar of the predilections of the people in creating improvements over the land.

As may befit a region where both short and long travel is generally 24 by air, nearly every street in Anchorage seems to be the road to the airport. Dense groves of plastic stand on either side—flashing, whirling, flaky. HOOSIER BUDDY'S MOBILE HOMES. WINNEBAGO SALES & SERVICE. DISCOUNT LIQUORS OPEN SUNDAY. GOLD RUSH AUTO SALES. PROMPT AC-TION LOCKSMITHS. ALASKA REFRIGERATION & AIR CONDITION. DENALI FUEL . . .

"Are the liquor stores really open Sundays?" 25

"Everything in Anchorage is open that pays." 26

Almost all Americans would recognize Anchorage, because Anchor- 27 age is that part of any city where the city has burst its seams and extruded Colonel Sanders.

"You can taste the greed in the air." 28

BELUGA ASPHALT. 29

Anchorage is sometimes excused in the name of pioneering. Build 30 now, civilize later. But Anchorage is not a frontier town. It is virtually unrelated to its environment. It has come in on the wind, an American spore. A large cookie cutter brought down on El Paso could lift something like Anchorage into the air. Anchorage is the northern rim of Trenton, the center of Oxnard, the ocean-blind precincts of Daytona Beach. It is con-densed, instant Albuquerque.

PANCHO'S VILLA, MEXICAN FOOD. BULL SHED, STEAK HOUSE AND   31
SONIC LOUNGE. SHAKEY'S DRIVE-IN PIZZA. EAT ME SUBMARINES.

Anchorage has developed a high-rise city core, with glass-box offices   32
for the oil companies, and tall Miamian hotels. Zonelessly lurching outward, it has made of its suburbs a carnival of cinder block, all with a
speculative mania so rife that sellers of small homesites—of modest lots
scarcely large enough for houses—retain subsurface rights. In vacant lots,
queen-post trusses lie waiting for new buildings to jump up beneath them.
Roads are rubbled, ponded with chuckholes. Big trucks, graders, loaders,
make the prevailing noise, the dancing fumes, the frenetic beat of the
town. Huge rubber tires are strewn about like quoits, ever ready for the
big machines that move hills of earth and gravel into inconvenient lakes,
which become new ground.

FOR LEASE. WILL BUILD TO SUIT.   33

Anchorage coins millionaires in speculative real estate. Some are   34
young. The median age in Anchorage is under twenty-four. Every three
or four years, something like half the population turns over. And with
thirty days of residence, you can vote as an Alaskan.

POLAR REALTY. IDLE WHEELS TRAILER PARK. MOTEL MUSH INN.   35

Anchorage has a thin history. Something of a precursor of the mod-   36
ern pipeline camps, it began in 1914 as a collection of tents pitched to
shelter workers building the Alaska Railroad. For decades, it was a
wooden-sidewalked, gravel-streeted town. Then, remarkably early, as cities go, it developed an urban slum, and both homes and commerce began
to abandon its core. The exodus was so rapid that the central business
district never wholly consolidated, and downtown Anchorage is even
more miscellaneous than outlying parts of the city. There is, for example,
a huge J. C. Penney department store filling several blocks in the heart of
town, with an interior mall of boutiques and restaurants and a certain
degree of chic. A couple of weedy vacant lots separate this complex from
five log cabins. Downtown Anchorage from a distance displays an
upreaching skyline that implies great pressure for land. Down below,
among the high buildings, are houses, huts, vegetable gardens, and bunga-
lows with tidy front lawns. Anchorage burst out of itself and left these
incongruities in the center, and for me they are the most appealing sights
in Anchorage. Up against a downtown office building I have seen cord-
wood stacked for winter.

In its headlong, violent expansion, Anchorage had considerable, but   37
not unlimited, space to fill. To an extent unusual among cities, Anchorage
has certain absolute boundaries, and in that sense its growth has been a
confined explosion. To the north, a pair of military bases establish, in
effect, a Roman wall. To the west and south, fjordlike arms of the
Pacific—Knik Arm, Turnagain Arm—frame the city. Behind Anchorage,
east, stand the Chugach Mountains, stunning against the morning and in
the evening light—Mount Magnificent, Mount Gordon Lyon, Temptation

Peak, Tanaina Peak, Wolverine Peak, the Suicide Peaks. Development has gone to some extent upward there. Houses are pushpinned to the mountainsides—a Los Angelized setting, particularly at night, above the starry lights of town. But the mountains are essentially a full stop to Anchorage, and Anchorage has nowhere else to go.

Within this frame of mountains, ocean, and military boundaries are 38 about fifty thousand acres (roughly the amount of land sought by the Capital Site Selection Committee), and the whole of it is known as the Anchorage Bowl. The ground itself consists of silt, alluvium, eolian sands, glacial debris—material easy to rearrange. The surface was once lumpy with small knolls. As people and their businesses began filling the bowl, they went first to the knolls, because the knolls were wooded and well drained. They cut down the trees, truncated the hills, and bestudded them with buildings. They strung utility lines like baling wire from knoll to knoll. The new subdivisions within the bowl were thus hither and yon, random, punctuated with bogs. Anchorage grew like mold.

WOLVERINE ALUMINUM SIDING. ALASKA FOUR-WHEEL DRIVE. JACK 39 BENNY'S RADIO-DISPATCHED CESSPOOL PUMPING.

Low ground is gradually being filled. The bowl has about a hundred 40 and eighty thousand people now, or almost half of human Alaska. There are some in town—notably, Robert Atwood, of the *Times*—who would like to see Anchorage grow to seven hundred thousand. Atwood is a big, friendly, old-football-tackle sort of man, with whitening hair and gold-rimmed glasses. Forty years on the inside, this impatient advocate of the commercial potentialities of Alaska is said to be one of the two wealthiest people in the state, the other being his brother-in-law. "Idealists here in town see a need for a park in every housing development," Atwood told me one day. "They want to bury utility lines, reserve green belts, build bicycle paths. With these things, the bowl could only contain three hundred and fifty thousand. They're making it very difficult for man, these people. They favor animals, trees, water, flowers. Who ever makes a plan for man? Who ever *will* make a plan for man? That is what *I* wonder. I am known among conservationists as a bad guy."

In Anchorage, if you threw a pebble into a crowd, chances are you 41 would not hit a conservationist, an ecophile, a wilderness preserver. In small ghettos, they are there—living in a situation lined with irony. They are in Alaska—many of them working for the federal government—because Alaska is everything wild it has ever been said to be. Alaska runs off the edge of the imagination, with its tracklessness, its beyond-the-ridgeline surprises, its hundreds of millions of acres of wilderness—this so-called "last frontier," which is certainly all of that, yet for the most part is not a frontier at all but immemorial landscape in an all but unapproached state. Within such vastness, Anchorage is a mere pustule, a dot, a minim—a walled city, wild as Yonkers, with the wildlife riding in a hundred and ninety-three thousand trucks and cars. Yet the city—where people are, where offices are—is perforce the home address of wilderness planners, of wildlife biologists, of Brooks Range guides.

The first few days I spent in Alaska were spent in Anchorage, and I 42 remember the increasing sense of entrapment we felt (my wife was with me), knowing that nothing less than a sixth of the entire United States, and almost all of it wilderness, was out there beyond seeing, while immediate needs and chores to do were keeping us penned in this portable Passaic. Finally, we couldn't take it any longer, and we cancelled appointments and rented a car and revved it up for an attempted breakout from town. A float plane—at a hundred and ten dollars an hour—would have been the best means, but, like most of the inmates of Anchorage, we could not afford it. For a great many residents, Anchorage is about all they ever see of Alaska, day after day after year. There are only two escape routes—a road north, a road south—and these are encumbered with traffic and, for some miles anyway, lined with detritus from Anchorage. We went south, that first time, and eventually east, along a fjord that would improve Norway. Then the road turned south again, into the mountains of Kenai— great tundra balds that reminded me of Scotland and my wife of parts of Switzerland, where she had lived. She added that she thought these mountains looked better than the ones in Europe. Sockeyes, as red as cardinals, were spawning in clear, shallow streams, and we ate our cheese and chocolate in a high meadow over a torrential river of green and white water. We looked up to the ridges for Dall sheep, and felt, for the moment, about as free. Anchorage shrank into perspective. It might be a sorry town, but it has the greatest out-of-town any town has ever had.

BIG RED'S FLYING SERVICE. BELUGA STEAM & ELECTRIC THAWING. 43 DON'T GO TO JAIL LET FRED GO YOUR BAIL.

There is a street in Anchorage—a green-lights, red-lights, busy 44 street—that is used by automobiles and airplanes. I remember an airplane in someone's driveway—next door to the house where I was staying. The neighbor started up its engine one night toward eleven o'clock, and for twenty minutes he ran it flat out while his two sons, leaning hard into the stabilizers, strained to hold back the plane. In Alaska, you do what you feel like doing, or so goes an Alaskan creed.

There is, in Anchorage, a somewhat Sutton Place. It is an enclave, 45 actually, with several roads, off the western end of Northern Lights Boulevard, which is a principal Anchorage thoroughfare, a neon borealis. Walter Hickel lives in the enclave, on Loussac Drive, which winds between curbs and lawns, neatly trimmed, laid out, and landscaped, under white birches and balsam poplars. Hickel's is a heavy, substantial home, its style American Dentist. The neighbors' houses are equally expensive and much the same. The whole neighborhood seems to be struggling to remember Scarsdale. But not to find Alaska.

I had breakfast one morning in Anchorage with a man who had come 46 to Alaska from The Trust for Public Land, an organization whose goal is to buy potential parkland in urban areas and hold it until the government, whose legislative machinery is often too slow for the land market, can get up the funds for the purpose. In overbuilt urban settings—from Watts to Newark and back to Oakland—The Trust for Public Land will acquire whatever it can, even buildings under demolition, in order to create small parks and gardens that might relieve the compressed masses. And now The Trust for Public Land had felt the need to come to Anchorage— to the principal city of Alaska—to help hold a pond or a patch of green for the people in the future to have and see.

Books were selling in Anchorage, once when I was there, for forty-   47
seven cents a pound.

There are those who would say that the only proper place for a new   48
capital of Alaska—if there has to be a new one—is Anchorage, because anyone who has built a city like Anchorage should not be permitted to build one anywhere else.

At Anchorage International Airport, there is a large aerial photo-   49
graph of Anchorage formed by pasting together a set of pictures that were made without what cartographers call ground control. This great aerial map is one of the first things to confront visitors from everywhere in the world, and in bold letters it is titled "ANCHORAGE, ALASKA. UNCONTROLLED MOSAIC."

Questions

Rereading and Independent Analysis

1. The situation that provides the background for McPhee's comments on Anchorage is the building of the Alaskan pipeline, which caused many changes in the state's population and economy. Reread this selection, underlining words and phrases that create a feeling of change and energy. What patterns and themes do McPhee's word choices demonstrate?

2. Do a little research in your library to discover whether Alaska changed as much as this description predicted that it would. Is it a booming place now? What major changes have occurred there since 1975?

3. List the public signs McPhee inserts in this selection so you can examine them apart from the rest of the text. What is their tone? Are they different from signs you might see in your own town? What effect does McPhee achieve by including these signs?

Suggested Discussion and Group Activities

1. Have you thought of moving to a remote place like Alaska? What are your reasons? Why do you think people make such moves? Cite examples of similar moves that you have read or heard about. Were the people involved satisfied with the change? Why?

2. One of McPhee's themes is the opposition of the "Sierra Club syndrome and the Dallas scenario." Define what he means by these refer-

ences. Have you experienced a similar tension between conservation and change in your community? Is McPhee's theme now dated because such tensions have been resolved? Give examples to support your points.

3. Discuss the material you found (Question 2, "Rereading") about actual changes in Alaska. In groups, share your findings. What forces have influenced that state since McPhee wrote? Are there other "Alaskas" undergoing active change now? What do you know about these changes?

Writing Suggestions

Response

Write a short account of a change you have experienced in a place or group you knew well before the change began. What were your feelings? Were you ambivalent or confused about the results of the change? What specific conditions changed for you? Next, draw an inference about the possible distinctions between "progress" and "change."

Analysis

In the last paragraph of this selection, McPhee describes a picture in the Anchorage airport, "formed by pasting together a set of pictures that were made without what cartographers call ground control." He implies that it is possible to form images (maps) of places and events without conventionally controlling "ground" (background, single perspective).

After carefully noting McPhee's techniques, write an essay in which you adopt his ways of combining observations to create a "picture" of a place you know. Try to communicate a sense of the predominant energy and direction of the place without discussing them directly in a "thesis" generalization. Rely on specific but scattered concrete observations that fit together to create a dominant impression. Ask some of your classmates to judge your success in creating this impression, and revise as they suggest.

Finding a Purpose

Write a proposal to your state legislature for a new city or town in your state that will be a new location for the state capital, a university, or another old or new public facility. Use McPhee's essay to find strategies to establish good reasons for your dream of a well-planned city that will open new patterns of movement and commerce in your state.

CHAPTER 4

Written Worlds

INTRODUCTION

The invention of print from movable type in 1450 revolutionized human interactions. Print made it possible to duplicate exact copies of books, maps, money, and engravings. The human world became, for the first time, a world joined by the widespread availability of printed texts. Knowing a poem or a biblical passage no longer depended on whether a traveling poet had passed through a community reciting the poem or a local church owned an expensive, hand-copied Bible.

Consequently, national and regional culture gradually also became written culture, to be read and handed down in books as stories and legends had been spoken and handed down through repetition. Purposes for speaking and remembering also became purposes for writing. Within newly "written" cultures, silent writing in local languages took on the authority and trustworthiness that had previously belonged to prominent people who spoke directly to their communities. People slowly came to "trust" writing, as they saw they could depend on it to stand in for distant and often unknown people. A set of popular or specialized texts, defined by a common subject, a common genre (form), or a common approach, could create and build on its own widely known traditions.

Special communities of written words are common now, so it is important as a reader and writer to realize that distinct purposes created them. To understand a poem, for instance, we identify an individual accomplishment partially by making comparisons with common patterns and commonly used figures of speech. As we read any piece of writing, we ask questions about the particular customs in its community. We ask how it is a distinct member of a group of similar forms (e.g., poems), of similar topics (e.g., distant places), or of similar methods and questions (e.g., an academic field). And as we begin to write, we identify other writing that has established a similar context for understanding our own new contribution.

This chapter is organized to show how distinct communities of texts may be formed around problems and ideas that have always concerned humankind. The sections of the chapter show how writing can create its own "places" in our imagination and in our organization of knowledge. The selections invite you to compare and contrast treatments of (1) idealized and frightening places; (2) "character" (a customary name for our usually disorganized individual selves, to which writing helped give a label); and (3) written history, science, and social sciences.

The last group contains writing from three broad disciplines, the organized subjects commonly addressed in education. Within these regions and others like them, there are many locales. "Science," for instance, includes physics, chemistry, biology, and mathematics—and within them, subsidiary fields such as microbiology, organic chemistry, or astrophysics. Introductions to these scholarly disciplines show their special methods of observation, their acceptable kinds of evidence, their preferred formats, and especially their specialized vocabularies. To take a course is not only to learn information about a subject but to become familiar with these elements of the subject's written tradition. As a student reader and writer, you need to be alert to the different methods, problems, evidence, and forms of writing that make up the subjects you will study. Choices about these matters determine the context around each contribution to a field. An individual contribution's right to "speak" among its peers depends largely on its conformity to the elements of context that a small world of writing has agreed to share.

IMAGINED PLACES

 # From the Constitution of the Brook Farm Association

Sometimes an imagined place where life can be lived according to idealistic principles becomes a reality, if only briefly, as communities form to experiment with new ways of life. One of the first impulses of the inhabitants of such communities is to write a statement of the principles that have brought them together and to make those principles "real," even if they are difficult to establish and maintain. Such places usually exist longer in the ideals and reading of those who know about them than they do in fact, but their formulation for brief times keeps their possibility alive. In the time immediately before the American Civil War began in 1861, many of these idealistic experiments in community living sprang up.

The Brook Farm Association expressed the literary and intellectual climate of New England at that time. Its supporters included Ralph Waldo Emerson and Henry David Thoreau (see Chapter 3), Amos Bronson Alcott (the educator and father of Louisa May Alcott, author of *Little Women*),

Margaret Fuller (a supporter of women's rights), William Ellery Channing (a Unitarian minister), and Nathaniel Hawthorne (author of *The Scarlet Letter*). This group had formed a Transcendental Club in 1836, which met to discuss the "new thought" of the time—developments in literature, philosophy, and religion. As a group they believed in the dignity of work, the need for intellectual and spiritual companionship, individual spiritual determination, common brotherhood, and self-reliance. They were against slavery and in favor of the right of women to vote. To allow this group to live by these beliefs, Brook Farm was established in 1841 in West Roxbury, Massachusetts, nine miles from Boston. Those who lived at Brook Farm (including, for a brief time, Hawthorne) wanted a low-cost community that would allow them leisure so that they could spend their time reading, writing, and discussing important ideas. They were to support these goals by shared responsibility for the farm.

The project lasted for five years, but it had to be closed for a number of practical reasons: dissension among the members, the discovery that the soil of the farm would not support enough crops to provide an income, and a final crushing blow—a fire that destroyed their "phalanstery," the communal building.

The section of the Constitution of the Brook Farm Association included here states the members' important values and establishes procedures for implementing their way of life. The document imitates the form of the American Constitution, beginning with a preamble and continuing with articles of governance. It establishes a contract among members who own stock in Brook Farm, describes the governance system they all will agree to, and provides for members' support. The language of the document is common in precise, contractual documents. (See Chapter 2.) You may find this selection to be a sort of quaint relic unless you try to imagine this place, or one like it, for yourself. What kinds of rules and conditions do you think would be necessary today to provide an idealistic communal setting? How is this constitution like other charters and formal agreements to form groups that you belong to or know of? Contrast the precision and specificity in this agreement with the actual problems that disbanded the farm.

In order more effectually to promote the great purposes of human culture; to establish the external relations of life on a basis of wisdom and purity; to apply the principles of justice and love to our social organization in accordance with the laws of Divine Providence; to substitute a system of brotherly cooperation for one of selfish competition; to secure to our children and those who may be entrusted to our care, the benefits of the highest physical, intellectual, and moral education, which in the progress of knowledge the resources at our command will permit; to institute an attractive, efficient, and productive system of industry; to prevent the exercise of wordly anxiety by the competent supply of our necessary wants; to diminish the desire of excessive accumulation, by making the acquisition of individual property subservient to upright and disinterested uses; to guarantee to each other forever the means of physical support, and of spiritual progress; and thus to impart a greater freedom, simplicity, truthfulness, refinement, and moral dignity, to our mode of life;—we the undersigned do unite in a voluntary Association, and adopt and ordain the following articles of agreement, to wit:

Article I

Sec. 1. The name of this Association shall be "THE BROOK-FARM AS-SOCIATION FOR INDUSTRY AND EDUCATION." All persons who shall hold one or more shares in its stock, or whose labor and skill shall be considered an equivalent for capital, may be admitted by the vote of two-thirds of the Association, as members thereof.

Sec. 2. No member of the Association shall ever be subjected to any religious test; nor shall any authority be assumed over individual freedom of opinion by the Association, nor by any one member over another; nor shall any one be held accountable to the Association, except for such overt acts, omissions of duty, as violate the principles of justice, purity, and love, on which it is founded; and in such cases the relation of any member may be suspended or discontinued at the pleasure of the Association.

Article II

Sec. 1. The members of this Association shall own and manage such real and personal estate in joint stock proprietorship, divided into shares of one hundred dollars, each, as may from time to time be agreed on . . .

Sec. 4. The shareholders on their part for themselves, their heirs and assigns, do renounce all claim on any profits accruing to the Association for the use of their capital invested in the stock of the Association, except five per cent, interest on the amount of stock held by them, payable in the manner described in the preceding section.

Article III

Sec. 1. The Association shall provide such employment for all its members as shall be adapted to their capacities, habits, and tastes; and each member shall select and perform such operations of labor, whether corporal or mental, as shall be deemed best suited to his own endowments, and the benefit of the Association.

Sec. 2. The Association guarantees to all its members, their children, and family dependents, house-rent, fuel, food, and clothing, and the other necessaries of life, without charge, not exceeding a certain fixed amount to be decided annually by the Association; no charge shall ever be made for support during inability to labor from sickness or old age, or for medical or nursing attendance, except in case of shareholders, who shall be charged therefor . . . but no charge shall be made to any members for education or the use of library and public rooms. . . .

Article V

Sec. 1.   The government of the Association shall be vested in a board of Directors, divided into four departments as follows; 1st., General Direction; 2d, Direction of Education; 3d., Direction of Industry; 4th, Direction of Finance; consisting of three persons each. . . .

Sec. 5.   The departments of Education and Finance shall be under the control each of its own Direction, which shall select, and in concurrence with the General Direction, shall appoint such teachers, officers, and agents, as shall be necessary to the complete and systematic organization of the department. No Directors or other officers shall be deemed to possess any rank superior to the other members of the Association, nor shall they receive any extra remuneration for their official services.

Sec. 6.   The department of Industry shall be arranged in groups and series, as far as practicable, and shall consist of three primary series; to wit, Agricultural, Mechanical, and Domestic Industry. The chief of each series shall be elected every two months by the members thereof. . . .

Questions

Rereading and Independent Analysis

1. Read the preamble to this constitution again. Notice the words that its authors use to define their goals: "culture," etc. What view of life outside Brook Farm do these words reveal? Compare this preamble with the briefer Preamble to the American Constitution (Chapter 2). How do the specific purposes stated in each document differ?

2. List the general topics in each article of this document. Why does every organization need to address these issues and provide for their regulation? Are any important provisions absent that are addressed in the American Constitution or the Bill of Rights? (See Chapter 2.)

Suggested Discussion and Group Activities

1. During the 1960s and 1970s, many experimental "communes" were started by young people who wanted to leave their ordinary surroundings and become self-reliant, removed from materialism and politics they did not approve of. Keeping this trend in mind, review the Brook Farm document to discover what it *excludes* from its community. What would these early farming dropouts have left behind, in both habits and experiences? Do you approve of this sort of divorce from the broader community? Why?

2. Do you see how a sick, weak, or very young shareholder could have been excluded from this plan? Was this document designed to fit only a certain kind of person? Who else might have been excluded? Is exclusion a flaw in such a plan? Why?

3. Bring in examples of similar writing in legal documents and contracts that you find difficult to understand. In groups, agree about the definitions of terms, using other examples that have been brought in—if they are helpful—to explain what is meant. Identify any of the language that is confusing. Explain what these terms mean, reading aloud to help you get the sense of the document under discussion. Experiment with ways to rewrite the documents for clarity without lessening their effects.

Writing Suggestions

Response
Can you imagine leaving your present circumstances to go to another place—perhaps even another planet—with only the people you would like to have with you? Write a reaction to the escape implied by Brook Farm, describing your own imaginary community and your reasons for wanting to join it, if only in fantasy.

Analysis
Imagine that you and the members of your class want to start an ideal university, without the problems that you see in the organization and administration of your present school. After you have discussed the nature of this new ideal place of learning, divide your class into groups. One group will prepare a preamble; the others will each prepare an article by separately addressing the topics taken up in the articles of the Brook Farm constitution.

Write the parts and then, as a class, edit and compile them into one document that is unified in its purposes and concepts. Use language that will firmly establish your new ideal and be easily understood by all.

Finding a Purpose
Imagine that you are living in the Brook Farm community. Write a letter to a friend who has refused to join the association, attempting to persuade him or her to join you. Use the Constitution to supply specific details of points in favor of joining.

 # A Voyage to Lilliput
Jonathan Swift

Gulliver's Travels (1726) humorously imitates a whole genre of travel stories that stretched the truth at a time when world exploration still meant reporting unknown societies and customs. The imagined places in Jonathan Swift's writing are vivid symbols of actual social attitudes and human pride so common that we can understand why Swift gave them geography and populations.

Swift (1667–1745) was an Anglican clergyman, dean of St. Patrick's Cathedral in Dublin, and an active participant in political affairs, but he is most often remembered now as a foremost British satirist. His poetry, treatises (*A Modest Proposal,* Chapter 5), and "fiction" *(Gulliver's Travels)* were among the first widely published and popularly read ironic writing. They made sharp points against the vanity, selfishness, and tyranny of individual and governmental practices in Swift's time. Swift said that he wrote "to vex the world rather than divert it." The travels of Lemuel Gulliver were designed to comment on human pride and on the self-deception that results from it, as well as to parody the printed tales of travel, adventure, and exploration that misled people. (This misleading practice has continued; see "Sebastian Cabot and the Northwest Passage" by David Roberts.)

In his way, Swift attempted "to vex the world" by hiding his identity as the author of *Gulliver,* as he did in much of his other writing. A legend says that someone (in the story it was a friend and contemporary poet, Alexander Pope) dropped the manuscript of *Gulliver* from a coach window at the door of the publisher. But it was widely known that Swift was the author, and as Samuel Johnson said in his criticism of Swift, the work "was read by the high and low; the lettered and illiterate. Criticism was for a while lost in wonder." Swift's bizarre tale surely impressed the "unlettered," those who were not familiar with other uses of a false voice in earlier travel tales such as Thomas More's *Utopia* (1516). Inexperienced readers might well have believed in the improbable existence of the peculiar Gulliver and of his obviously impossible visits, especially when actual travel was yielding genuine information about foreign wonders.

Gulliver's tales were published in two volumes, consisting of four books—the voyage to Lilliput presented here, the voyage to Brobdingnag (where everything is quite large), the voyage to Laputa (where contemporary "learning" has gone mad and the people live only by intellectual systems), and the voyage to the Houyhnhnms (the most perfect society on earth, populated only by horses). By maintaining Gulliver's innocent curiosity and by changing the author's perspective in each section of the *Travels,* Swift presents a consistent unraveling of human pride that is still applicable today. As you read, imagine what it would be like to believe what you are reading. What does Swift do to make the tale believable? What clues are there that he is *not* serious?

The Publisher to The Reader

THE AUTHOR of these Travels, Mr. Lemuel Gulliver, *is my an-* 1
tient and intimate Friend; there is likewise some Relation be-
tween us by the Mother's Side. About three Years ago Mr. Gulliver *growing weary of the Concourse of curious People coming*
to him at his House in Redriff, *made a small Purchase of Land,*
with a convenient House, near Newark, *in* Nottinghamshire,
his native Country; where he now lives retired, yet in good
Esteem among his Neighbours.

ALTHOUGH Mr. Gulliver *were born in* Nottinghamshire, 2 *where his Father dwelt, yet I have heard him say, his Family came from* Oxfordshire; *to confirm which, I have observed in the Church-Yard at* Banbury, *in that County, several Tombs and Monuments of the* Gullivers.

BEFORE *he quitted* Redriff, *he left the Custody of the* 3 *following Papers in my Hands, with the Liberty to dispose of them as I should think fit. I have carefully perused them three Times; The Style is very plain and simple; and the only Fault I find is, that the Author, after the Manner of Travellers, is a little too circumstantial. There is an Air of Truth apparent through the whole; and indeed the Author was so distinguished for his Veracity, that it became a Sort of Proverb among his Neighbours at* Redriff, *when any one affirmed a Thing, to say, it was as true as if Mr.* Gulliver *had spoke it.*

BY *the Advice of several worthy Persons, to whom, with* 4 *the Author's Permission, I communicated these Papers, I now venture to send them into the World; hoping they may be, at least for some time, a better Entertainment to our young Noblemen, than the common Scribbles of Politicks and Party.*

THIS *Volume would have been at least twice as large, if* 5 *I had not made bold to strike out innumerable Passages relating to the Winds and Tides, as well as to the Variations and Bearings in the several Voyages; together with the minute Descriptions of the Management of the Ship in Storms, in the Style of Sailors: Likewise the Account of the Longitudes and Latitudes; wherein I have Reason to apprehend that Mr.* Gulliver *may be a little dissatisfied: But I was resolved to fit the Work as much as possible to the general Capacity of Readers. However, if my own Ignorance in Sea-Affairs shall have led me to commit some Mistakes, I alone am answerable for them: And if any Traveller hath a Curiosity to see the whole Work at large, as it came from the Hand of the Author, I will be ready to gratify him.*

As *for any further Particulars relating to the Author, the* 6 *Reader will receive Satisfaction from the first Pages of the Book.*

Richard Sympson

Chapter I.

THE AUTHOR GIVETH SOME ACCOUNT OF HIMSELF AND FAMILY; HIS FIRST INDUCEMENTS TO TRAVEL. HE IS SHIPWRECKED, AND SWIMS FOR HIS LIFE; GETS SAFE ON SHOAR IN THE COUNTRY OF LILLIPUT; IS MADE A PRISONER, AND CARRIED UP THE COUNTRY.

My Father had a small Estate in *Nottinghamshire;* I was the Third of five
Sons. He sent me to *Emanuel-College* in *Cambridge,* at Fourteen Years
old, where I resided three Years, and applied my self close to my Studies:
But the Charge of maintaining me (although I had a very scanty Allowance) being too great for a narrow Fortune; I was bound Apprentice to Mr. 5
James Bates, an eminent Surgeon in *London,* with whom I continued four
Years; and my Father now and then sending me small Sums of Money, I
laid them out in learning Navigation, and other Parts of the Mathematicks,
useful to those who intend to travel, as I always believed it would be some
time or other my Fortune to do. When I left Mr. *Bates,* I went down to 10
my Father; where, by the Assistance of him and my Uncle *John,* and some
other Relations, I got Forty Pounds, and a Promise of Thirty Pounds a Year
to maintain me at *Leyden:* There I studied Physick two Years and seven
Months, knowing it would be useful in long Voyages.

SOON after my Return from *Leyden,* I was recommended by my
good Master Mr. *Bates,* to be Surgeon to the *Swallow,* Captain *Abraham* 15
Pannell Commander; with whom I continued three Years and a half,
making a Voyage or two into the *Levant,* and some other Parts. When I
came back, I resolved to settle in *London,* to which Mr. *Bates,* my Master,
encouraged me; and by him I was recommended to several Patients. I took
Part of a small House in the *Old Jury;* and being advised to alter my 20
Condition, I married Mrs. *Mary Burton,* second Daughter to Mr. *Edmond*
Burton, Hosier, in *Newgate-street,* with whom I received four Hundred
Pounds for a Portion.

BUT, my good Master *Bates* dying in two Years after, and I having
few Friends, my Business began to fail; for my Conscience would not suffer
me to imitate the bad Practice of too many among my Brethren. Having 25
therefore consulted with my Wife, and some of my Acquaintance, I determined to go again to Sea. I was Surgeon successively in two Ships, and
made several Voyages, for six Years, to the *East* and *West-Indies;* by which
I got some Addition to my Fortune. My Hours of Leisure I spent in reading
the best Authors, ancient and modern; being always provided with a good 30
Number of Books; and when I was ashore, in observing the Manners and
Dispositions of the People, as well as learning their Language; wherein I
had a great Facility by the Strength of my Memory.

THE last of these Voyages not proving very fortunate, I grew weary
of the Sea, and intended to stay at home with my Wife and Family. I
removed from the *Old Jury* to *Fetter Lane,* and from thence to *Wapping,* 35
hoping to get Business among the Sailors; but it would not turn to account.
After three Years Expectation that things would mend, I accepted an
advantageous Offer from Captain *William Prichard,* Master of the *Ante-*
lope, who was making a Voyage to the *South-Sea.* We set sail from *Bristol,*
May 4th, 1699, and our Voyage at first was very prosperous.   40

IT would not be proper for some Reasons, to trouble the Reader with
the Particulars of our Adventures in those Seas: Let it suffice to inform
him, that in our Passage from thence to the *East-Indies,* we were driven

by a violent Storm to the North-west of *Van Diemen's* Land. By an Observation, we found ourselves in the Latitude of 30 Degrees 2 Minutes South. Twelve of our Crew were dead by immoderate Labour, and ill Food; the rest were in a very weak Condition. On the fifth of *November,* which was the beginning of Summer in those Parts, the Weather being very hazy, the Seamen spyed a Rock, within half a Cable's length of the Ship; but the Wind was so strong, that we were driven directly upon it, and immediately split. Six of the Crew, of whom I was one, having let down the Boat into the Sea, made a Shift to get clear of the Ship, and the Rock. We rowed by my Computation, about three Leagues, till we were able to work no longer, being already spent with Labour while we were in the Ship. We therefore trusted ourselves to the Mercy of the Waves; and in about half an Hour the Boat was overset by a sudden Flurry from the North. What became of my Companions in the Boat, as well as of those who escaped on the Rock, or were left in the Vessel, I cannot tell; but conclude they were all lost. For my own Part, I swam as Fortune directed me, and was pushed forward by Wind and Tide. I often let my Legs drop, and could feel no Bottom: But when I was almost gone, and able to struggle no longer, I found myself within my Depth; and by this Time the Storm was much abated. The Declivity was so small, that I walked near a Mile before I got to the Shore, which I conjectured was about Eight o'Clock in the Evening. I then advanced forward near half a Mile, but could not discover any Sign of Houses or Inhabitants; at least I was in so weak a Condition, that I did not observe them. I was extremely tired, and with that, and the Heat of the Weather, and about half a Pint of Brandy that I drank as I left the Ship, I found myself much inclined to sleep. I lay down on the Grass, which was very short and soft; where I slept sounder than ever I remember to have done in my Life, and as I reckoned, above Nine Hours; for when I awaked, it was just Day-light. I attempted to rise, but was not able to stir: For as I happened to lie on my Back, I found my Arms and Legs were strongly fastened on each Side to the Ground; and my Hair, which was long and thick, tied down in the same Manner. I likewise felt several slender Ligatures across my Body, from my Armpits to my Thighs. I could only look upwards; the Sun began to grow hot, and the Light offended my Eyes. I heard a confused Noise about me, but in the Posture I lay, could see nothing except the Sky. In a little time I felt something alive moving on my left Leg, which advancing gently forward over my Breast, came almost up to my Chin; when bending my Eyes downwards as much as I could, I perceived it to be a human Creature not six Inches high, with a Bow and Arrow in his Hands, and a Quiver at his Back. In the mean time, I felt at least Forty more of the same Kind (as I conjectured) following the first. I was in the utmost Astonishment, and roared so loud, that they all ran back in a Fright; and some of them, as I was afterwards told, were hurt with the Falls they got by leaping from my Sides upon the Ground. However, they soon returned; and one of them, who ventured so far as to get a full Sight of my Face, lifting up his Hands and Eyes by way of Admira-

tion, cryed out in a shrill, but distinct Voice, *Hekinah Degul:* The others
repeated the same Words several times, but I then knew not what they   90
meant. I lay all this while, as the Reader may believe, in great Uneasiness:
At length, struggling to get loose, I had the Fortune to break the Strings,
and wrench out the Pegs that fastened my left Arm to the Ground; for,
by lifting it up to my Face, I discovered the Methods they had taken to
bind me; and, at the same time, with a violent Pull, which gave me   95
excessive Pain, I a little loosened the Strings that tied down my Hair on
the left Side; so that I was just able to turn my Head about two Inches. But
the Creatures ran off a second time, before I could seize them; whereupon
there was a great Shout in a very shrill Accent; and after it ceased, I heard
one of them cry aloud, *Tolgo Phonac;* when in an Instant I felt above an   100
Hundred Arrows discharged on my left Hand, which pricked me like so
many Needles; and besides, they shot another Flight into the Air, as we
do Bombs in *Europe;* whereof many, I suppose, fell on my Body, (though
I felt them not) and some on my Face, which I immediately covered with
my left Hand. When this Shower of Arrows was over, I fell a groaning with   105
Grief and Pain; and then striving again to get loose, they discharged
another Volly larger than the first; and some of them attempted with
Spears to stick me in the Sides; but, by good Luck, I had on me a Buff
Jerkin, which they could not pierce. I thought it the most prudent Method
to lie still; and my Design was to continue so till Night, when my left Hand   110
being already loose, I could easily free myself: And as for the Inhabitants,
I had Reason to believe I might be a Match for the greatest Armies they
could bring against me, if they were all of the same Size with him that I
saw. But Fortune disposed otherwise of me. When the People observed
I was quiet, they discharged no more Arrows: But by the Noise increasing,   115
I knew their Numbers were greater; and about four Yards from me, over-
against my right Ear, I heard a Knocking for above an Hour, like People
at work; when turning my Head that Way, as well as the Pegs and Strings
would permit me, I saw a Stage erected about a Foot and a half from the
Ground, capable of holding four of the Inhabitants, with two or three   120
Ladders to mount it: From whence one of them, who seemed to be a
Person of Quality, made me a long Speech, whereof I understood not one
Syllable. But I should have mentioned, that before the principal Person
began his Oration, he cryed out three times *Langro Dehul san:* (these
Words and the former were afterwards repeated and explained to me.)   125
Whereupon immediately about fifty of the Inhabitants came, and cut the
Strings that fastened the left side of my Head, which gave me the Liberty
of turning it to the right, and of observing the Person and Gesture of him
who was to speak. He appeared to be of a middle Age, and taller than any
of the other three who attended him; whereof one was a Page, who held   130
up his Train, and seemed to be somewhat longer than my middle Finger;
the other two stood one on each side to support him. He acted every part
of an Orator; and I could observe many Periods of Threatnings, and others
of Promises, Pity, and Kindness. I answered in a few Words, but in the
most submissive Manner, lifting up my left Hand and both my eyes to the   135

Sun, as calling him for a Witness; and being almost famished with Hunger, having not eaten a Morsel for some Hours before I left the Ship, I found the Demands of Nature so strong upon me, that I could not forbear shewing my Impatience (perhaps against the strict Rules of Decency) by putting my Finger frequently on my Mouth, to signify that I wanted Food. 140 The *Hurgo* (for so they call a great Lord, as I afterwards learnt) understood me very well: He descended from the Stage, and commanded that several Ladders should be applied to my Sides, on which above an hundred of the Inhabitants mounted, and walked towards my Mouth, laden with Baskets full of Meat, which had been provided, and sent thither by the King's 145 Orders upon the first Intelligence he received of me. I observed there was the Flesh of several Animals, but could not distinguish them by the Taste. There were Shoulders, Legs, and Loins shaped like those of Mutton, and very well dressed, but smaller than the Wings of a Lark. I eat them by two or three at a Mouthful; and took three Loaves at a time, about the bigness 150 of Musket Bullets. They supplyed me as fast as they could, shewing a thousand Marks of Wonder and Astonishment at my Bulk and Appetite. I then made another Sign that I wanted Drink. They found by my eating that a small Quantity would not suffice me; and being a most ingenious People, they slung up with great Dexterity one of their largest Hogsheads; 155 then rolled it towards my Hand, and beat out the Top; I drank it off at a Draught, which I might well do, for it hardly held half a Pint, and tasted like a small Wine of *Burgundy,* but much more delicious. They brought me a second Hogshead, which I drank in the same Manner, and made Signs for more, but they had none to give me. When I had performed these 160 Wonders, they shouted for Joy, and danced upon my Breast, repeating several times as they did at first, *Hekinah Degul.* They made me a Sign that I should throw down the two Hogsheads, but first warned the People below to stand out of the Way, crying aloud, *Borach Mivola;* and when they saw the Vessels in the Air, there was an universal Shout of *Hekinah* 165 *Degul.* I confess I was often tempted, while they were passing backwards and forwards on my Body, to seize Forty or Fifty of the first that came in my Reach, and dash them against the Ground. But the Remembrance of what I had felt, which probably might not be the worst they could do; and the Promise of Honour I made them, for so I interpreted my submissive 170 Behavior, soon drove out those Imaginations. Besides, I now considered my self as bound by the Laws of Hospitality to a People who had treated me with so much Expence and Magnificence. However, in my Thoughts I could not sufficiently wonder at the Intrepidity of these diminutive Mortals, who durst venture to mount and walk on my Body, while one of 175 my Hands was at Liberty, without trembling at the very Sight of so prodigious a Creature as I must appear to them. After some time, when they observed that I made no more Demands for Meat, there appeared before me a Person of high Rank from his Imperial Majesty. His Excellency having mounted on the Small of my Right Leg, advanced forwards up to 180 my Face, with about a Dozen of his Retinue; And producing his Credentials under the Signet Royal, which he applied close to my Eyes, spoke about ten Minutes, without any Signs of Anger, but with a kind of determinate Resolution; often pointing forwards, which, as I afterwards found, was towards the Capital City, about half a Mile distant, whither it was agreed 185 by his Majesty in Council that I must be conveyed. I answered in few Words, but to no Purpose, and made a Sign with my Hand that was loose, putting it to the other, (but over his Excellency's Head, for Fear of hurting him or his Train) and then to my own Head and Body, to signify that I desired my Liberty. It appeared that he understood me well enough; for 190 he shook his Head by way of Disapprobation, and held his Hand in a Posture to shew that I must be carried as a Prisoner. However, he made other Signs to let me understand that I should have Meat and Drink enough, and very good Treatment. Whereupon I once more thought of attempting to break my Bonds; but again, when I felt the Smart of their 195 Arrows upon my Face and Hands, which were all in Blisters, and many of the Darts still sticking in them; and observing likewise that the Number of my Enemies encreased; I gave Tokens to let them know that they might do with me what they pleased. Upon this, the *Hurgo* and his Train withdrew, with much Civility and chearful Countenances. Soon after I heard 200 a general Shout, with frequent Repetitions of the Words, *Peplom Selan,* and I felt great Numbers of the People on my Left Side relaxing the Cords to such a Degree, that I was able to turn upon my Right, and to ease my self with making Water; which I very plentifully did, to the great Astonishment of the People, who conjecturing by my Motions what I was going to 205 do, immediately opened to the right and left on that Side, to avoid the Torrent which fell with such Noise and Violence from me. But before this, they had dawbed my Face and both my Hands with a sort of Ointment very pleasant to the Smell, which in a few Minutes removed all the Smart of their Arrows. These Circumstances, added to the Refreshment I had 210 received by their Victuals and Drink, which were very nourishing, disposed me to sleep. I slept about eight Hours as I was afterwards assured; and it was no Wonder; for the Physicians, by the Emperor's Order, had mingled a sleeping Potion in the Hogsheads of Wine.

It seems that upon the first Moment I was discovered sleeping on the Ground after my Landing, the Emperor had early Notice of it by an 215 Express; and determined in Council that I should be tyed in the Manner I have related, (which was done in the Night while I slept) that Plenty of Meat and Drink should be sent me, and a Machine prepared to carry me to the Capital City.

This resolution perhaps may appear very bold and dangerous, and I am confident would not be imitated by any Prince in *Europe* on the like 220 Occasion; however, in my Opinion it was extremely Prudent as well as Generous. For supposing these People had endeavoured to kill me with their Spears and Arrows while I was asleep; I should certainly have awaked with the first Sense of Smart, which might so far have rouzed my Rage and Strength, as to enable me to break the Strings wherewith I was tyed; after 225 which, as they were not able to make Resistance, so they could expect no Mercy.

These People are most excellent Mathematicians, and arrived to a great Perfection in Mechanicks by the Countenance and Encouragement of the Emperor, who is a renowned Patron of Learning. This Prince hath several Machines fixed on Wheels, for the Carriage of Trees and other great Weights. He often buildeth his largest Men of War, whereof some are Nine Foot long, in the Woods where the Timber grows, and has them carried on these Engines three or four Hundred Yards to the Sea. Five Hundred Carpenters and Engineers were immediately set at work to prepare the greatest Engine they had. It was a Frame of Wood raised three Inches from the Ground, about seven Foot long and four wide, moving upon twenty two Wheels. The Shout I heard, was upon the Arrival of this Engine, which, it seems, set out in four Hours after my Landing. It was brought parallel to me as I lay. But the principal Difficulty was to raise and place me in this Vehicle. Eighty Poles, each of one Foot high, were erected for this Purpose, and very strong Cords of the bigness of Packthread were fastened by Hooks to many Bandages, which the Work-men had girt round my Neck, my Hands, my Body, and my Legs. Nine Hundred of the strongest Men were employed to draw up these Cords by many Pullies fastened on the Poles; and thus in less than three Hours, I was raised and slung into the Engine, and there tyed fast. All this I was told; for while the whole Operation was performing, I lay in a profound Sleep, by the Force of that soporiferous Medicine infused into my Liquor. Fifteen hundred of the Emperor's largest Horses, each about four Inches and a half high, were employed to draw me towards the Metropolis, which, as I said, was half a Mile distant.

About four Hours after we began our Journey, I awaked by a very ridiculous Accident; for the Carriage being stopt a while to adjust something that was out of Order, two or three of the young Natives had the Curiosity to see how I looked when I was asleep; they climbed up into the Engine, and advancing very softly to my Face, one of them, an Officer in the Guards, put the sharp End of his Half-Pike a good way up into my left Nostril, which tickled my Nose like a Straw, and made me sneeze violently: Whereupon they stole off unperceived; and it was three Weeks before I knew the Cause of my awaking so suddenly. We made a long March the remaining Part of the Day, and rested at Night with Five Hundred Guards on each Side of me, half with Torches, and half with Bows and Arrows, ready to shoot me if I should offer to stir. The next Morning at Sunrise we continued our March, and arrived within two Hundred Yards of the City-Gates about Noon. The Emperor, and all his Court, came out to meet us; but his great Officers would by no Means suffer his Majesty to endanger his Person by mounting on my Body.

AT the Place where the Carriage stopt, there stood an ancient Temple, esteemed to be the largest in the whole Kingdom; which having been polluted some Years before by an unnatural Murder, was, according to the Zeal of those People, looked upon as Prophane, and therefore had been applied to common Uses, and all the Ornaments and Furniture carried away. In this Edifice it was determined I should lodge. The great Gate

fronting to the North was about four Foot high, and almost two Foot wide,
through which I could easily creep. On each Side of the Gate was a small
Window not above six Inches from the Ground: Into that on the Left Side,
the King's Smiths conveyed fourscore and eleven Chains, like those that   275
hang to a Lady's Watch in *Europe,* and almost as large, which were locked
to my Left Leg with six and thirty Padlocks. Over against this Temple, on
the other Side of the great Highway, at twenty Foot Distance, there was
a Turret at least five Foot high. Here the Emperor ascended with many
principal Lords of his Court, to have an Opportunity of viewing me, as I   280
was told, for I could not see them. It was reckoned that above an hundred
thousand Inhabitants came out of the Town upon the same Errand; and
in spight of my Guards, I believe there could not be fewer than ten
thousand, at several Times, who mounted upon my Body by the Help of
Ladders. But a Proclamation was soon issued to forbid it, upon Pain of   285
Death. When the Workmen found it was impossible for me to break loose,
they cut all the Strings that bound me; whereupon I rose up with as
melancholy a Disposition as ever I had in my Life. But the Noise and
Astonishment of the People at seeing me rise and walk, are not to be
expressed. The Chains that held my left Leg were about two Yards long,   290
and gave me not only the Liberty of walking backwards and forwards in
a Semicircle; but being fixed within four Inches of the Gate, allowed me
to creep in, and lie at my full Length in the Temple.

Questions

Rereading and Independent Analysis

1. Reread "The Publisher to the Reader," making a list of the details
about Gulliver that are revealed in their order. How would a reader who
does not know what you do about Swift be persuaded by these details?
Why are they believable?

2. The text of the travels printed here uses conventions of written
English that were standard at the time Swift published. Choose any section of the selection and make a list of the features of punctuation, spelling,
mechanics, and vocabulary that you think distinguish it from present-day
writing. Then separate the section into shorter paragraphs. In class, compare these divisions with the ones your classmates made. Where do you
agree and disagree about the best places to begin and end the paragraphs?

Suggested Discussion and Group Activities

1. As a class, analyze the first section of Book I. What clues predict
the nature of Lilliput? At what point in the chapter does it become clear
that Lilliput differs from Gulliver's world? How does Swift ensure that you
will maintain the same perspective that Gulliver has on size?

2. Imagine that you want to publish a work that is entirely imaginary, but you want people to believe you actually have seen what you
describe. How would you, considering present-day media and stories, go
about ensuring that you would be absolutely trusted? In groups, create the

character of this imaginary "author" and specify details that would make your story convincing.

3. What are the social lessons taught by Book I? Are Swift's criticisms applicable now? How do the differences between current and past politics make a difference in the purpose and results of satire? If you wanted to satirize current politics, what are some of the possible settings and observers you might use?

Writing Suggestions

Response

Gulliver's encounter with the Lilliputians demonstrates typical ways we react to people who are very different from us. Describe such an encounter you have had and your reactions to it.

Analysis

1. Imagine a person whom you want to appear to have written a document or essay. Then write a brief letter to be placed before the actual body of this writing, establishing the existence and believability of this fictitious person. Your letter should serve the same purpose that Swift's opening letter does for *Gulliver's Travels,* so analyze his letter carefully before you begin to write. Use details to make the experience, identity, and attitudes of your chosen person believable.

2. Write an essay in which you explain the success of Swift's device of using differences in size and physical powers to demonstrate reactions to strange but still familiar people. In what ways does this device allow the reader to identify with Gulliver? In what ways does it make Swift's social criticism more pointed? You might compare the reactions of both Gulliver and the Lilliputians to your own responses in similar situations.

Finding a Purpose

Write an essay for other students in which you explain why Swift's writing is still appealing to us. If you wish, include *A Modest Proposal* (Chapter 5) as another example of his continuing appeal. What universal problems and situations does his work address, and how does his satiric treatment of them succeed for us as it did for his first readers?

 # From *Nineteen Eighty-four*
George Orwell

Anyone reading this selection is aware that the year 1984 was often judged, and at times lived, in the shadow of George Orwell's disturbing fiction of a future time, *Nineteen Eighty-four* (1949). His construction of life in that year has often been compared to actual and imagined realities of the present time. Orwell (1903–1950), whose real name was Eric Blair, was born in India of English parents, at a time when Britain still controlled a large colonial empire.

He won a scholarship to Eton, an upper-class boys' school in England, but went to Burma before completing his university education and served with the Indian police from 1922 to 1927. Orwell wrote from his experience. Moving from job to job on the Continent, he gathered the material for *Down and Out in Paris and London* (1933). He fought in the Spanish Civil War and afterwards wrote *Homage to Catalonia* (1938).

Orwell was a strong anti-imperialist with many antiestablishment views about the desirable form of government, and he was extraordinarily firm and prescient in his opposition to totalitarianism and thus to Nazism and Communism. *Animal Farm* (1945) expresses his revulsion at Hitler's treatment of the Jewish people. We owe to Orwell the distorted slogan, "Some animals are more equal than others."

Nineteen Eighty-four is a futuristic exploration of life under an extreme form of Communism that destroys and flattens individuality. The book demonstrates the power of a written world. At first, it was published as a cautionary tale warning against the dangers of reshaping human society, but it has since become the standard by which recent actual events and ways of life are evaluated. Fortunately, his prediction was not realized. In this section of the book, Winston Smith describes the new language devised by the state ("Big Brother") to control the mindless masses it creates. As you read it, think about uses of language you know of, or participate in, that divert us from the realities of events by giving them supposedly harmless names.

It was a bright cold day in April, and the clocks were striking thirteen. 1
Winston Smith, his chin nuzzled into his breast in an effort to escape the vile wind, slipped quickly through the glass doors of Victory Mansions, though not quickly enough to prevent a swirl of gritty dust from entering along with him.

The hallway smelt of boiled cabbage and old rag mats. At one end 2
of it a colored poster, too large for indoor display, had been tacked to the wall. It depicted simply an enormous face, more than a meter wide: the face of a man of about forty-five, with a heavy black mustache and ruggedly handsome features. Winston made for the stairs. It was no use trying the lift. Even at the best of times it was seldom working, and at present the electric current was cut off during daylight hours. It was part of the economy drive in preparation for Hate Week. The flat was seven flights up, and Winston, who was thirty-nine and had a varicose ulcer above his right ankle, went slowly, resting several times on the way. On each landing, opposite the lift shaft, the poster with the enormous face gazed from the wall. It was one of those pictures which are so contrived that the eyes follow you about when you move. BIG BROTHER IS WATCHING YOU, the caption beneath it ran.

Inside the flat a fruity voice was reading out a list of figures which 3
had something to do with the production of pig iron. The voice came from an oblong metal plaque like a dulled mirror which formed part of the surface of the right-hand wall. Winston turned a switch and the voice sank somewhat, though the words were still distinguishable. The instrument

(the telescreen, it was called) could be dimmed, but there was no way of shutting it off completely. He moved over to the window: a smallish, frail figure, the meagerness of his body merely emphasized by the blue overalls which were the uniform of the Party. His hair was very fair, his face naturally sanguine, his skin roughened by coarse soap and blunt razor blades and the cold of the winter that had just ended.

Outside, even through the shut window pane, the world looked cold. 4 Down in the street little eddies of wind were whirling dust and torn paper into spirals, and though the sun was shining and the sky a harsh blue, there seemed to be no color in anything except the posters that were plastered everywhere. The black-mustachio'd face gazed down from every commanding corner. There was one on the house front immediately opposite. BIG BROTHER IS WATCHING YOU, the caption said, while the dark eyes looked deep into Winston's own. Down at street level another poster, torn at one corner, flapped fitfully in the wind, alternately covering and uncovering the single word INGSOC. In the far distance a helicopter skimmed down between the roofs, hovered for an instant like a bluebottle, and darted away again with a curving flight. It was the Police Patrol, snooping into people's windows. The patrols did not matter, however. Only the Thought Police mattered.

Behind Winston's back the voice from the telescreen was still bab- 5 bling away about pig iron and the overfulfillment of the Ninth Three-Year Plan. The telescreen received and transmitted simultaneously. Any sound that Winston made, above the level of a very low whisper, would be picked up by it; moreover, so long as he remained within the field of vision which the metal plaque commanded, he could be seen as well as heard. There was of course no way of knowing whether you were being watched at any given moment. How often, or on what system, the Thought Police plugged in on any individual wire was guesswork. It was even conceivable that they watched everybody all the time. But at any rate they could plug in your wire whenever they wanted to. You had to live—did live, from habit that became instinct—in the assumption that every sound you made was overheard, and, except in darkness, every movement scrutinized.

Winston kept his back turned to the telescreen. It was safer; though, 6 as he well knew, even a back can be revealing. A kilometer away the Ministry of Truth, his place of work, towered vast and white above the grimy landscape. This, he thought with a sort of vague distaste—this was London, chief city of Airstrip One, itself the third most populous of the provinces of Oceania. He tried to squeeze out some childhood memory that should tell him whether London had always been quite like this. Were there always these vistas of rotting nineteenth-century houses, their sides shored up with balks of timber, their windows patched with cardboard and their roofs with corrugated iron, their crazy garden walls sagging in all directions? And the bombed sites where the plaster dust swirled in the air and the willow herb straggled over the heaps of rubble; and the places where the bombs had cleared a larger patch and there had sprung up sordid colonies of wooden dwellings like chicken houses? But it was no use, he could not remember: nothing remained of his childhood except a series of bright-lit tableaux, occurring against no background and mostly unintelligible.

The Ministry of Truth—Minitrue, in Newspeak*—was startlingly 7 different from any other object in sight. It was an enormous pyramidal structure of glittering white concrete, soaring up, terrace after terrace, three hundred meters into the air. From where Winston stood it was just possible to read, picked out on its white face in elegant lettering, the three slogans of the Party:

WAR IS PEACE

FREEDOM IS SLAVERY

IGNORANCE IS STRENGTH.

The Ministry of Truth contained, it was said, three thousand rooms above ground level, and corresponding ramifications below. Scattered about London there were just three other buildings of similar appearance and size. So completely did they dwarf the surrounding architecture that from the roof of Victory Mansions you could see all four of them simultaneously. They were the homes of the four Ministries between which the entire apparatus of government was divided: the Ministry of Truth, which concerned itself with news, entertainment, education, and the fine arts; the Ministry of Peace, which concerned itself with war; the Ministry of Love, which maintained law and order; and the Ministry of Plenty, which was responsible for economic affairs. Their names, in Newspeak: Minitrue, Minipax, Miniluv, and Miniplenty.

The Ministry of Love was the really frightening one. There were no 8 windows in it at all. Winston had never been inside the Ministry of Love, nor within half a kilometer of it. It was a place impossible to enter except on official business, and then only by penetrating through a maze of barbed-wire entanglements, steel doors, and hidden machine-gun nests. Even the streets leading up to its outer barriers were roamed by gorilla-faced guards in black uniforms, armed with jointed truncheons.

Winston turned round abruptly. He had set his features into the 9 expression of quiet optimism which it was advisable to wear when facing the telescreen. He crossed the room into the tiny kitchen. By leaving the Ministry at this time of day he had sacrificed his lunch in the canteen, and he was aware that there was no food in the kitchen except a hunk of dark-colored bread which had got to be saved for tomorrow's breakfast. He took down from the shelf a bottle of colorless liquid with a plain white label marked VICTORY GIN. It gave off a sickly, oily smell, as of Chinese rice-spirit. Winston poured out nearly a teacupful, nerved himself for a shock, and gulped it down like a dose of medicine.

---

* Newspeak was the official language of Oceania.

Instantly his face turned scarlet and the water ran out of his eyes. The 10
stuff was like nitric acid, and moreover, in swallowing it one had the
sensation of being hit on the back of the head with a rubber club. The next
moment, however, the burning in his belly died down and the world
began to look more cheerful. He took a cigarette from a crumpled packet
marked VICTORY CIGARETTES and incautiously held it upright, whereupon the tobacco fell out onto the floor. With the next he was more
successful. He went back to the living room and sat down at a small table
that stood to the left of the telescreen. From the table drawer he took out
a penholder, a bottle of ink, and a thick, quarto-sized blank book with a
red back and a marbled cover.

For some reason the telescreen in the living room was in an unusual 11
position. Instead of being placed, as was normal, in the end wall, where
it could command the whole room, it was in the longer wall, opposite the
window. To one side of it there was a shallow alcove in which Winston was
now sitting, and which, when the flats were built, had probably been
intended to hold bookshelves. By sitting in the alcove, and keeping well
back, Winston was able to remain outside the range of the telescreen, so
far as sight went. He could be heard, of course, but so long as he stayed
in his present position he could not be seen. It was partly the unusual
geography of the room that had suggested to him the thing that he was
now about to do.

But it had also been suggested by the book that he had just taken out 12
of the drawer. It was a peculiarly beautiful book. Its smooth creamy paper,
a little yellowed by age, was of a kind that had not been manufactured for
at least forty years past. He could guess, however, that the book was much
older than that. He had seen it lying in the window of a frowsy little junk
shop in a slummy quarter of the town (just what quarter he did not now
remember) and had been stricken immediately by an overwhelming desire to possess it. Party members were supposed not to go into ordinary
shops ("dealing on the free market," it was called), but the rule was not
strictly kept, because there were various things such as shoelaces and razor
blades which it was impossible to get hold of in any other way. He had
given a quick glance up and down the street and then had slipped inside
and bought the book for two dollars fifty. At the time he was not conscious
of wanting it for any particular purpose. He had carried it guiltily home
in his brief case. Even with nothing written in it, it was a compromising
possession.

The thing that he was about to do was to open a diary. This was not 13
illegal (nothing was illegal, since there were no longer any laws), but if
detected it was reasonably certain that it would be punished by death, or
at least by twenty-five years in a forced-labor camp. Winston fitted a nib
into the penholder and sucked it to get the grease off. The pen was an
archaic instrument, seldom used even for signatures, and he had procured
one, furtively and with some difficulty, simply because of a feeling that the
beautiful creamy paper deserved to be written on with a real nib instead

of being scratched with an ink pencil. Actually he was not used to writing by hand. Apart from very short notes, it was usual to dictate everything into the speak-write, which was of course impossible for his present purpose. He dipped the pen into the ink and then faltered for just a second. A tremor had gone through his bowels. To mark the paper was the decisive act. In small clumsy letters he wrote:

April 4th, 1984.

He sat back. A sense of complete helplessness had descended upon 14 him. To begin with, he did not know with any certainty that this *was* 1984. It must be round about that date, since he was fairly sure that his age was thirty-nine, and he believed that he had been born in 1944 or 1945; but it was never possible nowadays to pin down any date within a year or two.

For whom, it suddenly occurred to him to wonder, was he writing 15 this diary? For the future, for the unborn. His mind hovered for a moment round the doubtful date on the page, and then fetched up with a bump against the Newspeak word *doublethink.* For the first time the magnitude of what he had undertaken came home to him. How could you communicate with the future? It was of its nature impossible. Either the future would resemble the present, in which case it would not listen to him, or it would be different from it, and his predicament would be meaningless.

For some time he sat gazing stupidly at the paper. The telescreen 16 had changed over to strident military music. It was curious that he seemed not merely to have lost the power of expressing himself, but even to have forgotten what it was that he had originally intended to say. For weeks past he had been making ready for this moment, and it had never crossed his mind that anything would be needed except courage. The actual writing would be easy. All he had to do was to transfer to paper the interminable restless monologue that had been running inside his head, literally for years. At this moment, however, even the monologue had dried up. Moreover, his varicose ulcer had begun itching unbearably. He dared not scratch it, because if he did so it always became inflamed. The seconds were ticking by. He was conscious of nothing except the blankness of the page in front of him, the itching of the skin above his ankle, the blaring of the music, and a slight booziness caused by the gin.

Suddenly he began writing in sheer panic, only imperfectly aware of 17 what he was setting down. His small but childish handwriting straggled up and down the page, shedding first its capital letters and finally even its full stops:

April 4th, 1984. Last night to the flicks. All war films. One very good 18 *one of a ship full of refugees being bombed somewhere in the Mediterranean. Audience much amused by shots of a great huge fat man trying to swim away with a helicopter after him. first you saw him wallowing along in the water like a porpoise, then you saw him through the helicopters gunsights, then he was full of holes and the sea round him turned pink and he sank as suddenly as though the holes had let in the water. audience shouting with laughter when he sank. then you saw a lifeboat full of children with a helicopter hovering over it. there was a middleaged woman might have been a jewess sitting up in the bow with a little boy about three years old in her arms. little boy screaming with fright and hiding his head between her breasts as if he was trying to burrow right into her and the woman putting her arms round him and comforting him although she was blue with fright herself. all the time covering him up as much as possible as if she thought her arms could keep the bullets off him. then the helicopter planted a 20 kilo bomb in among them terrific flash and the boat went all to matchwood. then there was a wonderful shot of a childs arm going up up up right up into the air a helicopter with a camera in its nose must have followed it up and there was a lot of applause from the party seats but a woman down in the prole part of the house suddenly started kicking up a fuss and shouting they didnt oughter of showed it not in front of kids they didnt it aint right not in front of kids it aint until the police turned her turned her out i dont suppose anything happened to her nobody cares what the proles say typical prole reaction they never—*

. . . .

"Just the man I was looking for," said a voice at Winston's back.　　19

He turned round. It was his friend Syme, who worked in the Re-　20
search Department. Perhaps "friend" was not exactly the right word. You did not have friends nowadays, you had comrades; but there were some comrades whose society was pleasanter than that of others. Syme was a philologist, a specialist in Newspeak. Indeed, he was one of the enormous team of experts now engaged in compiling the Eleventh Edition of the Newspeak dictionary. He was a tiny creature, smaller than Winston, with dark hair and large, protuberant eyes, at once mournful and derisive, which seemed to search your face closely while he was speaking to you.

"I wanted to ask you whether you'd got any razor blades," he said.　21

"Not one!" said Winston with a sort of guilty haste. "I've tried all over　22
the place. They don't exist any longer."

Everyone kept asking you for razor blades. Actually he had two　23
unused ones which he was hoarding up. There had been a famine of them for months past. At any given moment there was some necessary article which the Party shops were unable to supply. Sometimes it was buttons, sometimes it was darning wool, sometimes it was shoelaces; at present it was razor blades. You could only get hold of them, if at all, by scrounging more or less furtively on the "free" market.

"I've been using the same blade for six weeks," he added untruth-　24
fully.

The queue gave another jerk forward. As they halted he turned and　25
faced Syme again. Each of them took a greasy metal tray from a pile at the edge of the counter.

"Did you go and see the prisoners hanged yesterday?" said Syme.   26

"I was working," said Winston indifferently. "I shall see it on the   27
flicks, I suppose."

"A very inadequate substitute," said Syme.   28

His mocking eyes roved over Winston's face. "I know you," the eyes   29
seemed to say, "I see through you. I know very well why you didn't go to
see those prisoners hanged." In an intellectual way, Syme was venomously
orthodox. He would talk with a disagreeable gloating satisfaction of helicopter raids on enemy villages, the trials and confessions of thought-crimi-
nals, the executions in the cellars of the Ministry of Love. Talking to him
was largely a matter of getting him away from such subjects and entan-
gling him, if possible, in the technicalities of Newspeak, on which he was
authoritative and interesting. Winston turned his head a little aside to
avoid the scrutiny of the large dark eyes.

"It was a good hanging," said Syme reminiscently. "I think it spoils   30
it when they tie their feet together. I like to see them kicking. And above
all, at the end, the tongue sticking right out, and blue—a quite bright blue.
That's the detail that appeals to me."

"Nex', please!" yelled the white-aproned prole with the ladle.   31

Winston and Syme pushed their trays beneath the grille. Onto each   32
was dumped swiftly the regulation lunch—a metal pannikin of pinkish-
gray stew, a hunk of bread, a cube of cheese, a mug of milkless Victory
Coffee, and one saccharine tablet.

"There's a table over there, under that telescreen," said Syme. "Let's   33
pick up a gin on the way."

The gin was served out to them in handleless china mugs. They   34
threaded their way across the crowded room and unpacked their trays
onto the metal-topped table, on one corner of which someone had left a
pool of stew, a filthy liquid mess that had the appearance of vomit. Winston
took up his mug of gin, paused for an instant to collect his nerve, and
gulped the oily-tasting stuff down. When he had winked the tears out of
his eyes he suddenly discovered that he was hungry. He began swallowing
spoonfuls of the stew, which, in among its general sloppiness, had cubes
of spongy pinkish stuff which was probably a preparation of meat. Neither
of them spoke again till they had emptied their pannikins. From the table
at Winston's left, a little behind his back, someone was talking rapidly and
continuously, a harsh gabble almost like the quacking of a duck, which
pierced the general uproar of the room.

"How is the dictionary getting on?" said Winston, raising his voice to   35
overcome the noise.

"Slowly," said Syme. "I'm on the adjectives. It's fascinating."   36

He had brightened up immediately at the mention of Newspeak. He   37
pushed his pannikin aside, took up his hunk of bread in one delicate hand
and his cheese in the other, and leaned across the table so as to be able
to speak without shouting.

"The Eleventh Edition is the definitive edition," he said. "We're   38 getting the language into its final shape—the shape it's going to have when nobody speaks anything else. When we've finished with it, people like you will have to learn it all over again. You think, I dare say, that our chief job is inventing new words. But not a bit of it! We're destroying words—scores of them, hundreds of them, every day. We're cutting the language down to the bone. The Eleventh Edition won't contain a single word that will become obsolete before the year 2050."

He bit hungrily into his bread and swallowed a couple of mouthfuls, 39 then continued speaking, with a sort of pedant's passion. His thin dark face had become animated, his eyes had lost their mocking expression and grown almost dreamy.

"It's a beautiful thing, the destruction of words. Of course the great 40 wastage is in the verbs and adjectives, but there are hundreds of nouns that can be got rid of as well. It isn't only the synonyms; there are also the antonyms. After all, what justification is there for a word which is simply the opposite of some other word? A word contains its opposite in itself. Take 'good,' for instance. If you have a word like 'good,' what need is there for a word like 'bad'? 'Ungood' will do just as well—better, because it's an exact opposite, which the other is not. Or again, if you want a stronger version of 'good,' what sense is there in having a whole string of vague useless words like 'excellent' and 'splendid' and all the rest of them? 'Plusgood' covers the meaning, or 'doubleplusgood' if you want something stronger still. Of course we use those forms already, but in the final version of Newspeak there'll be nothing else. In the end the whole notion of goodness and badness will be covered by only six words—in reality, only one word. Don't you see the beauty of that, Winston? It was B.B.'s idea originally, of course," he added as an afterthought.

A sort of vapid eagerness flitted across Winston's face at the mention 41 of Big Brother. Nevertheless Syme immediately detected a certain lack of enthusiasm.

"You haven't a real appreciation of Newspeak, Winston," he said 42 almost sadly. "Even when you write it you're still thinking in Oldspeak. I've read some of those pieces that you write in the *Times* occasionally. They're good enough, but they're translations. In your heart you'd prefer to stick to Oldspeak, with all its vagueness and its useless shades of meaning. You don't grasp the beauty of the destruction of words. Do you know that Newspeak is the only language in the world whose vocabulary gets smaller every year?"

Winston did know that, of course. He smiled, sympathetically he 43 hoped, not trusting himself to speak. Syme bit off another fragment of the dark-colored bread, chewed it briefly, and went on:

"Don't you see that the whole aim of Newspeak is to narrow the 44 range of thought? In the end we shall make thoughtcrime literally impossible, because there will be no words in which to express it. Every concept that can ever be needed will be expressed by exactly *one* word, with its meaning rigidly defined and all its subsidiary meanings rubbed out and forgotten. Already, in the Eleventh Edition, we're not far from that point. But the process will still be continuing long after you and I are dead. Every year fewer and fewer words, and the range of consciousness always a little smaller. Even now, of course, there's no reason or excuse for committing thoughtcrime. It's merely a question of self-discipline, reality-control. But in the end there won't be any need even for that. The Revolution will be complete when the language is perfect. Newspeak is Ingsoc and Ingsoc is Newspeak," he added with a sort of mystical satisfaction. "Has it ever occurred to you, Winston, that by the year 2050, at the very latest, not a single human being will be alive who could understand such a conversation as we are having now?"

"Except—" began Winston doubtfully, and then stopped.   45

It had been on the tip of his tongue to say "Except the proles," but 46
he checked himself, not feeling fully certain that this remark was not in some way unorthodox. Syme, however, had divined what he was about to say.

"The proles are not human beings," he said carelessly. "By 2050— 47
earlier, probably—all real knowledge of Oldspeak will have disappeared. The whole literature of the past will have been destroyed. Chaucer, Shakespeare, Milton, Byron—they'll exist only in Newspeak versions, not merely changed into something different, but actually changed into something contradictory of what they used to be. Even the literature of the Party will change. Even the slogans will change. How could you have a slogan like 'freedom is slavery' when the concept of freedom has been abolished? The whole climate of thought will be different. In fact there will *be* no thought, as we understand it now. Orthodoxy means not thinking—not needing to think. Orthodoxy is unconsciousness."

One of these days, thought Winston with sudden deep conviction, 48
Syme will be vaporized. He is too intelligent. He sees too clearly and speaks too plainly. The Party does not like such people. One day he will disappear. It is written in his face.

. . . .

It was after twenty-two hours when he got back to the flat. The lights 49
would be switched off at the main at twenty-three thirty. He went into the kitchen and swallowed nearly a teacupful of Victory Gin. Then he went to the table in the alcove, sat down, and took the diary out of the drawer. But he did not open it at once. From the telescreen a brassy female voice was squalling a patriotic song. He sat staring at the marbled cover of the book, trying without success to shut the voice out of his consciousness.

It was at night that they came for you, always at night. The proper 50
thing was to kill yourself before they got you. Undoubtedly some people did so. Many of the disappearances were actually suicides. But it needed desperate courage to kill yourself in a world where firearms, or any quick and certain poison, were completely unprocurable. He thought with a kind of astonishment of the biological uselessness of pain and fear, the

treachery of the human body which always freezes into inertia at exactly the moment when a special effort is needed. He might have silenced the dark-haired girl if only he had acted quickly enough; but precisely because of the extremity of his danger he had lost the power to act. It struck him that in moments of crisis one is never fighting against an external enemy but always against one's own body. Even now, in spite of the gin, the dull ache in his belly made consecutive thought impossible. And it is the same, he perceived, in all seemingly heroic or tragic situations. On the battle-field, in the torture chamber, on a sinking ship, the issues that you are fighting for are always forgotten, because the body swells up until it fills the universe, and even when you are not paralyzed by fright or screaming with pain, life is a moment-to-moment struggle against hunger or cold or sleeplessness, against a sour stomach or an aching tooth.

He opened the diary. It was important to write something down. The 51 woman on the television had started a new song. Her voice seemed to stick into his brain like jagged splinters of glass. He tried to think of O'Brien, for whom, or to whom, the diary was written, but instead he began thinking of the things that would happen to him after the Thought Police took him away. It would not matter if they killed you at once. To be killed was what you expected. But before death (nobody spoke of such things, yet everybody knew of them) there was the routine of confession that had to be gone through: the groveling on the floor and screaming for mercy, the crack of broken bones, the smashed teeth and bloody clots of hair. Why did you have to endure it, since the end was always the same? Why was it not possible to cut a few days or weeks out of your life? Nobody ever escaped detection, and nobody ever failed to confess. When once you had succumbed to thoughtcrime it was certain that by a given date you would be dead. Why then did that horror, which altered nothing, have to lie embedded in future time?

He tried with a little more success than before to summon up the 52 image of O'Brien. "We shall meet in the place where there is no darkness," O'Brien had said to him. He knew what it meant, or thought he knew. The place where there is no darkness was the imagined future, which one would never see, but which, by foreknowledge, one could mystically share in. But with the voice from the telescreen nagging at his ears he could not follow the train of thought further. He put a cigarette in his mouth. Half the tobacco promptly fell out on to his tongue, a bitter dust which was difficult to spit out again. The face of Big Brother swam into his mind, displacing that of O'Brien. Just as he had done a few days earlier, he slid a coin out of his pocket and looked at it. The face gazed up at him, heavy, calm, protecting, but what kind of smile was hidden beneath the dark mustache? Like a leaden knell the words came back at him:

WAR IS PEACE

FREEDOM IS SLAVERY

IGNORANCE IS STRENGTH.

Questions

Rereading and Independent Analysis

1. Reread this selection, making a list of each of the words and phrases that are identified as "Newspeak." Then rewrite each of the items on your list, using clear and accurate descriptive terms to show what these elements of Newspeak mean.

2. Make a list of each of the slogans and labels (e.g., "Victory Gin") in this selection. What is the purpose of such language? Can you think of examples now in use that rename an item or idea to make its characteristics either more or less clear?

Suggested Discussion and Group Activities

1. Although Orwell's fearsome predictions for 1984 did not materialize, we can find examples in American culture of many of the things he criticizes. Identify similarities between this written version of 1984 and our time. Then comment on Winston Smith's thought that "either the future would resemble the present, in which case it would not listen to him, or it would be different from it, and his predicament would be meaningless." Is either alternative correct? Explain why you think so.

2. The most emphasized tyranny in Orwell's *Nineteen Eighty-four* is control and modification of the language people use to do away with "vagueness and . . . useless shades of meaning." How can the use of simple slogans, distortions, and vague generalities modify people's behavior? Bring to your group similar examples of simplistic language in common use now. Discuss how these jargonistic simplifications affect our power to analyze facts and the implications of words. Can you cite examples of your own mistakes or misunderstandings caused by labels that substitute for complete explanations?

Writing Suggestions

Response

Choose an example of the kind of repression suggested by Orwell's vision of 1984 that you think controls your life. Write a few paragraphs in which you describe this force and the way it affects you.

Analysis

Write a warning to people who write advertising and news, using examples from Orwell to show how jargon and labels can create dangerous distortions. Show how Orwell uses images of writing, vocabulary, and slogans to demonstrate his point about the individual in a totalitarian state. Make it clear to writers of ads and news copy that preserving individualism is in the best interests of both their readers' and their own freedom.

Finding a Purpose

Write an essay entitled "Two Thousand Eighty-four." Your essay should serve Orwell's purpose—to warn people about the dangers that may result from current social trends. You may imagine the future as you wish, but one option would be to describe individual life in a world that is dominated by computer and fast-food companies that have joined in a conspiracy to become indispensable in everyone's daily activities. Imagine that this conglomerate has gained significant influence over social customs, politics, religion, and patterns of family life. You may wish to use one person's activities and thoughts to convey the general quality of life.

 # I Discover America
Abraham Cahan

In the earlier part of this century, thousands of immigrants arrived each year on the east coast of the United States after leaving their homes throughout Europe to establish new lives in the land of opportunity that they vividly imagined. It required courage to leave an ancestral home for an unknown, storybook land where they might—but might not—have friends or family. This courage was developed, as Abraham Cahan (1860–1951) shows in *The Rise of David Levinsky* (1917), by imaginatively creating a new world. The Polish, Russian, Greek, Italian, Turkish, and other immigrants all discovered a new America, multiplying Columbus's geographic America in their own versions of the new land. Their individual dreams gave form to the reality of open opportunity.

This immigrant experience, because it has created millions of individual new worlds, has become a common subject for many writers. (Mark Helprin's *Ellis Island* (1976) is a similar, more recent example of such an individual world.) The incidents and characters Cahan describes have become stock devices for representing the anxiety, fear, and excitement of the first taste of a new life. Cahan takes us from an imagined to a real America, shifting frequently between Levinsky's expectations before he came and the actual experiences he had. As you read, compare his story to other representations of arrivals and discoveries (for instance, in science fiction) that you have read or seen. How are Cahan's techniques similar to strategies used in other such accounts? Why do you think people often write about this kind of experience?

Two weeks later I was one of the multitude of steerage passengers on a 1
Bremen steamship on my way to New York. Who can depict the feeling of desolation, homesickness, uncertainty, and anxiety with which an emigrant makes his first voyage across the ocean? I proved to be a good sailor, but the sea frightened me. The thumping of the engines was drumming a ghastly accompaniment to the awesome whisper of the waves. I felt in the embrace of a vast, uncanny force. And echoing through it all were the heart-lashing words:

"Are you crazy? You forget your place, young man!" 2

When Columbus was crossing the Atlantic, on his first great voyage, 3
his men doubted whether they would ever reach land. So does many an
American-bound emigrant to this day. Such, at least, was the feeling that
was lurking in my heart while the Bremen steamer was carrying me to
New York. Day after day passes and all you see about you is an unbroken
waste of water, an unrelieved, a hopeless monotony of water. You know
that a change will come, but this knowledge is confined to your brain. Your
senses are skeptical.

In my devotions, which I performed three times a day, without 4
counting a benediction before every meal and every drink of water, grace
after every meal and a prayer before going to sleep, I would mentally
plead for the safety of the ship and for a speedy sight of land. My scanty
luggage included a pair of phylacteries and a plump little prayer-book,
with the Book of Psalms at the end. The prayers I knew by heart, but I
now often said psalms, in addition, particularly when the sea looked angry
and the pitching or rolling was unusually violent. I would read all kinds
of psalms, but my favorite among them was the 104th, generally referred
to by our people as "Bless the Lord, O my soul," its opening words in the
original Hebrew. It is a poem on the power and wisdom of God as manifes-
ted in the wonders of nature, some of its verses dealing with the sea. It is
said by the faithful every Saturday afternoon during the fall and winter:
so I could have recited it from memory; but I preferred to read it in my
prayerbook. For it seemed as though the familiar words had changed their
identity and meaning, especially those concerned with the sea. Their
divine inspiration was now something visible and audible. It was not I who
was reading them. It was as though the waves and the clouds, the whole
far-flung scene of restlessness and mystery, were whispering to me:

"Thou who coverest thyself with light as with a garment, who 5
stretches out the heavens like a curtain: who layeth the beams of his
chambers in the waters: who maketh the clouds his chariot: who walketh
upon the wings of the wind. . . . So is this great and wide sea wherein are
things creeping innumerable, both small and great beasts. There go the
ships: there is that leviathan whom thou hast made to play therein. . . ."

The relentless presence of Matilda in my mind worried me im- 6
measurably, for to think of a woman who is a stranger to you is a sin, and
so there was the danger of the vessel coming to grief on my account. And,
as though to spite me, the closing verse of Psalm 104 reads, "Let the
sinners be consumed out of the earth and let the wicked be no more." I
strained every nerve to keep Matilda out of my thoughts, but without
avail.

When the discoverers of America saw land at last they fell on their 7
knees and a hymn of thanksgiving burst from their souls. The scene, which
is one of the most thrilling in history, repeats itself in the heart of every
immigrant as he comes in sight of the American shores. I am at a loss to
convey the peculiar state of mind that the experience created in me.

When the ship reached Sandy Hook I was literally overcome with the 8
beauty of the landscape.

The immigrant's arrival in his new home is like a second birth to 9 him. Imagine a new-born babe in possession of a fully developed intellect. Would it ever forget its entry into the world? Neither does the immigrant ever forget his entry into a country which is, to him, a new world in the profoundest sense of the term and in which he expects to pass the rest of his life. I conjure up the gorgeousness of the spectacle as it appeared to me on that clear June morning: the magnificent verdure of Staten Island, the tender blue of sea and sky, the dignified bustle of passing craft—above all, those floating, squatting, multitudinously windowed palaces which I subsequently learned to call ferries. It was all so utterly unlike anything I had ever seen or dreamed of before. It unfolded itself like a divine revelation. I was in a trance or in something closely resembling one.

"This, then, is America!" I exclaimed, mutely. The notion of some- 10 thing enchanted which the name had always evoked in me now seemed fully borne out.

In my ecstasy I could not help thinking of Psalm 104, and, opening 11 my little prayer-book, I glanced over those of its verses that speak of hills and rocks, of grass and trees and birds.

My transport of admiration, however, only added to my sense of 12 helplessness and awe. Here, on shipboard, I was sure of my shelter and food, at least. How was I going to procure my sustenance on those magic shores? I wished the remaining hour could be prolonged indefinitely.

Psalm 104 spoke reassuringly to me. It reminded me of the way God 13 took care of man and beast: "Thou openest thine hand and they are filled with good." But then the very next verse warned me that "Thou hidest thy face, they are troubled: thou takest away their breath, they die." So I was praying God not to hide His face from me, but to open His hand to me; to remember that my mother had been murdered by Gentiles and that I was going to a strange land. When I reached the words, "I will sing unto the Lord as long as I live: I will sing praise to my God while I have my being," I uttered them in a fervent whisper.

My unhappy love never ceased to harrow me. The stern image of 14 Matilda blended with the hostile glamour of America.

One of my fellow-passengers was a young Yiddish-speaking tailor 15 named Gitelson. He was about twenty-four years old, yet his forelock was gray, just his forelock, the rest of his hair being a fine, glossy brown. His own cap had been blown into the sea and the one he had obtained from the steerage steward was too small for him, so that gray tuft of his was always out like a plume. We had not been acquainted more than a few hours, in fact, for he had been seasick throughout the voyage and this was the first day he had been up and about. But then I had seen him on the day of our sailing and subsequently, many times, as he wretchedly lay in his berth. He was literally in tatters. He clung to me like a lover, but we spoke very little. Our hearts were too full for words.

As I thus stood at the railing, prayer-book in hand, he took a look at 16 the page. The most ignorant "man of the earth" among our people can read holy tongue (Hebrew), though he may not understand the meaning of the words. This was the case with Gitelson.

"Saying, 'Bless the Lord, O my soul'?" he asked, reverently. "Why 17 this chapter of all others?"

"Because—Why, just listen." With which I took to translating the 18 Hebrew text into Yiddish for him.

He listened with devout mien. I was not sure that he understood it 19 even in his native tongue, but, whether he did or not, his beaming, wistful look and the deep sigh he emitted indicated that he was in a state similar to mine.

When I say that my first view of New York Bay struck me as some- 20 thing not of this earth it is not a mere figure of speech. I vividly recall the feeling, for example, with which I greeted the first cat I saw on American soil. It was on the Hoboken pier, while the steerage passengers were being marched to the ferry. A large, black, well-fed feline stood in a corner, eyeing the crowd of new-comers. The sight of it gave me a thrill of joy. "Look! there is a cat!" I said to Gitelson. And in my heart I added, "Just like those at home!" For the moment the little animal made America real to me. At the same time it seemed unreal itself. I was tempted to feel its fur to ascertain whether it was actually the kind of creature I took it for.

We were ferried over to Castle Garden. One of the things that caught 21 my eye as I entered the vast rotunda was an iron staircase rising diagonally against one of the inner walls. A uniformed man, with some papers in his hands, ascended it with brisk, resounding step till he disappeared through a door not many inches from the ceiling. It may seem odd, but I can never think of my arrival in this country without hearing the ringing footfalls of this official and beholding the yellow eyes of the black cat which stared at us at the Hoboken pier.

The harsh manner of the immigration officers was a grievous surprise 22 to me. As contrasted with the officials of my despotic country, those of a republic had been portrayed in my mind as paragons of refinement and cordiality. My anticipations were rudely belied. "They are not a bit better than Cossacks," I remarked to Gitelson. But they neither looked nor spoke like Cossacks, so their gruff voices were part of the uncanny scheme of things that surrounded me. These unfriendly voices flavored all America with a spirit of icy inhospitality that sent a chill through my very soul.

The stringent immigration laws that were passed some years later 23 had not yet come into existence. We had no difficulty in being admitted to the United States, and when I was I was loath to leave the Garden.

Many of the other immigrants were met by relatives, friends. There 24 were cries of joy, tears, embraces, kisses. All of which intensified my sense of loneliness and dread of the New World. The agencies which two Jewish charity organizations now maintain at the Immigrant Station had not yet been established. Gitelson, who like myself had no friends in New York, never left my side. He was even more timid than I. It seemed as though he were holding on to me for dear life. This had the effect of putting me on my mettle.

"Cheer up, old man!" I said, with bravado. "America is not the place 25 to be a ninny in. Come, pull yourself together."

In truth, I addressed these exhortations as much to myself as to him: 26 and so far, at least, as I was concerned, my words had the desired effect.

I led the way out of the big Immigrant Station. As we reached the 27 park outside we were pounced down upon by two evil-looking men, representatives of boarding-houses for immigrants. They pulled us so roughly and their general appearance and manner were so uninviting that we struggled and protested until they let us go—not without some parting curses. Then I led the way across Battery Park and under the Elevated railway to State Street. A train hurtling and panting along overhead produced a bewildering, a daunting effect on me. The active life of the great strange city made me feel like one abandoned in the midst of a jungle. Where were we to go? What were we to do? But the presence of Gitelson continued to act as a spur on me. I mustered courage to approach a policeman, something I should never have been bold enough to do at home. As a matter of fact, I scarcely had an idea what his function was. To me he looked like some uniformed nobleman—an impression that in itself was enough to intimidate me. With his coat of blue cloth, starched linen collar, and white gloves, he reminded me of anything but the policemen of my town. I addressed him in Yiddish, making it as near an approach to German as I knew how, but my efforts were lost on him. He shook his head. With a witheringly dignified grimace he then pointed his club in the direction of Broadway and strutted off majestically.

"He's not better than a Cossack, either," was my verdict. . 28

At this moment a voice hailed us in Yiddish. Facing about, we beheld 29 a middle-aged man with huge, round, perpendicular nostrils and a huge, round, deep dimple in his chin that looked like a third nostril. Prosperity was written all over his smooth-shaven face and broad-shouldered, stocky figure. He was literally aglow with diamonds and self-satisfaction. But he was unmistakably one of our people. It was like coming across a human being in the jungle. Moreover, his very diamonds somehow told a tale of former want, of a time when he had landed, an impecunious immigrant like myself; and this made him a living source of encouragement to me.

"God Himself has sent you to us," I began, acting as the spokesman: 30 but he gave no heed to me. His eyes were eagerly fixed on Gitelson and his tatters.

"You're a tailor, aren't you?" he questioned him. 31

My steerage companion nodded. "I'm a ladies' tailor, but I have 32 worked on men's clothing, too," he said.

"A ladies' tailor?" the well-dressed stranger echoed, with ill-concealed delight. "Very well; come along. I have work for you." 33

That he should have been able to read Gitelson's trade in his face and 34 figure scarcely surprised me. In my native place it seemed to be a matter of course that one could tell a tailor by his general appearance and walk. Besides, had I not divined the occupation of my fellow-passenger the moment I saw him on deck?

As I learned subsequently, the man who accosted us on State Street 35
was a cloak contractor, and his presence in the neighborhood of Castle
Garden was anything but a matter of chance. He came there quite often,
in fact, his purpose being to angle for cheap labor among the newly
arrived immigrants.

We paused near Bowling Green. The contractor and my fellow- 36
passenger were absorbed in a conversation full of sartorial technicalities
which were Greek to me, but which brought a gleam of joy into Gitelson's
eye. My former companion seemed to have become oblivious of my existence.

As we resumed our walk up Broadway the bejeweled man turned to 37
me.

"And what was your occupation? You have no trade, have you?"   38
"I read Talmud," I said confusedly.   39
"I see, but that's no business in America," he declared. "Any relatives 40
here?"
"No."   41
"Well, don't worry. You will be all right. If a fellow isn't lazy nor a 42
fool he has no reason to be sorry he came to America. It'll be all right."

"All right" he said in English, and I conjectured what it meant from 43
the context. In the course of the minute or two which he bestowed upon
me he uttered it so many times that the phrase engraved itself upon my
memory. It was the first bit of English I ever acquired.

The well-dressed, trim-looking crowds of lower Broadway impressed 44
me as a multitude of counts, barons, princes. I was puzzled by their preoccupied faces and hurried step. It seemed to comport ill with their baronial
dress and general high-born appearance.

In a vague way all this helped to confirm my conception of America 45
as a unique country, unlike the rest of the world.

When we reached the General Post-Office, at the end of the Third 46
Avenue surface line, our guide bade us stop. "Walk straight ahead," he said
to me, waving his hand toward Park Row. "Just keep walking until you see
a lot of Jewish people. It isn't far from here." With which he slipped a silver
quarter into my hand and made Gitelson bid me good-by.

The two then boarded a big red horse-car.   47
I was left with a sickening sense of having been tricked, cast off, and 48
abandoned. I stood watching the receding public vehicle, as though its
scarlet hue were my last gleam of hope in the world. When it finally
disappeared from view my heart sank within me. I may safely say that the
half-hour that followed is one of the worst I experienced in all the thirty-
odd years of my life in this country.

The big, round nostrils of the contractor and the gray forelock of my 49
young steerage-fellow haunted my brain as hideous symbols of treachery.

With twenty-nine cents in my pocket (four cents was all that was left 50
of the sum which I had received from Matilda and her mother) I set forth
in the direction of East Broadway.

Questions

Rereading and Independent Analysis

1. Throughout this selection, Cahan refers to the *difference* between reality and his thoughts or imagination. Reread this piece, marking these references. What pattern do they establish? Does this contrast change as new experiences accumulate?

2. Cahan frequently relies on metaphors and similes to explain the new and strange experiences he is relating in this narrative. Make a list of these comparisons. As you look over the list, identify their function. How do they combat Levinsky's "bewilderment"?

Suggested Discussion and Group Activities

1. This selection moves through stages—imagined America, new America, and a "real" America are all described. Find places in the selection that indicate shifts from one stage to another in the narrator's experiences. How are these stages common in adjusting to all new experiences? Explain your answers.

2. In groups, brainstorm to come up with lists of the things you look for when visiting any new locale. What do you expect to be the same as at home? What do you think will probably be different? How is Cahan's writing valuable to you as a way to make you feel more comfortable about novelty and change? What other resources do you use?

3. The United States is still one of the most frequently adopted countries in the world. Do you think recent immigrants would have experiences like Levinsky's? Imagine a young newcomer from a particular country and list ways his or her first encounters would probably differ from those described in this selection. How have new technologies and media made coming to this country a less startling process than it once was? What are the advantages and disadvantages of knowing more about a country or any new place before moving there?

Writing Suggestions

Response

Write a brief account of your own "discovery" of a new setting, perhaps of coming to your university. What were your primary feelings? Did it live up to your previous expectations?

Analysis

Write an essay in which you use the experience of immigrating to a new country to explain another sort of shocking change. This will require that you write an extended comparison, showing how a sudden change was *like* an immigration experience. Review the narrative form of Cahan's account, and use it as a model for your comparison.

Finding a Purpose

Cahan's piece explains a process of arrival and discovery. Write an essay in which you tell about a similar process you have experienced while adapting to new surroundings. (Use your "Response" answer if you wish.) Your readers are those you left behind, so they know you well but do not know the place you are describing or how you have changed to adapt to it. Make the new place and your changes vivid to them.

Congo on My Mind
Alberto Moravia

Translated by William Weaver

This description of a place that few of us have seen, but that has both actual and imaginary associations, was written by Alberto Moravia (b. 1907), whose long career as a novelist has made him one of Italy's foremost authors. Moravia began his writing career while hospitalized for tuberculosis. At 22, he published his first successful novel, *The Indifferent Ones* (1929). Moravia wrote and traveled in Europe until the increasingly powerful Fascist party took over in Italy. Mussolini read his satire *The Fancy Dress Party* (trans., 1947) and refused to allow its publication. During World War II, Moravia hid in the mountains until the Allies invaded.

His many novels and stories—*Wheel of Fortune* (1937), *Woman of Rome* (1949), *Two Adolescents* (1950), *The Conformist* (1951), and *Roman Tales* (1957)—broke new ground in psychological realism in literature. His work was taken up by the existential movement in Europe, which focused on life as it is actually experienced. He has remained a source for understanding the limited, impoverished, crude world in which the majority of postwar Europeans lived while they worked out universal personal problems.

Moravia himself is a witness to the power of places to influence imagination. His name (originally Pincherle) is the name of a region in Czechoslovakia where he and his family originated. In this essay, published in a special travel section of the *New York Times* in 1984, Moravia describes a trip to Zaire and explores the creation of written worlds such as the literary Congo of Joseph Conrad's novel *Heart of Darkness* (1902), about an explorer who becomes absorbed by the jungle and its "uncivilized" culture. Conrad's purely literary place provides the background for descriptions of the actual places Moravia saw on his trip as they are now.

This essay is a model for understanding the interaction of observation and interpretation. It shows us alternatives for interpreting our actual experiences by comparing and contrasting them to places that already "exist" for us in another form. As you read it (even if you have not read its implied source, Conrad's novel), you will be able to see how actual experiences can refer to other experiences we have had only in reading, with which we stock our imagination. Watch for shifts between the events taking place and Moravia's references to another, imagined version of this place. This interaction between event and imagination helps us understand the new events we witness, giving them significance beyond their immediate impact.

A word gives a name to a place and can also transform the place into 1
literature—which, in turn, is substituted for the place. After Homer, in
certain parts of the Mediterranean you are no longer traveling in Italy or
Greece but in the Iliad or the Odyssey. And it could be said that today,
after Conrad, you are not just in Zaire, or Malaysia, but in "Heart of
Darkness" or in "Lord Jim." These things come to my mind while I am
seated on the deck of the Colonel Ebeya, a small and ancient steamer that
in eight days travels up the River Zaire (it was called the Congo in Conrad's time) from Kinshasa to Kisangani.

I have been traveling to Africa, a continent that fascinates me and 2
to which I always long to return, for 15 years. It is my third voyage on this
river, whose immensity is worthy of the country through which it flows.

Before me, immobile as a swamp under the gray winter sky, stretches 3
the river, plum colored, pocked as far as the eye can see by floating clumps
of water hyacinths. In the distance, you can discern the hazy, melancholy
outline of the forest. The day is hot, humid and oppressive. In the silence
the regular, labored sound of the ship's engines suggests a heart that is
giving out. Everything is still, inert, exhausted, like the first day of Creation. But this endless swamp is actually a gigantic stream that, with imper-
ceptible movement, is flowing to the sea. I can sense the movement as I
look at one clump of water hyacinths, bigger than the others. A few
moments ago it was to the right of my eyes; now it's to the left.

So this is the river of "Heart of Darkness." But there are significant 4
differences between the river that I see and the river described by Conrad. For example, Conrad says that the boat, at a certain moment, comes
upon a kind of sandy island that divides the river into two narrow channels. Conrad's ship enters one of these channels; and then, as it proceeds,
very close to the shore (a distance of 10 feet, according to Conrad), Africa
suddenly bursts out. Savage and threatening faces appear amid the foliage,
and a hissing rain of arrows falls on the deck.

Now none of these details seem exact. At this moment, the Colonel 5
Ebeya is advancing along one of the channels, where an island, just as in
Conrad's novel, divides the river; a short time ago we passed through
another, similar passage. In fact, the entire river, at more or less regular
intervals, is divided into two channels by long, narrow, sandy islands. But
this doesn't make us navigate close to the forest; on the contrary, we are
so far from it that we could never see faces among the leaves or be struck
by arrows. At most, sharpening our eyes considerably, we could glimpse
acrobatic monkeys over there, swinging from branch to branch. Ten feet,
indeed! Between us and the forest, the shallow water must stretch for at
least 150 feet. But why does Conrad exaggerate? Why does he transform
the vast, majestic river into a narrow, menacing canal?

At this point I am distracted from my reflections by something that 6
is happening before my eyes. Yesterday, at a stop, my cabin mates bought
a monkey, already dressed, which is to say, headless, its fur singed, its arms
and legs trussed up. Now a young woman crouching on the deck is chop-

ping the monkey into pieces with great blows of a machete, and as she does this she throws hands, feet, legs, arms and sections of the belly into a pot boiling on a Primus stove. This sight fascinates me. I ask her if monkey is good to eat. She answers, laughing, that it is very good. I remember then that yesterday, in the captain's cabin, I saw a little alligator tied with a rope running between its jaws. The captain assured me that alligator, too, is very good to eat.

So Conrad exaggerates the narrowness of the river and makes it a 7 cramped passage. Why? I think about it a bit and conclude that there's no understanding Conrad unless you bear in mind that he was a man of the 19th century, a former Pole, an Anglophile, or rather an Anglomaniac and, moreover, an old-fashioned gentleman with a strict code of honor. And, naturally, a great writer, of acute moral sensitivity. So then, once these qualities are taken into consideration . . .

Another interruption. All of a sudden, there in the immense expanse 8 of water, I see something surprising on this river where only our steamer and the pirogues are usually seen. Here is a great white vessel, apparently brand-new, all decked out with flags, proceeding slowly in the direction opposed to ours. It looks like a pleasure ship, and, in fact, when I question the captain, who comes along the deck at this moment, he tells me it is the private yacht of Mobutu Sese Seko, the president of Zaire. Then my imagination pictures the luxury of that ship, and I cannot help comparing it with the squalor of ours: drab cabins, with worn linoleum and noisy, inefficient air-conditioners; bath full of spiders, broken mirrors and rusty faucets; stifling dining room, the radio blaring at full volume, army mess food (today it's water buffalo with potatoes, tomorrow potatoes with water buffalo).

As to Mobutu and his yacht, I recall a brief dialogue in Kinshasa: 9 "Mobutu? He's filling his pockets with money that belongs to Zaire. When the revolution comes, we'll settle accounts."

"How?"   10
"We'll kill his whole tribe!"   11
Obviously in Zaire, even today, revolution is a matter not of class but 12 of tribe.

But back to Conrad. He transforms the difficult navigation on the 13 Congo River into a kind of descent into the Underworld: ambushes, arrows, natural obstacles of every kind and, at the end, after two months of sinister journeying, the bloodied nest of Kurtz, the superman slaver and colonialist. All this has been said before, but it's worth repeating: The voyage of "Heart of Darkness" is a voyage to the depths of colonialism, which takes the form of an Inferno in which Conrad is the dubious and horrified Dante. And, as in the Inferno of Dante, at the end, there is the cave of Lucifer, so in the Inferno of Conrad, at the end, there is Kurtz's stronghold, surrounded by stakes on which the heads of disobedient natives are impaled.

I am distracted again. On the expanse of water a great raft appears; 14 it seems to be made of huge logs bound together. Little black figures cluster on the raft around a hut from which a thread of smoke is rising.

I ask a fellow passenger what this raft is; she answers that those are 15 trees cut down in the heart of the forest and then entrusted, in the form of a raft, to the river, which will carry them to the sea, where they will be loaded onto ships bound for Europe. The little black figures are pygmies who, for a pittance, are willing to spend several weeks on the river, as guardians of the raft. Sometimes the raft comes undone, the pygmies fall into the river, and the logs, adrift, are lost to the ocean until, finally, like Rimbaud's Bateau Ivre, they run aground on a beach where they rot undisturbed.

In short, when everything has been said, we have to admit that in 16 "Heart of Darkness" Conrad demonized Africa, Zaire, the river, the forest and, especially, colonialism. But why this demonization? Why didn't Conrad confine himself to denouncing the evils of colonialism, as Gide was to do later? You might say this was because of an interior conflict that was then translated into an unconscious sense of guilt. On the one hand, as we have said, Conrad was an Anglophile by habit and culture, but on the other hand he was not unaware that colonialism, in its horrors, involved the entire white race, including the English. And so colonialism seemed to him not a historic fact, which after all was not his concern, but rather an indelible stain on that white honor that is the basis of so many events in his novels. It was impossible, in other words, to concede that the crimes of colonialism were part of history, particularly of that white history of which the Europeans, and Conrad himself, were so proud. But what was evil? Conrad has Kurtz say it, not in the manner of a philosopher or a man of religion, but as the poet: "the horror, the horror."

Another distraction, this one longer than the others: We are landing. 17 The steamer has turned its prow toward the shore; the forest, with its great elegiac trees, is coming closer and closer; the howl of a siren is born and dies in the dazed silence. And to our stunned eyes a little clearing appears, cramped between the river and the forest, with some little huts, and all the inhabitants, probably fishermen and seasonal woodsmen, lined up on the bank in two rows, like the chorus in a Verdi opera. They are wearing holiday dress, with the familiar bright colors; in the first row are those who will come aboard to barter the natural products of the river and forest for the industrial products of the city; in the second are those who want to enjoy the spectacle of the ship's arrival, after days and days of savage solitude. The gangplank goes down, and immediately the vendors of cassava swarm up, the sellers of smoked monkey, fruit, fish and counterfeit fetishes for tourists.

On the decks all the passengers crowd the railings and exchange 18
laughter, calls and gestures with the men who have come alongside the
ship in their pirogues. Meanwhile, the river is alive with heads of swimmers, who out of sheer vanity perform reckless feats of diving. This display
of explosive sociability is not new to me. It occurs at every stop. Are these
people happy and thriving? It's hard to say, but there can be no doubt that
on this same river, formerly described by Conrad as the place of "horror,"
life seems to be easier than in the city or in the interior of the forest.

As our stop is prolonged, my mind inevitably returns to Kurtz. What 19
is the significance of Kurtz? Despite his claims to supermanhood, or
rather, precisely because of them, he symbolizes the maleficent heart of
colonialism. Kurtz is in the depths of the forest, two months' navigation
from the ocean, and not by chance. The heart, as everyone knows, is a vital
organ, but deep and hidden. The heart of the state? But in this use of the
metaphor of the heart, there is also an odd motivation, typical of Conrad's
perplexity in the face of the grand phenomenon of European expansion
throughout the whole world. According to Conrad, colonialism has not
one heart but two: what we might call the evil heart, personified by Kurtz,
and what we might call the good heart, personified by Lord Jim.

Another interruption. A beautiful gigantic woman arrives, with swell- 20
ing breasts, solid abdomen, massive thighs and colossal buttocks, all en-
wrapped in one of those multicolored fabrics manufactured especially for
Africa in Holland and England. The giantess advances regally; she has a
huge basket on her head and with one hand she is dragging along a tiny
little girl. On her arm and around her neck she wears copper circlets. She
has come to occupy an empty cabin on our deck. Her face is good humored
and yet involuntarily menacing because of the awesome size of her eyes,
nose and lips. She reminds me of something, and all of a sudden I realize
what it is: the giantess who appears in "Heart of Darkness," in the remote
spot where Kurtz seeks refuge. I even remember the sentence with which
Conrad introduces her: "She was savage and superb, wild eyed and magnificent; there was something ominous and stately in her deliberate progress. . . ."

Yes, for Conrad colonialism does have two hearts, a heart of darkness, 21
evil and a heart of light, good. The heart of darkness harbors Kurtz; the
heart of light, Lord Jim, first mate of the Patna, who displayed cowardice
(or perhaps it was unconscious racism; the passengers of the Patna were
all Mecca pilgrims, dark-skinned people) by abandoning the ship entrusted to him. He then redeems himself through the rest of his life. And
how does he redeem himself? Ending up in Malaya, in the sultanate of
Patusan, instead of exploiting and slaughtering the natives, as Kurtz does,
with analogous authority Jim tries to protect them, to save them, and in
the end he sacrifices himself for them. And yet Kurtz and Lord Jim resemble each other in many ways. Both flee Europe to hide in barbarous places,

secret and inaccessible; both manage to establish absolute dominion over the natives; both are persecuted by an obscure conscience, which they try to elude; and finally, both rightfully belong to the historic moment of pervasive colonialism.

And further there is that identical, Conradian obsession with dark, confined passages, viscera, where refuge is sought as in the maternal womb . . . 22

We are leaving again. The siren shrieks, the vendors lazily go ashore, the pirogues and the swimmers move off, the crowd on the bank breaks up. The Colonel Ebeya moves, heading toward the middle of the river. Ah, yes, Conrad. Colonialism, for him, did indeed have two hearts, the bad one of Kurtz and the good one of Lord Jim. Kurtz oppressed the natives; Lord Jim bore on his back the white man's famous burden. But today Kurtz and Lord Jim do not exist. Or rather, they may still exist, but they are no longer symbolic as they were in Conrad's time. The symbols are dead. As, in fact, Eliot says in the epigraph of a poem of his, quoting "Heart of Darkness": "Mistah Kurtz . . . he dead." We can add also: "Lord Jim . . . he dead." 23

I have finished re-reading "Heart of Darkness" and put it in my suitcase. Now I am reading another book on the Congo of earlier times: "Stanley's Way" by Thomas Sterling. While I am reading this book, I arrive at Kisangani, once known as Stanleyville. From the deck, leaning over the rail with the other passengers, I see the dock, the usual cranes, the usual piles of crates and packages, the usual loafers who look like policemen and customs officers and the usual customs officers and policemen who look like loafers. The gangplanks are thrown down; all the passengers get off. We get off, too. We have reached the end of our voyage, as in "Heart of Darkness," as in "Lord Jim." But we know we will find neither Kurtz nor Lord Jim, neither the bad colonialist nor the good. What will we find then? 24

Our answer comes the next day when we walk under a fine rain down some of the long avenues flanked by gigantic trees that extend from the center of the city, the nucleus of tropical supermarkets and emporiums, toward the endless brush. Among the trees we glimpse houses, villas, blackened by the dampness. But sometimes the black has another explanation. This is where the former Belgian masters lived, and the houses were set afire in the now distant, murky days of early independence. We walk for a while on broad, grassy pavement; we are looking for police headquarters, where we have been told to collect our passports. Our expedition has a strange background, and it is this: 25

Last night in the bar of the hotel an African in civilian clothes came over to us and said: "Will you buy me a beer?" 26

"Happily," we said at once, and ordered it. When the beer came, the African didn't introduce himself, didn't tell us his name but began to inveigh against colonialism and colonialists in a strange fashion, at once violent and insincere, as if he were repeating a familiar part. We pointed out to him that none of us were Belgian; he answered that we're white and 27

that's enough. A tense argument developed, threatening to end badly. My
traveling companions were irritated. The African laid it on thicker and
thicker. All of a sudden he said to us: "You know who I am? I'm the chief
of police in Kisangani. If I want, I can hold you in Kisangani as long as two
weeks. Now give me your passports."

Alarmed at the prospect of a forced stay in Kisangani, we handed 28
over our passports. He took them, stood up and told us we must come to
his office tomorrow morning. And that is what we are doing now.

Finally, tired and wet, we arrive at police headquarters, which we 29
find is one of the usual villas, blackened by dampness, at the end of a
melancholy tropical garden. A sentry blocks our way with his submachine
gun, another directs us toward a hut, which is apparently a kind of waiting
room.

We sit down and wait. There is nothing we can do but silently suffer 30
the heat and perhaps look at the few visible objects, which are: (1) two
submachine guns propped in a corner; (2) a little table with a ledger bound
in black oilcloth and a pad of paper, for announcing visitors; (3) a portrait
of Mobutu, wearing the well-known leopard skin hat; (4) the gray cement
floor; (5) the walls, painted green; (6) a little salamander, perfectly motion-
less in a corner of the ceiling, and a fly, which unaware that the salamander
is studying it, adjusts its wings with its legs; (7) some chairs covered with
peeling plastic. We wait, we wait a long time, in exhausting heat, boredom
and conjecture about the reason for our waiting. How long do we wait?
Two hours, let's say. And yet in the garden and all around the villa there
is no sign of life. What can the police chief be doing? Why is he making
us wait?

And we learn the answer after our two enervating hours. The same 31
armed sentry directs us toward a door of the villa. We enter an ordinary
room; the police chief is seated there behind an ordinary desk. He barely
glances at us. It all takes a few seconds. He invites us to have a seat, we
sit down, he takes out our passports, examines them one after the other,
compares the photographs with the originals, hands over the passports.
Now we are on our feet again. We take our leave and go out into the fine,
hot, silent rain.

What did the police chief want of us? He wanted nothing beyond 32
asserting and making us feel his authority. You have to admit: Since the
days of Kurtz and Lord Jim considerable progress has been made!

Questions

Rereading and Independent Analysis

1. Make a topical outline of this essay, listing the subjects Moravia
takes up in order. Your outline should show how Moravia moves between
fictional and actual experiences to compare and contrast them.

2. Make a list of the specific points of contrast between Moravia's observations of the jungle and those he tells us that Conrad described. How are these details significant for the point Moravia wants to make? How is his point different, as he sees it, from Conrad's?

Suggested Discussion and Group Activities

1. How have your experiences of a strange city or other place differed from the expectations you had when you first read about it, saw pictures of it, or heard about it? As a class, generalize about a common pattern in these differences. Did your expectations help or hinder your new experience? Why?

2. What is the main point of Moravia's essay? How does he go beyond simply contrasting two versions of the details of this African river to draw another inference? How do the themes of black vs. white and good vs. evil contribute to his point? As a class, write a statement that expresses Moravia's point.

Writing Suggestions

Response

Why do you think Moravia wrote this essay? Put yourself in his place and write a few paragraphs about the reasons you would have for telling about an exotic place and for using a literary comparison as you describe it. You needn't describe the place; focus on the benefits to you and to readers from writing about a trip in this way.

Analysis

Write an essay in which you compare and contrast two experiences, one based on immediate observations and firsthand knowledge and the other based on reading, other media, or hearsay. Use one of these experiences to explain and interpret the other. You might, for example, compare your reading about or television experience of a region of the country to your actual experience as a visitor there. Your audience should be readers of a magazine you like to read. Use your comparisons and contrasts to support a generalization for these readers.

Finding a Purpose

Write an essay, suitable for publication in the Sunday magazine of your local paper, in which you describe a trip you have taken or a new place you have explored. Tell your experience so that your local readers will be able to understand and identify with it. Show your draft to your writing group or a classmate before finishing so you know the questions for which a reader may need more detailed answers.

CREATING CHARACTER

From *Rhetoric*
Aristotle

Translated by W. Rhys Roberts

Ideas about human nature have always occupied a prominent place in the religion and philosophy of any culture. We have a long tradition in the West of characterizing people in ways that allow us to predict what they will think and do, what they will achieve, and how others will react to them. Aristotle (384–322 B.C.) was a student of Plato's at the ancient Academy in Athens and the tutor of Alexander the Great. As both a student and a teacher, he made unparalleled contributions to the Western world's systematic explanations of human knowledge and human nature. His many philosophical works, some of which we have now only in the form of the notes his students took, address ethics, physics, statecraft, natural sciences, logic, poetics, and rhetoric—the art of composing persuasive discourse.

     This selection from Aristotle's *Rhetoric* characterizes the important qualities of men at various ages in typical Aristotelian fashion. He is explaining at this point in the *Rhetoric* how a speaker should imagine the qualities of his listeners in order to present arguments that will appeal to their most basic desires and fears without offending them. It is possible, for instance, that a good reason to fight an enemy would persuade young men to go to war, but this same reason might sound rash and ill-considered to older men. Like the other ancient Greeks engaged in systematizing thought, Aristotle groups these and similar possibilities in categories, which are determined in this selection by whether an audience is predominantly young, old, or middle-aged. In this way, Aristotle arrives at definitions of his terms, pinning down individual details in general patterns that can be used to explain individual characteristics. He also, as you will see, imposes on these categories the principle of moderation and balance by which he defined "the good" in his work. You may find this piece difficult to read if you do not pause as you go along to think of examples that verify, or contradict, Aristotle's categories and generalizations. Supply some of your own experience to overcome this difficulty.

Young men have strong passions, and tend to gratify them indiscriminately. Of the bodily desires, it is the sexual by which they are most swayed and in which they show absence of self-control. They are changeable and fickle in their desires, which are violent while they last, but quickly over: their impulses are keen but not deep-rooted, and are like sick people's 5 attacks of hunger and thirst. They are hot-tempered and quick-tempered, and apt to give way to their anger; bad temper often gets the better of them; for owing to their love of honour they cannot bear being slighted, and are indignant if they imagine themselves unfairly treated. While they

love honour, they love victory still more; for youth is eager for superiority 10
over others, and victory is one form of this. They love both more than they
love money, which indeed they love very little, not having yet learnt what
it means to be without it—this is the point of Pittacus' remark about
Amphiaraus. They look at the good side rather than the bad, not having
yet witnessed many instances of wickedness. They trust others readily, 15
because they have not yet often been cheated. They are sanguine; nature
warms their blood as though with excess of wine; and besides that, they
have as yet met with few disappointments. Their lives are mainly spent
not in memory but in expectation, for expectation refers to the future,
memory to the past, and youth has a long future before it and a short past 20
behind it: on the first day of one's life one has nothing at all to remember,
and can only look forward. They are easily cheated, owing to the sanguine
disposition just mentioned. Their hot tempers and hopeful dispositions
make them more courageous than older men are; the hot temper prevents
fear, and the hopeful disposition creates confidence; we cannot feel fear 25
so long as we are feeling angry, and any expectation of good makes us
confident. They are shy, accepting the rules of society in which they have
been trained, and not yet believing in any other standard of honour. They
have exalted notions, because they have not yet been humbled by life or
learnt its necessary limitations; moreover, their hopeful disposition makes 30
them think themselves equal to great things—and that means having
exalted notions. They would always rather do noble deeds than useful
ones: their lives are regulated more by moral feeling than by reasoning;
and whereas reasoning leads us to choose what is useful, moral goodness
leads us to choose what is noble. They are fonder of their friends, inti- 35
mates, and companions than older men are, because they like spending
their days in the company of others, and have not yet come to value either
their friends or anything else by their usefulness to themselves. All their
mistakes are in the direction of doing things excessively and vehemently.
They disobey Chilon's precept by overdoing everything; they love too 40
much and hate too much, and the same with everything else. They think
they know everything, and are always quite sure about it; this, in fact, is
why they overdo everything. If they do wrong to others, it is because they
mean to insult them, not to do them actual harm. They are ready to pity
others, because they think every one an honest man, or somehow better 45
than he is: they judge their neighbor by their own harmless natures, and
so cannot think he deserves to be treated in that way. They are fond of
fun and therefore witty, wit being well-bred insolence.

Such, then, is the character of the Young. The character of Elderly
Men—men who are past their prime—may be said to be formed for the
most part of elements that are the contrary of all these. They have lived 50
many years; they have often been taken in, and often made mistakes; and
life on the whole is a bad business. The result is that they are sure about
nothing and *under-do* everything. They 'think', but they never 'know';

and because of their hesitation they always add a 'possibly' or a 'perhaps', putting everything this way and nothing positively. They are cynical; that is, they tend to put the worse construction on everything. Further, their experience makes them distrustful and therefore suspicious of evil. Consequently they neither love warmly nor hate bitterly, but following the hint of Bias they love as though they will some day hate and hate as though they will some day love. They are small-minded, because they have been humbled by life: their desires are set upon nothing more exalted or unusual than what will help them to keep alive. They are not generous, because money is one of the things they must have, and at the same time their experience has taught them how hard it is to get and how easy to lose. They are cowardly, and are always anticipating danger; unlike that of the young, who are warm-blooded, their temperament is chilly; old age has paved the way for cowardice; fear is, in fact, a form of chill. They love life; and all the more when their last day has come, because the object of all desire is something we have not got, and also because we desire most strongly that which we need most urgently. They are too fond of themselves; this is one form that small-mindedness takes. Because of this, they guide their lives too much by considerations of what is useful and too little by what is noble—for the useful is what is good for oneself, and the noble what is good absolutely. They are not shy, but shameless rather; caring less for what is noble than for what is useful, they feel contempt for what people may think of them. They lack confidence in the future; partly through experience—for most things go wrong, or anyhow turn out worse than one expects; and partly because of their cowardice. They live by memory rather than by hope; for what is left to them of life is but little as compared with the long past; and hope is of the future, memory of the past. This, again, is the cause of their loquacity; they are continually talking of the past, because they enjoy remembering it. Their fits of anger are sudden but feeble. Their sensual passions have either altogether gone or have lost their vigour: consequently they do not feel their passions much, and their actions are inspired less by what they do feel than by the love of gain. Hence men at this time of life are often supposed to have a self-controlled character; the fact is that their passions have slackened, and they are slaves to the love of gain. They guide their lives by reasoning more than by moral feeling; reasoning being directed to utility and moral feeling to moral goodness. If they wrong others, they mean to injure them, not to insult them. Old men may feel pity, as well as young men, but not for the same reason. Young men feel it out of kindness; old men out of weakness, imagining that anything that befalls any one else might easily happen to them, which, as we saw, is a thought that excites pity. Hence they are querulous, and not disposed to jesting or laughter—the love of laughter being the very opposite of querulousness.

Such are the characters of Young Men and Elderly Men. People always think well of speeches adapted to, and reflecting, their own character: and we can now see how to compose our speeches so as to adapt both them and ourselves to our audiences.

As for Men in their Prime, clearly we shall find that they have a character between that of the young and that of the old, free from the 100 extremes of either. They have neither that excess of confidence which amounts to rashness, nor too much timidity, but the right amount of each. They neither trust everybody nor distrust everybody, but judge people correctly. Their lives will be guided not by the sole consideration either of what is noble or of what is useful, but by both; neither by parsimony nor 105 by prodigality, but by what is fit and proper. So, too, in regard to anger and desire; they will be brave as well as temperate, and temperate as well as brave; these virtues are divided between the young and the old; the young are brave but intemperate, the old temperate but cowardly. To put it generally, all the valuable qualities that youth and age divide between 110 them are united in the prime of life, while all their excesses or defects are replaced by moderation and fitness.

Questions

Rereading and Independent Analysis

1. This selection does not contain modern paragraph separations that frequently lead the reader's attention from one topic to another. Reread the selection, inserting paragraph markers at places you think they might belong in a modern text. Then compare your divisions with those of your classmates. Do their choices agree with yours? What principles about paragraphs can you draw from your similar and different results?

2. This text presents difficulties in reading because, while it is very clearly organized, it does not rely on examples to repeat its points and make them clear. Choose one of the divisions in the selection and rewrite it, inserting examples that support its generalizations. Then reread the whole selection, inserting examples for yourself when you become confused.

Suggested Discussion and Group Activities

1. Do you think Aristotle's characterizations of youth and age are accurate? What evidence can you find to confirm or deny his definitions? Divide your class into three groups to list examples of qualities of the young, middle-aged, and older people you know. Then, as a class, see if your lists actually exemplify Aristotle's generalizations.

2. As a class, analyze the structure of this selection. Do the three divisions follow the same pattern from topic to topic? As a class, make an outline of the selection that shows the progress of Aristotle's points. What is the effect of this organization?

3. Aristotle's *Rhetoric* is a record of lectures he gave as a teacher.

Compare his pattern of organization to lectures you have heard on the subjects you are studying now. How can you tell from reading the passage that it is written notes from what a teacher said in classes rather than an exact record of his spoken words?

Writing Suggestions

Response
In Aristotle's time and for long time after, education and philosophy were the province of men. Reread this selection and make notes about how well you think it applies to both men and women. Are there changes or additions you would make in order for this classification to be applicable to all people? What are they?

Analysis
Aristotle's characterizations accomplish the purpose of *defining* their subjects. Write a similar definition of your choice of subject, using categories and classifications to explain its nature. First write a general statement that indicates the purpose of your definition. Then classify parts of the subject, showing the distinct characteristics of each group within it.

Finding a Purpose
Imagine that it is up to you to write the next brief section of the *Rhetoric,* and that it will address the particular characteristics of women at these stages of life. Write the section, using attitudes toward specific life events and changes, as Aristotle has done in his descriptions of men. In your definition, include examples that explain your categories. (Use your notes from your answer to "Response," above, as a resource.) When you have completed a draft of your new section of the *Rhetoric,* compare it to the drafts written by your group members. Work together on writing one collaborative version of this new contribution.

 # Dashiell Hammett
Lillian Hellman

This character sketch of Dashiell Hammett, the successful crime writer, cannot be read without noticing the relationship between Lillian Hellman (1905–1983) and her subject. Hellman was one of the most successful playwrights of this century, the author of *The Children's Hour* (1934), *The Little Foxes* (1939), *Watch on the Rhine* (1941), and other plays that work out interpersonal relations. She often used Southern settings remembered from her girlhood in New Orleans. Hellman also wrote journalistic reviews and memoirs—*An Unfinished Woman* (1969), *Pentimento* (1973), and the memoir/story *Maybe* (1980). For much of her adult life, Hellman lived with the crime writer and ex-policeman Dashiell Hammett and supported him through the devastating witch-hunts for Communists in the 1950s, which left him and many other writers and screen figures without work because they had been blacklisted. (See J. Robert Oppenheimer's "Prospects in the Arts and Sciences," Chapter 1.) She wrote eloquently of this period, as she did of her attempts to help Jews suffering under Hitler's tyranny before World War II.

In all her prose, Hellman creates impressionistic pictures that make us doubt writing's power actually to re-present reality. Her portrayal of Hammett, whom she wrote about only reluctantly, exploits this technique. She links specific memories rather than making explanations or drawing conclusions. Her characterization of him is a collection of incidents and stories of her own dependence on him as she wrote, but it presents a vivid picture of the man as he knew himself and as she knew him. Hellman has been accused, most notably by the equally prominent writer Mary MacCarthy, of making up events, not just representing them in an impressionistic way. As you read, keep in mind the "test of truth" you usually bring to personal accounts. What elements in this piece allow you to believe it is an actual account? What did Hellman do to create a sense of vagueness? Why do you think she used these devices?

For years we made jokes about the day I would write about him. In the 1 early years, I would say, "Tell me more about the girl in San Francisco. The silly one who lived across the hall in Pine Street."

And he would laugh and say, "She lived across the hall in Pine Street 2 and was silly."

"Tell more than that. How much did you like her and how—?" 3

He would yawn. "Finish your drink and go to sleep." 4

But days later, maybe even that night, if I was on the find-out kick, 5 and I was, most of the years, I would say, "O.K., be stubborn about the girls. So tell me about your grandmother and what you looked like as a baby."

"I was a very fat baby. My grandmother went to the movies every 6 afternoon. She was very fond of a movie star called Wallace Reid and I've told you all this before."

I would say I wanted to get everything straight for the days after his 7 death when I would write his biography and he would say that I was not to bother writing his biography because it would turn out to be the history of Lillian Hellman with an occasional reference to a friend called Hammett.

The day of his death came on January 10, 1961. I will never write that 8 biography because I cannot write about my closest, my most beloved friend. And maybe, too, because all those questions through all the thirty-one on and off years, and the sometime answers, got muddled, and life changed for both of us and the questions and answers became one in the end, flowing together from the days when I was young to the days when I was middle-aged. And so this will be no attempt at a biography of Samuel

Dashiell Hammett, born in St. Mary's County, Maryland, on May 27, 1894. Nor will it be a critical appraisal of his work. In 1966 I edited and published a collection of his stories. There was a day when I thought all of them very good. But all of them are not good, though most of them, I think, are very good. It is only right to say immediately that by publishing them at all I did what Hammett did not want to do: he turned down all offers to republish the stories, although I never knew the reason and never asked. I did know, from what he said about "Tulip," the unfinished novel that I included in the book, that he meant to start a new literary life and maybe didn't want the old work to get in the way. But sometimes I think he was just too ill to care, too worn out to listen to plans or read contracts. The fact of breathing, just breathing, took up all the days and nights.

In the First World War, in camp, influenza led to tuberculosis and 9 Hammett was to spend years after in army hospitals. He came out of the Second World War with emphysema, but how he ever got into the Second World War at the age of forty-eight still bewilders me. He telephoned me the day the army accepted him to say it was the happiest day of his life, and before I could finish saying it wasn't the happiest day of mine and what about the old scars on his lungs, he laughed and hung up. His death was caused by cancer of the lungs, discovered only two months before he died. It was not operable—I doubt that he would have agreed to an operation even if it had been—and so I decided not to tell him about the cancer. The doctor said that when the pain came, it would come in the right chest and arm, but that the pain might never come. The doctor was wrong: only a few hours after he told me, the pain did come. Hammett had had self-diagnosed rheumatism in the right arm and had always said that was why he had given up hunting. On the day I heard about the cancer, he said his gun shoulder hurt him again, would I rub it for him. I remember sitting behind him, rubbing the shoulder and hoping he would always think it was rheumatism and remember only the autumn hunting days. But the pain never came again, or if it did he never mentioned it, or maybe death was so close that the shoulder pain faded into other pains.

He did not wish to die and I like to think he didn't know he was 10 dying. But I keep from myself even now the possible meaning of a night, very late, a short time before his death. I came into his room, and for the only time in the years I knew him there were tears in his eyes and the book was lying unread. I sat down beside him and waited a long time before I could say, "Do you want to talk about it?"

He said, almost with anger, "No. My only chance is not to talk about 11 it."

And he never did. He had patience, courage, dignity in those last, 12 awful months. It was as if all that makes a man's life had come together to prove itself: suffering was a private matter and there was to be no invasion of it. He would seldom even ask for anything he needed, and so the most we did—my secretary and Helen, who were devoted to him, as most women always had been—was to carry up the meals he barely touched, the books he now could hardly read, the afternoon coffee, and the martini that I insisted upon before the dinner that wasn't eaten.

One night of that last year, a bad night, I said, "Have another martini. It will make you feel better." 13

"No," he said, "I don't want it." 14

I said, "O.K., but I bet you never thought I'd urge you to have another drink." 15

He laughed for the first time that day. "Nope. And I never thought I'd turn it down." 16

Because on the night we had first met he was getting over a five-day drunk and he was to drink very heavily for the next eighteen years, and then one day, warned by a doctor, he said he would never have another drink and he kept his word except for the last year of the one martini, and that was my idea. 17

We met when I was twenty-four years old and he was thirty-six in a restaurant in Hollywood. The five-day drunk had left the wonderful face looking rumpled, and the very tall thin figure was tired and sagged. We talked of T. S. Eliot, although I no longer remember what we said, and then went and sat in his car and talked at each other and over each other until it was daylight. We were to meet again a few weeks later and, after that, on and sometimes off again for the rest of his life and thirty years of mine. 18

Thirty years is a long time, I guess, and yet as I come now to write about them the memories skip about and make no pattern and I know only certain of them are to be trusted. I know about that first meeting and the next, and there are many other pictures and sounds, but they are out of order and out of time, and I don't seem to want to put them into place. (I could have done a research job, I have on other people, but I didn't want to do one on Hammett, or to be a bookkeeper of my own life.) I don't want modesty for either of us, but I ask myself now if it can mean much to anybody but me that my second sharpest memory is of a day when we were living on a small island off the coast of Connecticut. It was six years after we had first met: six full, happy, unhappy years during which I had, with help from Hammett, written *The Children's Hour,* which was a success, and *Days to Come,* which was not. I was returning from the mainland in a catboat filled with marketing and Hammett had come down to the dock to tie me up. He had been sick that summer—the first of the sicknesses—and he was even thinner than usual. The white hair, the white pants, the white shirt made a straight, flat surface in the late sun. I thought: Maybe that's the handsomest sight I ever saw, that line of a man, the knife for a nose, and the sheet went out of my hand and the wind went out the sail. Hammett laughed as I struggled to get back the sail. I don't know why, but I yelled angrily, "So you're a Dostoevsky sinner-saint. So you are." The laughter stopped, and when I finally came in to the dock we didn't speak as we carried up the packages and didn't speak through dinner. 19

Later that night, he said, "What did you say that for? What does it 20
mean?"

I said I didn't know why I had said it and I didn't know what it meant. 21

Years later, when his life had changed, I did know what I had meant 22
that day: I had seen the sinner—whatever is a sinner—and sensed the
change before it came. When I told him that, Hammett said he didn't
know what I was talking about, it was all too religious for him. But he did
know what I was talking about and he was pleased.

But the fat, loose, wild years were over by the time we talked that 23
way. When I first met Dash he had written four of the five novels and was
the hottest thing in Hollywood and New York. It is not remarkable to be
the hottest thing in either city—the hottest kid changes for each winter
season—but in his case it was of extra interest to those who collect people
that the ex-detective who had bad cuts on his legs and an indentation in
his head from being scrappy with criminals was gentle in manner, well
educated, elegant to look at, born of early settlers, was eccentric, witty,
and spent so much money on women that they would have liked him even
if he had been none of the good things. But as the years passed from 1930
to 1948, he wrote only one novel and a few short stories. By 1945, the
drinking was no longer gay, the drinking bouts were longer and the moods
darker. I was there off and on for most of those years, but in 1948 I didn't
want to see the drinking anymore. I hadn't seen or spoken to Hammett
for two months until the day when his devoted cleaning lady called to say
she thought I had better come down to his apartment. I said I wouldn't,
and then I did. She and I dressed a man who could barely lift an arm or
a leg and brought him to my house, and that night I watched delirium
tremens, although I didn't know what I was watching until the doctor told
me the next day at the hospital. The doctor was an old friend. He said, "I'm
going to tell Hammett that if he goes on drinking he'll be dead in a few
months. It's my duty to say it, but it won't do any good." In a few minutes
he came out of Dash's room and said, "I told him. Dash said O.K., he'd go
on the wagon forever, but he can't and he won't."

But he could and he did. Five or six years later, I told Hammett that 24
the doctor had said he wouldn't stay on the wagon.

Dash looked puzzled. "But I gave my word that day."   25

I said, "Have you always kept your word?"   26

"Most of the time," he said, "maybe because I've so seldom given it."   27

He had made up honor early in his life and stuck with his rules, fierce 28
in the protection of them. In 1951 he went to jail because he and two other
trustees of the bail bond fund of the Civil Rights Congress refused to
reveal the names of the contributors to the fund. The truth was that
Hammett had never been in the office of the Congress, did not know the
name of a single contributor.

The night before he was to appear in court, I said, "Why don't you 29
say that you don't know the names?"

"No," he said, "I can't say that." 30

"Why?" 31

"I don't know why. I guess it has something to do with keeping my 32 word, but I don't want to talk about that. Nothing much will happen, although I think we'll go to jail for a while, but you're not to worry because"—and then suddenly I couldn't understand him because the voice had dropped and the words were coming in a most untypical nervous rush. I said I couldn't hear him, and he raised his voice and dropped his head. "I hate this damn kind of talk, but maybe I better tell you that if it were more than jail, if it were my life, I would give it for what I think democracy is, and I don't let cops or judges tell me what I think democracy is." Then he went home to bed, and the next day he went to jail.

Questions

Rereading and Independent Analysis

1. Hellman's essay does not begin at the beginning either of Hammett's life or of her relationship with him but moves forward and backward through time. Make a chronological table representing this essay's movement through actual time. In your table, list a number that represents the place of each item in the narrative as it is told so that you can see both the time periods included and the narration of them. These numbers should indicate what is told first, last, etc. What pattern of arrangement do you see?

2. Make a list of topics and themes, like writing and drinking, that come up repeatedly in this essay. Which themes and habits tie Hellman's memories together for you as you read?

Suggested Discussion and Group Activities

1. How does Hellman convey her feelings about Hammett in this essay? Does she reveal any information about him by what she does *not* write about? What periods of time are not mentioned? How does the order of the events in her narrative, not in actual time, tell you about her feelings?

2. How true is it that Hellman's memoir is, as Hammett said it would be, about her and not about him? What do we learn about her from this essay? Could we know her fully without knowing how she thought of Hammett? Why?

3. In groups, decide what *themes* you would use if you were writing to characterize the members of your group. Do you and your classmates share the same thematic ideas? Do you have habits or other common characteristics that give a general impression of you? If you were your parents, what themes would you pick out to describe you? How would they differ from your own choices?

Writing Suggestions

Response

Quickly write down impressions you have of your relationship with a particular person who is important to you. Try to capture moments and conversations that characterize this relationship.

Analysis

Write a critical analysis of this essay, explaining how its control of the time sequence and of Hellman's voice as an author makes a coherent picture of a real, rather than only a "famous," person. (Use your notes from your answer to Question 1, "Rereading.") Explain how the author's point of view and personal comments influence the essay's picture of Hammett. Your analysis should be suitable to introduce the essay to readers who are doing research about Hammett's life, so it should indicate Hellman's specific perspective on him.

Finding a Purpose

Write a character sketch of a person you know well, using specific details and moments from your memory to make his or her important qualities vivid. Your sketch should make this person vivid to a reader who will never know him or her. It should show how the person shaped and contributed to your own life. Choose a specific reader for this sketch. Your reader should know you and your subject better after reading it.

 # On Self-Respect
Joan Didion

This essay describes an elusive personal quality that is often equated with "character" in its sense of integrity. Its author has written about character in many forms. Joan Didion (b. 1934) is an essayist, novelist, literary journalist, and screenwriter who often writes dry, personalized commentary on events, movements, or political situations that receive media attention. Her novels include *Run River* (1963), *Play It as It Lays* (1970), and *A Book of Common Prayer* (1977). They treat women whose personal situations are embedded in contemporary "scenes"—the movie culture of California and a famous person's disappearance. The essay collections *Slouching Toward Bethlehem* (1968) and *The White Album* (1979) include both personal reminiscences about Didion's origins in California and her observations of events that shaped the culture of the 1960s and 1970s. "On Self-Respect," from *Slouching Toward Bethlehem,* was first published in *Vogue* magazine, where she was a feature editor.

The essay demonstrates Didion's characteristically distinct prose style, which is rhythmic, terse, and full of references to history and literature. As you read, you will notice that her images and phrasing, which often imitate

other well-known styles, show us a writer's mind at work. She writes as
though she is struggling to define a quality that she does not want to oversim-
plify or reduce to pat definitions that would distort it. Why do you think it
was important for Didion to write about this subject? Is she successful at
making her description universally applicable?

Once, in a dry season, I wrote in large letters across two pages of a note- 1
book that innocence ends when one is stripped of the delusion that one
likes oneself. Although now, some years later, I marvel that a mind on the
outs with itself should have nonetheless made painstaking record of its
every tremor, I recall with embarrassing clarity the flavor of those particular ashes. It was a matter of misplaced self-respect.

I had not been elected to Phi Beta Kappa. This failure could scarcely 2
have been more predictable or less ambiguous (I simply did not have the
grades), but I was unnerved by it; I had somehow thought myself a kind
of academic Raskolnikov, curiously exempt from the cause-effect relationships which hampered others. Although even the humorless nineteen-
year-old that I was must have recognized that the situation lacked real
tragic stature, the day that I did not make Phi Beta Kappa nonetheless
marked the end of something, and innocence may well be the word for
it. I lost the conviction that lights would always turn green for me, the
pleasant certainty that those rather passive virtues which had won me
approval as a child automatically guaranteed me not only Phi Beta Kappa
keys but happiness, honor, and the love of a good man; lost a certain
touching faith in the totem power of good manners, clean hair, and proven
competence on the Stanford-Binet scale. To such doubtful amulets had my
self-respect been pinned, and I faced myself that day with the nonplused
apprehension of someone who has come across a vampire and has no
crucifix at hand.

Although to be driven back upon oneself is an uneasy affair at best, 3
rather like trying to cross a border with borrowed credentials, it seems to
me now the one condition necessary to the beginnings of real self-respect.
Most of our platitudes notwithstanding, self-deception remains the most
difficult deception. The tricks that work on others count for nothing in that
very well-lit back alley where one keeps assignations with oneself: no
winning smiles will do here, no prettily drawn lists of good intentions. One
shuffles flashily but in vain through one's marked cards—the kindness
done for the wrong reason, the apparent triumph which involved no real
effort, the seemingly heroic act into which one had been shamed. The
dismal fact is that self-respect has nothing to do with the approval of
others—who are, after all, deceived easily enough; has nothing to do with
reputation, which, as Rhett Butler told Scarlet O'Hara, is something people with courage can do without.

To do without self-respect, on the other hand, is to be an unwilling 4
audience of one to an interminable documentary that details one's failings,
both real and imagined, with fresh footage spliced in for every screening.

There's the glass you broke in anger, there's the hurt on X's face; watch now, this next scene, the night Y came back from Houston, see how you muff this one. To live without self-respect is to lie awake some night, beyond the reach of warm milk, phenobarbital, and the sleeping hand on the coverlet, counting up the sins of commission and omission, the trusts betrayed, the promises subtly broken, the gifts irrevocably wasted through sloth or cowardice or carelessness. However long we postpone it, we eventually lie down alone in that notoriously uncomfortable bed, the one we make ourselves. Whether or not we sleep in it depends, of course, on whether or not we respect ourselves.

To protest that some fairly improbable people, some people who 5 *could not possibly respect themselves,* seem to sleep easily enough is to miss the point entirely, as surely as those people miss it who think that self-respect has necessarily to do with not having safety pins in one's underwear. There is a common superstition that "self-respect" is a kind of charm against snakes, something that keeps those who have it locked in some unblighted Eden, out of strange beds, ambivalent conversations, and trouble in general. It does not at all. It has nothing to do with the face of things, but concerns instead a separate peace, a private reconciliation. Although the careless, suicidal Julian English in *Appointment in Samarra* and the careless, incurably dishonest Jordan Baker in *The Great Gatsby* seem equally improbable candidates for self-respect, Jordan Baker had it, Julian English did not. With that genius for accommodation more often seen in women than in men, Jordan took her own measure, made her own peace, avoided threats to that peace: "I hate careless people," she told Nick Carraway. "It takes two to make an accident."

Like Jordan Baker, people with self-respect have the courage of their 6 mistakes. They know the price of things. If they choose to commit adultery, they do not then go running, in an access of bad conscience, to receive absolution from the wronged parties; nor do they complain unduly of the unfairness, the undeserved embarrassment, of being named co-respondent. In brief, people with self-respect exhibit a certain toughness, a kind of moral nerve; they display what was once called *character,* a quality which, although approved in the abstract, sometimes loses ground to other, more instantly negotiable virtues. The measure of its slipping prestige is that one tends to think of it only in connection with homely children and United States senators who have been defeated, preferably in the primary, for reelection. Nonetheless, character—the willingness to accept responsibility for one's own life—is the source from which self-respect springs.

Self-respect is something that our grandparents, whether or not they 7 had it, knew all about. They had instilled in them, young, a certain discipline, the sense that one lives by doing things one does not particularly want to do, by putting fears and doubts to one side, by weighing immediate comforts against the possibility of larger, even intangible, comforts. It seemed to the nineteenth century admirable, but not remarkable, that Chinese Gordon put on a clean white suit and held Khartoum against the Mahdi; it did not seem unjust that the way to free land in California involved death and difficulty and dirt. In a diary kept during the winter of 1846, an emigrating twelve-year-old named Narcissa Cornwall noted coolly: "Father was busy reading and did not notice that the house was being filled with strange Indians until Mother spoke about it." Even lacking any clue as to what Mother said, one can scarcely fail to be impressed by the entire incident: the father reading, the Indians filing in, the mother choosing the words that would not alarm, the child duly recording the event and noting further that those particular Indians were not, "fortunately for us," hostile. Indians were simply part of the *donnée*.

In one guise or another, Indians always are. Again, it is a question of recognizing that anything worth having has its price. People who respect themselves are willing to accept the risk that the Indians will be hostile, that the venture will go bankrupt, that the liaison may not turn out to be one in which *every day is a holiday because you're married to me*. They are willing to invest something of themselves; they may not play at all, but when they do play, they know the odds. 8

That kind of self-respect is a discipline, a habit of mind that can never be faked but can be developed, trained, coaxed forth. It was once suggested to me that, as an antidote to crying, I put my head in a paper bag. As it happens, there is a sound physiological reason, something to do with oxygen, for doing exactly that, but the psychological effect alone is incalculable: it is difficult in the extreme to continue fancying oneself Cathy in *Wuthering Heights* with one's head in a Food Fair bag. There is a similar case for all the small disciplines, unimportant in themselves; imagine maintaining any kind of swoon, commiserative or carnal, in a cold shower. 9

But those small disciplines are valuable only insofar as they represent larger ones. To say that Waterloo was won on the playing fields of Eton is not to say that Napoleon might have been saved by a crash program in cricket; to give formal dinners in the rain forest would be pointless did not the candlelight flickering on the liana call forth deeper, stronger disciplines, values instilled long before. It is a kind of ritual, helping us to remember who and what we are. In order to remember it, one must have known it. 10

To have that sense of one's intrinsic worth which constitutes self-respect is potentially to have everything: the ability to discriminate, to love and to remain indifferent. To lack it is to be locked within oneself, paradoxically incapable of either love or indifference. If we do not respect ourselves, we are on the one hand forced to despise those who have so few resources as to consort with us, so little perception as to remain blind to our fatal weaknesses. On the other, we are peculiarly in thrall to everyone we see, curiously determined to live out—since our self-image is untena- 11

ble—their false notions of us. We flatter ourselves by thinking this compul-
sion to please others an attractive trait: a gist for imaginative empathy,
evidence of our willingness to give. *Of course* I will play Francesca to your
Paolo, Helen Keller to anyone's Annie Sullivan: no expectation is too
misplaced, no role too ludicrous. At the mercy of those we cannot but hold
in contempt, we play roles doomed to failure before they are begun, each
defeat generating fresh despair at the urgency of divining and meeting
the next demand made upon us.

It is the phenomenon sometimes called "alienation from self." In its   10
advanced stages, we no longer answer the telephone, because someone
might want something; that we could say *no* without drowning in self-
reproach is an idea alien to this game. Every encounter demands too
much, tears the nerves, drains the will, and the specter of something as
small as an unanswered letter arouses such disproportionate guilt that
answering it becomes out of the question. To assign unanswered letters
their proper weight, to free us from the expectations of others, to give us
back to ourselves—there lies the great, the singular power of self-respect.
Without it, one eventually discovers the final turn of the screw: one runs
away to find oneself, and finds no one at home.

Questions

Rereading and Independent Analysis

1. Didion's essay is an extended definition of a concept. Make a list,
paragraph by paragraph, of her methods of developing and elaborating
this definition. What question about self-respect does each paragraph answer? How does Didion rely on "negative details" (defining a thing by
saying what it is *not*) to establish what self-respect is?

2. Make a list of the references in the essay that you do not immediately recognize: perhaps, for example, Raskolnikov, Jordan Baker, Chinese
Gordon, or Stanford-Binet scale. Using reference works and your own
sense of their meaning from the context, make notes explaining each of
these allusions. Didion frequently relies on fictionalized situations and
characters to establish the emotional tone of this essay. Make a list of these
sources as well. Would you have to have read or seen them to understand
the essay? Write a statement of her point about self-respect. Why do you
think she wrote as she did for the readers of *Vogue?*

Suggested Discussion and Group Activities

1. Do you think that having self-respect as Didion defines it would
necessarily separate you from others? Find passages in the essay that
suggest how self-respect might do this. Is self-respect a quality that others
can perceive? Cite examples of people whose self-respect is made clear to
those who know them. How has it been revealed?

2. Didion frequently refers to situations in which things do not "go

well," despite surface characteristics that we rely on: clean hair, high IQ, and good intentions. Can you think of similar situations you have experienced? How does Didion suggest that self-respect benefits us in these situations? Does it make things go better or does it accomplish something else?

3. In groups, compare Didion's definition of self-respect to the character definitions in another essay from this section, such as the selection from Aristotle's *Rhetoric* or Jane O'Reilly's "Three Faces of Greed." What similar and different techniques of characterization can you identify? Which selection do you find more effective in giving you a sense of the writer's subject? Why?

Writing Suggestions

Response

Didion's essay refers to times when our self-respect is in question, either by ourselves or others. In your journal, describe a time when you questioned your own integrity. What happened? How did you resolve the situation?

Analysis

Write a definition of a personal quality (e.g., honesty, courage, loyalty). Use well-known examples, negative details (that is, what this quality is *not*), and your own experience. Begin by noting examples of this quality in action. Then use examples to illustrate your own growing understanding of the quality. Your essay explaining this quality should be suitable for publication in your student newspaper as an editorial or feature column.

Finding a Purpose

1. Didion suggests in her essay that self-respect, or "character," is a quality that "our grandparents" had more access to than we do. Write an essay in which you take a position about this judgment. Either support or refute her sense of declining self-respect in the present generation, and explain your position. If you refute her view, give examples that illustrate how common self-respect still is. Think of your essay as a letter that you will send to Didion, and be sure to include specific references to her statements as points and illustrations you either agree or disagree with.

2. Write a brief introduction to the selections in "Creating Character" in which you explain to a reader the lessons they offer about adulthood. Make specific references to selections you think are especially useful, and refer to the reasons these writers continue to explore "character" long after Aristotle wrote about it. How do writers learn from writing about this subject?

Three Faces of Greed
Jane O'Reilly

It is notable that contemporary views of "character" often focus on its less admirable along with its most excellent manifestations. This essay explores, from a number of perspectives, one of the most common characterizations of contemporary goals. Its author, Jane O'Reilly, a freelance writer who lives in New York and Key West, Florida, writes for national magazines and is currently working on a novel. She typically writes to characterize contemporary life and manners. This essay appeared in *Vogue* magazine, which publishes reviews, summaries, and interviews that keep its readers informed about current trends in visual, cinematic, and literary events. *Vogue* devotes most of its pages to promoting contemporary high fashion and to information about health and beauty trends. Its readers are generally affluent women who have time and money to devote to personal improvement.

O'Reilly's thesis is that "a kind of avid acquisitiveness is going on these days, and it is something beyond mere showing off." She contrasts this "something else" with earlier definitions of "success," like the "self-respect" described in Joan Didion's essay "On Self-Respect." O'Reilly's title, a play on the title of a popular book and film about a woman who had multiple personalities, *The Three Faces of Eve,* suggests the instability of social classes and personal values in her new 1980's definition of "success." As you read, notice the kinds of evidence—from economic theories, examples, and reasoning—O'Reilly uses to support her case. What do these sources of support say about her expectations of her readers? What additional message do you take from this essay when you consider the readership for which it was first published?

1   I saw some pictures in the newspaper of a kitchen that cost $100,000 to build. It belongs to a woman who does not cook. Ever. But she does entertain a lot. She serves crab meat, yam slices, unborn lamb, goat curry—all wheeled in, ready-to-eat, by the caterers. This woman has constructed for herself a $100,000 warming oven. I call that greedy. She would probably call it success.

2   Greed is almost solipsistic. "Rivalry is 'look at ME, not at her.' " says New York City psychoanalyst Peter Neubauer, M.D. "Jealousy is a yearning for acceptance and love that is denied. Envy is wanting to gain something that can never be achieved, like being able to sing. But greed has to do with insatiability; because there is no gratification, the craving continues beyond satisfaction of the function. It is not, 'I want to have it because *you* have it.' It's I WANT IT."

3   Tolstoy wrote a short story, "How Much Land Does a Man Need?" in which a man is offered all the land he can run across in a day. He runs and runs, beyond any possibility of utility, across another stream, another meadow. And he drops dead. "That is greed," Dr. Neubauer says. "It is irrational, limitless, with no social component to give it grace."

A kind of avid acquisitiveness is going on these days, and it is some- 4
thing beyond mere showing off. *"I want, I want, I want"* is the mantra of
the 'eighties. *People cannot get enough*—even the ones who already have
everything that can be got in exchange for money. Their febrile mood is
the social manifestation of a peculiar definition of "success" that has
emerged as the overriding esthetic of the 'eighties. The word no longer
describes a fluctuating process of life, such as "being happy," or "becoming depressed." No one needs to consider the question "success at what?"
when success means only one thing: success at making money. The word
no longer implies anything beyond itself, such as "hardworking" or "intelligent." Instead, it is used the way "kind" or "honest" or "generous" once
were used, to describe a virtue. And the outward sign of grace indicating
this modern attribute is wealth.

Ideas of the 'Eighties # 1: "They say life is a game, but you keep score in 5
money."—former United States Senator George Smathers.

But, I keep asking, what is the social benefit of a $100,000 kitchen 6
to someone who does not cook? In a city where an estimated forty thousand homeless people sleep in parks and doorways? Who exactly, in that
city, will be helped by a twenty-eight story condo project next to the "21"
Club, filled with one- and two-bedroom units "designed for corporate
ownership and part-time New York residents"? The point is that there is
no social benefit. The point is that money will be spent and money will be
made. It is a system American novelist Frank Norris and British economic
historian Richard H. Tawney as well as Friedrich Engels and Thorstein
Veblen have been trying to explain for the last hundred years. The new
and frightening thing about our extravagant tunnel vision is that nowadays
the getting and the spending are ends in themselves. Even the kitchen
and the condos are incidental.

Ideas of the 'Eighties # 2: "He who dies with the most toys *wins.* "—motto 7
on brass plaque advertised in *The Robb Report.* The same issue of this
journal for big spenders carried an ad for a recovery hotline: 1-800-CO-
CAINE. Spending frenzy is part of the short-circuited sensibility of the
cocaine age.

Addicted is another word that explains today's idea of success. Spend- 8
ing and/or getting can become uncontrollable habits. I went through a
short bout of aerobic spending last winter, and after a week or two, I edged
up on a great insight: it would never have an end. One day, I spent a
preposterous fortune on a knitted cap designed with a Scottie dog. Outside
the store, I saw the same cap on a three-year-old Yuppie tot. I retired from
the field and redirected my yearnings toward chocolate. Some people
choose alcohol, or drugs, or gambling, or sex. Even earning money is
addictive. Who knows if the M.B.A. doing conspicuous leisure with two

weeks of helicopter skiing is working to support his spending, or spending to justify his earning? The one sure thing is that none of these fixes satisfies our undefined longings. Whatever it is we want, we cannot name it, and we cannot buy it.

Ideas of the 'Eighties # 3: "Without children I would be comfortable with 9 $200,000 a year. Money means a lot to my happiness."—Laurie Gilbert, twenty-eight, a lawyer, in *Newsweek*'s story on Yuppies.

It is a commonplace that capitalism makes greed supreme. Its de- 10 mand that we accept the making of money as the basic good of society corrupts everything: religion, art, individual integrity. Nothing is worth doing for the satisfaction of doing it, or because it needs doing. There are no higher goals or larger responsibilities. For example:

Ideas of the 'Eighties # 4: "I don't think you can say someone has too much 11 if he's worked for it. If he's earned it, well, it's his to do with as he pleases."—William Kennedy, Pawtucket, Rhode Island, businessman, reacting to a letter from the American Catholic bishops urging changes in the economy to help the poor.

Ideas of the 'Eighties # 5: "Medical school would be a poor return on my 12 investment."—Marion Ryder, honors senior at Bowdoin College, in *The New York Times*.

Ideas of the 'Eighties # 6: "It means millions."—Bill Johnson, first Ameri- 13 can gold medalist in Alpine downhill skiing, when asked what the medal meant to him.

We are watching capitalism cannibalize itself. The middle class—the 14 foundation of a stable economy—is being devoured as more and more money goes to the rich. Downward mobility is the real trend behind the Yuppie flash: the median income for young families fell 14 percent in the last five years. And at the same time the people who are supposed to be giants of industry and commerce are nibbling at their own noses and fingertips. Take, for example, the Hunt brothers, two of the richest men in the world. They had an insatiable craving for silver. And they nearly brought down the banking system.

Consider also the corporate raiders: it is hard to find their productive 15 contribution to society. T. Boone Pickens and Carl Icahn make their millions and millions by simply threatening to take over the management of companies. After an hysterical flurry in which defensive chief executive officers protect their perks, bonuses, and golden parachutes, the stockholders and such people that care about the actual stated purpose or product of the company are left with the bill. Icahn, for example, in just one of his deals, was left with a $33 million profit after he *failed* to take over Marshall Field's in 1982. This kind of paper chase is not an industry, it is an activity: self-propelling, functionless, and—apparently—addictive.

David Riesman, author of *The Lonely Crowd,* once summed up the 16 momentum of human behavior by offering a rule: "The more, the more." But consider—if you dare—the arms race, and you begin to get an idea of where it will all end. In a mushroom cloud. No theories of security or power make rational the obliteration of our resources by the military budget. The arms race has an insatiable life of its own, and its greedy appetite will eventually want to be fed by a war, or two.

This present period of graceless extravagance is not new. It echoes 17 the Gilded Age (which inspired Veblen's ever-fresh term "conspicuous consumption" in 1899), the Jazz Age, and the 'fifties. The more altruistic 'thirties and 'sixties followed the latter eras of excess—not, perhaps, because of virtue, or even because greed became boring, but because of necessity. Nonetheless, the cycle turned. The 'nineties, if history is our guide, will be an improvement on the 'eighties. If we live that long.

Questions

Rereading and Independent Analysis

1. Reread O'Reilly's introduction, the first four paragraphs of the essay. Outline these paragraphs as a whole by listing the major point made in each one and the kind of evidence (e.g., examples, authorities, etc.) O'Reilly used to support them. What does she mean by calling greed the "overriding *esthetic* of the 'eighties"? How does she establish the believability of this thesis?

2. Each of this essay's "ideas of the 'eighties" is cited with a source for the quotation attached to it. Make a mental list of these sources. What does their variety imply? Is O'Reilly's characterization of the 1980s applicable nationally? Why?

3. In preparation for class discussion, make your own list of "ideas of the 'eighties." Using popular writing and other media, select a current attitude or position stated in a number of sources and write your examples. (If you wish, you may look for further examples to support O'Reilly's thesis.)

Suggested Discussion and Group Activities

1. Divide your class or small group into two groups. In one, list examples from your own experience, reading, or television viewing that support O'Reilly's characterization of the contemporary idea of "success." In the other, list examples of other kinds of success valued today that contradict her view. Then, as a whole class or group, contrast these two lists. Can you agree that she has accurately characterized the 1980s?

2. Compare the examples that support O'Reilly's argument to your own lists of "Ideas of the 'eighties." Try to state your examples in the same precise language O'Reilly uses to make her points vividly and quickly.

3. What conditions of life in the 1980s make it possible for greed to be an "overriding esthetic"? How does O'Reilly's evidence about increased separations between upper and lower levels of income contribute to this possibility? What examples does she use to remind her readers of contrasts between rich and poor?

Writing Suggestions

Response

In your journal, make notes about the ways you experience greed in yourself and others. What objects and activities exemplify greed for you? How do you justify this impulse when you become aware of it?

Analysis

O'Reilly's essay raises serious questions about the morality of contemporary views of "success." Write an essay for your classmates in which you give your personal definition of "success" and defend its appropriateness. In your essay, explain O'Reilly's points about how definitions of achievement change from one period to another and her attitudes toward people like the woman who never prepares meals in her $100,000 kitchen.

Finding a Purpose

1. Imagine that you are one of the regular readers of *Vogue*. Write a letter to the editor in which you explain why the magazine should not have published O'Reilly's essay because it is offensive to you. (You may want to look at a copy of the magazine before you write so that you will have an idea of the tastes of its presumed audience.)

2. Write an essay aimed at the readers of a national magazine of your choice in which you imitate O'Reilly's purpose. Choose a contemporary attitude to define, and develop your definition with examples from sources like those she uses. Your essay should reveal your approval or disapproval of an "idea of the 'eighties."

DISCIPLINED WORLDS

History

What Is History?
R. G. Collingwood

In the first paragraph of this selection from *The Idea of History* (1957), R. G. Collingwood (1889–1943) says, "History, like theology or natural science, is a special form of thought." Collingwood was a professor of philosophy and a historian at Oxford University earlier in this century. At that time, strict specialization in only one field of study was less common than it is now. Borders that divide fields had not been so firmly established as they later became, when subfields multiplied and scholars produced specialized works devoted to them. Collingwood found many connections between philosophy and history. His publications were controversial because they demanded that historians see how philosophical movements and concepts dominant at any time shape the "facts" of history. He also called on philosophers to recognize the "facts" that shape philosophies. Collingwood's writing demonstrates that he was what is commonly referred to as "an educated man"; his wide-ranging learning and research are evident throughout it.

This selection is particularly valuable, however, because it not only defines "history" as a way of thinking but also introduces the idea that ways of thinking and categories of study define the boundaries of any particular discipline or field. By examining the definition, purpose, method, and results of history, Collingwood provides a framework for examining any of the "special kinds of thought" that are studied discretely as "subjects." You should notice how his essay relies on a particular kind of evidence—examples and logical analysis—to support its points. Also notice the particular group of readers he is writing for. What do they know and think of as important? What level of diction does he employ to persuade this group? Have you previously thought of history as a specialized way of thinking or as hard "facts"?

What history is, what it is about, how it proceeds, and what it is for, are 1 questions which to some extent different people would answer in different ways. But in spite of differences there is a large measure of agreement between the answers. And this agreement becomes closer if the answers are subjected to scrutiny with a view to discarding those which proceed from unqualified witnesses. History, like theology or natural science, is a special form of thought. If that is so, questions about the nature, object, method, and value of this form of thought must be answered by persons having two qualifications.

First, they must have experience of that form of thought. They must 2 be historians. In a sense we are all historians nowadays. All educated persons have gone through a process of education which has included a certain amount of historical thinking. But this does not qualify them to give an opinion about the nature, object, method, and value of historical thinking. For in the first place, the experience of historical thinking which they have thus acquired is probably very superficial and the opinions based on it are therefore no better grounded than a man's opinion of the French people based on a single week-end visit to Paris. In the second place, experience of anything whatever gained through the ordinary educational channels, as well as being superficial, is invariably out of date. Experience of historical thinking, so gained, is modelled on text-books, and text-books always describe not what is now being thought by real live historians, but what was thought by real live historians at some time in the past when the raw material was being created out of which the text-book has been put together. And it is not only the results of historical thought which are out of date by the time they get into the text-book. It is also the principles of historical thought: that is, the ideas as to the nature, object, method, and value of historical thinking. In the third place, and connected with this, there is a peculiar illusion incidental to all knowledge acquired in the way of education: the illusion of finality. When a student is *in statu pupillari* [under instruction] with respect to any subject whatever, he has to believe that things are settled because the text-books and his teachers regard them as settled. When he emerges from that state and goes on studying the subject for himself he finds that nothing is settled. The dogmatism which is an invariable mark of immaturity drops away from him. He looks at so-called facts with a new eye. He says to himself: 'My teacher and text-books told me that such and such was true; but is it true? What reasons had they for thinking it true, and were these reasons adequate?' On the other hand, if he emerges from the status of pupil without continuing to pursue the subject he never rids himself of this dogmatic attitude. And this makes him a person peculiarly unfitted to answer the questions I have mentioned. No one, for example, is likely to answer them worse than an Oxford philosopher who, having read Greats in his youth, was once a student of history and thinks that this youthful experience of historical thinking entitles him to say what history is, what it is about, how it proceeds, and what it is for.

The second qualification for answering these questions is that a man 3 should not only have experience of historical thinking but should also have reflected upon that experience. He must be not only an historian but a philosopher; and in particular his philosophical thought must have included special attention to the problems of historical thought. Now it is possible to be a quite good historian (though not an historian of the highest order) without thus reflecting upon one's own historical thinking. It is even easier to be a quite good teacher of history (though not the very best kind of teacher) without such reflection. At the same time, it is important to remember that experience comes first, and reflection on that experience second. Even the least reflective historian has the first qualification. He possesses the experience on which to reflect; and when he is asked to reflect on it his reflections have a good chance of being to the point. An historian who has never worked much at philosophy will probably answer our four questions in a more intelligent and valuable way than a philosopher who has never worked much at history.

I shall therefore propound answers to my four questions such as I 4 think any present-day historian would accept. Here they will be rough and ready answers, but they will serve for a provisional definition of our subject-matter and they will be defended and elaborated as the argument proceeds.

(a) The definition of history. Every historian would agree, I think, 5 that history is a kind of research or inquiry. What kind of inquiry it is I do not yet ask. The point is that generically it belongs to what we call the sciences: that is, the forms of thought whereby we ask questions and try to answer them. Science in general, it is important to realize, does not consist in collecting what we already know and arranging it in this or that kind of pattern. It consists in fastening upon something we do not know,

and trying to discover it. Playing patience with things we already know may be a useful means towards this end, but it is not the end itself. It is at best only the means. It is scientifically valuable only in so far as the new arrangement gives us the answer to a question we have already decided to ask. That is why all science begins from the knowledge of our own ignorance: not our ignorance of everything, but our ignorance of some definite thing—the origin of parliament, the cause of cancer, the chemical composition of the sun, the way to make a pump work without muscular exertion on the part of a man or a horse or some other docile animal. Science is finding things out: and in that sense history is a science.

(b) The object of history. One science differs from another in that it 6 finds out things of a different kind. What kind of things does history find out? I answer, *res gestae:* actions of human beings that have been done in the past. Although this answer raises all kinds of further questions many of which are controversial, still, however they may be answered; the answers do not discredit the proposition that history is the science of *res gestae,* the attempt to answer questions about human actions done in the past.

(c) How does history proceed? History proceeds by the interpretation 7 of evidence: where evidence is a collective name for things which singly are called documents, and a document is a thing existing here and now, of such a kind that the historian, by thinking about it, can get answers to the questions he asks about past events. Here again there are plenty of difficult questions to ask as to what the characteristics of evidence are and how it is interpreted. But there is no need for us to raise them at this stage. However they are answered, historians will agree that historical procedure, or method, consists essentially of interpreting evidence.

(d) Lastly, *what is history for?* This is perhaps a harder question than 8 the others; a man who answers it will have to reflect rather more widely than a man who answers the three we have answered already. He must reflect not only on historical thinking but on other things as well, because to say that something is 'for' something implies a distinction between A and B, where A is good for something and B is that for which something is good. But I will suggest an answer, and express the opinion that no historian would reject it, although the further questions to which it gives rise are numerous and difficult.

My answer is that history is 'for' human self-knowledge. It is gener- 9 ally thought to be of importance to man that he should know himself, where knowing himself means knowing not his merely personal peculiarities, the things that distinguish him from other men, but his nature as man. Knowing yourself means knowing, first, what it is to be a man; secondly, knowing what it is to be the kind of man you are; and thirdly, knowing what it is to be the man *you* are and nobody else is. Knowing yourself means knowing what you can do; and since nobody knows what he can do until he tries, the only clue to what man can do is what man has done. The value of history, then, is that it teaches us what man has done and thus what man is.

Questions

Rereading and Independent Analysis

1. Make a topical outline of this selection, indicating the major and minor divisions of Collingwood's argument. Then in each section of this outline list the *kinds* of evidence he uses to support his statements. Where is he reasoning logically? Where does he use examples?

2. Reread the selection, marking each transitional and connective word Collingwood uses to connect his ideas in a way that makes them easy for the reader to follow and remember. What is the thought process that these connections reveal? How does this process suggest that history (which Collingwood is "doing" in this essay) is a way of thinking?

Suggested Discussion and Group Activities

1. One of Collingwood's most important assertions about history is that it is a "science." After examining definitions of "science" in a good dictionary and reviewing your own uses of the word, outline a class definition of "science" that includes its most narrow and its broadest implications. Apply this definition to Collingwood's meaning to see if the two fit well together.

2. In groups, decide how Collingwood's description of a "historian" differs from your definitions of other kinds of specialists—psychologists, sociologists, biologists, or mathematicians. What specific qualities in Collingwood's description would these people, and others like them, share? How would they differ in specific ways?

Writing Suggestions

Response

Write a few paragraphs telling how you became interested in a particular school subject and what sense you have of what you will be doing with that subject in five to ten years.

Analysis

On the basis of your class analysis of Collingwood's definition of history, construct a questionnaire with which to interview one of your professors about what it means to him or her to be, for example, a chemist or a professor of literature. You may want to work on your questionnaire in a group in class so that you can predict the results of your questions. After you have scheduled and conducted your interview, write a brief essay that explains the answers to your questions and draws a conclusion from them.

Finding a Purpose

One of a student's most common tasks is to write a proposal to a group asking to be admitted to a course of study or other training program. On the basis of your answer to "Response," prepare to submit such a statement to a group you choose.

   Your proposal is for a panel who are reviewing applications for admission to further study in a particular field or to a job-training program. They will want to know your educational background, your qualities as a student, and your plans for further study and work in this field or job. Before you write, make lists of the points you want to include and group them in categories.

   Finally, write a brief character sketch of yourself, listing the qualities you have that would be important in a good student or trainee. Write your proposal and this personal statement as a package about you that will persuade the panel that you should be admitted to a competitive program.

Sebastian Cabot and the Northwest Passage
David Roberts

David Roberts (b. 1943) is a mountain explorer who has written *The Mountain of My Fear, Deborah: A Wilderness Narrative,* and a novella, *Like Water and Like Wind.* This essay from his *Great Exploration Hoaxes* (1982) is one of ten essays in that collection that reviews—and exposes—the facts behind some usually accepted historical myths. One of these famous and generally accepted stories is the tale of Sebastian Cabot's 1508 voyage to "discover" Hudson Bay 100 years before Henry Hudson. (Others include Cook's supposed climb of Mt. McKinley, Peary's location of the North Pole, and Byrd's supposed flight over it.)

   Roberts's essay raises serious questions about the ways that reports become the "facts" of history. He shows ways of unraveling reported facts and narratives to determine their credibility. By calling into question events that we may accept as "true history," Roberts shows that history is like all other fields. It is a way of making believable cases in support of claims as much as it is a way of thinking about facts. (See Thomas Kuhn, "Crisis and the Emergence of Scientific Theories.") As you read, notice how careful Roberts is to establish his own credibility by referring often to his sources and to their agreement among themselves. What was his purpose for writing this essay? Think of other popular reports you may have read that appeared unbelievable to you—for instance, about the "Bermuda triangle." How does Roberts address his readers to ensure they will believe his debunking of popularly accepted untruths?

In 1508, Sebastian Cabot set sail from Bristol with three hundred men in two ships. He crossed the Atlantic quickly, visited the great fishing grounds of the Newfoundland Banks, familiar to Bristol men for about a decade, and made a landfall. Cabot had more serious exploratory ambitions, however, and soon pushed on toward the northwest, coasting along the shores of Labrador. He found the ice-clogged passage that would come to be called Hudson Strait, drifted through it, and entered the open water of Hudson Bay, a full century before Henry Hudson would "discover" it. Cabot wanted to push on, but his men were on the verge of mutiny.

He turned back, sailed south past the Newfoundland Banks, and 2 continued along the coast of the present United States, still searching for a westward passage through the American landmass. He may have wintered along this coast. Having explored the Atlantic shore all the way to the tip of Florida, he turned home, arriving in Bristol in April 1509 to find that his monarch, Henry VII, had died and a new Henry, who would turn out to be far less interested in geographical discovery than his father, was on the throne. Though he had not found a route to Cathay, Sebastian Cabot had completed the most significant voyage yet undertaken by English ships.

Or had he?   3

The leading 20th-century Cabot expert, James A. Williamson, be- 4 lieves that the 1508–9 expedition took place much as described above. But there are strong grounds for concluding—and sound scholars who argue— that Cabot's whole voyage was fictitious, that in fact he never left England.

To a modern observer, it may seem incredible that the true facts 5 about a voyage of such importance remain so conjectural. Surely such a pioneering venture would be bound to leave in its wake dozens of authentic records, even eyewitness accounts. Surely no man, no matter how clever, could fake a voyage that had supposedly involved three hundred men under the patronage of the King of England.

The uncertainty about Cabot's Northwest expedition originates in 6 two sources. One is primarily historical. Although the Spanish, the Portuguese, and the Italians took pains to chronicle their great nautical voyages during the late 15th and early 16th centuries, on the whole the English did not—until Richard Hakluyt began to collect and publish firsthand accounts of his countrymen's discoveries in 1582. Before Hakluyt, English voyages were recorded mainly in the memories of living seamen or in obscure Continental compendia of knowledge. Many great deeds and adventures slipped irrevocably into the dark hiding places of historical ignorance. Of the great mariner John Cabot, Sebastian's father, on whose 1497 voyage England's whole claim to North America rested, no portrait exists today, nor a single scrap of his handwriting. By the middle of the 16th century the facts of John Cabot's life had passed completely out of common memory.

The second cause of confusion surrounding Sebastian's Northwest 7 expedition lies in the very makeup of the man's character. Whether or not the 1508 voyage was a hoax, Sebastian Cabot seems to have been a thoroughgoing confidence artist. He managed to build successful careers in both Spain and England as an adviser on northern navigations mainly by fostering the illusion that he was the sole possessor of vast funds of secret geographical lore. He seems to have taken full credit for everything his father accomplished, letting John Cabot's reputation dwindle to that of a mere merchant, while his own burgeoned as the man who had discovered North America. At the peril of his own life, he played the conflicting interests of Spain, England, and Venice off against each other, entering into cabals and intrigues in which he promised worlds but avoided delivering much of real substance. He died on dry land with a comfortable pension, well liked and reputable.

The 16th-century sources for Cabot's expedition—probably all the 8 evidence scholars will ever have upon which to base their judgments—consist of some seventeen documents in Latin, Italian, Spanish, Portuguese, French, and English. They tend to be fragments only, some mere offhand allusions a sentence or two long. They contain among them so many mutual contradictions that there is no possible way of reconciling their details in a coherent account of a single voyage. By themselves, however, such discrepancies do not amount to evidence against Cabot. Many of the documenters were sloppy guardians of truth, and nearly all were writing down stories they had heard third- or fourth-hand, sometimes at a remove of seventy years from the events they describe. The closest thing we have to an account by Cabot himself appears in 1556 in a volume of navigations by a Venetian named Ramusio, who claims to have received a letter from the navigator, which he was summarizing.

Cabot's English service ended abruptly in 1512 when, on a visit to 9 Spain, he was invited by King Ferdinand to enter the Spanish marine as a *capitán de mar.* He did not serve an English king again until 1548, when Edward VI appointed him as a maritime adviser to the Admiralty. The long hiatus is no doubt responsible for the absence of any English sources for the 1508 expedition until the last years of Cabot's life, when a man named Richard Eden, who claimed to know the aged pilot, recorded a few skimpy details of that voyage. In 1555 Eden was writing at a distance of forty-seven years from the alleged embarkation from Bristol; and if he did receive the story from Cabot's lips, he may have been listening—so his detractors would insist—to an old man who had never been a reliable source aggrandize a myth of his own deeds that he had spent a lifetime concocting.

Faced with the fragmentary nature of the Renaissance sources and 10 the unlikelihood that new evidence will turn up, the modern student is reduced to choosing among scholars' portraits of Sebastian Cabot. Surprisingly, because of the extreme variation among those portraits, this effort amounts to a fascinating pastime. Thanks to the labors of James A. Williamson, any student can read the original texts of the seventeen sources translated into English. Williamson in fact invites the reader to decide for himself about Sebastian Cabot (see Bibliography).

The full range of judgment can be comprehended by looking at the 11 likenesses that three scholars, each the leading expert of his day, have unveiled for our scrutiny. Richard Biddle, a Pittsburgh lawyer, was the first man to try to assemble all the known documents bearing on Cabot; his 1831 *Memoir* represents the pinnacle of Cabot idolatry. In the last decade of the 19th century, the indefatigable Frenchman Henry Harrisse issued a stream of memoirs and monographs on Cabot, the general import of which was to debunk the explorer as a wholesale fraud. In our own century, James A. Williamson has spent over thirty years studying the controversy, and his works represent the effort, to use his own metaphor, to steady the pendulum of Cabot's reputation. Williamson acknowledges the navigator's shady and dubious sides, but expresses faith in the reality of the bold Northwest expedition.

Biddle's Cabot. It would not be fair to hold Richard Biddle responsi- 12
ble for exaggerations that only subsequent scholarship has corrected. The "rediscovery" of John Cabot was a triumph of late-19th-century research, and crucial documents have been unearthed as recently as 1956. To the Pennsylvania lawyer in 1831, John Cabot was merely a merchant sailor from Venice who had settled in Bristol, and to whom, with his three sons, in 1496 Henry VII had issued a patent for the discovery of lands "unknown to all Christians." Biddle took it for granted that Sebastian Cabot was the man who had discovered the mainland of North America in 1497. Whether or not the father even went on the voyage was a question Biddle briefly entertained, concluding that if John Cabot was on board, it was "merely for the purpose of turning to account his mercantile skill and sagacity."

Thus by 1508, in the American scholar's view, Sebastian Cabot was 13
already an accomplished and experienced mariner, whose "simple, but bold proposition" of 1497 had actually represented his first attempt to find a northwest route to Cathay. When Biddle turns his mind to the 1508 expedition, then, he harbors not the slightest suspicion that the journey may have been a hoax. The only question is just how far Sebastian actually penetrated along the Northwest Passage. His answer is, well into Hudson Bay. To buttress this conclusion, it is an easy matter for him to discover that the 16th-century sources that give Cabot the most northerly latitude at the point where he turned around, notably Ramusio and the Englishman Richard Willes, also happen to have been the work of the soberest chroniclers. The sources that limit Cabot's penetration to more southerly latitudes were the work of historical hacks, or of interested parties such as "Spaniards . . . jealous of the reputation of Cabot."

The most specious piece of Biddle's reasoning springs from a vague 14
similarity between the earliest source for Cabot's voyage, a Latin text by Peter Martyr from 1516, and a very recent traveler's account of the terrain around Hudson Bay. Only six years before Biddle was writing, Captain Edward Parry, as part of the Admiralty's vigorous new attack on the Northwest Passage, had led an expedition that attempted the route by pushing into the northwest corner of Hudson Bay. Biddle turns to Parry and finds:

Very little snow was now lying upon the ground, and numerous streams of water rushing down the hills and sparkling in the beams of the morning sun, relieved in some measure the melancholy stillness which otherwise reigned on this desolate shore.

Three hundred and seventeen years earlier, in the same latitude, according to Peter Martyr (as Englished by Hakluyt), Cabot had "found monstrous heaps of ice swimming on the sea, and in manner continual daylight; yet saw he the land in that tract free from ice, which had been molten by the heat of the sun." Such evidence convinces Biddle that the two sailors must have visited the same place. (In other exploration controversies, comparisons like this one are a favorite resort of the credulous.)

Biddle's enthusiasm seduces him into building a model hero. The 15 epithets with which he decorates Cabot again and again are "enterprising and intrepid," "accomplished and enthusiastic." The 1508 decision to turn back south, then, was a simple matter of nerve versus cowardice, of "the dauntless intrepidity that found a new impulse in perils before which his terrified companions gave way."

The full flavor of Biddle's idolatry may be tasted in his handling of 16 Cabot's 1526–30 Spanish expedition to the La Plata River in South America, the only voyage we can be sure Sebastian actually led. The accounts by which we know about this expedition are those of Cabot's underlings and financers, who filed lawsuits against their former commander and tried to have him arrested when he got back to Spain; thus our view of it may be one-sided. But it is hard not to picture the La Plata venture as a four-year disaster. Stimulated by the successful circumnavigation performed by one of Magellan's ships, Charles V put Cabot in command of an expedition "for the discovery of Tharsis, Ophir, and Eastern Cathay." The plan was to explore the coasts of South America in search of a more northerly passage to the Pacific than the one Magellan had found.

Soon after reaching Brazil, Cabot let himself be distracted by Por- 17 tuguese rumors of great treasures of gold and silver in the interior. He apparently gave up any intention of searching for the passage to Cathay and concentrated much of his next three years on fortune-hunting up the La Plata. As a result of the switch in plans, several of Cabot's officers threatened revolt. Even before he had reached the mouth of the river, he had put the troublemakers under arrest; then he set them on shore, although some were sick with fever, and sailed away, leaving them to die. (The officers managed to befriend the natives and eventually made their way to the Portuguese settlements to the north.) In the harbor near Santa Catalina, Cabot's flagship ran upon a submerged rock. Later allegations reported that the commander was the first man to abandon ship, which so demoralized the crew that the vessel ended up a complete wreck.

Cabot pushed up the La Plata and its tributaries, building forts as he 18 went. Chasing a rumor of gold, he led his men westward up the Paraguay River, despite failing provisions and hostile natives. When a few Indians approached the straggling band of Spaniards and offered to show them where they could find food, Cabot dispatched thirty men to follow the guides, who led them into an ambush in which they were all killed or wounded

In 1528 Cabot sent one of his ships home to request a relief expedi- 19
tion. Upon its arrival in Seville, the merchant backers of the expedition decided at once they wanted nothing more to do with Cabot. The king, steadfastly loyal, ordered a relief expedition at his own expense; but his instructions apparently were never carried out. Meanwhile Cabot had housed his men in a new fort on the Paraná River. While he was away, Indians attacked and burned the fort, killing most of its defenders. The native victory encouraged further attacks, and even though he had retreated with the remainder of his force to the coast, in the following months Cabot lost another thirty men while they were out fishing or foraging for roots. Late in 1529 the survivors decided to flee for Spain, which they did not reach until the following July.

Cabot returned to face seven years of judicial inquiry. It took the 20
scribes of the Council for the Indies three months simply to draw up the accusations and interrogations brought against the commander by his former subordinates. After two years Cabot was found guilty of maladministration and disobedience. He was sentenced to four years' banishment to Morocco as well as heavily fined. For some reason (perhaps the loyalty of Charles V) the banishment was never put into effect, and, amazingly, Cabot was allowed to continue in his office as pilot-major of Spain.

George Parker Winship, a scholar otherwise sympathetic to the ex- 21
plorer, sums up the La Plata expedition by remarking that Cabot "discovered only one thing—that he was not qualified for the leadership of a maritime adventure." Yet Biddle sees it differently. The La Plata voyage was a four-year conspiracy against a brave man, a "dark treachery" enacted by opportunistic and cowardly subordinates. He finds that some of the incriminating testimony "has that air of vagueness so characteristic of falsehood," yet discovers in the same documents proof of Cabot's "remarkable gentleness of deportment" and the "affectionate attachment" binding his men to him.

Biddle excuses the abandonment on shore of Cabot's officers as "the 22
daring exercise of . . . rightful authority," a bold step necessary to quell a mutiny. "The effect was instant. Discord vanished with this knot of conspirators." Nowhere does Biddle mention the great hurry in which Cabot allegedly fled his own grounded ship. He regards the massacres of Cabot's men by Indians as unfortunate mishaps, denies claims that they were provoked in part by Cabot's barbarous treatment of the natives, and in general assails "the disingenuousness of the Spanish historians." Glossing over the judicial aftermath of the expedition, Biddle resumes his narrative with the bland observation that Cabot took up again his functions as pilot-major. This uninterrupted service goes to demonstrate that "the defence submitted to the Emperor must have been completely successful."

At the end of his biography Biddle sums up his subject's importance 23
by saying, "The English language would probably be spoken in no part of
America but for Sebastian Cabot." Lamenting the fact that Cabot's burying place remains unknown, the lawyer concludes, "He gave a Continent
to England: yet no one can point to the few feet of earth she has allowed
him in return!"

Harrisse's Cabot. In 1897, with Britain at the height of Empire, the 24
four hundredth anniversary of (as it was now known to be) John Cabot's
discovery of America was widely celebrated. Buildings were constructed,
tablets mounted, a commemorative tower planned, statues commissioned,
and orations delivered, not only in Bristol but in Newfoundland, where it
was supposed the elder Cabot had made his landfall. The tenor of the
celebrations was on the whole honorific to both John and Sebastian Cabot,
as evinced by the Bristol statue that portrayed an eager, standing youth
being sent out to sea by a bearded, seated patriarch. (In 1937 it was
discovered that John Cabot, far from living to be an old man, had vanished
on his second expedition in 1498.) Ironically, coinciding with the outburst
of commemorative works, the monumental labors of a shrewd French
scholar were putting Sebastian Cabot's reputation into the deepest shade
it had ever known.

The culmination of Henry Harrisse's work was a large volume that 25
appeared in 1896, entitled *John Cabot the Discoverer of North-America
and Sebastian His Son,* in which the scholar declared his purpose to be "to
set forth a true history . . . based exclusively on authentic documents" of
the explorer "now held by many to have been one of the greatest naviga-
tors and cosmographers that ever lived." Winship, an admiring dissenter
from Harrisse's conclusions, said of the work, which he thought "magnificent," that it "is not a history; it is rather a laboratory manual." With the
painstaking zeal of a born iconoclast, Harrisse examines one by one all of
Sebastian Cabot's purported achievements and pokes holes in each of
them. Arguing from Sebastian's alleged friendship with chroniclers like
Peter Martyr, Harrisse blames the explorer not only for neglecting to
mention his father's deeds, but for willfully misrepresenting him as "a sort
of itinerant merchant, who had come to England solely to sell his goods,"
and for deliberately attributing to himself his father's navigations. Harrisse
is the first scholar to doubt that Sebastian, who must have been a youth
in his teens, was even along on the epochal 1497 voyage.

Underlining a sentence in Peter Martyr which other scholars had 26
tended to overlook, Harrisse begins to build his case: " 'Sume of the Span-
yards denye that [Sebastian] Cabot was the fyrst fynder of the lande of
Baccallaos [the Newfoundland Banks]: and affirme that he went not so far
westwarde.' " Detail by detail the revised portrait takes shape, of a man
"capable of disguising the truth, whenever it was in his interest to do so."
The numerous inaccuracies and inconsistencies in reports from sources
supposedly in contact with Cabot, even about basic matters like the country of his birth, derive, the French scholar concludes, not from careless
historians but from Cabot's own "usual manner of speaking, vainglorious

and erratic." Erratic like a fox, Harrisse means; for the method behind Cabot's unreliability was to gain power by being "constantly engaged in plotting and corresponding in secret with foreign rulers to advance his own interest." Thus the question of whether or not the 1508 Northwest expedition ever took place is inextricably bound up with the possible advantages Cabot might later have gained, first with the Spanish crown, then with the Venetian senate, by pretending he had led such an expedition.

The main source for dating the voyage in 1508–9 is a sentence in a 1536 report to the Venetian senate by the ambassador to Spain, one Marc-Antonio Contarini: "But upon his return he found the King dead, and his son caring little for the enterprise." Harrisse argues, from an allusion by the same author to Columbus, that the voyage he mistakenly records is actually John Cabot's 1497 expedition. All the earliest sources, though they disagree about the latitude reached and other details, repeat the "fact" that Sebastian sailed in two ships with three hundred men. To Harrisse this is proof only that after he had moved to Spain in 1512 Cabot kept telling the same story to different men. Tracing the swift rise in Cabot's fortunes at the Spanish court, Harrisse points to the documents that indicate that the Venetian kept trading on his supposedly unique knowledge of the Baccalaos fishing industry, and possibly of the Northwest Passage, which was widely theorized to exist. "This hyd secreate of nature," as one Italian source puts it, would have been extremely valuable information for the Spanish, who had explored no farther north than 40°.

Harrisse analyzes the remaining sources for the Northwest voyage, and tries to show that they merely borrow from the earlier Italian ones. Though he stops short of declaring that the expedition was entirely imaginary, the French writer's verdict is implicit: there is no evidence other than Cabot's own "vainglorious and erratic" boasts that he ever set sail from Bristol, much less reached Hudson Bay. And there was everything— a lucrative career as maritime adviser to kings—to be gained by misrepresenting himself as a sailor with unmatched experience in the North Atlantic.

The same sharp scrutiny is brought to every phase of Sebastian Cabot's life, and the cumulative effect is devastating. Two details are worth mentioning, as bearing retrospectively on the 1508 expedition. In 1521, though still in Spanish service, Cabot visited England and may have entered into an agreement with Henry VIII to lead a major English expedition of discovery. We know about the plan because the king ordered the twelve great livery companies of London to make a large contribution, and the Drapers objected, in an official protest.

> And we thynk it were to sore aventour to joperd v shipps wt men & goodes unto the said Iland [the Newefound Iland] upon the singuler trust of one man, callyd as we understand, Sebastyan, whiche Sebastyan, as we here say, was never in that land hym self, all if he makes reporte of

many thinges as he hath hard his Father and other men speke in tymes past.

As Winship later pointed out, we cannot be certain that the "Sebastyan" of the Drapers' protest is Cabot himself, let alone what the ostensible object of the expedition was. But to Harrisse the resemblances are too close to be coincidental. Whatever posterity had to say, the merchants of London in 1521 knew a fraud when they saw one, and his nine years' absence from the country had not diminished their memory of the man who took credit for his father's expeditions. 30

A 1544 "planisphere," supposedly executed by Sebastian Cabot, on which the Newfoundland "prima vista" is located and the mouth of the St. Lawrence indicated with great accuracy, was held for centuries to be evidence of Cabot's firsthand knowledge of the New World. Harrisse proves convincingly that the information on the planisphere derives from Jacques Cartier's expeditions, the nomenclature plagiarized from a 1541 French map that incorporated Cartier's discoveries. Thus in Harrisse's view Cabot was a shrewd student of his own hoaxes, and knew how to ransack sources of which the English and the Spanish might be largely ignorant to bolster his claims to knowledge. 31

In 1522 Cabot entered upon his most dangerous intrigue. At a time when he was privy to all the exploratory plans of the Spanish government, and when the balance of power in the New World was extremely delicate, he sent an agent secretly to Venice to promise to the Council of Ten that he was ready to travel to the Italian city to reveal a confidence on which, he claimed, the future greatness of the Venetian Republic depended. Even to promise this was, of course, high treason. Venice was quite interested, and sent Contarini to Valladolid to feel out Cabot further. Cabot, Contarini reported, grew terrified that the secret might get out. Obviously disconcerted at being approached so openly while he was in Spain, the pilot-major offered vague promises and delays. It may well be that at the very time that he was (probably openly) consulting with Henry VIII about a western expedition, Cabot was secretly offering Venice a slice of the pie. In any event, nothing came of the intrigue. 32

Harrisse's portrait, while it demolishes Cabot's pretensions as a navigator and cosmographer, establishes a Machiavellian schemer at least as interesting in human terms, however deceitful and self-centered he must have been. Cabot emerges as a kind of three-way double agent, playing Venice against England against Spain, all in the interests of his own power and wealth. To Harrisse, the intrigue and treachery were simply part of the man's "natural disposition." The marvel is that he got away with it all—and escaped banishment to Morocco to boot. 33

Williamson's Cabot. Despite Harrisse's decimation, the 20th century has been relatively kind to Sebastian Cabot. Winship, the influential bibliographer, writing only a few years after Harrisse, expresses his faith in the 1508 expedition, reasoning that it represented Cabot's attempt to sail 34 north to Cathay along the hypothetical "Great Circle" route. Summing up Cabot's achievement in 1973, the historian David Beers Quinn asserts that "modern scholarship—itself a fickle thing—has narrowed down his individual contribution to Bristol voyaging to a single venture, apparently made in the years 1508–9."

Much of the restitution depends on a kind of argument from the absence of evidence—at best a shaky business. Quinn, for example, suggests that Cabot's reason for leaving England in 1512 to serve the Spanish crown may have been the disgrace of having failed to complete the Northwest Passage three years before. Similarly, he argues from the absence of any Bristol records of the financing of the 1508 expedition that it most likely was launched from London instead. 35

More than any other scholar, James A. Williamson has swayed modern opinion back to a belief in the reality of the Northwest voyage. Williamson is no Biddle. A clear-headed skeptic, he himself casts doubt on details in the sources that even Harrisse left unattacked, as in his lucid demonstration that the ships that would have been available to Cabot could simply not have borne 150 men each. His argument in favor of the 1508 expedition is subtle and logical, well worth an open-minded appraisal. 36

An outline of the argument follows. In the earliest source, Peter Martyr's *Decades* of 1516, there is no mention of Cabot's purpose in sailing north, nor any northernmost latitude reached—despite the fact that Peter said that Cabot had been a frequent guest in his house. To Williamson the omissions are significant. In 1515 the Spanish were hoping to seize upon a direct passage to the Pacific through the unexplored Gulf of Mexico. The waters farther north they conceded to the Portuguese. It would have been injudicious, then, Williamson argues, for an Englishman in the service of Spain to let on publicly that he knew of a northern route to the Pacific, which would threaten Spain's potential supremacy in the New World. This would have been all the more true after the conquests of Mexico and Peru. 37

In 1520–1 when Cabot was in England negotiating with Henry VIII for the command of an Atlantic expedition, it would have presented no threat to Charles V if the project were merely a voyage to the Newfoundland fishery, by then a regular milk run for British ships. But the vehemence of the Drapers' protest, with its vague allusion to a "Newefound Iland," must, in Williamson's eyes, indicate a far more ambitious project: the Northwest Passage itself, treason against Spain. 38

The imprudence of conniving at the same time with Venice was exacerbated by the high ambition of Cabot's project. Contarini's report describing Cabot's reaction to the letter brought him in Valladolid gives a vivid picture of a man mortally frightened by the possible consequences of his own rashness: 39

At dinner time I withdrew with him, and delivered the letter, which he read, his colour changing completely during its perusal. Having finished

> reading it, he remained a short while without saying anything, as if
> alarmed and doubtful. . . . [At last he said] "I most earnestly beseech you
> to keep the thing secret, as it would cost me my life."

Williamson argues from the extremity of this reaction that Cabot was not
simply bluffing, that he must have believed in the existence of the Northwest Passage because he had already, fourteen years before, discovered it.

In Ramusio's 1556 collection of voyages we hear for the first time that 40
Cabot reached 67°30′N and found open sea, and that "he firmly believed
that by that way he could pass toward Eastern Cathay," and would have
done so but for his mutinous crew. Ramusio claims to be summarizing a
letter from Cabot, and therefore this story ought to be nearly a firsthand
account. Williamson believes that by now Cabot could be open and frank
about his earlier secrets because in 1548 he had returned to English
service, removing himself from the danger of treason. This theory requires
that Williamson reinterpret Ramusio's phrase "as was written to me, many
years ago, by Signor Sebastian Cabot our Venetian" as actually meaning
not many years ago.

In this manner the modern scholar examines each of the seventeen 41
sources for reliability, building up the argument that even their contradictions can be squared with a genuine voyage. The proof that Cabot not only
embarked, but sailed as far as the entrance to Hudson Bay, hinges on the
1577 testimony of Richard Willes, who wrote that Cabot had reached a
strait between 61° and 64°N, sailed west for 10° of longitude, then turned
south into a large body of open water which (Williamson suggests) he
thought was the Pacific. Willes's account is the most detailed English
source, and refers to a map made by one Gemma Frisius in or before 1537,
a copy of which is extant today. The crude outlines of a northern water
route show on this map, and though most of the place names are attributed
to the Portuguese, the south side of the passageway is inscribed, *"Terra per
britannos inventa"* (Land found by the Britons). Some scholars have regarded this as a confused record of the Breton Jacques Cartier's discovery
of the St. Lawrence. But to Williamson the coincidences are too striking
to ignore—including the rough accuracy of Willes's geography when compared to the actual Arctic. In 1508, he concludes, Sebastian Cabot discovered Hudson Bay.

The argument is indeed a possible one; it condenses the mature 42
deliberations of our century's leading Cabot scholar. Yet at half a dozen
crucial turns, its logic requires a little tug of rereading here, an extrapolation there. In Williamson's pages one senses the man's lifelong ambiva-
lence toward the Venetian adventurer of four centuries before. Under-
standably, he would like to see himself as ending a long line of Cabot
misrepresentations:

> He was no sooner dead than the English made a legend of his name. His
> reputation grew until it reached exaggeration in the eighteenth century
> and had scarcely declined a century ago [1829]. John Cabot was forgot-

ten, and Sebastian was revered as the father of English commerce and naval supremacy. Modern research has bred disillusionment and swung the pendulum too far in the other direction. It is time to steady it to rest.

But such is always the scholar's delusion, that he has at last steadied   43 the pendulum of fluctuating error. To shift the metaphor: trying to know the final truth about Cabot's alleged Northwest expedition is like trying to reconstruct a whole tapestry from a few shreds of cloth. We simply know too little. The 1508 expedition will remain eternally an unsolved question.

It is worth pointing out, however, how crucially Quinn and William-   44 son, in their relatively generous treatment of Cabot, rely on a kind of inverse reasoning. *If* Cabot had indeed been in Hudson Bay, then his behavior at such and such a juncture makes sense. For hard evidence they must resort to sources who themselves undoubtedly got entangled in Sebastian Cabot's web of deceitful boasts. As we shall see, it is not often that an explorer with a known record of misrepresentation and secrecy suddenly goes "straight" and pulls off a major achievement. Williamson and Quinn may themselves have fallen prey to the ironic temptations of 20th-century revisionism. It is Harrisse's debunking, in the last analysis, that has the ring of probability. Whether Sebastian Cabot left England at all is one question; but there seems no alternative to the conclusion that the 1508 expedition was in some—probably large—part a hoax.

None of which makes the man himself any less interesting; and we   45 are free to indulge in speculation as to just what kind of fellow Sebastian Cabot was. The only surviving portrait, an engraving copied from a con-temporary painting, shows an old man with a doubly forked beard, cove-tously clasping a globe, his right hand spreading a compass across its northern regions. The face looks shrewd and private, and gives off a sense of great power. Quinn sees Cabot in the Italian Renaissance tradition of businessmen-mystics: "A man of many talents, competent and far-seeing in many respects, he was also vain, and in action arbitrary, while he lived a fantasy life of mysteries and dark secrets alongside his more prosaic everyday activities." Williamson himself emphasizes the "lonely and mys-terious figure, a man without a country, deprived of patriotism yet able to simulate it, of ingratiating manners and secret mind, admired by schol-ars and respected by the great, successful to the outward view, but a failure by the measure of his own ambitions."

In his last years, with a comfortable pension, Cabot advised the cap-   46 tains of English expeditions attempting to sail by the Northeast Passage, up past Scandinavia and Russia, toward Cathay. The liveliest glimpse we have of him during his whole life comes from these years, when Stephen Borough, one of the captains, setting sail from Gravesend, remarked that Cabot had seen him off.

The good olde Gentleman Master Cabota gave to the poore most liberal almes, wishing them to pray for the good fortune, and prosperous suc-

cesse of the Serchthrift, our Pinnesse. And then at the signe of the Christopher, hee and his friends banketted, and made me, and them that
were in the company great cheere: and for the very joy that he had to
see the towardnes of our intended discovery, he entred into the dance
himselfe, amongst the rest of the young and lusty company.

In old age, apparently, even the inveterate schemer and loner could   47
raise a glass to hearten a young navigator about to pave his own perilous
way north into the frozen unknown.

Bibliography

Biddle, Richard. *A Memoir of Sebastian Cabot; with a Review of Maritime Discovery.*
    Philadelphia, 1831.
Harrisse, Henry. *John Cabot the Discoverer of North-America and Sebastian His Son.* Lon-
    don, 1896.
Porter, Rev. Edward G. "The Cabot Quadri-Centenary Celebrations at Bristol, Halifax, and
    St. John's in June 1897," *New England Magazine,* February 1898.
Quinn, David Beers. *England and the Discovery of America, 1481–1620.* New York, 1974.
———. *Sebastian Cabot and Bristol Exploration.* Bristol, 1968.
Williamson, James A. *The Cabot Voyages and Bristol Discovery Under Henry VII.* Cam-
    bridge, England, 1962.
———. *The Voyages of the Cabots and the English Discovery of North America under Henry
    VII and Henry VIII.* London, 1929.
Winship, George Parker. *Cabot Bibliography with an Introductory Essay on the Careers of
    the Cabots.* London, 1900.

Questions

Rereading and Independent Analysis

1. Roberts carefully points out that many people still think Cabot
accomplished what has traditionally been claimed for him. Make two lists
of the facts Roberts presents, one that shows evidence in favor of Cabot's
success and another that gives the evidence against it.

2. The bibliography at the end of Roberts's essay lists the works he
consulted. Use your library to find one of these sources about Cabot or one
that is not listed. Does Roberts's essay accurately report the information
in other sources?

Suggested Discussion and Group Activities

1. What did you know about Sebastian Cabot, Hudson Bay, and the
Northwest Passage before you read this selection? How surprising did you
find it?

2. Look up and review the three "versions" of Cabot that Roberts
reviews. On the basis of these three sources, check to discover which parts
of the three accounts Roberts used are verified by the other two. Which
are not? What reasons does Roberts suggest for discrepancies among
them? What does this tell you about how cases are made on the basis of
research?

3. After reading and analyzing this essay, are you convinced by it? Referring to specific passages in the essay, tell why you are or are not persuaded to Roberts's point of view.

Writing Suggestions

Response

Have you ever become disappointed in someone who was a public or private hero to you at first? Write about this experience, describing what made you change your mind about this person and the feelings you experienced.

Analysis

Choose a recent story from a news magazine—*Time* or *Newsweek,* for example—or a national newspaper such as the *Wall Street Journal* or the *New York Times.* Write an analysis of the report. Explain any questions you have about the facts, the explanations of causes, and the results of the event. From the internal evidence alone, how reliable do you think the report was? Why?

Finding a Purpose

Choose a recent, newsworthy event you have heard about in radio and television reports. Then use your library's resources—the *Readers' Guide to Periodical Literature* and any recent books you can find—to expand your knowledge of the event. Write an essay for your classmates in which you describe the difference between your first impression of the facts of the event and your understanding of it now that you have looked more deeply into the available information.

 # A History of the New History
Gertrude Himmelfarb

This review of a book by historian Lawrence Stone demonstrates how specialized fields of study monitor their contributors, holding them responsible for new works, which are carefully scrutinized for accuracy and explained so that others will know their authors' perspectives. Gertrude Himmelfarb (b. 1922), the reviewer, is also an historian, author of *On Liberty and Liberalism* (1974), and a professor at the Graduate School of the City University of New York. This essay reviewing Stone's book, *The Past and the Present* (1981), was published in the *New York Times Book Review.* As you read, you will discover Stone's many contributions to establishing other historians' current critical methods and his own research interests. It will also become clear that Himmelfarb admires and respects Stone's research and that she has learned much from him about how to write a review that both describes and evaluates a work.

This review is valuable, then, because it both informs readers about the content of a new book and "places" this new contribution to a subject. It shows how Stone's work fits into the development of history as a field and how he participates in internal disagreements about its proper boundaries, questions, and methods. This review also offers a useful summary of the development and methods of historical studies, showing how complex the field and its methods are now. As you read, take note of Himmelfarb's specific word choices. As any reviewer does, she uses evaluative language to reveal her opinions.

Only a decade ago, it was still possible to speak of the "new history." Today 1 the new history has become so thoroughly familiar, so firmly entrenched in the academy, that it threatens to become as conventional and academic as the old. This volume of essays by Lawrence Stone, a founding father of the new history, is a memorial to a "Golden Age" that, he tells us, is already in the past. If the memorial sometimes sounds more like a dirge than a eulogy, that is a tribute to the candor of one "old revolutionary" who knows when the revolution is over.

The first part of "The Past and the Present" defines the methodology 2 and subject matter of the new history: It is analytic rather than narrative; it relies on such techniques as quantification, model-building and psychoanalysis; it focuses upon groups more often than individuals, and the masses more often than elites; and it addresses itself to such subjects as the material basis of existence (demography, geography, economics, technology), the patterns and institutions of socialization (the family and school, prisons and asylums, factories and sports), the processes of social change (mobility, conflict and consensus) and the social aspects of popular culture, beliefs and attitudes. The "old history," by contrast, typically concerns itself with political events, diplomacy, revolutions and wars; its customary method is narrative; and its most prominent characters are kings, politicians and public figures. Strictly speaking, the new and the old are not mutually exclusive. Political historians have always found room for some cultural and social history. And some new historians have applied their new methods to the old subjects, quantifying and analyzing, for example, data about Members of Parliament and legislative issues, in order to correlate their voting records with their economic interests or with the class composition of their constituencies. But the emphasis and intent are so different as to warrant the distinction between new and old.

Whatever reservations Mr. Stone has about the new history, his own 3 commitment to it is firm; for him it is the only exciting kind of history, the "cutting edge of innovation." Yet his reservations are so considerable that his colleagues may well suspect him of giving comfort to the enemy. Certainly no humanist has so effectively exposed the fallacies, pretensions and assumptions of "quantohistory," or been so harshly critical of the "disaster area" of "psychohistory." This is not to say that Mr. Stone rejects quantification or psychoanalysis—in their appropriate places and to an appropriate degree. But he does insist upon their limitations. Above all, he warns of the dangerous reductivism inherent in the attempt to make of history a social science. Contemplating the sad state of the social sciences these days, he suggests that "it might be time for the historical rats to leave rather than to scramble aboard the social scientific ship which seems to be leaking and undergoing major repair."

In counseling these "historical rats" to leave the sinking ship of social 4 science, Mr. Stone is not urging them to return to the old history, but rather to board the newest ship in the armada of the new history, the flagship, as it now seems, sailing under the banner of *mentalités collectives.* Devoted to the study of popular beliefs, attitudes, customs, sentiments and modes of behavior, *mentalité* history models itself not on the social sciences but on a humanistic anthropology. Mr. Stone himself has embarked on just this course. His book, "The Family, Sex and Marriage in England 1500–1800," published in 1977, has an epigraph from Clifford Geertz, the anthropologist who is the guru of this school: "The problems, being existential, are universal; their solutions, being human, are diverse. . . . The road to the grand abstractions of science winds through a thicket of singular facts." The more famous phrase of Mr. Geertz, quoted in the present volume, is "thick description," the technique of bringing to bear upon a single episode a mass of facts of every kind and subjecting them to intensive analysis so as to elicit every possible cultural meaning, the exemplar of that method being Mr. Geertz's account of a Balinese cockfight in his "Interpretation of Cultures."

In espousing this kind of cultural-social history, Mr. Stone repudiates 5 not only the pseudo-scientific methodology of much of the new history but its ideology as well: the materialistic determinism (economic, geographic and demographic) of the French historians of the *Annales* school and the more familiar economic and social determinism of the Marxists. "The culture of the group," Mr. Stone asserts, "and even the will of the individual, are potentially at least as important causal agents of change as the impersonal forces of material output and demographic growth." And not only as important but, on occasion, primary and determinant. Thus contraception is "as much a product of a state of mind as it is of economic circumstances or technological inventions," and the puritan ethic was a "by-product of an unworldly religious movement" long before there was any economic need for a new work ethic. Moreover, in this cultural-social realm, elites and even individuals are often more influential than the masses in shaping history, and shaping it in political ways as well. "Civilizations have risen and fallen due to fluctuations in political authority and shifts in the fortunes of war"—a fact curiously overlooked, Mr. Stone observes, by those who preen themselves on being in the vanguard of the historical profession.

Mr. Stone even goes so far as to suggest that there is under way, 6 among some new historians, a "revival of narrative," one example being Emmanuel Le Roy Ladurie's "Montaillou," an account of life in a village in the Pyrenees in the early 14th century. But here Mr. Stone seems to be playing with words, for this example of the "narration of a single event" could more properly be characterized as analytic or structural. Certainly it is not what Gibbon, Macaulay or Ranke would have understood by narration, a story developed chronologically through a dramatic movement of events, so that the end is significantly different from the beginning. In "Montaillou" we have exactly the opposite, not so much a story as a "moment" in the Hegelian sense, in which the course of history is stopped in order to capture its essence, as in a still photograph.

If Mr. Stone, who normally chooses his words carefully, here seems   7 to be violating the obvious meaning of "narrative," it is to dramatize the break, as he sees it, of *mentalité* history from the other forms of the new history. "Narrative," he explains, is meant as a "shorthand code-word" to signify the rejection of the analytic methodology, the scientific pretensions and the economic and materialistic determinism of the new history. We have come, he says to "the end of an era," the end of the revolution. As in many a revolution, the end is being heralded not by some malcontent of the old guard but by one of the fathers of the revolution. In his own historical work—"The Crisis of the Aristocracy," "The Causes of the English Revolution," "Family and Fortune," "The Family, Sex and Marriage"—Mr. Stone has established himself as one of the most skillful and reputable practitioners of the new history. In the present volume he emerges as its most thoughtful critic.

The methodological essays in the first part of this book will attract the   8 most attention, and deservedly so. Yet in some respects the review essays that make up the second part are even more revealing. For these, written in the course of the past two decades, are reviews of books that Mr. Stone regarded at the time as prime exemplars of the new history. Rereading these reviews today, one is impressed by the rigor of his criticism from the beginning. Even in the first flush of revolution, his zeal was tempered by a vigilant, skeptical intelligence.

It is curious to find the same pattern repeating itself in one review   9 after another. The book is first placed in its largest framework and pronounced a major contribution to a most important subject. The reviewer then professes to be overwhelmed by the imaginativeness and boldness of the thesis, the number of facts and the variety of sources brought to bear upon it and the ingenuity of the author in weaving them all together. But before long that glowing tribute has given way to a detailed critique of thesis, facts, sources and reasoning, by the end of which little is left of that "flawed masterpiece." Some of Mr. Stone's most devastating critiques, moreover, are not of the social-science type of history but of the *mentalité* genre. In the case of Philippe Ariés' "History of Childhood" and David Fischer's "Growing Old in America," it is the methodology and data that are at fault; in E. P. Thompson's "Whigs and Hunters" and Christopher Hill's "Society and Puritanism in Pre-Revolutionary England," it is the

Marxist or neo-Marxist ideology that selects and distorts the evidence to
fit the preconceived thesis; in Barrington Moore's "Social Origins of Dicta-
torship and Democracy," it is the wrong question that is asked; in J. Bossy's
"English Catholic Community," it is the absence of all the "external
events" of the old history that can be ignored by the new only at the risk
of throwing out the baby with the bathwater.

One does not want to leave the impression that Mr. Stone is unduly   10
harsh. Indeed he seems often to go out of the way to be generous, to give
the book, at least at the outset, the benefit of the doubt, to credit it with
serious intentions. Those high expectations are themselves an invitation to
disillusionment. But even were it not for that, his criticisms would be fully
justified. Again and again, towards the end of his reviews, Mr. Stone puts
the question his reader must be asking: Where are we now? And all too
often he regretfully concludes that we are not all that much further along
than we were before—except, and here Mr. Stone does not falter, that an
important subject has been raised, one that would not have been raised
by the traditional historian and that some day may be dealt with more
satisfactorily than it has been so far.

Mr. Stone has raised so many issues and has dealt with them so   11
candidly that it may be churlish to ask even more of him. He has made
a large point, for example, of the role of ideology in general, and of
Marxism in particular, in the new history. This is all the more noteworthy
because Mr. Stone is not only a new historian but a man of the left; his
heart, he makes it clear, is still with his mentor, the Socialist historian R.
H. Tawney, even though he can no longer subscribe to most of Tawney's
historical theses. It is also clear that in his own work he has not been cowed
by the animus against "elitist" history. His "Crisis of the Aristocracy" is
largely devoted to one such elite, 382 noblemen by his count. And his
more recent "Family, Sex and Marriage" deals mainly with the gentry and
upper-middle classes, his contention being that modern feelings about the
family ("affective individualism," as he calls it) originated with them and
filtered down to the lower classes—a thesis that has been predictably and
bitterly attacked as paternalistic, elitist and "culture-bound."

Yet perhaps more can be said about the ideological impulse behind   12
the new history. If the new history does not quite illegitimize political,
constitutional and diplomatic histories, it does demean and belittle them,
in part because of a populist ideology that sees them as the instruments
of elites, in part because of a Marxist ideology that relegates them to the
realm of "epiphenomena" or "superstructure." By the same token, the
new history tends to scorn intellectual history. And here Mr. Stone joins
the pack, deriding "traditional intellectual history" as a "kind of paper-
chase of ideas back through the ages (which usually ends up with either
Aristotle or Plato)," and complaining that "great books" (in quotation
marks) are studied in an "historical vacuum." This is a bit of philistinism
unworthy (and untypical) of Mr. Stone. But it is all too typical of the
historian who is suspicious of "elitist" ideas that may indeed trace their

lineage to Plato or Aristotle, and of a discipline that does presume to characterize some books as great books (without the invidious quotation marks).

In this respect *mentalité* history is one of the worst offenders. Not 13 content to establish itself as an independent discipline devoted to the study of "mental structures"—"feelings, emotions, behavior patterns, values, and states of mind"—it feels obliged to denigrate those other mental structures known as "ideas," especially ideas that emanated from the best minds of the time. Mr. Stone elsewhere complains of the "hubris" of the new historian. But surely it is the grossest kind of hubris for the historian to be so dismissive of great books and great thinkers, to think that reality is better reflected in second-rate and third-rate thinkers than first-rate ones. And it is surely a peculiar sense of historical relevance to think that everything about a book is worth studying—the economics and technology of the publishing industry, or the sociology of the reading public—except the book itself, the ideas contained in it.

There is, finally, a methodological question. Mr. Stone has brilliantly 14 diagnosed the tendency of quantitative history to let the data dictate the subject, which all too often produces subjects that are trivial or trite. But the *mentalité* historian falls into the opposite trap of choosing a subject regardless of the availability or reliability of the data. It takes no great imagination, even for the conventional historian, to formulate wonderful questions to which he would dearly love to have answers. But the historical record, like the geological record, is notoriously faulty, full of gaps and flaws, infuriatingly lacking in the missing links we are always seeking. This is a problem for all historians, old and new. But the old historian minimizes it by deliberately focusing on those subjects—political, institutional, diplomatic, intellectual—which do have more or less adequate records, and which can be subjected to what was once called (the very expression now seems archaic) "canons of evidence." The new history, on the other hand, has a penchant for subjects that, by definition, produce few such records: the attitudes of the "inarticulate masses," or "states of mind" too subtle and private to lend themselves to the kind of evidence that survives the ages.

It is a challenging task that confronts the new history, and one can 15 understand why the brightest and most ambitious are attracted to it. It is an exciting game to ferret out whatever facts one can, however and wherever one can, and to make of them whatever one can, by way of deduction, generalization, extrapolation, supposition, intuition, imagination. Only a crotchety old historian would throw a damper on the festivities by pointing out that the results, more often than not, are thoroughly speculative and problematic. But even among the new historians there is evidence that the game is turning sour. Where the largest theses can be contrived out of the smallest facts (and of the most tenuous of facts), there is obviously much room for controversy, and it is no wonder that the new historians are even more contentious than the old.

As Mr. Stone would say, at this point in one of his reviews: Where 16 does this leave us? Mr. Stone thinks it leaves us with a chastened new history, less arrogant about what it can accomplish, less intolerant of the old history, more rigorous methodologically and more pluralistic ideologically. He also predicts that with the revolution over, the new history will consolidate its gains and make some overtures to the opposition. Some of the rest of us, mindful of the course of other revolutions, may be less sanguine. Several generations of historians (as generations go in the university) have a stake in the new history as they have come to know it. What others may criticize as methodological laxity, they regard as creativity; what others look upon as ideological indulgence, they take pride in as an act of moral commitment. Professor Stone may think that they have captured the commanding heights of the profession and carried out the basic objectives of their revolution. But like successful revolutionaries everywhere, they still see themselves as embattled and besieged, having to fend off the forces of darkness and reaction.

It will take many more voices like Mr. Stone's, voices from within 17 their own ranks, to convince the new historians that the new history is not necessarily admirable simply because it is new, nor the old contemptible simply because it is old. In the meantime, Mr. Stone, by the example of his own work and by his reflections in the present volume, may succeed in reassuring some old historians that the new and the old are not the mortal enemies they appeared to be in the bloody days of the revolution.

Questions

Rereading and Independent Analysis

1. Make a formal outline of Himmelfarb's review, indicating the topics she takes up in their order. Then compare your outline to her description of reviews by Stone, which are republished in his book. Does her review share the patterns of development that she says he uses? What are the differences?

2. Make an outline of the second paragraph of Himmelfarb's review, listing the points that contrast "new" and "old" history. Then mark places in the rest of her piece that develop these contrasts.

Suggested Discussion and Group Activities

1. Throughout this review, Himmelfarb shifts from "objective" description of the contents of Stone's work to interpretation of his, and others', motives and particular biases. In groups, review the essay, noting where Himmelfarb's own interpretations and evaluations are inserted. What distinguishes this essay as a review? On the basis of your class reading, make a list of a review's characteristics and the form it should take. What is the first information that should be included? What other points should a good reviewer make?

2. In groups, analyze examples of other reviews specifically to list the words that show their authors' opinions of the works reviewed. Make a list of the words that are emotional, colorful, and evaluative. As a group,

rewrite some of the most vivid statements of opinion in more neutral terms. What is gained and lost in a flatter, dispassionate version?

Writing Suggestions

Response

On your own, examine some reviews from your local school or town paper. Underline each instance of evaluative language in these reviews. These are words (usually adjectives, adverbs, and vivid verbs) that imply or announce an opinion. Try to supply alternatives for these words that change the favorable or unfavorable opinion of the reviewer to its opposite. Then write a few paragraphs in which you talk about how reviews influence your decisions to attend movies, watch certain television programs, and go to concerts. How is their language important?

Analysis

Reread Himmelfarb's review to list the causes of events that she says historians may include or exclude from their writing, depending on their particular methods and biases. List the evidence that various "schools" of history will consider, the methods they use to gather and analyze this data, and their sense of the purpose of history. Then choose a newsworthy local or school event whose facts you know intimately and write a brief explanation of its causes. Your explanation should analyze the causes from two perspectives—that of the old and of the new historians. Do not convey that there was only one reason that the event occurred.

Finding a Purpose

Choose a book you have read within the last few months and write a review of it for a publication whose readers need to know about the book and its quality. Your review should give details about the book's publication and author, should summarize its contents, and should include interpretation and evaluation from your own point of view as a reader of other books of this type. As you revise and edit, be sure you have chosen vocabulary that conveys your opinion and clearly reveals your evaluation of the work reviewed.

 # From "New Vietnam Scholarship"
Fox Butterfield

Fox Butterfield (b. 1939) is the *New York Times* Boston bureau chief. A correspondent in Vietnam from 1971 to 1973, he was one of the chief contributors to the *New York Times* articles that analyzed the Pentagon Papers about Vietnam released at the end of the war, and he was in Saigon covering its fall in 1975. Butterfield's essay was first published in the *New York Times Sunday Magazine,* but it resembles a term paper you might write for a history course. His purpose is to clarify and correct impressions and reports about the Vietnamese War, opinions that dominated public opinion about what was actually happening there during the time of the war itself.

His method is to "report," as though it were news, the new scholarship that has resulted from historical research conducted since the war ended in 1975. But he presents this revised picture of the war and its facts as a historian might, using carefully researched evidence from sources rather than observation and immediate inference, the usual methods of journalistic reporting.

Butterfield's essay is much longer than the parts presented here. Its clearly divided sections include (1) a lengthy introduction establishing his credentials and listing the new conclusions resulting from recent study; (2) "Fresh Perspectives on the Early Days," a description of the earliest conflicts in Vietnam and their inevitable implications; (3) "Political Compromises," which describes the conflict's progress through every President since Truman; (4) "The Military Confusion," which describes the consequences of fighting without a strategic plan; (5) "The Victories Ignored" and (6) "The Antiwar Movement," which reevaluate U.S. military success and the impact of strong protests against the war; and (7) "The Lessons of Vietnam," which draws summary conclusions from the whole group of scholars Butterfield has investigated. (Sections 1, 3, and 7 are included here.)

Butterfield's essay is a masterful example of how specific details gathered by a community who share various interests in a subject can be woven together to make one writer's own case, not just to show "what others say." His organization and clarity strongly support his thesis—that new information gathered after the prejudiced period that surrounded the conflict itself will create a new "history" of the Vietnamese War. As you read, you will need to recreate that prejudice from your own knowledge of the internal divisions this war caused in the United States. At the same time, look for Butterfield's corrective tone as he presents this carefully gathered information.

Ten years ago today, I stood on the floodlit tarmac of Tan Son Nhut air base 1 and watched as a group of 27 American prisoners of war were delivered to freedom by United States Army helicopters. The men had been picked up from a Communist-controlled rubber plantation near the Cambodian border, and their arrival was the first tangible benefit for Americans of the Paris peace accords, signed in late January.

It was an emotional moment. Gen. Frederick C. Weyand, the last 2 commander of United States forces in Vietnam, draped his arm around an Air Force colleague and confided, in tones just loud enough for me to hear, "It's the greatest day we've ever had in Vietnam."

There was a kind of resignation and finality about the remark, like 3 a losing football team salvaging a share of its pride with a meaningless touchdown in the final moments of the game. So it was with Vietnam. With the signing of the Paris agreement and the return of our P.O.W.'s, we withdrew not only the last American combat forces from Vietnam, but also our slender remaining interest in the country.

The war itself, of course, sputtered on for another two years, until 4
Saigon's stunning collapse in April 1975. But Americans went into a trance
of collective amnesia. The Vietnam War was such an agonizing, divisive
and baffling experience that we somehow resolved simply to forget it.
Unlike the fall of Nationalist China to Mao Zedong in 1949, there were no
postwar recriminations, no blame for who lost Vietnam. The shock had
been so great that nobody wanted to know. As a result, Vietnam became
not only the longest war in our history and the first war the United States
had lost—it was also the most misunderstood war.

The big questions went unasked and unanswered: How did we get 5
involved in Vietnam? Why did 57,939 Americans die there? Why did the
Communists win? What were the lessons of the war?

But now, a decade after the last American troops left Saigon, Viet- 6
nam is sparking renewed interest—though without the explosive rancor
of the 1960's and early '70's. The hottest star on television is Tom Selleck,
who plays Magnum, an amiable private eye and Vietnam veteran whose
exploits often involve flashbacks to his combat days in "Nam." Public
Television is planning an ambitious 13-hour series on the war, which it will
show within a year. The dedication of the polished black granite Vietnam
Veterans Memorial in Washington last November finally gave Vietnam
veterans a respected if ambiguous place alongside the monuments to
Jefferson, Lincoln and Washington.

Ultimately, the most important development may be the emergence 7
of a small group of scholars, journalists and military specialists who have
started to look afresh at the war. Drawing on new disclosures from Hanoi,
the opening of documents in the Presidential libraries, the Pentagon Papers (which are still the best published source material on the war) and
memoirs of some of the participants in the war, these writers have worked
quietly, with the general public largely unaware of their research.

For most of these scholars, their re-examination is not to prove 8
whether Vietnam was or was not a "noble cause," in President Reagan's
phrase, but to find out what really happened and why. In the process, they
are challenging some of the most cherished beliefs of both the right and
the left.

Among the new findings are the following: 9

- As opposed to the public caricature of him as a warmonger, 10
  Lyndon Johnson was actually reluctant to become more
  deeply involved in Vietnam. He sent American troops to
  Vietnam not out of *machismo,* but out of fear that if he "lost"
  South Vietnam, Congress would not pass his Great Society
  programs.
- Contrary to the American popular assumption that we could 11
  easily win, American Presidents from John Kennedy to Richard Nixon were never confident about our chances and, in
  fact, never had a plan to win in Vietnam. Instead, they did

only the minimum necessary not to lose Vietnam during their own tenure in the White House. They tried to fight a war on the cheap against a foe, North Vietnam, whose commitment was total.

- Under the restrictions imposed by the Presidents, some American generals knew almost from the start that they could not win the war. Without permission to cut off Hanoi's use of Laos and Cambodia, they realized, the critical strategic initiative remained in Hanoi's hands. Many officers now believe the Joint Chiefs of Staff should have resigned in protest. 12

- Both hawks and liberals were wrong about the Communists in Vietnam. While successive Administrations did not understand that the Communists' appeal had its roots in centuries of Vietnamese xenophobia, many antiwar critics—like Frances FitzGerald in her best-selling "Fire in the Lake"—over-glamorized the Vietcong, the Southern insurgents, and underestimated the role that North Vietnam played in leading the war in the South. 13

- The 1968 Tet offensive was a disastrous military defeat for the Communists, as Gen. William C. Westmoreland claimed, though most Americans regarded it as a setback for the United States. It was particularly brutal for the Vietcong, who bore the brunt of the fighting and who suffered such losses that thereafter they had to be replaced by North Vietnamese regulars, turning the conflict into a war between North and South. 14

- After Tet—though most Americans at home had given up on the war—the cumulative weight of American firepower and spending in Vietnam dramatically undercut support for the Communists. As a result, the United States was probably in a stronger position in Vietnam in 1972, just before the Paris peace accords, than at any previous point in the war. 15

- The antiwar movement did not have as much impact on American policy as is popularly thought. Lyndon Johnson's decision in March 1968 to de-escalate the war was not so much a response to the peace movement as a result of disaffection within his Administration over the disastrous costs of the war. The protesters' main contribution, in fact, may have been to help elect Richard Nixon twice—in 1968 over Hubert Humphrey and in 1972 over George McGovern. 16

A New Generation Decries Scholarly Arrogance

The picture of the Vietnam conflict that is emerging from the new research shows a war that was more complex, more morally ambiguous, than either the doves or the hawks had maintained. Of the war's many ironical twists, few match the postwar predicament of Communist Vietnam. 17

"It was a war nobody won," says Stanley Karnow, a syndicated 18 columnist, who covered Vietnam for several national publications. "North Vietnam won, of course, but it also lost." Mr. Karnow—who is chief correspondent for Public Television's series on Vietnam and who is writing a book to accompany it—was in Hanoi in 1981 to film some interviews for the series. He remembers asking Prime Minister Pham Van Dong what Vietnam's main problem now is. "He laughed," recalls Mr. Karnow. " 'That's a stupid question. Look around, you can see for yourself what problems we're having.' "

Hanoi's grim postwar record has raised a serious problem for schol- 19 ars. How much should it be taken into account when the war is analyzed? Can events during the war be interpreted in the light of the Communists' postwar detention of 50,000 to 100,000 former supporters of the Saigon regime in "re-education" camps, the corruption and economic misman-agement by Communist officials, the invasion of Cambodia, the persecu-tion of Vietnam's large Chinese ethnic minority and the flight of the boat people?

David W. P. Elliott, an assistant professor of political science at 20 Pomona College in California, believes that Vietnam's postwar record is irrelevant to understanding the war. "We shouldn't commit the historicist fallacy of reading the present into the past," says Mr. Elliott. "In 1975, the people wanted peace." Like many of the new scholars, Mr. Elliott's inter-est in Vietnam goes back to the 1960's. He learned Vietnamese in the Army and later did research on the Vietcong for the Rand Corporation, a private research organization working mostly for the Defense Depart-ment.

One of the few Vietnamese now teaching in the United States, Hue 21 Tam Ho Tai, an assistant professor of history at Harvard, agrees that the Communists' postwar failures "do not vindicate America's crusade in Viet-nam." For a part of Vietnam's troubles today were caused by the disloca-tions of the war. But Mrs. Tai, who came to the United States as a student at Brandeis, maintains that what has happened since 1975 offers an impor-tant perspective.

"During the war," she says, "people looked at the Communists and 22 said they were dedicated, driven and omnicompetent. Now we see them as corrupt and incompetent." Did the Communists change so much after 1975 or were Americans grossly mistaken in their earlier impressions?

Mrs. Tai believes that many Americans allowed their political pas- 23 sions to cloud their intellect. At the time of the war, she says, "it was fashionable to think that a guerrilla movement needed popular support to succeed, and that if the Vietcong survived, therefore they must have popular support." But that, Mrs. Tai contends, was a fallacious argument. "You can see how wrong it was now, because the Communists certainly aren't popular in the South." Or, she suggests, look at Cambodia. "Pol Pot came to power as a guerrilla, but looking at what he did to his country, you'd think twice before saying he was popular."

Mrs. Tai herself cannot be accused of being an inveterate anti-Com- 24 munist. Her father was a founder of the Trotskyite party in Vietnam; an aunt was a senior official in the Vietcong's Provisional Revolutionary Government. But she has long had reservations about those antiwar protesters who were too ready to turn the Vietnamese Communists into paragons of virtue and who refused to accept a view of the war that was not black and white.

At Brandeis, she remembers, a professor asked her in class what the   25
Vietnamese thought of the war. When she said that it was a difficult question to answer, since the view of an intellectual was probably very different from that of a peasant, the professor became angry. "Later," she says, "a student told me that my views didn't count because I was a bourgeois. I said, 'I'm sorry; I'm a human being. There are several hundred thousand members of the middle class in Vietnam.' "

This kind of academic narrow-mindedness, in Mrs. Tai's view, con-   26
tributed to American misunderstanding of Vietnam just as much as ignorance in the White House and the State Department.

Until quite recently, Vietnam has been a giant black hole in Ameri-   27
can academia. A survey by The New York Times in 1970 found that there was no scholar in the United States who devoted most of his or her time to studying North Vietnam; there was no American university with a tenured professorship in Vietnamese studies, and there were fewer than 30 students in the country studying the Vietnamese language. By comparison, there were three times that many studying Thai. According to the Social Science Research Council in New York, from 1951 to 1981 a total of 820 Americans applied to it for financial aid to work on Ph.D. dissertations in Southeast Asia. Of these, only 33 were for Vietnam, almost the same number as for Burma.

John K. Fairbank, professor emeritus of history at Harvard and the   28
man generally recognized as the founder of modern Chinese studies in the United States, refers to this lack of expertise on Vietnam as an academic Pearl Harbor. One reason for this blind spot, he suggests, was that the French excluded American missionaries and businessmen from Vietnam, and Americans therefore did not have a personal stake in Vietnam.

However, by the time the United States became militarily involved,   29
many academics considered the war so immoral that dispassionate analysis of the conflict became almost impossible. Only a handful of scholars actually went to Vietnam to do research there.

One of them was Samuel L. Popkin, now an associate professor of   30
political science at the University of California at San Diego. After he spent time in 1966 conducting interviews in Vietnamese villages, he was treated as a pariah when he returned to Harvard, where he was then an assistant professor.

His problem: He had returned from Vietnam with a complex view.   31
He did not approve of the way the Americans were fighting the war—"this crazy chasing around in the villages with our massive firepower looking for body counts"—but he did not find that the Communists were the popular good guys of American antiwar mythology.

Mr. Popkin's friends in Cambridge didn't want to hear about this. He 32
got back in his colleagues' good graces only after he was jailed in 1972 for
refusing to testify before a special grand jury set up by the White House
to find out who leaked the Pentagon Papers—the Pentagon's massive
top-secret study of American involvement in Indochina from World War
II to May 1968—to The New York Times.

Douglas Pike, who throughout the war years was the resident expert 33
in the United States Embassy in Saigon on the Vietnamese Communists,
remembers a similar encounter with academic close-mindedness when he
was on leave in Cambridge, Mass., in 1964 to write a book about the
Vietcong. He had been invited to take part in an antiwar teach-in and
found himself debating with a professor from the Harvard Dental School.
"The professor really didn't have his facts straight, so I asked him if he had
ever been to Vietnam," Mr. Pike recalls.

" 'No, that's not necessary,' the professor replied. 34

"So I said, 'I've never been to dental school, but suppose I give you 35
a root canal.'

" 'That's different,' he said. 36

"I replied, 'How at Harvard, of all places, can you say knowledge is 37
not important?' "

Mr. Pike has now retired from the Government and is the first direc- 38
tor of the Indochina studies program at the University of California at
Berkeley—an appointment that would have been unthinkable a decade
ago at a campus that was in the vanguard of the antiwar movement. Mr.
Pike has just completed a book on the North Vietnamese Army, which he
wrote after discovering to his amazement that there was no comparable
study. "We never even knew the names of North Vietnam's generals or
what their strategic thinking was," he says. "It shows how ignorant and
arrogant we were. We just assumed we would win." Mr. Pike's presence
at Berkeley, where he is setting up a two-million-page archive on Indochina, is testament to Vietnam's having quietly made the transition from
controversial public issue to history.

. . . .

Political Compromises

What went wrong on the American side? Today, the one common note 39
sounded by virtually all scholars is the need to start searching for the
answer with President Truman's decision in 1945 to reverse Washington's
earlier support for Ho Chi Minh. It was a choice made out of concern for
bolstering France in Europe against the looming Soviet menace.

"In class," says Robert A. Scalapino, director of the Institute of East 40
Asian Studies at the University of California at Berkeley, "I always stress
that the history of American involvement in Vietnam was a series of
decisions which cumulatively narrowed the choices for each succeeding
President. No President was able to begin afresh with Vietnam."

Professor Scalapino had a reputation as a conservative during the 41
war, but Professor George Kahin, who was an outspoken critic of the war,
and was until recently director of Cornell's Southeast Asia program, shares
his view. In a new study of American involvement in Vietnam from 1945
to 1967—which he says is based on trips to Vietnam in the 60's and
extensive original research in Government files—Professor Kahin claims
he will prove that Washington actually began giving secret military aid to
the French for Vietnam in the late 1940's.

"This aid was officially shown in the records as going to Europe, but 42
it was subverted to Vietnam by the French with U.S. understanding," says
Professor Kahin. Most history books date the origin of American involvement in Vietnam from a decision by President Truman's National Security
Council in 1950 to provide military aid for the French war in Indochina.

Another key turning point whose significance was not appreciated at 43
the time, historians now believe, was the 1963 coup against President
Diem. Because the Kennedy Administration sanctioned the coup, Washington became morally and politically responsible for all the regimes that
succeeded it, wrote Larry Berman in a new book, "Planning a Tragedy:
The Americanization of the War in Vietnam" (1982).

Mr. Berman, an associate professor of political science at the Univer- 44
sity of California at Davis, is one of several writers now offering a more
sympathetic portrait of Lyndon Johnson's role in the war. His book focuses
on the decision-making process that led up to President Johnson's announcement on July 28, 1965, that he was increasing the number of
American troops in Vietnam from 75,000 to 125,000, with additional
forces to be deployed as necessary. This move is generally regarded as the
critical decision that led to open-ended escalation.

Like a number of the new scholars, Mr. Berman was not trained in 45
Vietnamese studies but is a specialist on the American Presidency. His
book is based on recently declassified White House documents he found
while doing other research in the Johnson Library in Austin, Tex.

Nowhere in the documents was there evidence that President John- 46
son had a plan either for winning the war or for getting out. The reason
for the absence of any coherent strategic plan is that President Johnson
was trying to save his Great Society, not Vietnam. By an accident of
history, in July 1965 both Medicare and the Civil Rights Act of 1965 were
at crucial stages in Congressional committees; the Model Cities Act and
the Higher Education Act were soon to follow. Lyndon Johnson was
caught in a dilemma.

"He didn't want to do anything to jeopardize them," Mr. Berman 47
wrote. "He really wanted to be the next face on Mount Rushmore." But
the Communists were close to victory in Vietnam in early 1965, and
President Johnson could not leave himself open to a charge by conserva-
tives that he lost the war. On the other hand, if he took the steps the
Pentagon urged—mobilizing the Reserves, for instance—Congressional
liberals might have retaliated by withdrawing support for his Great Society programs.

"So Johnson chose a middle course, to fight the war at the lowest 48
possible cost, on the cheap," Mr. Berman went on. "And he lied about
what he was doing. He staged a debate to create a war climate, so that
when he announced the number of troops was only going up from 75,000
to 125,000, he looked like a moderate. But he knew there would be
300,000 troops in Vietnam in 1966."

"We get a tragic historical figure who had to choose between guns 49
and butter and couldn't," Mr. Berman continued. "In the end, he neither
settled the war nor got his Great Society, since as he fought in Vietnam,
it drained the money needed for his domestic programs."

Mr. Berman's thesis is similar to that in a book widely regarded by 50
scholars as a seminal study of America's role in Vietnam—"The Irony of
Vietnam: The System Worked" (1979), by Leslie H. Gelb, now a correspondent for The New York Times, and Richard K. Betts, a senior fellow
at the Brookings Institution. For this work, the authors drew heavily on
the Pentagon Papers, which provided critical new groundwork for analyzing Washington's decision-making process. Mr. Gelb himself was director
of the Pentagon Papers project within the Defense Department.

Mr. Gelb and Mr. Betts challenge the old liberal view put forward 51
in books, such as David Halberstam's best seller "The Best and the Brightest," that the United States stumbled into a quagmire in Vietnam through
hubris and miscalculation.

Instead, they argue, Washington's planning machinery worked well, 52
providing facts and options for the President. Rarely were the policymak-
ers deluded that the odds for success in Vietnam were high. The trouble
was that the Presidents, from Harry Truman to Richard Nixon, were afraid
both to risk losing Vietnam to the Communists and to accept the decisive
recommendations of their military advisers, which could lead to war with
China or a domestic backlash. So they chose the in-between option, doing
only what was necessary to stave off a Communist takeover at the time.
This prevented a Communist victory till 1975. But their policies of gradual
escalation played into the hands of the North Vietnamese, whose strategy
was to drag out the war and make it increasingly costly to the United
States.

In effect, the Presidents chose to "nibble the bullet rather than bite 53
it," Mr. Betts said at a conference on "The U.S. Experience in Vietnam"
held last month at the Woodrow Wilson International Center for Scholars
in Washington.

Another factor in Washington's decision making, scholars now say, 54
was that in the 1960's American political scientists were fascinated by
theories of how the United States could effectively fight limited wars, as
opposed to all-out conventional or nuclear war. Theorists explored the
question of how a nation could use force or the threat of force to compel
its adversary to back down. Implicit in their theories was the idea that it
was possible to signal your opponent by gradually increasing threats.

In another new study, "When Governments Collide: Coercion and 55
Diplomacy in the Vietnam Conflict, 1964–1968" (1980), Wallace J. Thies

has shown how President Johnson and his advisers believed they could "fine-tune" the bombing and their peace offers to "signal" Hanoi to abandon its support for the Vietcong. But President Johnson's program suffered from two serious flaws, argues Mr. Thies, a professor of political science at Berkeley.

First of all, in a bureaucracy as large as the American Government, 56 it proved impossible to "orchestrate" our bombing and diplomacy. For example, the selection and timing of bombing targets often depended on extraneous factors like the weather; coordination between the Air Force and diplomats was difficult. As a result, what Washington intended to be a show of firmness often appeared to Hanoi to be vacillation or weakness.

Second, Mr. Thies contends, Washington had little understanding of 57 politics in Hanoi and did not realize that the dominant group in the leadership, headed by Le Duan, the party First Secretary, had staked their careers on victory in the South after prolonged factional debate. By 1965, these men had already worked at infiltration and organizing the war in the South for many years. Like their American counterparts, they could not afford to be charged with losing South Vietnam.

Compared with the numerous new studies on the origins of Ameri- 58 can involvement in Vietnam, there has been little written on the war after 1966, and especially after the Tet offensive in 1968, largely because of the unavailability of materials. At the Johnson Library, relatively few documents have been declassified for the period after 1965, and given Federal budget cutbacks and the Reagan Administration's tightened procedures for declassification, library officials say further progress will be slow.

The situation is even worse for the Nixon years. There is no equiva- 59 lent of the Pentagon Papers for Mr. Nixon's Presidency and there is no Nixon Presidential library yet. So scholars are heavily dependent on the memoirs of Mr. Nixon and his Secretary of State Henry Kissinger.

One of the best accounts, however, has been pieced together by 60 George C. Herring, a professor of American history at the University of Kentucky and author of "America's Longest War: The United States and Vietnam, 1950–1975" (1979). Mr. Herring believes that President Nixon, like his predecessors, early on rejected calls for withdrawal—which he saw as dishonorable—and appealed for sharply increased escalation, feeling that he could solve a riddle that had baffled other Presidents.

Mr. Nixon's eventual strategy—Vietnamization—emerged on an im- 61 provised basis without a thorough policy review, Mr. Herring contends. In a paper written for the recent conference on Vietnam in Washington, Mr. Herring charged that during the first year of his Administration Mr. Nixon's policy may have been "a classic case of the President appeasing various bureaucratic constituencies by giving them a bit of what they wanted." The military got to bomb North Vietnam's sanctuaries in Cambodia; Secretary of Defense Melvin Laird got a speeded-up pull-out of American troops from Vietnam to appease American opinion (with Vietnamization, the war was turned over to the South Vietnamese Army—

ARVN—which was given new training and improved weapons) and the State Department got negotiations with Hanoi. But Mr. Herring concludes that President Nixon's plan did not provide either enough force to compel North Vietnam to negotiate or sufficient concessions to entice Hanoi to the table. Like the improvised strategies of the Johnson era, "it offered only extended stalemate."

That there could be a negotiated end to the fighting was, throughout 62 the war, one of the most consistent beliefs of both policy makers in Washington and their critics. But Allan E. Goodman, a professor at Georgetown University, believes this was naïve. In another of the new books, "The Lost Peace: America's Search for a Negotiated Settlement of the Vietnam War" (1978), he argues that "The real obstacle to a negotiated settlement was probably not Washington's diplomacy," but "as Hanoi maintained ever since its first direct conversation with Washington in 1962, the liberation of South Vietnam was an absolutely indispensable prerequisite" for a settlement.

In other words, North Vietnam was not prepared to compromise. 63 Hanoi was further encouraged when American spokesmen assured it that American bombing of North Vietnam was not intended to destroy the country. The North Vietnamese were aware that the longer the war went on the more painful it was for the United States. So Hanoi waited for Washington to make the concessions.

In the end, this was what happened. "Nearly every time Washington 64 made a negotiating offer to Hanoi, the U.S. terms softened," Mr. Goodman wrote, until finally, in the Paris talks in 1972, Mr. Kissinger agreed that the United States would withdraw from Vietnam without obtaining a comparable pledge from Hanoi.

Without access to more documents from the period, it is impossible 65 to judge if President Nixon and Mr. Kissinger believed the Paris accords gave South Vietnam a real chance to survive or whether they felt the agreement was merely a face-saving "decent interval" during which the United States could disentangle itself from Vietnam. Either way, America's exit from Vietnam proved as stumbling as its entry.

. . . .

The Lessons of Vietnam

Are there lessons Americans can learn from Vietnam? The question is 66 important, because it was one of the supposed lessons of World War II— not to appease aggression—that helped get the United States into Vietnam. There is little consensus, however, on what can be gleaned from Vietnam. James C. Thomson Jr., curator at the Nieman Foundation at Harvard, who was a member of President Johnson's National Security Council staff and who opposed American involvement in Vietnam, has proposed that the "central lesson" is that we should never again "take on the job of trying to defeat a nationalist anticolonial movement under indigenous Communist control in former French Indochina." This is, notes Mr. Thomson wryly, "a lesson of less than universal significance."

But Robert E. Osgood, a professor of American foreign policy at the 67 Johns Hopkins School of Advanced International Studies, believes Americans have learned the danger of intervening in a revolutionary war where the local government is weak. In such cases, the United States must commit so many troops to compensate for the regime's shortcomings that it ends up only undermining the government. El Salvador is an example, says Professor Osgood, who was one of the most important theorists on limited war in the 1960's.

"But this is not necessarily a lesson you can apply in every revolution- 68 ary war," he adds. In the Philippines after World War II, American aid provided a critical "missing component" that stopped a Communist insurgency. So to exclude American intervention in every contingency "is probably overdrawing the lesson," he says.

The problem, in Professor Osgood's view, is that there are many 69 variables for Washington to ponder: the strength of the local regime, the resolve of its adversary, the possibilities for getting out if American intervention proves unsuccessful.

The real issue is the magnitude of American interests and the threat 70 to them. "That was a mistake in Vietnam—our greatly inflated rhetoric about falling dominoes turned out to be wrong," Professor Osgood points out. But American foreign policy is still wedded to containment, and questions may arise again about combating a Communist-led revolution or takeover in the Middle East or Central America, he notes.

If that prospect arises, says Mr. Betts, we have not really learned 71 what to do except that the United States can fight only if the war is kept short. "We know more now," he believes, but we do not know how to avoid a disastrous war except at the possible price that Presidents Kennedy and Johnson foresaw—disastrous acceptance of defeat.

Another lesson is the need for better leadership, says Ernest R. May, 72 a professor of history at Harvard. At the Washington conference on Vietnam, he recalled that in 1948 George C. Marshall, then Secretary of State, opposed a military proposal to send 10,000 American advisers to aid the Chinese Nationalists because it involved a commitment of uncertain magnitude and indefinite duration. "What we did not have in 1965 was an individual of Marshall's stature and independent judgment," Mr. May said.

There are also lessons for small states that might look to the United 73 States for help. At the Washington meeting, Bui Diem, who served as South Vietnam's Ambassador to the United States, issued a warning. "My advice to small nations considering U.S. aid is that they should be wary of the United States," he said. "They should pay very close attention to the American domestic political system, because U.S. policies can change quickly. We small nations can end up losing higher stakes than the United

States itself because, for the American, you can turn the page and say, 'Well, it is an unhappy chapter for U.S. history.' But that is not the same now for the South Vietnamese."

And there are lessons for the military. The most important, Colonel 74 Summers believes, is that "we must relearn that public support is critical to American military strategy." To make his point, Colonel Summers quotes from General Weyand, the man who welcomed the P.O.W.'s to Saigon in 1973. "The American Army really is a people's army in the sense that it belongs to the American people," the general said. "When the American people lose their commitment, it is futile to try to keep the Army committed. In the final analysis, the American Army is not so much an arm of the executive branch as it is an arm of the American people."

Questions

Rereading and Independent Analysis

1. As a primary technique of development, this essay uses catalogs of a series of controversies among scholars and their interpretations of the war. Identify these controversies, classifying their areas of interest (for example, causes, results, class struggles, misinformation). Does Butterfield use all of these topics in each section? Why do you think he chose the method he did?

2. Make an outline of the sections of this essay in which you identify each part's subsections (introduction, development, conclusion) and locate its thesis statement. Then, based on your first general outline, indicate the progression of the content in these sections. What topics does Butterfield take up? How does he logically control their order?

3. If you are interested, look up the full version of this essay in the *New York Times Magazine,* Sunday, February 13, 1983. Read the whole essay to discover whether you think Butterfield's case is more persuasive when it is presented as a whole. What are your reasons?

Suggested Discussion and Group Activities

1. From the information you have about Butterfield, why do you think he took the time to write this essay? What are his purposes? What does the essay accomplish for you?

2. One way to understand Butterfield's purpose is to notice the difference between what he says people in the United States once believed and what they should conclude now on the basis of new evidence. As a class, or in groups, make a list of the changes in belief that Butterfield discusses. Then classify these changes: Do they concern facts, opinions, interpretations of motives, and other shifts from one perspective to another? What kind of evidence does Butterfield think is most important? Is his faith in "scholarship" too uncritical, or does he show that he has evaluated his sources?

3. This essay has an unstated but important subtopic—the ways that public opinion can be shaped and the influence public opinion has on the actions of the government. Do you agree with Butterfield's description of how public opinion is formed and how it changes? In your experience, does public opinion change suddenly? What causes it to change? Give examples.

Writing Suggestions

Response

Use what you have learned from Butterfield to comment on your own knowledge of the Vietnamese War, either as you learned it firsthand or as you have learned about it from movies, television, and other sources. Write a few paragraphs explaining how Butterfield's essay changed, or did not change, your mind about this conflict.

Analysis

In research writing, arguments are generally stated in the following way:

1. "Many people have thought . . ."
2. "But [however, despite, although] . . ."
3. "The [new] evidence shows . . ."
4. "So people should now believe [or consider, or remember] . . ."

Examine Butterfield's introduction and conclusion to see if they follow this pattern. Then choose other examples of research writing from this book (for instance, "Sebastian Cabot and the Northwest Passage" by David Roberts, or "Talking Like a Lady" by Robin Lakoff), or from your library, and examine the pattern of the arguments they present. As you read, make notes about the form of the essays you investigate—their persuasive organization, the context they establish for the cases they make, and their distinct points. Write a brief summary of the results of your investigation, explaining how this form is used to introduce new information and new perspectives into written "conversations" on a subject.

Finding a Purpose

Although you may have been too young to have any memories of the Vietnamese War, its impact on the United States was great enough to influence music, customs, and attitudes toward politics that are still held. Write an essay to a younger person in which you tell about the war from your own perspective, describing your first impressions when you were younger and your knowledge now, in a "personal history." What lessons have you learned from this war that you were not immediately involved in? What has it taught you about the impact of any war after it is over?

Daily Bread
Fernand Braudel

Translated by Sian Reynolds

Fernand Braudel (b. 1902), an eminent French historian, wrote his renowned *The Mediterranean and the Mediterranean World* (1949) during his five years as a prisoner of war in Germany. *The Structures of Everyday Life,* Vol. 1 (1981), from which this selection comes, was translated from the 1979 French text by Sian Reynolds. This internationally important work's subtitle, "The Limits of the Possible," reveals Braudel's position that specific social and economic contexts determine the ways historians can plausibly interpret the past. His book details sixteenth-to-eighteenth-century European measuring systems, agricultural production and trade, domestic customs, technological achievements, money systems, and urbanization. Braudel's preface identified his particular difficulty in writing this enormous project as having to move information from one context to another, a problem common to all writers who draw on research from many sources.

In a comment that applies to writing in any new field of study (for example, computer science, women's studies), Braudel points out a special "complication" that creates the refreshing perspective in this selection from his work, an account of earlier eating habits and some of their specific implications. It is "the painful uncovering of unusual themes which must all be incorporated into a coherent history, in short the difficult assembling of a number of *parahistoric* languages . . . which are usually kept separate . . . and which develop in the margin of traditional history." Other examples of these "uncovered" themes have been the role of women in the traditional versions of history that have usually excluded their contributions, and the tremendous influence that the invention of printing had on trade, exploration, and other activities that were transformed by the capacity to make multiple exact copies of maps and engravings. (See, for example, Gerda Lerner, *The Creation of Patriarchy* and Elizabeth Eisenstein, *The Printing Press as an Agent of Change.*) Traditional history, with its focus on great heroes and intellectual "movements," has made new work like Braudel's exciting, for it introduces readers to new conceptualizations of the past.

Grain and Calories

A man today requires 3500 to 4000 calories a day if he belongs to a rich 1 country and a privileged class. These levels were not unknown before the eighteenth century. But they were less frequently the norm than today. None the less as we need a reference point for our calculations we will use this figure of 3500 calories. Earl J. Hamilton in fact arrives at the same high level in his calculations of the nutritive value of the meals intended for the crews of the Spanish fleet in the Indies in about 1560.[112] This was certainly a record, that is if we are prepared to accept without hesitation (despite Courteline's warnings about listening to the bureaucracy) the official figures given by the Administration, in whose eyes the rations were always satisfactory.

We know of even higher levels at the tables of princes or privileged 2 classes (for example at Pavia at the Collegio Borromeo at the beginning of the seventeenth century); but such isolated cases should not deceive us. As soon as we begin to calculate the averages (for the great urban masses, for example) the level often falls to around 2000 calories. This was the case in Paris just before the Revolution. Of course the few figures we possess never hold the exact answer to the problems that concern us, especially as there is dispute over the reliability of calories as the test of a healthy diet (which demands a balance between carbohydrates, fats and protein). For example, should wine and alcohol be included in the calory intake? It has become established practice never to attribute more than 10% of the calory intake to drink. What is drunk over and above that percentage is not included in the calculations—which does not mean that the surplus did not count as far as the health and expenditure of the drinker were concerned.

None the less general rules do become apparent (Figure 12). For 3 example, the distribution of the various types of foodstuffs reveals the diversity or, much more often, the monotony of diet. Monotony is obvious whenever the share of carbohydrates (cereals in nearly every case) is *far* in excess of 60% of intake expressed in calories. The share of meat, fish and dairy products is then fairly limited and monotony sets in. Eating consists of a lifetime of consuming bread, more bread, and gruel.

On these criteria, it would appear that northern Europe was charac- 4 terized by a larger consumption of meat, and southern Europe by a larger share of carbohydrates, except obviously in the case of military convoys when meals were improved by barrels of salted meat and tunny fish.

Not surprisingly the tables of the rich were more varied than those 5 of the poor, the difference being marked by quality rather than quantity.[113] Cereals only represented 53% of calories on the Spinolas' luxurious table at Genoa around 1614–15. At the same date they formed 81% of the diet of the poor at the Hospital for Incurables (one kilogram of wheat is equivalent to 3000 calories and one kilogram of bread to 2500). If other dietary categories are compared, the Spinolas ate hardly any more meat and fish, but twice as much dairy produce and fats as the inmates of the hospital, and their much more varied diet included plenty of fruit, vegetables and sugar (3% of expenditure). Similarly we can be sure that if the boarders at the Collegio Borromeo (1609–18) were overfed (their almost incredibly large intake of food amounted to between 5500 and 7000 calories daily) they were not overfed in a particularly varied way. Cereals represented up to 73% of the total. Their food was not, could not be, particularly interesting.

Sooner or later a more varied diet became common in towns every- 6 where where assessment is possible, at the very least more varied than in the countryside. In Paris, where as we have seen, per capita consumption

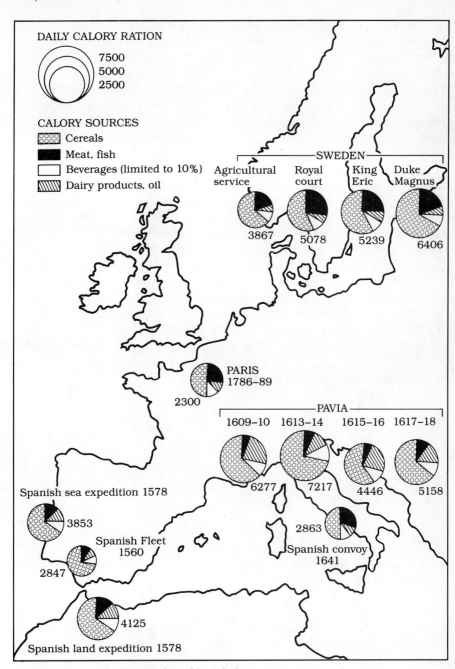

DAILY CALORY RATION

7500
5000
2500

CALORY SOURCES
Cereals
Meat, fish
Beverages (limited to 10%)
Dairy products, oil

— SWEDEN —

Agricultural service — 3867
Royal court — 5078
King Eric — 5239
Duke Magnus — 6406

PARIS 1786–89 — 2300

— PAVIA —

1609–10 — 6277
1613–14 — 7217
1615–16 — 4446
1617–18 — 5158

Spanish sea expedition 1578 — 3853

Spanish Fleet 1560 — 2847

Spanish convoy 1641 — 2863

Spanish land expedition 1578 — 4125

12 Some Diets of the Past, Reckoned in Calories
The map is based on a few relatively privileged menus. It would be necessary to find thousands
of examples, from different periods and every social level, to establish a valid map for Europe.
(From F. Spooner, *Régimes alimentaires d'autrefois.*)

in 1780 was about 2000 calories, only 58% of the total was accounted for
by cereals: about a pound of bread a day.[114] And this corresponds to figures
(both earlier and later) for average Parisian bread consumption: 540 grams
in 1637; 556 in 1728–30; 462 in 1770; 587 in 1788; 463 in 1810; 500 in
1820; and 493 in 1854.[115] We certainly cannot vouch for these quantities—
any more than we can vouch for the figure of 180 kilograms per person,
which *seems* (though the calculation is doubtful) to have been the annual
consumption in Venice at the beginning of the seventeenth century.[116]
However, other indications suggest that the Venetian working class was
both well paid and demanding, and that the better-off had the extravagant
habits of long-standing town-dwellers. [See figure 13.]

In general there is no doubt whatsoever that bread was consumed on
a substantial scale in the country, much more so than in the town, and
amongst the lowest levels of the working classes. According to Le Grand
d'Aussy in 1782, a working man or a peasant in France ate two or three
pounds of bread a day, 'but people who have anything else to eat do not
consume this quantity'. However, one can see construction workers in
southern Italy even today dining on enormous loaves accompanied, almost
as a flavouring, by a few tomatoes and onions significantly called the
companatico: something to go with the bread.

The triumph of bread arose of course because grain—and also alcohol

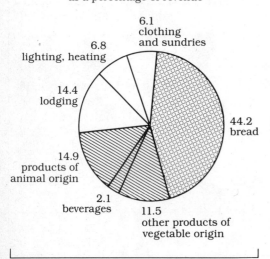

BUDGET OF A MASON'S FAMILY
(5 persons) in Berlin around 1800
as a percentage of revenue

6.1
clothing
and sundries

6.8
lighting, heating

14.4
lodging

44.2
bread

14.9
products of
animal origin

2.1
beverages

11.5
other products of
vegetable origin

food 72.7

13 Budget of a Mason's Family in Berlin about 1800
Compare it with the calculations of the *average* expenditure on food of the Parisian in 1788
and 1854. Bread here represents considerably more than half the family's food budget, an
enormous proportion in view of the relative price of cereals. So this is a precise example of
what a monotonous and difficult diet was like.

made from grain, as a Polish historian has pointed out[117] thus vindicating
the propensity of peasants in his country to drink and not only eat their
grain—was the least expensive foodstuff in relation to its calorific content.
In about 1780 it cost eleven times less than meat, sixty-five times less than
fresh sea fish, nine times less than fresh-water fish, six times less than eggs,
three times less than butter and oil. Grain, the primary source of energy,
came only third in expenditure, after meat and wine, in budgets calculated for the average Parisian in 1788 and 1854 (only 17% of total
expenditure in both cases).[118]

So grain is rehabilitated, after we have spoken so dismissively of it. 9
It was the manna of the poor, and 'its price was the most sensitive general
index of the food market'. 'This,' wrote Sébastien Mercier in 1770, 'is the
third consecutive winter when bread has been dear. During the past year,
half the peasants needed public charity and this winter will be the last
straw, because those who until now have lived by selling their effects now
have nothing left to sell.'[119] For the poor, if the cereal supply gave out,
everything gave out. We should not forget this dramatic aspect of the
problem: the slavery in which grain held producers, middlemen, tran-
sporters and consumers. There were constant mobilizations and alarms.
'The grain which feeds man has also been his executioner,' as Sébastien
Mercier said, or rather repeated.

The Price of Grain
and the Standard of Living

Mercier's remark is hardly an exaggeration. In Europe, grain represented 10
approximately half man's daily existence. Its price varied incessantly, at
the mercy of stocks, transport, bad weather preceding and therefore governing harvests, at the mercy of the harvests themselves, and finally according to the time of year. Our retrospective graphs of grain prices look
like the oscillations of a seismograph. The lives of the poor were all the
more affected by these variations, because they were rarely able to escape
seasonal increases in price by laying in large stocks at the right time. Can
we take the variations in grain prices as a sort of barometer of the standard
of living of the masses in the short and long term?

We have the choice of few, invariably imperfect, methods of working 11
this out. We can compare the price of grain with wages, but many wages
were paid in kind or partly in kind, partly in money. We can calculate
wages in terms of wheat or rye as Abel has, in the graph in Figure 14. We
can fix the average price of one typical 'shopping basket', as Phelps Brown
and Sheila Hopkins have.[120] Or we can adopt as our unit the hourly wage
of the most underprivileged workers, usually hodmen or plasterers' la-
bourers. This last method, employed by Jean Fourastié and his pupils,
notably René Grandamy, has its advantages. What do these 'real' prices
ultimately show? They certainly indicate that a quintal of grain (if we

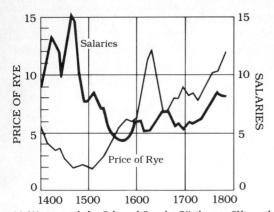

14 Wages and the Price of Rye in Göttingen, Fifteenth to Nineteenth Century
The price of rye is calculated in silver reichmarks, and wages (based on those of a woodcutter-joiner) are expressed in kilograms of rye. There is an obvious correlation between the rise in the price of rye and the drop in real wages, and vice versa. (After W. Abel.)

convert the old measures for this purpose) cost the equivalent of 100 hours' work until about 1543, then remained above that critical line until about 1883. This, in very general terms, is what French conditions (and conditions outside France, in the West, which were similar) suggest. A worker does approximately 3000 hours of work every year; his family (of four) consumes approximately twelve quintals a year. It is always serious when the 100-hours-for-one-quintal line is crossed; to cross the 200 is a danger signal; 300 is famine. In René Grandamy's opinion the 100 line was always crossed because of some sharp fluctuation, either by a rocketing rise, as in the middle of the sixteenth century, or by a sharp drop, as in 1883. Once the line was crossed in either direction the movement always proceeded rapidly. Thus for the centuries covered by this book, real prices moved in an unfavourable direction. The only favourable period seems to have followed the Black Death; this discovery makes it necessary to revise systematically all previous assumptions.

The conclusion therefore points to a low level of town wages, and to the poverty of the people in the country, where wages in kind fluctuated to almost the same rhythm. The rule for the poor was therefore fairly plain: they were obliged to fall back on secondary cereals, 'on less expensive products which still provided a sufficient number of calories, to abandon foods rich in protein in order to consume foodstuffs based on starch'. In Burgundy, on the eve of the French Revolution, 'the peasant, apart from the small farmer, eats little wheat. This luxury cereal is reserved for sale, for small children and for a few rare celebrations. It supplies the purse rather than the table ... Secondary cereals make up the main part of the peasant's food: *conceau* or maslin, rye in fairly rich homes, barley and oats in the poorest, maize in Bresse and in the Saône valley, rye and buckwheat in Morvan.'[121] Average consumption in Piedmont in about 1750 was as follows (in hectolitres): wheat 0.94; rye 0.91; other grains 0.41; chestnuts

0.45,[122] a total of 2.71 hectolitres a year. In this rather inadequate diet, wheat played only a modest part.

Bread of the Rich, Bread and Gruel of the Poor

There are different grades of bread just as there are various types of corn. [13] In Poitiers in December 1362, 'when the price of a *setier* of wheat reached twenty-four sous, there were four types of bread: *choyne* bread without salt, salted *choyne* bread, *safleur* bread and *reboulet* bread'. *Choyne* bread, with or without salt, was superior-quality white bread made from sifted flour. *Safleur* bread (the name is still used) contained the full flour, not subjected to sifting. *Reboulet* was probably made from 90% whole flour, and contained that fine bran 'which is still called *riboulet* in the Poitou dialect'. These four qualities corresponded to calm periods of moderate grain prices. Only three categories were authorized when prices were low, or rather reasonable, but seven widely different qualities could be manufactured when they rose; which meant in effect a whole range of inferior bread.[123] Nothing is more typical of the extent to which social inequality was the general rule (we have taken Poitiers from amongst thousands of other examples). Bread was sometimes bread in name alone. Often there was none at all.

Europe remained faithful to an old tradition and continued to feed [14] on coarse soups and gruels until the eighteenth century. These were older than Europe itself. The *puls* of the Etruscans and ancient Romans were basically millet. *Alica,* another gruel, had a starch or bread basis; there was also something known as Punic *alica,* a luxury dish containing cheese, honey and eggs.[124] Before it was made with maize, *polenta* was a gruel of barley grains, toasted and then ground and often mixed with millet. Oats were used in Artois in the fourteenth century (probably earlier and certainly later) 'to prepare a sort of porridge or gruel very common among the rural population'.[125] A gruel made of millet was current in Sologne, Champagne and Gascony in the fourteenth century and until the eighteenth. In Brittany there was also a thick gruel called *grou* made from buckwheat and water or milk.[126] Doctors in France at the beginning of the eighteenth century recommended gruel on condition that it was 'made with rich oats'.

These old practices have not entirely disappeared today. Scots and [15] English porridge is a gruel made from oats; *kasha* in Poland and Russia is made from ground and toasted rye, cooked like rice. A British grenadier in the Peninsula campaign in 1809 cooking a makeshift dinner was unwittingly linked to an old tradition: 'We prepared this wheat,' he tells, 'by boiling it like rice or, if it were more convenient, we crushed the grain between two flat stones and then boiled it so that we had a sort of thick dough.'[127] A young Turkish *sipahi,* Osman Aga, captured by the Germans at the time of the taking of Limova near Temesvar in 1688, was even more resourceful, much to his guards' surprise. The regular bread, the *kommis-sbrot,* being exhausted, the quartermaster distributed rations of flour to the soldiers (they had been without supplies for two days). Osman Aga was the only person who knew how to knead it with a little water and cook it under the hot ashes of the fire, having been, he said, in similar circumstances before.[128] It was almost like bread—or at any rate the unleavened bread, kneaded and cooked under ashes that is often eaten in Turkey and Persia.

White bread was therefore a rarity and a luxury. 'In all French, Spanish and English homes,' wrote Dupré de Saint-Maur, 'there are not more than two million men eating wheaten bread,'[129] If the statement is accurate it would mean that no more than 4% of the European population ate white bread. Even at the beginning of the eighteenth century, half the rural population fed on non-bread-making cereals and rye, and a lot of bran was left in the mixture of grains that went to make the bread for the poor. Wheaten bread and white bread, *choyne* bread (probably the bread eaten by canons, the word being a corruption of *chanoine*), remained a luxury for a long time. A French proverb says 'Don't eat the *choyne* bread first'.[130] It existed early on, but for the exclusive use of the rich. In 1581, young Venetians on the road to Compostela in Spain broke into an isolated house near the Duero to appease their hunger. There they found 'neither real bread, nor wine, nothing but five eggs and a large loaf made of rye and other mixtures which we could scarcely bear to look at, and of which some of us were able to eat one or two mouthfuls'.[131]

Of even higher quality than white bread, 'soft bread' became popular in Paris fairly early on. It was made from the finest flour, with the addition of brewer's yeast (in place of 'true' yeast). When milk was added to the mixture it became the 'Queen's bread' that Maria de Medici adored.[132] In 1668 the Faculty of Medicine vainly condemned the use of brewer's yeast but it continued to be used for 'rolls'. Women carried bushels full of them 'balanced on their heads in the manner of milkmaids' to the bakers' shops each morning. Soft bread of course remained a luxury. As a Parisian said (1788): 'with its firm golden crust it seems to rebuke the Limousin cob . . . it looks like a noble amongst rustics'.[133] These luxuries, however, were only available in times of abundance. In times of dearth, as in Paris in September 1740, two decrees of the Parlement promptly forbade 'the making of any types of bread except second quality'. Soft bread and rolls were prohibited; so was the use of powder with a flour base, widely used on wigs at that period.[134]

The real revolution in white bread only occurred between 1750 and 1850. At that period wheat took the place of other cereals (as in England) and bread was increasingly made from flours that had had most of the bran removed. At the same time the view gained ground that only bread, a fermented foodstuff, suited the health of the consumer. Diderot considered all gruel indigestible 'not having yet been fermented'.[135] In France, where the revolution in white bread began early, a National School of Bakery was founded in 1780.[136] Shortly afterwards Napoleon's soldiers introduced this 'previous commodity, white bread' all over Europe. None the less, taking the continent as a whole, the revolution was amazingly slow and not completed before 1850. But its influence on what kind of crops were grown was felt well before its final success, because of the traditional demand of the rich and the new demand of the poor. Wheat was predominant near Paris in the Multien and the Vexin, from the beginning of the seventeenth century, but not until the end of the century in the Valois, Brie and Beauvaisis. And western France remained loyal to rye.

The French led the way then, on the matter of white bread. Where is good bread eaten if not in Paris? asked Sébastien Mercier: 'I like good bread, I know it and I can tell it at a glance.'[137]

To Buy Bread, or Bake it at Home?

The price of bread did not vary; its weight did. Roughly speaking, variable weight was the general rule throughout the Western world. The average weight of bread sold in the bakers' shops in Saint Mark's Square or on the Rialto in Venice varied in an inverse ratio to the price of grain as Figure [15] demonstrates. Regulations published at Cracow in 1561, 1589 and 1592 indicate the same practices: unvarying prices and variable weights. They fixed what must have been the equivalents in bread, of variable quality and weight, of one *grosz* (a coin)—six pounds of rye bread or two pounds of wheaten bread in 1592.[138]

There were exceptions to this, including Paris. The regulation of July

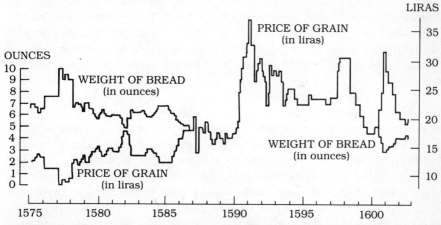

[15] Bread Weights and Grain Prices in Venice at the End of the Sixteenth Century
(From F. Braudel, 'La Vita economica di Venezia nel secolo XVI', in *La Civiltà veneziana del Rinascimento.*)

1371 distinguished three types of bread: *Chailli* bread, blistered or *bour-geois* bread and *brode* bread (a brown bread). Their respective weights for the same price were one, two and four *onces*. At this period, therefore, the usual system of constant prices and variable weights was in force. But after 1439[139] the respective weights of the three types of bread were fixed once and for all at half a pound, one pound and two pounds. 'After that, it was the price of bread that changed with a price of grain.' This was probably because of the authorization to sell 'cooked bread' by weight granted at a very early date to bakers working outside the capital—at Gonesse, Pontoise, Argenteuil, Charenton, Corbeil, etc. Bread in Paris, as in London, was bought at one of the ten to fifteen markets in the town much more than at bakers' shops.[140]

Bakers throughout Europe were then important people, more important even than the millers, because they bought grain direct and therefore played the part of merchants. But their production was intended only for a part of the consuming public. Domestic ovens, even in towns, must be taken into account in the production and public sale of household bread. In Cologne in the fifteenth century, in Castile in the sixteenth and even today, peasants from the neighbouring countryside arrived in the towns at daybreak to sell bread. In Venice it was the ambassadors' privilege to be supplied with country bread from the outskirts. It was reputed to be superior to the produce of the Venetian bakers. And numerous wealthy houses in Venice, Genoa and elsewhere had their own granaries and ovens. Even more modest householders often baked their own bread, judging by a painting of the town market in Augsburg in the sixteenth century: grain is being sold in small measures (which can indeed still be seen in the town museum).

In Venice in 1606, according to perfectly credible official calculations, bakers only handled 182,000 *stara* of the city's total grain consumption of 483,000. Markets accounted for another 109,500, and 'households which buy their own provisions'[141] for 144,000. The rest was used for the manufacture of biscuit for the fleet. So the bread sold by bakers amounted to only a little more than the total of bread baked at home—even in Venice.[142]

There was much commotion in Genoa in August 1673, when there was talk of forbidding domestic baking. 'The people are grumbling,' explained the French consul. 'It seems that [the nobles of the town] want to force everyone to buy bread at the markets and it is said that there are gentlemen [i.e. local businessmen] who offer one hundred and eighty thousand écus a year to have this privilege of making bread because . . . the custom is that everyone makes his own bread at home, and with this law passed no one will be able to do so, which will be a very great expense because bread is sold at the markets . . . at a price of forty lires a *mina* and is only worth about eighteen, besides which the aforesaid bread sold is good on the day it is made and is bitter and cannot be eaten on the next. This affair is causing a great stir and yesterday morning a notice was found stuck up on Saint-Sire Square where the ancient nobility assemblies, which spoke strongly against the government and threatened that its tyranny would be evaded.'[143]

According to Parmentier, it was only in the 1770s that the practice 26 of baking bread at home died out 'in most of the large towns in France'.[144] Jean Meyer notes that home-baking had entirely disappeared in Nantes by 1771, and puts it down to the adoption of white wheatmeal bread.[145]

We may wonder where the grain bought for family baking was 27 ground. In fact all towns had mills close at hand, for if grain kept fairly well (even so it was often stored on the ear and several threshings took place throughout the year) flour hardly kept any time. It had to be ground almost daily then, all through the year, in the mills which were then to be seen on the outskirts of every village and town, and sometimes even in the centre, wherever there was a stream. Any breakdown in the mills—such as happened in Paris, for instance, when the Seine froze or even flooded—brought immediate supply problems. So it is hardly surprising that windmills were built on the fortifications of Paris and that hand-powered mills still survived and had their advocates.

[These notes, numbered as they appear in this selection from a larger chapter, demonstrate the wide diversity of Braudel's methods and the extent of his scholarship.]

112. Earl J. HAMILTON, 'Wages and Subsistence on Spanish Treasure Ships, 1503–1660', in *Journal of Political Economy*, 1929.
113. All the following figures were calculated by F. C. SPOONER, 'Régimes alimentaires d'autrefois: proportions et calculs en calories', in *Annales E.S.C.*, 1961, pp. 568–74.
114. Robert PHILIPPE, 'Une opération pilote: L'étude du ravitaillement de Paris au temps de Lavoisier', in *Annales E.S.C.*, XVI, 1961, tables between pages 572 and 573. NB an error in the last table: read 58% for 50%.
115. Armand HUSSON, *Les Consommations de Paris*, 1856, pp. 79–106.
116. Calculations based on the documents in the Museo Corer, Donà delle Rose, 218, f°s 142 ff. From calculations made for the farming years 1603–4, 1604–5 and 1608–9, and allowing for records of the stocks of cereals, average consumption in Venice would have been about 450,000 stara. Since the city's population was 150,000, per capita consumption was 3 stara (at 60 kg to the stara = 180 kg). And these are in fact the figures arrived at by an official inquiry of 1760 (3 stara of wheat or 4.5 of maize). P. GEORGELIN, *op. cit.*, p. 209.
117. Witold KULA, '*Théorie économique du système féodal . . ., XVIe–XVIIIe s.*, 1970.
118. Robert PHILIPPE, 'Une opération pilote: l'étude du ravitaillement de Paris au temps de Lavoisier' in *Pour une histoire de l'alimentation*, ed. Jean-Jacques HEMARDINQUER, 1970, p. 65, table 5; A. HUSSON, *op. cit.*, p. 106.
119. Louis-Sébastien MERCIER, *Tableau de Paris*, 1782, IV, p. 132.
120. E. H. PHELPS BROWN and Sheila V. HOPKINS, 'Seven Centuries of Building Wages', in *Economica*, August 1955, pp. 195–206.
121. P. DE SAINT-JACOB, *op. cit.*, p. 539.
122. Giuseppe PRATO, *La Vita economica in Piemonte in mezzo a secolo XVIII*, 1908.
123. Paul RAVEAU, *Essai sur la situation économique et l'état social en Poitou au XVIe siècle*, 1931, pp. 63–5.
124. Jacques ANDRÉ, *Alimentation et cuisine à Rome*, 1961, pp. 62–3.
125. J.-M. RICHARD, *art. cit.*, p. 21.
126. Jean MEYER, *La Noblesse bretonne au XVIIIe siècle*, 1966, p. 449, note 3.
127. Reference mislaid.

128. O. AGA, *op. cit.*, pp. 64–5.

129. N.F. DUPRÉ DE SAINT-MAUR, *op. cit.*, p. 23.

130. Alfred FRANKLIN, *La Vie privée d'autrefois*, vol. III. *La cuisine*, 1888, p. 91.

131. London, P.R.O., 30, 25, 157, Giornale autografo di Francesco Contarini da Venezia a Madrid.

132. J. SAVARY, *Dictionnaire . . ., op. cit.*, IV, col. 10.

133. L.-S. MERCIER, *op. cit.*, XII, p. 242.

134. A.N., AD XI, 38, 225.

135. Denis DIDEROT, article 'bouillie', *Supplément à l'Encyclopédie*, II, 1776, p. 34.

136. L.-S. MERCIER, *op. cit.*, VIII, p. 154.

137. L.-S. MERCIER, *ibid.*, XII, p. 240.

138. According to documents I have consulted in the Cracow archives.

139. N. DELAMARE, *Traité de police*, II, 1710, p. 895.

140. *Ibid.*, 1772 edn., II, pp. 246–7; A. HUSSON, *op. cit.*, pp. 80–1.

141. A.d.S. Venice, Papadopoli, 12, f° 19 v°.

142. Museo Correr, Donà delle Rose, 218, f° 140 v°.

143. Correspondence of M. de Compans, French Consul in Genoa, A.N., A.E., B¹, 511.

144. Antoine PARMENTIER, *Le Parfait Boulanger*, 1778, pp. 591–2.

145. Jean MEYER, *La Noblesse bretonne au XVIIIe siècle, op. cit.*, p. 447 and note.

Questions

Rereading and Independent Analysis

1. Historians gather and organize information to demonstrate a "hypothesis," their position about the meaning of past facts. Reread the first paragraph of this chapter, "Daily Bread," to identify the hypothesis that Braudel supports. Write your understanding of his point in a sentence or two.

2. Reread the selection to identify the periods of time Braudel treats as major points of division in his treatment of eating habits. Then write brief notes to characterize the information about each of these major sections. Notice how he handles both divisions of time and continuity within them—for example, "As the centuries passed, . . ." Mark similar references to change.

3. The second section of this selection supplies details about commercial and domestic baking that specify implications of Braudel's title, "Daily Bread." How is this treatment of baking related to Braudel's links between economic class and food choices in the first section?

Suggested Discussion and Group Activities

1. In groups, make a list of the kinds of evidence Braudel uses to support his generalizations. Where does he find support for his points? How does he make his sources appear to be trustworthy? Why do you find them convincing? Notice the use of charts and diagrams as evidence.

2. Drawing on your knowledge of American history and geography, review what you know about population density in the United States. Try brainstorming as a group to write down everything you know collectively

about patterns of development and important changes in population grouping. Then make a list of causes you can identify. How do domestic needs and desires—food, clothing, comfort, social life—contribute to these patterns?

3. Choose a personal habit or a commodity you use every day—for example, daily bathing, soft drinks, or music. How does obtaining this feature of your life affect your general patterns of social interaction, learning and spending, and daily movements? As a class, think of ways that some of the habits you take for granted influence larger social patterns in your community.

Writing Suggestions

Response

In your journal, keep track of the ordinary commodities—such as food, soap, paper—that you use in a day. Then write a few paragraphs about how an accurate history of our time would have to include some important details (for instance, McDonald's hamburgers) that traditional histories omit.

Analysis: Personal and Group Research

1. In small groups, gather information for a report to the class on the eating habits of your group and the reasons for their choices. Keep logs of everything you eat and drink for a few days and classify these choices according to categories like time available, expense, family tradition, weight control, or any others that determine your group's patterns of eating. Organize your report and assign parts of it to individuals for writing and editing.

2. Choose an aspect of everyday life that interests you and a specific location and time period in which you want to explore it. Then gather information from sources like Braudel's—collections of letters, pictures, literature, biography, or other historical accounts—and write an essay in which you explain the significance of your chosen topic to major events and patterns of change in the context you are investigating. You might, for instance, look into the effects of public transportation on your city. Write an essay explaining your findings, using Braudel's work as a model for presenting your analysis of causes and effects.

Finding a Purpose

Braudel quotes elsewhere a typical prejudice about food: "Vigour and Fortitude of Heart are much more generally found in Persons that live on Flesh, than in such as live on lighter Meat." Make a list of similar current attitudes about the relation between food and the "kind" of person who eats it. Then write an essay in which you explain these attitudes, classifying groups according to the ways they associate choices of food and drink with personality and actions. Define a specific readership for your essay and make it clear from your presentation who those readers are.

Crisis and the Emergence of Scientific Theories
Thomas Kuhn

Thomas Kuhn (b. 1922) began his career as a physicist and became a historian of science at Princeton University. His book *The Structure of Scientific Revolutions* (1962) explained what appear to be sudden changes in the ways scientists think. But on publication it was taken to be a "revolution" itself, offering a startling new view of science. Kuhn claimed that "science" is *not* an objective and progressive development of truth but the work of groups of people, "scientific communities," who are trying to solve consciously chosen problems by testing hypotheses that they favor at any given time.

Kuhn used the term "paradigm" to explain the structures of belief with which scientific communities work. He showed that "paradigm shifts" have occurred when old beliefs no longer explain scientists' observations or solve their chosen problems. For instance, astronomy changed radically when telescopes became available to permit better observations. And microscopes were necessary before bacteria and viruses became interesting problems for medicine. Before each of these inventions, observers and doctors used explanations that they no longer consider applicable, worked with hypotheses that appear irrelevant to us now, and looked into entirely different kinds of problems. Consequently, Kuhn made it necessary to think of "truth" and "importance" as depending on a complex social context, which innovation may suddenly change.

In Kuhn's argument, science is comprised of available tools, specific interested people, and the possibility of convincing others that established beliefs are not adequate. Kuhn defined science as *persuasion* and said that persuasiveness in science depends on communities who share, and reform, the same general strategies of problem solving. He showed that "truth" is defined according to a specific community's accepted laws and rules.

Kuhn's book was widely influential—and widely criticized. His critics have complained especially that he reduced science to an intuitive, personal activity and did not see it as a rule-governed set of procedures, protected from individual agendas. In a new postscript to the book in 1969, Kuhn answered both critics and supporters who misinterpreted him. He said that if he could start writing the book again, seven years later, he would have begun with a more precise definition of scientific communities as *users of a shared language who are persuaded to the same point of view*. Thus the postscript demonstrates what Kuhn meant from the start: "knowledge" depends on shared definitions and direction in a community of people interested in the same problems.

This selection from Kuhn's book tells what he meant by "crisis" before a paradigm shift. Kuhn uses examples from astronomy, the study of gases, and Newtonian physics. You may not be specifically interested in "science," but most subjects you study have been changed in the last few decades by the ideas Kuhn stated. There is a new "paradigm," or structure of belief, about what knowledge is and how we organize it for study. As you read, keep firmly in mind that Kuhn thinks of his examples as *ways of thinking about a subject,* not as "absolute truths." (For instance, Einstein's theory of relativity [below] gave us "another way of thinking" about the problems Newton tried to solve.) Do you accept the views in any course as a "way of thinking" or as simple information? Refer to the advice in "To the Student" for help if you need it.

All the discoveries considered in Section VI were causes of or contributors 1 to paradigm change. Furthermore, the changes in which these discoveries were implicated were all destructive as well as constructive. After the discovery had been assimilated, scientists were able to account for a wider range of natural phenomena or to account with greater precision for some of those previously known. But that gain was achieved only by discarding some previously standard beliefs or procedures and, simultaneously, by replacing those components of the previous paradigm with others. Shifts of this sort are, I have argued, associated with all discoveries achieved through normal science, excepting only the unsurprising ones that had been anticipated in all but their details. Discoveries are not, however, the only sources of these destructive-constructive paradigm changes. In this section we shall begin to consider the similar, but usually far larger, shifts that result from the invention of new theories.

Having argued already that in the sciences fact and theory, discovery 2 and invention, are not categorically and permanently distinct, we can anticipate overlap between this section and the last. (The impossible suggestion that Priestley first discovered oxygen and Lavoisier then invented it has its attractions. Oxygen has already been encountered as discovery; we shall shortly meet it again as invention.) In taking up the emergence of new theories we shall inevitably extend our understanding of discovery as well. Still, overlap is not identity. The sorts of discoveries considered in the last section were not, at least singly, responsible for such paradigm shifts as the Copernican, Newtonian, chemical, and Einsteinian revolutions. Nor were they responsible for the somewhat smaller, because more exclusively professional, changes in paradigm produced by the wave theory of light, the dynamical theory of heat, or Maxwell's electromagnetic theory. How can theories like these arise from normal science, an activity even less directed to their pursuit than to that of discoveries?

If awareness of anomaly plays a role in the emergence of new sorts 3 of phenomena, it should surprise no one that a similar but more profound awareness is prerequisite to all acceptable changes of theory. On this point historical evidence is, I think, entirely unequivocal. The state of Ptolemaic astronomy was a scandal before Copernicus' announcement.[1] Galileo's

---

[1] A. R. Hall, *The Scientific Revolution, 1500–1800* (London, 1954), p. 16.

contributions to the study of motion depended closely upon difficulties discovered in Aristotle's theory by scholastic critics.[2] Newton's new theory of light and color originated in the discovery that none of the existing pre-paradigm theories would account for the length of the spectrum, and the wave theory that replaced Newton's was announced in the midst of growing concern about anomalies in the relation of diffraction and polarization effects to Newton's theory.[3] Thermodynamics was born from the collision of two existing nineteenth-century physical theories, and quantum mechanics from a variety of difficulties surrounding black-body radiation, specific heats, and the photoelectric effect.[4] Furthermore, in all these cases except that of Newton the awareness of anomaly had lasted so long and penetrated so deep that one can appropriately describe the fields affected by it as in a state of growing crisis. Because it demands large-scale paradigm destruction and major shifts in the problems and techniques of normal science, the emergence of new theories is generally preceded by a period of pronounced professional insecurity. As one might expect, that insecurity is generated by the persistent failure of the puzzles of normal science to come out as they should. Failure of existing rules is the prelude to a search for new ones.

Look first at a particularly famous case of paradigm change, the emergence of Copernican astronomy. When its predecessor, the Ptolemaic system, was first developed during the last two centuries before Christ and the first two after, it was admirably successful in predicting the changing positions of both stars and planets. No other ancient system had performed so well; for the stars, Ptolemaic astronomy is still widely used today as an engineering approximation; for the planets, Ptolemy's predictions were as good as Copernicus'. But to be admirably successful is never, for a scientific theory, to be completely successful. With respect both to planetary position and to precession of the equinoxes, predictions made with Ptolemy's system never quite conformed with the best available observations. Further reduction of those minor discrepancies constituted many of the principal problems of normal astronomical research for many of Ptolemy's successors, just as a similar attempt to bring celestial observation and Newtonian theory together provided normal research problems for Newton's eighteenth-century successors. For some time astronomers had every reason to suppose that these attempts would be as successful as

[2] Marshall Clagett, *The Science of Mechanics in the Middle Ages* (Madison, Wis., 1959), Parts II–III. A. Koyré displays a number of medieval elements in Galileo's thought in his *Etudes Galiléennes* (Paris, 1939), particularly Vol. I.

[3] For Newton, see T. S. Kuhn, "Newton's Optical Papers," in *Isaac Newton's Papers and Letters in Natural Philosophy,* ed. I. B. Cohen (Cambridge, Mass., 1958), pp. 27–45. For the prelude to the wave theory, see E. T. Whittaker, *A History of the Theories of Aether and Electricity,* I (2d ed.; London, 1951), 94–109; and W. Whewell, *History of the Inductive Sciences* (rev. ed.; London, 1847), II, 396–466.

[4] For thermodynamics, see Silvanus P. Thompson, *Life of William Thomson Baron Kelvin of Largs* (London, 1910), I, 266–81. For the quantum theory, see Fritz Reiche, *The Quantum Theory,* trans. II. S. Hatfield and H. L. Brose (London, 1922), chaps. i–ii.

those that had led to Ptolemy's system. Given a particular discrepancy, astronomers were invariably able to eliminate it by making some particular adjustment in Ptolemy's system of compounded circles. But as time went on, a man looking at the net result of the normal research effort of many astronomers could observe that astronomy's complexity was increasing far more rapidly than its accuracy and that a discrepancy corrected in one place was likely to show up in another.[5]

Because the astronomical tradition was repeatedly interrupted from outside and because, in the absence of printing, communication between astronomers was restricted, these difficulties were only slowly recognized. But awareness did come. By the thirteenth century Alfonso X could proclaim that if God had consulted him when creating the universe, he would have received good advice. In the sixteenth century, Copernicus' coworker, Domenico da Novara, held that no system so cumbersome and inaccurate as the Ptolemaic had become could possibly be true of nature. And Copernicus himself wrote in the Preface to the *De Revolutionibus* that the astronomical tradition he inherited had finally created only a monster. By the early sixteenth century an increasing number of Europe's best astronomers were recognizing that the astronomical paradigm was failing in application to its own traditional problems. That recognition was prerequisite to Copernicus' rejection of the Ptolemaic paradigm and his search for a new one. His famous preface still provides one of the classic descriptions of a crisis state.[6]

Breakdown of the normal technical puzzle-solving activity is not, of course, the only ingredient of the astronomical crisis that faced Copernicus. An extended treatment would also discuss the social pressure for calendar reform, a pressure that made the puzzle of precession particularly urgent. In addition, a fuller account would consider medieval criticism of Aristotle, the rise of Renaissance Neoplatonism, and other significant historical elements besides. But technical breakdown would still remain the core of the crisis. In a mature science—and astronomy had become that in antiquity—external factors like those cited above are principally significant in determining the timing of breakdown, the ease with which it can be recognized, and the area in which, because it is given particular attention, the breakdown first occurs. Though immensely important, issues of that sort are out of bounds for this essay.

If that much is clear in the case of the Copernican revolution, let us turn from it to a second and rather different example, the crisis that preceded the emergence of Lavoisier's oxygen theory of combustion. In the 1770's many factors combined to generate a crisis in chemistry, and historians are not altogether agreed about either their nature or their relative importance. But two of them are generally accepted as of first-rate

[5] J. L. E. Dreyer, *A History of Astronomy from Thales to Kepler* (2d ed.; New York, 1953), chaps. xi–xii.

[6] T. S. Kuhn, *The Copernican Revolution* (Cambridge, Mass., 1957), pp. 135–43.

significance: the rise of pneumatic chemistry and the question of weight relations. The history of the first begins in the seventeenth century with development of the air pump and its deployment in chemical experimentation. During the following century, using that pump and a number of other pneumatic devices, chemists came increasingly to realize that air must be an active ingredient in chemical reactions. But with a few exceptions—so equivocal that they may not be exceptions at all—chemists continued to believe that air was the only sort of gas. Until 1756, when Joseph Black showed that fixed air (CO_2) was consistently distinguishable from normal air, two samples of gas were thought to be distinct only in their impurities.[7]

After Black's work the investigation of gases proceeded rapidly, most 8 notably in the hands of Cavendish, Priestley, and Scheele, who together developed a number of new techniques capable of distinguishing one sample of gas from another. All these men, from Black through Scheele, believed in the phlogiston theory and often employed it in their design and interpretation of experiments. Scheele actually first produced oxygen by an elaborate chain of experiments designed to dephlogisticate heat. Yet the net result of their experiments was a variety of gas samples and gas properties so elaborate that the phlogiston theory proved increasingly little able to cope with laboratory experience. Though none of these chemists suggested that the theory should be replaced, they were unable to apply it consistently. By the time Lavoisier began his experiments on airs in the early 1770's, there were almost as many versions of the phlogiston theory as there were pneumatic chemists.[8] That proliferation of versions of a theory is a very usual symptom of crisis. In his preface, Copernicus complained of it as well.

The increasing vagueness and decreasing utility of the phlogiston 9 theory for pneumatic chemistry were not, however, the only source of the crisis that confronted Lavoisier. He was also much concerned to explain the gain in weight that most bodies experience when burned or roasted, and that again is a problem with a long prehistory. At least a few Islamic chemists had known that some metals gain weight when roasted. In the seventeenth century several investigators had concluded from this same fact that a roasted metal takes up some ingredient from the atmosphere. But in the seventeenth century that conclusion seemed unnecessary to most chemists. If chemical reactions could alter the volume, color, and texture of the ingredients, why should they not alter weight as well? Weight was not always taken to be the measure of quantity of matter. Besides, weight-gain on roasting remained an isolated phenomenon. Most

[7] J. R. Partington, *A Short History of Chemistry* (2d ed.; London, 1951), pp 48–51, 73–85, 90–120.

[8] Though their main concern is with a slightly later period, much relevant material is scattered throughout J. R. Partington and Douglas McKie's "Historical Studies on the Phlogiston Theory," *Annals of Science,* II (1937), 361–404; III (1938), 1–58, 337–71; and IV (1939), 337–71.

natural bodies (e.g., wood) lose weight on roasting as the phlogiston theory was later to say they should.

During the eighteenth century, however, these initially adequate responses to the problem of weight-gain became increasingly difficult to maintain. Partly because the balance was increasingly used as a standard chemical tool and partly because the development of pneumatic chemistry made it possible and desirable to retain the gaseous products of reactions, chemists discovered more and more cases in which weight-gain accompanied roasting. Simultaneously, the gradual assimilation of Newton's gravitational theory led chemists to insist that gain in weight must mean gain in quantity of matter. Those conclusions did not result in rejection of the phlogiston theory, for that theory could be adjusted in many ways. Perhaps phlogiston had negative weight, or perhaps fire particles or something else entered the roasted body as phlogiston left it. There were other explanations besides. But if the problem of weight-gain did not lead to rejection, it did lead to an increasing number of special studies in which this problem bulked large. One of them, "On phlogiston considered as a substance with weight and [analyzed] in terms of the weight changes it produces in bodies with which it unites," was read to the French Academy early in 1772, the year which closed with Lavoisier's delivery of his famous sealed note to the Academy's Secretary. Before that note was written a problem that had been at the edge of the chemist's consciousness for many years had become an outstanding unsolved puzzle.[9] Many different versions of the phlogiston theory were being elaborated to meet it. Like the problems of pneumatic chemistry, those of weight-gain were making it harder and harder to know what the phlogiston theory was. Though still believed and trusted as a working tool, a paradigm of eighteenth-century chemistry was gradually losing its unique status. Increasingly, the research it guided resembled that conducted under the competing schools of the pre-paradigm period, another typical effect of crisis.

Consider now, as a third and final example, the late nineteenth century crisis in physics that prepared the way for the emergence of relativity theory. One root of that crisis can be traced to the late seventeenth century when a number of natural philosophers, most notably Leibniz, criticized Newton's retention of an updated version of the classic conception of absolute space.[10] They were very nearly, though never quite, able to show that absolute positions and absolute motions were without any function at all in Newton's system; and they did succeed in hinting at the considerable aesthetic appeal a fully relativistic conception of space and motion would later come to display. But their critique was purely logical. Like the early Copernicans who criticized Aristotle's proofs of the earth's

[9] H. Guerlac, *Lavoisier—the Crucial Year* (Ithaca, N.Y., 1961). The entire book documents the evolution and first recognition of a crisis. For a clear statement of the situation with respect to Lavoisier, see p. 35.

[10] Max Jammer, *Concepts of Space: The History of Theories of Space in Physics* (Cambridge, Mass., 1954), pp. 114–24.

stability, they did not dream that transition to a relativistic system could have observational consequences. At no point did they relate their views to any problems that arose when applying Newtonian theory to nature. As a result, their views died with them during the early decades of the eighteenth century to be resurrected only in the last decades of the nineteenth when they had a very different relation to the practice of physics.

The technical problems to which a relativistic philosophy of space   12 was ultimately to be related began to enter normal science with the acceptance of the wave theory of light after about 1815, though they evoked no crisis until the 1890's. If light is wave motion propagated in a mechanical ether governed by Newton's Laws, then both celestial observation and terrestrial experiment become potentially capable of detecting drift through the ether. Of the celestial observations, only those of aberration promised sufficient accuracy to provide relevant information, and the detection of ether-drift by aberration measurements therefore became a recognized problem for normal research. Much special equipment was built to resolve it. That equipment, however, detected no observable drift, and the problem was therefore transferred from the experimentalists and observers to the theoreticians. During the central decades of the century Fresnel, Stokes, and others devised numerous articulations of the ether theory designed to explain the failure to observe drift. Each of these articulations assumed that a moving body drags some fraction of the ether with it. And each was sufficiently successful to explain the negative results not only of celestial observation but also of terrestrial experimentation, including the famous experiment of Michelson and Morley.[11] There was still no conflict excepting that between the various articulations. In the absence of relevant experimental techniques, that conflict never became acute.

The situation changed again only with the gradual acceptance of   13 Maxwell's electromagnetic theory in the last two decades of the nineteenth century. Maxwell himself was a Newtonian who believed that light and electromagnetism in general were due to variable displacements of the particles of a mechanical ether. His earliest versions of a theory for electricity and magnetism made direct use of hypothetical properties with which he endowed this medium. These were dropped from his final version, but he still believed his electromagnetic theory compatible with some articulation of the Newtonian mechanical view.[12] Developing a suitable articulation was a challenge for him and his successors. In practice, however, as has happened again and again in scientific development, the required articulation proved immensely difficult to produce. Just as Copernicus' astronomical proposal, despite the optimism of its author, created an increasing crisis for existing theories of motion, so Maxwell's

[11] Joseph Larmor, *Aether and Matter . . . Including a Discussion of the Influence of the Earth's Motion on Optical Phenomena* (Cambridge, 1900), pp. 6–20, 320–22.
[12] R. T. Glazebrook, *James Clerk Maxwell and Modern Physics* (London, 1896), chap. ix. For Maxwell's final attitude, see his own book, *A Treatise on Electricity and Magnetism* (3d ed.; Oxford, 1892), p. 470.

theory, despite its Newtonian origin, ultimately produced a crisis for the paradigm from which it had sprung.[13] Furthermore, the locus at which that crisis became most acute was provided by the problems we have just been considering, those of motion with respect to the ether.

Maxwell's discussion of the electromagnetic behavior of bodies in [14] motion had made no reference to ether drag, and it proved very difficult to introduce such drag into his theory. As a result, a whole series of earlier observations designed to detect drift through the ether became anomalous. The years after 1890 therefore witnessed a long series of attempts, both experimental and theoretical, to detect motion with respect to the ether and to work ether drag into Maxwell's theory. The former were uniformly unsuccessful, though some analysts thought their results equivocal. The latter produced a number of promising starts, particularly those of Lorentz and Fitzgerald, but they also disclosed still other puzzles and finally resulted in just that proliferation of competing theories that we have previously found to be the concomitant of crisis.[14] It is against that historical setting that Einstein's special theory of relativity emerged in 1905.

These three examples are almost entirely typical. In each case a [15] novel theory emerged only after a pronounced failure in the normal problem-solving activity. Furthermore, except for the case of Copernicus in which factors external to science played a particularly large role, that breakdown and the proliferation of theories that is its sign occurred no more than a decade or two before the new theory's enunciation. The novel theory seems a direct response to crisis. Note also, though this may not be quite so typical, that the problems with respect to which breakdown occurred were all of a type that had long been recognized. Previous practice of normal science had given every reason to consider them solved or all but solved, which helps to explain why the sense of failure, when it came, could be so acute. Failure with a new sort of problem is often disappointing but never surprising. Neither problems nor puzzles yield often to the first attack. Finally, these examples share another characteristic that may help to make the case for the role of crisis impressive: the solution to each of them had been at least partially anticipated during a period when there was no crisis in the corresponding science; and in the absence of crisis those anticipations had been ignored.

The only complete anticipation is also the most famous, that of [16] Copernicus by Aristarchus in the third century B.C. It is often said that if Greek science had been less deductive and less ridden by dogma, heliocentric astronomy might have begun its development eighteen centuries earlier than it did.[15] But that is to ignore all historical context. When

---

[13] For astronomy's role in the development of mechanics, see Kuhn, *op. cit.*, chap. vii.

[14] Whittaker, *op. cit.*, I, 386–410; and II (London, 1953), 27–40.

[15] For Aristarchus' work, see T. L. Heath, *Aristarchus of Samos: The Ancient Copernicus* (Oxford, 1913), Part II. For an extreme statement of the traditional position about the neglect of Aristarchus' achievement, see Arthur Koestler, *The Sleepwalkers: A History of Man's Changing Vision of the Universe* (London, 1959), p. 50.

Aristarchus' suggestion was made, the vastly more reasonable geocentric system had no needs that a heliocentric system might even conceivably have fulfilled. The whole development of Ptolemaic astronomy, both its triumphs and its breakdown, falls in the centuries after Aristarchus' proposal. Besides, there were no obvious reasons for taking Aristarchus seriously. Even Copernicus' more elaborate proposal was neither simpler nor more accurate than Ptolemy's system. Available observational tests, as we shall see more clearly below, provided no basis for a choice between them. Under those circumstances, one of the factors that led astronomers to Copernicus (and one that could not have led them to Aristarchus) was the recognized crisis that had been responsible for innovation in the first place. Ptolemaic astronomy had failed to solve its problems; the time had come to give a competitor a chance. Our other two examples provide no similarly full anticipations. But surely one reason why the theories of combustion by absorption from the atmosphere—theories developed in the seventeenth century by Rey, Hooke, and Mayow—failed to get a sufficient hearing was that they made no contact with a recognized trouble spot in normal scientific practice.[16] And the long neglect by eighteenth- and nineteenth-century scientists of Newton's relativistic critics must largely have been due to a similar failure in confrontation.

Philosophers of science have repeatedly demonstrated that more than one theoretical construction can always be placed upon a given collection of data. History of science indicates that, particularly in the early developmental stages of a new paradigm, it is not even very difficult to invent such alternates. But that invention of alternates is just what scientists seldom undertake except during the pre-paradigm stage of their science's development and at very special occasions during its subsequent evolution. So long as the tools a paradigm supplies continue to prove capable of solving the problems it defines, science moves fastest and penetrates most deeply through confident employment of those tools. The reason is clear. As in manufacture so in science—retooling is an extravagance to be reserved for the occasion that demands it. The significance of crises is the indication they provide that an occasion for retooling has arrived.

Questions

Rereading and Independent Analysis

1. Kuhn's argument is carefully controlled by frequent references to what he has already said and where he is going next. To follow what he says, underline these references to show how they control the logical progression of his points for his readers. How do these underlined passages create an outline of the selection? What do they tell you about the readers Kuhn had in mind and the thesis he wanted them to accept?

2. Make a list of the words Kuhn uses that you do not immediately

---

[16] Partington, *op. cit.*, pp. 78–85.

understand. Look them up in a good dictionary and reread the sentences in which you found them, reflecting on your new understanding. Rewrite any of the sentences you still find difficult in your own words to make their meaning clearer.

Suggested Discussion and Group Activities

1. As a class, work as observers with the examples Kuhn uses to develop his thesis. Find the elements of "insecurity" in his examples. How can you connect these methodological, procedural, or factual problems to other instances in your experience where new facts did not fit old beliefs and hypotheses? In your experience, how do people react when they cannot fit a familiar answer, method, or process to a new problem? Cite some examples.

2. In groups, explain why you think Kuhn's book drew criticism. What sort of "paradigm," or structure of belief, was his thesis requiring scientists to give up? Why would his argument create insecurity among scientists and historians of science? How is this chapter itself an example of persuasion? That is, how does he establish credibility, make a case based on evidence, and suggest alternatives? Did he foresee possible opposition to his case? Find specific instances in the text.

Writing Suggestions

Response

Remember a time when new information or new methods required you to change your perspective, beliefs, or ways of acting in a particular social or private activity. For instance, how did learning to drive change your life? Learning to use a computer? Write a narration describing this change. Then go on to draw some general conclusions about how easy or difficult it is for us to change our ways of acting and thinking.

Analysis

Using this selection or another one you choose as your example, write an essay in which you show someone else how to read new, unfamiliar material clearly and with understanding. Adapt the advice in the introduction to this book ("To the Student"), the questions in any "Rereading" section, and any other methods that have worked for you. Demonstrate a clear, step-by-step process of reading that someone else could follow.

Finding a Purpose

In your experience as a student, you have been exposed to a number of communities of knowledge—the different fields in which school courses are offered. Make notes on your observations of the vocabularies and methods that are commonly used in two or three of the subjects you have studied. For instance, how are students expected to think and use language in physical education, physics, psychology, and English classes?

Write an essay to a new student explaining the differences in approach among these different fields. Your essay should be a bit of friendly advice, telling this new student how to prepare to succeed in various fields that have different purposes, methods, and vocabularies. Use a friendly voice (second person) and give specific examples of how to act in class, the questions that are relevant, and ways of writing and studying that have worked well for you.

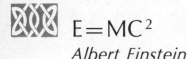

$E = MC^2$
Albert Einstein

Albert Einstein (1879–1955) was not a promising student in his early years. After leaving Zurich Polytechnic Institute, he became a clerk in the Patent Office in Berne, Switzerland. He had a difficult time getting this job and had had to postpone his marriage because he could not find work. He returned to his native Germany at the time of Hitler's rise to power and, as a Jew, had to leave his country in 1933. He went to the United States.

Einstein was a formidable mathematician, but, more importantly, he was a scientist with great intuitive power. Already during his earlier work as a clerk, he had developed theories that radically changed both scientific and popular perceptions of the world we live in. At the turn of the century, theoretical and experimental advances in understanding electricity and magnetism had led to inconsistencies and paradoxes. It was Einstein who realized that the only cure for these difficulties was a revolution in the way we viewed the space and time of the physical world.

Einstein reluctantly contributed to the development of atomic weapons in the United States out of concern that the Nazis might develop them first. In a letter to President Franklin D. Roosevelt in 1939, he represented the scientific community's view that it might be possible to create nuclear chain reactions in the near future. He asked Roosevelt to consider speeding experimental research and to acquire uranium quickly because Germany was making progress in the same direction. The results of these suggestions are well known.

Einstein's explanation of the equivalence of mass and energy was first published in 1946. It appeared in *Scientific Illustrated,* a magazine for people who are interested in science but not professionally involved in it. Einstein consequently wrote this explanation for nonscientists, taking care to find language and examples that could be understood by as many people as possible. Where he could, he used analogies to clarify his points, explaining his ideas by comparing them to more familiar processes. As you read, notice this strategy. Does it succeed in helping you understand Einstein's ideas? Why do you think he wanted nonspecialists to understand him?

In order to understand the law of the equivalence of mass and energy, we   1
must go back to two conservation or "balance" principles which, independent of each other, held a high place in pre-relativity physics. These were the principle of the conservation of energy and the principle of the conservation of mass. The first of these, advanced by Leibnitz as long ago as the

seventeenth century, was developed in the nineteenth century essentially as a corollary of a principle of mechanics.

Consider, for example, a pendulum whose mass swings back and 2 forth between the points A and B. At these points the mass m is higher by the amount h than it is at C, the lowest point of the path (see drawing). At C, on the other hand, the lifting height has disappeared and instead of it the mass has a velocity v. It is as though the lifting height could be converted entirely into velocity, and vice versa. The exact relation would be expressed as $mgh = \frac{m}{2}v^2$, with g representing the acceleration of gravity. What is interesting here is that this relation is independent of both the length of the pendulum and the form of the path through which the mass moves.

The significance is that something remains constant throughout the 3 process, and that something is energy. At A and at B it is an energy of position, or "potential" energy; at C it is an energy of motion, or "kinetic" energy. If this concept is correct, then the sum $mgh + m\frac{v^2}{2}$ must have the same value for any position of the pendulum, if h is understood to represent the height above C, and v the velocity at that point in the pendulum's path. And such is found to be actually the case. The generalization of this principle gives us the law of the conservation of mechanical energy. But what happens when friction stops the pendulum?

The answer to that was found in the study of heat phenomena. This 4 study, based on the assumption that heat is an indestructible substance which flows from a warmer to a colder object, seemed to give us a principle of the "conservation of heat." On the other hand, from time immemorial it has been known that heat could be produced by friction, as in the fire-making drills of the Indians. The physicists were for long unable to account for this kind of heat "production." Their difficulties were overcome only when it was successfully established that, for any given amount of heat produced by friction, an exactly proportional amount of energy had to be expended. Thus did we arrive at a principle of the "equivalence of work and heat." With our pendulum, for example, mechanical energy is gradually converted by friction into heat.

In such fashion the principles of the conservation of mechanical and 5

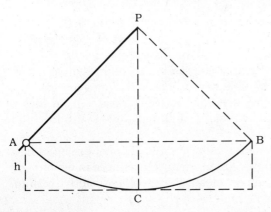

thermal energies were merged into one. The physicists were thereupon persuaded that the conservation principle could be further extendcd to take in chemical and electromagnetic processes—in short, could be applied to all fields. It appeared that in our physical system there was a sum total of energies that remained constant through all changes that might occur.

Now for the principle of the conservation of mass. Mass is defined by 6 the resistance that a body opposes to its acceleration (inert mass). It is also measured by the weight of the body (heavy mass). That these two radically different definitions lead to the same value for the mass of a body is, in itself, an astonishing fact. According to the principle—namely, that masses remain unchanged under any physical or chemical changes—the mass appeared to be the essential (because unvarying) quality of matter. Heating, melting, vaporization, or combining into chemical compounds would not change the total mass.

Physicists accepted this principle up to a few decades ago. But it 7 proved inadequate in the face of the special theory of relativity. It was therefore merged with the energy principle—just as, about 60 years before, the principle of the conservation of mechanical energy had been combined with the principle of the conservation of heat. We might say that the principle of the conservation of energy, having previously swallowed up that of the conservation of heat, now proceeded to swallow that of the conservation of mass—and holds the field alone.

It is customary to express the equivalence of mass and energy 8 (though somewhat inexactly) by the formula $E = mc^2$, in which c represents the velocity of light, about 186,000 miles per second. E is the energy that is contained in a stationary body; m is its mass. The energy that belongs to the mass m is equal to this mass, multiplied by the square of the enormous speed of light—which is to say, a vast amount of energy for every unit of mass.

But if every gram of material contains this tremendous energy, why 9 did it go so long unnoticed? The answer is simple enough: so long as none of the energy is given off externally, it cannot be observed. It is as though a man who is fabulously rich should never spend or give away a cent; no one could tell how rich he was.

Now we can reverse the relation and say that an increase of E in the 10 amount of energy must be accompanied by an increase of $\frac{E}{c^2}$ in the mass. I can easily supply energy to the mass—for instance, if I heat it by 10 degrees. So why not measure the mass increase, or weight increase, connected with this change? The trouble here is that in the mass increase the enormous factor c^2 occurs in the denominator of the fraction. In such a case the increase is too small to be measured directly; even with the most sensitive balance.

For a mass increase to be measurable, the change of energy per mass 11 unit must be enormously large. We know of only one sphere in which such amounts of energy per mass unit are released: namely, radioactive disintegration. Schematically, the process goes like this: an atom of the mass M splits into two atoms of the mass M' and M", which separate with tremendous kinetic energy. If we imagine these two masses as brought to rest—that is, if we take this energy of motion from them—then, considered together, they are essentially poorer in energy than was the original atom. According to the equivalence principle, the mass sum M' + M" of the disintegration products must also be somewhat smaller than the original mass M of the disintegrating atom—in contradiction to the old principle of the conservation of mass. The relative difference of the two is on the order of $\frac{1}{10}$ of one percent.

Now, we cannot actually weigh the atoms individually. However, there are indirect methods for measuring their weights exactly. We can likewise determine the kinetic energies that are transferred to the disintegration products M' and M". Thus it has become possible to test and confirm the equivalence formula. Also, the law permits us to calculate in advance, from precisely determined atom weights, just how much energy will be released with any atom disintegration we have in mind. The law says nothing, of course, as to whether—or how—the disintegration reaction can be brought about.

What takes place can be illustrated with the help of our rich man. The atom M is a rich miser who, during his life, gives away no money *(energy)*. But in his will he bequeaths his fortune to his sons M' and M", on condition that they give to the community a small amount, less than one thousandth of the whole estate *(energy or mass)*. The sons together have somewhat less that the father had *(the mass sum M' + M" is somewhat smaller than the mass M of the radioactive atom)*. But the part given to the community, though relatively small, is still so enormously large *(considered as kinetic energy)* that it brings with it a great threat of evil. Averting that threat has become the most urgent problem of our time.

Questions

Rereading and Independent Analysis

1. Reread this essay, underlining the references, examples, and comparisons that Einstein uses so that a nonscientist can understand his points. What sense of Einstein's personality do you get from these examples and references? What relationship with his reader does he want to establish?

2. Reread the last sentence of this essay. Clearly identify Einstein's purpose in it. Then look again at the essay as whole. Do you see any clues along the way that he will end with this persuasive appeal, or does the last paragraph completely break with what has gone before it?

Suggested Discussion and Group Activities

1. Analogy, or extended comparison, has been called the weakest form of proof. Does Einstein's use of the analogy with a miser clearly

explain the difference between kinetic and potential energy to you? What purposes might he have had for choosing this particular analogy? (Notice the date of this essay.) Suggest other comparisons that might explain the concept as well as this one does. Would they have served Einstein's special purposes as well in his time?

2. Review the content of this essay in groups, making sure you understand Einstein's explanation. How does the theory of the equivalence of mass and energy change the theories he used to explain this equivalence? Give examples of how his new theory would modify other theories.

Writing Suggestions

Response

Einstein had little to do with developing nuclear weapons, but he knew what their results might be. In your journal, write a few paragraphs about the ways potential nuclear disaster affects your feelings about the future. Do you usually ignore this potential? Do you think some people worry about it too much?

Analysis

1. Choose a problem or idea that you are more expert about than others in your class. Write an explanation of it, using comparisons and examples to clarify this subject for those who know little about it. Then show your explanation to classmates and revise it to answer any questions they have after reading.

2. Read J. Robert Oppenheimer's "Prospects in the Arts and Sciences" (Chapter 1) and write a brief introduction to it and this selection in which you explain the public contributions of these two men, the changes in our vision of the world that their work made over a relatively short time, and the value of understanding their personal as well as their scientific influence on our time. Use examples from these selections and other material about these scientists to support your points.

Finding a Purpose

Einstein's work and life clearly support the claim that "knowledge is power." Write an essay to a group of younger students supporting this statement. Use other examples of the relation of new knowledge to power to persuade them that new knowledge is worth pursuing because it determines who will be able to control a situation.

Use Einstein and other well-known scientists as examples of individuals who demonstrate your point. Begin with an example that younger students will understand and be able to relate to their own lives to persuade them that you are writing with their best interests in mind.

The Problem of the Four Colors
George Gamow

This brief selection is an example of the special way of thinking that defines the boundaries of scientific activity. This problem, set by George Gamow (1904–1968), demands solving, but none of many attempts has succeeded. In 1976 two mathematicians at the University of Illinois gave the problem to a computer, which came up with an answer that has been widely criticized for not meeting one of the important criteria that scientists use to evaluate solutions to problems. The computer's answer to this puzzle in map making was too complex, its critics say, for humans to understand its reasoning.

Thus the solution was not "elegant"; it was not the best solution to the problem because it did not appear to answer the most questions with the fewest steps. In other words, an elegant solution to a mathematical problem or to any problem is not lengthy and involved. It is not impractical to apply. This criterion for judging the value of solutions has been important in many contexts. In the ancient study of persuasion (rhetoric), it was one of the ways to *refute,* or argue against, proposals. (See The Declaration of Independence, Chapter 2.)

Gamow's essay is also a well-executed example of the common five-paragraph scheme. Gamow uses five paragraphs in a problem-and-solution pattern of explanation. As you read, notice the function of each paragraph in creating a whole explanation. Gamow states two problems: how to color a map and how to demonstrate mathematically (prove) that the way to do this coloring is universal in all situations. He closes with alternative methods of coloring and their results.

Suppose we have a surface of a sphere subdivided into a number of separate regions, and we are asked to color these regions in such a way that no two adjacent regions (that is, those having a common boundary) will have the same color. What is the smallest number of different colors we must use for such a task? It is clear that two colors only will in general not suffice since, when three boundaries come together in one point (as, for example, those of Virginia, West Virginia, and Maryland on a map of the United States, Figure 1) we shall need different colors for all of the three states. 1

It is also not difficult to find an example (Switzerland during the German annexation of Austria) where four colors are necessary. 2

But try as you will, you never will be able to construct an imaginary map, be it on the globe or on a flat piece of paper, for which more than four colors would be necessary. It seems that no matter how complicated we make the map, four colors always suffice to avoid any confusion along the boundaries. 3

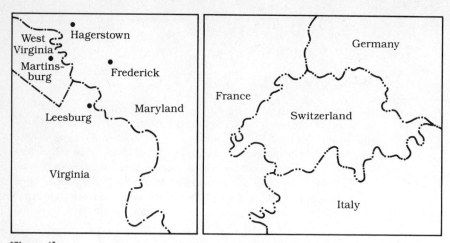

[Figure 1]
Topological maps of Maryland, Virginia, and West Virginia (on the left) and Switzerland, France, Germany, and Italy (on the right).

Well, if this last statement is true one should be able to prove it 4 mathematically, but in spite of the efforts of generations of mathematicians this has not yet been done. Here is a typical case of a mathematical statement that practically nobody doubts, but that nobody has been able to prove. The best that has been accomplished mathematically has been to prove that five colors are always sufficient. That proof is based on the Euler relationship, which has been applied to the number of countries, the number of their boundaries, and the number of triple, quadruple, etc. points in which several countries meet.

We do not demonstrate this proof, since it is fairly complicated and 5 would lead us away from the main subject of the discussion, but the reader can find it in various books on topology and spend a pleasant evening (and perhaps a sleepless night) in contemplating it. Either he can try to devise the proof that not only five, but even four colors are sufficient to color any map, or, if he is skeptical about the validity of this statement, he can draw a map for which four colors are not enough. In the event of success in either of the two attempts his name will be perpetuated in the annals of pure mathematics for centuries to come.

Questions

Rereading and Independent Analysis

1. Outline Gamow's essay, showing how each paragraph relates to the one following it. Since he cannot move from problem to final solution in this essay, how does Gamow present the problem of the four colors? How does he connect one paragraph to another?

2. Analyze each of the paragraphs of the essay to show its internal structure. Do they begin with topic sentences? Do the sentences following

the first sentence restrict its scope, give an example, or develop the first sentence in another way? When you have finished, apply your analysis to the whole essay. Does it follow the pattern found in each paragraph?

Suggested Discussion and Group Activities

1. Would it matter to you as a mapmaker or a person on a trip in strange territory whether there is "proof" that only four colors are necessary to distinguish boundaries on a map? What particular kind of truth are people who have worked on this problem seeking?

2. If no acceptable solution to this problem has been found, "try as [mathematicians] will," why do people still devote themselves to solving it? What is gained by these attempts? When do you think people should suspend their efforts to solve a problem?

3. In groups, choose a particular problem and come up with solutions that demonstrate both "elegant" and "inelegant" ways of solving it. You can use ordinary household problems as well as problems in any subject you have studied.

Writing Suggestions

Response

Use Gamow's essay to revise one of your own essays. That is, reread an essay you have written and make changes in it that clarify its reasoning, make it easier to follow from part to part, and place it in the argumentative form of Gamow's presentation. Imitate Gamow's ways of arranging and connecting the parts of a whole, and rearrange sentences in your paragraphs where necessary so that they follow the patterns he used. When you are finished, show a classmate your two versions for an opinion about whether the second version is easier to read and understand than the first.

Analysis

From your own experience, choose a problem or puzzle that you have at some time attempted to solve. Write an essay in which you explain the problem, the methods that you used to solve it step by step, and the nature of the solution you found. Your essay should be a model that your classmates can read in order to learn more about problem solving for themselves.

Finding a Purpose: Imitation

Write an essay for a popular magazine or journal on any puzzle of your choice. Begin with an example of the problem, show the difficulties it creates, and then describe the solution and any difficulties there are with the most common way of solving this problem. You might want to describe a particular product designed for one use, a situation in a sport or other kind of performance that requires attention to detail, or a household difficulty that requires special equipment.

On Societies as Organisms
Lewis Thomas

Lewis Thomas (b. 1913), a physician and educator, has been dean of both the Yale and New York University medical schools and president of the Memorial Sloan–Kettering Cancer Center. But he is better known as a leading popular writer about the links between science and the humanities. His essay collection *The Lives of a Cell* (1974) won the National Book Award in Arts and Letters. In this chapter from it, he expresses a profound theme that appears in all his writing, the interdependence and connectedness of living things. Since writing *Lives of a Cell,* Thomas has also published other collections you may want to read: *The Medusa and the Snail* (1979) and *The Youngest Science: Notes of Medicine Watcher* (1983).

This essay about the organic qualities of human societies is a vivid example of the theme Thomas wants to make us aware of. His strategies of presentation and his language both embody the interconnectedness that makes up his content. Thomas manages perspectives on his subject as though he were making a film. He looks at human and insect communities from various distances and angles to persuade his reader that there are multiple explanations for observations. He takes the point of view of a "bystander" who can shift his vision readily. He also demonstrates his point by using extended comparisons to identify human life with insect life. Thomas is a master of paragraph construction. His sentence units regulate the movement from one idea to another so that each becomes a composite, interrelated piece of the whole essay. As you read, remain aware of these fits between Thomas's point and the language he chooses to make it. Why do you think he wants to make this idea widely accepted? What are the results when we separate human from other life in strict compartments?

Viewed from a suitable height, the aggregating clusters of medical scien- 1 tists in the bright sunlight of the boardwalk at Atlantic City, swarmed there from everywhere for the annual meetings, have the look of assemblages of social insects. There is the same vibrating, ionic movement, interrupted by the darting back and forth of jerky individuals to touch antennae and exchange small bits of information; periodically, the mass casts out, like a trout-line, a long single file unerringly toward Childs's. If the boards were not fastened down, it would not be a surprise to see them put together a nest of sorts.

It is permissible to say this sort of thing about humans. They do 2 resemble, in their most compulsively social behavior, ants at a distance. It is, however, quite bad form in biological circles to put it the other way round, to imply that the operation of insect societies has any relation at all to human affairs. The writers of books on insect behavior generally take pains, in their prefaces, to caution that insects are like creatures from another planet, that their behavior is absolutely foreign, totally unhuman, unearthly, almost unbiological. They are more like perfectly tooled but crazy little machines, and we violate science when we try to read human meanings in their arrangements.

It is hard for a bystander not to do so. Ants are so much like human 3 beings as to be an embarrassment. They farm fungi, raise aphids as livestock, launch armies into wars, use chemical sprays to alarm and confuse enemies, capture slaves. The families of weaver ants engage in child labor, holding their larvae like shuttles to spin out the thread that sews the leaves together for their fungus gardens. They exchange information ceaselessly. They do everything but watch television.

What makes us most uncomfortable is that they, and the bees and 4 termites and social wasps, seem to live two kinds of lives: they are individuals, going about the day's business without much evidence of thought for tomorrow, and they are at the same time component parts, cellular elements, in the huge, writhing, ruminating organism of the Hill, the nest, the hive. It is because of this aspect, I think, that we most wish for them to be something foreign. We do not like the notion that there can be collective societies with the capacity to behave like organisms. If such things exist, they can have nothing to do with us.

Still, there it is. A solitary ant, afield, cannot be considered to have 5 much of anything on his mind; indeed, with only a few neurons strung together by fibers, he can't be imagined to have a mind at all, much less a thought. He is more like a ganglion on legs. Four ants together, or ten, encircling a dead moth on a path, begin to look more like an idea. They fumble and shove, gradually moving the food toward the Hill, but as though by blind chance. It is only when you watch the dense mass of thousands of ants, crowded together around the Hill, blackening the ground, that you begin to see the whole beast, and now you observe it thinking, planning, calculating. It is an intelligence, a kind of live computer, with crawling bits for its wits.

At a stage in the construction, twigs of a certain size are needed, and 6 all the members forage obsessively for twigs of just this size. Later, when outer walls are to be finished, thatched, the size must change, and as though given new orders by telephone, all the workers shift the search to the new twigs. If you disturb the arrangement of a part of the Hill, hundreds of ants will set it vibrating, shifting, until it is put right again. Distant sources of food are somehow sensed, and long lines, like tentacles, reach out over the ground, up over walls, behind boulders, to fetch it in.

Termites are even more extraordinary in the way they seem to ac- 7 cumulate intelligence as they gather together. Two or three termites in a chamber will begin to pick up pellets and move them from place to place, but nothing comes of it; nothing is built. As more join in, they seem to reach a critical mass, a quorum, and the thinking begins. They place pellets atop pellets, then throw up columns and beautiful, curving, symmetrical arches, and the crystalline architecture of vaulted chambers is created. It is not known how they communicate with each other, how the chains of termites building one column know when to turn toward the crew on the adjacent column, or how, when the time comes, they manage the flawless joining of the arches. The stimuli that set them off at the outset, building collectively instead of shifting things about, may be pheromones released when they reach committee size. They react as if alarmed. They become agitated, excited, and then they begin working, like artists.

Bees live lives of organisms, tissues, cells, organelles, all at the same 8 time. The single bee, out of the hive retrieving sugar (instructed by the dancer: "south-southeast for seven hundred meters, clover—mind you make corrections for the sundrift") is still as much a part of the hive as if attached by a filament. Building the hive, the workers have the look of embryonic cells organizing a developing tissue; from a distance they are like the viruses inside a cell, running off row after row of symmetrical polygons as though laying down crystals. When the time for swarming comes, and the old queen prepares to leave with her part of the population, it is as though the hive were involved in mitosis. There is an agitated moving of bees back and forth, like granules in cell sap. They distribute themselves in almost precisely equal parts, half to the departing queen, half to the new one. Thus, like an egg, the great, hairy, black and golden creature splits in two, each with an equal share of the family genome.

The phenomenon of separate animals joining up to form an organism 9 is not unique in insects. Slime-mold cells do it all the time, of course, in each life cycle. At first they are single amebocytes swimming around, eating bacteria, aloof from each other, untouching, voting straight Republican. Then, a bell sounds, and acrasin is released by special cells toward which the others converge in stellate ranks, touch, fuse together, and construct the slug, solid as a trout. A splendid stalk is raised, with a fruiting body on top, and out of this comes the next generation of amebocytes, ready to swim across the same moist ground, solitary and ambitious.

Herring and other fish in schools are at times so closely integrated, 10 their actions so coordinated, that they seem to be functionally a great multi-fish organism. Flocking birds, especially the seabirds nesting on the slopes of offshore islands in Newfoundland, are similarly attached, connected, synchronized.

Although we are by all odds the most social of all social animals— 11 more interdependent, more attached to each other, more inseparable in our behavior than bees—we do not often feel our conjoined intelligence. Perhaps, however, we are linked in circuits for the storage, processing, and retrieval of information, since this appears to be the most basic and universal of all human enterprises. It may be our biological function to build a certain kind of Hill. We have access to all the information of the biosphere, arriving as elementary units in the stream of solar photons. When we have learned how these are rearranged against randomness, to make, say, springtails, quantum mechanics, and the late quartets, we may have a clearer notion how to proceed. The circuitry seems to be there, even if the current is not always on.

The system of communications used in science should provide a neat, 12 workable model for studying mechanisms of information-building in human society. Ziman, in a recent *Nature* essay, points out, "the invention of a mechanism for the systematic publication of *fragments* of scientific work may well have been the key event in the history of modern science." He continues:

> A regular journal carries from one research worker to another the vari-
> ous . . . observations which are of common interest. . . . A typical scien-
> tific paper has never pretended to be more than another little piece in a
> larger jigsaw—not significant in itself but as an element in a grander
> scheme. *This technique, of soliciting many modest contributions to the
> store of human knowledge, has been the secret of Western science since
> the seventeenth century, for it achieves a corporate, collective power that
> is far greater than any one individual can exert* [italics mine].

With some alternation of terms, some toning down, the passage could 13 describe the building of a termite nest.

It is fascinating that the word "explore" does not apply to the search- 14 ing aspect of the activity, but has its origins in the sounds we make while engaged in it. We like to think of exploring in science as a lonely, medita- tive business, and so it is in the first stages, but always, sooner or later, before the enterprise teaches completion, as we explore, we call to each other, communicate, publish, send letters to the editor, present papers, cry out on finding.

Questions

Rereading and Independent Analysis

1. What is the thesis of this essay? Is it stated explicitly, or must it be inferred from the whole piece? Once you have determined its thesis, make an outline of the essay that shows how Thomas's development sup- ports it. How are each of his points related to one idea?

2. Thomas often employs a "periodic" sentence style, postponing important information in his sentences until their end. Choose a para- graph from the essay and analyze its sentences to show the locations of their subjects, verbs, and complements. What is his characteristic method of linking information within sentences? Notice particularly the effect of the last sentence in the essay.

Suggested Discussion and Group Activities

1. What is the progression of Thomas's choice of specific examples in this essay? How are examples used to move toward a particular view of the essay's most important issue?

2. Have you witnessed human beings change their behavior when they become parts of large groups or organizations? Cite some positive and negative examples of this change. Can you tell what Thomas thinks would be the nature of the "certain kind of Hill" humans may have been designed to build? Who or what does he imply is the "designer"?

3. In groups, make an outline of the changes in perspective or point

of view in this essay. From where is the author viewing his subject? Bring in examples from your own and other writing to show changes and controls on perspective as a successful strategy. Show how these pieces do this. (You might want to use selections from this chapter: Lillian Hellman, "Dashiell Hammett" and Abraham Cahan, "I Discover America".)

Writing Suggestions

Response

Using examples and statements from Thomas's essay in your introduction, write a response to his essay in which you extend his point. Show that many activities that we commonly imagine to be individual and separate achievements are "parts of a giant jigsaw puzzle" that reveal the aims of a larger group. Use observations and specific examples that show how individuals contribute to universal patterns of action that preserve society. Thomas is very much interested in student writing, so you might mail your response to him and ask for his comments on your ideas.

Analysis: Imitation

Copy a few of Thomas's sentences that demonstrate the "periodic" pattern of withholding information until the end. Then write your own sentences imitating these. Use the same location of subject, verb, and complement, the same method of elaborating on the sentence's idea, and language like Thomas's.

Finding a Purpose

Write a report on human beings (if you wish, from the perspective of an observer from another planet), telling how their behavior in groups differs from their behavior when they are alone. Describe the situations you see humans in from the point of view of someone who observes as Thomas observes ants or termites. Your purpose is to demonstrate only what you can see from observation, not prior knowledge, so you may want to prepare by taking notes in specific situations as though you were a bystander, not a participant.

 # Unlocking the Genetic Mystery
Judith M. Shapiro

This essay by Judith M. Shapiro, a public health practitioner, was published in *Mothers' Manual Magazine* in 1980. It is an example of writing to share scientific research with readers who are not interested in scientific details but who need to apply new research in their lives. Shapiro's report describes two methods of determining the health of a fetus before birth, methods that were developed in the decade before she wrote. She gives this information in a question-and-answer form. Her report answers questions about who needs such tests, the problems that these tests diagnose, and the possibilities and problems of developing other tests and making them widely available.

Shapiro's article is a useful example of clearly reported scientific information. She divides the report's parts into sections that have separate titles. By presenting her information this way, she makes it suitable for the internal divisions and headlines often used in magazines. But she also provides an example of the kind of presentation that is characteristic of summaries of biological information. In each section, she tells about research that was current at the time she wrote in a way that makes this information useful to a potential parent with questions about having a child. Shapiro also uses a tone that will persuade the reader of the importance and relevance of this information. As you read, imagine her reasons for wanting to make this information widely available and notice how her tone accomplishes this purpose. Can you think of other specialized topics that you would like to see summarized in this way?

"Do you want a boy or a girl?" is the question most frequently put to 1 expectant parents. "It doesn't matter as long as it is healthy," is the usual response. It is also the usual outcome—well over 90 percent of babies born in this country are healthy and normal in all regards.

For those couples, however, who fall in the so-called "high-risk" 2 category, whether because of age or family medical histories, the concern about a healthy baby is even more poignant. Now, thanks to a decade of tremendous progress in prenatal testing and, especially, clinical diagnostic techniques, these couples can be informed about the health of their unborn child. The vast majority of these diagnoses give the reassurance of a normal fetus (more than 95 percent of amniocentesis diagnoses do not contain the feared-for results), and the relief of having an anxiety-free pregnancy.

Prenatal Testing

The two major tools of prenatal testing are amniocentesis and chromo- 3 some banding. While amniocentesis has been with us more than 10 years, the recently developed technique of chromosome banding, developed initially in 1970, has made amniocentesis a much more sophisticated diagnostic procedure.

Amniocentesis, performed by a qualified obstetrician between the 4 15th [and] 18th weeks of pregnancy, involves inserting a hollow needle into the uterus through the abdomen to withdraw a small amount of the amniotic fluid surrounding the fetus. It is usually preceded by ultrasound examination, a painless procedure using high-frequency sound waves to transmit a picture of the fetus onto a television screen. With this picture the physician can precisely locate the fetus and the placenta to avoid touching them with the needle and to find the largest free area of amniotic fluid. (Ultrasound is also used to detect certain severe malformation in the developing fetus, multiple pregnancies, and fetal age.)

Once the amniotic fluid is obtained, it is sent to a laboratory where 5 fetal cells are removed and allowed to multiply in a nutrient bath. After a few weeks the cells are analyzed for chromosome abnormalities or inherited disorders of body chemistry. Chromosomes are microscopic packages of vital hereditary information. Normal humans have 23 pairs of chromosomes in each of their body cells, including one pair of sex chromosomes—two X chromosomes in females, or an X plus a Y in males.

Chromosomes come in different shapes and sizes. When they were 6 first looked at in the late 1950's and 1960's, it was hard to distinguish some of them from others. The chromosome banding technique, a process through which chromosomes are stained with chemicals, was the vital breakthrough which enabled technicians to see differences and similarities much more clearly. This revealed chromosomal causes of many birth defects whose origins had previously been a mystery.

The most common serious chromosome abnormality is Down's syn- 7 drome, detectable only in some cases before chromosome bonding. Most children with Down's syndrome are born with an extra number-21 chromosome in every cell of their body and therefore have 47 chromosomes instead of the normal 46. These children exhibit varying degrees of mental retardation and usually have other health problems.

There are a wide range of inherited disorders of body chemistry that 8 cannot be identified as chromosome defects can by bonding techniques, but reveal themselves as chemical abnormalities in amniotic fluid cells. Today, about 100 such defects are detectable prenatally. "But most of these disorders are rare and are tested for only if there is a specific reason for suspicion, such as family history or screening of carriers," explains Sara Finley, M.D. of the laboratory of Medical Genetics, University of Alabama in Birmingham.

Tay-Sachs disease, which disables and kills within the first five years 9 of life, is the best-known example of a disorder which can be prevented by genetic screening of adults who may carry the abnormal gene. One in every 25 Jews of Eastern European descent carries it, and if two carriers marry, there is a one in four chance with each pregnancy that the child will be affected. Carriers for this disease can be identified by a simple blood test, but for a woman at risk, who is already pregnant, prenatal diagnosis is possible.

A third major birth defect for which amniocentesis is useful is an 10 open malformation of the skull or spine, called a neural tube defect. Its effects include stillbirth, death in infancy, brain damage and paralysis. It can be detected by measuring the amount of a specific substance, called alpha-fetoprotein, in the amniotic fluid. Fortunately, the neural tube defect is rare; and although it is not hereditary, the test for it is performed primarily on women who have had a child or close relative with the defect.

Since it is virtually impossible to screen all pregnant women by 11 amniocentesis, new testing procedures are being searched for. These would be to determine if there are indicators that the woman should indeed pursue amniocentesis. In the mid-1970's a few laboratories in this country and around the world began to explore the possibility of measuring the level of alpha-fetoprotein in the mother's blood as an initial screen.

"On the basis of the blood levels, we could focus down on a high-risk 12 subgroup within that large, unselected pregnant population," reports Dr. James Macri, director of the Neural Tube Defect Laboratory at the State University of New York in Stony Brook.

Researchers are hopeful that in the 1980's this type of testing will be 13 implemented via a network of regionalized centers. Ideally these would not only provide the service to a large population of pregnant women, but also have the necessary associated services, such as ultrasound, amniocentesis, highly reliable laboratory services and professional counselors.

Why Genetic Counseling

Many couples come to a genetic counselor because of a family history of 14 birth defects which they believe to be hereditary. In these cases prenatal diagnosis should be preceded by counseling with a person trained in medical genetics. Often the fears of these couples are allayed and prenatal diagnosis is not recommended.

"All patients have different ethnic, moral and ethical backgrounds, 15 as do most counselors. Counseling should be a vehicle of transmission of scientific knowledge at a level that can be understood by each patient. It should not be used to direct a decision which has moral or ethical implications," notes Garver. In the case of amniocentesis results that do show a defect, the affected couple is referred for further counseling to explore their options.

A Success Story

Today there may be positive options thanks to the many research scientists 16 who are actively involved in devising in-utero treatment for some birth defects. To date, one case stands out in the medical journals. It concerns a child named April Murphy who was born with a rare vitamin metabolism defect called methymalonic adidemia (MMA). April's older sister had died of this shortly after birth and when her mother became pregnant again, she was offered prenatal diagnosis.

Test results showed that her second baby would also have MMA, but 17 that the family's form of the disorder was responsive to vitamin B_{12}. It was decided to give Terry huge intramuscular injections of the vitamin—5,000 times the normal adult dose. The idea was to force the vitamin across the placenta to saturate both the mother's and the unborn baby's tissues, thus preventing possible prenatal damage.

Although April is kept on a controlled B_{12}-supplemented diet, in 18

every other respect she is a healthy 6-year-old. And she has a new baby
sister who was shown to be unaffected when Terry again had amniocentesis.

Looking Ahead

In spite of the rapid advances in prenatal testing, many genetic disorders 19
remain undiagnosable prenatally. A link, however, may exist between the
gene that causes such diseases and another gene whose product can be
detected, making an indirect diagnosis possible. Gene mapping (determining where certain genes are located in a specific part of a chromosome)
is a new scientific tool for researchers actively investigating classic hemo-
philia—an x-linked disorder—and juvenile diabetes, among others, for
potentially useful gene linkages. Success will have a great impact on the
future of clinical genetics.

It is hoped that major advances also will occur in this decade in the 20
prenatal diagnosis of sickle cell anemia and cystic fibrosis. Sickle cell anemia, a blood disorder that affects primarily people of African descent, can
presently be detected by a complicated and somewhat risky procedure of
testing fetal blood. Researchers in California are now testing a new technique to diagnose the disease in amniotic fluid cells; this would make
diagnosis safer and much more widely available.

Cystic fibrosis, the most common severe birth defect of body chemis- 21
try among Caucasians, is a hereditary disorder that appears in childhood
and causes chronic lung infections, digestive problems, growth retardation and often death in young adulthood. Although scientists have tried to
find a prenatal test for this disease, none has worked so far. But many
experts believe that work going on at the present will eventually lead to
a prenatal test for the disease as well as a carrier detection test.

While amniocentesis is a proven, safe, medical procedure, it is never- 22
theless "invasive"—that is, it involves entering the fetal environment.
Consequently, its use is limited to women considered as potentially at high
risk of giving birth to children with serious, prenatally detectable defects.
To simplify prenatal testing—giving the same information as amniocentesis without invading the uterus—research is currently under way at Stan-
ford University to develop a simple blood test that can also be used to
determine fetal abnormalities. Dr. Leonard Herzenberg has found that a
few fetal cells are present in the maternal bloodstream as early as the 15th
week of pregnancy. These can be separated from maternal blood cells by
using a very high-speed fluorescence-activated cell sorter. This technique,
when perfected, could lead to widespread screening of pregnant women.

The future possibilities of medical genetics are exciting, but says 23
Arthur J. Salisbury, M.D., vice president for medical services of the March
of Dimes, "We are faced with the disturbing fact that, despite the increased number of families who are helped by counseling services, 80
percent of the people who could be helped are not being reached."

One way to reach these people is to increase the number of "satellite 24 clinics," staffed by genetic experts from major medical centers. These clinics, which are held periodically in community hospitals or public health facilities, bring modern genetic information to people who would have difficulty traveling long distances to a regional medical center.

The major problem in the future of clinical genetics is in funding. 25 During the 1970's the March of Dimes had been the major source of funds to clinical centers in the United States which practice medical genetics. Currently the federal government is beginning to recognize the importance of genetic counseling services. The National Genetic Disease Act, which was passed in 1978, received an appropriation of $4 million; an additional $4 million has been tentatively added by the Congress to bring total federal funding to $8 million by 1979–80.

"Genetic services development in the 1980's is going to be strained 26 financially unless there is more federal or other funding," adds Dr. Salisbury. "It's not so much that more major genetic centers are needed, but the increase in demand is so critical that they need more personnel and should be seeing more patients."

The gift of a precious life in health, prayed for by all parents, is the 27 goal of hundreds of genetic scientists. Much has been done and, with the nation's support, more will be done during the next 10 years in solving one of life's greatest mysteries—life itself.

Questions

Rereading and Independent Analysis

1. Identify the thesis of this essay. Then, after noticing the essay's progression from part to part, make a note of how each part helps accomplish the purpose established in the introduction. Could the purpose of the whole have been accomplished if any of these parts had been omitted?

2. Compress this report into its fewest essential statements. To find out what they are, read it again, placing brackets around every sentence and phrase that could be left out of the essay without diminishing its informative content. Copy out the statements that are left into one paragraph. Does this paragraph give a clear picture of the contents?

Suggested Discussion and Group Activities

1. This essay takes the form of a technical report of specialized information. As a class, identify the methods Shapiro used to make that information accessible to a general reader. How do her voice as a writer, pattern of organization, and choice of vocabulary make this technical information accessible? Give specific examples of these strategies.

2. Is this essay only "factual," or does it have persuasive purposes as well? Using evidence from the essay itself, explain what you think the essay is persuading its readers to do and think. How effective do you think

this persuasion is for these readers? What different choices would have made it ineffective?

Writing Suggestions

Response

Write a response to Shapiro's report in which you tell how the information in this essay might be followed up by reports on other tests you would like to know about. Give your reasons for wanting further information and ask questions like the questions she used in her report.

Analysis

1. Based on your answer to Question 2, "Rereading," write an *abstract* of this essay. An *abstract* is the briefest possible version of the essay in its author's words, so use language that Shapiro uses. Your abstract should tell what the essay *does* and should be not much longer than 75 words. Tell what information the essay gives readers.

2. Write a *summary* of this essay. Your summary should compress the essay's major and minor points in the most direct way. Make statements without qualifications or evaluations. Begin with "This essay defines. . . ." The technique of deletion that you used earlier to analyze may help you remove unnecessary statements from the essay before you write your summary. Your summary should be no longer than 300 words—a little more than one typed, double-spaced page.

Finding a Purpose: Library Work

Choose one of the other essays in this section and write both an *abstract* and a *summary* of it. After writing, go to your library to find periodicals that publish abstracts of research in the subject of your chosen essay. Compare your abstract to another one. Write a brief comparison between your own writing and the published abstract, showing differences and evaluating your effectiveness at achieving the same purpose.

Social Sciences

 # Case 4: Katharina
Sigmund Freud

Translated by James Strachey

The publication of *Studies in Hysteria,* by Sigmund Freud and Josef Breuer, in May 1895 marked the beginning of an entirely new study of human feelings and behavior. The study of psychology has contributed greatly to the complex area of studies involving social relations that we now call "social sciences." After more than ten years of carefully considering a few cases of inexplicable neurotic symptoms they had treated, Freud and Breuer only cautiously published their findings. It is clear that the two doctors were working at the beginning of a new "science," for they assumed that readers would not see their work as meaningful without extensive justifications for their points.

These published cases may appear to be crude examples from an era before psychiatry and psychology flowered into their present status as established fields that help treat troublesome mental states. But at the time, suggesting that the human mind responded to memories that it had been unable to absorb creatively or confront directly was a radical and disturbing suggestion. Freud and Breuer hypothesized that unabsorbed memories become *hysteria,* a condition in which a physical symptom takes the visible place of the inwardly suppressed memory.

Freud (1856–1939) was born in Freiberg, Moravia (now part of Czechoslovakia). He worked in Vienna, where his family had moved early in his life, until he was arrested by the Nazis as a Jew. He was released and moved to London in 1938, where he continued his painstaking research. Freud's new ideas caused a furor. He used new methods such as dream analysis, hypnosis, and psychoanalysis, and conceived the theories of infantile sexuality and the three-part personality: ego, superego, and id. Because of the impact of his new visions of human beings and his experiments in ways to help them, it is tempting to think of Freud as an aggressive thinker who acted on intuition. But as this early case study of Katharina shows, Freud published only after long consideration of the implications of his work. He probably had worked with this patient in the early 1890s, years before his report appeared.

His greatest quality was his patience, for he slowly developed methods to free his clients' memories for open analysis and meticulously interpreted their statements. A sensitive, extremely well-read analyst, he understood how symbolism and allusions (associated but digressive references) can explain behaviors that would otherwise remain inexplicable. In particular, by linking a client's remembered descriptions with his or her own insights, he found a key to helping people repair the otherwise irreparable damages caused by traumas. As you read, notice how Freud writes as a creator of fiction, telling a story that explains a physical reality in terms of hidden mental processes.

In the summer vacation of the year 189– I made an excursion into the 1
Hohe Tauern[1] so that for a while I might forget medicine and more particularly the neuroses. I had almost succeeded in this when one day I turned aside from the main road to climb a mountain which lay somewhat apart and which was renowned for its views and for its well-run refuge hut. I reached the top after a strenuous climb and, feeling refreshed and rested, was sitting deep in contemplation of the charm of the distant prospect. I was so lost in thought that at first I did not connect it with myself when these words reached my ears: "Are you a doctor, sir?" But the question was addressed to me, and by the rather sulky-looking girl of perhaps eighteen who had served my meal and had been spoken to by the landlady as

[1] [One of the highest ranges in the Eastern Alps.]

"Katharina." To judge by her dress and bearing, she could not be a servant, but must no doubt be a daughter or relative of the landlady's.

Coming to myself I replied: "Yes, I'm a doctor: but how did you know 2 that?"

"You wrote your name in the Visitors' Book, sir. And I thought if you 3 had a few moments to spare . . . The truth is, sir, my nerves are bad. I went to see a doctor in L——— about them and he gave me something for them; but I'm not well yet."

So there I was with the neuroses once again—for nothing else could 4 very well be the matter with this strong, well-built girl with her unhappy look. I was interested to find that neuroses could flourish in this way at a height of over 6,000 feet; I questioned her further therefore. I report the conversation that followed between us just as it is impressed on my memory and I have not altered the patient's dialect.[1]

"Well, what is it you suffer from?"   5

"I get so out of breath. Not always. But sometimes it catches me so 6 that I think I shall suffocate."

This did not, at first sight, sound like a nervous symptom. But soon 7 it occurred to me that probably it was only a description that stood for an anxiety attack: she was choosing shortness of breath out of the complex of sensations arising from anxiety and laying undue stress on that single factor.

"Sit down here. What is it like when you get 'out of breath'?"   8

"It comes over me all at once. First of all it's like something pressing 9 on my eyes. My head gets so heavy, there's a dreadful buzzing, and I feel so giddy that I almost fall over. Then there's something crushing my chest so that I can't get my breath."

"And you don't notice anything in your throat?"   10

"My throat's squeezed together as though I were going to choke."   11

"Does anything else happen in your head?"   12

"Yes, there's a hammering, enough to burst it."   13

"And don't you feel at all frightened while this is going on?"   14

"I always think I'm going to die. I'm brave as a rule and go about 15 everywhere by myself—into the cellar and all over the mountain. But on a day when that happens I don't dare to go anywhere; I think all the time someone's standing behind me and going to catch hold of me all at once."

So it was in fact an anxiety attack, and introduced by the signs of a 16 hysterical "aura"[2]—or, more correctly, it was a hysterical attack the content of which was anxiety. Might there not probably be some other content as well?

"When you have an attack do you think of something? and always the 17 same thing? or do you see something in front of you?"

---

[1] [No attempt has been made in the English translation to imitate this dialect.]
[2] [The premonitory sensations preceding an epileptic or hysterical attack.]

"Yes. I always see an awful face that looks at me in a dreadful way, 18 so that I'm frightened."

Perhaps this might offer a quick means of getting to the heart of the 19 matter.

"Do you recognize the face? I mean, is it a face that you've really 20 seen some time?"

"No." 21

"Do you know what your attacks come from?" 22

"No." 23

"When did you first have them?" 24

"Two years ago, while I was still living on the other mountain with 25 my aunt. (She used to run a refuge hut there, and we moved here eighteen months ago.) But they keep on happening."

Was I to make an attempt at an analysis? I could not venture to 26 transplant hypnosis to these altitudes, but perhaps I might succeed with a simple talk. I should have to try a lucky guess. I had found often enough that in girls anxiety was a consequence of the horror by which a virginal mind is overcome when it is faced for the first time with the world of sexuality.[1]

So I said: "If you don't know, I'll tell you how *I* think you got your 27 attacks. At that time, two years ago, you must have seen or heard something that very much embarrassed you, and that you'd much rather not have seen."

"Heavens, yes!" she replied, "that was when I caught my uncle with 28 the girl, with Franziska, my cousin."

"What's this story about a girl? Won't you tell me all about it?" 29

"You can say *anything* to a doctor, I suppose. Well, at that time, you 30 know, my uncle—the husband of the aunt you've seen here—kept the inn on the ————kogel.[2] Now they're divorced, and it's my fault they were divorced, because it was through me that it came out that he was carrying on with Franziska."

"And how did you discover it?" 31

"This way. One day two years ago some gentlemen had climbed the 32 mountain and asked for something to eat. My aunt wasn't at home, and Franziska, who always did the cooking, was nowhere to be found. And my

---

[1] I will quote here the case in which I first recognized this causal connection. I was treating a young married woman who was suffering from a complicated neurosis and, once again [cf. p. 150 *n.*], was unwilling to admit that her illness arose from her married life. She objected that while she was still a girl she had had attacks of anxiety, ending in fainting fits. I remained firm. When we had come to know each other better she suddenly said to me one day: "I'll tell you now how I came by my attacks of anxiety when I was a girl. At that time I used to sleep in a room next to my parents'; the door was left open and a night-light used to burn on the table. So more than once I saw my father get into bed with my mother and heard sounds that greatly excited me. It was then that my attacks came on."—[Two cases of this kind are mentioned by Freud in a letter to Fliess of May 30, 1893 (Freud, 1950*a*, Letter 12). Cf. also Section II of the first paper on anxiety neurosis (1895*b*).]

[2] [The name of the "other" mountain.]

uncle was not to be found either. We looked everywhere, and at last Alois, the little boy, my cousin, said: 'Why, Franziska must be in Father's room!' And we both laughed; but we weren't thinking anything bad. Then we went to my uncle's room but found it locked. That seemed strange to me. Then Alois said: 'There's a window in the passage where you can look into the room.' We went into the passage; but Alois wouldn't go to the window and said he was afraid. So I said: 'You silly boy! I'll go. I'm not a bit afraid.' And I had nothing bad in my mind. I looked in. The room was rather dark, but I saw my uncle and Franziska; he was lying on her."

"Well?" 33

"I came away from the window at once, and leant up against the wall 34 and couldn't get my breath—just what happens to me since. Everything went blank, my eyelids were forced together and there was a hammering and buzzing in my head."

"Did you tell your aunt that very same day?" 35

"Oh no, I said nothing." 36

"Then why were you so frightened when you found them together? 37 Did you understand it? Did you know what was going on?"

"Oh no. I didn't understand anything at that time. I was only sixteen. 38 I don't know what I was frightened about."

"Fräulein Katharina, if you could remember now what was happen- 39 ing in you at that time, when you had your first attack, what you thought about it—it would help you."

"Yes, if I could. But I was so frightened that I've forgotten every- 40 thing."

(Translated into the terminology of our "Preliminary Communica- 41 tion" this means: "The affect itself created a hypnoid state, whose products were then cut off from associative connection with the ego-conscious- ness.")

"Tell me, Fräulein. Can it be that the head that you always see when 42 you lose your breath is Franziska's head, as you saw it then?"

"Oh no, she didn't look so awful. Besides, it's a man's head." 43

"Or perhaps your uncle's?" 44

"I didn't see his face as clearly as that. It was too dark in the room. 45 And why should he have been making such a dreadful face just then?"

"You're quite right." 46

(The road suddenly seemed blocked. Perhaps something might turn 47 up in the rest of her story.)

"And what happened then?" 48

"Well, those two must have heard a noise, because they came out 49 soon afterwards. I felt very bad the whole time. I always kept thinking about it. Then two days later it was a Sunday and there was a great deal to do and I worked all day long. And on the Monday morning I felt giddy again and was sick, and I stopped in bed and was sick without stopping for three days."

We [Breuer and I] had often compared the symptomatology of hys- 50 teria with a pictographic script which has become intelligible after the discovery of a few bilingual inscriptions. In that alphabet being sick means disgust. So I said: "If you were sick three days later, I believe that means that when you looked into the room you felt disgusted."

"Yes, I'm sure I felt disgusted," she said reflectively, "but disgusted 51 at what?"

"Perhaps you saw something naked? What sort of state were they 52 in?"

"It was too dark to see anything; besides they both of them had their 53 clothes on. Oh, if only I knew what it was I felt disgusted at!"

I had no idea either. But I told her to go on and tell me whatever 54 occurred to her, in the confident expectation that she would think of precisely what I needed to explain the case.

Well, she went on to describe how at last she reported her discovery 55 to her aunt, who found that she was changed and suspected her of concealing some secret. There followed some very disagreeable scenes between her uncle and aunt, in the course of which the children came to hear a number of things which opened their eyes in many ways and which it would have been better for them not to have heard. At last her aunt decided to move with her children and niece and take over the present inn, leaving her uncle alone with Franziska, who had meanwhile become pregnant. After this, however, to my astonishment she dropped these threads and began to tell me two sets of older stories, which went back two or three years earlier than the traumatic moment. The first set related to occasions on which the same uncle had made sexual advances to her herself, when she was only fourteen years old. She described how she had once gone with him on an expedition down into the valley in the winter and had spent the night in the inn there. He sat in the bar drinking and playing cards, but she felt sleepy and went up to bed early in the room they were to share on the upper floor. She was not quite asleep when he came up; then she fell asleep again and woke up suddenly "feeling his body" in the bed. She jumped up and remonstrated with him: "What are you up to, Uncle? Why don't you stay in your own bed?" He tried to pacify her: "Go on, you silly girl, keep still. You don't know how nice it is."—"I don't like your 'nice' things; you don't even let one sleep in peace." She remained standing by the door, ready to take refuge outside in the passage, till at last he gave up and went to sleep himself. Then she went back to her own bed and slept till morning. From the way in which she reported having defended herself it seems to follow that she did not clearly recognize the attack as a sexual one. When I asked her if she knew what he was trying to do to her, she replied: "Not at the time." It had become clear to her much later on, she said; she had resisted because it was unpleasant to be disturbed in one's sleep and "because it wasn't nice."

I have been obliged to relate this in detail, because of its great 56 importance for understanding everything that followed.—She went on to tell me of yet other experiences of somewhat later date: how she had once again had to defend herself against him in an inn when he was completely drunk, and similar stories. In answer to a question as to whether on these occasions she had felt anything resembling her later loss of breath, she answered with decision that she had every time felt the pressure on her eyes and chest, but with nothing like the strength that had characterized the scene of discovery.

Immediately she had finished this set of memories she began to tell 57 me a second set, which dealt with occasions on which she had noticed something between her uncle and Franziska. Once the whole family had spent the night in their clothes in a hay loft and she was woken up suddenly by a noise; she thought she noticed that her uncle, who had been lying between her and Franziska, was turning away, and that Franziska was just lying down. Another time they were stopping the night at an inn at the village of N———; she and her uncle were in one room and Franziska in an adjoining one. She woke up suddenly in the night and saw a tall white figure by the door, on the point of turning the handle: "Goodness, is that you, Uncle? What are you doing at the door?"—"Keep quiet. I was only looking for something."—"But the way out's by the *other* door."—"I'd just made a mistake" . . . and so on.

I asked her if she had been suspicious at that time. "No, I didn't 58 think anything about it; I only just noticed it and thought no more about it." When I enquired whether she had been frightened on these occasions too, she replied that she thought so, but she was not so sure of it this time.

At the end of these two sets of memories she came to a stop. She was 59 like someone transformed. The sulky, unhappy face had grown lively, her eyes were bright, she was lightened and exalted. Meanwhile the understanding of her case had become clear to me. The later part of what she had told me, in an apparently aimless fashion, provided an admirable explanation of her behavior at the scene of the discovery. At that time she had carried about with her two sets of experiences which she remembered but did not understand, and from which she drew no inferences. When she caught sight of the couple in intercourse, she at once established a connection between the new impression and these two sets of recollections, she began to understand them and at the same time to fend them off. There then followed a short period of working-out, of "incubation," after which the symptoms of conversion set in, the vomiting as a substitute for moral and physical disgust. This solved the riddle. She had not been disgusted by the sight of the two people but by the memory which that sight had stirred up in her. And, taking everything into account, this could only be the memory of the attempt on her at night when she had "felt her uncle's body."

So when she had finished her confession I said to her: "I know now 60 what it was you thought when you looked into the room. You thought: 'Now he's doing with her what he wanted to do with me that night and those other times.' That was what you were disgusted at, because you remembered the feeling when you woke up in the night and felt his body."

"It may well be," she replied, "that that was what I was disgusted at 61 and that that was what I thought."

"Tell me just one thing more. You're a grown-up girl now and know 62 all sorts of things . . ."

"Yes, now I am." 63

"Tell me just one thing. What part of his body was it that you felt that 64 night?"

But she gave me no more definite answer. She smiled in an embar- 65 rassed way, as though she had been found out, like someone who is obliged to admit that a fundamental position has been reached where there is not much more to be said. I could imagine what the tactile sensation was which she had later learnt to interpret. Her facial expression seemed to me to be saying that she supposed that I was right in my conjecture. But I could not penetrate further, and in any case I owed her a debt of gratitude for having made it so much easier for me to talk to her than to the prudish ladies of my city practice, who regard whatever is natural as shameful.

Thus the case was cleared up.—But stop a moment! What about the 66 recurrent hallucination of the head, which appeared during her attacks and struck terror into her? Where did it come from? I proceeded to ask her about it, and, as though *her* knowledge, too, had been extended by our conversation, she promptly replied: "Yes, I know now. The head is my uncle's head—I recognize it now—but not from *that* time. Later, when all the disputes had broken out, my uncle gave way to a senseless rage against me. He kept saying that it was all my fault: if I hadn't chattered, it would never have come to a divorce. He kept threatening he would do some-thing to me; and if he caught sight of me at a distance his face would get distorted with rage and he would make for me with his hand raised. I always ran away from him, and always felt terrified that he would catch me some time unawares. The face I always see now is his face when he was in a rage."

This information reminded me that her first hysterical symptom, the 67 vomiting, had passed away; the anxiety attack remained and acquired a fresh content. Accordingly, what we were dealing with was a hysteria which had to a considerable extent been abreacted. And in fact she had reported her discovery to her aunt soon after it happened.

"Did you tell your aunt the other stories—about his making advances 68 to you?"

"Yes. Not at once, but later on, when there was already talk of a 69 divorce. My aunt said: 'We'll keep that in reserve. If he causes trouble in the Court, we'll say that too.'"

I can well understand that it should have been precisely this last 70 period—when there were more and more agitating scenes in the house and when her own state ceased to interest her aunt, who was entirely occupied with the dispute—that it should have been this period of accumulation and retention that left her the legacy of the mnemic symbol [of the hallucinated face].

I hope this girl, whose sexual sensibility had been injured at such an 71 early age, derived some benefit from our conversation. I have not seen her since.

Discussion

If someone were to assert that the present case history is not so much an 72 analyzed case of hysteria as a case solved by guessing, I should have nothing to say against him. It is true that the patient agreed that what I interpolated into her story was probably true; but she was not in a position to recognize it as something she had experienced. I believe it would have required hypnosis to bring that about. Assuming that my guesses were correct, I will now attempt to fit the case into the schematic picture of an "acquired" hysteria on the lines suggested by Case 3. It seems plausible, then, to compare the two sets of erotic experiences with "traumatic" moments and the scene of discovering the couple with an "auxiliary" moment. The similarity lies in the fact that in the former experiences an element of consciousness was created which was excluded from the thought-activity of the ego and remained, as it were, in storage, while in the latter scene a new impression forcibly brought about an associative connection between this separated group and the ego. On the other hand there are dissimilarities which cannot be overlooked. The cause of the isolation was not, as in Case 3, an act of will on the part of the ego but *ignorance* on the part of the ego, which was not yet capable of coping with sexual experiences. In this respect the case of Katharina is typical. In every analysis of a case of hysteria based on sexual traumas we find that impressions from the pre-sexual period which produced no effect on the child attain traumatic power at a later date as memories, when the girl or married woman has acquired an understanding of sexual life. The splitting-off of psychical groups may be said to be a normal process in adolescent development; and it is easy to see that their later reception into the ego affords frequent opportunities for psychical disturbances. Moreover, I should like at this point to express a doubt as to whether a splitting of consciousness due to ignorance is really different from one due to conscious rejection, and whether even adolescents do not possess sexual knowledge far oftener than is supposed or than they themselves believe.

A further distinction in the psychical mechanism of this case lies in 73 the fact that the scene of discovery, which we have described as "auxiliary," deserves equally to be called "traumatic." It was operative on account of its own content and not merely as something that revived previous traumatic experiences. It combined the characteristics of an "auxiliary" and a "traumatic" moment. There seems no reason, however, why this coincidence should lead us to abandon a conceptual separation which in other cases corresponds also to a separation in time. Another peculiarity of Katharina's case, which, incidentally, has long been familiar to us, is seen in the circumstance that the conversion, the production of the hysterical phenomena, did not occur immediately after the trauma but after an interval of incubation. Charcot liked to describe this interval as the "period of psychical working out" [*élaboration*].

The anxiety from which Katharina suffered in her attacks was a 74 hysterical one; that is, it was a reproduction of the anxiety which had appeared in connection with each of the sexual traumas. I shall not here comment on the fact which I have found regularly present in a very large number of cases—namely that a mere suspicion of sexual relations calls up the affect of anxiety in virginal individuals.[1]

Questions

Rereading and Independent Analysis

1. Underline or put brackets around those parts of Freud's "story" about Katharina that contain only his reactions and responses to her approach to him and their conversations. Then reread only these sections of this case-study report. How does Freud reveal his own personality in his shaping of her story? Does this revelation decrease his trustworthiness? What vision of Freud do you get from the report?

2. Reread Freud's "Discussion" of this case, noting the specific parts of the case history that are referred to directly and indirectly. Are the points he stresses in the "Discussion" clear in the first part of this study, where they make up the narrative of the case? How does your attention to them change after reading the "Discussion"?

Suggested Discussion and Group Activities

1. There are two "stories" in this case history: the narrative of Katharina's experience and the narrative of Freud's encounter with Katharina. What familiar fictional techniques does Freud introduce into these narrations? In what ways is this case study like a detective story? What is the purpose, for instance, of suspense about the explanation of the face Katharina sees? What is the purpose of the last footnote, added in 1924?

2. According to data from current therapists and analysts, clients now infrequently exhibit symptoms of "hysterical conversion" like Katharina's anxiety attacks or other physical symptoms such as unexplained

---

[1] (*Footnote added* 1924:) I venture after the lapse of so many years to lift the veil of discretion and reveal the fact that Katharina was not the niece but the daughter of the landlady. The girl fell ill, therefore, as a result of sexual attempts on the part of her own father. Distortions like the one which I introduced in the present instance should be altogether avoided in reporting a case history. From the point of view of understanding the case, a distortion of this kind is not, of course, a matter of such indifference as would be shifting the scene from one mountain to another.

paralysis or blindness. Using the theories Freud himself suggested, how would you explain this change? Is it possible that Freud's work could have cured a general hysteria? How?

3. In groups, plan a similar case study—a narrative of a patient's encounter with a doctor or of some other professional relationship that helped an individual. Outline the specific information you would have to include to make the individual case vivid while making it useful for other doctors or professionals.

Writing Suggestions

Response

1. Write for yourself or someone else a brief narration of an actual event in which you show how a memory was needed to explain something that would otherwise have seemed strange. You need not delve into sensitive problems in this account, but try to make it clear that you needed a missing connection to unravel a mysterious cause.

2. How do you react to Freud's views of human feelings and actions? Write a few paragraphs in which you apply these views to yourself. Do they make you uncomfortable? Can you determine why?

Analysis

Write an essay in which you analyze Freud's strategies in this case study. Explain how his techniques were designed to appeal to a dubious, if not hostile, reader. Show how he establishes his believability by demonstrating precise observation, emphasizing his objectivity, and showing his unwillingness to draw conclusions that are based on anything but the evidence he has gathered. Show how Freud's choice of fictional, mystery-story techniques was suitable for the work he was doing at the time.

Finding a Purpose

1. Imagine that you are one of the earliest reviewers of *Studies in Hysteria* and that you have had very negative reactions to the book. Write a review for publication in one of your favorite magazines. Describe the book's contents, using "Katharina" as an example, and show how its fictional characteristics should warn readers away from this new and dangerous approach to human problems. (See Himmelfarb's "A History of the New History," above, as a model for writing reviews.)

2. Freud's work exemplifies a common method in social scientific research, the case study. Choose a specific behavior (an action or response) that you observe in yourself and in others. (Do not choose one that strikes you as neurotic but an ordinary, harmless one.) Observe this behavior over a period of time, taking notes about the setting where it occurs, motives for it, results of this action, and any variations you notice.

After you gather data, write a report to share your observations with others interested in this behavior. Take care to establish your reliability as an observer and your lack of a personal motive for drawing your conclusions. You may wish to use Freud's case study of Katharina as a model or Judith M. Shapiro's report on genetic research, "Unlocking the Genetic Mystery."

 # From *Male and Female*
Margaret Mead

Margaret Mead's energy and willingness to explore cultural settings in person made her one of the foremost scholars in the field of anthropology. Mead (1901–1978) spent her childhood in Philadelphia and studied anthropology at Barnard College in New York. She wrote 25 books, including *Coming of Age in Samoa* (1928), a study based on observations from field work in Samoa, which she did to obtain her Ph.D. Some of her other books are *Male and Female* (1949), *A Way of Seeing* (1970), and *Blackberry Winter: My Early Years* (1972). Mead also became an influential speaker on social issues, arguing against pollution, racism, sexual stereotypes, and environmental destruction.

Mead's life was as fluid and changing as her diverse scholarly interests. She refused to adopt stereotypical roles as a woman, wife, or mother, and raised her children while working as a scholar and public figure at a time when this combination was very unusual. Her anthropological methods have recently become controversial within the field, but her ground-breaking studies of South Sea Islanders remain influential models for reporting observations of the actual patterns of domestic life.

This selection, from *Male and Female,* looks at American domestic life as an anthropologist would look, describing its distinctive character. In it, Mead distinguishes American from tribal family patterns. As you read, look for places where Mead's values about family life appear to shape her attitudes toward her observations. This essay is an example of a five-paragraph treatment, with the author using comparisons and contrasts to make her points. Notice how she controls the information she reports and explains her assessment of it in a clearly organized presentation.

In the United States the striking characteristic is that each set of parents 1 is different from each other set, that no two have exactly the same memories, that no two families could be placed side by side and it could be said: "Yes, these four parents ate the same food, played the same games, heard the same lullabies, were scared by the same bogeys, taught that the same words were taboo, given the same picture of what they would be as men and women, made ready to hand on unimpaired the tradition they received, whole, unravelled, unfaded, from their parents."

Every home is different from every other home, every marriage, 2 even within the same class, in the same clique, contains contrasts between the partners as superficially striking as the difference between one New

Guinea tribe and another. "In our family we never locked the bathroom door." "In our family you never entered another person's room without knocking." "Mother always asked to see our letters, even after we were grown." "The smallest scrap of paper on which one had written something was returned unread." "We were never allowed to mention our legs." "Father said that 'sweat' was a good deal honester word than 'perspiration,' but to be careful not to say it when we went to Aunt Alice's." "Mother said my hands would get rough if I climbed trees." "Mother said girls ought to stretch their legs and get some exercise while they were young." Side by side, next-door neighbours, children of first cousins, sometimes children of sisters or brothers, the ways of each household diverge, one family bringing up the children to prudery, privacy, and strongly marked sex roles, another to an open give-and-take that makes the girls seem tomboys. Then again comes marriage between the children with the different upbringings, and again the clash, the lack of timing, the lack of movement in step, of the new set of parents. Every home is different from every other home; no two parents, even though they were fed their cereal from silver porringers of the same design, were fed it in quite the same way. The gestures of the feeding hands, whether of mother, grandmother, Irish cook, English nurse, Negro mammy, country-bred hired girl, are no longer the assured, the highly patterned gestures of the member of a homogeneous society. The recently come foreigner's hand is unsure as it handles unfamiliar things and tries to thrust a spoon into the mouth of a child who acts and speaks strangely; the old American's hand bears marks of such uncertainties in former generations, and may tremble or clench anew over some recent contact with some newly arrived and little-understood stranger.

But just because every home is different from every other home, 3 because no husband and wife can move effortlessly in step to the same remembered cradle-songs, so also is every home alike. The anthropologist who has studied a New Guinea tribe can often predict down to the smallest detail what will go on in each family if there is a quarrel, what will be said when there is a reconciliation, who will make it, with what words and what gestures. No anthropologist can ever hope to do the same thing for the United States. What the quarrel will be, who will make up and how, will differ in every home; what the highest moment between parents and child will be will differ. But the form, the kind of quarrel, the kind of reconciliation, the kind of love, the kind of misunderstandings, will be alike in their very difference. In one home the husband will indicate his importunate desire by bringing flowers, in another by kicking the cat playfully as he enters, in a third by making a fuss over the baby, in a fourth by getting very busy over the radio, while the wife may indicate her acceptance or rejection of his erotic expectation by putting on more lipstick or by rubbing off the lip-stick she has on, by getting very busy tidying up the room or by sinking in a soft dream into the other overstuffed chair, playing idly with her baby's curly hair. There is no pattern, no simple word or gesture that has been repeated by all husbands in the presence of all the small children who are to be future husbands, and all the small girls who are to be wives, so that when they grow up they will be letter-perfect in a ballet of approach or retreat.

In America the language of each home is different, there is a code 4 in each family that no one else knows. And that is the essential likeness, the essential regularity, among all these apparent differences. For in each American marriage there is a special code, developed from the individual pasts of the two partners, put together out of the accidents of honeymoon and parents-in-law, finally beaten into a language that each understands imperfectly. For here is another regularity. When a code, a language, is shared by every one in the village, spoken by the gracious and the grim, by the flexible-tongued and the stubborn, by the musical voice and the halting and stammering voice, the language becomes beautifully precise, each sound sharply and perfectly differentiated from each other sound. The new-born baby, first babbling happily through his whole possible range of lovely and unlovely noise, listens, and narrows his range. Where he once babbled a hundred nuances of sound, he limits himself to a bare half-dozen, and practices against the perfection, the sureness, of his elders. Later, he too, however stumbling his tongue or poor his ear, will speak the language of his people so that all can understand him. The perfected model made by the lips and tongues of many different sorts of people speaking the same words holds the speech of each new-comer clear and sharp enough for communication. And as with speech, so with gesture, so with the timing of initiative, of response, of command and obedience. The toddler falls in step with the multitude around him and cannot fail to learn his part.

But in a culture like modern America, the child does not see any such 5 harmonious, repetitive behaviour. All men do not cross their legs with the same assured masculinity, or squat on wooden stools to protect themselves from a rear-guard attack. All women do not walk with little mincing steps, or sit and lie with thighs drawn close together, even in sleep. The behavior of each American is itself a composite, an imperfectly realized version, of the behavior of others who in turn had, not a single model—expressed in many voices and many ways, but still a single model—but a hundred models, each different, each an individually developed style, lacking the authenticity, the precision, of a group style. The hand held out in greeting, to still a tear, or to help up a strange child that has stumbled, is not sure that it will be taken, or if taken, taken in the sense in which it is offered. Where patterns of courtship are clear, a girl knows the outcome if she smiles, or laughs, casts down her eyes, or merely walks softly by a group of harvesting youths cradling a red ear of corn in her arms. But in America, the same smile may evoke a casual answering grin, embarrassed averted eyes, an unwelcome advance, or may even mean being followed home along a deserted street, not because each boy who answers feels differently about the girl, but because each understands differently the cue that she gives.

Questions

Rereading and Independent Analysis

1. This excerpt is a model for a five-paragraph essay developed by comparison and contrast. Make an outline of it, copying the thesis sentence and showing how the essay systematically distinguishes between American ("A") and tribal ("B") family codes.

2. Choose one of the middle three paragraphs in this selection and analyze its method of development. Does it begin with a topic sentence? Is it divided according to subtopics? Do the sentences limit and specify the topic, exemplify it, or restate it? Describe how the paragraph you have chosen is a self-contained unit of composition. How does it support Mead's central point?

Suggested Discussion and Group Activities

1. What is Mead's thesis in this excerpt? How is it relevant to your family? How does it characterize American life outside the family and distinguish the United States from other countries? How would you generalize Mead's thesis to describe the American "character"?

2. In groups or in pairs, choose a particular behavior that operates according to "codes"—for instance, showing respect for someone, disagreeing, or expressing friendship. Then test Mead's thesis about Americans by making notes on the ways that individual members of your group communicate their own ideas about these codes. Note your personal responses to these signals. If you wish, expand this limited "field work" by interviewing others outside your class.

Writing Suggestions

Response

Recall a personal experience in which you misunderstood a person or were misunderstood yourself. Write a few paragraphs in your journal about this experience. Did it result from your having an expressive code that differed from the one of the person or group who misunderstood you? Can you generalize about this experience in a brief statement?

Analysis

1. Pretend briefly to be an anthropologist preparing a report on your family that verifies or disputes Mead's view of American family codes. Write a five-paragraph essay that imitates hers. Gather information by making notes about specific family interactions. Then show how the signals and codes of your parents are different depending on particular situations, and how they affect all of the family's members.

2. On the basis of the field work you and your classmates conducted (Question 2, "Discussion"), write an essay in which you show how your class is a microcosm of American differences. Your purpose is to explain American groups like yours to a class of students in another country. Show that your class is very diverse, explaining how it includes people with differing family communication patterns that help them understand what simple gestures and words mean.

First make an outline as a class, then divide work on sections of the report among groups. Explain in the last section of this report how it is that even with such diversity, members of your class and other similar groups can get along well, do business with one another, and share the same government. Is there one "code" that all share?

 # Young Observers
Robert Coles

Robert Coles (b. 1929) is a pediatrician and professor of psychiatry at Harvard Medical School. By virtue of his ability to write for both expert and popular audiences, he has greatly influenced social reform in recent decades. His five-volume *Children in Crisis* (1967–1978), a study of the effects of poverty and family problems on the young, won the Pulitzer Prize. Coles has also written about literature in *William Carlos Williams: The Knack of Survival in America* (1975), *Walker Percy: An American Search* (1978), and *Flannery O'Connor's South* (1980).

The selection included here is from *Privileged Ones: The Well-Off and the Rich in America* (1977), which is the fifth volume of his *Children in Crisis*. It tells about changes in the lives of Helen and Geoff, two privileged children who were interviewed as they grew up. In it, Coles clearly demonstrates the difference between "telling" and "showing" in writing. He allows Helen to speak for herself within the loose threads of his interpretations. Like all social scientists, Coles believes that the words and actions of individuals and groups are rich sources of data that show us the designs and patterns in our lives. You may wish to compare this report to Coles's interview with the Eskimo woman in "The Madness of Dark" (the first selection in this book).

Children like Helen play right in the heart of Boston and talk about their 1 houses, their yards, even their streets. The houses are town houses, the yards are small, though sometimes quite lovely, with potted plants everywhere, or a small patch of land quite nicely used to support flowers. There are slate terraces, lights that can banish the dark completely, and outdoor furniture that is as handsome as it is practical. The streets sometimes are really small alleys; or a group of houses may make up a "square" or a "court," or something called a "landing." That is to say, there is privacy amid the urban press of traffic and crowds.

Not that Helen is a stranger to the country; her parents own what they call a "country house," as a matter of fact. It is a "farm" on Martha's Vineyard and is near the ocean. But the child doesn't want to leave the city when her parents do, on weekends. Often her parents have asked her to draw a picture of their country home, but Helen has been reluctant. When she obliged, at the age of nine, her parents were dismayed. How could an artist able to evoke city life so carefully and sympathetically fail to be similarly responsive to a familiar and pleasant rural setting? Helen was at the time able to answer that question: "I don't want to go away from home. This is my home. There's only one reason I like to go to our country house—because Daddy is there. All week we don't see much of him. Sometimes I'm lucky if I see him for five minutes in the morning, before I go to school. There are days when he's away. There are other days when he's been at a meeting the night before, and he just can't get up to say hello. Then when I come home, he's at work. And a lot of times he doesn't get home before we go to bed. I miss him. So does my brother, Geoff. He says he wishes Daddy would lose his job, then we'd have him here at home. Geoff says he even *prays* that Daddy will lose his job. Geoff is only seven, and he doesn't realize that if Daddy loses his job, we might be in trouble, because we wouldn't have all the money we do now. Then we might have to sell that country house—but Daddy would at least be home more. Maybe he could get a new job right away, and it would be a better one.

"I once had a bad dream in the middle of the night. I think I was talking in my sleep, and Mommy overheard me. She was still awake. When I woke up, she was standing beside the bed, and she wanted to know if I was okay. I said yes. She asked me what I'd been dreaming about. I remembered; I told her it was about Daddy, and he was in the house we have in the country, and he had to get out, to go back to Boston, but the door wouldn't open. So he climbed out through a window, and then he got in the car, and he drove off; but he left us behind, and we didn't know how to get back to Boston, and we all started crying, even Mommy. She told me I was being silly to have a dream like that; and then I went back to sleep. The trouble with our country home is that you're away from everyone. We've gone there on some weekends when Daddy is in Texas, on some business trip, and then we have the worst time ever, because Mommy is unhappy when Daddy is away. Geoff starts crying and says that he's afraid Daddy may never get back, and then we couldn't get away from here, because he's the one who knows how to close up the house before we leave. But I tell Geoff not to worry, because Mommy knows how to close up the house, too."

Her father is an important young executive in a real estate firm that develops land sites for commercial buyers and also arranges for the construction of all sorts of buildings as well as the rental of space in them once they are completed. He went to Grinnell College, in Iowa, came East to the Harvard Business School, and, as Helen puts it, "fell in love with Boston." He has been on the rise ever since he graduated from the business school. He worked for three other companies before he got a chance to return to Boston: first Procter & Gamble in Cincinnati, then a real estate company in Houston, and finally a textile company in North Carolina. He grabbed the opportunity to return to "real estate development," and swore to his wife that they would not move again, having done so four times in six years of marriage. He has poured his heart and soul into his work since then, and will undoubtedly be able to keep his promise. He has become one of the firm's most successful executives—a planner, a salesman, a coordinator of projects, a shrewd observer of the entire nation's business climate, and a man very much liked by the firm's president.

When he does have time to be with his children, they are grateful 5 and happy—though they ask him, right off, how long it will be until he leaves. They also ask him when they will *next* see him. His wife often tries to prevent those questions, but unsuccessfully. She has known her husband since they were both in the same classroom in high school and has built her life around him and his work as well as her two children. Her older child was able, at nine, to indicate how the family's life works: "My mother keeps Daddy steady. He says so. She became a nurse before they got married, and he says it's a good thing she did. He'll come home late, and he has a headache or a stomachache, and she knows what medicine to give him. If they go out together, she'll go up to him and pinch him on the arm, and that means he's been drinking too much, and he should stop, unless he wants to get sick. Then he usually stops; but sometimes he doesn't, and there's trouble the next morning. Daddy will be sick. He has to watch out, or he'll drink more and more, and then he'll be in bad trouble.

"He's the one who decides whether we'll go to the country or 6 whether we'll stay home because he and Mommy have to go to a party. Sometimes he tells her he's sick in his stomach and he has a bad headache. But when she tells him she'll call up and explain to the people, he says no, it's important to go out. I wish some weekend we could just stay here and they wouldn't go out, and we could visit the Aquarium. I've never been there with my parents. I came home from school one afternoon and asked Mommy if we could go there with her and Daddy, and she said yes, but it depends on what Daddy has to do. We haven't gone yet. When Daddy comes home, we have to keep quiet. Mommy makes sure of that. She tells us that if we don't help out, Daddy will be upset, and he works very hard. She says that later, when we're older, Daddy will be with us a lot, and we can look forward to the day. But by that time Geoff and I may be all grown up!"

If she had a wish, with respect to her future, what would it be? What 7 about her present life—how pleased is she with it, and what about it would she want different? She is a talkative and speculative child, at times annoyingly so. Her father does not like her questions, or her social and political

observations. Her mother may enjoy them, but she also has been embarrassed by what she has heard. She has been described by her husband as
"the source" of Helen's inspiration. But Helen is quite capable of developing her own ideas, sharing them with her brother Geoff, and surprising
both parents by the vivid originality (and emotional power) of her mind.
Her teachers, too, consider Helen quite bright and perceptive. At the age
of ten she wrote a composition which her teacher found almost unbearably personal, and so did not post on the bulletin board, though she ordinarily did display especially worthwhile writing. The title was "My Parents."
It went as follows: "My Daddy is going to be president of his company one
of these days. I heard him tell my mother that. He said he had to work day
and night, but in the end it would be worth it. My mother is not so sure.
My brother Geoff and I are not so sure, either. My brother and I wish our
father could be home with us, and not at the office or traveling all day and
half the night. My mother wants him to keep his job, but she is afraid he
could get sick. My grandfather has a farm, and many are the days when
Geoff and I say that it's too bad that Daddy doesn't own a farm, and then
we'd see him a lot more than we do. But we love our house here in Boston,
and it is because Daddy has such a good job that we can have all the toys
and live where we do. You can't have everything. Our mother tells us that.
I know what she means."

Helen has some ideas about her future. She wants to marry a man 8
who already has a lot of money. Such a person, she is sure, will not have
to work as hard as her father does. Such a person, she believes, would be
able to spend long hours at home. Perhaps he would work in the Aquarium
or the Science Museum in Boston; or in its Museum of Fine Arts. She goes
to those places often with friends, and notices not only fish, or wonderfully
intricate machinery, or paintings, but grown-up men who work. She is not
sure about the kind of work her future husband might do in one of those
places; perhaps be the director—"the one who makes the decisions." She
has heard her father talk about "decisions," about how hard they sometimes are to make. She hopes her husband will have an easier job of
making decisions; but she is not about to consign him to the gendarmes,
the sanitation department, or the ranks of salespeople. Her brother has
suggested that standing guard in a museum, or selling things in a museum
store, or operating one of the rather elaborate and inviting floor waxing
and polishing machines would be acceptable jobs for himself in the future.
Why not for his sister's husband, too?

Helen refuses to go along with those recommendations. She keeps 9
reminding her brother that they are "fairly rich," and that it would be
"very bad" to live a relatively "poor" life. What is that kind of life like?
She has a few ideas on the subject: "We wouldn't be able to go to our
school. We'd be in a public school. The black kids and the white kids would
fight. And we wouldn't have very good teachers. And we wouldn't live on
this nice street. And we wouldn't have our friends. And we wouldn't be

able to take trips. It wouldn't be a very fun life. Daddy may be away a lot, but he's given us a fun life. Our mother keeps telling Geoff and me that we have to be grateful for the success Daddy has become."

Helen is grateful. She is also compassionate toward others whose 10 parents have been less successful. She has helped her mother wrap presents to be sent to churches in the city's ghetto. She has received Girl Scouts at her home, and gone to their homes—in the ghetto. Each time—a matter of a few hours—she has been eager and outgoing, quite anxious to get along with the black girl. She has told her parents often that she likes black children, that she cannot understand why others of her age who are white don't feel the same way. At ten she drew a picture of her "favorite black girl," who was almost exactly, to the day, Helen's age. The black girl is shown sitting on the steps of the six-family wooden house where she lives. The house is located on a street that once was fairly pleasant but now has deteriorated considerably. The particular building Helen drew was in fact grayish green, but Helen made it brown. The front stairs were dangerous to use, and appear so in the picture. The girl sits on them, small in size, her head tilted forward. Her arms are short, her feet thin. She is not given a dress. The windows are not drawn as they appear in life, but are given an irregular, haphazard arrangement. To the side of the building we see some nondescript bodies of youths (not identified by name) who are huddled together. They are using drugs, the artist says.

Helen has seen such young people several times "passing a cigarette 11 around," and been told by her host Girl Scout what was happening. When she told her parents, on return home, what she had witnessed, they were surprised and dismayed. They were also worried. Her father has several city planners for friends, has been enthusiastically in favor of various urban renewal projects, and has told his children that he wished that "a few blacks" lived in their neighborhood. But stories of drug use made the father change his mind: "One day Daddy will like the black people, and he'll tell us how he'd like to help them, and sometimes he does. But another day will come when he's changed his mind. Then he's all against them. He says it'll soon be so bad in the city, because of the black people, that we'll have to go live in our country home, or in one of the tall apartment houses that Daddy's company owns; they have police guarding them all the time, and they have to, because if they didn't, everyone would be robbed. We have an alarm system, and if someone tries to break in, the police will come right away. I think they hear the alarm, or a detective does. I don't know where he is. He might be sitting in an office someplace. There are a lot of black kids around who steal. They use drugs, and they need money to buy the drugs. One girl I know, she's black, and she came here for an afternoon. She told me all about the bad people she knew. She says Geoff and I are lucky. She told us why. Geoff said he felt real sorry for her. I felt sorry for her, too. But she's pretty tough. She says she can take care of herself. She says she wouldn't want to be anyone else but who she is. That's what she told me when we were playing with my dolls. She said she didn't like my dolls. She said my room had too much stuff in it, and if she had all that stuff, she'd want to throw it out.

"I didn't like her too much. She may be poor, but she's not so nice. 12 The minister tells us that poor people are very good, and we should be nice to them; and they told us that at the Scout meetings. But Daddy says it's the poor who make a lot of trouble in the city, and that girl might turn out to be a robber one day. She kept on picking up things in my room, and putting them down again. I thought to myself that she should stop that, but I didn't dare say anything to her.

"She said she was tough, and I believed her. She *was* tough! Maybe 13 she stole some of my things. I have a lot of dolls, and things for my dollhouses, and she could have taken something and I might not even miss it. A black boy came here, to visit my brother, and he took three of Geoff's Corgi cars, we're pretty sure, but we can't prove it, and we don't want to cause any trouble for the kid. He's the only black boy in Geoff's class. He's poor, but the school gave him a scholarship. We've got five or six black kids in our school. Our parents say it's important to have some blacks going to school with you, but they should do good work. If they don't, then the teacher has to take a lot of time to help them, and she can't teach the other kids, and it's not fair."

She began to worry a lot, at the age of eleven, about what was fair 14 and what wasn't at all fair. She thought that her brother Geoff was being pushed too much—and at a distance or remove, no less—by her father. Geoff was expected to be at the top of his class and a successful athlete and popular. He was none of those three; he was, at nine, nearly ten, an average student, average at sports, neither a leader nor a popular companion. He was, in fact, a rather shy boy, interested in guinea pigs (of which he had four) and highways—he had many road maps—and airplanes, models of which he constructed endlessly then stored in a large walk-in closet. The boy also tended to pay attention to "current events," about which he felt inclined to talk during his social studies course. He knew a lot about Presidents, senators, governors. He liked geography, and could point out nations others of his age didn't know existed. His sister was also a companion; *they* had guinea pigs, looked at AAA maps, talked about various kinds of jet plane, watched the evening news, or looked at an enormous wall map of the world, located in Helen's room.

A month after her eleventh birthday Helen stared at that map and 15 wondered out loud about others her age, in America and abroad: "They tell us in school that we should give our pennies to UNICEF, and then a lot of kids won't go hungry. The next thing you know we're eating lunch, and there's so much food, and we all go get seconds, and sometimes we even go get thirds, and there are a lot of kids who say they're not going to tell their parents how much they ate, because they're getting fat and they're not supposed to eat so much. I told the teacher we should skip lunch, and the food should go to Africa, where millions of people are starving to death. My mother is trying to lose weight. My father is always trying, but he doesn't have the willpower, he says. They both tell Geoff and me that they wish they could eat as much as we do! I told my mother the other day, and so did Geoff, that it's not right for us to buy so much food and then throw a lot away. She said I was worrying too much about everyone in the world, and you can't do that. Geoff spoke up for me! He said: 'Why not?' Daddy told him not to talk like that to our mother. Then I said it—the same thing: 'Why not?' He told us both to go to our rooms for five minutes.

"When we came back the maid brought us our suppers again, but I 16 didn't want to eat anything. They made me finish some of the food on the plate. When the dessert came, I said I didn't want any. Then Mother said I had to eat it, because the maid would be offended; she made it. I said no, I wasn't hungry. Geoff said he wasn't hungry, either. Daddy lost his temper. He said we're spoiled brats. He said we talk back to him and Mommy, and we act as if we're a prince and princess, and entitled to get our way all the time. He said we'd better 'cut it out.' When he says those words, he's angry. He gave us a long lecture on how hard he worked, and it's all for us, but we don't say thank you, we just 'pick and choose.'

"He said that he never could eat the kind of supper we had that night 17 when he was a boy. He remembers saving up pennies to go buy an Oh Henry bar, or an ice cream cone. Once he dropped the candy bar while unwrapping it, and he picked it up and was going to eat it, anyway, but it was dirty, and his father took it away and threw it down a sewer, and told Daddy he'd learn to be more careful after that. Daddy said Geoff and I need some discipline, and if we don't watch out, we'll get so soft we'll never amount to anything. Then he decided to stop talking. Geoff and I ate the dessert, and when the maid came and cleared the table, and asked us how we liked what she'd made, we told her we liked it a lot. Then Geoff and I asked to be excused. When we went upstairs we looked at a *National Geographic* magazine, and there were some kids from India shown, and it said they didn't eat very much, and a lot of the kids there would die. I told Geoff I had a stomachache; and he said he had one, too. But we got better, and we went to bed, and the next day we went to our country house, and Daddy came with us, and we all had a good time."

When Helen was twelve she had slimmed down, was preoccupied 18 with the French language, which she had begun to study in earnest, and with France as a nation. She read books about its history, geography, culture. She had on the walls of her rooms pictures of Paris and of the rural landscape to the south. She listened a lot to records of spoken French and to French music. And she dreamed of going to France. She would do so upon turning thirteen—six weeks there with her mother and brother. They were joined by her father in Paris for the last week. That trip did it—the conversion of an interest into a love affair. Upon her return to America Helen became known to the French consulate in Boston, and she loved going to a patisserie not far from her home. She excelled in French, was the best at speaking as well as reading and writing the language. And, after reading an article or two in the newspapers about contemporary problems in the formerly French-dominated parts of Africa, she began to understand the nostalgia of the colonialists: "The French are so smart, and they must have helped the native people in Africa. When the French left, I read, there was trouble, and now there's starvation. If the French had only stayed, then the people there would be better off. I joked with my French teacher; I said I wouldn't mind if the United States became part of the French empire! I like our flag, but I like the tricolor better; and I like 'La Marseillaise' better than our 'Star-Spangled Banner.' In Africa the French tried to bring the tribes together, but then when the countries became independent there, the tribes started fighting with each other, and there's been trouble ever since. It's too bad."

She was no longer worried about the "trouble" hundreds of thou- 19 sands of utterly impoverished men, women, and children face daily; her worry was directed at the notion of "progress." When is it genuine, when a prelude to disaster? The result was lively talk at the table, especially at suppertime. Those talks encouraged Helen's parents, who saw her as a girl who was fast growing up and becoming responsible and thoughtful. Helen also spoke highly of her parents: "I used to think my father didn't care enough about us at home, but now I realize how hard he works, and it's all for us. He helps a lot of other people, too. Geoff says that when he grows up he doesn't want to work as hard as Daddy, but I hope Geoff will change his mind later on. That's what happened in the French empire. It wasn't 'progress' when the French left Africa. It was the beginning of a lot of trouble. My mother says I'm not being fair to the natives, because they don't have the education that the French have. But that's why the French should have stayed there, so they could keep educating the natives.

"If France still had its empire, I would try to go to Africa and teach 20 the natives. Maybe I could still go; but it wouldn't be as interesting now. According to our teacher, a lot of the African countries have very poor governments. And if you're white, you can get into a lot of trouble. My mother says there's a real problem they have, the natives: they'd like our help, but they don't always like us! That's not fair; a lot of white people just want to be generous, and they don't want to take anything away from the natives. Geoff and I argue a lot; he says that if he lived in Africa and was a native, he'd want to be the boss and not have to salute my French flag! I told him it didn't make any difference which flag the natives salute. Geoff says he wishes he could have been in the French Foreign Legion, and so do I, but there weren't any women allowed."

She wrote a story for her English class—responded eagerly to her 21 teacher's request that the imagination be used to the fullest. She told her readers about the French Foreign Legion, then had a woman cooking meals for Legionnaires, and finally, becoming their leader—after saving them all from ambush at the hands of some natives, whom she had spotted. Only in France, or among Frenchmen, was such an outcome possible, she insisted, at the end of her composition; after all, France is the nation of

Jeanne d'Arc. The teacher was pleased, praised the author highly—but with one reservation. The description of the natives was called "not quite fair, even for a story." The author was asked to discuss the matter further with the teacher, and did.

Helen remembered vividly, even months later, what went on: "We 22 had an argument. I told her the natives were always stealing, and the French had to watch them, and that was the job of the Legionnaires. She said I was being too critical of the natives. That's when I told her that I thought the French are smarter than the natives, and there's been a lot of trouble since the empire ended. She asked where I got my facts. I said from reading magazines and the newspaper. Then I told her to look at our school, and how the black kids aren't doing very well. There are three in our class, and they're all getting special help, and they get bad marks. (We see their papers; they even show their papers to us.) I guess I shouldn't have brought up the subject of our black kids, because the teacher got upset and told me she had another appointment.

"I left the room, and one of the black kids and her mother came in. 23 When I got home and told my mother, she said I should be careful about what I say outside the house. Mom told me a lot of people in the school are beginning to worry about the scholarship students. I said the scholarship students are all black. Mom said it's best to call them the scholarship students, and not the black students. I asked why there aren't any *white* scholarship students, and she said because we don't need any—since everyone is already white in our school. That's when I said maybe there shouldn't be *any* scholarship students anymore, if they're all having trouble in our school. And my mother said, yes, she was beginning to agree with me, though she told me we'd both better wait and see what happens, and not 'go advertising' what we think. Daddy has told us, a lot of times, not to 'go advertising' what we think; he says you should let the other person tell you what is on his mind first."

By the age of thirteen and a half her mind was taken up with schools: 24 would she go away to X or Y boarding school? France remained a preoccupation, if not an obsession—the latter a word her father used, half jokingly, to describe the continuing concern of both his children, actually, with "les affaires françaises." He was not by inclination or habit one to use a psychologically pejorative word, like "obsession," but he had begun to get annoyed with what he regarded as the excessive Gallic pride of his daughter. She had responded with a gradual diminution of interest in "that foreign nation." She would never see eye to eye with him. But she did find it hard to disagree with him outright. And besides, they really did agree "on most important things," as she came to realize quite clearly when they had their first long personal talk, a couple of months short of her fourteenth birthday. He asked her what she anticipated doing with her life. She told him that she no longer thought she would live in Paris and become an actress or live someplace in the French Alps, where she would try to be a "champion skier." Nor was she anymore taken up with dreams of geographic expeditions to central Africa. She wanted to stay in New England and nourish a rapidly developing hobby of hers—one she envisioned turning into a career: photography.

She had received a Polaroid camera when eleven and had largely 25 ignored it for over a year. At twelve she took many pictures, asked for a conventional camera, began to use that, too. At thirteen she felt increasingly competent with the two cameras, and began to learn how to develop her own pictures. She was taught how to do so at school and by a neighbor who was a rather experienced amateur photographer. Helen was becoming known as such herself by her classmates, and her photographs of Boston, of the rural landscape near her parents' country home, were displayed in the school's library. She was in the eighth grade at the time, and it was then that she announced, in another one of her compositions, her intention to become a fashion photographer. She had for a year or so been taking notice of *Vogue* and *Mademoiselle,* both regularly present in her mother's sitting room. Maybe someday she might be a fashion photographer, and roam the world—combining thereby a life of travel and photography. And maybe she would, in the course of such a life, meet a Frenchman she liked, or maybe an Englishman; eventually she would marry, she speculated, a European.

However, when her brother said that he too might want to go to 26 Europe, and maybe live there, she expressed disapproval. She would in time decide to come back to this country. Europe was fine, but America is best, she told Geoff. He did, as he got older, take up the camera with an enthusiasm to match hers, but he was interested in less romantic pictures. In the country he photographed (at twelve and thirteen) the men who worked on the road, or the local policeman at work. In the city, Geoff walked away from the well-to-do enclave he considered home; he reached other streets, far less attractive, took pictures of stores and storekeepers and ordinary working people. His finest work was done with the firemen who were assigned to a location a few blocks away from his home. He asked the men if he could photograph the engines, then asked them if they minded standing near those engines. He built up a portfolio of photographs that the school judged worthy of highest honors in its annual hobby show.

Geoff was rather more critical of himself than others were of him. His 27 sister was quite upset with him, as a matter of fact, when she heard what he had to say about the fire station series of pictures: "He told me he was worried, because there's a kid in his room who is black, and he told Geoff that his father can't find a job, and he keeps trying, and he applied for a job as a policeman and a fireman, but he still hasn't heard anything. I told Geoff not to worry; it was silly to worry. If the father wanted a job bad enough, according to our Daddy, then there are plenty of jobs to be found. Daddy showed us once how many pages there are in the newspaper full of advertisements for people to come and apply for a job. Geoff isn't old enough to understand a lot of things. He feels sorry for everyone! I used to be like him. But when you get older you know that people have to help themselves. It's not fair, though, about the black people. They've had a bad time. But they're having a better time."

She thought she might try to follow her brother's lead, do some 28
documentary photographs. Why not go to a black neighborhood and take
pictures there? If Geoff could win a prize for his pictures of firemen and
their engines, she could win the same prize a year later with the project
she had in mind. Her mother offered to drive her to a black neighborhood
and stay with her while she used her camera. Her father said no, they
might both get in trouble. Helen decided to go see—to drive with her
mother down a street where one black classmate lives and see what was
there waiting for the camera to catch hold of. But just as they were ready
to go, she told her mother that she had reconsidered, had no further
interest in the idea, and wanted instead to take some pictures of the houses
and people in her own neighborhood. She liked cats, had an idea about
what she would do: photographic portraits of cats sitting on the steps of
town houses.

Questions

Rereading and Independent Analysis

1. Reread this selection, marking the narrative of Helen's childhood
at each year that is reported. Then underline or put brackets around
Coles's comments and interpretations. Copy his comments separately, in
a long paragraph. As a separate statement, do his comments create a
"composition"? What is this paragraph's stated or implied thesis? What
patterns of development does it use? What would you infer from reading
only this compression of the selection?

2. As you review this selection, notice the themes that are repeated
throughout to unify Helen's and Geoff's changes during the period reported. Do any of these repeated ideas become less or more important
over time? Why do you think so?

Suggested Discussion and Group Activities

1. As you read this selection, did your attitude toward Helen and her
family change? If so, explain how you are led to draw inferences from the
report that create your attitudes toward this family. Are your attitudes a
result of the ways the information is reported? What favorable or unfavorable judgments about the children does Coles make himself?

2. Are any of the problems that bother Helen and Geoff also problems for you or your friends? How did you and your friends change your
responses to such problems over your years of childhood and young adulthood?

Writing Suggestions

Response
Imagine that you are Helen or Geoff but ten years older than they were
at the end of this report. Write an introduction to Coles's report from the

point of view of one of the children. Tell the reader how the experiences discussed in the report influence you and your family now.

Analysis

Write an analysis of this selection, explaining how Coles arranged and controlled the materials from taped interviews to create the effect of this report on its readers. Begin by discussing the impression the essay makes on you. Then explain how the essay creates that result by referring to specific passages from it, specific ways Coles controlled the reader's responses, and your own reactions as you read.

Finding a Purpose

Reread this selection and a few of those before it in the section "Social Sciences." Imagine that you are writing an introduction to a textbook for a beginning course in psychology and other social sciences. Your task, using these essays and any others you want to include as examples, is to explain to students what some of the methods of the social sciences are.

How do researchers gather information, sift it, organize it, and report it? What problems concern them? Use specific examples from your reading to make your points. You should conclude with some comments on the suitability of these methods and on their dangers. Is privacy ever invaded? How are this and other dangers taken into account in these essays?

 # The Human Being
Erving Goffman

This selection raises some interesting questions about the nature of the "object" that is studied by social scientists—the human being. It takes a point of view about people and their "character" or "spirit" that differs from our common understandings of these ideas. Its author, Erving Goffman (b. 1922), studied at the University of Toronto and the University of Chicago, and wrote his Ph.D. dissertation about material he gathered from a community he lived in on the Shetland Islands. He has worked at the National Institute of Mental Health and is a professor of sociology at the University of California, Berkeley. His numerous books include *The Presentation of Self in Every-day Life* (1956), *Encounters: Two Studies in the Sociology of Interaction* (1961), *Stigmas: Notes on the Management of Spoiled Identity* (1964), and *Relations in Public: Microstudies of the Public Order* (1971).

As these titles show, Goffman studies the ways people present themselves and are perceived in public and social, rather than interior or solitary, situations. His major work, *Frame Analysis* (1974), is the source of the short definition of the "human being" presented here. In it, Goffman argues that the "individual" is a construction whose "identity" is a fiction. This identity is, he says, actually a story we tell to achieve continuity and "plot," or significance, in our lives. He thinks that the individual self is created by a number of encounters, not by an unchanging set of predispositions. It is not a product of fixed internal qualities. As you read, you will probably find yourself unable to remain neutral about his ideas, for they question some deeply held assumptions about a sense of identity.

As in much of his work, Goffman wrote this definition by drawing heavily on examples from literature and popular media. He uses the situation of the theater, with its "actors," "roles," "scenes," and "audiences," to exemplify his points. He also explains an analysis that is often applied to literary writing, showing how the person writing is not the same person whom we take to be the "author" or "voice" in particular pieces we read. From his first sentence, we are aware of his energy and experience as a sociologist who is concerned about public, social human behaviors. Notice his specialized vocabulary, which characterizes much of the writing in his field. Basing his ideas on his catalog of evidence, he takes a conclusive stance about a controversial subject.

It is hardly possible to talk about the anchoring of doings in the world 1 without seeming to support the notion that a person's acts are in part an expression and outcome of his perduring self, and that this self will be present behind the particular roles he plays at any particular moment. After all, from any and all of our dealings with an individual we acquire a sense of his personality, his character, his quality as a human being. We come to expect that all his acts will exhibit the same style, be stamped in a unique way. If every strip of activity is enmeshed and anchored in its environing world so that it necessarily bears the marks of what produced it, then surely it is reasonable to say that each utterance or physical doing that the individual contributes to a current situation will be rooted in his biographical, personal identity. Behind current role, the person himself will peek out. Indeed, this is a common way of framing our perception of another. So three cheers for the self. Now let us try to reduce the clatter.

Start with a simple case. A popular radio comedy series features a 2 small, permanent cast of players, each of whom, as the series progresses and settles down to an effective formula, acquires a colorful personality, a cast identity all his own. Each becomes as familiar and human as living individuals need to be for us. It is these radio personages who are given particular parts to play in the skits which make up each week's show. The accent and mode of speaking each cast personality has developed and become identified with is each week partly submerged in the character he is obliged that week to play. Part of the humor of the show will be to see how the personality we know so well must bend himself to the particularities of a particular part, yet will be constitutionally unable to bend very far. Parts but not "casting" will often be announced in advance, so that the first spoken word will tell listeners "who" is going to do that part and what strains on credulity are to be joyfully expected. Broad comedy will be achieved when such a personality finds that he has been saddled with a part that is too uncongenial for him and finds a comic reason to drop his mask and petulantly revert back to his true self—if only for a moment—before he regains his self-control and disappears again into the appointed part.

Now it happens that knowing followers of the show come to appreci- 3
ate that the personality sustained by each player across his several parts
may itself be somewhat put on, or at least tailored to increase its power
as a typification of a possible way of being. And, in fact, closer examination
of the show credits proves that something not unlike the Standwell puppet
show is involved, for it turns out that the whole show is put on by three
or four actual performers, each of whom plays two or more members of
the cast. And the accents that show through a character's accents are
themselves put on. Once again we are reminded that a sense of the humanity of a performer is somehow generated by discrepancy between role
and character, which discrepancy itself can be manufactured for the effect
it produces. If such is true of role-character contrasts, what about person-
role contrasts?

Look now at fiction—the novel and the short story. As suggested, the 4
writer can choose how openly intrusive he will be; he can obviously speak
through a particular character and, if he wants, provide a running comment in an impersonal voice that can only be his "own." Just as the manner
in which his characters saying what they say will convey their personality,
so the manner in which he handles the author's task will—so it seems—
convey his personality and beliefs. And an important part of what the
reader gets out of his reading is the experience of contact with the writer.
For the latter turns out to be (and indeed must be or he would not be much
read) a person of fine spirit, broad knowledgeability, and deep moral
feeling, who incidentally implies that the reader is just the sort to appreciate such quality, else the author would not be writing in the first place.
Here the theatrical frame is different from the fictional one, since in plays
the writer must work through his characters entirely, and their virtues
tend to be attributed to them, not to him.[1] All of this is also true, perhaps
to a lesser degree, of nonfiction writers.[2]

---

[1] As Patrick Cruttwell remarks in a useful paper, "Makers and Persons," *Hudson Review,* XII
(Spring 1959–Winter 1960):

> . . . the drama's characters must be self-explanatory in their actions and their sayings—
> whereas in the novel, or the narrative poem, the opportunity is always there for the
> writer to comment and explain and tell the reader how such and such a character or
> episode ought to be taken: and that is where, in narrative, the personal usually enters.
> [p. 495]

[2] Cruttwell extends the argument to personal journals, even those not written (apparently)
with publication in mind (*ibid.,* pp. 487–489). In a very useful article Walter Gibson,
"Authors, Speakers, Readers, and Mock Readers," *College English,* XI (1950): 265–269,
took up the case in regard to book reviewing, suggesting how much of that literary form
consists of using the works of others as a target of response which will confirm for the reader
that he has found a brilliant, many-sided critic who appreciates that the reader is the
appropriate recipient for this response. Writing, then, breeds a presumed (Gibson calls him
mock) writer who, in fact, is likely to be vastly different from the actual writer, and a
presumed reader, who on the same grounds is likely to be vastly different from the actual
one. The posturing of the writer, Gibson argues, calls out a posturing from the reader—a
mutually affirmed affectation.

But this sense of the author can only be a facilitated delusion. With 5 only the text to draw on, at best a partial picture can be adduced, for there will be a great deal about the writer that never gets into his print. But more to the point, whatever does get in is not some sort of spontaneous unschooled expression. After all, the writer and his editors have the text to work on at their leisure. Lapses in taste and knowledgeability can be corrected. Spelling errors, grammatical mistakes, repetitiveness, bad puns, "too" frequent use of particular words, and other mannerisms can be caught in time. Phrases can be turned, tuned, and tempered. If in one draft he seems to be striving for an effect, then in the next draft he can strive to remove this impression. False notes must be caught during rehearsal and played again right. Indeed, it is apparent that if this polishing has not been done, critics will be quick to note the fact disapprovingly. So the quality of mind and feeling the writer's writing implies he has is no less a labored artifact than the quality of self a playwright's words generate for one of his characters. Yet although we readers are prepared to see that the characters an author presents to us are fictional, along with their personal qualities, this very mindfulness on our part seems to lead us to assume that what we sense to be the writer is the real thing; we respond to what we sense is spontaneous, to what we sense is uncalculated, to what is therefore organically characteristic of the way the writer is as a person. Which means that the work a writer does ends up being work through which he cuts a figure, and that the materials provided him in fictional plots, topics of public interest, and the efforts of other writers become disguises for some sort of exhibitionism. That he who might write this last sentence would still take some editorial care over it does not deny what it says.[3]

The argument, then, is that in fiction and even nonfictional writing, 6 the sort of person the author is emerges from the writing, but that this is an artifact of writing—certainly so in part—and not a result of some organic expressive carry-over from actor to actions. It should also be apparent that the channel through which this projection is accomplished is not

---

[3] Which is but to mimic Gibson. In extracting the pretensions contained in quoted bits of two book reviews he presents—and I think effectively—a statement in one paragraph followed then by a next paragraph which applies to the first paragraph the analysis that paragraph recommends. To wit:

> It will surprise no one to learn that the first passage was taken from a recent issue of *Partisan Review*, and that the second is from the *New Yorker*. Perhaps it is fair to say that the mock reader addressed by these speakers represents ideal audiences of the two periodicals. In any case it seems plain that the job of an editor is largely the definition of his magazine's mock reader and that an editorial "policy" is a decision or prediction as to the role or roles in which one's customers would like to imagine themselves. Likewise, a man fingering the piles at a magazine stand is concerned with the corollary question, Who do I want to pretend I am today?
>
> (The mock reader of this article numbers among his many impressive accomplishments the fact of having participated at various times as mock reader of both the *New Yorker* and the *Partisan Review*.) [*Ibid.*, p. 267.]

the one that carries the story line; rather the writer in effect relies on the subordinated channels, namely, aspects of discourse that need not be directly attended. So the fact that impressions of the author are somehow indirectly delivered, there to be sensed, certainly not something for the author to lay claim to directly, is a feature of the channeling of communication as much as it is a feature of man.

Now turn to real face-to-face interaction among persons. Again 7 one finds that a discrimination is made between the individual as a continuing selfsame entity and the role he happens to be playing at the moment. It is, in addition, this difference that carries the burden of conveying personality.[4] And this "role distance" will be carried largely in the subordinate tracks. But although this stylistic carry-over from personal identity to current role can be treated as another aspect of the sense in which an individual's behavior is grounded or anchored in something beyond itself, I do not think this should be the first place to look for an accounting.

Perhaps the lead can be given to us again by looking at written 8 productions. Follow Gibson's argument:

> Most teachers agree that the attitudes expressed by the "lover" in the love sonnet are not to be crudely confused with whatever attitudes the sonneteer himself may or may not have manifested in real life. Historical techniques are available for a description of the sonneteer, but the literary teacher's final concern must be with the speaker, that voice or disguise through which someone (whom we may well call "the poet") communicates with us. It is this speaker who is "real" in the sense most useful to the study of literature, for the speaker is made of language alone, and his entire self lies on the page before us in evidence.[5]

As with sonneteers, so with makers or writers of fiction. Obviously, the author cannot be identified with a particular character in his story if for no other reason than he has managed to produce more than one character, and each of these presumably has its own claim to reflect a little of him. But just as we obtain an impression of each character, so we obtain an impression, or rather glean an impression, of the author. And just as we rely on what is said and done by or in regard to a particular character for our impression of that character, so we tend to rely on the whole content of the fictional work itself to gain an impression of the author. Of course, the reputation of the writer may well precede our response to a given particular product, but this prior preparation is not in one sense necessary. For the kind of conclusion we come to can be arrived at solely from what the printed world makes available to us. We learn about the *writer* from

---

[4] Argued in "Role Distance," *E.*, p. 152.
[5] Gibson, "Authors, Speakers," p. 265.

literary gossip, published and unpublished; we learn about the *author* from his books.[6]

And so it is during actual dealings between actual persons. Again 9 there will be a response to the role that each presents as his mantle for the moment. Again something will glitter or smolder or otherwise make itself apparent beyond the covering that is officially worn. And again, the sense of otherness that is created, the sense of the person beyond the role, is, or certainly can be, a product of what becomes locally available. Again, of course, externally established information will be brought to bear. But again, this is not necessary for the *kind* of response that is produced. A sense of the person *can* be generated locally. And this discrepancy between person and role, this interstice through which a self peers, this human effect, need no more depend upon the world beyond the current situation than does the role itself. Whatever a participant "really is," is not really the issue. His fellow participants are not likely to discover this if indeed it is discoverable. What is important is the sense he provides them through his dealings with them of what sort of person he is behind the role he is in. In Gibson's terms, they are concerned with the poet, not the sonneteer. They are concerned with the author, not the writer. They are concerned with something that is generated in the contrasting streams of his immediate behavior. What they discover from their gleanings will apparently point to what this fellow is like beyond the current situation. But every situation he is in will provide his others with such an image. That is what situations can do for us. That is a reason why we find them (as we find novels) engrossing. But that is no reason to think that all these gleanings about himself that an individual makes available, all these pointings from his current situation to the way he is in his other occasions, have anything very much in common. Gleanings about an individual point beyond the situation to what presumably will be found in all other gleanings of him, but one cannot say that they point in the same direction, for it is their very nature to make themselves felt as pointing in a same direction.

The function of a striking remark, ironic, witty, or learned, is not to 10 disclose or conceal the perduring nature of its maker, for a remark (or a novel) can hardly do that: its function is to generate the notion that an interactant brings a personage along with him, a poet or an author of whom such sentiments can be characteristic. And of poets and authors and personages they certainly can be.

---

[6] Book dedication is a possible exception, for here there is a sense in which the writer exploits the authorial channel to convey—nay, to broadcast—a personal message in a voice different from the one he will immediately take up. A Durkheimian twist. As if the self-demanding labor of doing the book gave the writer the privilege and obligation to show publicly that he has a separate, private life and is committed to it, while at the same time those who make up this life have a right to be so recognized. One is reminded of the presence of hand-held wives when husbands accept success or defeat in their effort to win an election.

You will note that the characters a playwright designs have a local 11
setting, visible to us, in which to stride, lounge, and bubble. They are given
things to say and do so that they can be directed to say and do them with
particular style. What results is the creative mystery of the dramatic arts.
For somehow or other stage characters known to be stage characters can
end up giving the realest possible impression of possessing real personal
qualities, indeed quite striking ones. But why shouldn't a stage scene be
sufficient for the production of these effects? Those materials are just what
we employ to create ours.

So once again one is faced with the recursive character of framing. 12
The resources we use in a particular scene necessarily have some continuity, an existence before the scene occurs and an existence that continues
on after the scene is over. But just as this is part of reality, so conceptions
that this is so become part of reality, too, and thus have an additional effect.
There is no "objective" reason why a flag or any other piece of ritual
equipment should not be treated as sacred while it is functioning within
a ceremony but be treated in an everyday way while being manufactured
or, after being in use, while in storage awaiting the next ceremonial occasion. And that, by and large, is what occurs. But close examination will
disclose that although flags and the like are treated in a relatively matter-
of-fact way when not in ritual use, some small circumspection will continue to be displayed.[7] And *this* continuity of character is not forced upon
us by the continuity of material things but by our *conceptions* about the
continuity of spiritual ones. Sacred relics, mementos, souvenirs, and locks
of hair do sustain a physical continuity with what it is they commemorate;
but it is our cultural beliefs about resource continuity which give to these
relics some sentimental value, give them their personality. Just as it is
these beliefs that give us ours.

Questions

Rereading and Independent Analysis

1. Make a list of the words Goffman uses that indicate he is writing
within the field of sociology—for example, "interactant." Then look up
these words or translate them into your own, more familiar vocabulary.
Reread the sentences in which you found them, inserting your substitu-
tions. What is changed in your view of the meaning? Do you become
another sort of "mock reader" than the one Goffman says he is imagining
for this piece? What does he mean by that term? Who is his ideal reader?

---

[7] In the case of national flags, this examination need not be very close. Nation-states are our
really sacred entities, and most members of this club lay down a "flag etiquette" to deal
with offstage handling and "flag desecration" statutes to deal with violations of the rules.
Here, see Sasha R. Weitman, "National Flags: A Sociological Overview," *Semiotica*, VIII
(1973): 337. A close study of offstage management of sacred religious objects is available in
Samuel Heilman, "*Kehillat Kidesh:* Deciphering a Modern Orthodox Jewish Synagogue"
(Ph.D. diss., Department of Sociology, University of Pennsylvania, 1973), esp. pp. 101–115.

2. Make a careful outline of this selection to show how it systematically attempts to "reduce the clatter" about the self. List the points Goffman makes. How does he use a process of elimination to persuade his readers?

Suggested Discussion and Group Activities

1. Goffman's position about the self in this essay is highly controversial. To test his position, describe the roles you play in your life. Do you agree that roles are not something you "play" but the only ways you are known by others or can know yourself? If not, what is your evidence of a "perduring self"?

2. In groups, list the roles you play during a typical week. Do you have more than one identity? What similarities are there among your group members? What is your evidence for your answer? Is it based primarily on your experience or on the way others treat you?

3. Can you tell that one person named Goffman wrote the selection you have just read? Give reasons why you think you can.

Writing Suggestions

Response

One of Shakespeare's most famous comparisons states that "all the world's a stage" and that men and women are actors. Shakespeare says that people play "parts" determined by their age, in changing stages of life. Write a personal essay in which you describe a time or times in your life when you have managed a difficult or unpleasant task by playing "a part." Clearly identify the role or character you imitated, and evaluate the results of your acting, both for yourself and for those who made up your audience.

Analysis

Write an essay in which you apply to any work you have read Goffman's analysis of the difference between the "writer," "author," and "person" who wrote a piece of writing. Point out where the "voice" of the "author" is visible in your choice. Distinguish it from the voice of other characters, and show how these distinct voices contributed to your reading experience. What evidence do you have that one person—the writer—controlled this experience?

Finding a Purpose

Write an essay in which you explain to classmates why Goffman's view of the "self" is controversial. To supply specific evidence, read Joan Didion's essay "On Self-Respect" (in this chapter). Then explain the controversy around Goffman's ideas by comparing and contrasting these two views of the "self"—the one that Goffman argues for and the "self" Didion assumes she is writing about. Can you distinguish these views of what human beings are only on the basis of whether human beings are alone or are acting in social settings and relationships? What other distinctions are important?

Writing About Writing: Diversions and Dangers

INTRODUCTION

Writing that depends on other writing offers us a special kind of enjoyment. It is a mirror on both the reader's and the writer's worlds. It shows us as readers that we can easily misread by overlooking subtle intentions and effects, and it points out both amusing and disturbing results if we do. It shows writers to themselves, powerfully suggesting that they look carefully at their processes, the words on their pages, and the possible results their writing may have. In this chapter, the selections are grouped to show the playfulness, the risks, and the competitions that occur in a distinctly written world. These selections self-consciously depend on other writing for their forms and themes, so they are a way to monitor reading and writing, to keep it honest.

Writing about writing is both recreative and re-creative. It is playful, full of games and contests that are won by using a new angle of interest, testing another writer. Critiques, satires, and parodies like those included here rely entirely on a sense of context. They reexamine an already considered topic, tone, or purpose from a new perspective. As we observe how writers criticize, imitate, or analyze the implications of words and names, we see that we can enjoy similar pleasure in our own uses of language.

Writing about writing is also re-creative. It allows us to construct and temporarily to inhabit new frames of mind. By giving us this freedom, writing's generative powers renew the actual world of experience as often as they continue it. As readers and writers, we use texts to explore, analyze, and experiment. They help us reinform our individual and community experiences. A full participant in the written world actively looks for pleasure and risks in the possible uncertainty of the imaginative spaces that written words create.

Writers have traditionally understood this playfulness and also a darker side of the game, the danger that written words will be divorced from the writer the moment they are written and will lose contact with meaningful "reality." The selections here that portray the "dangers" of writing demonstrate that we cannot question the writers of most of our reading about their intentions. We are never sure that we read as the writer thought we would. And even when we know a writer's intention, we must still ask if a piece of writing is "true." Does it allow us to place it accurately in the context that produced it? Or does it adopt a mask that hides its writer's voice, its sources, and its purposes?

Well-constructed texts appear to be solid and well grounded. But if their authors are dishonest about the relations of these texts to the writers' and readers' worlds, they can undermine the believability of all written words. On a spectrum from the irony whose joke we cannot "get" to the crime of plagiarism, such writing can endanger our ability to interpret experience. The constructed "fictional realities" that writing allows us to consider can become more powerful than everyday experience and can distort our values.

These selections therefore show relations between written and "actual" worlds. By demonstrating written playfulness and by warning us not to lose our sense of possible distortions in writing, they raise intriguing questions about what we think "reality" is. In the final section, this commentary is extended by showing competition between reading and writing and other media. Some reports indicate that reading and writing are, or soon will be, lost to a new visual and electronic "literacy." But the processes of self-examination, statement, and re-vision that reading and writing offer become more, not less, necessary in newly complex technological worlds. Predictions of an end to writing simply generate more reading and writing—new expeditions to unmapped portions of the written world.

PLAYING WITH WORDS

 Fenimore Cooper's
Literary Offenses
Mark Twain

American readers have many special reasons to be grateful to Samuel Langhorne Clemens (1835–1910), whose pen name, Mark Twain, is itself an
amusing gift. In Twain's playfulness with the language of his name we see
both an American use of pragmatic language ("twain" means "two fathoms
deep") and greater implications ("two fathoms deep" indicates "safe
water"). This essay is a satiric critique of James Fenimore Cooper (1789–
1851), who wrote popular but unrealistic historical novels about the nineteenth-century frontier. It calls attention to some misuses of language that we
can appreciate without having read either Cooper or his earliest reviewers'
high praise.

This essay was published first in North American Review in 1895. At
the time, interest in literary writing was replacing traditional attention to the
art of public speaking and the history of language in a recently developed
university study called "English." Twain is imitating, and making fun of, a
new tradition of forming simplistic textbook lists of rules for good writing.
Yet the purpose of these rules was of great concern to him; he was quite
serious about good, sound writing and thought that Cooper had omitted
some of its important elements.

Twain also calls into question ways of deciding which pieces of writing
will be elevated to the status of "Great Literature." The "tree-calf, hand-
tooled, seven-dollar Friendship's Offering" of the time was an expensive
popular compilation. It was an early form of packaging "acceptable" literature analogous to the *Reader's Digest Condensed Books* today. As you read,
try to identify how Twain's humor still attracts us, even though we are not
familiar with the particular situation he was addressing. What techniques
does he use to insure his readers' cooperation with his humor?

The Pathfinder and The Deerslayer stand at the head of Cooper's novels as artistic creations.
There are others of his works which contain parts as perfect as are to be found in these, and
scenes even more thrilling. Not one can be compared with either of them as a finished whole.

The defects in both of these tales are comparatively slight. They were pure works of
art.—*Prof. Lounsbury.*

The five tales reveal an extraordinary fulness of invention.

. . . One of the very greatest characters in fiction, Natty Bumppo. . . .

The craft of the woodsman, the tricks of the trapper, all the delicate art of the forest,
were familiar to Cooper from his youth up.—*Prof. Brander Matthews.*

Cooper is the greatest artist in the domain of romantic fiction yet produced by America.—*Wilkie Collins.*

It seems to me that it was far from right for the Professor of English 1
Literature in Yale, the Professor of English Literature in Columbia, and

Wilkie Collins to deliver opinions on Cooper's literature without having read some of it. It would have been much more decorous to keep silent and let persons talk who have read Cooper.

Cooper's art has some defects. In one place in *Deerslayer,* and in the 2 restricted space of two-thirds of a page, Cooper has scored 114 offences against literary art out of a possible 115. It breaks the record.

There are nineteen rules governing literary art in the domain of 3 romantic fiction—some say twenty-two. In *Deerslayer* Cooper violated eighteen of them. These eighteen require:

1. That a tale shall accomplish something and arrive somewhere. But the *Deerslayer* tale accomplishes nothing and arrives in the air.

2. They require that the episodes of a tale shall be necessary parts of the tale, and shall help to develop it. But as the *Deerslayer* tale is not a tale, and accomplishes nothing and arrives nowhere, the episodes have no rightful place in the work, since there was nothing for them to develop.

3. They require that the personages in a tale shall be alive, except in the case of corpses, and that always the reader shall be able to tell the corpses from the others. But this detail has often been overlooked in the *Deerslayer* tale.

4. They require that the personages in a tale, both dead and alive, shall exhibit a sufficient excuse for being there. But this detail also has been overlooked in the *Deerslayer* tale.

5. They require that when the personages of a tale deal in conversation, the talk shall sound like human talk, and be talk such as human beings would be likely to talk in the given circumstances, and have a discoverable meaning, also a discoverable purpose, and a show of relevancy, and remain in the neighborhood of the subject in hand, and be interesting to the reader, and help out the tale, and stop when the people cannot think of anything more to say. But this requirement has been ignored from the beginning of the *Deerslayer* tale to the end of it.

6. They require that when the author describes the character of a personage in his tale, the conduct and conversation of that personage shall justify said description. But this law gets little or no attention in the *Deerslayer* tale, as Natty Bumppo's case will amply prove.

7. They require that when a personage talks like an illustrated, gilt-edged, tree-calf, hand-tooled, seven-dollar Friendship's Offering in the beginning of a paragraph, he shall not talk like a negro minstrel in the end of it. But this rule is flung down and danced upon in the *Deerslayer* tale.

8. They require that crass stupidities shall not be played upon the reader as "the craft of the woodsman, the delicate art of the forest," by either the author or the people in the tale. But this rule is persistently violated in the *Deerslayer* tale.

9. They require that the personages of a tale shall confine themselves to possibilities and let miracles alone; or, if they venture a miracle, the author must so plausibly set it forth as to make it look possible and reasonable. But these rules are not respected in the *Deerslayer* tale.

10. They require that the author shall make the reader feel a deep interest in the personages of his tale and in their fate; and that he shall make the reader love the good people in the tale and hate the bad ones. But the reader of the *Deerslayer* tale dislikes the good people in it, is indifferent to the others, and wishes they would all get drowned together.

11. They require that the characters in a tale shall be so clearly defined that the reader can tell beforehand what each will do in a given emergency. But in the *Deerslayer* tale this rule is vacated.

In addition to these large rules there are some little ones. These 4 require that the author shall

12. *Say* what he is proposing to say, not merely come near it.

13. Use the right word, not its second cousin.

14. Eschew surplusage.

15. Not omit necessary details.

16. Avoid slovenliness of form.

17. Use good grammar.

18. Employ a simple and straightforward style.

Even these seven are coldly and persistently violated in the *Deer-* 5 *slayer* tale.

Cooper's gift in the way of invention was not a rich endowment; but 6 such as it was he liked to work it, he was pleased with the effects, and indeed he did some quite sweet things with it. In his little box of stage properties he kept six or eight cunning devices, tricks, artifices for his savages and woodsmen to deceive and circumvent each other with, and he was never so happy as when he was working these innocent things and seeing them go. A favorite one was to make a moccasined person tread in the tracks of the moccasined enemy, and thus hide his own trail. Cooper wore out barrels and barrels of moccasins in working that trick. Another stage-property that he pulled out of his box pretty frequently was his broken twig. He prized his broken twig above all the rest of his effects, and worked it the hardest. It is a restful chapter in any book of his when somebody doesn't step on a dry twig and alarm all the reds and whites for two hundred yards around. Every time a Cooper person is in peril, and absolute silence is worth four dollars a minute, he is sure to step on a dry twig. There may be a hundred handier things to step on, but that wouldn't satisfy Cooper. Cooper requires him to turn out and find a dry twig; and if he can't do it, go and borrow one. In fact, the Leather Stocking Series ought to have been called the Broken Twig Series.

I am sorry there is not room to put in a few dozen instances of the 7 delicate art of the forest, as practised by Natty Bumppo and some of the other Cooperian experts. Perhaps we may venture two or three samples. Cooper was a sailor—a naval officer; yet he gravely tells us how a vessel, driving towards a lee shore in a gale, is steered for a particular spot by her skipper because he knows of an *undertow* there which will hold her back against the gale and save her. For just pure woodcraft, or sailorcraft, or whatever it is, isn't that neat? For several years Cooper was daily in the society of artillery, and he ought to have noticed that when a cannon-ball strikes the ground it either buries itself or skips a hundred feet or so; skips again a hundred feet or so—and so on, till finally it gets tired and rolls. Now in one place he loses some "females"—as he always calls women—in the edge of a wood near a plain at night in a fog, on purpose to give Bumppo a chance to show off the delicate art of the forest before the reader. These mislaid people are hunting for a fort. They hear a cannon-blast, and a cannon-ball presently comes rolling into the wood and stops at their feet. To the females this suggests nothing. The case is very different with the admirable Bumppo. I wish I may never know peace again if he doesn't strike out promptly and *follow the track* of that cannon-ball across the plain through the dense fog and find the fort. Isn't it a daisy? If Cooper had any real knowledge of Nature's ways of doing things, he had a most delicate art in concealing the fact. For instance: one of his acute Indian experts, Chingachgook (pronounced Chicago, I think), has lost the trail of a person he is tracking through the forest. Apparently that trail is hopelessly lost. Neither you nor I could ever have guessed out the way to find it. It was very different with Chicago. Chicago was not stumped for long. He turned a running stream out of its course, and there, in the slush in its old bed, were that person's moccasin-tracks. The current did not wash them away, as it would have done in all other like cases—no, even the eternal laws of Nature have to vacate when Cooper wants to put up a delicate job of woodcraft on the reader.

We must be a little wary when Brander Matthews tells us that 8 Cooper's books "reveal an extraordinary fulness of invention." As a rule, I am quite willing to accept Brander Matthew's literary judgments and applaud his lucid and graceful phrasing of them; but that particular statement needs to be taken with a few tons of salt. Bless your heart, Cooper hadn't any more invention than a horse; and I don't mean a high-class horse, either; I mean a clothes-horse. It would be very difficult to find a really clever "situation" in Cooper's books, and still more difficult to find one of any kind which he has failed to render absurd by his handling of it. Look at the episodes of "the caves"; and at the celebrated scuffle between Maqua and those others on the table-land a few days later; and at Hurry Harry's queer water-transit from the castle to the ark; and at Deerslayer's half-hour with his first corpse; and at the quarrel between Hurry Harry and Deerslayer later; and at—but choose for yourself; you can't go amiss.

If Cooper had been an observer his inventive faculty would have 9 worked better; not more interestingly, but more rationally, more plausibly. Cooper's proudest creations in the way of "situations" suffer noticeably from the absence of the observer's protecting gift. Cooper's eye was splendidly inaccurate. Cooper seldom saw anything correctly. He saw nearly all things as through a glass eye, darkly. Of course a man who cannot see the commonest little every-day matters accurately is working at a disadvantage when he is constructing a "situation." In the *Deerslayer* tale Cooper has a stream which is fifty feet wide where it flows out of a lake; it presently narrows to twenty as it meanders along for no given reason, and yet when a stream acts like that it ought to be required to explain itself. Fourteen pages later the width of the brook's outlet from the lake has suddenly shrunk thirty feet, and become "the narrowest part of the stream." This shrinkage is not accounted for. The stream has bends in it, a sure indication that it has alluvial banks and cuts them; yet these bends are only thirty and fifty feet long. If Cooper had been a nice and punctilious observer he would have noticed that the bends were oftener nine hundred feet long than short of it.

Cooper made the exit of that stream fifty feet wide, in the first place, for no particular reason; in the second place, he narrowed it to less than twenty to accommodate some Indians. He bends a "sapling" to the form of an arch over this narrow passage, and conceals six Indians in its foliage. They are "laying" for a settler's scow or ark which is coming up the stream on its way to the lake; it is being hauled against the stiff current by a rope whose stationary end is anchored in the lake; its rate of progress cannot be more than a mile an hour. Cooper describes the ark, but pretty obscurely. In the matter of dimensions "it was little more than a modern canal-boat." Let us guess, then, that it was about one hundred and forty feet long. It was of "greater breadth than common." Let us guess, then, that it was about sixteen feet wide. This leviathan had been prowling down bends which were but a third as long as itself, and scraping between banks where it had only two feet of space to spare on each side. We cannot too much admire this miracle. A low-roofed log dwelling occupies "two-thirds of the ark's length"—a dwelling ninety feet long and sixteen feet wide, let us say—a kind of vestibule train. The dwelling has two rooms—each forty-five feet long and sixteen feet wide, let us guess. One of them is the bedroom of the Hutter girls, Judith and Hetty; the other is the parlor in the daytime, at night it is papa's bedchamber. The ark is arriving at the stream's exit now, whose width has been reduced to less than twenty feet to accommodate the Indians—say to eighteen. There is a foot to spare on each side of the boat. Did the Indians notice that there was going to be a tight squeeze there? Did they notice that they could make money by climbing down out of that arched sapling and just stepping aboard when the ark scraped by? No, other Indians would have noticed these things, but Cooper's Indians never notice anything. Cooper thinks they are marvelous creatures for noticing, but he was almost always in error about his Indians. There was seldom a sane one among them.

The ark is one hundred and forty feet long; the dwelling is ninety feet long. The idea of the Indians is to drop softly and secretly from the arched sapling to the dwelling as the ark creeps along under it at the rate of a mile an hour, and butcher the family. It will take the ark a minute and a half to pass under. It will take the ninety foot dwelling a minute to pass under. Now, then, what did the six Indians do? It would take you thirty years to guess, and even then you would have to give it up, I believe. Therefore, I will tell you what the Indians did. Their chief, a person of quite extraordinary intellect for a Cooper Indian, warily watched the canal-boat as it squeezed along under him, and when he had got his calculations fined down to exactly the right shade, as he judged, he let go and dropped. And *missed the house!* That is actually what he did. He missed the house, and landed in the stern of the scow. It was not much of a fall, yet it knocked him silly. He lay there unconscious. If the house had been ninety-seven feet long he would have made the trip. The fault was Cooper's, not his. The error lay in the construction of the house. Cooper was no architect.

There still remained in the roost five Indians. The boat has passed 12 under and is now out of their reach. Let me explain what the five did—you would not be able to reason it out for yourself. No. 1 jumped for the boat, but fell in the water astern of it. Then No. 2 jumped for the boat, but fell in the water still farther astern of it. Then No. 3 jumped for the boat, and fell a good way astern of it. Then No. 4 jumped for the boat, and fell in the water *away* astern. Then even No. 5 made a jump for the boat—for he was a Cooper Indian. In the matter of intellect, the difference between a Cooper Indian and the Indian that stands in front of the cigar-shop is not spacious. The scow episode is really a sublime burst of invention; but it does not thrill, because the inaccuracy of the details throws a sort of air of fictitiousness and general improbability over it. This comes of Cooper's inadequacy as an observer.

The reader will find some examples of Cooper's high talent for inac- 13 curate observation in the account of the shooting-match in *The Pathfinder.*

> "A common wrought nail was driven lightly into the target, its head having been first touched with paint."

The color of the paint is not stated—an important omission, but 14 Cooper deals freely in important omissions. No, after all, it was not an important omission; for this nail-head is *a hundred yards from* the marksmen, and could not be seen by them at that distance, no matter what its color might be. How far can the best eyes see a common house-fly? A hundred yards? It is quite impossible. Very well; eyes that cannot see a house-fly that is a hundred yards away cannot see an ordinary nail-head at that distance, for the size of the two objects is the same. It takes a keen eye to see a fly or a nail-head at fifty yards—one hundred and fifty feet. Can the reader do it?

The nail was lightly driven, its head painted, and game called. Then 15 the Cooper miracles began. The bullet of the first marksman chipped an edge of the nail-head; the next man's bullet drove the nail a little way into the target—and removed all the paint. Haven't the miracles gone far enough now? Not to suit Cooper; for the purpose of this whole scheme is to show off his prodigy, Deerslayer-Hawkeye-Long-Rifle-Leather-Stocking-Pathfinder-Bumppo before the ladies.

> " 'Be all ready to clench it, boys!' cried out Pathfinder, stepping
> into his friend's tracks the instant they were vacant. 'Never mind a new
> nail; I can see that, though the paint is gone, and what I can see I can hit

at a hundred yards, though it were only a mosquito's eye. Be ready to clench!'

"The rifle cracked, the bullet sped its way, and the head of the nail was buried in the wood, covered by the piece of flattened lead."

There, you see, is a man who could hunt flies with a rifle, and com- 16 mand a ducal salary in a Wild West show to-day if we had him back with us.

The recorded feat is certainly surprising just as it stands; but it is not 17 surprising enough for Cooper. Cooper adds a touch. He has made Pathfinder do this miracle with another man's rifle; and not only that, but Pathfinder did not have even the advantage of loading it himself. He had everything against him, and yet he made that impossible shot; and not only made it, but did it with absolute confidence, saying, "Be ready to clench." Now a person like that would have undertaken that same feat with a brickbat, and with Cooper to help he would have achieved it, too.

Pathfinder showed off handsomely that day before the ladies. His 18 very first feat was a thing which no Wild West show can touch. He was standing with the group of marksmen, observing—a hundred yards from the target, mind; one Jasper raised his rifle and drove the centre of the bull's-eye. Then the Quartermaster fired. The target exhibited no result this time. There was a laugh. "It's a dead miss," said Major Lundie. Pathfinder waited an impressive moment or two; then said, in that calm, indifferent, know-it-all way of his, "No, Major, he has covered Jasper's bullet, as will be seen if anyone will take the trouble to examine the target."

Wasn't it remarkable! How *could* he see that little pellet fly through 19 the air and enter that distant bullet-hole? Yet that is what he did; for nothing is impossible to a Cooper person. Did any of those people have any deep-seated doubts about this thing? No; for that would imply sanity, and these were all Cooper people.

> "The respect for Pathfinder's skill and for his *quickness and accu-*
> *racy of sight*" (the italics are mine) "was so profound and general, that
> the instant he made this declaration the spectators began to distrust their
> own opinions, and a dozen rushed to the target in order to ascertain the
> fact. There, sure enough, it was found that the Quartermaster's bullet
> had gone through the hole made by Jasper's, and that, too, so accurately
> as to require a minute examination to be certain of the circumstance,
> which, however, was soon clearly established by discovering one bullet
> over the other in the stump against which the target was placed."

They made a "minute" examination; but never mind, how could they 20 know that there were two bullets in that hole without digging the latest one out? for neither probe nor eyesight could prove the presence of any more than one bullet. Did they dig? No; as we shall see. It is the Pathfinder's turn now; he steps out before the ladies, takes aim, and fires.

But, alas! here is a disappointment; an incredible, an unimaginable 21 disappointment—for the target's aspect is unchanged; there is nothing there but that same old bullet-hole!

> " 'If one dared to hint at such a thing,' cried Major Duncan, 'I should say that the Pathfinder has also missed the target!' "

As nobody had missed it yet, the "also" was not necessary; but never 22 mind about that, for the Pathfinder is going to speak.

> " 'No, no, Major,' said he, confidently, 'that *would* be a risky decla-ration. I didn't load the piece, and can't say what was in it; but if it was lead, you will find the bullet driving down those of the Quartermaster and Jasper, else is not my name Pathfinder.'
> "A shout from the target announced the truth of this assertion."

Is the miracle sufficient as it stands? Not for Cooper. The Pathfinder 23 speaks again, as he "now slowly advances towards the stage occupied by the females":

> " 'That's not all, boys, that's not all; if you find the target touched at all, I'll own to a miss. The Quartermaster cut the wood, but you'll find no wood cut by that last messenger."

The miracle is at last complete. He knew—doubtless *saw*—at the 24 distance of a hundred yards—that his bullet had passed into the hole *without fraying the edges.* There were now three bullets in that one hole—three bullets embedded processionally in the body of the stump back of the target. Everybody knew this—somehow or other—and yet nobody had dug any of them out to make sure. Cooper is not a close observer, but he is interesting. He is certainly always that, no matter what happens. And he is more interesting when he is not noticing what he is about than when he is. This is a considerable merit.

The conversations in the Cooper books have a curious sound in our 25 modern ears. To believe that such talk really ever came out of people's mouths would be to believe that there was a time when time was of no value to a person who thought he had something to say; when it was the custom to spread a two-minute remark out to ten; when a man's mouth was a rolling-mill, and busied itself all day long in turning four-foot pigs of thought into thirty-foot bars of conversational railroad iron by attenua-tion; when subjects were seldom faithfully stuck to, but the talk wandered all around and arrived nowhere; when conversations consisted mainly of irrelevancies, with here and there a relevancy, a relevancy with an embar-rassed look, as not being able to explain how it got there.

Cooper was certainly not a master in the construction of dialogue. 26 Inaccurate observation defeated him here as it defeated him in so many other enterprises of his. He even failed to notice that the man who talks corrupt English six days in the week must and will talk it on the seventh, and can't help himself. In the *Deerslayer* story he lets Deerslayer talk the showiest kind of book-talk sometimes, and at other times the basest of base dialects. For instance, when some one asks him if he has a sweetheart, and if so, where she abides, this is his majestic answer:

> " 'She's in the forest—hanging from the boughs of the trees, in a soft rain—in the dew on the open grass—the clouds that float about in the blue heavens—the birds that sing in the woods—the sweet springs where I slake my thirst—and in all the other glorious gifts that come from God's Providence!' "

And he preceded that, a little before, with this: 27

> " 'It consarns me as all things that touches a fri'nd consarns a fri'nd.' "

And this is another of his remarks: 28

> " 'If I was Injin born, now, I might tell of this, or carry in the scalp and boast of the expl'ite afore the whole tribe; or if my inimy had only been a bear' "—and so on.

We cannot imagine such a thing as a veteran Scotch Commander-in-   29
Chief comporting himself in the field like a windy melodramatic actor, but Cooper could. On one occasion Alice and Cora were being chased by the French through a fog in the neighborhood of their father's fort:

> " *'Point de quartier aux coquins!'* cried an eager pursuer, who seemed to direct the operations of the enemy.
> " 'Stand firm and be ready, my gallant 60ths!' suddenly exclaimed a voice above them; 'wait to see the enemy; fire low, and sweep the glacis.'
> " 'Father! father!' exclaimed a piercing cry from out the mist; 'it is I! Alice! thy own Elsie! spare, O! save your daughters!'
> " 'Hold!' shouted the former speaker, in the awful tones of parental agony, the sound reaching even to the woods, and rolling back in solemn echo. ' 'Tis she! God has restored me my children! Throw open the sally-port; to the field, 60ths, to the field! pull not a trigger, lest ye kill my lambs! Drive off these dogs of France with your steel!' "

Cooper's word-sense was singularly dull. When a person has a poor   30
ear for music he will flat and sharp right along without knowing it. He keeps near the tune, but it is *not* the tune. When a person has a poor ear for words, the result is a literary flatting and sharping; you perceive what he is intending to say, but you also perceive that he doesn't *say* it. This is Cooper. He was not a word-musician. His ear was satisfied with the *approximate* word. I will furnish some circumstantial evidence in support of this charge. My instances are gathered from half a dozen pages of the tale called *Deerslayer*. He uses "verbal," for "oral"; "precision," for "facility"; "phenomena," for "marvels"; "necessary," for "predetermined"; "unsophisticated," for "primitive"; "preparation," for "expectancy"; "rebuked," for "subdued"; "dependent on," for "resulting from"; "fact," for "condition"; "fact," for "conjecture"; "precaution," for "caution"; "explain," for "determine"; "mortified," for "disappointed"; "meretricious," for "factitious"; "materially," for "considerably"; "decreasing," for "deep-

ening"; "increasing," for "disappearing"; "embedded," for "enclosed"; "treacherous," for "hostile"; "stood," for "stopped"; "softened," for "replaced"; "rejoined," for "remarked"; "situation," for "condition"; "different," for "differing"; "insensible," for "unsentient"; "brevity," for "celerity"; "distrusted," for "suspicious"; "mental imbecility," for "imbecility"; "eyes," for "sight"; "counteracting," for "opposing"; "funeral obsequies," for "obsequies."

There have been daring people in the world who claimed that Cooper 31 could write English, but they are all dead now—all dead but Lounsbury. I don't remember that Lounsbury makes the claim in so many words, still he makes it, for he says that *Deerslayer* is a "pure work of art." Pure, in that connection, means faultless—faultless in all details—and language is a detail. If Mr. Lounsbury had only compared Cooper's English with the English which he writes himself—but it is plain that he didn't; and so it is likely that he imagines until this day that Cooper's is as clean and compact as his own. Now I feel sure, deep down in my heart, that Cooper wrote about the poorest English that exists in our language, and that the English of *Deerslayer* is the very worst that even Cooper ever wrote.

I may be mistaken, but it does seem to me that *Deerslayer* is not a 32 work of art in any sense; it does seem to me that it is destitute of every detail that goes to the making of a work of art; in truth, it seems to me that *Deerslayer* is just simply a literary *delirium tremens*.

A work of art? It has no invention; it has no order, system, sequence, 33 or result; it has no lifelikeness, no thrill, no stir, no seeming of reality; its characters are confusedly drawn, and by their acts and words they prove that they are not the sort of people the author claims that they are; its humor is pathetic; its pathos is funny; its conversations are—oh! indescribable; its love-scenes odious; its English a crime against the language.

Counting these out, what is left is Art. I think we must all admit that. 34

Questions

Rereading and Independent Analysis

1. Outline the grounds on which Twain objects to Cooper and to the critics' praise for him. Does the essay follow the list of "rules" at its beginning? What is the purpose of the list? What major objections does Twain explain in the rest of the essay? How does he support them?

2. How does Twain's choice of words and phrasing establish his *persona* (role for the person writing) in this essay? Make a list of specific examples from the essay that show you that his "voice" was supposedly a "spoken" response to literary writing.

Suggested Discussion and Group Activities

1. What kinds of expertise does Twain demonstrate to establish his own right to judge Cooper? Where does he use his own experience as a writer and a reader to make his case? What is the effect of these choices about presenting himself?

2. As a reader, how does your opinion of Cooper change as you read? Keeping in mind that this essay was published at a time when Cooper's reputation was good, describe how Twain convinces the reader of the justice of his case.

3. In groups, choose an example of your disagreement with other people or with the "establishment" view of the quality of a book or film. What are your grounds? How did you learn to appreciate and to criticize this kind of book or film?

Writing Suggestions

Response

Write a serious personal response to Twain's essay in which you argue that the "true-to-life" qualities of fiction, or their absence, are not grounds for evaluating it. Explain why readers and other audiences do not object to flaws in an author's factual details. Use an example of a piece of fiction or a film in which the "facts" were not your reason for liking or disliking it. If you have read Cooper and liked his books, explain why Twain's criticism does not change your mind.

Analysis

Using Twain's essay as a model, write an explanation of why following "rules" does not guarantee the quality of any special activity. Cite the accepted "rules" for writing, performing well at a sport, or any other activity you choose, and then show how a particular successful person does not follow these rules. What may be successful alternatives to following rules?

Finding a Purpose

Write an evaluation of a popular film or novel for your student newspaper. In your review, take an unusual point of view, demonstrating that praise for this work has been misplaced. Be sure to establish your personality and expertise in a way that will assure readers of your credibility.

 # The Declaration of Independence in American
H. L. Mencken

H. L. Mencken (1880–1956) was a dominant force in American journalism and a fearsome watchdog over the American language. He growled at every banality he noticed in writing and speech. He particularly disliked complacent, middle-class attitudes that allow language and culture to lose their freshness. Mencken edited the *Baltimore Evening Herald,* wrote for the *Baltimore Sun* from 1906 until his death, and founded the *American Mercury,* a literary magazine. His detailed scholarly work, *The American Lan-*

guage, was first published in 1919. He set a style in popular American attitudes, supporting the "common man," criticizing "intellectuals," and railing against the stupidity of mass culture, the electorate, and group thought.

"The Declaration of Independence in American," a parody of the Declaration (see Chapter 2), is written in "Common Speech." It was reprinted in *A Mencken Chrestomathy* (a collection of literary passages used for studying language and literature) with the following explanatory note by Mencken:

"From THE AMERICAN LANGUAGE, THIRD EDITION, 1923, pp. 398–402. First printed, as Essay in American, in the Baltimore *Evening Sun*, Nov. 7, 1921. Reprinted in THE AMERICAN LANGUAGE, SECOND EDITION, 1921, pp. 388–92. From the preface thereof: 'It must be obvious that more than one section of the original is now quite unintelligible to the average American of the sort using the Common Speech. What would he make, for example, of such a sentence as this one: "He has called together bodies at places unusual, uncomfortable, and distant from the depository of their public records, for the sole purpose of fatiguing them into compliance with his measures"? Or of this: "He has refused for a long time, after such dissolutions, to cause others to be elected, whereby the legislative powers, incapable of annihilation, have returned to the people at large for their exercise." Such Johnsonian periods are quite beyond his comprehension, and no doubt the fact is at least partly to blame for the neglect upon which the Declaration has fallen in recent years. When, during the Wilson Palmer saturnalia of oppressions [1918–20], specialists in liberty began protesting that the Declaration plainly gave the people the right to alter the government under which they lived and even to abolish it altogether, they encountered the utmost incredulity. On more than one occasion, in fact, such an exegete was tarred and feathered by shocked members of the American Legion, even after the Declaration had been read to them. What ailed them was simply that they could not understand its Eighteenth Century English.' This jocosity was denounced as seditious by various patriotic Americans, and in England it was accepted gravely and deplored sadly as a specimen of current Standard American."

When things get so balled up that the people of a country got to cut loose 1 from some other country, and go it on their own hook, without asking no permission from nobody, excepting maybe God Almighty, then they ought to let everybody know why they done it, so that everybody can see they are not trying to put nothing over on nobody.

All we got to say on this proposition is this: first, me and you is as good 2 as anybody else, and maybe a damn sight better: second, nobody ain't got no right to take away none of our rights: third, every man has got a right to live, to come and go as he pleases, and to have a good time whichever way he likes, so long as he don't interfere with nobody else. That any government that don't give a man them rights ain't worth a damn; also, people ought to choose the kind of government they want themselves, and nobody else ought to have no say in the matter. That whenever any government don't do this, then the people have got a right to give it the bum's rush and put in one that will take care of their interests. Of course, that don't mean having a revolution every day like them South American yellowbellies, or every time some jobholder goes to work and does something he ain't got no business to do. It is better to stand a little graft, etc., than to have revolutions all the time, like them coons, and any man that wasn't a anarchist or one of them I.W.W.'s would say the same. But when things get so bad that a man ain't hardly got no rights at all no more, but you might almost call him a slave, then everybody ought to get together and throw the grafters out, and put in new ones who won't carry on so high and steal so much, and then watch them. This is the proposition the people of these Colonies is up against, and they have got tired of it, and won't stand it no more. The administration of the present King, George III, has been rotten from the start, and when anybody kicked about it he always tried to get away with it by strong-arm work. Here is some of the rough stuff he has pulled:

He vetoed bills in the Legislature that everybody was in favor of, and 3 hardly nobody was against.

He wouldn't allow no law to be passed without it was first put up to 4 him, and then he stuck it in his pocket and let on he forgot about it, and didn't pay no attention to no kicks.

When people went to work and gone to him and asked him to put 5 through a law about this or that, he give them their choice: either they had to shut down the Legislature and let him pass it all by himself, or they couldn't have it at all.

He made the Legislature meet at one-horse tank towns, so that 6 hardly nobody could get there and most of the leaders would stay home and let him go to work and do things like he wanted.

He give the Legislature the air, and sent the members home every 7 time they stood up to him and give him a call-down or bawled him out.

When a Legislature was busted up he wouldn't allow no new one to 8 be elected, so that there wasn't nobody left to run things, but anybody could walk in and do whatever they pleased.

He tried to scare people outen moving into these States, and made 9 it so hard for a wop or one of these here kikes to get his papers that he would rather stay home and not try it, and then, when he come in, he wouldn't let him have no land, and so he either went home again or never come.

He monkeyed with the courts, and didn't hire enough judges to do 10 the work, and so a person had to wait so long for his case to come up that he got sick of waiting, and went home, and so never got what was coming to him.

He got the judges under his thumb by turning them out when they 11 done anything he didn't like, or by holding up their salaries, so that they had to knuckle down or not get no money.

He made a lot of new jobs, and give them to loafers that nobody 12 knowed nothing about, and the poor people had to pay the bill, whether they could or not.

Without no war going on, he kept an army loafing around the coun- 13 try, no matter how much people kicked about it.

He let the army run things to suit theirself and never paid no atten- 14 tion whatsoever to nobody which didn't wear no uniform.

He let grafters run loose, from God knows where, and give them the 15
say in everything, and let them put over such things as the following:

Making poor people board and lodge a lot of soldiers they ain't got 16
no use for, and don't want to see loafing around.

When the soldiers kill a man, framing it up so that they would get 17
off.

Interfering with business.   18

Making us pay taxes without asking us whether we thought the things 19
we had to pay taxes for was something that was worth paying taxes for or
not.

When a man was arrested and asked for a jury trial, not letting him 20
have no jury trial.

Chasing men out of the country, without being guilty of nothing, and 21
trying them somewheres else for what they done here.

In countries that border on us, he put in bum governments, and then 22
tried to spread them out, so that by and by they would take in this country
too, or make our own government as bum as they was.

He never paid no attention whatever to the Constitution, but he 23
went to work and repealed laws that everybody was satisfied with and
hardly nobody was against, and tried to fix the government so that he
could do whatever he pleased.

He busted up the Legislatures and let on he could do all the work 24
better by himself.

Now he washes his hands of us and even goes to work and declares 25
war on us, so we don't owe him nothing, and whatever authority he ever
had he ain't got no more.

He has burned down towns, shot down people like dogs, and raised 26
hell against us out on the ocean.

He hired whole regiments of Dutch, etc., to fight us, and told them 27
they could have anything they wanted if they could take it away from us,
and sicked these Dutch, etc., on us.

He grabbed our own people when he found them in ships on the 28
ocean, and shoved guns into their hands, and made them fight against us,
no matter how much they didn't want to.

He stirred up the Indians, and give them arms and ammunition, and 29
told them to go to it, and they have killed men, women and children, and
don't care which.

Every time he has went to work and pulled any of these things, we 30
have went to work and put in a kick, but every time we have went to work
and put in a kick he has went to work and did it again. When a man keeps
on handing out such rough stuff all the time, all you can say is that he ain't
got no class and ain't fitten to have no authority over people who have got
any rights, and he ought to be kicked out.

When we complained to the English we didn't get no more satisfac- 31
tion. Almost every day we give them plenty of warning that the politicians
over there was doing things to us that they didn't have no right to do. We

kept on reminding them who we was, and what we was doing here, and how we come to come here. We asked them to get us a square deal, and told them that if this thing kept on we'd have to do something about it and maybe they wouldn't like it. But the more we talked, the more they didn't pay no attention to us. Therefore, if they ain't for us they must be agin us, and we are ready to give them the fight of their lives, or to shake hands when it is over.

Therefore be it resolved, That we, the representatives of the people 32 of the United States of America, in Congress assembled, hereby declare as follows: That the United States, which was the United Colonies in former times, is now a free country, and ought to be; that we have throwed out the English King and don't want to have nothing to do with him no more, and are not taking no more English orders no more; and that, being as we are now a free country, we can do anything that free countries can do, especially declare war, make peace, sign treaties, go into business, etc. And we swear on the Bible on this proposition, one and all, and agree to stick to it no matter what happens, whether we win or we lose, and whether we get away with it or get the worst of it, no matter whether we lose all our property by it or even get hung for it.

Questions

Rereading and Independent Analysis

1. Compare this version of the Declaration with the original, printed in Chapter 2. List the words and formal features that the two have in common. Find what exactly tells you that this version also actually *is* the Declaration?

2. List all of the words, grammar, and mechanical devices of Mencken's "Declaration" that you think of as poor or nonstandard English. Next to each, write the words of the original that correspond to them. What evaluation do you make when you compare the two lists?

Suggested Discussion and Group Activities

1. When you review the original Declaration next to Mencken's, do you think of the original as "snobbish"? What was the purpose of the original? To whom is it addressed? What was the educational background of the people who wrote it? Where was Mencken's version first published? What was its purpose? What generalizations can you make about the fit between a level of language and the context in which it is used?

2. Was Mencken accurate about the "Common Speech" of most Americans? Does his "Declaration" intend to make fun of the average person? What does he say his intention is? Why does he think it important that all Americans understand the original Declaration?

3. In groups, choose another important American document and rewrite part of it so that any American could understand it.

Writing Suggestions

Response

How do you react when you hear or read language that you cannot understand? Do you "switch off" and lose the sense of it? Does it offend you? Write a few paragraphs about these responses, using particular examples to show what you mean.

Analysis

1. Write a "translation" of any piece of writing that you think most people would not understand, using language that would make it clear to them. Then write a parody (a humorous imitation) of the piece of writing you rewrote, indicating by your choice of words and other features of your "voice" that you do not mean it to be taken seriously.

2. Find examples of writing where the author has obscured the meaning by using inflated diction, awkward sentence structure, and confusion about who is acting and what is being done. Analyze this writing, explaining *why* you think the author chose to write this way. Show an alternative by rewriting all or part of the piece.

Finding a Purpose

Write a feature article for a local paper in which you explain the meaning of an important document or group of documents. Your audience is readers who you think do not understand the language used or have forgotten the purpose of it. Choose a public document like those in Chapter 2 of this book or statements by companies, utilities, and other organizations about their rules, procedures, or policies. You might look especially for notices about changes in traditional policies. Explain why it is important that your readers know what the document means.

 # The Macbeth Murder Mystery
James Thurber

James Thurber (1894–1961) was one of the greatest humor writers in the English language, according to his own judgment and that of many others who were not put off by his need for recognition. His many contributions to the *New Yorker* magazine (where this light humor about Macbeth first appeared) and his cartoons have an edge of social commentary. They often take up family relations in ways that suggest they have instructive as well as entertaining purposes. Thurber was a master of the "casual," a short piece of humorous observation that appears to have been written at one sitting. He wrote critical humor pieces about many experiences we all share: family; football players; troubles with using a microscope; and college professors, particularly faculty members at Ohio State University, the home-town school that he attended but neither liked nor graduated from.

Thurber began his career in New York, writing for the *New Yorker.* Then he moved to France, where he worked at the American Embassy from 1918 to 1920. After his first marriage ended, he returned to New York and the *New Yorker,* where he shared an office with E. B. White (who is well known for his children's books, especially *Charlotte's Web,* and for contributing to *The Elements of Style*). By this time Thurber was almost totally blind as a result of a childhood accident; as his health declined in later life, he wrote children's books and fantasy. Collections of his writings appeared regularly throughout the 1930s, 1940s, and 1950s: *The Seal in the Bedroom and Other Predicaments* (1932); *My Life and Hard Times* (1933); *Fables for Our Time* (1940); *My World and Welcome to It* (1942); *The Thurber Carnival* (1945); *The Thurber Album* (1952); and *The Owl in the Attic and Other Perplexities* (1959). Thurber's humor was the basis for a television comedy series in the late 1960s. His short story "The Secret Life of Walter Mitty" created a classic fantasizing male character whose strange imagination and peculiar perspective were true of Thurber himself.

In "The Macbeth Murder Mystery" Thurber uses the device of innocently questioning a woman mystery fan, which results in his playing with the plot of Shakespeare's play. As in much of his work, a woman is portrayed as unreasonable, an object of humor, willing to question the most established opinions. But Thurber's primary reason for writing this, as you will see, is to make fun of complex interpretations of literature. Before reading, you may want to look up the plot and characters of *Macbeth,* but any reader who has read or seen mystery stories will be able to appreciate Thurber's wit in this piece.

"It was a stupid mistake to make," said the American woman I had met 1 at my hotel in the English lake country, "but it was on the counter with the other Penguin books—the little sixpenny ones, you know, with the paper covers—and I supposed of course it was a detective story. All the others were detective stories. I'd read all the others, so I bought this one without really looking at it carefully. You can imagine how mad I was when I found it was Shakespeare." I murmured something sympathetically. "I don't see why the Penguin-books people had to get out Shakespeare plays in the same size and everything as the detective stories," went on my companion. "I think they have different-colored jackets," I said. "Well, I didn't notice that," she said. "Anyway, I got real comfy in bed that night and all ready to read a good mystery story and here I had 'The Tragedy of Macbeth'—a book for high-school students. Like 'Ivanhoe.' " "Or 'Lorna Doone,' " I said. "Exactly," said the American lady. "And I was just crazy for a good Agatha Christie, or something. Hercule Poirot is my favorite detective." "Is he the rabbity one?" I asked. "Oh, no," said my crime-fiction expert. "He's the Belgian one. You're thinking of Mr. Pinkerton, the one that helps Inspector Bull. He's good, too."

Over her second cup of tea my companion began to tell the plot of 2 a detective story that had fooled her completely—it seems it was the old family doctor all the time. But I cut in on her. "Tell me," I said. "Did you read 'Macbeth'?" "I *had* to read it," she said. "There wasn't a scrap of anything else to read in the whole room." "Did you like it?" I asked. "No,

I did not," she said, decisively. "In the first place, I don't think for a moment that Macbeth did it." I looked at her blankly. "Did what?" I asked. "I don't think for a moment that he killed the King," she said. "I don't think the Macbeth woman was mixed up in it, either. You suspect them the most, of course, but those are the ones that are never guilty—or shouldn't be, anyway." "I'm afraid," I began, "that I—" "But don't you see?" said the American lady. "It would spoil everything if you could figure out right away who did it. Shakespeare was too smart for that. I've read that people never *have* figured out 'Hamlet,' so it isn't likely Shakespeare would have made 'Macbeth' as simple as it seems." I thought this over while I filled my pipe. "Who do you suspect?" I asked, suddenly. "Macduff," she said, promptly. "Good God!" I whispered, softly.

"Oh Macduff did it, all right," said the murder specialist. "Hercule Poirot would have got him easily." "How did you figure it out?" I demanded. "Well," she said, "I didn't right away. At first I suspected Banquo. And then, of course, he was the second person killed. That was good right in there, that part. The person you suspect of the first murder should always be the second victim." "Is that so?" I murmured. "Oh, yes," said my informant. "They have to keep surprising you. Well, after the second murder I didn't know *who* the killer was for a while." "How about Malcolm and Donalbain, the King's sons?" I asked. "As I remember it, they fled right after the first murder. That looks suspicious." "Too suspicious." said the American lady. "Much too suspicious. When they flee, they're never guilty. You can count on that." "I believe," I said, "I'll have a brandy," and I summoned the waiter. My companion leaned toward me, her eyes bright, her teacup quivering. "Do you know who discovered Duncan's body?" she demanded. I said I was sorry, but I had forgotten. "Macduff discovers it," she said, slipping into the historical present. "Then he comes running downstairs and shouts, 'Confusion has broke open the Lord's anointed temple' and 'Sacrilegious murder has made his masterpiece' and on and on like that." The good lady tapped me on the knee. "All that stuff was rehearsed," she said. "You wouldn't say a lot of stuff like that, offhand, would you—if you had found a body?" She fixed me with a glittering eye. "I—" I began. "You're right!" she said. "You wouldn't! Unless you had practiced it in advance. 'My God, there's a body in here!' is what an innocent man would say." She sat back with a confident glare.

I thought for a while. "But what do you make of the Third Murderer?" I asked. "You know, the Third Murderer has puzzled 'Macbeth' scholars for three hundred years." "That's because they never thought of Macduff," said the American lady. "It was Macduff, I'm certain. You couldn't have one of the victims murdered by two ordinary thugs—the murderer always has to be somebody important." "But what about the banquet scene?" I asked, after a moment. "How do you account for Macbeth's guilty actions there, when Banquo's ghost came in and sat in his chair?" The lady leaned forward and tapped me on the knee again. "There wasn't any ghost," she said. "A big, strong man like that doesn't go around seeing ghosts—especially in a brightly lighted banquet hall with

dozens of people around. Macbeth was *shielding somebody!*" "Who was
he shielding?" I asked. "Mrs. Macbeth, of course," she said. "He thought
she did it and he was going to take the rap himself. The husband always
does that when the wife is suspected." "But what," I demanded, "about
the sleepwalking scene, then?" "The same thing, only the other way
around," said my companion. "That time *she* was shielding *him*. She
wasn't asleep at all. Do you remember where it says, 'Enter Lady Macbeth
with a taper'?" "Yes," I said. "Well, people who walk in their sleep *never
carry lights!*" said my fellow-traveler. "They have a second sight. Did you
ever hear of a sleepwalker carrying a light?" "No," I said, "I never did."
"Well, then, she wasn't asleep. She was acting guilty to shield Macbeth."
"I think," I said, "I'll have another brandy," and I called the waiter. When
he brought it, I drank it rapidly and rose to go. "I believe," I said, "that
you have got hold of something. Would you lend me that 'Macbeth'? I'd
like to look it over tonight. I don't feel, somehow, as if I'd ever really read
it." "I'll get it for you," she said. "But you'll find that I am right."

    I read the play over carefully that night, and the next morning, after 5
breakfast, I sought out the American woman. She was on the putting
green, and I came up behind her silently and took her arm. She gave an
exclamation. "Could I see you alone?" I asked, in a low voice. She nodded
cautiously and followed me to a secluded spot. "You've found out something?" she breathed. "I've found out," I said, triumphantly, "the name of
the murderer!" "You mean it wasn't Macduff?" she said. "Macduff is as
innocent of those murders," I said, "as Macbeth and the Macbeth woman."
I opened the copy of the play, which I had with me, and turned to Act II,
Scene 2. "Here," I said, "you will see where Lady Macbeth says, 'I laid
their daggers ready. He could not miss 'em. Had he not resembled my
father as he slept, I had done it.' Do you see?" "No," said the American
woman, bluntly, "I don't." "But it's simple!" I exclaimed. "I wonder I
didn't see it years ago. The reason Duncan resembled Lady Macbeth's
father as he slept is that *it actually was her father!*" "Good God!" breathed
my companion, softly. "Lady Macbeth's father killed the King," I said,
"and, hearing someone coming, thrust the body under the bed and
crawled into the bed himself." "But," said the lady, "you can't have a
murderer who only appears in the story once. You can't have that." "I
know that," I said, and I turned to Act II, Scene 4. "It says here, 'Enter
Ross with an old Man.' Now, that old man is never identified and it is my
contention he was old Mr. Macbeth, whose ambition it was to make his
daughter Queen. There you have your motive." "But even then," cried
the American lady, "he's still a minor character!" "Not," I said, gleefully,
"when you realize that he was also *one of the weird sisters in disguise!*"
"You mean one of the three witches?" "Precisely," I said. "Listen to this
speech of the old man's. 'On Tuesday last, a falcon towering in her pride
of place, was by a mousing owl hawk'd at and kill'd.' Who does that sound
like?" "It sounds like the way the three witches talk," said my companion,
reluctantly. "Precisely!" I said again. "Well," said the American woman,
"maybe you're right, but . . ." "I'm sure I am," I said. "And do you know

what I'm going to do now?" "No," she said. "What?" "Buy a copy of 'Hamlet,'" I said, "and solve *that!*" My companion's eye brightened. "Then," she said, "you don't think Hamlet did it?" "I am," I said, "absolutely positive he didn't." "But who," she demanded, "do you suspect?" I looked at her cryptically. "Everybody," I said, and disappeared into a small grove of trees as silently as I had come.

Questions

Rereading and Independent Analysis

1. Make notes about the *exposition* (information) and its delivery in this humorous essay. What details are given that allow any reader, even one who has read neither Shakespeare nor detective fiction, to understand what the two speakers are talking about? Where are these bits of information revealed?

2. If you have read *Macbeth,* choose a classmate who has not read it and read Thurber's piece together. Discuss the difference that knowing the play made in your two readings of this story.

Suggested Discussion and Group Activities

1. What is the implied thesis of this piece? In groups, write thesis sentences that suggest that this essay is about observing evidence from different perspectives, travel encounters, judging books by their covers, or detective stories. As a class, decide which of these possible theses for the essay has the most evidence to support it.

2. One of the issues that this essay tells us about is a reader's power to create the meaning in his or her reading. What does the American woman use reading for? What are some other examples of special uses of reading?

Writing Suggestions

Response

Write an essay in which you explain the humor of a misunderstanding that you or someone you know had. Explain how the misunderstanding happened and tell whether it was corrected or left as it was.

Analysis

In many ways, Thurber's piece is about analyzing and interpreting. Choose a work you have read with whose "standard reading" you are familiar. (If you like, choose one of the selections in this collection and the interpretation suggested by its headnote and questions.) Then write an explanation to a classmate of how the standard interpretation missed one or more details that must be included to understand the piece's "true" meaning. Explain what that "true" meaning becomes when these details are noticed. If you wish, take a humorous perspective on this unusual explanation.

Finding a Purpose: Further Reading
Read one or two of Thurber's other essays and write a review of them for
the class in which you summarize and give examples of his most frequently
used humorous techniques and themes. Your review should serve to encourage your classmates to read more of Thurber.

 # Hobbitry
Guy Davenport

Considering his experience in many fields of writing and literature, it is not
surprising that Guy Davenport (b. 1927), who sometimes writes under the
name Max Montgomery, enjoys the play among words and their contexts.
He clearly appreciates continuing traditions, including his own Southern
tradition. Born in South Carolina, he attended Duke University, went to
Oxford as a Rhodes Scholar, and received his Ph.D. at Harvard. He is a
sophisticated man of letters who has taught at the University of Kentucky and
has written short stories, poetry, essays, librettos, and translations of the
classics. He also writes, sometimes under his pseudonym, critical essays and
reviews. His books include two collections of short stories (*Da Vinci's Bicycle* [1979] and *Eclogues* [1981]) and the collection of essays from which
"Hobbitry" comes, *The Geography of the Imagination* (1981).

　　The tradition and importance of naming things, addressed in this
essay, are as ancient and well documented as the Book of Genesis in the Old
Testament. The biblical story of creation tells about God's naming the parts
of creation and continues with Adam naming all living creatures. What
something is "called," its unique name, is a powerful totem. In the Old
Testament, God refuses to allow the Jews to use his name, an indication of
the power of a name to fix identity. (See the section "Letters of the Law"
in Chapter 2.) Davenport's use of more than one name himself shows how
we associate versatile personalities and roles with particular names. We are
not necessarily adopting only a written *persona* (mask) to obscure our
identities when we use another name, as Jonathan Swift and many others
have done to hide the sources of political writing. (See "A Modest Proposal"
and the excerpt from the trial of Yuli Daniel later in this chapter.) Writers who
play with names may, in fact, be claiming another actual identity by using
another name. This essay is about the sources of the names that have
charmed the many readers of the Ring Trilogy, a three-volume account of
a fictional world of small creatures. The hobbits are mixtures of Anglo-Saxon
simplicity and contemporary determination to remain free, so the sources
Davenport identifies for their names are not surprising.

In the sad list of things that will always be beyond me, philology is toward　1
the top, up with my inability to drive an automobile or pronounce the
word "mirroring." The well-meant efforts of two universities to teach me
to read (and in a recurring nightmare, to write and speak) Old English, or

Anglo-Saxon as they sometimes called it, I have no intention of forgiving. Some grudges are permanent. On Judgment Day I shall proudly and stubbornly begrudge learning how to abandon a sinking ship, how to crawl under live machine-gun fire, and Anglo-Saxon.

The first professor to harrow me with the syntax and morphology of 2 Old English had a speech impediment, wandered in his remarks, and seemed to think that we, his baffled scholars, were well up in Gothic, Erse, and Welsh, the grammar of which he freely alluded to. How was I to know that he had one day written on the back of one of our examination papers, "In a hole in the ground there lived a hobbit"?

Not until years later could I know that this vague and incomprehensi- 3 ble lecturer, having poked around on a page of the dread "Anglo-Saxon Chronicle" for an hour, muttering place names and chuckling over variant readings, biked out to Sandfield Road in Headington and moved Frodo and Sam toward Mordor.

Even when I came to read *The Lord of the Rings* I had trouble, as 4 I still do, realizing that it was written by the mumbling and pedantic Prof. J. R. R. Tolkien.

Nor have I had much luck in blending the professor and the author 5 in my mind. I've spent a delicious afternoon in Tolkien's rose garden talking with his son, and from this conversation there kept emerging a fond father who never quite noticed that his children had grown up, and who, as I gathered, came and went between the real world and a world of his own invention. I remembered that Sir Walter Scott's son grew up in ignorance that his father was a novelist, and remarked as a lad in his teens when he was among men discussing Scott's genius, "Aye, it's commonly him is first to see the hare."

Nor, talking with his bosom friend H. V. G. ("Hugo") Dyson, could 6 I get any sense of the Tolkien who invented hobbits and the most wonderful adventures since Ariosto and Boiardo. "Dear Ronald," Dyson said, "writing all those silly books with three introductions and ten appendixes. His was not a true imagination, you know: He made it all up." I have tried for fifteen years to figure out what Dyson meant by that remark.

The closest I have ever gotten to the secret and inner Tolkien was 7 in a casual conversation on a snowy day in Shelbyville, Kentucky. I forget how in the world we came to talk of Tolkien at all, but I began plying questions as soon as I knew that I was talking to a man who had been at Oxford as a classmate of Ronald Tolkien's. He was a history teacher, Allen Barnett. He had never read *The Hobbit* or *The Lord of the Rings.* Indeed, he was astonished and pleased to know that his friend of so many years ago had made a name for himself as a writer.

"Imagine that! You know, he used to have the most extraordinary 8 interest in the people here in Kentucky. He could never get enough of my tales of Kentucky folk. He used to make me repeat family names like Barefoot and Boffin and Baggins and good country names like that."

And out the window I could see tobacco barns. The charming anach- 9

ronism of the hobbits' pipes suddenly made sense in a new way. The Shire
and its settled manners and shy hobbits have many antecedents in folklore
and in reality—I remember the fun recently of looking out of an English
bus and seeing a roadsign pointing to Butterbur. Kentucky, it seems,
contributed its share.

Practically all the names of Tolkien's hobbits are listed in my Lexing- 10
ton phone book, and those that aren't can be found over in Shelbyville.
Like as not, they grow and cure pipe-weed for a living. Talk with them,
and their turns of phrase are pure hobbit: "I hear tell," "right agin," "so
Mr. Frodo is his first and second cousin, once removed either way," "this
very month as is." These are English locutions, of course, but ones that are
heard oftener now in Kentucky than in England.

I despaired of trying to tell Barnett what his talk of Kentucky folk 11
became in Tolkien's imagination. I urged him to read *The Lord of the
Rings* but as our paths have never crossed again, I don't know that he did.
Nor if he knew that he created by an Oxford fire and in walks along the
Cherwell and Isis the Bagginses, Boffins, Tooks, Brandybucks, Grubbs,
Burrowses, Goodbodies, and Proudfoots (or Proudfeet, as a branch of the
family will have it) who were, we are told, the special study of Gandalf the
Grey, the only wizard who was interested in their bashful and countrified
ways.

Questions

Rereading and Independent Analysis

1. The effect of Davenport's essay relies partially on its *allusions*,
references to specific names or concepts you may not know. Use a good
dictionary to look up "syntax," "morphology," "Gothic," "Erse," "anach-
ronism," "locution," and any other words you do not recognize.

2. Make a list of the specific facts Davenport reveals about himself,
about Tolkien, and about the hobbits, in the order they are revealed. What
is the effect of arranging his material in this way? How do these separate
bits of information unify the essay?

Suggested Discussion and Group Activities

1. This essay depends on surprise for its impact on the reader. What
is its central revelation? What are the ways that Davenport (the "I" of the
essay) is surprised as he leads up to this revelation? How does he employ
other surprises throughout the essay? For instance, how do you react to
the three instances of "learning" that he says he will begrudge on Judgment Day (paragraph 1)?

2. What is the effect of beginning this essay with a description of
Davenport's failure to learn Old English? How is that failure related to the
purpose of the whole piece?

3. In groups, list other examples of names taken from "real life" and
applied to fictional characters or places. Then list examples of the reverse

process, where fictional names identify actual things. Why do you think we more often use words from fiction to name places and people? What effects do such names have?

4. Explain Davenport's use of three quotations from Scott's son, Dyson, and Bennett. What qualities do these quotations share? How do they "speak" for Davenport?

Writing Suggestions

Response

Write a brief account of a teacher you remember whom you revered as much as Davenport did Tolkien. What specific habits of this person stick in your memory? How did you feel in his or her classes? What did you learn beyond the subject matter you were taught?

Analysis

1. Imagine that you are writing a dictionary of names for children. Choose at least five names for boys and five for girls and write "entries" that explain what a child with each name will be like and be able to do in life.

2. Write a "philological" analysis of Davenport's essay. Explain how the names he uses throughout serve the essay's purpose. You will need to use a historical dictionary (e.g., *The Oxford English Dictionary*) and a gazetteer (book of maps) to identify all of Davenport's allusions to people and places. How do the names in this piece help a reader to visualize Davenport's personal memories?

Finding a Purpose

Write an essay in which you offer a writer advice about using surprise effectively. In your essay, compare Davenport's use of surprise to the young William Allen's use of it in the two stories in "A Whole Society of Loners and Dreamers" (see the section "Writers Alone" in Chapter 3). Explain why he succeeds while the young Allen did not.

THE TROUBLE WITH WRITING

 ## From *Phaedrus*
Plato

It is unusual to focus on the "troubles" writing can cause, so it is useful to go to the first statement we have of these possible dangers of writing. The Greek philosopher Plato (429?–347 B.C.) is the best known ancient source for a doubtful attitude about the value of writing. Plato's written dialogue between his teacher Socrates and the young student of composition and speech making, Phaedrus, is most famous for its criticism of the art of public speaking (rhetoric). But it is equally important because it shows how early writing was perceived as it became an important way to record speech. The alphabet was just coming into common use in Plato's time, and like any new, revolutionary technology, it required thoughtful consideration of the changes it was liable to bring about. Socrates, the older man, never wrote down his thoughts, so we know his words only through Plato, who later became Aristotle's teacher.

The last part of the dialogue, from which this selection comes, begins after Socrates' sharp demonstration of the dangers of mechanical patterns of organization in speech. As he closes, Socrates associates the power of writing with legendary Greek myths and the creative power of the gods, who gave language to humankind. But Socrates demonstrates to Phaedrus that writing has a tricky, dual nature.

The Greek word he uses in reference to it, *pharmakon,* means both "medicine" and "poison." Writing will aid memory by preserving words, but it will destroy memory by making it unnecessary. Writing will settle questions about meanings by fixing language, but it will multiply questions because it will be around long after the person who used a word is gone and cannot tell us his intention. Writing will look like a physical body, but it will be only the ghost of knowledge, which resides in the human soul. Socrates insists that "dialectic," the process of conversation, is the better way to conduct inquiry. He stresses that writing is by nature playful rather than "serious" since neither its origins nor its intentions can be verified.

Socrates' comments on writing do hold out hope both for a "science of speech" and for the success of one of his young friends, Isocrates, who was the first writer of speeches for others to deliver. As in all of Plato's dialogues, Socrates' character is playful. The dialogue leaves us aware that all we know of Socrates' intentions must be known through someone else's writing. This selection shows that the problem of saying exactly what we mean in writing and having that meaning remain clear long after we have written was identified at the very beginning of Western thought on the subject. As you read, keep in mind your own frequent desires to ask writers you cannot reach what they meant. This unavailability of writers has two results for us: it prevents us from settling on one interpretation of writing for all time, but it also allows us to renew and revitalize writing in new situations, as Americans have with our Constitution (see Chapter 2).

SOCR: Then shall we take it for granted that the subject of science and the lack of it in the case of speech has been adequately treated?

PHAEDR: Surely.

SOCR: Yet there remains the matter of propriety and impropriety in writ-   5
      ing: what conditions make it proper or improper? Isn't that so?

PHAEDR: Yes.

SOCR: Now do you know how to act or speak about words so that you may best please the gods?

PHAEDR: Not in the least. Do you?

SOCR: At least I can tell you what I've heard from our ancestors. Whether   10
      it's true or not, only they know; but if we could find out the truth for ourselves, should we still bother about merely human opinions?

PHAEDR: A ridiculous question. But tell me what you say you heard.

SOCR: I heard, then, that at Naucratis in Egypt there lived one of the old
gods of that country, the one whose sacred bird is called the ibis; and 15
the name of the divinity was Theuth. It was he who first invented
numbers and arithmetic, geometry and astronomy, dicing, too, and
the game of draughts and, most particularly and especially, writing.
Now the King of all Egypt at that time was Thamus who lived in the
great city of the upper region which the Greeks call the Egyptian 20
Thebes; the god himself they call Ammon. Theuth came to him and
exhibited his arts and declared that they ought to be imparted to the
other Egyptians. And Thamus questioned him about the usefulness
of each one; and as Theuth enumerated, the King blamed or praised
what he thought were the good or bad points in the explanation. Now 25
Thamus is said to have had a good deal to remark on both sides of
the question about every single art (it would take too long to repeat
it here); but when it came to writing, Theuth said, "This discipline,
my King, will make the Egyptians wiser and will improve their
memories: my invention is a recipe for both memory and wisdom." 30
But the King said, "Theuth, my master of arts, to one man it is given
to create the elements of an art, to another to judge the extent of
harm and usefulness it will have for those who are going to employ
it. And now, since you are father of written letters, your paternal
goodwill has led you to pronounce the very opposite of what is their 35
real power. The fact is that this invention will produce forgetfulness
in the souls of those who have learned it. They will not need to
exercise their memories, being able to rely on what is written, calling
things to mind no longer from within themselves by their own
unaided powers, but under the stimulus of external marks that are 40
alien to themselves. So it's not a recipe for memory, but for reminding, that you have discovered. And as for wisdom, you're equipping
your pupils with only a semblance of it, not with truth. Thanks to you
and your invention, your pupils will be widely read without benefit
of a teacher's instruction; in consequence, they'll entertain the delu- 45
sion that they have wide knowledge, while they are, in fact, for the
most part incapable of real judgment. They will also be difficult to get
on with since they will have become wise merely in their own con-
ceit, not genuinely so."

PHAEDR: Now, Socrates, it's perfectly easy for you to make up tales from 50
Egypt or anywhere else you please.

SOCR: Yes, my friend, and the priests of Zeus' temple at Dodona used to
relate that the first prophetic words came from an oak. Now the men
of that age, unlike in their simplicity to you young sages, believed
that if they heard the truth even from "oak or rock," that was enough 55
for them. You, however, seem to think not of the truth, but are more
concerned with the identity of the speaker or the locale from which
the account comes.

PHAEDR: You're right to rebuke me. I do agree that the Theban is correct
    in what he says about writing.   60

SOCR: Then any man who imagines that he has bequeathed an art to
    posterity because he put his views in writing, and also anyone who
    inherits such an "art" in the belief that any subject will be clear or
    certain because it is couched in writing—such men will be utterly
    simple-minded. They must be really ignorant of Zeus Ammon's 65
    method of delivering prophetic truth[1] if they believe that words put
    in writing are something more than what they are in fact: a reminder
    to a man, already conversant with the subject, of the material with
    which the writing is concerned.

PHAEDR: Quite right.   70

SOCR: Writing, you know, Phaedrus, has this strange quality about it,
    which makes it really like painting: the painter's products stand
    before us quite as though they were alive; but if you question them,
    they maintain a solemn silence. So, too, with written words: you
    might think they spoke as though they made sense, but if you ask 75
    them anything about what they are saying, if you wish an explana-
    tion, they go on telling you the same thing, over and over forever.
    Once a thing is put in writing, it rolls about all over the place, falling
    into the hands of those who have no concern with it just as easily as
    under the notice of those who comprehend; it has no notion of whom 80
    to address or whom to avoid. And when it is ill-treated or abused as
    illegitimate, it always needs its father to help it, being quite unable
    to protect or help itself.

PHAEDR: You're quite right about that, too.

SOCR: Well then, are we able to imagine another sort of discourse, a 85
    legitimate brother of our bastard? How does it originate? How far is
    it better and more powerful in nature?

PHAEDR: What sort of discourse? What do you mean about its origin?

SOCR: A discourse which is inscribed with genuine knowledge in the soul
    of the learner; a discourse that can defend itself and knows to whom 90
    it should speak and before whom to remain silent.

PHAEDR: Do you mean the living, animate discourse of a man who really
    knows? Would it be fair to call the written discourse only a kind of
    ghost of it?

SOCR: Precisely. Now tell me this: take a sensible farmer who has seed he 95
    is anxious to tend properly and wants it to yield him a good full crop:
    would he seriously plant it during the summer, and in forcing-areas
    at that, and then take pleasure in the spectacle of a fine crop on the
    eighth day? If he ever did such a thing, wouldn't it be just for fun or
    to meet the needs of a special festival? But with seed that he was 100
    really serious about, wouldn't he make full use of scientific husbandry

---

[1] Spoken, not written.

and plant it in suitable soil and be perfectly satisfied if it came to maturity in the eighth month?

PHAEDR: As you know, Socrates, the latter would be a serious act, the former quite different, and motivated as you say. 105

SOCR: Shall we suppose that a man who has real knowledge of justice and beauty and goodness will have less intelligence about his own seeds than a farmer does?

PHAEDR: By no means.

SOCR: Then he will not, when he's in earnest, resort to a written form and 110 inscribe his seeds in water, and in inky water at that; he will not sow them with a pen, using words which are unable either to argue in their own defense when attacked or to fulfill the rôle of a teacher in presenting the truth.

PHAEDR: It certainly doesn't seem likely. 115

SOCR: No indeed. But when he does use writing, he will be sowing the forcing-areas of written expression, as it were, for the mere fun of it, even though he may be packing away a treasury of reminders against an old age of forgetfulness, if he ever reaches it—and not only for his own use, but for any other's whose goal is the same as his. 120 It will delight him to watch the delicate, forced bloom of his plants; and while others are engaged in various other amusements, refreshing themselves with banquets and the like, he will presumably prefer to spend the time he devotes to play in such activity as I have suggested. 125

PHAEDR: A splendid pastime, Socrates, and what a contrast to those other base ones! When a man can find his recreation in words, I mean, letting his imaginative discourse dwell on justice and the other subjects you mention.

SOCR: So it is, dear Phaedrus. But, in this regard, far more noble and 130 splendid is the serious pursuit of the dialectician, who finds a congenial soul and then proceeds with true knowledge to plant and sow in it words which are able to help themselves and help him who planted them; words which will not be unproductive, for they can transmit their seed to other natures and cause the growth of fresh words in 135 them, providing an eternal existence for their seed; words which bring their possessor to the highest degree of happiness possible for a human being to attain.

PHAEDR: Yes, this is indeed far more noble and splendid.

SOCR: And now, Phaedrus, since we agree about these matters, we are in 140 a position to decide the others.

PHAEDR: What others?

SOCR: Those that we wished to investigate, those that brought us to our present position: we wanted to look into the reproach brought against Lysias for writing out speeches, and also to examine speeches 145 themselves and see which were the products of art and which were not. Now I think we have pretty well cleared up the question of what is and what is not art.

PHAEDR: Yes, I did think so; but just remind me again how we did it.

SOCR: A man must first know the truth about every single subject on 150 which he speaks or writes. He must be able to define each in terms of a universal class that stands by itself. When he has successively defined his subjects according to their specific classes, he must know how to continue the division until he reaches the point of indivisibility. He must make the same sort of distinction with reference to the 155 nature of the soul. He must then discover the kind of speech that matches each type of nature. When that is accomplished, he must arrange and adorn each speech in such a way as to present complicated and unstable souls with complex speeches, speeches exactly attuned to every changing mood of the complicated soul—while the 160 simple soul must be presented with simple speech. Not until a man acquires this capacity will it be possible to produce speech in a scientific way, in so far as its nature permits such treatment, either for purposes of instruction or of persuasion. This is what our entire past discussion has brought to light. 165

PHAEDR: Yes, that was certainly what we came to see.

SOCR: And now, what about the question of whether it is honorable or disgraceful to write and deliver speeches? Under what circumstances may this properly involve reproach? Wasn't this made clear a little while ago when we said—? 170

PHAEDR: What did we say?

SOCR: That, whether Lysias or anyone else who has ever or will ever lay down laws in written form, either in private or in public, and think that in composing a document for a political maneuver he achieves thereby great certainty or clarity—this sort of composition is a dis- 175 grace to the writer, no matter whether one affirms or denies it. For ignorance, whether conscious or not, of justice and injustice, good and evil, cannot possibly fail to involve reproach of the most shameful sort, even though the whole mob applauds it.

PHAEDR: Quite so. 180

SOCR: On the other hand, there is the man who thinks that the written word on any subject necessarily contains much that is playful, and that no work, whether in verse or prose, has ever been written or recited that is worthy of serious attention—and this applies to the recitations of rhapsodes also, delivered for the sake of mere persua- 185 sion, which give no opportunity for questioning or exposition—the truth is that the best of these works merely serves to remind us of what we know already. However, complete lucidity and serious importance, he will think, belong only to those lessons in justice and beauty and goodness which are delivered for the sake of true instruc- 190 tion and are, in fact, inscribed in the soul; such discourses as these should be counted as his own legitimate children, a name to be applied first to those that take their source within himself, and secondarily to any of their offspring or brothers that may have worthily been implanted within the souls of others. To other kinds of discourse 195 he will pay no attention. Such a man as this, Phaedrus, is probably the sort of man that you and I might do well to pray we might become.

PHAEDR: With all my heart I wish and pray it may be so.

SOCR: Then enough of this amusement of ours with speeches—we have 200 given it its due. Do you go and tell Lysias that the two of us went down to the stream and the sanctuary of the Nymphs and there we heard voices instructing us to tell Lysias and all the other prose writers, and Homer and all the other poets who write to be recited or sung; and in the third place, Solon and all the other writers who 205 compose political tracts under the name of laws: "If a man composes his work with the full knowledge of the truth and can come to the aid of what he has written when he is challenged and has the power to demonstrate from his own mouth the poverty of his writings, he ought not to be designated by a name drawn from them, but by one 210 that indicates his serious pursuits."

PHAEDR: Then what names would you assign him?

SOCR: To call him wise, it seems to me, Phaedrus, is too overwhelming a term to be applied properly to any but a god. To call him a lover of wisdom or something similar would be more fitting and more seemly. 215

PHAEDR: And quite appropriate.

SOCR: Yes. On the other hand, a man who has nothing more worth while to show us than the works he has written, or rather put together, spending hours twisting phrases this way or that, pasting in this and pruning that—such a man you would, no doubt, be right to call a poet 220 or a speech-writer or a drafter of laws.

PHAEDR: Quite so.

SOCR: Then tell this to your friend.

PHAEDR: And what about you? What will you do? For you surely shouldn't pass up your own friend. 225

SOCR: What friend?

PHAEDR: The fair Isocrates. What message will you give him, Socrates? By what name shall we call him?

SOCR: Isocrates is still quite young, Phaedrus. But I don't mind telling you what I prophesy for him. 230

PHAEDR: Do tell me.

SOCR: It seems to me that his natural talents are too good to be judged by the standards of Lysias and his school; moreover, he appears to possess a nobler character. I should not be surprised, when he grows older, if in the kind of writing that he now essays he should surpass 235 all that have ever embraced the subject professionally, just as though they were mere children; and further still, if this is not enough for him, some more divine impulse may well lead him to greater heights;

for by his very nature, my friend, there is a tincture of philosophy in the man's thought. This, then, is the message I transmit from the 240 divinities of this place to Isocrates, my beloved. And do you convey a different one to your beloved Lysias.

PHAEDR: So it shall be. Let us go, then, since even the heat has grown milder.

SOCR: Wouldn't it be well to pray to the divinities here before we go? 245

PHAEDR: It would indeed.

SOCR: Beloved Pan and all the other gods who dwell here, grant me to be beautiful within. And as for my external possessions, may they befriend those I have within me. Let me believe that it is only the wise man who is rich. Let the mass of my gold be only what the temperate 250 man, and no other, can make his own.—Is there anything else we should ask, Phaedrus? I've prayed for all I want.

PHAEDR: Please include me in your prayer, for friends hold everything in common.

SOCR: Let us go. 255

Questions

Rereading and Independent Analysis

1. This portion of Plato's dialogue may be divided into the following sections: the origins of writing (lines 1–50); the effect of writing after it is written (51–84); another, "legitimate" kind of discourse (85–215); a true art of speech (216–254); and a summary. Reread the selection, making a list of Socrates' major points in each section.

2. Read each of Phaedrus' comments. How can you tell whether he is serious or ironic in his responses and questions? When you have doubts about his exact intentions, explain why.

Suggested Discussion and Group Activities

1. In groups, make a list of Socrates' charges against writing. List examples from your own experience that would support or deny these charges.

2. One of Socrates' most important points is that writing is a "bastard." Explain what qualities of writing he is referring to by this term. How does his extended metaphor about gardening and farming also apply to this literal image?

Writing Suggestions

Response

Remember one of your most important teachers, either in school or another setting. Make notes of what you can remember of his or her words to you. Then compose a dialogue between yourself and this teacher by adding to these notes. Your finished dialogue should show a reader the teacher's special qualities.

Analysis
Based on your class discussions of this dialogue and your own experience as a writer, write an essay about writing's dangers as you know them. Your readers are students of writing who have their doubts about its usefulness. They think it is better to talk to others about what they know and their ideas than to fix them in written words. Imagine yourself either taking Socrates' part in the twentieth century, or answering him with reasons that writing is worth the uncertainty it creates.

Finding a Purpose
Imagine that you need to explain a concept you have recently learned about to students who were not in the course where you learned it. Write a dialogue between a student and a teacher so that the student's questions and the teacher's explanations address any difficulties you and your classmates had in grasping the concept. You need not be as playful as Socrates and Phaedrus were, but have the student participate fully with questions and objections. You may choose any concept you wish to explain, but limit your choice so your dialogue will be thorough and clear. You may wish to draw on lecture notes and reading from this or another class.

 # A Modest Proposal
Jonathan Swift

Perhaps the most memorable example of satiric writing in English is this satire by Jonathan Swift (see Chapter 4) proposing an outrageous solution to food shortages in Ireland. As dean of St. Patrick's Cathedral in Dublin, Swift was a champion of Irish resistance to English policies. He is still celebrated in Ireland for his strong pro-Irish support. In 1724 he became the leader of Irish resistance to English oppression. He wrote numerous pamphlets and letters under the name of "M. B., Drapier," arguing for the Irish cause and against the exploitation that resulted in the commonplace judgment that "the English are devouring the Irish." Swift published almost all of his writing anonymously. Although many people knew who had written his inflammatory Drapier Letters, no one claimed the £300 offered for revealing M. B.'s identity.

We are always concerned about how our writing will be "taken," but this problem multiplies when we attempt to write with two meanings at once, as in satire. The greatest danger is that satire will, by some at least, be misread. It is the most difficult writing to stabilize for all readers. The problem is twofold: How can the writer stay in "character" without producing trite and obvious jokes? Will the pretense be so well conveyed that no one will understand its humor?

After the publication of this pamphlet, A Modest Proposal for Preventing the Children of Poor People in Ireland from Being a Burden to Their Parents or Country, and for Making Them Beneficial to the Public (1729), some people had a difficult time recognizing Swift's characteristic satire. He so successfully assumed the voice of a benevolent and entirely logical "projector" (a person who thinks up schemes, in this case humanitarian projects that forget humankind) that some were outraged at the pamphlet's seemingly serious suggestion. As you read, imagine that you are an eighteenth-century Irish reader of this anonymous pamphlet, surrounded by poverty and starvation. Look for clues that this pamphlet is satiric and for holes in its logical reasoning. If no one had told you that this is satire, would you recognize it as such on your own?

It is a melancholy object to those who walk through this great town or 1
travel in the country, when they see the streets, the roads, and cabin doors, crowded with beggars of the female-sex, followed by three, four, or six children, all in rags and importuning every passenger for an alms. These mothers, instead of being able to work for their honest livelihood, are forced to employ all their time in strolling to beg sustenance for their helpless infants, who, as they grow up, either turn thieves for want of work, or leave their dear native country to fight for the Pretender in Spain, or sell themselves to the Barbadoes.[1]

I think it is agreed by all parties that this prodigious number of 2
children in the arms, or on the backs, or at the heels of their mothers, and frequently of their fathers, is in the present deplorable state of the kingdom a very great additional grievance; and therefore whoever could find out a fair, cheap, and easy method of making these children sound, useful members of the commonwealth would deserve so well of the public as to have his statue set up for a preserver of the nation.

But my intention is very far from being confined to provide only for 3
the children of professed beggars; it is of a much greater extent, and shall take in the whole number of infants at a certain age who are born of parents in effect as little able to support them as those who demand our charity in the streets.

As to my own part, having turned my thoughts for many years upon 4
this important subject, and maturely weighed the several schemes of other projectors, I have always found them grossly mistaken in their computation. It is true, a child just dropped from its dam may be supported by her milk for a solar year, with little other nourishment; at most not above the value of two shillings, which the mother may certainly get, or the value in scraps, by her lawful occupation of begging; and it is exactly at one year old that I propose to provide for them in such a manner as instead of being a charge upon their parents or the parish, or wanting food and raiment for the rest of their lives, they shall on the contrary contribute to the feeding, and partly to the clothing, of many thousands.

---

[1] Make agreements to work in return for passage to a colony.

There is likewise another great advantage in my scheme, that it will 5 prevent those voluntary abortions, and that horrid practice of women murdering their bastard children, alas, too frequent among us, sacrificing the poor innocent babes, I doubt, more to avoid the expense than the shame, which would move tears and pity in the most savage and inhuman breast.

The number of souls in this kingdom being usually reckoned one 6 million and a half, of these I calculate there may be about two hundred thousand couples whose wives are breeders; from which number I subtract thirty thousand couples who are able to maintain their own children, although I apprehend there cannot be so many under the present distresses of the kingdom; but this being granted, there will remain an hundred and seventy thousand breeders. I again subtract fifty thousand for those women who miscarry, or whose children die by accident or disease within the year. There only remain an hundred and twenty thousand children of poor parents annually born. The question therefore is, how this number shall be reared and provided for, which, as I have already said, under the present situation of affairs, is utterly impossible by all the methods hitherto proposed. For we can neither employ them in handicraft nor agriculture; we neither build houses (I mean in the country) nor cultivate land. They can very seldom pick up a livelihood by stealing till they arrive at six years old, except where they are of towardly parts; although I confess they learn the rudiments much earlier, during which time they can however be looked upon only as probationers, as I have been informed by a principal gentleman in the county of Cavan, who protested to me that he never knew above one or two instances under the age of six, even in a part of the kingdom so renowned for the quickest proficiency in that art.

I am assured by our merchants that a boy or a girl before twelve years 7 old is no salable commodity; and even when they come to this age they will not yield above three pounds, or three pounds and half a crown at most on the Exchange; which cannot turn to account either to the parents or the kingdom, the charge of nutriment and rags having been at least four times that value.

I shall now therefore humbly propose my own thoughts, which I 8 hope will not be liable to the least objection.

I have been assured by a very knowing American of my acquaintance 9 in London, that a young healthy child well nursed is at a year old a most delicious, nourishing, and wholesome food, whether stewed, roasted, baked, or boiled; and I make no doubt that it will equally serve in a fricassee or a ragout.

I do therefore humbly offer it to public consideration that of the 10 hundred and twenty thousand children, already computed, twenty thousand may be reserved for breed, whereof only one fourth part to be males, which is more than we allow to sheep, black cattle, or swine; and my reason is that these children are seldom the fruits of marriage, a circumstance not much regarded by our savages, therefore one male will be sufficient to serve four females. That the remaining hundred thousand may at a year old be offered in sale to the persons of quality and fortune through the kingdom, always advising the mother to let them suck plentifully in the last month, so as to render them plump and fat for a good table. A child will make two dishes at an entertainment for friends; and when the family dines alone, the fore or hind quarter will make a reasonable dish, and seasoned with a little pepper or salt will be very good boiled on the fourth day, especially in winter.

I have reckoned upon a medium that a child just born will weigh 11 twelve pounds, and in a solar year if tolerably nursed increaseth to twenty-eight pounds.

I grant this food will be somewhat dear, and therefore very proper 12 for landlords, who, as they have already devoured most of the parents, seem to have the best title to the children.

Infant's flesh will be in season throughout the year, but more plenti- 13 ful in March, and a little before and after. For we are told by a grave author, an eminent French physician, that fish being a prolific diet, there are more children born in Roman Catholic countries about nine months after Lent than at any other season; therefore, reckoning a year after Lent, the markets will be more glutted than usual, because the number of popish infants is at least three to one in this kingdom; and therefore it will have one other collateral advantage, by lessening the number of Papists among us.

I have already computed the charge of nursing a beggar's child (in 14 which list I reckon all cottagers, laborers, and four fifths of the farmers) to be about two shillings per annum, rags included; and I believe no gentleman would repine to give ten shillings for the carcass of a good fat child, which, as I have said, will make four dishes of excellent nutritive meat, when he hath only some particular friend or his own family to dine with him. Thus the squire will learn to be a good landlord, and grow popular among the tenants; the mother will have eight shillings net profit, and be fit for work till she produces another child.

Those who are more thrifty (as I must confess the times require) may 15 flay the carcass; the skin of which artificially dressed will make admirable gloves for ladies, and summer boots for fine gentlemen.

As to our city of Dublin, shambles may be appointed for this purpose 16 in the most convenient parts of it, and butchers we may be assured will not be wanting; although I rather recommend buying the children alive, and dressing them hot from the knife as we do roasting pigs.

A very worthy person, a true lover of his country, and whose virtues 17 I highly esteem, was lately pleased in discoursing on this matter to offer a refinement upon my scheme. He said that many gentlemen of this kingdom having of late destroyed their deer, he conceived that the want of venison might be well supplied by the bodies of young lads and maidens, not exceeding fourteen years of age nor under twelve, so great a number of both sexes in every county being now ready to starve for want of work and service; and these to be disposed of by their parents, if alive, or otherwise by their nearest relations. But with due deference to so excellent a friend and so deserving a patriot, I cannot be altogether in his sentiments; for as to the males, my American acquaintance assured me from frequent experience that their flesh was generally tough and lean, like that of our schoolboys, by continual exercise, and their taste disagreeable; and to fatten them would not answer the charge. Then as to the females, it would, I think with humble submission, be a loss to the public, because they soon would become breeders themselves: and besides, it is not improbable that some scrupulous people might be apt to censure such a practice (although indeed very unjustly) as a little bordering upon cruelty; which, I confess, hath always been with me the strongest objection against any project, how well soever intended.

But in order to justify my friend, he confessed that this expedient was 18 put into his head by the famous Psalmanazar, a native of the island Formosa, who came from thence to London above twenty years ago, and in conversation told my friend that in his country when any young person happened to be put to death, the executioner sold the carcass to persons of quality as a prime dainty; and that in his time the body of a plump girl of fifteen, who was crucified for an attempt to poison the emperor, was sold to his Imperial Majesty's prime minister of state, and other great mandarins of the court, in joints from the gibbet, at four hundred crowns. Neither indeed can I deny that if the same use were made of several plump young girls in this town, who without one single groat to their fortunes cannot stir abroad without a chair, and appear at the playhouse and assemblies in foreign fineries which they never will pay for, the kingdom would not be the worse.

Some persons of a desponding spirit are in great concern about that 19 vast number of poor people who are aged, diseased, or maimed, and I have been desired to employ my thoughts what course may be taken to ease the nation of so grievous an encumbrance. But I am not in the least pain upon that matter, because it is very well known that they are every day dying and rotting by cold and famine, and filth and vermin, as fast as can be reasonably expected. And as to the younger laborers, they are now in almost as hopeful a condition. They cannot get work, and consequently pine away for want of nourishment to a degree that if at any time they are accidentally hired to common labor, they have not strength to perform it; and thus the country and themselves are happily delivered from the evils to come.

I have too long digressed, and therefore shall return to my subject. 20 I think the advantages by the proposal which I have made are obvious and many, as well as of the highest importance.

For first, as I have already observed, it would greatly lessen the 21 number of Papists, with whom we are yearly overrun, being the principal breeders of the nation as well as our most dangerous enemies; and who stay at home on purpose to deliver the kingdom to the Pretender, hoping to take their advantage by the absence of so many good Protestants, who have chosen rather to leave their country than to stay at home and pay tithes against their conscience to an Episcopal curate.

Secondly, the poorer tenants will have something valuable of their 22 own, which by law may be made liable to distress, and help to pay their landlord's rent, their corn and cattle being already seized and money a thing unknown.

Thirdly, whereas the maintenance of an hundred thousand children, 23 from two years old and upwards, cannot be computed at less than ten shillings a piece per annum, the nation's stock will be thereby increased fifty thousand pounds per annum, besides the profit of a new dish introduced to the tables of all gentlemen of fortune in the kingdom who have any refinement in taste. And the money will circulate among ourselves, the goods being entirely of our own growth and manufacture.

Fourthly, the constant breeders, besides the gain of eight shillings 24 sterling per annum by the sale of their children, will be rid of the charge of maintaining them after the first year.

Fifthly, this food would likewise bring great custom to taverns, 25 where the vintners will certainly be so prudent as to procure the best receipts for dressing it to perfection, and consequently have their houses frequented by all the fine gentlemen, who justly value themselves upon their knowledge in good eating; and a skillful cook, who understands how to oblige his guests, will contrive to make it as expensive as they please.

Sixthly, this would be a great inducement to marriage, which all wise 26 nations have either encouraged by rewards or enforced by laws and penalties. It would increase the care and tenderness of mothers toward their children, when they were sure of a settlement for life to the poor babes, provided in some sort by the public, to their annual profit instead of expense. We should see an honest emulation among the married women, which of them could bring the fattest child to the market. Men would become as fond of their wives during the time of their pregnancy as they are now of their mares in foal, their cows in calf, or sows when they are ready to farrow; nor offer to beat or kick them (as is too frequent a practice) for fear of a miscarriage.

Many other advantages might be enumerated. For instance, the ad- 27 dition of some thousand carcasses in our exportation of barreled beef, the propagation of swine's flesh, and improvement in the art of making good bacon, so much wanted among us by the great destruction of pigs, too frequent at our tables, which are no way comparable in taste or magnificence to a well-grown, fat, yearling child, which roasted whole will make a considerable figure at a lord mayor's feast or any other public entertainment. But this and many others I omit, being studious of brevity.

Supposing that one thousand families in this city would be constant 28 customers for infants' flesh, besides others who might have it at merry meetings, particularly weddings and christenings, I compute that Dublin would take off annually about twenty thousand carcasses, and the rest of the kingdom (where probably they will be sold somewhat cheaper) the remaining eighty thousand.

I can think of no one objection that will possibly be raised against this 29 proposal, unless it should be urged that the number of people will be thereby much lessened in the kingdom. This I freely own, and it was indeed one principal design in offering it to the world. I desire the reader will observe, that I calculate my remedy for this one individual kingdom of Ireland and for no other that ever was, is, or I think ever can be upon earth. Therefore let no man talk to me of other expedients: of taxing our absentees at five shillings a pound: of using neither clothes nor household furniture except what is of our own growth and manufacture: of utterly rejecting the materials and instruments that promote foreign luxury: of curing the expensiveness of pride, vanity, idleness, and gaming in our women: of introducing a vein of parsimony, prudence, and temperance: of learning to love our country, in the want of which we differ even from Laplanders and the inhabitants of Topinamboo: of quitting our animosities and factions, nor acting any longer like the Jews, who were murdering one another at the very moment their city was taken: of being a little cautious not to sell our country and conscience for nothing: of teaching landlords to have at least one degree of mercy toward their tenants: lastly, of putting a spirit of honesty, industry, and skill into our shopkeepers; who, if a resolution could now be taken to buy only our native goods, would immediately unite to cheat and exact upon us in the price, the measure, and the goodness, nor could ever yet be brought to make one fair proposal of just dealing, though often and earnestly invited to it.

Therefore I repeat, let no man talk to me of these and the like 30 expedients, till he hath at least some glimpse of hope that there will ever be some hearty and sincere attempt to put them in practice.

But as to myself, having been wearied out for many years with offer- 31 ing vain, idle, visionary thoughts, and at length utterly despairing of success, I fortunately fell upon this proposal, which, as it is wholly new, so it hath something solid and real, of no expense and little trouble, full in our own power, and whereby we can incur no danger in disobliging England. For this kind of commodity will not bear exportation, the flesh being of too tender a consistence to admit a long continuance in salt, although perhaps I could name a country which would be glad to eat up our whole nation without it.

After all, I am not so violently bent upon my own opinion as to reject 32 any offer proposed by wise men, which shall be found equally innocent, cheap, easy, and effectual. But before something of that kind shall be advanced in contradiction to my scheme, and offering a better, I desire the author or authors will be pleased maturely to consider two points. First, as things now stand, how they will be able to find food and raiment for an hundred thousand useless mouths and backs. And secondly, there being a round million of creatures in human figure throughout this kingdom, whose sole subsistence put into a common stock would leave them in debt two millions of pounds sterling, adding those who are beggars by profession to the bulk of farmers, cottagers, and laborers, with their wives and children who are beggars in effect; I desire those politicians who dislike my overture, and may perhaps be so bold to attempt an answer, that they will first ask the parents of these mortals whether they would not at this day think it a great happiness to have been sold for food at a year old in the manner I prescribe, and thereby have avoided such a perpetual scene of misfortunes as they have since gone through by the oppression of landlords, the impossibility of paying rent without money or trade, the want of common sustenance, with neither house nor clothes to cover them from the inclemencies of the weather, and the most inevitable prospect of entailing the like or greater miseries upon their breed forever.

I profess, in the sincerity of my heart, that I have not the least 33 personal interest in endeavoring to promote this necessary work, having no other motive than the public good of my country, by advancing our trade, providing for infants, relieving the poor, and giving some pleasure to the rich. I have no children by which I can propose to get a single penny; the youngest being nine years old, and my wife past childbearing.

Questions

Rereading and Independent Analysis

1. The effect of *A Modest Proposal* depends largely on the tight logic of its "author's" reasoning. Swift lays out the "author's" points formally, so that if we accept his observations and evidence in one part, we will have to reasonably agree with the inferences and judgments that follow. Make an outline of the piece, showing its logic. First divide it into sections and examine it to determine the progression of its parts. Then retrace the argument, making an outline that indicates premises, propositions, causes, effects, and conclusions. You should show how Swift moves from "if" to "then" throughout the piece.

2. Make a catalog of the kinds of evidence that Swift uses to develop his case. What are the sources of concrete details he supplies to give the impression that he has thought through a solution and its results very carefully, leaving no objections unanswered?

3. Swift carefully chooses his language in the *Proposal* to establish his *persona* (mask as "author"). Read aloud paragraphs 6, 10, and 17, as though you were genuinely the proposer of this scheme. How do your emphasis and tone sound? Try varying your "delivery" of important words and phrases to change the tone of each paragraph. Then make a list of the words in these paragraphs and others that you think are especially crucial to establishing the tone of the *Proposal*.

Suggested Discussion and Group Activities

1. What conditions in Ireland is Swift describing in the pamphlet? What sort of economic, social, and political facts are revealed? Cite information in the pamphlet that contributes to your understanding of what Ireland was like at the time.

2. The reasoning of the "author" of this plan depends on one premise (basic assumption), a connection the author makes automatically but that no one else would accept. Identify this premise. How does the language of the pamphlet reveal its "author's" assumption that one sort of life is identical to another?

3. In groups, brainstorm about an answer to the pamphlet that would object to it on its own terms. You want to show in your own pamphlet that this solution will not work on the very grounds that its "author" says that it will. Make a list of reasons why this solution is unsuitable without referring to your outrage at cannibalism.

Writing Suggestions

Response

Write a satiric essay on any subject you choose. Identify its purpose and best possible readers through your use of language, not by explanations outside your writing.

Analysis

1. Identify the purpose of Swift's pamphlet and the effect that the success of his actual desired outcome would have brought about. Then write an essay for the class in which you show how the techniques in a few of its paragraphs support, in every detail of their composition, this purpose and potential result. Compare your analysis with those of your classmates to see if you identify the same techniques.

2. Using Swift's writing in this collection and a few other examples, write an essay in which you analyze the problems of controlling a satiric "voice." (You may wish to include Mencken, Twain, and Thurber as examples.) How can a writer make two intentions clear at one time without falling into an overly obvious style? What is the importance of knowing who will read specific satiric writing? Is controlling the readership the only way to insure how writing will be taken, or is even this an inadequate method of communicating clearly?

Finding a Purpose

Imagine that you must write a section for a new textbook on writing in which you will explain to students like yourself the benefits and dangers of anonymous writing. Use Swift's writing as an example, but also consider other kinds of unsigned authorship and both their positive and negative potentials.

From the Transcript of the Trial of Yuli Daniel

Translated and edited by Max Hayward

In the 1950s and early 1960s, two Soviet story writers, Andrei Sinyavsky (b. 1925) and Yuli Daniel (b. 1925), sent some of their stories and essays criticizing the Stalinist period to Western European countries and the United States for publication. After these stories were published, the Soviet government charged both authors with defamation of the state—intentionally writing and publishing malicious lies about the government. This part of the transcript of their trial, which was secretly sent out of the Soviet Union, records part of the examination of Daniel. Both he and Sinyavsky decided to plead innocent; both were found guilty and sentenced to labor camps.

The stories that most aroused the prosecution in this case were published in *Dissonant Voices in Soviet Literature* (1964). Daniel was examined in this portion of the questioning about the works "This Is Moscow Speaking," "Hands," "The Man From Minap," and "Atonement." In the first, he portrays a "Public Murder Day," when adult citizens are allowed to murder anyone they want, except for some officials. In some places, mass slayings occur; in others, nothing is reported. The hero of the story first decides to kill the cruel leaders of this plan, then decides that all death is horrible and decides not to kill at all.

"Hands" describes the trembling hands of a secret police official who has gunned down "enemies of the state," including an old priest who walks toward him as he fires blanks that his friends have put in his weapon as a joke. "The Man From Minap" is about a man who can control the sex of the children he fathers by thinking of Karl Marx if he wants a boy and of Klara Zetkin (a German Communist) if he wants a girl. "Atonement" is about a man who suffers for the collective guilt of all who were forced to participate in and allow Stalinist terrorism.

This transcript portrays two dangers of writing. The first, obviously, is that a powerful government will suppress both the writer and the writing, imprisoning the one and censoring the other if the writer or writing is judged dangerous. Repression of this sort has plagued writers and artists in all times and places. Socrates, for example, was forced to take poison because his (unwritten) teaching was considered dangerous to the Athenian state.

The second danger is that the already dotted line between "truth" and "fiction" will become even more blurred. We must assume that the prosecutor in this case believed the charges against Daniel and that his questions showed, by his lights, true beliefs about Daniel's intentions. And we must equally assume that Daniel believed his own explanations of the difference between an author and his writing. Nonetheless, throughout this exchange we develop doubts about each man's firm separation of "literature" from "life." This transcript raises important questions about the politics of writing while it demonstrates how censorship can be defended by those who are convinced that they have "truth." Before reading, try to recall examples of censorship you have heard about or experienced. What issues do you think are important in determining the justice of censoring some writing? Is censorship ever justifiable? Why?

PROSECUTOR: And now, Daniel, will you explain the ideology of *This Is Moscow Speaking?*

DANIEL: For me there is a difference between content and ideology. First, I want to tell how and why this story was written. The idea was suggested by a friend. I was attracted by the notion that in describing 5 an imaginary Public Murder Day I could shed light on the psychology and behavior of people. The plot itself, a Public Murder Day, was what gave this particular story its political coloring. I must mention my own political position, leaving aside the literary aim I had set myself. In 1960–61, when I was writing this story, I—and not only I, 10 but any person who thought seriously about the situation in our country—was convinced that a new cult of personality was about to be established. Stalin had not been dead all that long. We all remembered well what were called "violations of socialist legality." And again I saw all the symptoms: there was again one man who knew 15 everything, again one person was being exalted, again one person was dictating his will to agricultural experts, artists, diplomats and writers. Again we saw one single name in the newspapers and on posters, and every utterance of this person, however crude or trivial, was again being held up to us as a revelation, as the quintessence of 20 wisdom. . . .

JUDGE: And so, in fear of a restoration of the cult of personality in our country, you decided to turn to the publishers Harper & Row in Washington?

DANIEL: I am not talking now about why I sent the story abroad, but about 25 why I wrote it.

JUDGE: Go ahead.

DANIEL: Well, seeing all this happen and remembering the horrors of the purges and violations of legality under Stalin, I concluded—and I am a pessimist by nature—that the terrible days of Stalin's cult could 30 come back. And, as you may recall, in those days things happened that were far more terrible than anything in my story. Remember the mass purges, the deportation and annihilation of entire peoples. What I wrote was child's play by comparison. . . .

JUDGE: I understand, of course, that the author's narrative and words 35 spoken by his characters are two different things. But here is what you wrote in *This Is Moscow Speaking*. (*He quotes the conversation with Volodya Margulis, including the passage, "But, do they expect to gain from this Decree?" etc.*)

DANIEL: You are quite right in saying that the attitude of the author is not 40 always identical with that of his characters. And the hero of my story objects to the words you have quoted. He says, "We must stand up

for the Soviet regime." So the passage you have just read is quite
clear.

JUDGE: Is that the same hero who fires his tommy gun "from the hip"? 45

DANIEL: That's right. And I'll explain this too. The idea of the story is,
briefly, that a human being should remain a human being, no matter
in what circumstances he may find himself, no matter under what
pressure and from what quarter. He should remain true to himself,
to himself alone, and have nothing to do with anything that his 50
conscience rejects, that goes against his human instinct. . . . Now
about this passage with the words "from the hip." The indictment
describes it as a call to settle accounts with the party leaders and the
government. It is true that my hero is speaking about the leaders; he
mentions them because he remembers the mass persecutions and 55
feels that those who are guilty should bear responsibility. But at this
point the indictment breaks off the quotation. The book does not stop
there, nor even does this particular soliloquy of my hero stop there.
He recalls scenes of killing and slaughter that he saw in the war. And
this mental image fills him with revulsion. The indictment obviously 60
gives a tendentious interpretation to this passage. After all, the same
hero says further on: "I want to kill no one." How can any reader then
say this character wants to kill? It should be clear to everyone that
he does not.

JUDGE: But you are by-passing the main point. Your hero is allowed to kill 65
by decree of the Soviet Government. In other words, we have a bad
government, and a good character who does not want to kill anyone
except the government?

DANIEL: That does not follow from the story. The hero says "no one." No
one means no one. 70

JUDGE: But you do have such a decree in the story?

DANIEL: Yes.

PROSECUTOR: I would like to ask Daniel to read the epigraph to Chapter
4.

JUDGE: I don't see any need for reading unprintable language in this 75
courtroom.

PROSECUTOR: I still would like permission to read the epigraph, with cuts,
without the bad language.[1]

JUDGE: Go ahead, but without the bad language.

PROSECUTOR: *(reading):* "I hate them so much I have spasms, I scream, 80
I tremble. Oh, if only all these ——— could be collected and destroyed at once!" Well, Daniel, how do you explain this epigraph?

DANIEL: It's an epigraph to the hero's thoughts. . . . *(Laughter in the
courtroom. Daniel looks around nervously.)*

PROSECUTOR: Who is it that you hate so? Who do you want to destroy? 85

---

[1] The "bad language" omitted is the Russian word for "whores." (The quotation is on p. 277
of *Dissonant Voices*.) [The footnotes in this selection are Hayward's.]

DANIEL: Who are you talking to? To me or to my hero, or to someone else?

PROSECUTOR: Who is your positive hero?[2] Who expresses your point of view in the story?

DANIEL: I have already told you once before in our preliminary talk that 90 the story has no entirely positive hero and that there doesn't have to be one.

PROSECUTOR: We had no preliminary talk. But who expresses the author's point of view? Where does it come in?

DANIEL: The characters do convey the author's attitudes, but only in part. 95 No single character is identical with the author. Maybe it's bad literature, but it is literature, and it doesn't divide everything into black and white.

PROSECUTOR: I would like to read out the findings of Glavlit[3] about Arzhak's story: *"This Is Moscow Speaking* is a monstrous lampoon." 100 . . . *(There follows an assessment of the story that agrees completely with the indictment, except that the Glavlit report finds that the story also has an element of anti-Semitism.)* Do you agree with this assessment, Daniel?

DANIEL: Certainly not. The report says that I express my ideas through 105 "the mouths of my characters." That is a naïve accusation, to put it mildly. That way you can accuse any Soviet writer of being anti-Soviet. Just take the White Guards in the works of Lavrenev, Sholokhov, Leonov—[4]

PROSECUTOR: *(interrupting):* Have the Western press comparisons of you 110 with Dostoyevsky gone to your head so much that you now compare yourself with leading Soviet writers?

DANIEL: I am not comparing myself with anyone. All I mean is that it is not what characters say but the author's own attitude toward what they say that is important. 115

---

[2] In the language of Soviet literary criticism the characters (referred to as "heroes") of novels and plays, etc., are divided into "positive" and "negative." It is implicit in the official doctrine of "socialist realism" that "positive" heroes should set a good example in their public and private lives, and that they should triumph over the "negative" characters, at least morally. In the last years of Stalin's life the rigid enforcement of this requirement resulted in a standard plot in which an inevitable "happy ending" was preceded by a "conflict" between the "negative" and "positive" characters.

[3] "Glavlit," a portmanteau word derived from: *"glavnoye upravlenie po delam literatury i izdatelstv"* (Chief Directorate on Matters of Literature and Publishing Houses), is the Soviet censorship agency originally set up by decree of the Council of People's Commissars in 1922. It is rarely referred to in public, but all works appearing in print in the Soviet Union have to be submitted to it. . . .

[4] Boris Lavrenev (1891–1959), Mikhail Sholokhov (born 1905), and Leonid Leonov (born 1899) are "classical" Soviet writers who had White Guardist characters in novels dealing with the Civil War. The portrayal of "counterrevolutionaries" in Soviet literature in the first years after the Revolution (e.g., in Leonov's *Badgers,* 1925) was often remarkably detached. The hero of Sholokhov's *And Quiet Flows the Don,* Grigori Melekhov, actually serves the White Guardist cause for considerable periods during the Civil War.

PROSECUTOR: In the preliminary investigation didn't you say you were in partial agreement with the Glavlit findings?

DANIEL: That is true, but only with the bare facts as given there.

PROSECUTOR: *(reading from the Glavlit report):* "In the author's view, the Soviet people blindly follow the party leadership." How would 120 you judge your story in the light of this?

DANIEL: I didn't mean to say anything so harsh. To some extent I agree with the idea that the political initiative of the masses . . . I don't believe in it very much. I consider the masses politically passive.

PROSECUTOR: In other words, if a "Public Murder Day" were proclaimed, 125 you would expect everyone simply to rush off to kill as they were told?

DANIEL: No, I don't say that in the story. The "Public Murder Day" is a literary device, chosen as a way of studying people's reactions.

JUDGE: There is something I want to clear up. Just imagine a communal 130 apartment where Ivanova is having a quarrel with Sidorova.[5] If Ivanova were to write that there is a certain lady who is making life difficult for another lady, then it would be an innuendo, a figure of speech. But if she were to write that Sidorova was throwing garbage into her soup, then we would have something like a libel, slander or 135 something else subject to legal proceedings. You were, after all, writing about the Soviet Government, not about ancient Babylon, but about a specific government that proclaimed a "Public Murder Day," and you name the date—August 10, 1960. Is that a device or outright slander?   140

DANIEL: Let me just use your example. If Ivanova were to write that Sidorova literally flies about on a broomstick or turns herself into an animal, that would be a literary device, not slander. I took an obviously fantastic situation.

JUDGE: But here is what B. Filippov wrote: "Can we say that what Arzhak 145 describes is all that far removed from reality?" So, you see, Daniel, it is not just a literary device, is it?

DANIEL: It is a literary device.

PROSECUTOR: Daniel, do you deny that the "Public Murder Day" supposedly proclaimed by the Soviet Government is in fact slander? 150

DANIEL: I hold that slander is something you can make people believe, at least theoretically. *(Laughter in the courtroom.)*

JUDGE: I want to clear this up. *(Reading from the law code:)* "Slander is the spreading of information known to be false and defamatory." That is the legal side of it.   155

DANIEL: What about imaginary situations, then?

JUDGE: I will go back to my example. If Ivanova were to assert that

[5] Sidorova and Ivanova are common Russian surnames in the feminine form.

Sidorova did something that Sidorova did not in fact do, then lawyers would call such a statement slander.

PROSECUTOR: You have slandered ordinary Soviet people. Just look how 160 Soviet people supposedly react to the proclamation of "Public Murder Day." *(He reads excerpts.)* These are supposed to be educated people. How can that be anything but slander? Take your conversation with Margulis—

DANIEL: *(interrupting):* That's not my conversation, it's my hero talking. 165

PROSECUTOR: But isn't that slander on the Soviet people?

DANIEL: In that case Mayakovsky's *Bathhouse* and *Bedbug* would also be slander on the Soviet people. Didn't Mayakovsky slander Pierre Skripkin?

PROSECUTOR: Let's not talk about that. Just show me a single Soviet per- 170 son in your story who seems like a real Soviet person. Just look at the picture you give of our intellectuals!

DANIEL: You talk about Soviet intellectuals as if they were all worthy of admiration.

PROSECUTOR: Just show me one person who is portrayed in a good light. 175 *(He reads excerpt.)* Isn't that slander on the Soviet people, on the Soviet Government?

DANIEL: Even the statutes of the Writers Union don't require writers to write only about noble, intelligent and good people. Why should I be obliged to write about good people in a work of satire? Satirists from 180 Aristophanes to Gogol—

PROSECUTOR: Your head has been turned!

DANIEL: May I make a statement? I am a writer. I cannot avoid referring to the history of literature, to the experience of other writers. That does not mean I put myself on a par with them. I don't, either as 185 regards wisdom or talent. I wish the prosecutor would stop saying that I do.

PROSECUTOR: In your story you mention *Izvestia* and *Literature and Life,* you mention the writers Bezymensky and Mikhalkov. You slander the entire Soviet press, all Soviet writers. What is it if not slander on 190 the Soviet press?

DANIEL: No, it is not slander on the Soviet press. I was alluding to individual writers, timeservers. It is a parody of the hackneyed style, the clichés that we often find in our papers.

PROSECUTOR: I expected that answer, and I am going back to the passage 195 about *Izvestia.* It says that "as usual, the paper printed an editorial calling for observance of 'Public Murder Day,'" etc. As usual! Isn't that slander on the entire Soviet press?

DANIEL: It's a gibe at the style of newspaper articles.

PROSECUTOR: Now, at last, you are speaking with your real voice. 200

JUDGE: There is no need for remarks that do not advance the case.

DANIEL: I always speak with my real voice.

PROSECUTOR: You write that the people are anti-Semitic and just waiting to start a pogrom. You compare its mood with what led to Babi Yar.[6] But there the killers were Fascists. Isn't it blasphemous to compare 205 our entire people with the Fascists?

DANIEL: It does not follow from the passage that the entire Soviet people is anti-Semitic; all that follows is that a few individuals are so inclined. I was talking about certain people, without mentioning names, who might want to settle private accounts; I said there might be a few 210 examples of such scum. Nothing more than this can be read into the text.

PROSECUTOR: A few individuals or the entire people—we will see right away. *(He reads a passage describing how Georgians killed Armenians, Armenians killed Georgians, and in Central Asia everyone* 215 *killed Russians.)* Isn't that slander on the entire Soviet people?

DANIEL: No. It is not slander on the entire Soviet people.

PROSECUTOR: And you say that all this happens under the direction of the Central Committee. Isn't that slander?

DANIEL: You keep forgetting that the starting point for all this is an imagi- 220 nary situation, not something that actually happened. *(Laughter in courtroom.)*

. . . .

PROSECUTOR: Why did you write works that could be interpreted as anti-Soviet?

DANIEL: Are you asking about them all or about any one in particular? 225

PROSECUTOR: You can tell us about any one of them.

DANIEL: I'll talk about "Hands." I know I don't have the right to put questions to the court. But can the prosecution point to a single sentence, a single word, a single syllable that could be interpreted as anti-Soviet? This story is a literary version of an actual event that was 230 recounted to me. There is nothing in the story to justify the charges against me. The indictment contradicts itself when it talks about this story. The indictment contends that the Soviet regime has never used force. But such a point of view is not scientific, it is not Marxist, it is not Leninist. According to Lenin, revolution is coercion, and the 235 state is coercive, and [in a revolutionary state there is] coercion of the minority by the majority. The indictment charges that I wrote: "The Soviet regime used violence against the Soviet people." There is nothing along these lines in the story, which is about the execution of counterrevolutionaries. There is nothing in the story to suggest 240 that this calls for retribution. It cannot be interpreted as in the indictment. Now, about "The Man from Minap." I don't like this

[6] A ravine in Kiev where the Germans massacred thousands of Jews in 1941. In his famous poem Evgeny Evtushenko complained that no monument had been put up there. The prosecutor's reference is to a passage on p. 273 of *Dissonant Voices.*

story; it is poorly written, crude, and in bad taste, but it contains
nothing anti-Soviet. It is a satire, a caricature, an extravaganza; all
this is in the tradition of satiric writing. Why is the portrayal of ten 245
bad persons passed off by the prosecution as a portrayal of the whole
of Soviet society? The characters of a satirical work are always negative, and the positive hero is always a conventional figure in such
writings. There is no basis for saying that the story is directed against
the morals and ethics of Soviet society. Why did I write it? Among 250
my friends there are many scientists, and one of them told me about
the fuss over Bashyan and Lepeshinskaya[7] (I don't equate these two
names) and that such sensational affairs have done harm to our science. The story dealt with that scandal and not with the branch of
science in question. Glavlit evidently feels I should have glorified the 255
events that I satirize.

The prosecutor and Daniel have a long argument about the "scientific theories" mentioned in the Glavlit report.
The judge reads a passage from the report describing the story as a
libel on "certain scientific theories."

JUDGE: Daniel, were you attacking Bashyan in this story?
DANIEL: No, I was attacking the practice of making sensational publicity
about scientific discoveries.
JUDGE: And if that is the main point of the story, why does your character 260
Volodya think about Karl Marx and Klara Zetkin at such an inappropriate time and in such a situation?
DANIEL: That can be explained by the haste with which the story was
written *(Disapproving murmur and coarse laughter in the courtroom.)* 265
JUDGE: Your story "Hands" is about the distant past. Why did you send this
story abroad instead of, say, "Escape"?
DANIEL: I wanted what I had written to be printed. I am convinced that
there is nothing anti-Soviet in my works. But I know that our editors
and publishers think that there are certain forbidden themes which 270
should not be dealt with in literature. There are a number of topics
on which writers do not write, or publishers do not publish them. The
subject of "Hands" is a taboo one which is passed over in silence. It
is about a kind of work which is bloody and difficult, but necessary.
The hero of the story is a worker who later serves in the Cheka. And 275
because of this work his hands tremble. *(Summarizes the story.)*

[7] Olga Lepeshinskaya (1871–1963) was a Soviet biologist who, like Lysenko, became notorious in the last years of Stalin's life for her attacks on genetics and strident advocacy of her
own dubious theories. In 1950 she received the Stalin prize for what was claimed to be "a
great discovery in biology." This consisted in a claim that there were noncellular forms of
life. One of her most active supporters was G. M. Boshyan (misspelled Bashyan in the
transcript). . . .

JUDGE: But why did you send this one abroad first?

DANIEL: Because I could assume that this story would not be published
here: it is about a forbidden subject that has not been dealt with in
our literature since the 1930's. . . .   280

JUDGE: But why this, and not "Escape" or some translations? It is written
in a gruesome style. *(Reads a passage.)* But that's not the point. Why
was the subject of the shooting of the priests so important to you at
this time? Why did you have to bring the subject up again at this
time? The *émigrés* made a lot of fuss about Tikhon.[8] Does this have   285
anything to do with literature?

DANIEL: But the hero does not know why he is executing people.

JUDGE: *(reads a passage, then says):* It is obvious that they would love to
publish this abroad.

DANIEL: I had no political purpose when I wrote this story. *(Laughter in*   290
the courtroom.)

. . . .

PROSECUTOR: You wrote things which, upon your own admission, could
be interpreted as anti-Soviet. You did this over a long period of time.
You knew how these things were interpreted in the West. Let us hear
how you yourself would describe your conduct.   295

DANIEL: I've always thought and I continue to think that my books were
not anti-Soviet and that I put no anti-Soviet meaning into them, since
I did not criticize or make fun of the basic principles of our life. I do
not equate individuals with the social system as such, or the government with the state, or a certain period with the Soviet epoch as a   300
whole. The state may exist for centuries but a government is often
short-lived and frequently inglorious. As regards my attitude to their
publication abroad, this is another matter—I regret it. Until my arrest I could only guess at the reaction to my works in the West.
During the investigation I understood that my works had been inter- 305
preted there as being attacks not on individual persons but on the
system, not as attacks on a certain period but as attacks on the cause
as a whole. None of my things is anti-Soviet in its basic idea—you
cannot say that it is anti-Soviet to suggest that a man should always
remain human, even if he finds himself in a situation like that of the   310
"Public Murder Day."

JUDGE: Even in the monstrous situation involving the Supreme Soviet of
the U.S.S.R.?

DANIEL: Yes, and I do not regard that as anti-Soviet.

JUDGE: And you sent these literary figments of your imagination abroad? 315

DANIEL: That I regret.

[8] Tikhon was the first Patriarch of the Russian Orthodox Church. . . . Many priests (like those
executed in Daniel's story) suffered because of their support of him. . . .

JUDGE: Your inventions involve one political idea after another. *(Repeats passages already quoted in the indictment.)*

DANIEL: Our literature and press are silent about the things on which I write. But literature is entitled to deal with any period and any 320 question. I feel that there should be no prohibited subjects in the life of society.

PROSECUTOR: But you took the year 1960. You thought up this decree!

. . . .

KISENISHSKY: Tell us how you got the idea for the story "Atonement."

DANIEL: In recent years we have often heard about people being exposed 325 as slanderers whose denunciations landed innocent people in jail. I wanted to show a rather different situation—how a man must feel if he has been falsely accused of doing something as terrible as this. This was something that actually happened to somebody I knew well. That's how the idea of the story came to me. The indictment says that 330 the underlying notion of the story is that everybody is to blame for the cult of personality and the mass persecutions. I agree with this interpretation, but not with the word "slanderous" used to describe the story. I feel that every member of society is responsible for what happens in society. And I make no exception for myself. I wrote that 335 "everybody is to blame" because there has been no reply to the question of who is to blame. Nobody has ever publicly stated who was to blame for these crimes, and I will never believe that three men— Stalin, Beria and Ryumin—could alone do such terrible things to the whole country. But nobody has yet replied to the question as to who 340 is guilty.

KISENISHSKY: When did you last send a manuscript abroad and why did you stop sending them?

DANIEL: In 1963.

KISENISHSKY: Give us the main facts about your life. 345

DANIEL: I was born in 1925. I went straight from school to the front line; during the war I fought on the second Ukrainian and third Byelorussian fronts. After being severely wounded, I was demobilized and received a pension as a war invalid. In 1946 I entered Kharkov University, and then transferred to the Moscow Province Teachers 350 Training College, from which I was graduated. Then I taught for two years at a school in Lyudinovo. After that I taught for four years in Moscow.

SOKOLOV: *(people's assessor):* Obviously you must have foreseen the impact of the publication of your manuscripts. What did you think it 355 would be?

DANIEL: If I had foreseen such an impact, I would not have sent my manuscripts abroad.

JUDGE: But you must have foreseen their political effect?

DANIEL: I did not think about how my works would be judged from a 360
political point of view. I thought only in terms of how they would
be judged from the point of view of their literary qualities or failings.

JUDGE: Then why did you have all these political details—that monstrous
decree, the execution of a priest because of Tikhon, and the Institute 365
of Scientific Profanation?

DANIEL: In *This Is Moscow Speaking* all these details are part and parcel
of the fantastic plot of the story.

JUDGE: All the people in it are moral degenerates—surely this has a political purpose, and has nothing to do with the plot. Why, for what 370
reason, did you have all this? Wasn't it in order to create a certain
impression?

DANIEL: It was not part of my intention to depict good people. The colors
are laid on rather thick in my story, but I was not trying to portray
good people. I was showing how bad people might behave in an 375
imaginary situation.

JUDGE: In the situation resulting from that decree of the Supreme Soviet!

DANIEL: I've already said that I would regard any excesses as possible if
the cult of personality were to return. 380

PROSECUTOR: You say that you didn't think about politics. But what about
this sentence here, for example, in your story *This Is Moscow Speaking:* "Anyway, to tell the truth, to be printed abroad, by anti-Soviet
publishers is not so good"? What are we to make of this?

DANIEL: It means exactly what it says—it's not very nice. I repeat once 385
more that I've already said what I think about the ethical side of the
matter.

JUDGE: Are there any points which you would like to make to the court?

DANIEL: Yes. The Prosecution constantly equates the author with his characters. This is particularly impermissible if the characters in ques- 390
tion, to put it mildly, are not quite right in the head. For instance in
"Atonement" the main character has gone out of his mind and it is
he who shouts: "Our prisons are within us!"

JUDGE: *(interrupts):* He only goes mad a page further on.

DANIEL: No. On the next page he is already in a mental hospital. Another 395
thing—quotations are always given without any reference to the
state of the characters who utter them. One has gone out of his mind,
another is an alcoholic.

JUDGE: All your intellectuals are drunkards.

DANIEL: I beg you, in the first place, not to quote out of context, and, in 400
the second place, to take account of the condition of the characters.
And if I have overdone things here and there, this should not be put
down to my being an anti-Soviet, but to my lack of literary skill.
(Laughter in the courtroom.)

Questions

Rereading and Independent Analysis

1. Reread the transcript, noticing the details of each of the stories mentioned. Make notes about each of the stories in which you portray their action, characters, and tone as well as you can. Can you imagine a message you would take from reading the stories?

2. What are the positions that each man takes on the relationship of art to life? How do they differ in important ways? Use specific passages from the transcript to answer these questions, copying their relevant words if you wish.

3. We do not know who made this transcript or how it was taken out of the Soviet Union. Whatever the circumstances, one of this transcript's important "characters" was the audience in the courtroom. Review each of the places where responses from the courtroom are mentioned. Do they appear to have had any effect on either Daniel or the prosecutor? Describe the effects you imagine and give reasons for them from what follows each audience response.

Suggested Discussion and Group Activities

1. Do you think there are circumstances when censorship should be established? Specify the circumstances in which you think limits on individual and group freedom must be imposed as well as your reasons for these opinions.

2. In groups, review some of the other readings you have completed (for example, those by Swift and Goffman) to specify the difference between the "author," or *persona,* and the person who wrote. What difference does it make whether the person writing and the voice in the piece of writing are one and the same? How does their separation or identity affect your interpretation of the writing?

3. Discuss instances in which writing or public speech were considered dangerous to a government, culture, or other group. How was this danger characterized? How was it prevented or allowed to have an influence? What was the final result of the "dangerous" communication?

Writing Suggestions

Response

Make notes on your responses as you read this transcript. What were your reactions to specific points made by both participants? Did you see the possible worth of the prosecutor's position in other situations? Do you think that Daniel was lying about his intentions?

Analysis: Further Reading

1. Find and read one of the stories that Daniel was questioned about in this trial. Then write an evaluation of it, supporting your conclusion that the story either was or was not expressing Daniel's negative opinions about Soviet government and life.

2. Investigate a case of censorship in America, using your library as a resource. Then write a report to the class that tells about the situation and its results. Your report should be factual and should end with a comparison between the case you investigated and the Daniel case and its outcome.

Finding a Purpose

To explain a social value that is important in your community, try writing a dialogue like this one, set in a courtroom. Make up a charge and its background; then write the crucial portion of the examination of the defendant. You may wish to focus on an extension of First Amendment rights in film making, other public speech, or private activities. If you wish, work with one or two others to establish the background of the mock trial and to write the parts of the dialogue.

Hey Kid, Wanna Buy
A Used Term Paper?
Phyllis Zagano

We usually think the relationship between the piece of writing we read and the name of its writer is clear. But as you know from writing, everything we read has innumerable sources, not just those we give credit to, but our entire stock of language. We praise successful imitations and parodies like Swift's *Gulliver's Travels* (Chapter 4) that would not be meaningful without the writing that they make fun of. We collaborate with others, rely on many sources we cannot specifically account for, and discuss our writing as we write it with anyone who will listen.

Nonetheless, we go out of our way to avoid falsely representing our participation in written conversations. Written words are simple marks on a page. They do not reveal their immediate origins, so they can be used to cheat a reader by misrepresenting the actual sources of their meanings. The danger of such misrepresentation was implied in Socrates' worries about writing in *Phaedrus*. Establishing a trustworthy written character is more complicated than establishing trust among friends who can rely on you to be honest with them. It is more complex than simply telling a truth as you know it because, to establish the value of what you write, you are not simply "telling" but are additionally clearly showing your part in the continuing written discussion of a topic.

Consequently, we have elaborate systems for citing references in footnotes, and we go out of our way to acknowledge the help we use. In writing, these are the only available ways to prevent readers from mistrusting everything they encounter in continuing written conversations. We need to indicate clearly whose ideas we are responding to if we are to monitor their results. The danger of plagiarism, implying that someone else's words are your own or that you have written alone when you have had help, in school research, or in any field, is that it distorts the subject and makes it impossible to verify or criticize new contributions.

As writers, we know when we are stealing in our writing, and Phyllis Zagano's editorial addresses such theft directly. Her comments on plagiarism appeared in *The Chronicle of Higher Education,* a national newspaper for university professors and administrators. In it, Zagano, a college professor at the time this essay was published, argues that buying term papers and research projects should be against federal law because state legislation is spotty and ineffective. Her argument is put in legal terms, and her case is focused and clear.

Plagiarism is considered one of the most serious academic crimes because written words have become the currency of education. They demonstrate a student's learning and thought and identify his or her contribution to a subject or field of interest (see Chapter 4). As you read, notice how the issue of writing's monetary value is connected to educational values. Have you ever made this connection before?

The term-paper companies that gained considerable notoriety in the early 1 1970's are neither gone nor forgotten. Ready-made term papers, once hawked from dingy storefronts near college campuses, are now offered for sale through the mails. Affluent students can purchase by mail papers that are written to their specifications.

During the past few months, I've completed the same procedure any 2 enterprising student with a Master Charge card can go through if he's unwilling to write an assigned paper. All it takes is a few weeks and between $14 and $35 to get any assignment, no matter how specialized, written by someone else.

Just days after I wrote to Research Assistance, Inc., in Los Angeles, 3 I held in my hands Volume 6 of the "Nation's Most Extensive Library of Research Material"—184 closely typed pages of merchandise with a table of contents running from Advertising to Women Studies *(sic)*. I had over 6,000 titles from which to choose. I chose two: No. 1439, "The Treatment of Death by Emily Dickinson" ("Contends that the poet's attitude toward death influenced her use of words in unconventional ways. Quotes from poems and critics. f.n. Bib. 5pp.") and No. 3473, "American Literature from Colonial Times to the 1860's" ("Reviews several books to illustrate their contrasting of Civilized (Old World) and Wilderness life (New World) 5pp."). Each retailed for $13.75. The unimpressive results seemed to be photocopies of papers previously submitted elsewhere. One had handwritten corrections and comments on it. But, undaunted, I continued with my plan.

Professors Miriam Baker and Peter Shaw, of the Stony Brook English 4 Department, had both agreed in advance to read "my" papers. Well, I got the papers back the other day, and it seems that the classic rip-off can be a rip-off itself. Shaw gave me a C-minus. Baker failed me. Baker, an assistant professor of English and a Dickinson scholar, wrote that "the writer failed utterly to make any genuine statement about the poet as an artist and instead falls back on commonplace and genuinely erroneous biographical ideas." An undergraduate who doesn't know anything about Emily Dickinson doesn't have to pay $13.75 for erroneous biographical ideas. He can make them up on his own.

All was not lost. I still had the C-minus from Shaw, an associate 5 professor of English and the author, most recently, of *The Character of John Adams.* The paper managed a C-minus only because it was marked as a freshman paper.

In essence, what I did was pay a company $28.20 ("Include 70¢ extra 6 for postage and handling") to help me pass two courses. While I really managed to pass only one, there are thousands of students across the country who regularly make use of these services and regularly pass courses using bought papers.

You really *can* get through school on a credit card. And it's not illegal. 7

Both New York and California have laws that regulate the sale of 8 term papers—but just the sale. I purchased my papers from a Los Angeles firm that is prohibited by California law from selling papers that will be presented for academic credit in the State of California. I'm in New York, and there is nothing outlawing my action. I am bound only by my own college's regulations (if I am caught). New York has a similar law, which classes the sale of term papers as a Class B misdemeanor. But a law firm specializing in criminal law has advised me that it would be difficult, if not impossible, to prove that Research Assistance, Inc., is doing business in New York.

The country's first legislation outlawing the sale of term papers came 9 in North Carolina in 1969. Since then, several other states besides New York and California—among them, Illinois, Massachusetts, Connecticut, Pennsylvania, and Maryland—have acted to try and prohibit an activity that seems tantamount to fraud.

The state legislatures are still at it. In Washington State, the Subcom- 10 mittee on Postsecondary Education of the House of Representatives' Higher Education Committee has drafted a law it hopes will end the state's problem with plagiarism. The law has passed the House, and is awaiting action in the Senate. Washington is the home of several typical term-paper mills, as well as of Research Unlimited, a more specialized firm.

Research Unlimited set up offices there in 1972, shortly after term- 11 paper laws were enacted in its home state, Illinois. Its brochure offers a complete line of individually written academic assignments, including doctoral dissertations: "In the case of larger and more complex projects, such as theses and dissertations, we offer a complete service, beginning with the proposal and ending with the abstract. In addition to preparing all of the written texts, we compile and assemble the bibliographic mate- rial required and perform any statistical analysis that may be involved." I found out about Research Unlimited through an ad in *The New York Times Book Review.* The Washington law is similar to those in other states; it will prevent such companies only from doing business within the state. It won't prevent their moving to another state, or advertising and doing business by mail in states where laws have yet to be enacted.

While the Washington State law is constitutionally defensible, the 12
nationwide pastiche of laws has not been effective in dealing with term-
paper companies. Probably the only thing that can put an end to them is
a national law.

It's fraud. It's fraud and conspiracy to commit fraud through inter- 13
state commerce. Injunctions have come out of the courts against term-
paper companies based on common-law fraud principles. And there is
nothing constitutional about fraud.

Those who say it is up to the university to protect itself against 14
plagiarism are begging the question. The recommended remedies—specialized assignments, more in-class writing, more examinations—forget
that it is the nature of the true scholar to find a topic and deal with it in
writing. The university is interested in fostering scholarship, and it is
hampered by the fact that honest students are competing against professionally written material that has been tailor-made and is therefore un-
traceable.

Congress should be willing to protect the reputation of an educa- 15
tional system it pours so many millions of dollars into. After all, while I've
completed a process that is seemingly illegal, it turns out that, in the State
of New York at least, I can't even get myself arrested for it.

Questions

Rereading and Independent Analysis

1. Zagano's editorial comment follows the topical form of a classical
argument. Its parts include (a) a narration of the problem, (b) a statement
of a thesis, (c) the "exposition" (emphasis on legal solutions and explanation
of current law), (d) a "digression" (an answer to alternative solutions), and
(e) a concluding restatement of the thesis. Make an outline of the essay,
showing where each of these parts begins and the transitions that lead
from one section to another.

2. Make a list of the details and examples that Zagano uses to support
her points in this editorial. Then classify them according to their sources.
What kinds of evidence does she use? Why would this evidence be particularly effective in persuading her readers? How does it ensure their trust
of her?

Suggested Discussion and Group Activities

1. Divide your class into opposing sides arguing for and against the
thesis that an individual's plagiarism affects everyone in a class or a school.
The people arguing *against* this thesis will be arguing that plagiarism is
a matter that only affects the person attempting it. List points in favor of
your position. Decide what sort of supporting investigation might be necessary to make your points trustworthy, fair, and believable. Then outline
an argument you would make for your side, either in writing or in spoken
debate.

2. Zagano's arguments against alternative solutions to the problem

of term-paper fraud is relatively brief. After rereading that section of her editorial, discuss additional arguments that would support her solution above others. What arguments would support finding other alternatives?

Writing Suggestions

Response
Write a few paragraphs in your journal in which you describe an event that made you feel cheated as a result of someone's dishonesty or misrepresentation.

Analysis
1. A "Saturday Night Live" TV skit once showed a college recruiter telling a high school class that "the deal" at his college was that the students would get to keep half the money their parents paid the school, and get a diploma, if they signed up for the nonexistent college and kept their mouths shut. Write an essay in which you take this ridiculous idea into a more serious realm: explain why it is easier for a rich student to get a college degree than for a poor student. Use concrete examples of the educational advantages affluent students have.
2. Write a persuasive essay in which you explain how each student's honesty—or tolerance of dishonesty in himself or herself and others—affects the quality of everyone's education. Use examples from your experience, your reading of this essay, and class discussion to support your points. Choose a specific group of readers for your essay and identify them as your implied readers.

Finding a Purpose
Based on your own and others' experiences with cheating of any kind, write an editorial for your school newspaper in which you support an internal solution (one from within your school, classes, or student groups) to the problem. Your editorial should follow the pattern of development in Zagano's, but it need not rely on legal solutions.

 # Janet Cooke's Pulitzer Prize–Winning Story
The Washington Post

In April every year, the national Pulitzer Prizes for outstanding writing of all kinds are announced. In April 1980 *Washington Post* reporter Janet Cooke was awarded the Pulitzer Prize in reporting local news for her story, "Jimmy's World," an expose of heroin use in the black community in the District of Columbia. Her news story told of an eight-year-old child shooting heroin and a family atmosphere defined by drug traffic.

A week after Cooke's prize was formally announced, the *Post* published the article below, which is the paper's self-analysis. It is an explanation, an accurate report, and a speculative evaluation of how the newspaper whose reporters exposed the Watergate scandal in the Nixon administration could also publish Cooke's absolutely dishonest, fictional account as featured "news."

The lengthy investigation of Cooke's dishonesty that is partially presented here was led and finally written by the *Post*'s ombudsman, Bill Green. It reveals how seriously a newspaper must take the question of its writers' authenticity. It also demonstrates how clues to dishonesty can be overlooked because we normally believe people and the stories they tell us about their lives, work, and experiences. This account reveals not only the damage that dishonest writing does to the credibility of its setting, but also the great impact a piece of writing may have on a group of people and a whole community. It also shows reporters' investigative and writing processes in action, revealing how their writing moves from observations to numerous drafts involving revisions and editing. The readers of Janet Cooke's story are major contributors to this account, for their responses first established the story's power, then slowly stripped it of all credibility.

At the same time, the character of Janet Cooke herself becomes a product of her own resume, where the claims she wrote about her own background are first reported positively, then negatively, as changing signs of her credibility. This account provides a complete descriptive model of a working community of writers and editors who share the responsibility—whether to their credit or blame—for any published piece of writing.

The Reporter: When She Smiled, She Dazzled; When She Crashed . . .

On July 12, 1979, 11 days before her 25th birthday, Janet Cooke, a reporter on the Toledo Blade, wrote a letter to Ben Bradlee. It was the kind of letter Bradlee receives daily.   1

"Dear Mr. Bradlee: 2

"I have been a full time reporter for The Blade for slightly more than two years, and I believe I am now ready to tackle the challenge of working for a larger newspaper in a major city. . . ."

Attached to the letter was a resume and copies of six stories Cooke   3 had written for The Toledo Blade. One thing caught Bradlee's eye: the resume said Cooke was a Phi Beta Kappa graduate of Vassar in 1976. Bradlee underlined those statements and sent the clippings and resume to Bob Woodward. On the letter, he scrawled to his secretary that he would see Cooke.

When Cooke visited The Post two weeks later, every interviewer was   4 impressed. She was a striking, smartly dressed, articulate black woman, precisely the kind of applicant editors welcome, given the pressures to hire minorities and women.

And she could write.   5

As is the usual practice, she was interviewed around the newsroom,   6 the city editor, the Style editor, the metro editor.

The written summary of impressions, compiled by Tom Wilkinson, 7
assistant managing editor for personnel, states:

"Janet Cooke came in and saw everyone and was pretty high on 8
everyone's list. What impressed me is that she had pretty well created
her own beat. She seems to be a pretty good self-starter. I found her to
be very smart." So did others. Only city editor Herb Denton questioned
whether she was tough enough. "There's a lot of Vassar still in her,"
Denton said.

Hiring is a group decision at The Post—the editors call it collegial— 9
and it takes time. Sometime in the next couple of months, nobody remembers the exact date, a memo went to Wilkinson from Woodward. It said,
"We're ready to offer her a job on the Weekly. Can we go ahead?"

They could, and Janet was employed as a reporter by The Post on Jan. 10
3, 1980. So impressed had the staff been with her and her writing that the
usual check of references was done in a cursory manner. Wilkinson
vaguely remembers talking with someone at The Blade. Others can't
remember any checks.

She was assigned to the District Weekly, where a staff prepares one 11
of the three local sections for zoned distribution every Thursday in Maryland, Virginia and the District of Columbia.

The editor, Stan Hinden, a veteran of 30 years in journalism, remem- 12
bers: "Janet was much like many reporters we get from smaller papers.
That is, she wrote and reported reasonably well. We tend to be detail-
conscious, and she needed to know how to get more detail, but she was
good and smart and better than most."

. . . .

Her first big article appeared on Feb. 21. It was a dramatic story of 13
Washington's drug-infested riot corridor, years after the 1968 disorders,
and an hour-by-hour account of a police patrol along 14th Street.

"It was a fine piece of journalism," Aplin-Brownlee [Vivian Aplin- 14
Brownlee was Cooke's immediate editor] said. "Masterfully written."

The editor had worked with her reporter all week. "She was not 15
really street-savvy," Aplin-Brownlee said. "She didn't know the kinds of
people she was dealing with, but she was tenacious and talented."

. . . .

"She had to learn the street. She didn't know what was happening 16
in the nitty-gritty. I was grooming her, training her. It was ironic that she
became a reporter of the drug culture."

Cooke grew up in a middle-class home in Toledo, where her father, 17
Stratman Cooke, worked for 35 years for Toledo Edison and is now secretary to the corporation. He remembers that he gave her her first typewriter when she was 5 and that a grade school teacher said she couldn't
believe the poetry Janet wrote. It was that good.

Janet learned quickly about life in an urban slum. Her 14th Street 18 story drew compliments not only from her colleagues, but also Bradlee and Richard Harwood, deputy managing editor, congratulated her.

Janet's ambition was taking shape. She wanted to move to the daily 19 Metro staff, which is responsible for seven-day coverage of local news. Strong, the Metro staff is a favorite of the publisher, Donald Graham.

Graham believes the quality of the metro staff has improved enor- 20 mously in the 10 years he has been with the paper. "The city staff particularly has begun to tell us things we didn't understand about this town," Graham said.

. . . .

Janet Cooke wanted to move quickly. She told Woodward so, and she 21 frequently talked with Milton Coleman, who had succeeded Herb Denton as district editor for the daily staff. Aplin-Brownlee knew of the conversations.

Once when the "Jimmy" story was developing, Cooke told a friend, 22 "This story is my ticket off the Weekly."

While she aspired to the Metro staff, she had bigger ambitions. "She 23 set enormous goals for herself," Karlyn Barker, a Metro reporter, said. "She wanted a Pulitzer Prize in three years, and she wanted to be on the national staff in three to five years," Barker said. "She had winner written all over her, although it was strange, every day she acted as though she was protecting her job. She was the last person who needed to do that."

. . . .

Sometime in August of last year, Aplin-Brownlee heard talk of a new 24 type of heroin on the streets of Washington. The drug was said, so she heard, to ulcerate the skin of its users. She asked Cooke to look into it.

During background interviews on the story, Cooke didn't find the 25 new type of heroin, but she found out a lot about the use of heroin in Washington.

Interviewing social workers and drug rehabilitation experts, Cooke 26 amassed extensive notes and taped interviews with intriguing leads. In all, there were two hours of tape-recorded interviews plus 145 pages of handwritten notes plus a collection of pamphlets and documents on drug abuse.

When Aplin-Brownlee saw what Cooke had collected, she immedi- 27 ately said, "This is a story for the daily."

"The daily" is Weekly jargon for the Metro section. Cooke took her 28 notebooks and her ideas to Milton Coleman. Aplin-Brownlee was not to see the story again until it appeared on the front page of The Washington Post of Sept. 28 under the headline, "Jimmy's World."

The Story: First the Idea, and Finally the Presses Rolled

Milton Coleman is a rangy, tall man. His quietness is deceptive. He pur- 29 sues news as though it's his quarry, and admiring colleagues regard him as highly competitive. When he sits, he sprawls. He likes to work in a vest. He is a relentless jogger, and finished last Sunday's Washington marathon in three hours and 25 minutes, 57 minutes behind the winner.

Coleman arrived at The Washington Post on May 12, 1976. He had 30
been on The Minneapolis Star for two years after Columbia Graduate School of Journalism, a stint in radio news, a job as Washington correspondent for a black news service and three years with the Student Organization for Black Unity. He majored in fine arts at the University of Wisconsin-Milwaukee.

At The Post he reported on Montgomery County and D.C. City Hall 31
before he was named assistant city editor in March of last year. On May 26, 1980, he took over the city desk. He is among the most respected of The Post's editing staff.

When Janet Cooke brought her reporting notes on heroin to Cole- 32
man, stories of heroin use in the city were running regularly. Four appeared in August and three in September before "Jimmy's World" was published.

. . . .

"I talked over Janet's materials with her," Coleman said. "She talked 33
about hundreds of people being hooked. And at one point she mentioned an 8-year-old addict. I stopped her and said, 'That's the story. Go after it. It's a front-page story.'

"It appeared that the kid was at RAP Inc., a service organization for 34
drug addicts. I went to Managing Editor [Howard] Simons' office . . . and we talked it through. If RAP gave us permission to talk with the boy, could we reveal the name? We agreed that we would not under any circumstances. Would RAP let us talk with the parents? We didn't know. Janet went back out."

Two weeks passed. On a story of this nature, it is common practice 35
at The Post to give a reporter all the time he or she needs.

Cooke returned to Coleman and said she couldn't find the boy, but 36
a week later she said she had found another young addict. He was 8 years old. "Jimmy's World" was born.

"She told me that she had gone out on the playgrounds, had asked 37
around and had left her cards in a number of places. One of them had found its way to the boy's mother, who had called Janet in anger and asked, 'Why are you looking for my boy?' "

Cooke told Coleman she had talked with the mother again but had 38
reached no agreement on an interview. In answer to her question, Coleman said she could promise the mother anonymity.

"I told her if the mother called again to keep her on the phone, keep 39
talking, talk it through. Be persistent," Coleman said.

Coleman did not ask the mother's name or the family's street ad- 40
dress. He had promised Cooke confidentiality for her sources. The jugular of journalism lay exposed—the faith an editor has to place in a reporter.

Simons says an editor can ask the name of a source and if a reporter 41
refuses to reveal it the editor has the option to reject a story. He did not
ask Cooke or Coleman to reveal any details on identity.

"Janet told me she had been back in touch with the mother and that 42
the two of them were to have dinner at Eastover Shopping Center,"
Coleman said.

Later Cooke told him she had had the dinner and that two days later 43
she visited the mother's house, the same imaginary house she was to
describe in great detail as "Jimmy's World."

There were no further interviews with "Jimmy" or his family, she 44
told Coleman. But she said she was worried. "Ron," the invented mother's
invented lover, had threatened Cooke, the reporter told her editor. All
during the interview, she said, Ron had paced the room with a knife in his
hand, and once had said to her, "If I see any police, Miss Lady, or if any
police come to see me, we [he glances again at the knife] will be around
to see you."

The threat was taken so seriously by Coleman and others at The Post 45
that when Richard Cohen wrote a column after "Jimmy's World" appeared, Coleman insisted that Cohen's reference to the knife be deleted.
It was. Simons, whose concern for the staff is nearly parental, wouldn't let
Cooke go home for two nights after her story was published. He arranged
for her to stay with another Post employe.

When Coleman heard her description of her "interview," he asked 46
her to do a memo on it. On this kind of story, Coleman wants the reporter
to write the story roughly but soon after the event, while details are fresh
in the reporter's mind.

Cooke's memo, her first draft on the subject, is 13½ pages long, 47
double-spaced on letter-size paper. It contains exhausting detail. "Jimmy"
wears a blue and green Izod T-shirt—"Bad, ain't it. I got me six of these."
There was an eight-foot plaid sofa against one living-room wall, a matching
love seat against the other. Both were covered in plastic. There was a color
television set in the room, along with a lot of Panasonic stereo equipment,
"receiver, tape deck." There was a rubber tree plant, fake bamboo blinds,
a brown shag rug, two lamps, a chrome and glass coffee table and a chrome
and glass end table.

At this point, Coleman saw the name "Tyrone" on the memo, and 48
determined that this was the fictitious child's "real" first name. He was also
told the elementary school "Tyrone" attended and the general neighborhood where he supposedly lived. This was reassuring at the time, and later
translated into general newsroom gossip that Coleman knew who the
child was.

Other editors did not ask, then or later. Managing editor Simons had 49
earlier given Cooke assurances that she could keep the family anonymous,
according to Coleman, who said, "Howard said she should deal with me
and tell me the child's identity. 'I don't want to know,' he said, somewhat
jokingly."

"None of them asked me for the name," Coleman remembers. "I 50
may have been asked, do you believe it?"

Cooke's descriptive language was convincing to Coleman, but 51
Woodward was to say later that if he had seen this first draft he might
have asked questions about the long and seemingly perfect quotations.
Woodward never looked at the first draft until Cooke's Pulitzer was in
question.

Coleman, who knows the streets better than Woodward, said he 52
found no reason to question the quotes. "Ron" is quoted as saying, for
example, "He'd be bugging me all the time about what the shots were,
what people was doin' and one day he said, 'When can I get off.' I said well
s———, you can have some now. I let him snort a little and damn, it was
wild. The little dude really did get off."

Coleman read it over, made suggestions on reworking it, suggested 53
how to write the "lead," the opening, how to rearrange the material.

"I wanted it to read like John Coltrane's music. Strong. It was a great 54
story, and it never occurred to me that she could make it up. There was
too much distance between Janet and the streets," Coleman said.

"I had no doubts," he said.   55

When the second draft came in, Coleman called in Bob Barkin, The 56
Post's art director, to illustrate the story. Obviously there would be no
photographs. It was Friday, Sept. 19, nine days before the story was to be
published.

Barkin selected illustrator Michael Gnatek Jr. for the drawing. Brad- 57
lee was later to find the full illustration so powerful in its horror that he
insisted it run inside the paper. "People are eating breakfast while they
read the paper, you know," he said.

The full drawing ran on page A9, only a smaller drawing of "Jimmy" 58
ran on the front page. It shows a young man, his face twisted in a half-
smile, huge eyes watching, his slender arm gripped by a huge fist as a
needle is injected.

Coleman did some checking of his own. He found someone who 59
knew, and asked if Janet's description of "shooting up" is the way it's done.
He wanted to know if, as the story said, liquid ebbs out of the syringe, and
is replaced by red blood, which is then reinjected. He was satisfied with
how the answers agreed with Janet's account.

Bo Jones is The Post's counsel. He and his associate, Carol Weisman, 60
are frequently called in to "lawyer" a story, particularly those dealing with
subjects that might have legal implications.

Jones suggested some changes. "Ron" was said to be from Atlanta. 61
Jones suggested making it "from the South," because "Ron" might be
traceable in Atlanta, and the promise of anonymity was absolute. Jones
also suggested striking out "public housing." That, also, could be traced,
he said.

Woodward saw the story for the first time. He divides stories into two 62
categories: possible libel or criminal charges and all others. "Jimmy" fell

into Woodward's category two. It could not libel because its subjects were anonymous.

"Janet had written a great piece," Woodward says. "In a way, both 63 she and the story were almost too good to be true. I had seen her go out on a complicated story and an hour later turn in a beautifully written piece. This story was so well-written and tied together so well that my alarm bells simply didn't go off. My skepticism left me. I was personally negligent."

Woodward called in Cooke and asked her to tell him about it. He 64 simply wanted to hear her story. "She was a terrific actress, terrific," he said. She related it all in the most disarming way. It was so personal, so dramatic, so hard in her tummy."

None of the Post's senior editors subjected Cooke's story to close 65 questioning. Simons was on vacation in Florida the week before it appeared. Deputy managing editor Richard Harwood had no role in its preparation. Ben Bradlee read the story that week and thought it was "a helluva job."

Are they satisfied with the preliminary screening on "Jimmy's 66 World"? Simons answered: "Yes, there was no reason to disbelieve the story." Bradlee said: "I am not satisfied now—but I was then."

Coleman, who was editing Cooke's copy, reflects on this: "Much of 67 my attention was concentrated on the story and formulating it. Subconsciously, I think I firmly believed that the extra eyes of the backup system would catch anything that I missed."

Now Coleman believes other editors were relying on him. "We 68 never really debated whether or not it was true," he said. "I think—if I can gore my own ox—they kind of took it for granted that Coleman should know."

. . . .

Janet Cooke had one last chance to change her mind. On Friday 69 night, before the story was to run on Sunday, Coleman called her in. Simons had gone out of town, but before he left, he insisted that Coleman have a talk with the reporter.

"I told her what Simons told me to say. He's almost romantic about 70 this kind of thing," Coleman said. "I said she had written a story that is certain to be controversial. You have seen a crime and you may be subpoenaed. We don't think so, but you may. You should know that The Post will stand behind you 100 percent. If you are subpoenaed, and you refuse to reveal your sources, you may be found in contempt of court and have to spend time in jail. Before the story goes, if you don't want to face that, we won't run it. Think it over, tell me in the morning."

Saturday morning Cooke told Coleman to let it go. 71

The article had been held for Sunday publication. There is more 72 space for long stories—"Jimmy's World" ran 2,256 words—and there are more readers—892,220 copies of the paper ran on Sunday, Sept. 28.

"Jimmy's World" was on the front page. The presses started running at 9:54 P.M.

The Publication: 'Jimmy' Hit Washington Like a Grenade, and Bounced

Jimmy's story struck at Washington's heart. The paper had no sooner 73 reached the streets than The Washington Post's telephone switchboard lit up like a space launch control room.

Readers were outraged. The story was described as racist and crimi- 74 nal. The concern was for Jimmy. "What about the boy?" was the central question. It was repeated for the next four days in as many versions as the human mind can invent.

By Monday, Washington Police Chief Burtell Jefferson had launched 75 a mammoth city-wide search. He had called on his youth division to get to work Sunday. Mayor Marion Barry was incensed. All schools, social services and police contacts were to be asked for "Jimmy's" whereabouts. The word went out on the streets that big reward money was available. Last week Assistant Chief Maurice Turner said the police had been prepared to offer up to $10,000.

The Los Angeles Times-Washington Post News Service moved the 76 story out to 300 clients. "Jimmy" was national, then international.

Much later, after Ronald Reagan was elected president, Donnie Rad- 77 cliffe of The Post's Style staff sent a copy of the story to the nation's first-lady-to-be. Radcliffe thought it would be useful information as the Reagans prepared to come to Washington.

Nancy Reagan wrote back ". . . How terribly sad to read it and to 78 know there are so many others like him out there. I hope with all my heart I can do something to help them. Surely there must be a way . . . ."

It would be difficult to overestimate Washington's compassion for 79 "Jimmy" or its anger when The Post refused to reveal his identity or address.

Police were receiving letters from all over the country, including one 80 signed by 30 students in a Richmond school, pleading that they find "Jimmy."

At one point, as Milton Coleman and Howard Simons had predicted, 81 police threatened to subpoena Janet Cooke in an effort to force her to reveal names and addresses.

At The Post, Simons sent out instructions that if the police got a 82 search warrant no member of the staff was to resist. Cooke, while not staying at her apartment, was to be at work, on the newsroom floor, and out on some part of the follow-up story.

Coleman established an 11-member reporting team for the follow- 83 up. Five of them were assigned to the breaking story. With these five, the other six were given a different assignment. They were to search for another "Jimmy," on the theory that if there is one, there must be others.

. . . .

By the following weekend, Coleman was uneasy. It was a slight feel- 84 ing, but it was real. "I thought the police would have found him in three days at the outside. I'm not one of those people who believe the police can't do anything right. They could find him. I knew it."

Courtland Milloy was also worried. He and Cooke had gone out to 85 find the second "Jimmy."

"We were supposed to be finding another kid," Milloy said. "But I'll 86 tell you the truth, I wanted to find Jimmy. Hell, that kid needed help. So as we drove around I circled through Condon Terrace, the general area where Janet said he lived.

"It didn't take long to see that she didn't know the area. It's one of 87 the toughest sections in town. I know it well. She said she didn't see the house. I asked her if it was to the right of us, the left of us, or had we passed it. She didn't know.

. . . .

Milloy's serious doubts about the story began there. When he and 88 Cooke had looked for seven hours they returned to the office. Milloy went to Coleman and said, "I think you ought to buy me a drink."

The next day, Coleman did, and Milloy told him about his growing 89 disbelief in Cooke's story.

Milloy went further. "I wanted to find 'Jimmy.' I mean, does The Post 90 sanction a reporter watching a kid getting shot up? Even the Condon Terrace people were calling offering to help.

"I got a call from the 'Queen of the Underworld' [about whom Milloy 91 had written on the same Sunday Cooke's story ran], and she asked if she could help. She wanted to find that kid, man."

. . . .

Four days after the story ran, the telephone calls to The Post 92 changed. They were now asking, in great numbers, what the police were doing. Why weren't they finding Jimmy, and what were they doing about the drug traffic?

The intense police search continued for 17 days. The city had been 93 finely combed. Nothing.

On Oct. 15, Mayor Barry said, "We're kind of giving up on that." It 94 remained an open case.

"I've been told the story is part myth, part reality," Barry said. "We 95 all have agreed that we don't believe that the mother or the pusher would allow a reporter to see them shoot up."

Were Bradlee and Simons worried by City Hall's claim that the story 96 was untrue? Both said they felt the weight of criticism, but were reassured by the fact that at one point the mayor had said city officials had found such a child.

. . . .

The Post stuck by its story and what it described as its First Amend- 97 ment rights to protect its sources.

"At any rate," Coleman recalls, "I voiced my concerns to Howard 98 [Simons], and he said in so many words that they were legitimate. But he urged me to find the most creative way to examine them, stressing that I more than anyone else had to stand by my reporter. At the point that I even began to hint to her that I thought she had not been truthful, her trust in me could be destroyed."

Simons says, "I have no memory of either Coleman or Woodward 99 discussing Milloy's disbelief with me at that point."

In the paper's newsroom, where doubts about the story were begin- 100 ning to thump faintly, there were congratulations and commendations for Cooke.

Publisher Don Graham wrote her a note on Oct. 7: "With all the 101 turmoil of the last week, it's important that one say the basic thing: not only was that a very fine story in Sunday's paper a week ago, it was only one of many you've done in the last year.

"The Post has no more important and tougher job than explaining 102 life in the black community in Washington. A special burden gets put on black reporters doing that job, and a double-special burden on black re- porters who try to see life through their own eyes instead of seeing it the way they're told they should. The Post seems to have many such reporters. You belong very high up among them.

"If there's any long-term justification for what we do, it's that people 103 will act a bit differently and think a bit differently if we help them under- stand the world even slightly better. Much of what we write fails that first test because we don't understand what we're writing about ourselves.

"You seem to have much more than the common measure of under- 104 standing and the ability to explain what you see. It's a great gift.

"And you went through your tests of last week with what seemed to 105 me world-class composure. Sincerely, Don."

On Monday morning after "Jimmy's World" appeared, Woodward 106 walked over to Vivian Aplin-Brownlee's desk and said Janet Cooke was now a member of the Metro daily staff. Aplin-Brownlee was furious. She had lost her most experienced reporter.

The Doubts: From the Very First Moment, Some Suspected the Worst

From the day "Jimmy's" story appeared there were doubts about it. Mil- 107 ton Coleman felt misgivings first when the police couldn't find the boy,

Courtland Milloy when he accompanied Janet Cooke on a trip through the area where the youngster was supposed to live.

There were others. Mayor Marion Barry was one. Dr. Alyce Gullat- 108 tee, director of Howard University's Institute for Substance Abuse and Addiction, was another. She was one of the people Cooke interviewed when she was gathering her original material.

In a telephone call with Pat Tyler, then of The Washington Post's 109 metro staff, Gullattee said the story had caused a panic in the community to the extent that addicts were hunkered down, afraid to go out to seek treatment out of fear that they will run afoul of swarms of police looking for the 8-year-old.

Gullattee also said she didn't believe any of those people "fired 110 up" in front of Cooke. Junkies, she said, just don't trust reporters like that.

Elsa Walsh, Cooke's roommate, doubted. She had gone through 111 Cooke's notes once and found nothing on "Jimmy."

But there was more. "She's the kind of person who has fears for her 112 own safety," Walsh said. "My own instincts told me it was wrong. She would have real trouble going into the 'Jimmy' setting. And then, when I tried to put what I know of Janet together with the story itself, they wouldn't fit." She did not express these misgivings to any editors.

Among the strongest doubters was Vivian Aplin-Brownlee of the 113 District Weekly, who was Janet's first editor at The Post. She had not been in touch with the story since it was turned over to the Metro staff.

"I had been tough on Janet. She knew it and I knew it," Aplin- 114 Brownlee said. "But when I first read the story I was astonished. I thought it was going to be about the use of heroin that causes skin ulcers. That's what it started out to be.

"I never believed it, and I told Milton that. I knew her so well and 115 the depth of her. In her eagerness to make a name she would write farther than the truth would allow.

"When challenged on facts in other stories, Janet would reverse 116 herself, but without dismay or consternation with herself.

"I knew she would be tremendously out of place in a 'shooting gal- 117 lery.' I didn't believe she could get access. No pusher would shoot up a child in her presence.

"Some of the language didn't ring true. What 8-year-old in 'Jimmy's' 118 circumstances would make a connection between math and drugs?" (As the story claimed.)

On the day Cooke's Pulitzer Prize was announced, Aplin-Brownlee 119 went to Coleman and said, "I hope she has committed the perfect crime."

When the hoax became known, Coleman went back to Aplin-Brown- 120 lee and said, "It wasn't the perfect crime after all."

. . . .

While Coleman had been troubled that the police were unable to 121
find the boy, Woodward found that unremarkable. "It seemed logical," he
said, "that his mother would take him away to Baltimore or wherever."

But Coleman was infuriated. He went to managing editor Simons 122
and spilled out his anger. For the first time, Simons felt misgivings about
the story. "But all I had was a hunch and the fact that she had ducked the
visit. [Simons had suggested that Coleman and Cooke visit "Jimmy's"
house, but Cooke said he had moved.] How do you prove a negative?" he
said.

The faith of an editor in his reporter that is a principal connector in 123
all the events of the episode was upheld. Skepticism was put aside.

Bradlee says that throughout he was unaware of the skepticism. 124
"Nobody ever came in this room and said, 'I have doubts about the story'—
before or after publication—and nobody said someone else had misgivings
about the story," Bradlee said.

One editor who had early misgivings was deputy metro editor David 125
Maraniss, who also serves as Maryland editor. He read the story on vacation and didn't feel it quite added up. Since it was not his territory and
criticism might be viewed as poaching, Maraniss did not take his questions
to Woodward until much later.

. . . .

When the hoax was exposed, their [the newsroom staff's] doubts 126
about the story and their frustration with management burst out in a
meeting of the Metro staff at Woodward's house last Thursday night.
Coleman says now:

". . . There was undoubtedly also some degree of pride—we had 127
published the story in the first place and stood by it. We probably put too
much faith in the hope that maybe things were not the way so many
indicators suggested they might be."

. . . .

Meanwhile, Aplin-Brownlee says that Cooke was having migraine 128
headaches and stayed out of the office more than usual.

The Ombudsman:
After the Agony, the Reappraisal

I wrote this story of "Jimmy's World" after being invited to do so by The 129
Washington Post's executive editor, Ben Bradlee. It is important to understand the verb, "invited," because if I had been assigned to do it, that
would have violated the relationship The Post has maintained with its
ombudsmen for over a decade.

The central idea is autonomy for the person who sits in this chair. 130
Without it, the ombudsman would be a fake, like "Jimmy." With it, The

Post takes its chances, as it should. I have been filling this role at The Post since September, and will return in August to my regular work in the administration of Duke University.

All of which is to say that this piece is my own. Twenty Post reporters 131 discussed the one-man undertaking Wednesday afternoon and didn't like it. They wanted the story staffed, as The Wall Street Journal did with its account of "Jimmy" that appeared Friday. I turned the reporters away, although it would have been great to have them share the work. But I am grateful that they volunteered.

There are omissions in this article, perhaps some errors too. The most 132 glaring omission is the absence of an interview with Janet Cooke. She refused to see me. I don't think she was trying to be evasive. I think she simply didn't want to go over it again with a stranger now. The pain has simply been too great. Where Cooke is quoted directly in this account, the words are attributed to the editors or reporters who were in conversation with her.

I regret her decision because her version of the whole episode should 133 be here. No doubt, it would differ in some respects from this account.

After the agony of this week, deputy metropolitan editor David 134 Maraniss, who has grown close to Cooke and feels protective of her, reports that she is doing better, seems to understand what she has done, and is feeling remorseful. "By Friday," he said, "she was beautiful again."

Four Post employees were involved in producing this story, all of 135 them at my request. Noel Epstein, assistant editor of Outlook, and Ron Shaffer of the Metro staff did some research, none of the writing. William Greider, assistant managing editor for national news, edited it. He changed nothing without my approval. Robin Gradison, a news aide, supplied research and good cheer and coffee for four days. She was terrific.

The Post's attitude toward this project was summarized in the catch 136 phrase, "full disclosure." That word went out to the staff from Bradlee and publisher Donald Graham.

The result was that every question I asked about The Post's handling 137 of "Jimmy" got an answer. Maraniss declined to relate his off-the-record conversations with Cooke. Other than that, no one refused to answer my questions.

The most impressive reaction was from the news staff members who 138 filed in and out of my office offering help. I am willing to lay odds that no sentence in this piece was written without interruption except those that were typed between midnight Friday and 8 A.M. yesterday.

The Prize: Of Fiefdoms and Their Knights and Ladies of Adventure

The Washington Post has 493 employees on its news staff. At the top of 139 the pyramid is the executive editor, Ben Bradlee. His second-in-command

and alter ego is the managing editor, Howard Simons. Third in line is the
deputy managing editor, Richard Harwood.

They constitute the presiding troika, and they split the duties of top 140
news administration, rotating, for example, weekend duties. They are the
last port of call for news decisions. Normally, Bradlee and Simons preside
over daily 2:30 P.M. and 6:30 P.M. story conferences. Harwood is responsible for the Sunday interpretative section, "Outlook," and The Washington
Post Magazine, among other duties.

Bradlee is luminescent, Simons and Harwood, philosophical. All 141
three are former reporters, a characteristic of most Post editors.

Below them are the archdukes and duchesses of the newsroom, the 142
assistant managing editors, 12 of them, nine with news staffs. The other
three are responsible for personnel, administration and special projects.
All are called AMEs.

Below them on the organization chart are various levels of other 143
editors: earls, counts, countesses, viscounts, barons.

Then there are the reporters, the knight adventurers or lady adven- 144
turers. They write the copy.

So prestigious is The Post among journalists and would-be journalists 145
in this country and abroad that one could feel comfortable betting that the
entire staff could be replaced, at least numerically, once a month by the
applications the paper receives.

The Post calls its news administration a federal system. That is in- 146
tended to indicate, and does, the enormous latitude and authority that is
given to the assistant managing editors, the archdukes.

They pull together budgets and administer them, decide on stories, 147
hire and fire (but only with the agreement from the troika), reward and
punish, and—importantly—congregate every day for the story conferences. When Bradlee or Simons wants to issue instructions, the assistant
managing editors get the word and pass it along.

. . . .

Among the rewards in which AMEs play a key role are nomina- 148
tions for the prizes of journalism. On Nov. 17, 1980, the AME for administration, Elsie Carper, sent out a memo asking for nominations. Her
list contained 73 award possibilities. Leading the list, as always, were
the Pulitzer Prizes, which are awarded in 12 categories. Winners become the nobility of American journalism. The Post has won Pulitzers
16 times.

On Woodward's Metro staff, there was competition for Pulitzer 149
nominations. It is not uncommon at The Post. David Maraniss, the Maryland editor, was pushing hard for a series by one of his Maryland reporters,
Neil Henry, as an entry in the feature category.

. . . .

Meanwhile, Milton Coleman, Woodward's city editor, was pushing 150
Janet Cooke's "Jimmy's World." In a memo to Woodward on Dec. 10 he
also suggested that the story be nominated for the Sigma Delta Chi award,
the Heywood Brown award, the Ellis Willis Scripps award and as one of
a package submission for the Robert F. Kennedy award.

· · · ·

"Jimmy's World" was also entered for a prize from the Maryland- 151
D.C. Press Association. It won second prize.

Before the entries were sent off, indeed while the nominations were 152
being considered, doubts among the staff about Cooke's story rose to new
intensity.

This time, even Maraniss was involved. After a dinner with investiga- 153
tive reporter Jonathan Neumann, Maraniss re-read the story, and this time
it didn't ring true. He found he couldn't believe it. He said that to Woodward, and suggested that Woodward re-read the story before it was nominated. In hindsight, he said he thinks he didn't put it as strongly as he
might have. He didn't want to appear to be knocking down a story Coleman liked so much.

Neumann, who had won a Pulitzer for investigative reporting for 154
The Philadelphia Inquirer, was a principal in discussions among other
reporters. "A number of people felt strongly that it should not be nominated because it could disgrace us," he said. "A couple of dozen people
talked about it but we didn't go to top editors. I think we felt it wouldn't
be fair to put her on the carpet when we couldn't prove anything."

With all the doubts about the "Jimmy" story, how could it have been 155
submitted, with The Post's full backing, to the Pulitzer committee?

Woodward, who accepted Coleman's urgings and strongly supported 156
the story to Bradlee, Simons and Harwood, says it most tellingly: "I have
used the phrase 'in for a dime, in for a dollar' to describe my overall
conclusion about submitting the Cooke story for a Pulitzer or any other
prize.

· · · ·

"I think that the decision to nominate the story for a Pulitzer is of 157
minimal consequence. I also think that it won is of little consequence. It
is a brilliant story—fake and fraud that it is.

"It would be absurd for me or any other editor to review the authen- 158
ticity or accuracy of stories that are nominated for prizes.

"If so, our posture would be as follows: we published the story and 159
said it was true, but now we are going to nominate it for a Pulitzer—now
that's serious business."

· · · ·

The Confession: At the End, There Were the Questions, Then the Tears

Pulitzer Prize decisions were made on April 3. Formal announcement was   160
scheduled 10 days later, but two members of the advisory board called
Ben Bradlee within hours after the decisions were final. He was elated,
and called both Bob Woodward and Milton Coleman.

Janet Cooke was in New Haven working on the Reagan shooting   161
story, and John W. Hinckley Jr. Woodward and Coleman reached her by
telephone.

Later, she told an interviewer, laughing, "It was right on deadline   162
when they called. I thought they were calling because I hadn't filed the
story yet, and all I could think of was, 'Oh, God, is it possible to get fired
from 600 miles away?' "

Executive editor Bradlee got on the telephone and repeated the   163
message. "Even then I wasn't convinced," she said.

Finally persuaded, she faced an evening alone. She said she bought   164
a bottle of champagne, called her mother and watched "Dallas" in her
motel room.

The public announcement of the awards was on April 13. At The   165
Toledo Blade that day, in the words of executive news editor Joe O'Conor,
"We have an edition that goes to press shortly after 8 A.M. In it, we had
a sidebar on Miss Cooke and her Toledo background.

"Sometime later that day, one of the editors showed me a copy of the   166
AP's biographical sketches on Pulitzer winners. The information in it did
not jibe with our information, so we did what we would normally do: we
pointed out to AP that our information and theirs didn't mesh."

At the Associated Press the story moved to Louis D. Boccardi, vice   167
president and executive editor in New York. He said:

"Tuesday morning, The Toledo Blade pointed out to our correspon-   168
dent in Toledo that there were discrepancies between our account of Miss
Cooke's educational background and what they knew to be the truth.

"More specifically, the background we carried, which was given by   169
The Post to the Pulitzer committee, said that she had a master's degree
from the University of Toledo, an undergraduate degree from Vassar, and
had studied at the Sorbonne."

Michael Holmes, the AP's correspondent in Toledo, started his own   170
checking, and confirmed the Blade's facts. He reported to his New York
office. From there a message went to Paris to check the Sorbonne connection, and a call was made to Cooke at The Post.

"Miss Cooke said, essentially, that the information in her official biog-   171
raphy was correct. At this point, it was quite clear that something was
wrong, and so we pressed our efforts on the story," Boccardi said.

The "official" biography released by the Pulitzer committee and   172
carried on the AP wire came from a standard Post biographical form that
had been attached to her nomination for the prize.

Cooke filled it out. Nobody on The Post checked it, yet it differed 173 significantly from the resume she had filed for the Post when she applied for a job.

The new resume claimed that she spoke or read French, Spanish, 174 Portuguese and Italian. Her original resume claimed only French and Spanish. The new form claimed she had won six awards from the Ohio Newspaper Women's Association and another from the Ohio AP. Her first resume claimed only a single award from the Ohio Newspaper Women's Association. The new form also showed that she graduated magna cum laude from Vassar in 1976, attended the Sorbonne in 1975 and received a master's degree from the University of Toledo in 1977. The original made no reference to the Sorbonne.

Vassar records show that she attended classes there for one year. She 175 was graduated from the University of Toledo, but received no master's degree.

Between 3 and 3:30 Tuesday afternoon telephones in managing edi- 176 tor Howard Simons' and Bradlee's office rang simultaneously. Boccardi was calling Simons, and Dixie Sheridan, assistant to the president of Vassar, was calling Bradlee. Sheridan's call was prompted by the AP queries she had received.

The callers asked Bradlee and Simons the same questions: what did 177 they know about the records discrepancies? Neither of the editors had an answer.

Simons summoned Woodward, Coleman and Tom Wilkinson to 178 Bradlee's office. Wilkinson, The Post's assistant managing editor for personnel, brought Janet's personnel folder and the Pulitzer biography.

"When we saw the papers, we knew we had a problem," Simons said. 179 He and Bradlee decided that the first thing to go after was the Vassar records discrepancies.

To do that, they dispatched Coleman to take Cooke for a walk around 180 the block and talk to her.

"Take her to the woodshed," Bradlee said, borrowing a phrase Lyn- 181 don B. Johnson once used on Hubert H. Humphrey. He meant: ask her every question, get it right.

Coleman and Cooke walked across L Street to the Capitol Hilton 182 Hotel. In the bar they ordered two ginger ales, and Coleman questioned her persistently on her background. Why was Vassar saying she only attended classes there one year when Cooke was saying she had been graduated?

Cooke said she didn't know. 183

"Okay, let's call Vassar," Coleman suggested at one point. It was 4:30 184 in the afternoon, and he was afraid the college's registrar's office might close.

"I don't see why it is so important," Cooke said. "The Vassar records 185 are just me. The 'Jimmy' story is something I did."

Coleman, after Cooke told him where Vassar is located, reached Judy 186

Blom, a clerk in the registrar's office. She informed Coleman that Cooke was never graduated from the school. Coleman asked to speak to her supervisor, and was transferred to Margaret Battistoni, administrative assistant to the registrar. She confirmed the clerk's response.

Coleman looked at Cooke, who said she had records to prove her claim, that her mother had the papers. 187

"Let's call Toledo," Coleman said, meaning the university. But Cooke wanted to talk to her mother, and did, for 15 or 20 minutes, while Coleman stood by. 188

After that conversation Cooke said, "Let's talk." They returned to the bar and ordered two more ginger ales. 189

Cooke told Coleman that Vassar was right, that she had gone there but had run into emotional problems and returned home the following year to enter the University of Toledo, where she had been graduated. 190

"Then that part of your resume is wrong," Coleman said. 191

"Yes." 192

"What about languages? Do you speak four languages?" 193

"Yes." 194

"And the Sorbonne, were you there?" 195

"Yes." 196

"And the 'Jimmy' story?" 197

"It's true." 198

When Coleman went to the telephone to call Woodward, a member of the city school board happened to be at the next pay phone, and Coleman told Woodward he would have to speak in code. 199

"Vassar?" Woodward asked. 200

"Not true," Coleman answered. 201

"Jimmy?" 202

"She says it's true." 203

At the Post, Bradlee suggested that Coleman be asked to bring Cooke back into The Post at the L Street entrance to avoid being conspicuous and to take her to the vacant eighth-floor office of The Post's corporate president. Bradlee and Woodward joined Cooke and Coleman there. Simons stayed in the fifth floor newsroom to conduct the daily 6:30 story conference. 204

When Bradlee and Woodward arrived, Cooke was seated on a sofa, crying and saying, "You get caught at the stupidest things." 205

Bradlee shook her hand, then came on strong. He, Simons and Woodward had decided while Coleman and Cooke were out that the record's discrepancies cast serious doubts on her honesty and that her honesty, or lack of it, was the only thing that held the "Jimmy" story together. 206

Janet was crying harder, and Bradlee began to check off her language proficiency. "Say two words to me in Portuguese," he said. She said she couldn't. 207

"Do you have any Italian?" Bradlee asked. 208

Cooke said no. 209

Bradlee, fluent in French, asked her questions in the language. Her   210
answers were stumbling. Bradlee said later that it sounded as if she had
once had some high school instruction.

. . . .

Bradlee asked about Jimmy's identity. Tuesday was the first time Post   211
editors had been told his full name, "Tyrone Davis." His mother and her
boyfriend, they were told, were named Candi Davis and Robert Jackson
Anderson, and they lived on Xenia Street. This was the first time any of
them had been told where "Jimmy" supposedly lived.

"You've got 24 hours to prove the 'Jimmy' story is true," Bradlee said.   212

. . . .

Bradlee, Simons, publisher Donald Graham and Woodward reassem-   213
bled in Bradlee's office. Graham asked if it was really safe to send Coleman
and Cooke to Xenia Street, and was told that it had to be done.

David Maraniss, deputy Metro editor and one of those who had   214
earlier doubted the story, joined the group. Maraniss had known Cooke
since shortly after she arrived at The Post, although he was never her
editor. Genial and respected as an editor, Maraniss develops close relationships with his staff. He and Cooke had had lunch several times, and he had
gone over her stories informally at times. His friendship was to prove
crucial during the evening.

Bradlee and Graham went to dinner at Mel Krupin's restaurant as   215
Cooke's notes and tapes for the Jimmy story arrived at The Post. The
documents had been held in safekeeping in the law offices of Williams &
Connolly since shortly after the story was published.

Woodward, Maraniss and Wilkinson began the laborious job of going   216
over 145 pages of hand-written notes and listening to her tape-recorded
interviews. It was the background for the "Jimmy" story, but this was the
first time that any editor at The Post had inspected her materials. Woodward said later that he saw "echoes" of the published story all through her
notes, but no indication that she had actually interviewed a child using
heroin.

While the three editors were poring over the tapes and notes, Cole-   217
man called. He said they couldn't find "Jimmy's" house, and Coleman later
said that when Cooke failed to identify a house, that fact convinced him
the story was a fake. Now, everybody dealing with Cooke believed she was
lying. But she stuck with her story.

The editors called Elsa Walsh, Cooke's roommate since mid-Decem-   218
ber, who was covering a city council meeting in Alexandria for the Virginia Weekly. She drove to The Post and told an editor, for the first time,
that she had never believed the "Jimmy" story. Once, she said, she had
looked through Cooke's "Jimmy" notes and found none about the boy. She
also recalled that Cooke had once told her that she was valedictorian at
Vassar. Walsh had not gone to an editor with her doubts.

While Coleman and Cooke drove back to the office, Bradlee and 219
Simons went home. It was 11:30 P.M. Both left instructions to be notified
if anything developed.

Coleman and Cooke joined Woodward, Maraniss and Wilkinson in 220
The Post's fifth floor conference room, and the questioning continued.

. . . .

Wilkinson told Cooke he was concerned for her. Woodward con- 221
tinued to say that he knew she had faked the story, even though she had
done it brilliantly.

"This is getting too cruel," Cooke said. "All I have left is my story." 222

But Maraniss was comforting. "Give up the Pulitzer," he said to her, 223
"and you can have yourself back."

The editors say she continued to deny that "Jimmy" didn't exist, 224
repeated it 15 or 20 times, and then a subtle change crept into her answers.

"I have to believe the story. 225

"What am I going to do?" 226

Coleman remained silent. Woodward tried one last time. "If a just 227
God were looking down, what would he say is the truth?"

"I don't know what you mean," Cooke said. 228

Coleman paced the floor. Maraniss sat at the table across from Cooke. 229

Woodward proposed a compromise. Would she sign a statement 230
saying she didn't deserve a Pulitzer Prize because she couldn't prove it?
Cooke replied that she didn't know why she should say that although she
understood it was necessary.

Woodward and Wilkinson left the room, and Coleman soon joined 231
them.

Maraniss sat alone with Cooke. Both were weeping. He held her 232
hand.

"I was afraid I was going to be left alone with you," Cooke said. "The 233
first time I saw you today I thought, 'Oh boy, he knows, and I'm going to
have to tell him.' I couldn't lie to you. I couldn't tell them. I never would
tell Woodward. The more he yelled, the more stubborn I was. Wilkinson
represents the corporation. It means so much to Milton. You guys are
smart, Woodward for the mind, you for the heart. Why were you smiling?"

"Because," said Maraniss, "I had a tremendous surge of empathy for 234
you, refusing to submit to the institution in an absurd situation. You were
so strong not to give in. The institution will survive."

"Oh, David, what am I going to do?" Cooke asked. 235

They talked for an hour, reviewing their childhoods. Each time an- 236
other editor opened the conference room door, Maraniss waved him
away.

They talked about the horror and the fear she had gone through, 237
especially when she was nominated for a Pulitzer.

She said she was rooting for a series by Neil Henry, a Metro reporter 238 whose articles were considered for a Post Pulitzer nomination in another category.

"I didn't think I had a chance," she said. "There were so many other great stories."   239

"You can recover and you will," Maraniss told her.   240

"The only thing I can do is write," Cooke said.   241

"That's not true," Maraniss replied.   242

Then he said, "You don't have to say anything to the others, I'll do it for you. What do I tell them?"   243

"There is no Jimmy and no family," she said. "It was a fabrication. I did so much work on it, but it's a composite. I want to give the prize back."   244

Woodward and Wilkinson had left the room to discuss the feasibility of putting Cooke on indefinite leave. They called Bradlee, and he decided against it. Bradlee said call off the questioning, it was beginning to sound like a "third degree."   245

But when Woodward, Wilkinson and Coleman went back into the conference room, Maraniss looked up and announced: "You can go home now, Jimmy is a composite."   246

Each editor hugged and kissed her.   247

. . . .

"You must have been in a panic for a year," Maraniss said, "after you lied on your resume. How did you feel the night you won the Pulitzer?"   248

"Awful," she said. "I prayed I wouldn't get it, but I never told anybody that."   249

Maraniss drove her to the Ontario apartments, where she stayed up all night, talking with friends.   250

At 7 o'clock Wednesday morning, Bradlee broke the news to Graham, who was, as usual, in his office by 6:30. Bradlee invited Graham to his house for breakfast, and they talked about what to do next.   251

After two hours of sleep at Woodward's house, Maraniss returned to the Ontario, where he and Cooke talked for two hours. Then he called Bradlee, who asked Maraniss to get Cooke's resignation and a written statement.   252

In longhand, she wrote: " 'Jimmy's World' was in essence a fabrication. I never encountered or interviewed an 8-year-old heroin addict. The September 28, 1980, article in The Washington Post was a serious misrepresentation which I deeply regret. I apologize to my newspaper, my profession, the Pulitzer board and all seekers of the truth. Today, in facing up to the truth, I have submitted my resignation. Janet Cooke."   253

Cooke's mother arrived from Toledo Wednesday, and her father flew to Washington on Friday. While Janet Cooke was being grilled by Washington Post editors, her father had spent the night of April 14 filling out his income tax returns.   254

"What did I do that went wrong?" Stratman Cooke asked. "I know   255

I was away from home a lot, had to travel a lot. But I couldn't have it both ways . . . . She was extremely ambitious, eager to prove herself. I encouraged that."

The Conclusions: Once Again, a Fail-Safe System Proves the Exception

So why did it all happen? And how? Milton Coleman and Bob Woodward 256 try to take the blame, and well they should. They had primary responsibility. But to place all the burden on them is a huge mistake. There's enough blame to go around.

Ben Bradlee, the executive editor, was wrong, and Howard Simons, 257 the managing editor, was wrong. Beginning, of course, with Janet Cooke, everybody who touched this journalistic felony—or who should have touched it and didn't—was wrong. It was a complete systems failure, and there's no excuse for it. These are brilliant people. The Post newsroom runs over with high-caliber talent and skills that weren't employed.

Other thoughts: 258

1) The system failed because it wasn't used, not because it is faulty. 259 Bradlee and Simons should have asked tough questions, so should Woodward and Coleman and others. And every staffer who had a serious doubt about "Jimmy" had an unavoidable responsibility to pursue it, hard.

2) This business of trusting reporters absolutely goes too far. Clearly 260 it did in this case. There is a point when total reliance on this kind of trust allows the editor to duck his own responsibility. Editors have to insist on knowing and verifying. That's one of the big reasons they hold their jobs.

3) There's a mythology hanging in the air of the newsroom. Some- 261 times it acts like a disease. Young reporters come onto the staff expecting to find another Watergate under every third rock they kick over. That is naive. Blockbusters are not everyday occurrences. Editors are somewhat infected too, but not to the degree that some of the reporters say they believe. Editors have to get all there is in a news story.

4) The Post did not invent Janet Cooke. That is a ridiculous idea. 262 Given its competitive nature, it may very well have unwittingly encouraged her success and thereby hastened her failure. Hers was an aberration that grew in fertile ground, according to one reporter. That's close to the mark.

5) While editors repeatedly talked about their trust in reporters, the 263 trust apparently only applies to written stories, not to reporters' opinions. Otherwise, somebody with authority would have heard something about those persistent doubts on the Cooke story and would have investigated.

6) The front page syndrome is a problem, and it may be insoluble. 264 Page one is the prestige position in the paper, and until the stories it is to carry have been selected, the rest of the paper can't take shape. And Bradlee is right. The paper has to get out, on schedule, every day. Some of the pressures reporters talk about come with the news business.

7) No reporter or other staff member should be employed without 265 a thorough check of his or her credentials.

8) The scramble for journalistic prizes is poisonous. The obligation is 266 to inform readers, not to collect frameable certificates, however prestigious. Maybe The Post should consider not entering contests.

9) News executives have a responsibility to resolve personnel hassles 267 quickly. Among the what-ifs: had Coleman and Vivian Aplin-Brownlee been on better terms, he might have asked her to look over the Cooke story before it ran, and she, given her instant disbelief of the story, might have challenged it effectively. And that Coleman-Maraniss disagreement should have been attended to promptly.

10) Young reporters are impatient. Even the best of them, among 268 whose ranks Janet Cooke appeared to be, profit by seasoning. To push them too fast is a high-risk undertaking.

11) Did race have anything to do with Cooke's ascendancy? Did she 269 get choice assignments and move up because she was handsome and black? Was she employed for the same reason?

There's some yes and some I-don't-know in any honest answer. If 270 there's an employer who says he wouldn't have hired her, he hasn't seen Cooke either in person or at work. There are white editors on this paper who want to report news on the black community but who know they can't get at some of it in the same way blacks can.

Milton Coleman, as good as any at The Post and Cooke's last editor, 271 is black. So are two of her strongest critics, Vivian Aplin-Brownlee, who was her first editor, and Courtland Milloy, who was among the first and most persistent doubters.

Race may have played some role, but professional pride and human 272 decency were deeply involved in this story and that has not a diddle to do with race.

12) To believe that this mistake, big as it was, challenges the honesty 273 of any other story in The Post or any other newspaper, is overreaching. It won't wash. There is no evidence whatsoever that this kind of thing is tolerated at this paper. To over-reach the other way, if this experience tightens discipline in the news process, it may have done some good.

13) When confidentiality is granted to a news source, by a reporter, 274 that promise cannot commit the supervising editor. If the reporter can't support the integrity of his or her story by revealing the name to his or her editor, the story shouldn't be published. And if that safeguard prevents some news stories from appearing, so be it.

14) To give the impression that The Post is staffed by disgruntled 275 people is nonsense. For every reporter or editor with a complaint, however legitimate, there is at least one other who is on a personal high because he or she works for this newspaper. Staff loyalty to The Post is so powerful that it borders on the absurd.

15) The Post is one of the very few great enterprises in journalism, 276 and everybody associated with it ought to be proud of it.

Questions

Rereading and Independent Analysis

1. In describing Janet Cooke, the *Post* mentions one editor saying "We tend to be detail-conscious, and she needed to know how to get more detail." Make a list of the details you notice in the telling of this story that show that the people writing it actually did see, talk to, or verify the truth of what they were describing. For instance, why do you think the writers included the time the presses started to roll, printing "Jimmy's World," and the names of the people they spoke to at Vassar?

2. Make a list of the "characters" in the *Post*'s story. What does the story tell you about each of them? List the details. Then form categories from your lists to come up with the ways that the *Post* uses "ethical proof," the information that establishes a person's trustworthiness. Does the *Post* emphasize achievements or "pieces of paper"? Why did Janet Cooke say that Vassar is "just me, but the 'Jimmy' story is something I did."

3. Review the sections into which the *Post* divides this story. How do these divisions contribute to the story's drama?

Suggested Discussion and Group Activities

1. In this story, who appears to have been responsible for Cooke's story? Why does the *Post* place responsibility as it does? What is the purpose of this story's treatment of Cooke's dishonesty?

2. What are the stages Janet Cooke went through as she wrote her story? Find places in this account that tell you how she must have gone through the process of writing it.

3. Compare the beginning and the end of the story. What effect is created by withholding the details about Janet Cooke's life that the newspaper had when it began to write this account? How does this technique support the purpose of the whole piece?

4. In groups, investigate a recent newsworthy event at your school. Assign each member a particular task of reporting, and then compare the notes you have taken to see how many verifiable facts there are for which you have more than one source.

Writing Suggestions

Response

How do you respond to the dishonesty revealed by this story? Do you have sympathy for Janet Cooke? Who do you think deserves the blame for her attempt? The story raises the issue of group responsibility. Do you agree that others share responsibility for the story's publication and impact?

Analysis

1. Using the event that you and your group investigated (Question 4, "Suggested Discussion"), write an account of what you discovered, using a narrative technique like the one in the *Post*. Explain how you as a reporter began, gathered information, wrote, and finally verified the report.

2. With your group, write the story you investigated in response to Question 4. Trade your completed collaborations with other groups, and then consult with your campus or local newspaper about the possibility of publishing your analysis of the news.

3. Write an account of your own writing processes, telling how you go about writing for school and in other situations. Be specific and detailed about what you do, how much time you spend doing it, the equipment you use, and how you vary your procedures for writing depending on your purpose, the time you have, and your expected readers. Have your classmates read your account to tell you if it is detailed enough to be believable and helpful.

Finding a Purpose
Choose an event you think is newsworthy and write a piece about it for your local paper. Imitate the detail, accuracy, and high visibility that the *Post* aimed for in this selection. Have your classmates read your report. If you wish, use it in a class newspaper that you share responsibility for publishing.

 # Talking Like a Lady
Robin Lakoff

There is a story that a new administrator in a university called a meeting of his faculty to explain his new programs for their departments. During the meeting, he referred to all of the men present as "Professor . . ." or "Mr. . . ." At the end of the meeting, the only woman present took him aside, pointing out that the only given name he had used was hers—Robin. The administrator's gaffe had just become more evidence for the thesis of Lakoff's research, that even our most ordinary uses of language reveal deeply held values.

Robin Lakoff is a professor of linguistics at the University of California, Berkeley. Lakoff has been a pioneer researcher into gender-related habits of language use. She began this study in 1971, supported by the Center for Advanced Study for the Behavioral Sciences and the National Science Foundation. By studying verifiable instances, the actual words that people say, she has provided empirical evidence that gender determines forms of address, expectations, and distinct vocabulary choices as people talk to each other. Her work moves from noting the parts of statements—the words people use—to noting the results that these words have in comparison with other choices of words in different contexts. This scientific, or empirical, approach to research has resulted in her numerous publications, including the source of this essay, *Language and Woman's Place* (1975). As you read this selection, you will probably have strong reactions (either positive or negative) to Lakoff's argument. Notice how you respond and try to keep an open, critical perspective on her points. Look for supporting and contrary evidence in your own experience.

"Women's language" shows up in all levels of the grammar of English. We   1
find differences in the choice and frequency of lexical items; in the situations in which certain syntactic rules are performed; in intonational and
other supersegmental patterns. As an example of lexical differences, imagine a man and a woman both looking at the same wall, painted a pinkish
shade of purple. The woman may say (2):

(2) The wall is mauve,

with no one consequently forming any special impression of her as a result
of the words alone; but if the man should say (2), one might well conclude
he was imitating a woman sarcastically or was a homosexual or an interior
decorator. Women, then, make far more precise discriminations in naming colors than do men; words like *beige, ecru, aquamarine, lavender,* and
so on are unremarkable in a woman's active vocabulary, but absent from
that of most men. I have seen a man helpless with suppressed laughter at
a discussion between two other people as to whether a book jacket was to
be described as "lavender" or "mauve." Men find such discussion amusing
because they consider such a question trivial, irrelevant to the real world.

We might ask why fine discrimination of color is relevant for women,   2
but not for men. A clue is contained in the way many men in our society
view other "unworldly" topics, such as high culture and the Church, as
outside the world of men's work, relegated to women and men whose
masculinity is not unquestionable. Men tend to relegate to women things
that are not of concern to them, or do not involve their egos. Among these
are problems of fine color discrimination. We might rephrase this point by
saying that since women are not expected to make decisions on important
matters, such as what kind of job to hold, they are relegated the noncrucial
decisions as a sop. Deciding whether to name a color "lavender" or
"mauve" is one such sop.

If it is agreed that this lexical disparity reflects a social inequity in   3
the position of women, one may ask how to remedy it. Obviously, no one
could seriously recommend legislating against the use of the terms
"mauve" and "lavender" by women, or forcing men to learn to use
them. All we can do is give women the opportunity to participate in the
real decisions of life.

Aside from specific lexical items like color names, we find differ-   4
ences between the speech of women and that of men in the use of particles that grammarians often describe as "meaningless." There may be
no referent for them, but they are far from meaningless: they define
the social context of an utterance, indicate the relationship the speaker
feels between himself and his addressee, between himself and what he
is talking about.

As an experiment, one might present native speakers of standard   5
American English with pairs of sentences, identical syntactically and in
terms of referential lexical items, and differing merely in the choice of
"meaningless" particle, and ask them which was spoken by a man, which
a woman. Consider:

(3) *(a)* Oh dear, you've put the peanut butter in the refrigerator
again.

(b) Shit, you've put the peanut butter in the refrigerator again.

It is safe to predict that people would classify the first sentence as part   6
of "women's language," the second as "men's language." It is true that
many self-respecting women are becoming able to use sentences like (3)
(b) publicly without flinching, but this is a relatively recent development,
and while perhaps the majority of Middle America might condone the use
of *(b)* for men, they would still disapprove of its use by women. (It is of
interest, by the way, to note that men's language is increasingly being used
by women, but women's language is not being adopted by men, apart
from those who reject the American masculine image [for example, homo-
sexuals]. This is analogous to the fact that men's jobs are being sought by
women, but few men are rushing to become housewives or secretaries.
The language of the favored group, the group that holds the power, along
with its nonlinguistic behavior, is generally adopted by the other group,
not vice versa. In any event, it is a truism to state that the "stronger"
expletives are reserved for men, and the "weaker" ones for women.)

Now we may ask what we mean by "stronger" and "weaker" exple-   7
tives. (If these particles were indeed meaningless, none would be stronger
than any other.) The difference between using "shit" (or "damn," or one
of many others) as opposed to "oh dear," or "goodness," or "oh fudge" lies
in how forcefully one says how one feels—perhaps, one might say, choice
of particle is a function of how strongly one allows oneself to feel about
something, so that the strength of an emotion conveyed in a sentence
corresponds to the strength of the particle. Hence in a really serious
situation, the use of "trivializing" (that is, "women's") particles constitutes
a joke, or at any rate, is highly inappropriate. (In conformity with current
linguistic practice, throughout this work an asterisk (*) will be used to
mark a sentence that is inappropriate in some sense, either because it is
syntactically deviant or used in the wrong social context.)

(4) *(a)* *Oh fudge, my hair is on fire.
(b) *Dear me, did he kidnap the baby?

As children, women are encouraged to be "little ladies." Little ladies   8
don't scream as vociferously as little boys, and they are chastised more
severely for throwing tantrums or showing temper: "high spirits" are
expected and therefore tolerated in little boys; docility and resignation are
the corresponding traits expected of little girls. Now, we tend to excuse
a show of temper by a man where we would not excuse an identical tirade
from a woman: women are allowed to fuss and complain, but only a man
can bellow in rage. It is sometimes claimed that there is a biological basis
for this behavior difference, though I don't believe conclusive evidence
exists that the early differences in behavior that have been observed are
not the results of very different treatment of babies of the two sexes from
the beginning; but surely the use of different particles by men and women

is a learned trait, merely mirroring nonlinguistic differences again, and again pointing out an inequity that exists between the treatment of men, and society's expectations of them, and the treatment of women. Allowing men stronger means of expression than are open to women further reinforces men's position of strength in the real world: for surely we listen with more attention the more strongly and forcefully someone expresses opinions, and a speaker unable—for whatever reason—to be forceful in stating his views is much less likely to be taken seriously. Ability to use strong particles like "shit" and "hell" is, of course, only incidental to the inequity that exists rather than its cause. But once again, apparently accidental linguistic usage suggests that women are denied equality partially for linguistic reasons, and that an examination of language points up precisely an area in which inequity exists. Further, if someone is allowed to show emotions, and consequently does, others may well be able to view him as a real individual in his own right, as they could not if he never showed emotion. Here again, then, the behavior a woman learns as "correct" prevents her from being taken seriously as an individual, and further is considered "correct" and necessary for a woman precisely because society does *not* consider her seriously as an individual.

Similar sorts of disparities exist elsewhere in the vocabulary. There 9 is, for instance, a group of adjectives which have, besides their specific and literal meanings, another use, that of indicating the speaker's approbation or admiration for something. Some of these adjectives are neutral as to sex of speaker: either men or women may use them. But another set seems, in its figurative use, to be largely confined to women's speech. Representative lists of both types are below:

neutral	*women only*
great	adorable
terrific	charming
cool	sweet
neat	lovely
	divine

As with the color words and swear words already discussed, for a man 10 to stray into the "women's" column is apt to be damaging to his reputation, though here a woman may freely use the neutral words. But it should not be inferred from this that a woman's use of the "women's" words is without its risks. Where a woman has a choice between the neutral words and the women's words, as a man has not, she may be suggesting very different things about her own personality and her view of the subject matter by her choice of words of the first set or words of the second.

(5) *(a)* What a terrific idea!
     (b) What a divine idea!

It seems to me that *(a)* might be used under any appropriate conditions by a female speaker. But *(b)* is more restricted. Probably it is used appropriately (even by the sort of speaker for whom it was normal) only in case the speaker feels the idea referred to to be essentially frivolous, trivial, or unimportant to the world at large—only an amusement for the speaker herself. Consider, then, a woman advertising executive at an advertising conference. However feminine an advertising executive she is, she is much more likely to express her approval with (5) *(a)* than with *(b)*, which might cause raised eyebrows, and the reaction: "That's what we get for putting a woman in charge of this company."

On the other hand, suppose a friend suggests to the same woman that she should dye her French poodles to match her cigarette lighter. In this case, the suggestion really concerns only her, and the impression she will make on people. In this case, she may use *(b)*, from the "woman's language." So the choice is not really free: words restricted to "women's language" suggest that concepts to which they are applied are not relevant to the real world of (male) influence and power.

One may ask whether there really are no analogous terms that are available to men—terms that denote approval of the trivial, the personal; that express approbation in terms of one's own personal emotional reaction, rather than by gauging the likely general reaction. There does in fact seem to be one such word: it is the hippie invention "groovy," which seems to have most of the connotations that separate "lovely" and "divine" from "great" and "terrific" excepting only that it does not mark the speaker as feminine or effeminate.

(6) *(a)* What a terrific steel mill!
    (b) *What a lovely steel mill! (male speaking)
    (c) What a groovy steel mill!

I think it is significant that this word was introduced by the hippies, and, when used seriously rather than sarcastically, used principally by people who have accepted the hippies' values. Principal among these is the denial of the Protestant work ethic: to a hippie, something can be worth thinking about even if it isn't influential in the power structure, or moneymaking. Hippies are separated from the activities of the real world just as women are—though in the former case it is due to a decision on their parts, while this is not uncontroversially true in the case of women. For both these groups, it is possible to express approval of things in a personal way—though one does so at the risk of losing one's credibility with members of the power structure. It is also true, according to some speakers, that upper-class British men may use the words listed in the "women's" column, as well as the specific color words and others we have categorized as specifically feminine, without raising doubts as to their masculinity among other speakers of the same dialect. (This is not true for lower-class Britons, however.) The reason may be that commitment to the work ethic need not necessarily be displayed: one may be or appear to be a gentleman of leisure, interested in various pursuits, but not involved in mundane (business or political) affairs, in such a culture, without incurring disgrace. This is rather analogous to the position of a woman in American middle-class society, so we should not be surprised if these special lexical items are usable by both groups. This fact points indeed to a more general conclusion. These words aren't, basically, "feminine"; rather, they signal "uninvolved," or "out of power." Any group in a society to which these labels are applicable may presumably use these words; they are often considered "feminine," "unmasculine," because women are the "uninvolved," "out of power" group *par excellence.*

Another group that has, ostensibly at least, taken itself out of the search for power and money is that of academic men. They are frequently viewed by other groups as analogous in some ways to women—they don't really work, they are supported in their frivolous pursuits by others, what they do doesn't really count in the real world, and so on. The suburban home finds its counterpart in the ivory tower: one is supposedly shielded from harsh realities in both. Therefore it is not too surprising that many academic men (especially those who emulate British norms) may violate many of these sacrosanct rules I have just laid down: they often use "women's language." Among themselves, this does not occasion ridicule. But to a truck driver, a professor saying, "What a lovely hat!" is undoubtedly laughable, all the more so as it reinforces his stereotype of professors as effete snobs.

When we leave the lexicon and venture into syntax, we find that syntactically too women's speech is peculiar. To my knowledge, there is no syntactic rule in English that only women may use. But there is at least one rule that a woman will use in more conversational situations than a man. (This fact indicates, of course, that the applicability of syntactic rules is governed partly by social context—the positions in society of the speaker and addressee, with respect to each other, and the impression one seeks to make on the other.) This is the rule of tag-question formation.[1]

---

[1] Within the lexicon itself, there seems to be a parallel phenomenon to tag-question usage, which I refrain from discussing in the body of the text because the facts are controversial and I do not understand them fully. The intensive *so,* used where purists would insist upon an absolute superlative, heavily stressed, seems more characteristic of women's language than of men's, though it is found in the latter, particularly in the speech of male academics. Consider, for instance, the following sentences:

(a) I feel *so* unhappy!
(b) That movie made me *so* sick!

Men seem to have the least difficulty using this construction when the sentence is unemotional, or nonsubjective—without reference to the speaker himself:

(c) That sunset is *so* beautiful!
(d) Fred is *so* dumb!

Substituting an equative like so for absolute superlatives (like *very, really, utterly*) seems to be a way of backing out of committing oneself strongly to an opinion, rather like tag questions (cf. discussion below, in the text). One might hedge in this way with perfect right in making aesthetic judgments, as in (c), or intellectual judgments, as in (d). But it is somewhat odd to hedge in describing one's own mental or emotional state: who, after all, is qualified to contradict one on this? To hedge in this situation is to seek to avoid making any strong statement: a characteristic, as we have noted already and shall note further, of women's speech.

A tag, in its usage as well as its syntactic shape (in English) is midway 15
between an outright statement and a yes-no question: it is less assertive
than the former, but more confident than the latter. Therefore it is usable
under certain contextual situations: not those in which a statement would
be appropriate, nor those in which a yes-no question is generally used, but
in situations intermediate between these.

One makes a statement when one has confidence in his knowledge 16
and is pretty certain that his statement will be believed; one asks a question when one lacks knowledge on some point and has reason to believe
that this gap can and will be remedied by an answer by the addressee. A
tag question, being intermediate between these, is used when the speaker
is stating a claim, but lacks full confidence in the truth of that claim. So
if I say

(7) Is John here?

I will probably not be surprised if my respondent answers "no"; but if I
say

(8) John is here, isn't he?

instead, chances are I am already biased in favor of a positive answer,
wanting only confirmation by the addressee. I still want a response from
him, as I do with a yes-no question; but I have enough knowledge (or think
I have) to predict that response, much as with a declarative statement. A
tag question, then, might be thought of as a declarative statement without
the assumption that the statement is to be believed by the addressee: one
has an out, as with a question. A tag gives the addressee leeway, not forcing
him to go along with the views of the speaker.

There are situations in which a tag is legitimate, in fact the only 17
legitimate sentence form. So, for example, if I have seen something only
indistinctly, and have reason to believe my addressee had a better view,
I can say:

(9) I had my glasses off. He was out at third, wasn't he?

Sometimes we find a tag question used in cases in which the speaker 18
knows as well as the addressee what the answer must be, and doesn't need
confirmation. One such situation is when the speaker is making "small
talk," trying to elicit conversation from the addressee:

(10) Sure is hot here, isn't it?

In discussing personal feelings or opinions, only the speaker normally 19
has any way of knowing the correct answer. Strictly speaking, questioning
one's own opinions is futile. Sentences like (11) are usually ridiculous.

(11) *I have a headache, don't I?

But similar cases do, apparently, exist, in which it is the speaker's opinions,
rather than perceptions, for which corroboration is sought, as in (12):

(12) The way prices are rising is horrendous, isn't it?

While there are of course other possible interpretations of a sentence 20
like this, one possibility is that the speaker has a particular answer in
mind—"yes" or "no"—but is reluctant to state it baldly. It is my impression, though I do not have precise statistical evidence, that this sort of tag
question is much more apt to be used by women than by men. If this is
indeed true, why is it true?

These sentence types provide a means whereby a speaker can avoid 21
committing himself, and thereby avoid coming into conflict with the addressee. The problem is that, by so doing, a speaker may also give the
impression of not being really sure of himself, of looking to the addressee
for confirmation, even of having no views of his own. This last criticism is,
of course, one often leveled at women. One wonders how much of it
reflects a use of language that has been imposed on women from their
earliest years.

Related to this special use of a syntactic rule is a widespread differ- 22
ence perceptible in women's intonational patterns.[2] There is a peculiar
sentence intonation pattern, found in English as far as I know only among
women, which has the form of a declarative answer to a question, and is
used as such, but has the rising inflection typical of a yes-no question, as
well as being especially hesitant. The effect is as though one were seeking
confirmation, though at the same time the speaker may be the only one
who has the requisite information.

(13) *(a)* When will dinner be ready?
     (b) Oh . . . around six o'clock . . . ?

It is as though *(b)* were saying, "Six o'clock, if that's OK with you, if you
agree." *(a)* is put in the position of having to provide confirmation, and
(b) sounds unsure. Here we find unwillingness to assert an opinion carried
to an extreme. One likely consequence is that these sorts of speech patterns are taken to reflect something real about character and play a part
in not taking a woman seriously or trusting her with any real responsibilities, since "she can't make up her mind" and "isn't sure of herself." And
here again we see that people form judgments about other people on the
basis of superficial linguistic behavior that may have nothing to do with
inner character, but has been imposed upon the speaker, on pain of worse
punishment than not being taken seriously.

Such features are probably part of the general fact that women's 23
speech sounds much more "polite" than men's. One aspect of politeness

---

[2] For analogues outside of English to these uses of tag questions and special intonation
patterns, ct. my discussion of Japanese particles in "Language in Context," *Language,* 48
(1972), 907–27. It is to be expected that similar cases will be found in many other languages
as well. See, for example, M. R. Haas's very interesting discussion of differences between
men's and women's speech (mostly involving lexical dissimilarities) in many languages, in
D. Hymes, ed., *Language in Culture and Society* (New York: Harper & Row, 1964).

is as we have just described: leaving a decision open, not imposing your mind, or views, or claims on anyone else. Thus a tag question is a kind of polite statement, in that it does not force agreement or belief on the addressee. A request may be in the same sense a polite command, in that it does not overtly require obedience, but rather suggests something be done as a favor to the speaker. An overt order (as in an imperative) expresses the (often impolite) assumption of the speaker's superior position to the addressee, carrying with it the right to enforce compliance, whereas with a request the decision on the face of it is left up to the addressee. (The same is true of suggestions: here, the implication is not that the addressee is in danger if he does not comply—merely that he will be glad if he does. Once again, the decision is up to the addressee, and a suggestion therefore is politer than an order.) The more particles in a sentence that reinforce the notion that it is a request, rather than an order, the politer the result. The sentences of (14) illustrate these points: (14) *(a)* is a direct order, *(b)* and *(c)* simple requests, and *(d)* and *(e)* compound requests.[3]

(14) *(a)* Close the door.
  (b) Please close the door.
  (c) Will you close the door?
  (d) Will you please close the door?
  (e) Won't you close the door?

Let me first explain why *(e)* has been classified as a compound request. (A sentence like *Won't you please close the door* would then count as a doubly compound request.) A sentence like (14) *(c)* is close in sense to "Are you willing to close the door?" According to the normal rules of polite conversation, to agree that you are willing is to agree to do the thing asked of you. Hence this apparent inquiry functions as a request, leaving the decision up to the willingness of the addressee. Phrasing it as a positive question makes the (implicit) assumption that a "yes" answer will be forthcoming. Sentence (14) *(d)* is more polite than *(b)* or *(c)* because it combines them: *please* indicating that to accede will be to do something for the speaker, and *will you,* as noted, suggesting that the addressee has the final decision. If, now, the question is phrased with a negative, as in (14) *(e),* the speaker seems to suggest the stronger likelihood of a negative response from the addressee. Since the assumption is then that the addressee is that much freer to refuse, (14) *(e)* acts as a more polite request than (14) *(c)* or *(d): (c)* and *(d)* put the burden of refusal on the addressee, as *(e)* does not.

Given these facts, one can see the connection between tag questions and tag orders and other requests. In all these cases, the speaker is not committed as with a simple declarative or affirmative. And the more one compounds a request, the more characteristic it is of women's speech, the

[3] For more detailed discussion of these problems, see Lakoff, "Language in Context."

less of men's. A sentence that begins *Won't you please* (without special emphasis on *please*) seems to me at least to have a distinctly unmasculine sound. Little girls are indeed taught to talk like little ladies, in that their speech is in many ways more polite than that of boys or men, and the reason for this is that politeness involves an absence of a strong statement, and women's speech is devised to prevent the expression of strong statements.

Questions

Rereading and Independent Analysis

1. In order to understand Lakoff's arguments fully, you need to understand the categories that she uses to classify examples. If you cannot be sure of her meaning from the context, use a dictionary to define "lexical features," "syntax," "declarative," "imperative," "intonational," and other words you are not sure of.

2. Reread this chapter, underlining the inferences and judgments Lakoff makes after describing her observations and evidence. Make a list of the words she uses to emphasize her caution in drawing conclusions— for example, "suggests" and "likely." What do these words tell you about her intended readers and the context in which she wrote this book?

Suggested Discussion and Group Activities

1. Do you agree with the conclusions that Lakoff has reached? Give reasons for and against them, based on evidence from the chapter itself. Then offer evidence from your own experience. Test your experience by reversing the gender of the sentences she uses as examples—have men read the sentences that she says women say, and the reverse. Are these reversals comfortable for the speaker? What responses do they create?

2. Comment on Lakoff's own language. For instance, how does she use passive verbs and personal pronouns in this chapter? What characteristics identify her research as belonging to the social sciences? (See the section "Social Sciences" in Chapter 4.) What characteristics identify it as a chapter in a book published for a popular audience? Does the chapter clearly show who its ideal readers are?

3. This method of investigating language could be extended to other groups based on race, class, employment, or another category. In groups, use the evidence of Lakoff's methods presented here to form a plan for doing research within one of these other categories. You might choose office workers, city employees, or people from a specific region.

Writing Suggestions

Response

Make notes over the period of a week on the terms of address, the adjectives, and other word choices you use when talking both to people who have authority over you and to those you might think of as your subordinates. Be accurate and objective, merely noting these choices. Then, at the end of the note taking, write a few generalizations about this language. Did your observations make you more aware of specific language?

Analysis

1. Lakoff's chapter makes the point that words are not separate from the people who use them but an integral part of "who we are" in the fullest sense. Write a personal essay in which you discuss how you control your own use of language depending on how you want people to respond to you in particular situations.

2. Choose one feature of language—adjectives, tag questions, personal pronouns, or another limited characteristic of ordinary speech. For a few days, keep a notebook with you in which you record examples of the ways a particular group of people use this feature in their speech. (You may observe students, teachers, or another category of people you see daily.) Then write a report to your class in which you present your evidence and draw from it some limited conclusions about this group's image of themselves and their relationships to others.

Finding a Purpose

Labeling and stereotyping are common ways to keep a person or a group in its "place." Write a confidential letter to the president of your (imagined) place of employment in which you explain why you think that many of your coworkers have been hired because they fit a popular stereotype of the kinds of people who should be doing those jobs.

RE-PLACEMENTS: WRITING A NEW WORLD

 # Tlön, Uqbar, Orbis Tertius
Jorge Luis Borges

Translated by James E. Irby

This complex story by Jorge Luis Borges (1899–1986) gives us a dual perspective on the "infrastructure" of the written world. We usually think of people who devote themselves to working with this infrastructure—its dictionaries, bibliographies, actual texts, and encyclopedias—as what Samuel Johnson called "harmless drudges." Their work seems boring, inconsequential, distant from the interesting meat of meaning and even further from everyday life. But, as this story shows, their attention to details could have an unsettling result for "reality"—the physical world we accept as the truth that is the subject of writing. Writing creates more, of course, than a record of actual reality. Borges's story tells of another world, an entirely written one, created by an encyclopedia and allowed to dominate the world of experience.

Borges was an Argentinian whose interests in poetry, philosophy, and fiction shaped many of his numerous publications after he began writing reviews (another part of the infrastructure) in 1919. His work has been collected in translations whose titles reveal the oblique perspective he chose, for example, *Labyrinths* (1962) and *Ficciones* [Fictions] (1962), which won the International Publishers' Prize. The editors of the Borges *Reader* (1981) say that the key to understanding anything Borges has written is that he viewed reading "as a form of writing—or rewriting." That is, his works insist that the reader become a collaborator in the writing. They are often thoroughly laden with notes, footnotes, and "editors" comments, all of which prevent readers from staying *in* the fictional, or science fictional, world of which these works might otherwise appear to be a part.

These issues are the theme of "Tlön, Uqbar, Orbis Tertius," which tells stories within stories in fractured sections, one "fact" at a time. We learn that Uqbar is the fictional creation of a seventeenth-century secret society. We learn that Tlön is a mirror image of our world, where all of our common assumptions about language, "reality," and subjectivity are reversed. We cannot be sure, but we also think we learn that Orbis Tertius will be, or has already been, produced by Tlön. We become absorbed in the details of these complicated facts as we also become increasingly aware of the sinister secrecy of these worlds and the motives of Ezra Buckley, a plain, aptly named American millionaire, who has (or so we guess) motivated their creation.

You should not, however, let the complexity of this science fiction prevent your enjoyment of its obvious playfulness. As you will see, Borges requires that you collaborate with him in understanding how complexly related written and actual worlds are. He enlists your cooperation by paying a great deal of attention to establishing the believability of this fiction. (As you read, notice how the matter-of-fact tone of the narrator is used to call all matters of fact into question.) But he also allows you to understand the implications when a piece of writing becomes "real" and determines the actions and interests of everyone whom it touches.

I

I owe the discovery of Uqbar to the conjunction of a mirror and an ency- 1
clopedia. The mirror troubled the depths of a corridor in a country house on Gaona Street in Ramos Mejía; the encyclopedia is fallaciously called *The Anglo-American Cyclopaedia* (New York, 1917) and is a literal but delinquent reprint of the *Encyclopaedia Britannica* of 1902. The event took place some five years ago. Bioy Casares had had dinner with me that evening and we became lengthily engaged in a vast polemic concerning the composition of a novel in the first person, whose narrator would omit or disfigure the facts and indulge in various contradictions which would permit a few readers—very few readers—to perceive an atrocious or banal reality. From the remote depths of the corridor, the mirror spied upon us.

We discovered (such a discovery is inevitable in the late hours of the night) that mirrors have something monstrous about them. Then Bioy Casares recalled that one of the heresiarchs of Uqbar had declared that mirrors and copulation are abominable, because they increase the number of men. I asked him the origin of this memorable observation and he answered that it was reproduced in *The Anglo-American Cyclopaedia,* in its article on Uqbar. The house (which we had rented furnished) had a set of this work. On the last pages of Volume XLVI we found an article on Upsala; on the first pages of Volume XLVII, one on Ural-Altaic Languages, but not a word about Uqbar. Bioy, a bit taken aback, consulted the volumes of the index. In vain he exhausted all of the imaginable spellings: Ukbar, Cedar, Ooqbar, Ookbar, Oukbahr . . . Before leaving, he told me that it was a region of Iraq or of Asia Minor. I must confess that I agreed with some discomfort. I conjectured that this undocumented country and its anonymous heresiarch were a fiction devised by Bioy's modesty in order to justify a statement. The fruitless examination of one of Justus Perthes' atlases fortified my doubt.

The following day, Bioy called me from Buenos Aires. He told me he 2 had before him the article on Uqbar, in Volume XLVI of the encyclopedia. The heresiarch's name was not forthcoming, but there was a note on his doctrine, formulated in words almost identical to those he had repeated, though perhaps literarily inferior. He had recalled: *Copulation and mirrors are abominable.* The text of the encyclopedia said: *For one of those gnostics, the visible universe was an illusion or (more precisely) a sophism. Mirrors and fatherhood are abominable because they multiply and disseminate that universe.* I told him, in all truthfulness, that I should like to see that article. A few days later he brought it. This surprised me, since the scrupulous cartographical indices of Ritter's *Erdkunde* were plentifully ignorant of the name Uqbar.

The tome Bioy brought was, in fact, Volume XLVI of the *Anglo-* 3 *American Cyclopaedia.* On the half-title page and the spine, the alphabetical marking (Tor-Ups) was that of our copy, but, instead of 917, it contained 921 pages. These four additional pages made up the article on Uqbar, which (as the reader will have noticed) was not indicated by the alphabetical marking. We later determined that there was no other difference between the volumes. Both of them (as I believe I have indicated) are reprints of the tenth *Encyclopaedia Britannica.* Bioy had acquired his copy at some sale or other.

We read the article with some care. The passage recalled by Bioy was 4 perhaps the only surprising one. The rest of it seemed very plausible, quite in keeping with the general tone of the work and (as is natural) a bit boring. Reading it over again, we discovered beneath its rigorous prose a fundamental vagueness. Of the fourteen names which figured in the geographical part, we only recognized three—Khorasan, Armenia, Erzerum—interpolated in the text in an ambiguous way. Of the historical names, only one: the impostor magician Smerdis, invoked more as a metaphor. The note seemed to fix the boundaries of Uqbar, but its nebulous reference points were rivers and craters and mountain ranges of that same region. We read, for example, that the lowlands of Tsai Khaldun and the Axa Delta marked the southern frontier and that on the islands of the delta wild horses procreate. All this, on the first part of page 918. In the historical section (page 920) we learned that as a result of the religious persecutions of the thirteenth century, the orthodox believers sought refuge on these islands, where to this day their obelisks remain and where it is not uncommon to unearth their stone mirrors. The section on Language and Literature was brief. Only one trait is worthy of recollection: it noted that the literature of Uqbar was one of fantasy and that its epics and legends never referred to reality, but to the two imaginary regions of Mlejnas and Tlön . . . The bibliography enumerated four volumes which we have not yet found, though the third—Silas Haslam: *History of the Land Called Uqbar,* 1874—figures in the catalogues of Bernard Quaritch's bookshop.[1] The first, *Lesbare und lesenswerthe Bemerkungen über das Land Ukkbar in Klein-Asien,* dates from 1641 and is the work of Johannes Valentinus Andreä. This fact is significant; a few years later, I came upon that name in the unsuspected pages of De Quincey (*Writings,* Volume XIII) and learned that it belonged to a German theologian who, in the early seventeenth century, described the imaginary community of Rosae Crucis—a community that others founded later, in imitation of what he had prefigured.

That night we visited the National Library. In vain we exhausted atlases, catalogues, annuals of geographical societies, travelers' and historians' memoirs: no one had ever been in Uqbar. Neither did the general index of Bioy's encyclopedia register that name. The following day, Carlos Mastronardi (to whom I had related the matter) noticed the black and gold covers of the *Anglo-American Cyclopaedia* in a bookshop on Corrientes and Talcahuano . . . He entered and examined Volume XLVI. Of course, he did not find the slightest indication of Uqbar.

II

Some limited and waning memory of Herbert Ashe, an engineer of the southern railways, persists in the hotel at Adrogué, amongst the effusive honeysuckles and in the illusory depths of the mirrors. In his lifetime, he suffered from unreality, as do so many Englishmen; once dead, he is not even the ghost he was then. He was tall and listless and his tired rectangular beard had once been red. I understand he was a widower, without children. Every few years he would go to England, to visit (I judge from some photographs he showed us) a sundial and a few oaks. He and my father had entered into one of those close (the adjective is excessive)

---

[1] Haslam has also published *A General History of Labyrinths.* [The footnotes in this story are Borges'.]

English friendships that begin by excluding confidences and very soon dispense with dialogue. They used to carry out an exchange of books and newspapers and engage in taciturn chess games . . . I remember him in the hotel corridor, with a mathematics book in his hand, sometimes looking at the irrecoverable colors of the sky. One afternoon, we spoke of the duodecimal system of numbering (in which twelve is written as 10). Ashe said that he was converting some kind of tables from the duodecimal to the sexagesimal system (in which sixty is written as 10). He added that the task had been entrusted to him by a Norwegian, in Rio Grande do Sul. We had known him for eight years and he had never mentioned his sojourn in that region . . . We talked of country life, of the *capangas,* of the Brazilian etymology of the word *gaucho* (which some old Uruguayans still pronounce *gaúcho*) and nothing more was said—may God forgive me—of duodecimal functions. In September of 1937 (we were not at the hotel), Herbert Ashe died of a ruptured aneurysm. A few days before, he had received a sealed and certified package from Brazil. It was a book in large octavo. Ashe left it at the bar, where—months later—I found it. I began to leaf through it and experienced an astonished and airy feeling of vertigo which I shall not describe, for this is not the story of my emotions but of Uqbar and Tlön and Orbis Tertius. On one of the nights of Islam called the Night of Nights, the secret doors of heaven open wide and the water in the jars becomes sweeter; if those doors opened, I would not feel what I felt that afternoon. The book was written in English and contained 1001 pages. On the yellow leather back I read these curious words which were repeated on the title page: *A First Encyclopaedia of Tlön. Vol. XI. Haler to Jangr.* There was no indication of date or place. On the first page and on a leaf of silk paper that covered one of the color plates there was stamped a blue oval with this inscription: *Orbis Tertius.* Two years before I had discovered, in a volume of a certain pirated encyclopedia, a superficial description of a nonexistent country; now chance afforded me something more precious and arduous. Now I held in my hands a vast methodical fragment of an unknown planet's entire history, with its architecture and its playing cards, with the dread of its mythologies and the murmur of its languages, with its emperors and its seas, with its minerals and its birds and its fish, with its algebra and its fire, with its theological and metaphysical controversy. And all of it articulated, coherent, with no visible doctrinal intent or tone of parody.

In the "Eleventh Volume" which I have mentioned, there are allu- 7 sions to preceding and succeeding volumes. In an article in the *N. R. F.* which is now classic, Néstor Ibarra has denied the existence of those companion volumes; Ezequiel Martínez Estrade and Drieu La Rochelle have refuted that doubt, perhaps victoriously. The fact is that up to now the most diligent inquiries have been fruitless. In vain we have upended the libraries of the two Americas and of Europe. Alfonso Reyes, tired of these subordinate sleuthing procedures, proposes that we should all undertake the task of reconstructing the many and weighty tomes that are lacking: *ex ungue leonem* [the lion is known by its claw]. He calculates, half in earnest and half jokingly, that a generation of *tlönistas* should be sufficient. This venturesome computation brings us back to the fundamental problem: Who are the inventors of Tlön? The plural is inevitable, because the hypothesis of a lone inventor—an infinite Leibniz laboring away darkly and modestly—has been unanimously discounted. It is conjectured that this brave new world is the work of a secret society of astronomers, biologists, engineers, metaphysicians, poets, chemists, algebraists, moralists, painters, geometers . . . directed by an obscure man of genius. Individuals mastering these diverse disciplines are abundant, but not so those capable of inventiveness and less so those capable of subordinating that inventiveness to a rigorous and systematic plan. This plan is so vast that each writer's contribution is infinitesimal. At first it was believed that Tlön was a mere chaos, an irresponsible license of the imagination; now it is known that it is a cosmos and that the intimate laws which govern it have been formulated, at least provisionally. Let it suffice for me to recall that the apparent contradictions of the Eleventh Volume are the fundamental basis for the proof that the other volumes exist, so lucid and exact is the order observed in it. The popular magazines, with pardonable excess, have spread news of the zoology and topography of Tlön; I think its transparent tigers and towers of blood perhaps do not merit the continued attention of *all* men. I shall venture to request a few minutes to expound its concept of the universe.

Hume noted for all time that Berkeley's arguments did not admit the 8 slightest refutation nor did they cause the slightest conviction. This dictum is entirely correct in its application to the earth, but entirely false in Tlön. The nations of this planet are congenitally idealist. Their language and the derivations of their language—religion, letters, metaphysics—all presuppose idealism. The world for them is not a concourse of objects in space; it is a heterogeneous series of independent acts. It is successive and temporal, not spatial. There are no nouns in Tlön's conjectural *Ursprache*, from which the "present" languages and the dialects are derived: there are impersonal verbs, modified by monosyllabic suffixes (or prefixes) with an adverbial value. For example: there is no word corresponding to the word "moon," but there is a verb which in English would be "to moon" or "to moonate." "The moon rose above the river" is *hlör u fang axaxaxas mlö*, or literally: "upward behind the on-streaming it mooned."

The preceding applies to the languages of the southern hemisphere. 9 In those of the northern hemisphere (on whose *Ursprache* there is very little data in the Eleventh Volume) the prime unit is not the verb, but the monosyllabic adjective. The noun is formed by an accumulation of adjectives. They do not say "moon," but rather "round airy-light on dark" or "pale-orange-of-the-sky" or any other such combination. In the example selected the mass of adjectives refers to a real object, but this is purely fortuitous. The literature of this hemisphere (like Meinong's subsistent world) abounds in ideal objects, which are convoked and dissolved in a moment, according to poetic needs. At times they are determined by mere simultaneity. There are objects composed of two terms, one of visual and another of auditory character: the color of the rising sun and the faraway cry of a bird. There are objects of many terms: the sun and the water on a swimmer's chest, the vague tremulous rose color we see with our eyes closed, the sensation of being carried along by a river and also by sleep. These second-degree objects can be combined with others; through the use of certain abbreviations, the process is practically infinite. There are famous poems made up of one enormous word. This word forms a *poetic object* created by the author. The fact that no one believes in the reality of nouns paradoxically causes their number to be unending. The languages of Tlön's northern hemisphere contain all the nouns of the Indo-European languages—and many others as well.

It is no exaggeration to state that the classic culture of Tlön comprises 10 only one discipline: psychology. All others are subordinated to it. I have said that the men of this planet conceive the universe as a series of mental processes which do not develop in space but successively in time. Spinoza ascribes to his inexhaustible divinity the attributes of extension and thought; no one in Tlön would understand the juxtaposition of the first (which is typical only of certain states) and the second—which is a perfect synonym of the cosmos. In other words, they do not conceive that the spatial persists in time. The perception of a cloud of smoke on the horizon and then of the burning field and then of the half-extinguished cigarette that produced the blaze is considered an example of association of ideas.

This monism or complete idealism invalidates all science. If we ex- 11 plain (or judge) a fact, we connect it with another; such linking, in Tlön, is a later state of the subject which cannot affect or illuminate the previous state. Every mental state is irreducible: the mere fact of naming it—i.e., of classifying it—implies a falsification. From which it can be deduced that there are no sciences on Tlön, not even reasoning. The paradoxical truth is that they do exist, and in almost uncountable number. The same thing happens with philosophies as happens with nouns in the northern hemisphere. The fact that every philosophy is by definition a dialectical game, a *Philosophie des Als Ob* [Philosophy of As If], has caused them to multiply. There is an abundance of incredible systems of pleasing design or sensational type. The metaphysicians of Tlön do not seek for the truth or even for verisimilitude, but rather for the astounding. They judge that metaphysics is a branch of fantastic literature. They know that a system is nothing more than the subordination of all aspects of the universe to any one such aspect. Even the phrase "all aspects" is rejectable, for it supposes the impossible addition of the present and of all past moments. Neither is it licit to use the plural "past moments," since it supposes another impossible operation . . . One of the schools of Tlön goes so far as to negate time: it reasons that the present is indefinite, that the future has no reality other than as a present hope, that the past has no reality other than as a present memory.[2] Another school declares that *all time* has already transpired and that our life is only the crepuscular and no doubt falsified and mutilated memory or reflection of an irrecoverable process. Another, that the history of the universe—and in it our lives and the most tenuous detail of our lives—is the scripture produced by a subordinate god in order to communicate with a demon. Another, that the universe is comparable to those cryptographs in which not all the symbols are valid and that only what happens every three hundred nights is true. Another, that while we sleep here, we are awake elsewhere and that in this way every man is two men.

Amongst the doctrines of Tlön, none has merited the scandalous reception accorded to materialism. Some thinkers have formulated it with less clarity than fervor, as one might put forth a paradox. In order to facilitate the comprehension of this inconceivable thesis, a heresiarch of the eleventh century[3] devised the sophism of the nine copper coins, whose scandalous renown is in Tlön equivalent to that of the Eleatic paradoxes. There are many versions of this "specious reasoning," which vary the number of coins and the number of discoveries; the following is the most common:

On Tuesday, X crosses a deserted road and loses nine copper coins. On Thursday, Y finds in the road four coins, somewhat rusted by Wednesday's rain. On Friday, Z discovers three coins in the road. On Friday morning, X finds two coins in the corridor of his house. The heresiarch would deduce from this story the reality—i.e., the continuity—of the nine coins which were recovered. *It is absurd* (he affirmed) *to imagine that four of the coins have not existed between Tuesday and Thursday, three between Tuesday and Friday afternoon, two between Tuesday and Friday morning. It is logical to think that they have existed—at least in some secret way, hidden from the comprehension of men—at every moment of those three periods.*

The language of Tlön resists the formulation of this paradox; most people did not even understand it. The defenders of common sense at first did no more than negate the veracity of the anecdote. They repeated that it was a verbal fallacy, based on the rash application of two neologisms not authorized by usage and alien to all rigorous thought: the verbs "find" and "lose," which beg the question, because they presuppose the identity of the first and of the last nine coins. They recalled that all nouns (man, coin, Thursday, Wednesday, rain) have only a metaphorical value. They denounced the treacherous circumstance "somewhat rusted by Wednesday's rain," which presupposes what is trying to be demonstrated: the

---

[2] Russell (*The Analysis of Mind*, 1921, page 159) supposes that the planet has been created a few minutes ago, furnished with a humanity that "remembers" an illusory past.

[3] A century, according to the duodecimal system, signifies a period of a hundred and forty-four years.

persistence of the four coins from Tuesday to Thursday. They explained that *equality* is one thing and *identity* another, and formulated a kind of *reductio ad absurdum:* the hypothetical case of nine men who on nine successive nights suffer a severe pain. Would it not be ridiculous—they questioned—to pretend that this pain is one and the same?[4] They said that the heresiarch was prompted only by the blasphemous intention of attributing the divine category of *being* to some simple coins and that at times he negated plurality and at other times did not. They argued: if equality implies identity, one would also have to admit that the nine coins are one.

Unbelievably, these refutations were not definitive. A hundred years 15 after the problem was stated, a thinker no less brilliant than the heresiarch but of orthodox tradition formulated a very daring hypothesis. This happy conjecture affirmed that there is only one subject, that this indivisible subject is every being in the universe and that these beings are the organs and masks of the divinity. X is Y and is Z. Z discovers three coins because he remembers that X lost them; X finds two in the corridor because he remembers that the others have been found . . . The Eleventh Volume suggests that three prime reasons determined the complete victory of this idealist pantheism. The first, its repudiation of solipsism; the second, the possibility of preserving the psychological basis of the sciences; the third, the possibility of preserving the cult of the gods. Schopenhauer (the passionate and lucid Schopenhauer) formulates a very similar doctrine in the first volume of *Parerga und Paralipomena.*

The geometry of Tlön comprises two somewhat different disciplines: 16 the visual and the tactile. The latter corresponds to our own geometry and is subordinated to the first. The basis of visual geometry is the surface, not the point. This geometry disregards parallel lines and declares that man in his movement modifies the forms which surround him. The basis of its arithmetic is the notion of indefinite numbers. They emphasize the importance of the concepts of greater and lesser, which our mathematicians symbolize as $>$ and $<$. They maintain that the operation of counting modifies quantities and converts them from indefinite into definite sums. The fact that several individuals who count the same quantity should obtain the same result is, for the psychologists, an example of association of ideas or of a good exercise of memory. We already know that in Tlön the subject of knowledge is one and eternal.

In literary practices the idea of a single subject is also all-powerful. 17 It is uncommon for books to be signed. The concept of plagiarism does not exist: it has been established that all works are the creation of one author, who is atemporal and anonymous. The critics often invent authors: they

---

[4] Today, one of the churches of Tlön Platonically maintains that a certain pain, a certain greenish tint of yellow, a certain temperature, a certain sound, are the only reality. All men, in the vertiginous moment of coitus, are the same man. All men who repeat a line from Shakespeare *are* William Shakespeare.

select two dissimilar works—the *Tao Te Ching* and the *1001 Nights,* say—
attribute them to the same writer and then determine most scrupulously
the psychology of this interesting *homme de lettres . . .*

Their books are also different. Works of fiction contain a single plot,   18
with all its imaginable permutations. Those of a philosophical nature invariably include both the thesis and the antithesis, the rigorous pro and
con of a doctrine. A book which does not contain its counterbook is considered incomplete.

Centuries and centuries of idealism have not failed to influence real-   19
ity. In the most ancient regions of Tlön, the duplication of lost objects is
not infrequent. Two persons look for a pencil; the first finds it and says
nothing; the second finds a second pencil, no less real, but closer to his
expectations. These secondary objects are called *hrönir* and are, though
awkward in form, somewhat longer. Until recently, the *hrönir* were the
accidental products of distraction and forgetfulness. It seems unbelievable
that their methodical production dates back scarcely a hundred years, but
this is what the Eleventh Volume tells us. The first efforts were unsuccessful. However, the *modus operandi* merits description. The director of one
of the state prisons told his inmates that there were certain tombs in an
ancient river bed and promised freedom to whoever might make an
important discovery. During the months preceding the excavation the
inmates were shown photographs of what they were to find. This first
effort proved that expectation and anxiety can be inhibitory; a week's
work with pick and shovel did not manage to unearth anything in the way
of a *hrön* except a rusty wheel of a period posterior to the experiment. But
this was kept in secret and the process was repeated later in four schools.
In three of them the failure was almost complete; in the fourth (whose
director died accidentally during the first excavations) the students
unearthed—or produced—a gold mask, an archaic sword, two or three
clay urns and the moldy and mutilated torso of a king whose chest bore
an inscription which it has not yet been possible to decipher. Thus was
discovered the unreliability of witnesses who knew of the experimental
nature of the search . . . Mass investigations produce contradictory objects;
now individual and almost improvised jobs are preferred. The methodical
fabrication of *hrönir* (says the Eleventh Volume) has performed prodigious services for archaeologists. It has made possible the interrogation
and even the modification of the past, which is now no less plastic and
docile than the future. Curiously, the *hrönir* of second and third degree—
the *hrönir* derived from another *hrön,* those derived from the *hrön* of a
hrön—exaggerate the aberrations of the initial one; those of fifth degree
are almost uniform; those of ninth degree become confused with those of
the second; in those of the eleventh there is a purity of line not found in
the original. The process is cyclical: the *hrön* of twelfth degree begins to
fall off in quality. Stranger and more pure than any *hrön* is, at times, the
ur: the object produced through suggestion, educed by hope. The great
golden mask I have mentioned is an illustrious example.

Things become duplicated in Tlön; they also tend to become effaced 20
and lose their details when they are forgotten. A classic example is the
doorway which survived so long as it was visited by a beggar and disappeared at his death. At times some birds, a horse, have saved the ruins of
an amphitheater.

Postscript (1947). I reproduce the preceding article just as it ap- 21
peared in the *Anthology of Fantastic Literature* (1940), with no omission
other than that of a few metaphors and a kind of sarcastic summary which
now seems frivolous. So many things have happened since then . . . I shall
do no more than recall them here.

In March of 1941 a letter written by Gunnar Erfjord was discovered 22
in a book by Hinton which had belonged to Herbert Ashe. The envelope
bore a cancellation from Ouro Preto; the letter completely elucidated the
mystery of Tlön. Its text corroborated the hypotheses of Martínez Estrada.
One night in Lucerne or in London, in the early seventeenth century, the
splendid history has its beginning. A secret and benevolent society
(amongst whose members were Dalgarno and later George Berkeley)
arose to invent a country. Its vague initial program included "hermetic
studies," philanthropy and the cabala. From this first period dates the
curious book by Andreä. After a few years of secret conclaves and prema-
ture syntheses it was understood that one generation was not sufficient to
give articulate form to a country. They resolved that each of the masters
should elect a disciple who would continue his work. This hereditary
arrangement prevailed; after an interval of two centuries the persecuted
fraternity sprang up again in America. In 1824, in Memphis (Tennessee),
one of its affiliates conferred with the ascetic millionaire Ezra Buckley.
The latter, somewhat disdainfully, let him speak—and laughed at the
plan's modest scope. He told the agent that in America it was absurd to
invent a country and proposed the invention of a planet. To this gigantic
idea he added another, a product of his nihilism[5]: that of keeping the
enormous enterprise secret. At that time the twenty volumes of the *Encyclopaedia Britannica* were circulating in the United States; Buckley suggested that a methodical encyclopedia of the imaginary planet be written.
He was to leave them his mountains of gold, his navigable rivers, his
pasture lands roamed by cattle and buffalo, his Negroes, his brothels and
his dollars, on one condition: "The work will make no pact with the
impostor Jesus Christ." Buckley did not believe in God, but he wanted to
demonstrate to this nonexistent God that mortal man was capable of
conceiving a world. Buckley was poisoned in Baton Rouge in 1828; in 1914
the society delivered to its collaborators, some three hundred in number,
the last volume of the First Encyclopedia of Tlön. The edition was a secret
one; its forty volumes (the vastest undertaking ever carried out by man)
would be the basis for another more detailed edition, written not in En-

[5] Buckley was a freethinker, a fatalist and a defender of slavery.

glish but in one of the languages of Tlön. This revision of an illusory world,
was called, provisionally, *Orbis Tertius* and one of its modest demiurgi was
Herbert Ashe, whether as an agent of Gunnar Erfjord or as an affiliate, I
do not know. His having received a copy of the Eleventh Volume would
seem to favor the latter assumption. But what about the others?

In 1942 events became more intense. I recall one of the first of these 23
with particular clarity and it seems that I perceived then something of its
premonitory character. It happened in an apartment on Laprida Street,
facing a high and light balcony which looked out toward the sunset. Princess Faucigny Lucinge had received her silverware from Poitiers. From
the vast depths of a box embellished with foreign stamps, delicate immobile objects emerged: silver from Utrecht and Paris covered with hard
heraldic fauna, and a samovar. Amongst them—with the perceptible and
tenuous tremor of a sleeping bird—a compass vibrated mysteriously. The
Princess did not recognize it. Its blue needle longed for magnetic north;
its metal case was concave in shape; the letters around its edge corresponded to one of the alphabets of Tlön. Such was the first intrusion of this
fantastic world into the world of reality.

I am still troubled by a stroke of chance which made me the witness 24
of the second intrusion as well. It happened some months later, at a
country store owned by a Brazilian in Cuchilla Negra. Amorim and I were
returning from Sant' Anna. The River Tacuarembó had flooded and we
were obliged to sample (and endure) the proprietor's rudimentary hospitality. He provided us with some creaking cots in a large room cluttered
with barrels and hides. We went to bed, but were kept from sleeping until
dawn by the drunken ravings of an unseen neighbor, who intermingled
inextricable insults with snatches of *milongas*—or rather with snatches of
the same *milonga*. As might be supposed, we attributed this insistent
uproar to the store owner's fiery cane liquor. By daybreak, the man was
dead in the hallway. The roughness of his voice had deceived us: he was
only a youth. In his delirium a few coins had fallen from his belt, along with
a cone of bright metal, the size of a die. In vain a boy tried to pick up this
cone. A man was scarcely able to raise it from the ground. I held it in my
hand for a few minutes; I remember that its weight was intolerable and
that after it was removed, the feeling of oppressiveness remained. I also
remember the exact circle it pressed into my palm. This sensation of a very
small and at the same time extremely heavy object produced a disagreeable impression of repugnance and fear. One of the local men suggested
we throw it into the swollen river; Amorim acquired it for a few pesos. No
one knew anything about the dead man, except that "he came from the
border." These small, very hard cones (made from a metal which is not of
this world) are images of the divinity in certain regions of Tlön.

Here I bring the personal part of my narrative to a close. The rest 25
is in the memory (if not in the hopes or fears) of all my readers. Let it suffice
for me to recall or mention the following facts, with a mere brevity of
words which the reflective recollection of all will enrich or amplify.
Around 1944, a person doing research for the newspaper *The American*

(of Nashville, Tennessee) brought to light in a Memphis library the forty volumes of the First Encyclopedia of Tlön. Even today there is a controversy over whether this discovery was accidental or whether it was permitted by the directors of the still nebulous *Orbis Tertius*. The latter is most likely. Some of the incredible aspects of the Eleventh Volume (for example, the multiplication of the *hrönir*) have been eliminated or attenuated in the Memphis copies; it is reasonable to imagine that these omissions follow the plan of exhibiting a world which is not too incompatible with the real world. The dissemination of objects from Tlön over different countries would complement this plan . . .[6] The fact is that the international press infinitely proclaimed the "find." Manuals, anthologies, summaries, literal versions, authorized re-editions and pirated editions of the Greatest Work of Man flooded and still flood the earth. Almost immediately, reality yielded on more than one account. The truth is that it longed to yield. Ten years ago any symmetry with a semblance of order—dialectical materialism, anti-Semitism, Nazism—was sufficient to entrance the minds of men. How could one do other than submit to Tlön, to the minute and vast evidence of an orderly planet? It is useless to answer that reality is also orderly. Perhaps it is, but in accordance with divine laws—I translate: inhuman laws—which we never quite grasp. Tlön is surely a labyrinth, but it is a labyrinth devised by men, a labyrinth destined to be deciphered by men.

The contact and the habit of Tlön have disintegrated this world. 26 Enchanted by its rigor, humanity forgets over and again that it is a rigor of chess masters, not of angels. Already the schools have been invaded by the (conjectural) "primitive language" of Tlön; already the teaching of its harmonious history (filled with moving episodes) has wiped out the one which governed in my childhood; already a fictitious past occupies in our memories the place of another, a past of which we know nothing with certainty—not even that it is false. Numismatology, pharmacology and archaeology have been reformed. I understand that biology and mathematics also await their avatars . . . A scattered dynasty of solitary men has changed the face of the world. Their task continues. If our forecasts are not in error, a hundred years from now someone will discover the hundred volumes of the Second Encyclopedia of Tlön.

Then English and French and mere Spanish will disappear from the 27 globe. The world will be Tlön. I pay no attention to all this and go on revising, in the still days at the Adrogué hotel an uncertain Quevedian translation (which I do not intend to publish) of Browne's *Urn Burial*.

[6] There remains, of course, the problem of the *material* of some objects.

Questions

Rereading and Independent Analysis

1. This story's complexities call for careful analysis. Form small groups in your class to work together on the story's chronology and to

make lists of the exact events that are known that show the characteristics of Tlön, Uqbar, and Orbis Tertius. When, in the story, did each of the events occur? Who participated in which events at what time? What are the precise details of the "interior" fiction, the story of the world of Tlön?

2. Borges's story depends on techniques for making fictitious events true-to-life, in order to call into question our subjectivity in all our views of "life." Review the story to find specific details that create this *verisimilitude*. Focus particularly on the narrator. Why do we believe him? What ordinary daily matters are stressed to make us accept the extraordinary content of the story?

Suggested Discussion and Group Activities

1. As a class, compile the information you gathered in groups about the "facts" of this story. Make a chronological chart that explains what happened in the order it happened.

2. Explain the joke on the philosopher in Tlön who tries to understand a world where things exist when they are not perceived. Identify other bits of humor that encourage you to take "reality" lightly. What is Borges's purpose in highlighting the ways we take experience to be unimportant? What is his political implication?

3. What is the significance of Ezra Buckley in this story? What principles does he represent? Is the narrator—or Borges—critical of Buckley's potential powers? Explain your answer.

Writing Suggestions

Response

As you read this story, are you persuaded to be skeptical about the "reality" you usually accept? Write a few paragraphs suggesting alternatives to our common beliefs about the relation of our senses to reality.

Analysis

1. Write an essay in which you explain how Borges's story comments on your own views of orderly, predictable "reality." Imagine that you are writing for readers who have read the story but who do not understand its relation to anything they believe. What does Borges tell us about how we usually establish "truth"?

2. The world of Tlön has reversed the rules of the world we live in. It has shifted from *materialism* (belief in the independent existence of things in space) to *idealism* (belief that reality consists of a series of mental processes in time). Try writing a description of a public sports event or other entertainment as it would take place in Tlön. Make it clear that the participants accept idealism as their version of reality.

Finding a Purpose

Write an entry for a fictional encyclopedia in which you precisely explain and document a concept, place, or thing that does not exist. Be sure to lend credibility to your entry by being precise in giving details about observations. Write with an "objective" point of view.

 # From *Riddley Walker*
Russell Hoban

Science fiction is one of the most recreative—and re-creative—kinds of writing. Authors who work in the genre rewrite our world, allowing us to live in other times and places beyond possibility in any other way. It contains its own landscapes—futurism, fantasy, transformations, social commentary, and many others. Science fiction writers freely reverse, distort, or turn inside out their pictures of our lives, changing physical laws, social customs, and conventional plots.

In *Riddley Walker* (1980), Russell Hoban (b. 1925) wrote of the world to come, 1500 years after a final nuclear holocaust. Hoban, who also wrote *Turtle Diary* (1982, 1986) and is well-known as an author of children's books, including *Bread and Jam for Frances* and the other Frances books, is like many other authors of science fiction who have created their own language. Like James Joyce in *Finnegan's Wake,* he tells this story of the future in a new language. It is a residue, made of leftover words and spellings from a world that slowly lost its history and culture after it blew itself apart. It then gradually restored an imitation language for speaking and writing that was heavily influenced by what people vaguely remembered of earlier written language.

Riddley Walker is both a riddle of language and a quest story. Its futuristic characters puzzle over the riddle of the atom's split, showing humankind's accidental yet inevitable desire to have the "powders" [powers] of explosion. Riddley is a picaresque hero whose journeys from one part of England to another in 2347 O.C. (Our Count) reveal his own quest to understand this leftover world, "what the idear of us myt be" [what the idea of us might be]. His book is prefaced with a map showing places in the England he travels—Cambry [Cambridge], Sams Itch [Sandwich], Do It Over [Dover], Fork Stoan [Folkestone]. Under the map he writes, "This here is mostly jus places Ive tol of in this writing. I don't have no room for the woal of everything there is in Inand." [This here is mostly just places I've told of in this writing. I don't have room for the whole of everything there is in England.]

The scene included here requires you to interpret word by word as Riddley and Goodparley negotiate over the stoans (charcoal and sulphur). They unravel the written legend (caption) that explains a fifteenth-century painting, *The Legend of St. Eustace,* which Hoban saw in its reconstructed form in Canterbury Cathedral in 1974 (A.D.—All Done). As you read, make notes to explain the words Riddley uses. You will find the message of the chapter worth unraveling and will probably think it needs repeating in all ages, in any form. Keep in mind how Hoban's observations of his own time and place are transformed in this fiction.

Wel Im telling Truth here aint I. Thats the woal idear of this writing which   1
I begun wylst thinking on what the idear of us myt be. Right then when
I got grabbit my 1st thot wer: Wel now may be I dont have to program
nothing for a littl.

   Who ever had a holt of me clamp me in a strangl holt with a arm like   2
iron and the other han stuck a knife agenst my belly. I thot: It aint even
that long since I had my E cut in me I dont hardly have no parper scab
on it yet.

   Any how this hevvy in charge of me he pushes me tords the doar of   3
the shelter and he says, 'Here he is Guvner.'

   The doar opens and of coarse theres Goodparley sitting there who   4
else wud it be. With his fit up. He dont have Orfing with him its jus him
and Belnot Phist which Phists face is even witern userel. Looking at poor
old Phist then I thot we myt even end up frends if the boath of us come
thru this littl rumpa a live.

   Goodparley he smyls his teef at me and his little eyes theyre near   5
dantsing wylst theyre peaping over the fents of his cheaks. He says to me,
'Wel Riddley yung Walker its ben a long day for you aint it. We bes change
your name from Walker to Runner you ben moving so fas 1 place to a
nother and back agen. All the way to Fork Stoan to meet a boat with a dead
sailer in it. Funny thing to do in the middl of the nite and such a stormy
nite and all. Dead sailer from the other side which he brung you some
thing for our friend Phist dint he. O yes he brung some kynd of treats what
myt they be myt they be honey sweets or what?'

   I dint say nothing.   6

   He says, 'You know Riddley Iwd cernly like to have a littl scan of   7
them sweets.'

   I dint say nothing I dint know what to say. The hevvy what brung   8
me in begun to smyl.

   Goodparley says, 'Wel you know Riddley weare going to tern your   9
up side down weare going to emty your pockits so what ever youve got
whynt you jus han it over.'

   Funny thing. I dint want him going thru my pockits I dint want him   10
getting his hans on that blackent figger whatd put me on the road to where
ever I wer going. There wernt no way I cud hide that bag of stoans so I
took it out of my pockit and I held it out to him.

   He jus lookit at that bag for a littl like he dint want that minim to go   11
a way from him. He says, 'Riddley what dyou think is in there dyou think
that myt be a littl salt now dyou think it myt be a littl saver what dyou
think it myt be?'

   Phist says to Goodparley, 'Abel he dont know nothing Ive tol you that   12
all ready he aint clevver.'

   Goodparley says, 'O no and in deed he aint hes bettern clevver hes   13
a mover hes a happener. Now Riddley Runner you jus tel me what you
think youve got in that bag. Iwd be interstit to know what you think it is.'

   I said, 'Truth is I dont have no idear what it is.'   14

He says, 'No you dont know do you I know wel a nuff thats Truth. 15
All you done wer grab it becaus youre a mover and a happener aint you.
Youve got to move about and make things happen o I sust that right a nuff
and early on. Realy I wunt have to do nothing only tern you luce and let
you run and youwd persoon get every thing all happent out and moving
I wunt have to stress my self and strain like I ben doing so long. Yes thats
all itwd take to get us moving frontwards agen is you and me working to
gether. Abel Goodparley and Riddley Runner. Riddley Orfing. Why cant
I have you for Shadder Mincer in stead of that dretful littl Orfing on my
back and dragging his feet all the time.'

He took me by the rist of my out stretcht arm and pult me to him. 16
He took the bag out of my han he said, 'You can feal it in there pecking
to get out cant you. Like a chick in a shel. Whatwl it hatch I wunner?' He
put his han in to the bag and brung it out ful of stoans. I hadnt seen them
in the lite befor. Yeller they wer. Broakin bits of yeller stoan.

Goodparley lookit over to Phist like he wer going to have his head 17
on a poal right soon. He said, 'Wel you foun your self a sweets place did
you and sweeter nor honey you foun your self the yellerboy stoan the Salt
4.'

Phist said, 'I dint fynd nothing Abel I aint no mover nor no hap- 18
pener.'

Goodparley said, 'No and for a true fack you aint my littl pink eyed 19
frend you aint no kynd of a mover nor happener thats jus what I come
plaining of this long time innit. "Tryl narrer," you told me. "Thats the way
to do it which wewl do it in the new working," you said. "Spare the
mending and tryl narrer." And all the time you ben waiting on your boat
with honey sweets your Salt 4 you clevver littl man you yellerboy stoaner
you. Whatm I going to do with you I wunner howm I going to put you strait
it looks to me like youve tyd your self in such a knot there aint no end to
it.'

Phist said, 'Abel I bint waiting on no boat I never knowit nothing 20
about no boat til you come in here with your hevvys and claiming Trubba
on me. I know I aint the frendyes bloak in the worl I know theres some
dont like me may be theres some in the Mincerywd like to put some
Trubba on me. I don't know what others myt be doing but *I* aint ben
running no stoans. Them Fork Stoan hevvys they can say what they like
that dont put nothing on me. You start beleaving that kynd of thing and
any I can bring down any 1 they like all they have to do is jus only sen them
some colourt stoans or powders or what ever.'

Goodparley said, 'What powders Belnot? What kynd of powders myt 21
you be talking about?'

Phist said, 'Eusas sake Abel you jump on every word I say and pro- 22
gramming for Trubba. I aint talking about no powders I dont have no
powders I jus only said stoans and powders sames you myt say sticks and
stoans it wernt nothing only a way of saying.'

Goodparley said, 'Yes wel leave it with me jus a little Belnot this 23 wants thinking on praps youwl be so kynd to leave us the loan of your shelter and have a nice cup of tea in the gate house wylst I have a word with this here dog frendy oansome travveler.'

The hevvy as brung me in took Phist out. Goodparley looking at me 24 and smyling hard then he said, 'Howd you get dog frendy Riddley?'

I said, 'I don't know it jus happent. I gone over that fents without 25 realy thinking it out I jus run with them dogs nor they dint arga warga.'

He said, 'You jus run with them dogs did you o youre a deap 1 theres 26 mor and mor to you aint there tel me whyd you go to Fork Stoan with Lissener?'

I said, 'I keap saying I dont know but its Truth it jus like come in to 27 my mynd I thot we bes not break the circel then.'

He said, 'O yes I beleave you parbly you dont even know your self 28 what levvils youre working. *Horny Boy* which is what you are the same as any yung man. *Rung Widders Bel* Ive heard about you and Lorna Elswint shes out livet moren 1 husbin and manys the time youve rung her bel. *Stoal his Fathers Ham as wel.* Which you took over your dads connexion when he got took off. Thats 3 blipful roun the circle nex you done your 1st acturel. *Bernt his Arse.* Bernt your arse here in the digging then over the fents you gone and running with them dogs to Bernt Arse where you bernt *my* arse killing 1 of my hevvys with your dogs. I sust youwd parbly hoal up til dark and I sust you myt do a nother acturel so on I gone to Fork Stoan a head of you. I wer there by The Warnings when you come *and Forkt a Stoan* which is that same and very bag of yeller stoans you brung here roading blipful agen bringing them stoans to Belnot Phist like I knowit you wud you *Done It Over.* You gone over this here fents in the morning and back you come doing it over agen at nite. Only this 2nd time you like *broak a boan* dint you in a way of saying. You got cawt by your old Nunkel Abel.'

My head begun to feal like it wer widening like circels on water I 29 dint know if it wud ever stop I dint know where the end of it wud be. The stranger it took me the mor I fealt at home with it. The mor I fealt like Iwd be long where ever it wer widening me to. I said, 'How can you work all that out of a kid rime? *Fools Circel 9wys* is a kid rime for a kid game.'

He said, 'O Riddley you known bettern that you know the same as 30 I do. What ben makes tracks for what wil be. Words in the air pirnt foot steps on the groun for us to put our feet in to. May be a nother 100 years and kids wil sing a rime of Riddley Walker and Abel Goodparley with their circel game.'

I said, 'What put *Fools Circel 9wys* in the air then?'   31

He said, 'Dint Lissener tel you who ben the 1st Ardship then?'   32

I said, 'He said it ben Eusa.'   33

He said, 'Dint he tel you how the Eusa folk stoand Eusa out of 34 Cambry for what he done? How they crowdit him roun the circel of Inland 1 town to a nother? Every town they come to they tol them on the gate,

"This is Eusa what done the clevver work for Bad Time." Them what wer lef in the towns them what wer the soar vivers of the barming they torchert Eusa then. Torchert him and past him on to the nex. Thats when the playgs come follering hot on Eusas road and wiping out each town he lef behynt him. 9 towns in the rime and 9 towns dead but Cambry shud be in it 2ce it ben the 1st it ben the las. Cambry where they stoand him out of starting him on to his circel and Cambry where they brung him back to blyn and bloody not a man no mor he ben cut off.

'To the gate they brung him lef a space all roun him come the dogs 35 then and licking his soars. Them on the gate they wer afeart they said, "Why dont you say Trubba not if you want in?" Eusa said, "I can't say that." They beat him to death then with col iron becaws it ben col iron he done Inland to death with. Mynd you this wer his oan folk done it to him.

'They took his head off then they put it on a poal for telling. Eusas 36 head tol them, "Onlyes part of Inland kep ther hands clean of this ben the Ram which is the head of Inland. You cut my head off my body now the body of Inland wil be cut off from the head." With that there come a jynt wave it wer a wall of water hyer nor a mountin. Dint it come tho. It come rushing it come roaring it come roaling down it cut acrost the lan right thru from Reakys Over down to Roaming Rune. It cut the Ram off sepert from the res of Inland that wer the day the Ram be come a nylan.

'That head of Eusa said to them what put it on the poal, "Now throw 37 me in the sea." Which they done that and the head wer swimming then agenst the tide it swum acrost that water from Inland to the Ram. Them on the Ram took in the head and this is what it tol them: "Make a show of me for memberment and for the answers to your askings. Make a show with han figgers put a littl woodin head of me on your finger in memberment of my real head on a poal. Keap the Eusa folk a live in memberment of the hardship they brung on. Out of that hardship let them bring a Ardship 12 years on and 12 years come agen. Let the head of Inland ask the Ardship then. Let the head of Inland road the circel ful and to the senter asking what he wants to know for all of Inland. When the right head of Inland fynds the right head of Eusa the answer wil come and Inland wil rise up out of what she ben brung down to." Then the head roalt back in to the water it swum out to sea.'

Goodparley wer all as cited telling that his littl eyes wer shyning you 38 cud see it wer hy telling for him. He said, 'Theres your Fools Circel Riddley its that ful circel Eusa gone his hevvy road on time back way back. Its that circel I ben roading looking for the answer as wil bring poor Inland up from what she ben brung down to.'

Dint say nothing for a littl nyther of us jus lissening to the hisper of 39 the rain. Finely I said, 'Why wernt all this in the *Eusa Story* then?'

Goodparley said, 'It ben Eusa wrote the *Eusa Story* he done it befor 40 they stoand him out of Cambry. After that he dint write nothing mor. Words! Theywl move things you know theywl do things. Theywl fetch. Put

a name to some thing and youre beckoning. Iwl write a message if I have
to but I wunt word nothing moren that on paper. Eusa ben fetcht by words
on paper you know.'

I said, 'What dyou mean?' With my head widening in circels and my   41
mynd sinking like the stoan what made the circels. Part of me where I wer
and part of me with Lissener and coming in to Cambry. Thinking:

> Never did the Good Luck brother
> Tern a round to help the other

With a sickish fealing as I myt be the Good Luck brother and I contrackt
I *wud* help the other Iwd get to him soon I cud and what ever Trubba he
wer in wewd boath be in it. Cursing my self for leaving him and coming
to Widders Dump which I hadn't done nothing only put them yeller stoans
in Goodparleys hans.

Goodparley had a peace of paper in his han and holding it in front   42
of me. He said, 'Have a read of this.'

This is what I read wrote down the same: 43

The Legend of St Eustace
The Legend of St Eustace dates from the year A.D. 120 and this XVth-   44
century wall painting depicts with fidelity the several episodes in his life.
The setting is a wooded landscape with many small hamlets; a variety of
wild creatures are to be seen and a river meanders to the open sea.

1. At the bottom of the painting St Eustace is seen on his knees before   45
his quarry, a stag, between whose antlers appears, on a cross of radiant
light, the figure of the crucified Saviour. The succeeding episodes lead up
to his martyrdom.

2. The Saint and his family appear before the Bishop of Rome renounc-   46
ing their worldly possessions and becoming outcasts.

3. His wife is taken off by pirates in a ship; on the right the father and   47
sons stand praying on the shore.

4. St Eustace and his boys reach a river swollen by torrents. Having   48
swum to the opposite side with one of the children, he returns for the
other. As he reaches the middle of the stream a wolf runs off with the
child he has left. He looks back and beholds a lion in the act of carrying
off the other child. We see St Eustace praying in the midst of the river.

5. Fifteen years pass by. St Eustace has recovered his wife and sons and   49
is the victorious general of the Emperor Hadrian, who orders a great sacrifice to the gods in honour of his victories. Eustace and his family refuse
to offer incense. We see them being roasted to death in a brazen bull.
The Emperor Hadrian stands on the left with a drawn sword in his hand.

6. At the top of the painting two angels hold a sheet containing the four   50
souls; the Spirit of God in the form of a dove descends to receive them
into heaven.

The date of the painting is about 1480; the work is highly skilled in an   51
English tradition and is a magnificent example of wall painting of this
date.

Wel soons I begun to read it I had to say, 'I dont even know ½ these 52
words. Whats a Legend? How dyou say a guvner S with a littl t?'

Goodparley said, 'I can as plain the most of it to you. Some parts is 53
easyer workit out nor others theres bits of it wewl never know for cern
jus what they mean. What this writing is its about some kynd of picter or
dyergam which we dont have that picter all we have is the writing. Parbly
that picter ben some kynd of a seakert thing becaws this here writing (I
dont mean the writing youre holding in your han I mean the writing time
back way back what this is wrote the same as) its cernly seakert. Its blipful
it aint jus only what it seams to be its the syn and foller of some thing else.
A Legend thats a picter what *depicted* which is to say pictert on a wall its
done with some kynd of paint callit *fidelity. St* is short for sent. Meaning
this bloak Eustace he dint jus tern up he wer sent. *A.D. 120* thats the year
count they use to have it gone from Year 1 right the way to Bad Time.
A.D. means All Done. 120 years all done theyre saying thats when they
begun this picter in 120 nor they never got it finisht til 1480 is what it says
here wel you know there aint no picter cud take 1360 years to do these
here year numbers is about some thing else may be wewl never know
what.'

I said, 'What year is it now by that count?' 54

He said, 'We dont know jus how far that count ever got becaws Bad 55
Time put a end to it. Theres a stoan in the Power Ring stannings has the
year number 1997 cut in to it nor we aint never seen no year number
farther on nor that. After Bad Time dint no 1 write down no year count
for a long time we dont know how long til the Mincery begun agen. Since
we startit counting its come to 2347 O.C. which means Our Count.'

I said, 'Dyou mean to tel me them befor us by the time they done 56
1997 years they had boats in the air and all them things and here we are
weve done 2347 years and mor and til slogging in the mud?'

He put his han on my sholder he said, 'Now youre talking jus like me 57
I dont know how many times Ive said that. Now you see the woal thing
what Im getting at its why Im all ways strest and straint Im just a woar
out man. *Riddley we aint as good as them befor us. Weve come way way
down from what they ben time back way back.* May be it wer the barms
what done it poysening the lan or when they made a hoal in what they
callit the O Zoan. Which that O Zoan you cant see it but its there its
holding in the air we breave. You make a hoal in it and Woosh! No mor
air. Wel word ben past down thats what happent time back way black. You
hear what I said? I said time back way *black.* You ever hear the story of
why the crow is black and curses all the time?

Thru the smoak hoal I cud see the nite thinning out and the day 58
coming on. I dint want to hear no storys about crows. I said, 'Wheres
Orfing is he gone after Lissener?'

He said, 'Gone a head of him to Cambry.' 59

I said, 'Waiting a jump on him.' 60

He said, 'Keaping a eye and a ear on him til I get there.' 61

I said, 'Whatwl you do when you get there?'   62

He said, 'Iwl do what I *ben* doing Iwl go on asking wont I. Do some 63
Cambry asking then its up to Horny Boy and begin that woal Fools Circel
over agen becaws it ben broak this time.'

I said, 'You going to help the qwirys on him?'   64

He said, 'Whats the use of helping qwirys on him that poor simpo I 65
dont think he knows nothing to tel no moren any of them ever do. I do
like other Pry Mincers done befor me becaws thats what the Mincery
wants. Im terning them frontwards in a woal lot of ways only I cant do it
all at 1ce. We aint none of us what you cud call qwick but mos of them
roun me theyre 2ce as unqwick as I am Iwl tel you that. May be you ben
thinking Im your nemminy but that aint how it is. You think like I do you
feal like I do we aint nemminys. Its them as cant think nor feal none of
them things theyre the nemminy. Them peopl as jus want to hol on to
what theyve got theyre afeart to chance any thing theyre afeart to move
even 1 littl step forit. I dont care if its Mincery or forms or fentses its them
as wont move theyre the nemminy. Riddley may be you dont know it but
you dont have no better frend nor me?'

I dint say nothing.   66

He give me a littl shake and took his han off my sholder. He said, 'Wel 67
never mynd les get on with this here writing. *XVth century* parbly that
old spel for some kynd of senter where they done this thing theyre telling
of in this blipful writing. *Episodes* thats when you do a thing 1 part at a
time youve got to get the 1st episode done before you go on to the nex.
Thats how youwl do if youre working chemistery or fizzics. Youwl do your
boyl ups and your try outs in episodes, *"Wooded landscape with many
small hamlets."* Wel thats littl pigs innit then theres a *variety* which thats
like a pack or a herd and *creatures* thats creachers parbly dogs. May be
Folleree and Folleroo in that pack who knows. May be them littl pigs is
the many cools and party cools weare looking for becaws this here is blipful
writing it aint strait. *"Meanders to the open sea."* Mazy ways to a open sea
meaning a look see is what I take that to mean. Whatre we follering them
mazy ways for? Have a look right here now weare coming on to the nuts
and balls of the thing weare coming to the hart of the matter and the Hart
of the Wud where them dogs is on the foller of them littl pigs. Whats at
the bottom of the thing and whats this sent bloaks name? Wel it says right
here: *"At the bottom of the painting St Eustace".* That name mynd you
of any other name?'

I said, 'Eusa.'   68

He said, 'Thats it. Its the very same name jus woar down a littl. Who 69
ever this bloak wer what wrote our *Eusa Story* he connectit his self to this
here Legend or dyergam and the chemistery and fizzics of it becaws this
here Legend writing and the *Eusa Story* the 2 of them ben past down to
gether in the Mincery. *"St Eustace is seen on his knees before his quarry."*
Which a *quarry* is a kynd of digging. Whys he on his knees? What brung

him down what knockt him off his feet? What come out of that digging?
A stag. Wel thats our Hart of the Wud innit we know him wel a nuff. Whats
he got be tween his antlers its *"a cross of radiant light".* Which is the same
as radiating lite or radiation which may be youve heard of.'

I said, 'No I never.'   70

He said, 'Youve seen wite shaders on stannings cernly you seen the   71
1 in that hoal in Bernt Arse where you foun Lissener.'

I said, 'Yes I seen that wite shadder.'   72

He said, 'Wel it ben radiant lite as made that shadder. Radiant lite.   73
Shyning. Wel we know from our oan *Eusa Story* where you fynd the Hart
of the Wud youwl fynd a shyning in be tween his horns. Which that
shyning is the Littl Shyning Man the Addom. Only in this Legend its callit
"the figure of the crucified Saviour". Figure is a word means moren 1
thing and 1 of the things it means is number. Number of the *crucified
Saviour.* Now Iwl tel you some thing intersting Riddley Walker son of
Brooder Walker you what put the yellerboy stoan the Salt 4 in my hands.
Iwl tel you theres a working in this thing theres a pattren theres more
connexions nor wewl ever fynd reveals of. You know who put me on to
what this woal things about? This woal blipful writing?'

I said, 'How cud I know that?'   74

He said, 'It wer your oan dad it were Brooder Walker the same. It   75
wer that reveal he done back when Dog Et largent in Little Salting. Orfing
and me we done a special show then your dad come a long Nex Nite he
done a connexion and a reveal the woal thing took lessen a minim. I wernt
there to hear it but I heard of it. Dyou have that 1 in memberment?'

I said, 'O yes I member that. "A littl salting and no saver." '   76

He said, 'That's the 1. "A little salting and no saver." Wel you know   77
every now and agen youwl hear some thing it means what ever it means
but youwl know theres more in it as well. Moren wer knowit by who ever
said it. So that reveal stayd in my mynd. You see how it wer up to then
I never thot this Legend ben anything moren a picter story about a bloak
with a name near the same as Eusa. Nor I dint know nothing of chemistery
nor fizzics then I hadnt payd no tension to it. Any how I wer reading over
this here Legend like I use to do some times and I come to *"the figure of
the crucified Saviour".* Number of the crucified Saviour and wunnering
how that be come the Little Shyning Man the Addom. Suddn it jumpt in
to my mynd "A little salting and no saver". I dint have no idear what
crucified myt be nor up to then I hadn't give *Saviour* much thot I thot it
myt mean some 1 as saves only that dint connect with nothing. Id never
put it to gether with saver like in *savery.* Not sweet. Salty. A salt crucified.
I gone to the chemistery working I askit 1 Stoan Phist that wer Belnots dad
what *crucified* myt be nor he wernt cern but he thot itwd be some thing
you done in a crucioboal. 1st time Id heard the word. Thats a hard firet boal
they use it doing a chemistery try out which you cud call that crucifrying
or crucifying. Which that crucified Saviour or crucifryd salt thats our Littl

Shyning Man him as got pult in 2 by Eusa. So *"the figure of the crucified Saviour"* is the number of the salt de vydit in 2 parts in the cruciboal and radiating lite coming acrost on it. The salt and the saver. 1ce youve got that salt youre on your way to the woal chemistery and fizzics of it. Right up to your las try out which is the *brazen bull* which is to say your brazing boal and the chard coal. But thats all tecker knowledging realy you wunt hardly unner stan it nor I wont wear you out with it. Youve got to do your take off and your run off and your carry off. Which its wrote in the story its the wife took off by pirates and the wolf run off with 1 littl boy and the lion carrit off the other. The wife is the sof and the sweet you see which is took off by the sharp and the salty. Them pirates and wolfs and lions theyre all assits theyre all sharp and biting its all chemistery in there. Them 2 littl boys theyre what they call "catwl twis" which is what you put in to qwicken on your episodes. Right thru that part of it Eusa hes what lef after the takings hes having his res and due. Finely after the brazing boal you get your *four souls* which is your 4 salts gethert. Man and wife and littl childer coming back to gether for the las time thats your new clear family it aint the 1 you startit with its the finement of it in to shyning gethert to the 1 Big 1. Mynd you all this what Im saying its jus theary which I mean we aint done nothing with it yet we cudnt cud we we aint had the parper salts and that. Wel now this here bag of yellerboy myt be the break and thru the barren year with a bang. I know itwl take tryl narrer and spare the mending but may be this time wewl do it.'

I dint say nothing I wer jus sitting there with my head widening in   78
them circels spreading to no where. It wer broad day looking in thru the smoak hoal. Goodparley looking at me suddn then he says, 'We never did emty your pockits did we whats that bulging in there? Trubba not Iwl jus have a littl look.' Which he reaches in to my pockit and puls out that blackent hook nose hump back figger.

He looks at it and his eyes get big then nex thing he begins to cry.   79
I dint know what to do I said, 'What is it?'

He wer snuffling and wiping his eyes he said, 'O how that takes me   80
back o how it twisses my hart. I tel you theres a working in this it aint jus happening random theres too many things be twean us.'

I said, 'Whatre you talking about? Whats that got to do with that   81
figger?'

'O,' he said. 'How them trees swayd in the morning wind that day   82
and the smoak going up from the berning!' He wer pulling me to him and hugging me and slubbering on my neck. I dint know what to do I pattit his back like you wud with any frend took greavis. Knowing wylst I done it he wernt my frend tho he wantit to be. Some thing else as wel. Dint know how I knowit but I knowit I had the upper of him some how I wer the stronger 1. He myt have me kilt if it come on him to do it yet I had a Power he dint. He knowit and I knowit yet I cudntve said right then what it wer. I dont mean the Power you have when some 1 craves for you I mean some thing else.

Questions

Rereading and Independent Analysis

1. Solving this riddle requires that you both understand the words and see through the action to its significance. Reread this selection a few times. Then read it aloud. As you recognize them, write down the spellings of words as we would write them.

2. Make an outline of the action in this selection, explaining in brief notes the significance of the characters' statements. What is the "Power" Riddley now has?

Suggested Discussion and Group Activities

1. In groups working on sections of this selection, translate its words so that you can read it clearly. Then list the principles of speech and writing that you think Hoban followed to construct this new language. Is he consistent in applying rules of transformation? How do you think he actually wrote the book's language?

2. Review the interpretation of the painting of St. Eustace. What misinterpretations does Goodparley make? Why would he make them? What does this scene tell you about the "meaning" of words? How do we determine what a group of letters "means"?

3. This scene describes the nuclear war's "cause" while it shows some of its effects. What "history" and actual science do you learn from this selection?

Writing Suggestions

Response

Try writing a few paragraphs giving your own view of what the future will be like in five centuries. Give details that make daily life clear, and refer to the past to demonstrate the changes you foresee.

Analysis

1. Write a paragraph or two imitating Hoban's language. Continue his description of the world Riddley lives in. Use the principles of "translation" you and the class determined earlier.

2. Misunderstandings often have to do with language differences or a person's ignorance of certain words. Write a short narrative piece in which you tell of a time when you witnessed or were part of such a misunderstanding. Describe a specific event where your lack of knowledge of a word interfered with your understanding. Then go on to generalize about ways that language both helps us to understand and causes us to misunderstand each other.

Finding a Purpose

1. Write a summary of this section of *Riddley Walker* for a reader who has not yet read it. Explain the language and give advice for under-

standing it; explain the social message in the passage and the reasons you think Hoban chose to state this message as he did.

2. Read *Riddley Walker* and write an explanatory review of it for the class. You may want to compare it to *Huckleberry Finn, A Clockwork Orange, Lord of the Flies,* or another book that tells of a young person's journeys and of initiations. Compare it to other science fiction that uses contrived languages. (See Gertrude Himmelfarb's "A History of the New History," in Chapter 4 for a model of a review.)

 # Forever and the Earth
Ray Bradbury

It is probably not an exaggeration to say that Ray Bradbury (b. 1920) educated a prespace generation about how it might feel to live in an open universe. His many science fiction stories and novels create a world in which we travel and raise families, worry about our careers, grow old and fall in love—on Mars, on the way to Venus, or in the middle of deep space. Bradbury is one of the most successful science fiction writers, perhaps because he relocates ordinary feelings and experience in laboratory situations, focusing on their possibilities in future times and places. His books include *The Illustrated Man* (1951), *Dandelion Wine* (1957), *The Martian Chronicles* (1958), and *Something Wicked This Way Comes* (1962). Many of his stories have been adapted for film and television.

In this story, Bradbury summarizes both the past and future of writing. He brings Henry William Field, a failed writer in A.D. 2257, together with the expansive, early twentieth-century American novelist Thomas Wolfe, whose novels are huge in both size and scope. This story is a tribute to what writers—and only writers—can accomplish in celebrating the expansiveness of new life. As you read it, you will learn about Wolfe and the energy of writing he embodies for Bradbury and the future.

After seventy years of writing short stories that never sold, Mr. Henry 1 William Field arose one night at eleven-thirty and burned ten million words. He carried the manuscripts downstairs through his dark old mansion and threw them into the furnace.

"That's that," he said, and thinking about his lost art and his misspent 2 life, he put himself to bed, among his rich antiques. "My mistake was in ever trying to picture this wild world of A.D. 2257. The rockets, the atom wonders, the travels to planets and double suns. Nobody can do it. Everyone's tried. All of our modern authors have failed."

Space was too big for them, and rockets too swift, and atomic science 3 too instantaneous, he thought. But at least the other writers, while failing, had been published, while he, in his idle wealth, had used the years of his life for nothing.

After an hour of feeling this way, he fumbled through the night 4
rooms to his library and switched on a green hurricane lamp. At random,
from a collection untouched in fifty years, he selected a book. It was a book
three centuries yellow and three centuries brittle, but he settled into it
and read hungrily until dawn. . . .

At nine the next morning, Henry William Field staggered from his 5
library, called his servants, televised lawyers, scientists, literateurs.

"Come at once!" he cried. 6

By noon, a dozen people had stepped into the study where Henry 7
William Field sat, very disreputable and hysterical with an odd, feeding
joy, unshaven and feverish. He clutched a thick book in his brittle arms
and laughed if anyone even said good morning.

"Here you see a book," he said at last, holding it out, "written by a 8
giant, a man born in Asheville, North Carolina, in the year 1900. Long
gone to dust, he published four huge novels. He was a whirlwind. He lifted
up mountains and collected winds. He left a trunk of penciled manuscripts
behind when he lay in bed at Johns Hopkins Hospital in Baltimore in the
year 1938, on September fifteenth, and died of pneumonia, an ancient and
awful disease."

They looked at the book. 9

Look Homeward, Angel. 10

He drew forth three more. *Of Time and the River. The Web and the* 11
Rock. You Can't Go Home Again.

"By Thomas Wolfe," said the old man. "Three centuries cold in the 12
North Carolina earth."

"You mean you've called us simply to see four books by a dead man?" 13
his friends protested.

"More than that! I've called you because I feel Tom Wolfe's the man, 14
the necessary man, to write of space, of time, huge things like nebulae and
galactic war, meteors and planets, all the dark things he loved and put on
paper were like this. He was born out of his time. He needed really *big*
things to play with and never found them on Earth. He should have been
born this afternoon instead of one hundred thousand mornings ago."

"I'm afraid you're a bit late," said Professor Bolton. 15

"I don't intend to be late!" snapped the old man. "I will *not* be 16
frustrated by reality. You, professor, have experimented with time-travel.
I expect you to finish your time machine as soon as possible. Here's a
check, a blank check, fill it in. If you need more money, ask for it. You've
done *some* traveling already, haven't you?"

"A few years, yes, but nothing like centuries—" 17

"We'll *make* it centuries! You others"—he swept them with a fierce 18
and shining glance—"will work with Bolton. I *must* have Thomas Wolfe."

"What!" They fell back before him. 19

"Yes," he said. "That's the plan. Wolfe is to be brought to me. We will 20
collaborate in the task of describing the flight from Earth to Mars, as only
he could describe it!"

They left him in his library with his books, turning the dry pages, 21
nodding to himself. "Yes. Oh, dear Lord yes, Tom's the boy, Tom is the
very boy for this."

The months passed slowly. Days showed a maddening reluctance to leave 22
the calendar, and weeks lingered on until Mr. Henry William Field began
to scream silently.

    At the end of four months, Mr. Field awoke one midnight. The phone 23
was ringing. He put his hand out in the darkness.

    "Yes?"   24

    "This is Professor Bolton calling."   25

    "Yes, Bolton?"   26

    "I'll be leaving in an hour," said the voice.   27

    "Leaving? Leaving where? Are you quitting? You can't do that!"   28

    "Please, Mr. Field, leaving means *leaving.*"   29

    "You mean, you're actually going?"   30

    "Within the hour."   31

    "To 1938? To September fifteenth?"   32

    "Yes!"   33

    "You're sure you've the date fixed correctly? You'll arrive before he 34
dies? Be sure of it! Good Lord, you'd better get there a good hour before
his death, don't you think?"

    "*Two* hours. On the way back, we'll mark time in Bermuda, borrow 35
ten days of free floating continuum, inject him, tan him, swim him, vitamin-
ize him, make him well."

    "I'm so excited I can't hold the phone. Good luck, Bolton. Bring him 36
through safely!"

    "Thank you, sir. Good-bye."   37

    The phone clicked.   38

Mr. Henry William Field lay through the ticking night. He thought of Tom 39
Wolfe as a lost brother to be lifted intact from under a cold, chiseled stone,
to be restored to blood and fire and speaking. He trembled each time he
thought of Bolton whirling on the time wind back to other calendars and
other days, bearing medicines to change flesh and save souls.

    Tom, he thought, faintly, in the half-awake warmth of an old man 40
calling after his favorite and long-gone child, Tom, where are you tonight,
Tom? Come along now, we'll help you through, you've got to come,
there's need for you. I couldn't do it, Tom, none of us here can. So the next
best thing to doing it myself, Tom, is helping you to do it. You can play
with rockets like jackstraws, Tom, and you can have the stars, like a
handful of crystals. Anything your heart asks, it's here. You'd like the fire
and the travel, Tom, it was made for you. Oh, we've a pale lot of writers
today, I've read them all, Tom, and they're not like you. I've waded in
libraries of their stuff and they've never touched space, Tom; we need *you*
for that! Give an old man his wish then, for God knows I've waited all my

life for myself or some other to write the really great book about the stars, and I've waited in vain. So, wherever you are tonight, Tom Wolfe, make yourself tall. It's that book you were going to write. It's that good book the critics said was in you when you stopped breathing. Here's your chance, will you do it, Tom? Will you listen and come through to us, will you do that tonight, and be here in the morning when I wake? Will you, Tom?

His eyelids closed down over the fever and the demand. His tongue 41
stopped quivering in his sleeping mouth.

The clock struck four.   42

Awakening to the white coolness of morning, he felt the excitement rising 43
and welling in himself. He did not wish to blink, for fear that the thing which awaited him somewhere in the house might run off and slam a door, gone forever. His hands reached up to clutch his thin chest.

Far away . . . footsteps . . .   44

A series of doors opened and shut. Two men entered the bedroom. 45

Field could hear them breathe. Their footsteps took on identities. 46
The first steps were those of a spider, small and precise: Bolton. The second steps were those of a big man, a large man, a heavy man.

"Tom?" cried the old man. He did not open his eyes.   47

"Yes," said a voice, at last.   48

Tom Wolfe burst the seams of Field's imagination, as a huge child 49
bursts the lining of a too-small coat.

"Tom Wolfe, let me look at you!" If Field said it once he said it a 50
dozen times as he fumbled from bed, shaking violently. "Put up the blinds, for God's sake, I want to see this! Tom Wolfe, is that *you?*"

Tom Wolfe looked down from his tall thick body, with big hands out 51
to balance himself in a world that was strange. He looked at the old man and the room and his mouth was trembling.

"You're just as they said you were, Tom!"   52

Thomas Wolfe began to laugh and the laughing was huge, for he must 53
have thought himself insane or in a nightmare, and he came to the old man and touched him and he looked at Professor Bolton and felt of himself, his arms and legs, he coughed experimentally and touched his own brow. "My fever's gone," he said. "I'm not sick anymore."

"Of course not, Tom."   54

"What a night," said Tom Wolfe. "It hasn't been easy. I thought I was 55
sicker than any man ever was. I felt myself floating and I thought, This is fever. I felt myself traveling, and thought, I'm dying fast. A man came to me. I thought, This is the Lord's messenger. He took my hands. I smelled electricity. I flew up and over, and I saw a brass city. I thought, I've arrived. This is the city of heaven, there is the Gate! I'm numb from head to toe, like someone left in the snow to freeze. I've got to laugh and do things or I might think myself insane. You're not God, are you? You don't look like Him."

The old man laughed. "No, no, Tom, not God, but playing at it. I'm 56

Field." He laughed again. "Lord, listen to me. I said it as if you should know who Field is. Field, the financier, Tom, bow low, kiss my ring finger. I'm Henry Field. I like your work, I brought you here. Come along."

The old man drew him to an immense crystal window.   57

"Do you see those lights in the sky, Tom?"   58

"Yes, sir."   59

"Those fireworks?"   60

"Yes."   61

"They're not what you think, son. It's not July Fourth, Tom. Not 62 in the usual way. Every day's Independence Day now. Man has declared his Freedom from Earth. Gravitation without representation has been overthrown. The Revolt has long since been successful. That green Roman Candle's going to Mars. That red fire, that's the Venus rocket. And the others, you see the yellow and the blue? Rockets, all of them!"

Thomas Wolfe gazed up like an immense child caught amid the 63 colorized glories of a July evening when the set-pieces are awhirl with phosphorus and glitter and barking explosion.

"What year is this?"   64

"The year of the rocket. Look here." And the old man touched some 65 flowers that bloomed at his touch. The blossoms were like blue and white fire. They burned and sparkled their cold, long petals. The blooms were two feet wide, and they were the color of an autumn moon. "Moon-flowers," said the old man. "From the other side of the moon." He brushed them and they dripped away into a silver rain, a shower of white sparks on the air. "The year of the rocket. That's a title for you, Tom. That's why we brought you here, we've need of you. You're the only man could handle the sun without being burnt to a ridiculous cinder. We want you to juggle the sun, Tom, and the stars, and whatever else you see on your trip to Mars."

"Mars?" Thomas Wolfe turned to seize the old man's arm, bending 66 down at him, searching his face in unbelief.

"Tonight. You leave at six o'clock."   67

The old man held a fluttering pink ticket on the air, waiting for Tom 68 to think to take it.

It was five in the afternoon. "Of course, of course I appreciate what you've 69 done," cried Thomas Wolfe.

"Sit down, Tom. Stop walking around."   70

"Let me finish, Mr. Field, let me get through with this, I've got to say 71 it."

"We've been arguing for hours," pleaded Mr. Field, exhaustedly.   72

They had talked from breakfast until lunch until tea, they had wan- 73 dered through a dozen rooms and ten dozen arguments, they had perspired and grown cold and perspired again.

"It all comes down to this," said Thomas Wolfe, at last. "I can't stay 74 here, Mr. Field. I've got to go back. This isn't my time. You've no right to interfere—"

"But, I—" 75

"I was deep in my work, my best yet to come, and now you run me 76 off three centuries. Mr. Field, I want you to call Mr. Bolton back. I want you to have him put me in his machine, whatever it is, and return me to 1938, my rightful place and year. That's all I ask of you."

"But, don't you *want* to see Mars?" 77

"With all my heart. But I know it isn't for me. It would throw my 78 writing off. I'd have a huge handful of experience that I couldn't fit into my other writing when I went home."

"You don't understand, Tom, you don't understand at all." 79

"I understand that you're selfish." 80

"Selfish? Yes," said the old man. "For myself, and for others, very 81 selfish."

"I want to go home." 82

"Listen to me, Tom." 83

"Call Mr. Bolton." 84

"Tom, I don't want to have to tell you this. I thought I wouldn't have 85 to, that it wouldn't be necessary. Now, you leave me only this alternative." The old man's right hand fetched hold of a curtained wall, swept back the drapes, revealing a large white screen, and dialed a number, a series of numbers. The screen flickered into vivid color, the lights of the room darkened, darkened, and a graveyard took line before their eyes.

"What are you doing?" demanded Wolfe, striding forward, staring at 86 the screen.

"I don't like this at all," said the old man. "Look there." 87

The graveyard lay in midafternoon light, the light of summer. From 88 the screen drifted the smell of summer earth, granite, and the odor of a nearby creek. From the trees, a bird called. Red and yellow flowers nodded among the stones, and the screen moved, the sky rotated, the old man twisted a dial for emphasis, and in the center of the screen, growing large, coming closer, yet larger, and now filling their senses, was a dark granite mass; and Thomas Wolfe, looking up in the dim room, ran his eyes over the chiseled words, once, twice, three times, gasped, and read again, for there was his name:

THOMAS WOLFE.

And the date of his birth and the date of his death, and the flowers 89 and green ferns smelling sweetly on the air of the cold room.

"Turn it off," he said. 90

"I'm sorry, Tom." 91

"Turn it off, turn it off! I don't believe it." 92

"It's there." 93

The screen went black and now the entire room was a midnight 94 vault, a tomb, with the last faint odor of flowers.

"I didn't wake up again," said Thomas Wolfe. 95

"No. You died that September of 1938. So, you see. O God, the 96
ironies, it's like the title of your book. Tom, you *can't* go home again."

"I never finished my book." 97

"It was edited for you, by others who went over it, carefully." 98

"I didn't finish my work, I didn't finish my work." 99

"Don't take it so badly, Tom." 100

"How else can I take it?" 101

The old man didn't turn on the lights. He didn't want to see Tom 102
there. "Sit down, boy." No reply. "Tom?" No answer. "Sit down, son; will
you have something to drink?" For answer there was only a sigh and a kind
of brutal moaning.

"Good Lord," said Tom, "it's not fair. I had so much left to do, it's 103
not fair." He began to weep quietly.

"Don't do that," said the old man. "Listen. Listen to me. You're still 104
alive, aren't you? Here? Now? You still *feel*, don't *you?*"

Thomas Wolfe waited for a minute and then he said, "Yes." 105

"All right, then." The old man pressed forward on the dark air. "I've 106
brought you here, I've given you another chance, Tom. An extra month
or so. Do you think *I* haven't grieved for you? When I read your books and
saw your gravestone there, three centuries worn by rains and wind, boy,
don't you imagine how it killed me to think of your talent gone away?
Well, it did! It killed me, Tom. And I spent my money to find a way to you.
You've a respite, not long, not long at all. Professor Bolton says that, with
luck, he can hold the channels open through time for eight weeks. He can
keep you here that long, and only that long. In that interval, Tom, you
must write the book you've wanted to write—no, not the book you were
working on for them, son, no, for they're dead and gone and it can't be
changed. No, this time it's a book for us, Tom, for us the living, that's the
book we want. A book you can leave with us, for you, a book bigger and
better in every way than anything you ever wrote; say you'll *do* it, Tom,
say you'll forget about that stone and that hospital for eight weeks and start
to work for us, will you, Tom, will you?"

The lights came slowly on. Tom Wolfe stood tall at the window, 107
looking out, his face huge and tired and pale. He watched the rockets on
the sky of early evening. "I imagine I don't realize what you've done for
me," he said. "You've given me a little more time, and time is the thing
I love most and need, the thing I always hated and fought against, and the
only way I can show my appreciation is by doing as you say." He hesitated.
"And when I'm finished, then what?"

"Back to your hospital in 1938, Tom." 108

"Must I?" 109

"We can't change time. We borrowed you for five minutes. We'll 110
return you to your hospital cot five minutes after you left it. That way, we
upset nothing. It's all been written. You can't hurt us in the future by living
here now with us, but, if you refused to go back, you could hurt the past,
and resultantly, the future, make it into some sort of chaos."

"Eight weeks," said Thomas Wolfe. 111

"Eight weeks."   112
"And the Mars rocket leaves in an hour?"   113
"Yes."   114
"I'll need pencils and paper."   115
"Here they are."   116
"I'd better go get ready. Good-bye, Mr. Field."   117
"Good luck, Tom."   118

Six o'clock. The sun setting. The sky turning to wine. The big house   119
quiet. The old man shivering in the heat until Professor Bolton entered.
"Bolton, how is he getting on, how was he at the port; tell me?"

Bolton smiled. "What a monster he is, so big they had to make a   120
special uniform for him! You should've seen him, walking around, lifting
up everything, sniffing like a great hound, talking, his eyes looking at
everyone, excited as a ten-year-old!"

"God bless him, oh, God bless him! Bolton, can you keep him here   121
as long as you say?"

Bolton frowned. "He doesn't belong here, you know. If our power   122
should falter, he'd be snapped back to his own time, like a puppet on a
rubber band. We'll try and keep him, I assure you."

"You've got to, you understand, you can't let him go back until he's   123
finished with his book. You've—"

"Look," said Bolton. He pointed to the sky. On it was a silver rocket.   124
"Is that him?" asked the old man.   125
"That's Tom Wolfe," replied Bolton. "Going to Mars."   126
"Give 'em hell, Tom, give 'em hell!" shouted the old man, lifting both   127
fists.

They watched the rocket fire into space.   128

By midnight, the story was coming through.   129

Henry William Field sat in his library. On his desk was a machine that   130
hummed. It repeated words that were being written out beyond the
moon. It scrawled them in black pencil, in facsimile of Tom Wolfe's fevered hand a million miles away. The old man waited for a pile of them
to collect and then he seized them and read them aloud to the room where
Bolton and the servants stood listening. He read the words about space
and time and travel, about a large man and a large journey and how it was
in the long midnight and coldness of space, and how a man could be
hungry enough to take all of it and ask for more. He read the words that
were full of fire and thunder and mystery.

Space was like October, wrote Thomas Wolfe. He said things about   131
its darkness and its loneliness and a man so small in it. The eternal and
timeless October, was one of the things he said. And then he told of the
rocket itself, the smell and the feel of the metal of the rocket, and the sense
of destiny and wild exultancy to at last leave Earth behind, all problems
and all sadnesses, and go seeking a bigger problem and a bigger sadness.
Oh, it was fine writing, and it said what had to be said about space and man
and his small rockets out there alone.

The old man read until he was hoarse, and then Bolton read, and 132
then the others, far into the night, when the machine stopped transcribing
words and they knew that Tom Wolfe was in bed, then, on the rocket,
flying to Mars, probably not asleep, no, he wouldn't sleep for hours yet, no,
lying awake, like a boy the night before a circus, not believing the big
jeweled black tent is up and the circus is on, with ten billion blazing
performers on the high wires and the invisible trapezes of space.

"There," breathed the old man, gentling aside the last pages of the 133
first chapter. "What do you think of that, Bolton?"

"It's good." 134

"Good hell!" shouted Field. "It's wonderful! Read it again, sit down, 135
read it again, damn you!"

It kept coming through, one day following another, for ten hours at 136
a time. The stack of yellow papers on the floor, scribbled on, grew immense in a week, unbelievable in two weeks, absolutely impossible in a
month.

"Listen to this!" cried the old man, and read. 137

"And this!" he said. 138

"And this chapter here, and this little novel here, it just came 139
through, Bolton, titled 'The Space War,' a complete novel on how it feels
to fight a space war. Tom's been talking to people, soldiers, officers, men,
veterans of space. He's got it all here. And here's a chapter called 'The
Long Midnight,' and here's one on the Negro colonization of Mars, and
here's a character sketch of a Martian, absolutely priceless!"

Bolton cleared his throat. "Mr. Field?" 140

"Yes, yes, don't bother me." 141

"I've some bad news, sir." 142

Field jerked his gray head up. "What? The time element?" 143

"You'd better tell Wolfe to hurry his work. The connection may 144
break sometime this week," said Bolton, softly.

"I'll give you anything, anything if you keep it going!" 145

"It's not money, Mr. Field. It's just plain physics right now. I'll do 146
everything I can. But you'd better warn him."

The old man shriveled in his chair and was small. "But you can't take 147
him away from me now, not when he's doing so well. You should see the
outline he sent through an hour ago, the stories, the sketches. Here, here's
one on spatial tides, another on meteors. Here's a short novel begun, called
'Thistledown and Fire'—"

"I'm sorry." 148

"If we lose him now, can we get him again?" 149

"I'd be afraid to tamper too much."   • 150

The old man was frozen. "Only one thing to do then. Arrange to have 151
Wolfe type his work, if possible, or dictate it, to save time; rather than have
him use pencil and paper, he's got to use a machine of some sort. See to
it!"

The machine ticked away by the hour into the night and into the 152 dawn and through the day. The old man slept only in faint dozes, blinking awake when the machine stuttered to life, and all of space and travel and existence came to him through the mind of another:

"... *the great starred meadows of space* ..." 153

The machine jumped. 154

"Keep at it, Tom show them!" The old man waited. 155

The phone rang. 156

It was Bolton. 157

"We can't keep it up, Mr. Field. The continuum device will absolute 158 out within the hour."

"Do something!" 159

"I can't." 160

The teletype chattered. In a cold fascination, in a horror, the old man 161 watched the black lines form.

"... *the Martian cities, immense and unbelievable, as numerous as* 162 *stones thrown from some great mountain in a rushing and incredible avalanche, resting at last in shining mounds* ..."

"Tom!" cried the old man. 163

"Now," said Bolton, on the phone. 164

The teletype hesitated, typed a word, and fell silent. 165

"Tom!" screamed the old man. 166

He shook the teletype. 167

"It's no use," said the telephone voice. "He's gone. I'm shutting off 168 the time machine."

"No! Leave it on!" 169

"But—" 170

"You heard me—leave it! We're not sure he's gone." 171

"He is. It's no use, we're wasting energy." 172

"Waste it, then!" 173

He slammed the phone down. 174

He turned to the teletype, to the unfinished sentence. 175

"Come on, Tom, they can't get rid of you that way, you won't let 176 them, will you, boy, come on. Tom, show them, you're big, you're bigger than time or space or their damned machines, you're strong and you've a will like iron, Tom, show them, don't let them send you back!"

The teletype snapped one key. 177

The old man bleated. "Tom! You *are* there, aren't you? Can you still 178 write? Write, Tom, keep it coming, as long as you keep it rolling, Tom, they *can't* send you back!"

"*The,*" typed the machine. 179

"More, Tom, more!" 180

Odors of, clacked the machine. 181

"Yes?" 182

Mars, typed the machine, and paused. A minute's silence. The ma- 183 chine spaced, skipped a paragraph, and began:

The odors of Mars, the cinnamons and cold spice winds, the winds 184
of cloudy dust and winds of powerful bone and ancient pollen—

"Tom, you're still alive!"   185

For answer the machine, in the next ten hours, slammed out six 186
chapters of "Flight Before Fury" in a series of fevered explosions.

"Today makes six weeks, Bolton, six whole weeks, Tom gone, on Mars, 187
through the Asteroids. Look here, the manuscripts. Ten thousand words
a day, he's driving himself, I don't know when he sleeps, or if he eats, I
don't care, he doesn't either, he only wants to get it done, because he
knows the time is short."

"I can't understand it," said Bolton. "The power failed because our 188
relays wore out. It took us three days to manufacture and replace the
particular channel relays necessary to keep the Time Element steady, and
yet Wolfe hung on. There's a personal factor here, Lord knows what, we
didn't take into account. Wolfe lives here, in this time, when he *is* here,
and can't be snapped back, after all. Time isn't as flexible as we imagined.
We used the wrong simile. It's not like a rubber band. More like osmosis;
the penetration of membranes by liquids, from Past to Present, but we've
got to send him back, can't keep him here, there'd be a void there, a
derangement. The one thing that really keeps him here now is himself,
his drive, his desire, his work. After it's over he'll go back as naturally as
pouring water from a glass."

"I don't care about reasons, all I know is Tom is finishing it. He has 189
the old fire and description, and something else, something more, a searching of values that supersede time and space. He's done a study of a woman
left behind on Earth while the damn rocket heroes leap into space that's
beautiful, objective, and subtle; he calls it 'Day of the Rocket,' and it is
nothing more than an afternoon of a typical suburban housewife who lives
as her ancestral mothers lived, in a house, raising her children, her life not
much different from a cavewoman's, in the midst of the splendor of science and the trumpetings of space projectiles; a true and steady and subtle
study of her wishes and frustrations. Here's another manuscript, called
'The Indians,' in which he refers to the Martians as Cherokees and Iroquois
and Blackfoots, the Indian nations of space, destroyed and driven back.
Have a drink, Bolton, have a drink!"

Tom Wolfe returned to Earth at the end of eight weeks.   190

He arrived in fire as he had left in fire, and his huge steps were 191
burned across space, and in the library of Henry William Field's house
were towers of yellow paper, with lines of black scribble and type on them,
and these were to be separated out into the six sections of a masterwork
that, through endurance, and a knowing that the sands were dwindling
from the glass, had mushroomed day after day.

Tom Wolfe came back to Earth and stood in the library of Henry 192
William Field's house and looked at the massive outpourings of his heart

and his hand and when the old man said, "Do you want to read it, Tom?"
he shook his great head and replied, putting back his thick mane of dark
hair with his big pale hand, "No. I don't dare start on it. If I did, I'd want
to take it home with me. And I can't do that, can I?"

"No, Tom, you can't."   193

"No matter *how* much I wanted to?"   194

"No, that's the way it is. You never wrote another novel in that year, 195
Tom. What was written here must stay here, what was written there must
stay there. There's no touching it."

"I see." Tom sank down into a chair with a great sigh. "I'm tired. I'm 196
mightily tired. It's been hard, but it's been good. What day is it?"

"This is the fifty-sixth day."   197

"The *last* day?"   198

The old man nodded and they were both silent awhile.   199

"Back to 1938 in the stone cemetery," said Tom Wolfe, eyes shut. "I 200
don't like that. I wish I didn't know about that, it's a horrible thing to
know." His voice faded and he put his big hands over his face and held
them tightly there.

The door opened. Bolton let himself in and stood behind Tom 201
Wolfe's chair, a small phial in his hand.

"What's that?" asked the old man.   202

"An extinct virus. Pneumonia. Very ancient and very evil," said 203
Bolton. "When Mr. Wolfe came through, I had to cure him of his illness,
of course, which was immensely easy with the techniques we know today,
in order to put him in working condition for his job, Mr. Field. I kept this
pneumonia culture. Now that he's going back, he'll have to be reinocu-
lated with the disease."

"Otherwise?"   204

"Otherwise, he'd get well, in 1938."   205

Tom Wolfe arose from his chair. "You mean, get well, walk around, 206
back there, be well, and cheat the mortician?"

"That's what I mean."   207

Tom Wolfe stared at the phial and one of his hands twitched. "What 208
if I destroyed the virus and refused to let you inoculate me?"

"You can't do that!"   209

"But—supposing?"   210

"You'd ruin things."   211

"What things?"   212

"The pattern, life, the ways things are and were, the things that can't 213
be changed. You can't disrupt it. There's only one sure thing, you're to die,
and I'm to see to it."

Wolfe looked at the door. "I could run off."   214

"We control the machine. You wouldn't get out of the house. I'd have 215
you back here, by force, and inoculated. I anticipated some such trouble
when the time came; there are five men waiting down below. One shout
from me—you see, it's useless. There, that's better. Here now."

Wolfe had moved back and now had turned to look at the old man 216
and the window and this huge house. "I'm afraid I must apologize. I don't
want to die. So very much I don't want to die."

The old man came to him and took his hand. "Think of it this way: 217
you've had two more months than anyone could expect from life, and
you've turned out another book, a last book, a fine book, think of that."

"I want to thank you for this," said Thomas Wolfe, gravely. "I want 218
to thank both of you. I'm ready." He rolled up his sleeve. "The inocula-
tion."

And while Bolton bent to his task, with his free hand Thomas Wolfe 219
penciled two black lines across the top of the first manuscript and went
on talking:

"There's a passage from one of my old books," he said, scowling to 220
remember it. "*. . . of wandering forever and the Earth . . . Who owns the
Earth? Did we want the Earth? That we should wander on it? Did we need
the Earth that we were never still upon it? Whoever needs the Earth shall
have the Earth; he shall be upon it, he shall rest within a little place, he
shall dwell in one small room forever . . .*"

Wolfe was finished with the remembering.   221

"Here's my last book," he said, and on the empty yellow paper facing 222
the manuscript he blocked out vigorous huge black letters with pressures
of the pencil:

FOREVER AND THE EARTH, by Thomas Wolfe.

He picked up a ream of it and held it tightly in his hands, against his 223
chest, for a moment. "I wish I could take it back with me. It's like parting
with my son." He gave it a slap and put it aside and immediately thereafter
gave his quick hand into that of his employer, and strode across the room,
Bolton after him, until he reached the door where he stood framed in the
late-afternoon light, huge and magnificent. "Good-bye, good-bye!" he
cried.

The door slammed. Tom Wolfe was gone.   224

They found him wandering in the hospital corridor.   225
    "Mr. Wolfe!"   226
    "What?"   227
    "Mr. Wolfe, you gave us a scare, we thought you were gone!"   228
    "Gone?"   229
    "Where did you go?"   230
    "Where? Where?" He let himself be led through the midnight corri- 231
dors. "Where? Oh, if I *told* you where, you'd never believe."

    "Here's your bed, you shouldn't have left it."   232

Deep into the white death bed, which smelled of pale, clean mortal- 233
ity awaiting him, a mortality which had the hospital odor in it; the bed
which, as he touched it, folded him into fumes and white starched coldness.

    "Mars, Mars," whispered the huge man, late at night. "My best, my 234

very best, my really fine book, yet to be written, yet to be printed, in
another year, three centuries away . . ."

"You're tired."   235

"Do you really think so?" murmured Thomas Wolfe. "Was it a   236
dream? Perhaps. A good dream."

His breathing faltered. Thomas Wolfe was dead.   237

In the passing years, flowers are found on Tom Wolfe's grave. And this is   238
not unusual, for many people travel there. But these flowers appear each
night. They seem to drop from the sky. They are the color of an autumn
moon, their blossoms are immense, and they burn and sparkle their cold,
long petals in a blue and white fire. And when the dawn wind blows they
drip away into a silver rain, a shower of white sparks on the air. Tom Wolfe
has been dead many, many years, but these flowers never cease. . . .

Questions

Rereading and Independent Analysis

1. List the details that Bradbury includes in the first page of this story
that make you accept its "truth" from the beginning.

2. Bradbury has written in this story about a world he says Mr. Field
cannot write about. Reread the story to note the language that Bradbury
and "Wolfe" use to capture the qualities of space. Then write a few sentences in imitation of this language, describing the sky, the ocean, or another infinitely expansive idea.

3. Make lists of the images of nature (e.g., flowers, meadows, suns)
and of technological devices. How do these images demonstrate the story's
theme? Note those places where Bradbury joins natural and mechanistic
descriptions together.

Suggested Discussion and Group Activities

1. This story's important science fiction "trick" is the use of time
travel. As a class, outline the story's references to time and its manipulations. How does Bradbury suggest that Wolfe's writing is more powerful
than the "rules" of time? Explain to the class any recent theories in physics
you know of that suggest we may be able to accomplish travel through
time.

2. What is Mr. Field's distinct character? He is an unpublished writer
but seems to be all-powerful. In what ways is he described? What are his
motives? How does Bradbury suggest that Field's character is an ironic
comment on the future? What is the significance of his name? Of Bolton's
name?

3. This story is "about" writing that is destroyed, unwritten, unpublished, and unseen. In groups, find the references to this unrealized writing. How do Bradbury's references to "absent" writing create a metaphor
for the future?

Writing Suggestions

Response

If you were Mr. Field, whom would you bring back to life for a time? What would this person do for you that no one alive now can do?

Analysis

1. As a class or in groups, make a plan for rewriting this story to cast Mr. Field and Thomas Wolfe as film directors. First divide the story into workable parts, based on changes in its perspectives and times. Then decide which details would have to be changed. Create a finished plan for the class to read as a whole.

2. Using this story and other readings from this collection as evidence, write a fictional "history" that summarizes some of the changes in writers' social and political roles through time. Write your history from the point of view of Mr. Field or someone living at his time. Tell the roles that writers fulfilled in different settings and writing communities, giving a sense of how these roles were added to and changed as writing became more common.

Finding a Purpose

Write an outline for a story in which you briefly bring back to life a particular person to accomplish a particular action or task that no one else can accomplish. Describe the characters, the setting, and the results of this temporary visit from another time. Then write the first few paragraphs of the story and show them and your outline to classmates for suggestions.

 # The New Literacy
Benjamin M. Compaine

Each selection in this book has demonstrated the power of written words to create worlds that grow increasingly complex over time. In this essay, Benjamin Compaine, a professor at Harvard University, explores the unpredictable future of reading and writing under the influence of new computer technologies. Although he is at times reluctant to do so, he makes many predictions about "new" literacy by using "old" literacy as evidence for his predictions in a summary of the history of uses of reading and writing.

Compaine insists that the Canadian communications expert Marshall McLuhan was incorrect when he claimed that "the medium is the message." (See McLuhan's books *The Medium is the Massage* or *The Gutenberg Galaxy.*) McLuhan said that a means of communication carries its own specific information, which controls any "message." Compaine disagrees, pointing out that a message is a message and a medium is a medium. He thinks that "writing" will be preserved as a human act, no matter what technology we use to create it. But he undermines this argument somewhat by also showing that economically important technologies have changed our ways of creating, storing, transmitting, and receiving messages, and *have* transformed the messages. New media have transformed messages; they are not limited to "containing" them. Compaine suggests that our primary ways of learning will be changed by virtue of the new access we will have to speedy, electronic tools for writing. Before you read, think of examples of the ways new technologies influence your own learning, reading, and writing. How has the computer changed not only *how* you accomplish these purposes but your goals and plans for doing them? Have any other technologies changed your image of the activity they serve?

I believe books will never disappear. It is
impossible for it to happen. Of all of mankind's
diverse tools, undoubtedly the most astonishing are
his books. . . . If books were to disappear, history
would disappear. So would men.

> Jorge Luis Borges[1]

Reading and writing will become obsolete skills.

> Sol Cornberg[2]

On any given work day, perhaps 7 million employed people are paid to spend their time in front of a television screen. They are not watching "General Hospital," but rather, are reading material produced by a computer. These people are airline reservations clerks and travel agents, stockbrokers, newspaper reporters and editors, catalog showroom order-takers, and customer service representatives at telephone, utility, and other sorts of firms. Among the 7 million, there are secretaries and, to a small but increasing extent, executives. They clearly have many different jobs and levels of responsibilities, but they all share one trait: more and more, they are using the computer for some portion of their information storage and retrieval. And instead of using a computer specialist as an intermediary, as they would have done only a few years ago, they are interacting directly with the computer. This means that much of what they read appears on a video display terminal—a VDT—instead of in ink on paper.　1

　This essay is about the implications of the skills these workers are developing. It is about the possible significance of the *$8 billion* spent on video games in 1981—more than was spent on movie theater admissions and record purchases combined. It is about the phenomenon of using microcomputers in elementary and secondary schools—often at the insistence of kids and their parents, before the curriculum supervisors know what's happening. It is about computer summer camps for kids. It concerns the wired university.　2

　My objective here is to describe several of the forces and trends at work in society—only in part a function of technology—and the implications of these for traditional concepts of literacy. Central to this discussion　3 is the role of the engine of this change, the computer, and hence "computer literacy."

In this essay, I do *not* predict the future. Nor do I advocate a course 4
of action: I aim to neither salute nor denigrate the idea of a new literacy. But change is clearly in the wind. This essay, then, suggests that factors may impinge on future developments in reading and literacy, and that those who consider themselves to be educated and, above all, literate will want to take heed.

The Old Literacy

We cannot talk about the future of reading or the book without reference 5
to their fellow traveler, literacy. Each generation tends to assume literacy is static, petrified, as it were, in their moment of time. Literacy, however, is dynamic, a bundle of culturally relevant skills. The appropriate skills for literacy, moreover, have changed over time. Before the written record came into wide use (in England, starting in the last half of the eleventh century), the oral tradition predominated. To be literate meant the ability to compose and recite orally. In the twelfth century, to make a "record" of something meant to bear oral witness, not to produce a document for others to read. Even if a treaty was in the form of sealed letters, "both parties also named witnesses who were to make legal record . . . in court if necessary." Despite the existence of written documents, "the spoken word was the legally valid record."[3]

Furthermore, at that time, to be *litteratus* meant to know Latin, 6
rather than having only the specific ability to read and write. To be sure, the vernacular replaced Latin for discourse. But even then, because of the difficulty of writing with a quill on parchment or with a stylus on wax, writing was considered a special skill that "was not automatically coupled with the ability to read."[4] The most common way of committing words to writing in twelfth century England was by dictating to a scribe, who was a craftsman and not necessarily himself able to compose. Thus, reading and dictating were typically paired, rather than reading and writing.

Although the basic skills of modern literacy—reading and writing— 7
had become relatively widespread in England by the mid-nineteenth century, the literati of the period seemed to impose a greater barrier for admission to full-fledged literacy. It was not merely the ability to read, they said, but the reading of the "right" materials that separated the truly literate from the great unwashed. How, if at all, they asked, did the spread of the printed word contribute to the spiritual enrichment and intellectual enlightenment of the English nation? "More people were reading than ever before; but in the opinion of most commentators, they were reading the wrong things, for the wrong reasons, and in the wrong way."[5]

All this is grist for the notion that today's standards of literacy are 8
rooted in the past, yet at the same time, should not be presumed to be the standard for the future. For example, at a recent meeting of "experts"

convened to discuss the status of books and reading, several participants indicated that when they referred to the status of "the book," they had in mind great literature and intellectual enrichment. They were not referring to the 38,000 other titles (out of about 40,000) published annually that range from cookbooks and "how-to" books to Harlequin romances. Thus they were carrying on the tradition of the nineteenth century literati, who idealized their own past. They felt that things were far different—and infinitely better—in the old days.

Similarly, the library, today's bastion of the book and reading, has not 9 always been held in such high regard by the literati. Free libraries for the common man in England were viciously criticized by the reading elite. Instead of encouraging "habits of study and self-improvement, they catered to the popular passion for light reading—above all, for fiction."[6] Indeed, one librarian told a meeting in 1879 that "schoolboys or students who took to novel reading to any great extent never made much progress in after life."[7] The irony of attitudes such as this should not be lost to the critics of video games as a corrupting influence on today's "schoolboys or students."

The New Literacy

"To describe our business as one that traffics in paper, ink, and type is to 10 miss the point entirely. Our real enterprise is ideas and information." A quote from a futurist? Perhaps. This is the strategic outlook of W. Bradford Wiley, chairman of John Wiley & Sons, one of the oldest publishing houses in New York City, and publisher, in the nineteenth century, of Herman Melville, Nathaniel Hawthorne, and Edgar Allen Poe, and most of the first American editions of John Ruskin. Wiley adds, "Until now, our medium has been the bound book; tomorrow our medium will expand to include [computer-stored] data banks and video discs."[8]

What evidence is there that Wiley is onto something? First, he has 11 recognized, at least implicitly, that Marshall McLuhan was off base. The medium, by and large, is *not* the message. The message is the content, and the medium is the way it is conveyed and displayed. *Content*— the ideas, knowledge, story, information, and so on—is the work of an author, a producer, a photographer. Technology, history, and even politics play a role in how this content is processed and the format in which it is ultimately displayed. *Process* incorporates the gathering, handling, storage, and transmission of the content; it may involve typewriters, computers, file cabinets; telephone lines, broadcasting towers, printing presses; and trucks and retail stores. *Format* is the manner of display—such as ink on paper, sound from a vibrating speaker cone, images on a cathode ray tube, light projected through a film, and so on.[9] Thus the content may be quite independent of the medium.

This article, for example, has been written at a standard typewriter 12 keyboard. But instead of paper as the format, the letters appear on a green television screen. Although you are now reading this in a conventional ink on paper format, the process for creating this bound version may be quite different from that used only ten or twenty years ago. Computerized phototypesetting equipment has substantially replaced all the old Linotype machines that used to produce lead slugs for galleys. Moreover, there is no technological or perhaps even economic reason to keep subscribers to *Daedalus* from reading this article the same way it was written—on a video screen. It may be argued that someday it will be. The major barrier to this may be cultural: most of us have been brought up to read print on paper. Many adults would today recoil in horror at the thought of losing the feel and portability of printed volumes. But, as Wiley indicated, print is no longer the only rooster in the barnyard.

There are more solid trends that support Wiley's approach. One is 13 the pervasive and perhaps long-run impact of video games. In short order, these have gone from barroom novelties to a worldwide phenomenon. In 1976 Atari's sales were $39 million; in 1981 they were $1.23 billion, and may double in 1982 to $2.4 billion (about the size of Kellogg or Gillette). Americans may spend about $2 billion in 1982 on cartridges for home video games, and they will likely drop into video game machines this year considerably more than the 22 billion quarters they did in 1981. That money is coming from somewhere, most likely, from the implicit budget people have for other media and entertainment. This includes movie admissions, records, and, to some extent, books.

Even if the video game craze itself is a fad, it nonetheless may have 14 considerable cultural significance, much as the dime novel or penny press had in earlier years. For the first time, it has made the video tube into something other than a passive format for the masses. Heretofore, only a handful of specialists, mostly computer programmers and some designers, used VDTs as an interactive medium. The rest of the world sat back and watched on their television tube what others provided.

Moreover, while critics of video games decry the presumed ill effects 15 of the video game parlors—much as their nineteenth century counterparts lamented the coming of literacy for the common reader—they may well prove to be myopic regarding the nature of the games themselves. As with much great literature, which can be appreciated on several levels of understanding, video games can be viewed on one level as simply entertainment. But in his book *How to Master Home Video Games,* Harvard undergraduate Tom Hirschfeld described these games as presenting players with a challenge. He notes that those who become the best at it are those who figure out the pattern programmed into the computer. The game players are becoming, almost painlessly, computer-literate. Without becoming computer experts, they may be intuitively learning the strengths and limitations of computer logic. The U.S. army, which must train large numbers of youngsters fresh from the video game rooms, understood the implications of the games almost immediately, and has already contracted for training exercises using video gamelike lessons played on microcomputers. The schools will no doubt follow.

The home video games are actually specialized personal computers. 16 They have made consumers familiar with the concept of a computerized console that plugs into a video tube. All that a computer adds is a keyboard. Of the approximately 1.5 million personal desktop computers in use by the end of 1981, about 500,000 of these were in homes. With the Timex 1000, the retail price for a real programmable computer has fallen to under $100. As a result, it is estimated that the number of computers in homes will triple by the end of 1982. Thus, unlike the situation in the 1960s when expensive computers in schools were imposed from the top— and computerized education failed miserably—we now see the development of grassroots interests in having microcomputers in the schools. It is the kids and their parents who are often in the forefront of this effort, with local PTAs holding bake sales and the like to raise the money when school districts are pinched for funds. (In the past, some of that effort went to buying books for the school library.)

Thus, although educators are still concerned primarily with how 17 students learn from print, young people today spend more time (about twenty-eight hours weekly by one study) using electronic devices, like television and electronic games, than with print (about twenty-five). Further, most of the discretionary time spent is with the electronic medium, while most of the time spent with printed material is involuntary.[10] Together with the video game trend, this suggests that schoolchildren of today are developing a new set of skills that may lead to a different standard for literacy.

But what about the 7 million or more adults working with VDTs as 18 part of their daily routine? How will they approach the prospect of adopting at home tools similar to those they use in the workplace? Besides home computers, there are already a few such opportunities to retrieve and manipulate content, with a great many more in prospect. Services such as those offered by CompuServe Information Service and Source Telecomputing have already offered portions of newspapers such as the *New York Times* and the *Los Angeles Times* via computer to home terminals, in addition to a wide range of other types of information. Houghton Mifflin has produced an interactive videodisk version of Roger Tory Peterson's venerable bird identification books.

Three "videotext"[11] services, Oracle, Ceefax, and Prestel, have been 19 commercially available in Great Britain since 1980. Prestel, the most ambitious, has been slow to achieve much popular interest, perhaps because of its cost, its strangeness, and the method required to access its voluminous information stores. Nonetheless, several videotext services that are in the prototype stage in the United States at this time may well be made available commercially by traditional publishing firms. These include Times Mirror Company (publisher of newspapers, books, and magazines),

Knight-Ridder Newspapers (publisher of newspapers and books), and CBS Inc. (which, in addition to being the largest television network, also owns the publishing company Holt, Rinehart, & Winston and many well-known magazines). While the services offered by these firms are likely to tie together home terminals with large computers by telephone lines, the country's largest book and magazine publisher, Time Inc., has also tested a text-on-the-video-screen service to be delivered via cable.

That nonpublishers are getting into the act is a fact not lost on 20 traditional publishers. Mead Corporation, one of the largest paper manufacturers, is also one of the most successful electronic publishers. On its NEXIS Service, it offers the full text of articles from the *Washington Post, Newsweek, U.S. News & World Report, Business Week*, UPI, Associated Press, Reuters news services, *Encyclopaedia Brittanica*, and scores of other publications. The company's LEXIS service is known by most lawyers and used by many. It provides nearly unlimited access to tens of thousands of laws and cases, at federal, state, and international levels, that often required days of work in a library. These services can be accessed by users who have received very little special training. Although the cost today restricts NEXIS and LEXIS to use in institutions, similar services may become as inexpensive over time as today's mainstream media.

The interest in "electronic publishing" is motivated by more than a 21 mere fascination with technological toys. In part, there are some significant economic trends involved. The price of the paper used in book and magazine publishing has jumped substantially since the early 1970s, following years of only minimal increases. The cost of newsprint jumped 200 percent between 1970 and 1981, well over twice the rate of increase for all commodities. In large measure, these huge increases reflect the high energy component in the manufacture of paper. The physical distribution of printed material, moreover, especially newspapers, is highly energy-intensive. These cost trends contrast dramatically with the costs of computer-stored information, which have been declining at a rate of about 25 percent annually for the last thirty years. (Consider the magnitude of this decline: if the price of a Rolls Royce had decreased in proportion to that of computer storage, a Rolls Royce today would cost about $2.50.) The outlook for the foreseeable future is for continued similar decreases in cost.

As a preliminary indicator of the changing demand for new informa- 22 tion skills in the workplace, Carolyn Frankel, a researcher with Harvard's Program on Information Resources Policy, surveyed the help-wanted ads in the *New York Times* for the same June day in 1977 through 1982. She counted all jobs or skills in those ads that mentioned some "computer literacy" skill, such as word processing, programming, data-entry, and so on. In 1977, 5.8 percent of the want ads specified those skills. The percentage increased regularly to 1982, when 10.3 percent of the jobs listed required such skills. Perhaps of equal significance is the way these jobs were described. Earlier in the period, the ads were for specific jobs that implied a computer skill, such as "Wang operator" or "word processor." By 1982 conventional job titles such as secretary specified the required skills as "experience with word processing" or "knowledge of Sabre" (a computer system for travel agents). From this apparent trend, we can conclude that, as new technology becomes more commonplace and skills in it more widespread, the skills become incorporated into traditional jobs. When the power saw was a novelty, building contractors sought out "power-saw operators." But later on, when most carpenters were expected to have some familiarity with this tool, builders again began to seek out carpenters as such, carpenters who had, among other skills, knowledge of the power saw.

In 1977 none of the help-wanted ads for travel agents in the *Times* 23 on the day surveyed mentioned any sort of computer skill; in 1980 one fifth mentioned a computer-related skill. By 1982, as a consequence of the implementation of computer reservations services by the industry, 71 percent required familiarity with such skills. Similarly, the number of bookkeeping jobs requiring computer-related skills doubled to 24 percent from 1977 to 1982; the proportion of secretary/typist want ads that required word processing skills went from zero in 1977 to 15 percent in 1982; and the number of jobs that were labeled "word processing" or that specified the ability to use a word processor, increased eightfold in that period, despite the recession in 1982 and a lower level of help-wanted ads overall.

The impact of all this in the workplace will be visible, if not profound. 24 About $25,000 of capital is invested for every worker in a manufacturing setting, compared to approximately $4,000 for every office—or knowledge—worker, but that may change soon. In 1980 even an information-intensive company such as Aetna Life & Casualty Company had only one video terminal for each six employees; by 1985 they expect to have one terminal for every two employees. The ubiquity of these terminals and the increased familiarity workers will have with them may result in expanded application, such as electronically transmitted and stored "mail" both within an office and from remote office sites, including overseas offices.

Other indices suggest that we are in the midst of a fundamental 25 change in the way we receive and process information. A taxi service in Ottawa has eliminated the crackling radio heretofore used to dispatch taxis and replaced it with a video screen in the cab on which the messages flash. When the driver is called, a buzzer sounds and a fare's location is printed on the screen. Since no other driver gets that message, no one can beat him (or her) to the fare. The head of one cab company using the system likes it, he explained, because voice dispatching causes noise and confusion, not to mention slips of paper everywhere.

We now see centers of higher learning using computers in the liberal 26 arts. Classics scholars at Princeton are studying Virgil with the help of a computer programmed to scan the text quickly, picking out passages that contain the same word used in different contexts. This reduces the drudgery, they claim, and allows them more time to study the meaning. Dartmouth applies similar analytical techniques to the Bible and Shakespeare. Apparently, students are integrating this technology into their academic lives as easily as they did the simpler calculator in the last decade.[12]

Even department stores and toy shops now carry computers so that 27 consumers do not have to go into the threatening territory of a specialty store. At the same time, advertising campaigns by computer manufacturers are using well-known entertainers such as Bill Cosby and Dick Cavett in prime time commercials to further demystify their product.

Combining the Old and the New

Historically, the development of a literacy has gone through identifiable 28 stages. Literacy starts with specialists, and then begins to have a wider impact on institutions, as it becomes the preferred medium of business, culture, and politics. Finally, it becomes so pervasive that even the masses are considered to be handicapped without it. We can trace modern notions of literacy from eleventh century England, in the movement from reliance on spoken words to written records, first in the Church and then in political institutions; to the introduction of the printing press in the fifteenth century; to the development of the newspaper and mass-consumed book along with popular education in the nineteenth.

History also suggests that one need not be fully literate to participate 29 in literacy. One measure of changing literacy in twelfth and thirteenth century England was possession of a seal. In the reign of Edward the Confessor, only the king possessed a seal to authenticate documents. By the reign of Edward I (1307), even serfs were required by statute to have one.[13] In colonial times in the United States, signing one's name was skill enough to be called literate.

In the thirty-five or so years since the development of modern com- 30 puters, we can identify trends similar to the much slower advance of traditional literacy. At first, computers were strictly for those who could read and write in the tongue of computer machine language, a "priestly" class whom all users of computers had to depend upon. As computers became more widespread and their application more pervasive, they began to have a greater impact on business and social institutions. The languages (COBOL, FORTRAN, BASIC, etc.) evolved into something closer to the vernacular, so that more people were able to learn to read and write computer language.

Today, we are perhaps at the threshold of an era where the computer 31 is becoming so simple to use and inexpensive that the masses can use it without having to understand how it works. They can thus participate in computer literacy without necessarily being computer-literate. That may come in time, as the computer becomes as commonplace as the book. Yet, if we look at the computer as a tool, it may be no more necessary for the mass of people to understand how a computer works in order to use it than it is to understand the mechanics of the automobile's internal combustion engine in order to drive. (This suggests a nice parallel. In the 1950s, when the automobile was king, many boys were born "with a wrench in their hand." Today, we see kids who are barely teenagers playing around with RAM chips in much the same way.)

Implications for Reading and the Book

It would be foolish, though perhaps fun, to speculate on the long-term 32 societal impacts that may grow out of the trends I have described. As someone must surely have once said, "Predicting is a hazardous occupation, especially when it deals with the future." Moreover, while I have tried to identify some forces and trends relative to literacy and reading, there are other trends—cultural, political, and technological—that have not been included or even recognized as yet.

In the long term, it is possible, even probable, that the computer, 33 combined with modern communications facilities, will be cited by historians of the future as a fundamental milestone for civilization, out of which many changes will be traced. What those changes will be cannot be foretold; it is difficult enough to understand the implications of our own historical antecedents. Elizabeth Eisenstein wrote: "It is one thing to describe how methods of book production changed after the mid-15th century. . . . It is another thing to decide how access to a greater abundance or variety of written records affected ways of learning, thinking, and perceiving among literate elites."[14]

In the near term, we might profitably think about computer skills as 34 additional proficiencies in the bundle we call literacy. Note that I have referred to computer skills as additional to, not replacements for, existing skills. Reading and writing will continue to be essential; computer memory may replace some paper and file draws; but we will still have to compose sentences for a documentary format. And although the text may appear on screen, it must still be read and, of course, understood. Thus the written word must be taught and learned. Slightly further out, however, writing—meaning composing with pen in hand or fingers on keyboard—may become less necessary. Although still far from perfected, work on voice recognition by computers is proceeding rapidly. Today, an increasing number of busy people dictate their letters, memos, and even books onto audio tape for later transcription by someone else. Ironically, this harks back to the Medieval era, when the educated composed orally to scribes, who made the written record. With reliable voice recognition computers, we could return to such an era of oral literacy.

There is an even greater likelihood of computer-generated voice 35 synthesis; that is, the output from a computer in the form of a voice—like Hal, in the movie *2001: A Space Odyssey*—rather than as text on a screen or printer. Yet it is unlikely that voice synthesis will totally replace reading, since we can assimilate information much faster with our eyes than with our ears.

Even that assertion, however, is subject to question. The current 36 adult generations, raised on print and the book, have a close cultural identity with both. We have *learned* how to use them, how to skim, how to use an index with ease, and so on. We associate certain pleasant emotions with the tactile sensation of the book. And, as one skeptic put it, could we imagine curling up in front of a fire with a Tolstoy novel on the video screen?

But these are largely learned cultural biases. The kids today playing 37 Pac-Man are learning to assimilate great amounts of information rapidly from a video screen. They are learning to manipulate the information on that screen at an intuitive level, using keyboards or "joysticks." If the technology results in the development of video screens with twice the resolution of today's (possible now, but prohibitively expensive), and with ever lower electronic storage costs (perhaps using a videodisk), it may not be all that farfetched to expect tomorrow's youngsters to carry their thin, high-resolution video screens with them when they travel or to sit in front of the fireplace reading from them. And, conceivably, an "oral" generation may also learn to absorb content at a faster rate from speech, with greater skill—or literacy—and with enjoyment equal to our pleasure in reading words from a book.

Such speculation should not obscure the robustness of older formats 38 in the face of new ones. Records, film, radio, and television have successively been feared as threats to print. Yet all have survived and thrived, though sometimes having to fill somewhat different functions. General interest mass audience magazines like *Look* and *Life* lost their national audiences to television, and as a result, magazines generally became largely a special-interest medium. Books, on the other hand, have shown remarkable resilience in the face of new informational and cultural formats. Indeed, new processes and formats frequently create opportunities for the older ones. Television spawned magazines such as *TV Guide,* and is widely credited with sparking interest in sports magazines and expanded newspaper sports pages. Cinema and television films based on books have increased sales of those books. In some cases, original scripts for films were later published as books. Examples range from *Star Wars* to *The Ascent of Man.* Computer magazines are thriving. And there are now books and magazines for video game enthusiasts.

There are few fears evoked today that were not previously heard 39 during the Victorian era. Today, the enemy of reading is television. But the doom of reading has been falsely prophesied ever since the invention of the pneumatic tire, when it was believed that the bicycle would put the whole family on wheels and thus spell the end of fireside reading.[15] On the other hand, there is a certain validity to the pessimism of Samuel Johnson—who, had he lived today, could have had in mind Atari's Pack-Man—when he wrote: "People in general do not willingly read, if they can have anything else to amuse them."[16]

It is likely that we are on the verge of yet another step in the evolu- 40 tion of literacy. Yet we can feel confident that whatever comes about will not replace existing skills, but supplement them. Neither the printing press nor the typewriter replaced either speech or handwriting. The electronic hand calculator has not replaced the need to understand mathematics, though it may reduce the need to memorize multiplication tables. The new literacy will likely involve a greater emphasis on the visual, but only as a continuation of the trend that has involved the improvements in photography, printing techniques, and television.

Above all, the new literacy, whatever it looks like, is not to be 41 feared—first, because it will come about regardless of what we think about it; second, because for any threat to some existing institution or relationship, the new literacy will provide equal or greater opportunity; third, because change brought about in part by technology takes place incrementally, and adjustments by society and individuals will evolve naturally.

I remain haunted, however, by how a sixteen-year-old reporter for 42 *Children's Express,* a newspaper published entirely by schoolchildren, characterized the Fourth Assembly of the World Future Society in July 1982, whose theme was the new world of telecommunications: "I think the message was clear that it's really our [young people's] world. I was kind of laughing at the people here. This technology, all they talked about, they really couldn't grasp. This belongs to us."[17]

Endnotes

The author gratefully acknowledges the contribution of Harvard graduate student Carolyn Frankel for the research and analysis incorporated into this article.

[1] From *Horizon,* in an article about the importance of books in an era of mass communication. Quoted on the editorial page of *The Wall Street Journal.* February 6, 1982.

[2] Quoted by Alvin Toffler in *Future Shock* (New York: Random House, 1970), p. 144. Mr. Cornberg is a communications system designer.

[3] M.T. Clanchy, *From Memory to Written Record: England, 1066–1307* (Cambridge: Harvard University Press, 1979), p. 56.

[4] Ibid., p. 88.

[5] Richard D. Altick, *The English Common Reader: A Social History of the Mass Reading Public,* 1800–1900 (Chicago: University of Chicago Press, 1974), p. 368.

[6] Ibid., p. 231.

[7] Ibid., p. 233.

[8] Jack Egan, "Publishing for the Future," *New York,* August 16, 1982, p. 10.

[9] Benjamin M. Compaine, *A New Framework for the Media Arena: Content, Process and Format* (Cambridge: Program on Information Resources Policy, Harvard University, 1980), pp. 6–17.

[10] Fred M. Hechinger, "About Education," *New York Times,* December 15, 1982, p. C-5.

[11] "Videotext" (sometimes videotex) is a term used to describe any service that provides text and graphics on a video screen in a "page" format. That is, each screenful of material is identified like a print page and can be viewed in its entirety by the user. Videotext (in a version sometimes called "view-data") may be transmitted from a computer to the user by a telephone connection, by cable, or, conceivably, by other electronic transmission techniques. It is considered "interactive" because each user determines which "pages" should be sent by some type of controlling mechanism, such as a numerical keypad or a full typewriterlike keyboard. Videotext may also provide opportunity for ordering goods

that are featured or advertised on the system, or even for certain financial functions, such as checking banking account balances or transferring funds. Teletext refers to systems that appear to be similar, but involve transmission of the video pages by cable or by broadcasting in a continuous stream. The user has a numerical keypad by which he can identify a particular page to view. The next time that page is transmitted (probably no longer than thirty seconds), it will be "grabbed" and held on the video screen until another page is requested. It is therefore not a truly interactive service, as the user never has access to the computer itself.

[12] "The Wired University Is on the Way," *Business Week,* April 26, 1982, p. 68.

[13] Clanchy, *From Memory to Written Record,* p. 2.

[14] Elizabeth L. Eisenstein, *The Printing Press as an Agent of Change* (Cambridge, England, and New York: Cambridge University Press, 1979), p. 8.

[15] Altick, *The English Common Reader,* p. 374.

[16] Ibid., p. 373.

[17] "Time Tripping at a Convention of World Futurists," *The Boston Globe,* August 4, 1982, p. 55.

Questions

Rereading and Independent Analysis

1. Compaine proceeds by stating, and supporting, two alternate theses. Identify the two theses he begins with; then outline the evidence he uses to support these and additional points throughout the essay. If you had to write a single, implied thesis for the essay, what would it be?

2. Review Compaine's use of his sources. In which parts of the essay do they predominate? What is the effect of their variety on your willingness to accept his points?

Suggested Discussion and Group Activities

1. One way to view this essay is as a story whose ending is in doubt. Examine Compaine's use of historical narrative. At what points in the essay do references to time appear? How does the implied history support the points he wants to make about the future?

2. In groups, characterize Compaine's view of the old literacy. What dangers does he suggest in the new literacy? Find evidence in the essay to support the claim that he prefers the new version of literacy.

3. Compaine's essay was written about 1982. From your own experience since then, explain how we may be moving toward restoring the "oral" world that he envisioned. Does it make sense to imagine everyone carrying personal VDTs for "reading" before the fire? What elements of the old literacy do you think are still necessary and will remain important? Can you think of other predictions about the future that did not turn out to be accurate?

Writing Suggestions

Response

Write a few paragraphs for your journal in which you explain how a new technology has changed your way of doing a daily activity. Has the new equipment changed your attitude toward this activity? How?

Analysis

Write a letter to a grandparent or another older person in which you explain the appeal of video games to young people today. Use analogies that your imagined reader will be able to relate to his or her own experience in order to make your explanation clear.

Finding a Purpose

Bill Gates, a Harvard dropout, was the founder of Microsoft, a successful computer software company. Steven Jobs, who left Reed University before graduation, and Stephen Wozniak, who did not finish at Berkeley, founded Apple Computers. Numerous accounts have circulated recently of high school students who infiltrate closed computer systems, sometimes stealing important information. On the basis of these accounts and others you know about, write a piece to contemporary students in which you make a case for "the importance of a *complete* education." What values and ways of making choices might be missed by leaving school before finishing, even if you are successful later?

You may use any *persona,* form, and evidence you think will be effective. Show your work to your classmates to test its persuasiveness.

Acknowledgments

William Allen, "A Whole Society of Loners and Dreamers." From *Saturday Review* (November 11, 1972). Copyright © 1972 by Saturday Review. Reprinted by permission.

Roger Angell, "The Old Folks Behind Home." From *The Summer Game* by Roger Angell. Copyright © 1962 by Roger Angell. All rights reserved. Reprinted by permission of Viking Penguin, Inc.

Aristotle, "Young Men and Elderly Men." Reprinted from *On the Contrary,* edited by Martha Rainbolt and Jane Fleetwood. By permission of the State University of New York Press. Copyright © 1984 by the State University of New York Press.

William Blake, "Proverbs of Hell." From *Blake's Poetry and Designs,* a Norton Critical Edition, selected and edited by Mary Lynn Johnson and John E. Grant. Reprinted by permission of W. W. Norton & Company, Inc. Copyright © 1979 by W. W. Norton & Company, Inc.

Jorge Luis Borges, "Tlön, Uqbar, Orbus Tertius." From Jorge Luis Borges, *Labyrinths.* Copyright © 1962, 1964 by New Directions Publishing Corporation. Reprinted by permission of the publisher.

Ray Bradbury, "Forever and the Earth." From *Long After Midnight* by Ray Bradbury. Copyright © 1950 by Ray Bradbury; renewed 1977 by Ray Bradbury. Reprinted by permission of Don Congdon Associates, Inc.

Dorothea Brande, "The Sources of Originality." From *Becoming A Writer* by Dorothea Brande. Copyright © 1934 by Harcourt Brace Jovanovich, Inc., renewed 1962 by Gilbert I. Collins and Justin Brande. Reprinted by permission of the publisher.

Fernand Braudel, "Daily Bread." From *The Structures of Everyday Life* by Fernand Braudel. Copyright © 1979 by Librarie Armand Colin Paris and English translation copyright © 1981 by William Collins Sons Limited and Harper & Row. Reprinted by permission of Harper & Row.

Fox Butterfield, "The New Vietnam Scholarship." From *The New York Times* (February 13, 1983). Copyright © 1983 by The New York Times Company. Reprinted by permission.

Abraham Cahan, "I Discover America." From *The Rise of David Levinsky* by Abraham Cahan. Copyright © 1917 by Harper & Row. Reprinted by permission of the publisher.

Robert Coles, selections from "The Madness of Dark." From *The Last and First Eskimos* by Robert Coles, Copyright © 1978 by Robert Coles. Reprinted by permission of the author.

Robert Coles, "Young Observers." From *Privileged Ones: The Well-Off and the Rich in America: Volume II of Children in Crisis* by Robert Coles, M.D. Copyright © 1977 by Robert Coles. By permission of Little, Brown and Company.

R. G. Collingwood, selections from "What Is History." Reprinted from *The Idea of History* by R. G. Collingwood. Copyright © 1946 by Oxford University Press. Reprinted by permission of Oxford University Press.

Benjamin M. Compaine, "The New Literacy." Reprinted by permission of *Daedalus*, Journal of the American Academy of Arts and Sciences, "Readings Old and New," Vol. 112, No. 1 (Winter 1983): Cambridge, MA.

Gloria Cooper, excerpts from *Squad Helps Dog Bite Victim and Other Flubs From the Nation's Press.* Compiled by Gloria Cooper. Copyright © 1965, 1966, 1967, 1968, 1969, 1970, 1971, 1972, 1973, 1974, 1975, 1976, 1977, 1978, 1979 by Graduate School of Journalism, Columbia University. Copyright © 1980 by Trustees of Columbia University, the City of New York. Reprinted by permission of Doubleday, a division of Bantam, Doubleday, Dell Publishing Group, Inc.

Guy Davenport, "Hobbitry." Excerpted from *The Geography of the Imagination.* Copyright © 1981 by Guy Davenport. Published by North Point Press and reprinted by permission.

Toi Derricotte, selection from *The Black Notebooks.* In Lyn Lifshin, ed., *Ariadne's Thread.* New York: Harper & Row, 1982.

Joan Didion, "On Self Respect." From *Slouching Towards Bethlehem* by Joan Didion. Copyright © 1961, 1964, 1965, 1966, 1967 by Joan Didion. Reprinted by permission of Farrar, Straus and Giroux, Inc.

Albert Einstein, "E = MC²." From *Science Illustrated* Magazine. Copyright © 1946.

Loren Eiseley, "The Letter." From *All the Strange Hours: The Excavation of A Life.* Copyright © 1975 Loren Eiseley. Reprinted with the permission of Charles Scribner's Sons, an imprint of Macmillan Publishing Company.

Sigmund Freud, "Case 4: Katharina." From *Studies on Hysteria* by Josef Breuer and Sigmund Freud. Translated from the German and edited by James Strachey, in collaboration with Anna Freud, assisted by Alix Strachey and Alan Tyson. Published in the United States of America by Basic Books, Inc., by arrangement with the Hogarth Press, Ltd. Reprinted by permission of Basic Books, Inc.

Paul Fussell, selections from "The Troglodyte World." From *The Great War and Modern Memory* by Paul Fussell. Copyright © 1975 by Oxford University Press, Inc. Reprinted by permission of the publisher.

George Gamow, "The Problem of the Four Colors." Reprinted from George Gamow: *One Two Three . . . Infinity,* © 1947, 1961, Viking Press. Dover Publications reprint, 1988. Reprinted by permission of the publisher.

Erving Goffman, "VI: The Human Being." Excerpts from *Frame Analysis* by Erving Goffman. Copyright © 1974 by Erving Goffman. Reprinted by permission of Harper & Row.

Gen. Ulysses S. Grant and Gen. Robert E. Lee, "Civil War Surrender Documents." From *Major Peace Treaties of Modern History, 1648–1967, Volume II,* edited by Fred L. Israel. Copyright © 1967 by Chelsea House Publishers. Reprinted by permission.

Bill Green, excerpts from "The Reporter . . .", "The Story . . .", "The Publication . . .", "The Doubts . . .", "The Ombudsman . . .", "The Prize . . .", "The Confession . . .", and "The Conclusions." From *The Washington Post* (April 19, 1981). Copyright © 1981 The Washington Post. Reprinted by permission.

Marina N. Haan and Richard B. Hammerstrom, selections from *Graffiti in the Big Ten.* Copyright © 1981 by Marina N. Haan and Richard B. Hammerstrom. Reprinted by permission of Warner Books, New York.

Lillian Hellman, "Dashiell Hammett." From *An Unfinished Woman: A Memoir* by Lillian Hellman. Copyright © 1969 by Lillian Hellman. By permission of Little, Brown and Company.

Gilbert Highet, "The Gettysburg Address." From *A Clerk of Oxenford: Essays on Literature and Life* by Gilbert Highet. Reprinted by permission of Curtis Brown, Ltd. Copyright © 1954 by Gilbert Highet.

Gertrude Himmelfarb, "A History of the New History." From *The New York Times* (January 10, 1982). Copyright © 1982 by The New York Times Company. Reprinted by permission.

Russell Hoban, selections from *Riddley Walker* by Russell Hoban. Copyright © 1980 by

Purposes: A Rhetorical Index

(This index lists patterns of organization, rhetorical modes, and purposes demonstrated in the selections.)

An Index of Assignments for Reading and Writing

This table catalogues many of the processes, organizational patterns, genres, and writing situations that are called for in the "writing" questions at the end of each selection. As aids to reading comprehension, the questions for analysis and discussion frequently call for sentence analysis, for topical or formal outlines, working with vocabulary, writing thesis statements, and listing and classification.

INTERPRETIVE ANALYSIS

PROBLEM/SOLUTION

PROCESS (CAUSAL)

PROCESS ANALYSIS

REPORTS

Experiments and Observations